TRUST THE LOCALS!

"Travelers swear by the recommendations in the *Best Places* guidebooks."

—*Sunset* magazine

OKS ARE SOLD

SASQUATCH BOOKS
www.sasquatchbooks.com

Praise for Best Places® Guidebooks

"Best Places *are the best regional restaurant and guide books in America.*"
—The Seattle Times

"Best Places *covers must-see portions of the West Coast with style and authority. In-the-know locals offer thorough info on restaurants, lodgings, and the sights.*"
—National Geographic Traveler

"*Travelers swear by the recommendations in the* Best Places *guidebooks.*"
—Sunset Magazine

"*Known for their frank yet chatty tone . . .*"
—Publishers Weekly

"*For travel collections covering the Northwest, the* Best Places *series takes precedence over all similar guides.*"
—Booklist

"*The best guide to Seattle is the locally published* Best Places Seattle *. . .*"
—Jonathan Raban, Money Magazine

"*Whether you're a Seattleite facing the winter doldrums or a visitor wondering what to see next, guidance is close at hand in* Best Places Seattle."
—Sunset Magazine

"Best Places Seattle *remains one of the best, most straightforward urban guidebooks in the country.*"
—The Seattle Times

"*This tome* [Best Places Seattle] *is one of the best practical guides to any city in North America.*"
—Travel Books Worldwide

"*Visitors to Washington, Oregon, and British Columbia would do well to pick up* Best Places Northwest *for an exhaustive review of food and lodging in the region . . . An indispensable glove-compartment companion.*"
—Travel and Leisure

TRUST THE LOCALS

The original insider's guides, written by local experts

EVERY PLACE STAR-RATED & RECOMMENDED

★★★★ The very best in the city

★★★ Distinguished; many outstanding features

★★ Excellent; some wonderful qualities

★ A good place

HELPFUL ICONS

Watch for these quick-reference symbols throughout the book:

 **FAMILY FUN**

 **GOOD VALUE**

 **ROMANTIC**

 **EDITORS' CHOICE**

BEST PLACES®

SEATTLE

The Locals' Guide to the Best Restaurants, Lodgings, Sights, Shopping, and More!

Edited by

MONICA FISCHER

Printed in the United States of America
Published by Sasquatch Books
Distributed by PGW/Perseus

Eleventh edition
15 14 13 12 11 10 09 08 9 8 7 6 5 4 3 2 1

ISBN-10: 1-57061-540-3
ISBN-13: 978-1-57061-540-5
ISSN: 1095-9734

Project editor: Kurt Stephan
Copy editor: Diane Sepanski
Cover design: Rosebud Eustace
Cover photograph: Narisa Spaulding/Stock.XCHNG
Interior composition/design: Scott Taylor/FILTER/Talent
Interior maps: GreenEye Design

SPECIAL SALES

Best Places guidebooks are available at special discounts on bulk purchases for corporate, club, or organization sales promotions, premiums, and gifts. For more information, contact your local bookseller or Special Sales, Best Places Guidebooks, 119 South Main Street, Suite 400, Seattle, Washington 98104, 800/775-0817.

SASQUATCH BOOKS

119 South Main Street, Suite 400
Seattle, WA 98104
(206) 467-4300
www.sasquatchbooks.com
custserv@sasquatchbooks.com

CONTENTS

Introduction

Shortly after wrapping up this edition of *Best Places Seattle*, I arranged a Super Seattle Day for my nephews.

Matthew and Riley, then 8 and 7, live in Puyallup, and don't spend much time in the city. Thus far, their urban travels have consisted primarily of the Zoo, the Aquarium, Safeco Field, and Qwest Field, where Matthew and I attend the first Seahawks home game every year.

Though they have never publicly dubbed me so, I am the boys' Cool Aunt, the one who buys them the best gifts, slips them cash when their parents aren't looking, wears Converse sneakers even as I approach my fourth decade, and inhabits an ever-lengthening list of neighborhoods in and around Seattle.

In the last few years, as my nephews have become more fluent in suburban team sports and chain-food dining, I have begun to realize that, though they live a mere 30 miles away, Seattle is becoming as foreign to them as the menu at Claim Jumper is to me. So to my list of Cool Aunt responsibilities, I have added Seattle Immersion 101.

Which was why, on a perfect summer Saturday in June, we embarked upon Super Seattle Day: an amphibious excursion on Ride the Ducks, the city's quackiest tourist attraction; lunch at the Center House food court; an afternoon ride to the Space Needle observation deck; and an early-evening viewing of *Ratatouille* at downtown's Meridian 16 cineplex.

As the boys chuckled over Captain Cody's corny Ride the Ducks jokes (huge underpants will *always* get a laugh from a 7-year-old), clambered to peer out the glass windows of the Space Needle elevator, and gazed in wonder at the bright red Mohawk of the hipster kid chilling outside the movie theater, I began to believe that our day had been a success. But it wasn't until we were driving out of the city that I knew it without a doubt.

As we left the skyscrapers of Seattle behind, Matthew wistfully asked, "Why does Seattle get all the good stuff?"

When you live and work in Seattle, it's easy to take the good stuff for granted, and I feel fortunate to have my nephews around to remind me what a wondrous place it can be.

I also feel lucky to have had the opportunity to work on this latest edition of *Best Places Seattle*, which—in the absence of nephews—can be another excellent reminder of all that our city has to offer: breathtaking views, stellar restaurants, abundant recreational opportunities, a thriving arts scene, and some of the best shopping west of the Mississippi.

I hope this guide will help you to discover some of our city's good stuff, whether you live here every day of the year, or have just one super day to spend in Seattle.

—Monica Fischer, Editor

Contributors and Acknowledgments

LARA FERRONI, who wrote a portion of our restaurant reviews, is a Seattle food photographer and writer with a not-so-small obsession with food. Where most people might simply cook and eat, she feels compelled to document each and every bite and sip. She has penned pieces for *Seattle* magazine and *Hungry? Seattle: Family!* in addition to her own blogs on food and photography, *Cook & Eat* and *Still Life With*.

Seattle native **MONICA FISCHER**, who wrote the Planning a Trip, Lay of the City, and Lodgings chapters, has been pounding the city's pavement for more than 15 years, writing about everything from rock to roller derby to retail therapy. She is a former editor of *Experience Hendrix – The Official Jimi Hendrix Magazine*, *Seattle Homes & Lifestyles*, *Seattle* magazine and *Seattle Bride*. Currently, she is the editor of NWsource.com, an online city guide, as well as this edition of *Best Places Seattle*.

Reviewing another portion of this edition's restaurants was **ANGELA GARBES**, who also lives to eat and write in Seattle. A graduate of Barnard College, she is the publicist for poetry publisher Copper Canyon Press and has worked at local independent bookstores, as well as Seattle's alternative weekly *The Stranger*, where her work still appears regularly. She enjoys reading, cooking, chatting, and watching sports.

ADRIANA GRANT has lived in Seattle since 1995. She writes about visual art, dance, theater, and food for *Seattle Weekly*. Her critical work on art and books has also appeared in *The Stranger*, *The American Book Review*, *Rain Taxi*, and *Art Access*. A poet and visual artist, her work has been published by *3rdbed*, LIT, *Monkey Puzzle*, and *Bird Dog*, and seen at the Henry Art Gallery, Western Bridge, Consolidated Works, CoCA, and Bumbershoot.

Recreation chapter contributor **YEMAYA MAURER** is happiest when she's playing, sweating, or in pursuit of adventure, only leaving the Northwest when an opportunity sounds too good to pass up—like leading canopy tours in Costa Rica; the three-month sea kayaking and mountaineering exhibition in Patagonia; or the summer she worked on backcountry campsite restoration in Yosemite. She's an avid tennis player, runner, cross country skier, kayaker, and hiker whose work has appeared in *Seattle* magazine. She is currently writing a book about winter hiking and camping.

AJA PECKNOLD has spent the better part of a decade working in the trenches of Seattle's thriving music scene. After putting in time getting her hands dirty as a venue booker, manager, and publicist, she is currently the clubs editor at *Seattle Weekly* and spends many of her evenings at the best venues, clubs, and bars in the city, reporting all the news that's fit to print (and some that probably isn't) about nightly happenings around town. She brings her bottomless wealth of nocturnal knowledge to this edition's Nightlife chapter (now smoke free!)—straight with no chaser.

LEI ANN SHIRAMIZU is a fervent journalist, copywriter, and, shop girl, having recently opened Momo, a boutique in Seattle's Japantown. The writer of our Shopping chapter, her words have appeared in *Seattle* magazine, *Seattle Bride*, *Seattle Business Monthly*, *Seattle Weekly*, NWsource.com, and the international textile glossy, *Textile View*. Her clients include nonprofits United Way of King County, Mockingbird Society, and Listen & Talk, as well as luxury purveyors Rosanna, Nordstrom, and The Bellevue Collection—with very little in between. She splits her days between a Hansel-and-Gretel woodland cottage where she lives with her husband, Tom Kleifgen (who lent a hand with the wine section), and her office/store in the International District, where shopping is exotic and there's always a good, cheap lunch.

When **PAT TANUMIHARDJA**, who wrote many of our restaurant reviews, as well as the Exploring chapter, first came to Seattle as an undergrad in 1992, she was in awe of this remarkable city and its take-your-breath-away-beautiful setting. Even after calling it home all these years (albeit with short stints elsewhere), she still is—in awe, that is. She writes about Seattle's vibrant cultural and culinary scene for various local publications, including *Seattle* magazine, *Seattle Woman*, and *Northwest Home + Garden*. Having lived on three continents, she has collected a treasure chest of global experiences that inform and influence her writing in myriad ways. Inevitably, her heart always leads her back to Seattle.

DAVID VOLK likes to keep the pot stirred. The author of *The Tribe Has Spoken: Life Lessons From Reality TV*, Volk is a freelance writer and humorist who enjoys covering food, travel, and popular culture. A columnist for *Seattle* magazine, he has also written for *Horizon Airlines Magazine* and *Washington Law & Politics*. When he isn't writing, he can be found searching for urban adventures, odd experiences, and kitschy places overlooked by locals. He is currently working on a book about funerals, death rites, and rituals gone horribly wrong.

Along with these talented writers, this edition of *Best Places Seattle* was skillfully crafted by a team of savvy wordsmiths and cat herders, including publisher Gary Luke and managing editor Kurt Stephan of Sasquatch Books, copy editor Diane Sepanski, compositor/designer Scott Taylor of FILTER/Talent, proofreader Grace Drone, and indexer Michael Ferreira.

About Best Places® Guidebooks

People trust us. Best Places guidebooks, which have been published continuously since 1975, represent one of the most respected regional travel series in the country. Our reviewers know their territory, and seek out the very best a city or region has to offer. We provide tough, candid reports about places that have rested too long on their laurels, and delight in new places that deserve recognition. We describe the true strengths, foibles, and unique characteristics of each establishment listed.

Best Places Seattle is written by and for locals, and is therefore coveted by travelers. It's written for people who live here and who enjoy exploring the city's bounty, including its out-of-the-way places of high character and individualism. It's these very characteristics that make *Best Places Seattle* ideal for tourists, too. The best places in and around the city are the ones that denizens favor: independently owned establishments of good value, touched with local history, run by lively individuals, and graced with natural beauty. With this 11th edition of *Best Places Seattle*, travelers will find the information they need: where to go and when, what to order, which rooms to request (and which to avoid), where the best music, art, nightlife, shopping, and other attractions are, and how to find the city's hidden secrets.

NOTE: *The reviews in this edition are based on information available at press time and are subject to change. Readers are advised that places listed in previous editions may have closed or changed management or may no longer be recommended by this series. The editors welcome information conveyed by users of this book. A report form is provided at the end of the book, and feedback is also welcome via email: BPFeedback@sasquatchbooks.com.*

How to Use This Book

This book is divided into ten chapters covering a wide range of establishments, destinations, and activities in and around Seattle. All evaluations are based on numerous reports from local and traveling inspectors. Final judgments are made by Sasquatch Books editors. **EVERY PLACE FEATURED IN THIS BOOK IS RECOMMENDED.**

STAR RATINGS *(for Top 200 Restaurants and Lodgings only)* Restaurants and lodgings are rated on a scale of one to four stars (with half stars in between), based on uniqueness, loyalty of local clientele, performance measured against the establishment's goals, excellence of cooking, cleanliness, value, and professionalism of service. Reviews are listed alphabetically, and every place is recommended.

★★★★	The very best in the region
★★★	Distinguished; many outstanding features
★★	Excellent; some wonderful qualities
★	A good place
UNRATED	New or undergoing major changes

(For more on how we rate places, see the Best Places Star Ratings sidebar.)

PRICE RANGE *(for Top 200 restaurants and Lodgings only)* Prices for restaurants are based primarily on dinner for two, including dessert and tip, but not alcohol. Prices for lodgings are based on peak season rates for one night's lodging for two people (i.e., double occupancy). Peak season is typically Memorial Day to Labor Day; off-season rates vary but often can be significantly less. Call ahead to verify, as all prices are subject to change.

BEST PLACES® STAR RATINGS

Any travel guide that rates establishments is inherently subjective—and Best Places is no exception. We rely on our professional experience, yes, but also on a gut feeling. And, occasionally, we even give in to soft spot for a favorite neighborhood hangout. Our star-rating system is not simply a checklist; it's judgmental, critical, sometimes fickle, and highly personal.

For each new edition, we send local food and travel experts out to review restaurants and lodgings and then rate them on a scale of one to four, based on uniqueness, loyalty of local clientele, performance measured against the establishment's goals, excellence of cooking, cleanliness, value, and professionalism or service. That doesn't mean a one-star establishment isn't worth dining or sleeping at. Far from it! When we say that all the places listed in our books are recommended, we mean it. That one-star pizza joint may be just the ticket for the end of a whirlwind day of shopping with the kids. But if you're planning something more special, the star ratings can help you choose an eatery or hotel

$$$$	Very expensive (more than $125 for dinner for two; more than $250 for one night's lodging for two)
$$$	Expensive (between $85 and $125 for dinner for two; between $150 and $250 for one night's lodging for two)
$$	Moderate (between $35 and $85 for dinner for two; between $85 and $150 for one night's lodging for two)
$	Inexpensive (less than $35 for dinner for two; less than $85 for one night's lodging for two)

RESERVATIONS *(for Top 200 Restaurants only)* We used one of the following terms for our reservations policy: reservations required, reservations recommended, or no reservations. No reservations means either reservations are not necessary or are not accepted.

PARKING We've indicated a variety of options for parking in the facts lines at the end of each review.

ADDRESSES AND PHONE NUMBERS Every attempt has been made to provide accurate information on an establishment's location and phone number, but it's always a good idea to call ahead and confirm. For establishments with two or more locations, we try to provide information on the original or most recommended branches.

CHECKS AND CREDIT CARDS Many establishments that accept checks also require a major credit card for identification. Note that some accept only local checks. Credit cards are abbreviated in this book as follows: American Express (AE), Carte that will wow your new clients or be a stunning, romantic place to celebrate an anniversary or impress a first date.

We award four-star ratings sparingly, reserving them for what we consider truly the best. And once an establishment has earned our highest rating, everyone's expectations seem to rise. Readers often write us specifically to point out the faults in four-star establishments. With changes in chefs, management, styles, and trends, it's always easier to get knocked off the pedestal than to ascend it. Three-star establishments, on the other hand, seem to generate healthy praise. They exhibit outstanding qualities, and we get lots of love letters about them. The difference between two and three stars can sometimes be a very fine line. Two-star establishments are doing a good, solid job and are gaining attention, while one-star places are often dependable spots that have been around forever.

The restaurants and lodgings described in *Best Places Seattle* have earned their stars from hard work and good service (and good food). They're proud to be included in this book: look for our Best Places sticker in their windows. And we're proud to honor them in this, the eleventh edition of *Best Places Seattle*.

Blanche (CB), Diners Club (DC), Discover (DIS), Japanese credit card (JCB), MasterCard (MC), and Visa (V).

E-MAIL AND WEB SITE ADDRESSES E-mail and Web site addresses have been included where available. Please note that the Web is a fluid and evolving medium, and that Web pages are often "under construction" or, as with all time-sensitive information, may no longer be valid.

MAP INDICATORS The letter-and-number codes appearing at the end of most listings refer to coordinates on the fold-out map included in the front of the book. Single letters (for example, F7) refer to the Downtown Seattle map; double letters (FF7) refer to the Greater Seattle map on the flip side. If an establishment does not have a map code listed, its location falls beyond the boundaries of these maps.

HELPFUL ICONS Watch for these quick-reference symbols throughout the book:

FAMILY FUN Places that are fun, easy, and great for kids.

GOOD VALUE While not necessarily cheap, these places offer a good deal within the context of the region.

ROMANTIC These spots offer candlelight, atmosphere, intimacy, or other romantic qualities—kisses and proposals are encouraged!

EDITORS' CHOICE These are places that are unique and special to the city, such as a restaurant owned by a beloved local chef or a tourist attraction recognized around the globe.

Appears after listings for establishments that have wheelchair-accessible facilities.

INDEXES In addition to the general index at the back of the book, there are five specialized indexes: restaurants are indexed by star rating, features, and location at the beginning of the Restaurants chapter, and nightspots are indexed by features and locations at the beginning of the Nightlife chapter.

READER REPORTS At the end of the book is a report form. We receive hundreds of reports from readers suggesting new places or agreeing or disagreeing with our assessments. They greatly help in our evaluations, and we encourage you to respond.

PLANNING A TRIP

PLANNING A TRIP

How to Get Here

BY PLANE

Like most cities, Seattle hides its bustling airport on the outskirts of town where it can't mar the pretty skyline. **SEATTLE-TACOMA INTERNATIONAL AIRPORT** (17801 International Blvd, SeaTac; 206/431-4444; portseattle.org/seatac; map:OO6), better known simply as Sea-Tac (there's also a city named SeaTac, sans hyphen), is located 13 miles south of Seattle, about a half-hour freeway ride from downtown. In 2006 Sea-Tac was the 17th busiest airport in the country, serving just shy of 30 million passengers.

The airport currently has just two runways, only one of which can be used when low clouds are present—a whopping 44 percent of the time. In order to alleviate flight delays, a third (all-weather) runway is under construction and expected to be completed in late 2008 or early 2009. Construction of the third runway can cause traffic delays, so allow plenty of time to get to the airport.

Sea-Tac's central terminal enjoyed a major renovation just a few years ago and is now home to more than 35 restaurants and stores, including the Body Shop, Borders Books, Made in Washington, Anthony's Seafood & Fish Bar, and Dilettante Chocolates & Mocha Café. The central terminal, which is bounded by a curved wall of windows, provides the airport's only opportunity to view arriving and departing airplanes—a big hit with kids, as is the terminal's children's play area.

Travelers who need information or directions should look for roaming airport volunteers in blue jackets or "pathfinders" in red blazers or purple shirts carrying matching clipboards. These folks, available between 6am and 11pm daily, will point you in the right direction. Throughout the airport, families will find restrooms with changing tables; nearly all men's and women's restrooms, as well as the family restrooms, have them. If you need to check your e-mail, Laptop Lane, located in the north satellite terminal near the United Airlines gates, provides Internet access, phones, fax machines, and photocopying. In addition, high-speed wireless Internet access is available everywhere at Sea-Tac except the subway and upper floors of the garage. The fee is $7.95 for 24 hours of access for non–AT&T subscribers. Ground transportation information is available at a staffed booth in the baggage claim near carousel 12 and on the third floor of the airport garage. An Airport Information booth is located in the baggage claim across from carousel 12 and offers local trip suggestions seven days a week, along with a plethora of splashy travel brochures. International visitors in need of information and services should proceed to the inspection booths at Customs and Immigration, located in the south satellite, or the Airport Information booth outside the exit from the B gates. There they will find special phones to link them up with interpreters for more than 150 languages. For exhaustive information on airport services and operating conditions, call the **AIRPORT INFORMATION LINE** (206/431-4444): you can listen to recorded messages on everything from parking, paging, hotels, and customs to lost and found. Or go to the **AIRPORT WEB SITE** (portseattle.org/seatac).

The **SEA-TAC PARKING COMPLEX**, which offers 8,300 daily and hourly parking spaces, is connected to the main terminal via sky bridges on the fourth floor. It's self-serve when it comes to paying for parking, with automated pay stations also located on the fourth floor of the garage, so tickets should be kept with the parker, not in the car. Machines take cash, credit, and debit cards. Short-term parkers can pick a spot on the garage's fourth floor and pay $2 for up to 30 minutes and $4 for an hour. Daily parking, located on the top four floors (5–8) of the garage, costs $7 for 1 to 2 hours; $9 for 2 to 3 hours; $10 for 3 to 4 hours; and $2 per additional hour, up to $22 maximum per day. The airport also offers a reduced weekly parking rate. Travelers headed out for more than four days, but not more than seven days, pay a flat $99 rate. Valet parking is not available.

A repeating recorded message will remind you that there is no parking allowed in the ticketing/departures and baggage claim/arrivals drives (drop and go, or load and go only), but a free **CELL PHONE LOT** just two minutes from baggage claim allows drivers to park nearby while they wait for arriving passengers. The lot is located on S 170th Street, just east of the airport expressway, adjacent to the Doug Fox long-term parking lot.

For less expensive long-term parking, try the numerous **COMMERCIAL PARKING LOTS** in the vicinity of the airport. The following operate 24 hours a day and offer free shuttle service for their parking and car rental patrons: Thrifty Airport Parking (18836 International Blvd, SeaTac; 206/242-7275; thriftynorthwest.com), Park 'n' Fly (17600 International Blvd, SeaTac; 206/433-6767; parknflyseattle.com), and Doug Fox Airport Parking (2626 S 170th St, SeaTac; 206/248-2956; dougfoxparking.com). You'll find the best customer service—and often the lowest rates—at Seattle SeaTac Airport Parking (2701 S 200th St, SeaTac; 206/824-2544; seatacpark.com). Check the Web site for specials a few days before your trip.

AIRPORT TRANSPORTATION

One of the easiest and least expensive ways of getting to Sea-Tac Airport from downtown (or vice versa) is on the **GRAY LINE OF SEATTLE DOWNTOWN AIRPORTER** (206/626-6088; graylineseattle.com). Going to the airport, the shuttle stops every 30 minutes at downtown hotels, including the Madison Renaissance, Crowne Plaza, Fairmont Olympic, Hilton, Sheraton, Grand Hyatt, Warwick, and Westin, from 5am to 11pm. Going from the airport to the hotels, it runs from 5:30am to 11pm at the same intervals, leaving from the north and south ends of the airport baggage claim area. The ride is about 30 to 45 minutes between the Madison Renaissance and the airport. Cost for adults is $17 round trip ($10.25 one way); children are $12 round trip ($7.25 one way); and children under 2 ride free.

SHUTTLE EXPRESS (425/981-7000 or 800/487-7433; shuttleexpress.com) provides door-to-door van service to and from the airport, serving the entire Greater Seattle area, from Everett to Tacoma. The company guarantees that if a rider misses a flight because of their service, Shuttle Express will cover any additional cost to rebook the flight. The cost ranges from $19 to $34 one way in the Greater Seattle area. Costs to and from outlying areas are higher, and groups traveling from a single pickup point pay reduced rates. You may share the ride with other passengers, so expect to stop elsewhere en route. To ensure availability, make reservations two to three days ahead for trips to the airport. The shuttle from Sea-Tac operates 24 hours a day and requires no advance notice; the service desk is located on the third floor of the parking garage.

Thanks to a King County ordinance, **TAXIS** to the airport from the downtown Seattle hotel district cost a flat fee of $28 for one or two people—"downtown" limits stretch from the waterfront at Pier 70 to the intersection of Broad and Mercer streets, east to Interstate 5 and Boren Avenue, and south to where the freeway meets S Dearborn Street. A ride from the airport to downtown runs about $33, not including tip. At the airport, catch a cab on the third floor of the parking garage.

Not surprisingly, public transit offers the cheapest ride to the airport. **KING COUNTY METRO TRANSIT** (206/553-3000; transit.metrokc.gov) delivers travelers to Sea-Tac via two routes: the number 174 (which can take up to an hour from downtown) and the number 194 (a 30-minute ride via I-5). Both buses run every half hour, seven days a week, and both stop on the baggage claim level of the airport. Fares are $1.25 one way, $2 during rush hour.

The long-awaited **LIGHT RAIL CONNECTION** between downtown Seattle and Sea-Tac Airport is expected to be completed in 2009, offering travelers a fast, convenient way to get to the airport. Trains will run to and from Sea-Tac every 6 to 10 minutes, dropping passengers at a station that is just a four-minute walk away from the main terminal. A pedestrian bridge will link the light rail station to the airport garage.

BY CHARTER OR PRIVATE AIRPLANE

Most **AIRPLANE AND HELICOPTER CHARTER COMPANIES** are based at King County International Airport/Boeing Field (206/296-7380; metrokc.gov/airport; map:KK6) south of downtown. Other airplane charters are located north of the city at Snohomish County Airport Paine Field in Everett (425/353-2110; painefield.com) and south of Seattle at Renton Municipal Airport Clayton Scott Field in Renton (425/430-7471; rentonwa.gov; map:MM3). Call the Seattle automated flight service station (206/767-2726) for up-to-date weather reports and flight-related information.

BY BUS

GREYHOUND (811 Stewart St, Downtown; 206/628-5526 or 800/231-2222; greyhound.com; map:I4) is usually the least expensive way to get to Seattle by bus. The station is within walking distance of the downtown retail core.

BY TRAIN

The wide seats inside and beautiful vistas outside make **AMTRAK** (800/872-7245, passenger information and reservations; 206/382-4128, baggage and package express; 206/382-4713, lost and found; amtrak.com) the most comfortable and scenic mode of transportation to Seattle. Especially eye catching is the Portland-to-Seattle route, some of which runs along the shores of Puget Sound. The Coast Starlight leaves Seattle headed south to Portland, San Francisco, and Los Angeles; the Amtrak Cascades travels north to Vancouver, British Columbia; and the Empire Builder heads east to Chicago via Spokane. The train pulls up to King Street Station (303 S Jackson St, Pioneer Square; map:P7) at the south end of downtown.

BEST PLACE
TO GET OUT OF THE RAIN?

"Theo Chocolates for a tour of the factory. You get to eat your weight in chocolate."

Rachel Hart, Seattle *magazine editorial director*

BY CAR

The primary north-south artery in Seattle is **INTERSTATE 5**, which runs south from Seattle through Tacoma and the state capital of Olympia to Portland, Oregon (185 miles south of Seattle), and on through California. To the north via I-5 lies Vancouver BC, just 143 miles away. More or less parallel to I-5 is the north-south route **HIGHWAY 99**, which becomes Aurora Avenue for a stretch through the city. Just south of downtown, I-5 meets **INTERSTATE 90**, Seattle's primary connection to all points east. From downtown, I-90 crosses a floating bridge over Lake Washington to the eastern suburbs, then crosses the Cascades at Snoqualmie Pass before dropping down to the Columbia plateau of Eastern Washington and curving its way toward Spokane, 280 miles east. The other link to the Eastside suburbs is **HIGHWAY 520**, which leaves I-5 just north of downtown, crosses a different floating bridge, and passes near the Bellevue and Kirkland town centers before ending in Redmond. Both east-west highways connect with **INTERSTATE 405**, which runs north-south through the suburbs east of Lake Washington. To go to and from the Olympic Peninsula to the west, take a scenic **FERRY RIDE** across Puget Sound (see the Ferry Rides sidebar in the Day Trips chapter).

A cautionary note: Seattle's rapid growth over the last decade has led to traffic that can be nerve defying, with commuters clogging both the freeways and arterials. The raising of the Ballard, Fremont, University, and Montlake bridges to let sailboats and barges pass through can also tack on extra time to a drive. Road warriors need to be on the defensive. Try to plan your arrival and departure times to avoid rush hours, generally 7am to 9am and 3pm to 7pm weekdays.

When to Visit

No doubt about it, the best time to visit Seattle is summer, when blue skies and sunshine chase away the winter gloom, and longer days mean there is finally enough time to take advantage of all the festivals, historic landmarks, natural resources, stunning views, and good eats the city has to offer. The baseball season is in full swing, and even if the Mariners are flailing, there's no better way to spend a day than soaking up the outfield sunshine with a cold local beer.

Late fall and winter do have their charms, however. Sure, there's more rain and considerably lower temperatures, but the city unites in support of the Seahawk and Husky football teams, and celebrates the return of the thriving theater and arts season. Plus, hotel rates, airfares, and admission fees are often lower that time of year.

WEATHER

Have mercy on the region's weather forecasters: between the mountains, the warm offshore currents, and the cold fronts sweeping down from the north, predicting weather here is an exercise in equivocation. Your best bet is to be prepared for anything, though clouds are the most common denominator. If you're trying to avoid rain on your visit, July and August are the warmest and driest months, though Seattleites often spend the Fourth of July under cover or wrapped in fleece. Even when it does finally warm up, temperatures rarely top 80 degrees. Since so few days are uncomfortably hot, air conditioners are notably absent. Things get wet in winter, with averages of around 5 to 6 inches of rain a month from November through January, but temperatures are mild enough that snow and ice are infrequent. On those rare days when the slick stuff does appear, though, watch out: the town grinds to a halt, and the streets become one big Roller Derby. The table below shows averages of temperature and precipitation.

AVERAGE TEMPERATURE AND PRECIPITATION BY MONTH

Month	Daily Maximum Temp. (degrees F)	Daily Minimum Temp. (degrees F)	Monthly Precipitation (inches)
JANUARY	46	36	5.13
FEBRUARY	50	37	4.18
MARCH	53	39	3.75
APRIL	58	42	2.59
MAY	64	47	1.78
JUNE	70	52	1.49
JULY	75	55	0.79
AUGUST	76	56	1.02
SEPTEMBER	70	52	1.63
OCTOBER	60	46	3.19
NOVEMBER	51	40	5.90
DECEMBER	46	36	5.62

Source: weather.com

Events to Plan Around

FEBRUARY

Northwest Flower and Garden Show

WASHINGTON STATE CONVENTION & TRADE CENTER, 9TH AVENUE AND PIKE STREET, DOWNTOWN; 800/569-2832; GARDENSHOW.COM/SEATTLE/INDEX/INDEX.ASP

This five-day horticultural extravaganza features nearly 300 exhibits and more than 6 acres of gardens. Held in early February, the show brings an early spring to the Northwest. General admission is $19 (half day $13).

APRIL

Skagit Valley Tulip Festival

MOUNT VERNON, 60 MILES NORTH OF SEATTLE VIA I-5; 360/428-5959; TULIPFESTIVAL.ORG

Washington's temperate climate makes it a viable, if less exotic, alternative to the Netherlands when it comes to raising tulips. During the entire month of April, Mount Vernon seizes the moment and entertains visitors with a street fair, parades, and thousands of acres of tulips. Admission prices vary from farm to farm.

MAY

Opening Day of Boating Season

ALONG THE MONTLAKE CUT BETWEEN LAKE WASHINGTON AND LAKE UNION; 206/325-1000; SEATTLEYACHTCLUB.ORG

Boat owners from the Northwest and beyond come to participate in this festive ceremonial regatta, which officially kicks off the nautical summer on the first Saturday in May. Parade entry and log boom moorage are free.

Seattle International Children's Festival

SEATTLE CENTER; 206/684-7338; SEATTLEINTERNATIONAL.ORG

Professional children's performers come from all over the world for this popular event. Crafts, storytelling, puppet shows, and musical and theater performances entertain kids and their parents for six days in mid-May. Tickets are $18 in advance, $20 at the door.

Seattle International Film Festival

NESHOLM FAMILY LECTURE HALL AT MARION OLIVER MCCAW HALL, 321 MERCER ST, SEATTLE CENTER, AND VARIOUS THEATERS AROUND TOWN; 206/464-5830; SEATTLEFILM.COM

Film buffs schedule vacation time around this cinematic bonanza, held over a 3½-week period from late May to mid-June. Tickets can be competitive to acquire, so plan ahead. The most recent festival boasted films from 60 countries, with 198 narrative films, 60 documentaries, and 141 shorts. Admission to each film is $9, $7.50 for SIFF group members and students with ID. Series passes are $200, $150 for SIFF group members.

JUNE

Fremont Fair

N 34TH STREET, ALONG THE FREMONT SHIP CANAL; 206/694-6706; FREMONTFAIR.COM

The artsy, eccentric Fremont neighborhood celebrates summer's beginning with a solstice parade, music, crafts booths, food, dance, and naked cyclists. This event gets bigger and crazier every year. Participation and ogling are free.

JULY

Seafair

VARIOUS LOCATIONS THROUGHOUT SEATTLE AND SURROUNDING COMMUNITIES; 206/728-0123; SEAFAIR.COM

Seattle's frenzied summer fete has been around since 1950. Highlights include milk carton boat races at Green Lake, numerous neighborhood street fairs and parades, a marathon in Bellevue, breathtaking performances by the Blue Angels, and hydroplane races on Lake Washington. Parades and street fairs are free; prices for athletic and sporting events vary.

Chinatown/International District Summer Festival

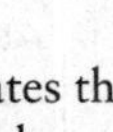

HING HAY PARK, 423 MAYNARD AVE S, INTERNATIONAL DISTRICT; 206/382-1197; CIDBIA.ORG

The Chinatown/International District's mid-July extravaganza celebrates the richness and diversity of Asian culture with dancing, instrumental and martial arts performances, food booths, arts and crafts, and the wildly popular Karaoke Idol contest. Admission is free.

AUGUST

Auction of Washington Wines

CHATEAU STE. MICHELLE WINERY, 14111 NE 145TH ST, WOODINVILLE; 206/667-9436; AUCTIONOFWASHINGTONWINES.ORG

This three-day event in mid-August attracts wine enthusiasts from around the state and raises hundreds of thousands of dollars for Children's Hospital and Regional Medical Center. Cost for individual events varies.

SEPTEMBER

Bumbershoot

SEATTLE CENTER; 206/281-7788; BUMBERSHOOT.ORG

Though a bumbershoot is an umbrella, the weather on Labor Day weekend, when this multi-arts festival is held, usually doesn't require one. Bumbershoot hosts craftspeople, writers, comedians, poets, and both big-name national (think R.E.M.) and local musical performers. The festival occurs in venues throughout the Seattle Center, and a $30 daily pass is all you need.

NOVEMBER

Seattle Marathon

FIFTH AVENUE, BETWEEN HARRISON AND MERCER STREETS; 206/729-3660; SEATTLEMARATHON.ORG
Each year on Thanksgiving weekend thousands of runners brave wind, rain, and chilly temperatures to participate in Seattle's most popular footrace. The 26.2-mile event begins downtown near Experience Music Project and wraps up in Seattle Center's Memorial Stadium. Registration fees vary.

DECEMBER

Christmas Ship Festival

VISITS BEACHES CITYWIDE; 206/623-1445; ARGOSYCRUISES.COM
Since *Sleepless in Seattle*, the rest of the world has associated Christmas in Seattle with lighted boats skimming along the water. Area musical groups climb aboard to serenade folks gathered at 45 different waterfront locations, and there's no charge to watch from shore. Call for a schedule.

Time

Seattle is on Pacific standard time, which is three hours behind New York, two hours behind Chicago, one hour behind Denver, one hour ahead of Anchorage, and two hours ahead of Honolulu. Currently, daylight saving time begins the second Sunday in March and ends the first Sunday in November. Because Seattle is located so far north (between the 47th and 48th latitudes), residents enjoy long daylight hours in summer, with sunrises before 6am and sunsets well after 9pm.

What to Bring

It isn't easy to pack lightly for a visit to Seattle. Our unpredictable weather means that you should be prepared for warm days, cool days, wet days, and everything in between, especially if you're visiting in spring or fall.

Bring layers that you can add or remove. Even summer evenings can be cool, so pack a sweater or light jacket. Sunglasses are a must year-round, and though most locals are too stubborn to carry an umbrella, it's a good idea to have one. Tuck a small one in your suitcase, borrow one from your hotel, or buy one at any of the tourist shops near Pike Place Market. If you plan to take walking tours of the city, wear water-resistant shoes and wool socks. When choosing what to wear, remember that Seattle pioneered the art of dressing casual. Suits and ties are mostly seen only in the downtown business district; otherwise, jeans, khakis, T-shirts, and fleece jackets are ubiquitous. With a few exceptions, even the most expensive restaurants and chichi clubs allow patrons to wear jeans, and only a few require a jacket.

If you want to stay connected while you're away from home, bring your laptop. You'll find hundreds of outposts—including coffee shops, stores, hotels, parks, and buses—offering wireless Internet access, much of it free (see the Unplugged sidebar in this chapter.)

Smoking

In December 2005 the state of Washington banned smoking in all public places, including hotels and bars. The only exception is Indian casinos, because they are exempt from state laws. In addition, smokers must stay 25 feet away from any door or window, so don't be surprised to see small groups of people lighting up outside office buildings and restaurants. Some restaurants in Seattle do have outdoor patios that allow smoking, but they are far less common than in cities with warmer climates.

General Costs

Seattle has shaken off its tech-bust hangover, and its economic outlook is quite rosy. As a result of the improved economy, numerous new restaurants, hotels, and clothing boutiques have popped up all over the city, and prices for amenities have climbed.

Housing costs, too, are extremely high. According to the National Association of Realtors, in the fourth quarter of 2006 the median home price in the Seattle-Tacoma-Bellevue area had risen to $372,000, lower than San Francisco, Los Angeles, New York City, and Washington DC, but well above Portland, Chicago, St. Louis, and Minneapolis.

Costs for quotidian items are in keeping with the region and are relative to any robust, big city.

AVERAGE COSTS FOR LODGING AND FOOD

Double room	
INEXPENSIVE	**$85–$150**
MODERATE	**$150–$250**
EXPENSIVE	**$250 AND UP**
Lunch for one (including beverage and tip)	
INEXPENSIVE	**$9–$13**
MODERATE	**$13–$20**
EXPENSIVE	**$20 AND UP**
Beverages in a restaurant	
GLASS OF WINE	**$6–$12**
PINT OF BEER	**$4–$6**

COCA-COLA	**$1.50**
DOUBLE TALL LATTE	**$3.50**

Other common items

MOVIE TICKET	**$9–$10**
ROLL OF FILM	**$5**
TAXI PER MILE	**$2**
RAIN JACKET FROM REI	**$70–$450**
SEATTLE SOUVENIR T-SHIRT	**$12–$15**

Tips for Special Travelers

FAMILIES WITH CHILDREN

In an emergency, call 911, 24 hours a day. For questions about your child's health, growth, or development, call the **CHILDREN'S RESOURCE LINE** (206/987-2500 or 866/987-2500), a service provided by Children's Hospital & Regional Medical Center. If you think your child has ingested a toxic substance, call the **WASHINGTON POISON CENTER** (800/222-1222; wapc.org). A local publication, **PARENTMAP** (206/709-9026; parentmap.com), serves as a resource for parents and is available free at many libraries, grocery stores, and other businesses catering to families.

BEST PLACE
TO LET THE KIDS RUN FREE?

"The Seattle Children's Museum—they've made it adult-proof."

Greg Nickels, mayor of Seattle

The majority of downtown hotels cater heavily to business travelers. This means that family-oriented amenities such as swimming pools, game rooms, and inexpensive restaurants are more readily found at hotels outside the downtown area. Many hotels allow kids to stay free when traveling with their parents, so ask when you make reservations. Most major restaurants have children's menus.

Watch for this icon throughout the book ; it indicates places and activities that are great for families.

SENIORS

SENIOR SERVICES OF SEATTLE–KING COUNTY (2208 2nd Ave, Belltown; 206/448-5757; seniorservices.org; map:H7) runs a referral service for seniors, offering information about health and welfare resources and transportation and mobility services. It also publishes a newsletter called *Passport* that lists upcoming events for seniors, including fairs, volunteer activities, opportunities for flu shots, and some happenings at neighborhood senior centers. For

PUBLIC TRANSIT, a Regional Reduced Fare Permit, or senior bus pass, is $3 for people 65 and older. The passes are good for life and reduce the fare to 25 cents on all buses or 50 cents during peak hours. Senior passes can be purchased in person at Metro's King Street Center customer service office (201 S Jackson St, Pioneer Square; 206/553-3060; map:O8) or the Transportation Connection customer service office (Rainier Square, 1301 5th Ave, Downtown; map:K6).

BEST PLACE
TO BE A LOCAL?

"The kitchenette counter at Oriental Mart. 'Aunties' Leila and Joy—the sisters who run this little Filipino lunch counter—will make you feel like family while you visit. Chatting over chicken adobo, you'll soon forget you're sitting in the heart of tourist central."

Nancy Leson, food critic for The Seattle Times

PEOPLE WITH DISABILITIES

For information about using public transportation, call the **KING COUNTY METRO ACCESSIBLE SERVICE REGISTRATION OFFICE** (206/263-3113). After registering for services, riders can then call the Access Ride Line for reservations (206/205-5000 or 206/749-4286 TTY). For tour companies and other private companies offering mobility services, call **SEATTLE'S CONVENTION & VISITORS BUREAU** (206/461-5840; visitseattle.org). **THE DEAF/BLIND SERVICE CENTER** (206/323-9178; seattledbsc.org) offers volunteers and helpers for hire who assist deaf or blind Washington state residents in taking walks, grocery shopping, or going to the bank. Visitors from elsewhere in Washington state can contact the center in advance of their trip for a list of volunteers to call directly for assistance. **THE WASHINGTON TALKING BOOK AND BRAILLE LIBRARY** (2021 9th Ave, Downtown; 206/615-0400 or 206/615-0418 TTY; wtbbl.org; map:G4) has thousands of recorded and Braille titles available for loan.

WOMEN

Seattle is known as a relatively safe city, but as in most cities, women travelers should take extra precautions at night, especially in Belltown, the University District, and Pioneer Square. **THE UNIVERSITY OF WASHINGTON WOMEN'S CENTER** (4014 University Wy NE, Cunningham Hall, University District; 206/685-1090; depts.washington.edu/womenctr; map:FF6) is open to students as well as the general public and offers an extensive library, job listings, a community bulletin board, and class information. For health and reproductive services, call **PLANNED PARENTHOOD** (2001 E Madison St, Capitol Hill; 206/328-7700; plannedparenthood.org; map:HH6).

PET OWNERS

Pet-friendly hotels are one of the hottest travel trends in Seattle, so visitors with pets will find themselves welcome just about everywhere—including the luxurious new **HOTEL 1000** and the artsy and very hip **HOTEL MAX**. Refer to guidebooks such as *The Dog Lover's Companion to the Pacific Northwest* by Val Mallinson (Avalon, 2005) and *The Dog Lover's Companion to Seattle* by Steve Giordano (Avalon, 2001) for other places your dog or cat is welcome to share your room.

Mid- to high-end pet supply stores are scattered throughout town, including **BARK** (5338 Ballard Ave N, Ballard; 206/783-4972; barknaturalpet.com; map:EE8), **PET ELEMENTS** (6701 California Ave SW, West Seattle; 206/932-0457; map:JJ9), and **THREE DOG BAKERY** (1408 1st Ave, Downtown; 206/364-9999; threedog.com; map:J7). There's also an in-city doggie day care, **THE BARKING LOUNGE** (500 Dexter Ave N, South Lake Union; 206/382-1600; barkinglounge.com; map:D3).

Seattle boasts 11 spacious and well-tended off-leash areas within the city limits. For overall information on Seattle's off-leash areas (listed below), call the **SEATTLE PARKS AND RECREATION DEPARTMENT** (206/684-4075; seattle.gov/parks).

BLUE DOG POND PARK (Martin Luther King Jr. Way at Massachusetts Street, Central District; map:II6) has a giant blue dog sculpture at the park's entrance.

GENESEE PARK (46th Avenue S and S Genesee Street, Columbia City; map: JJ5) has a fully fenced off-leash area east of the playfield.

GOLDEN GARDENS PARK (8498 Seaview Pl NW, Ballard; map:DD9) has a fenced 2.2-acre off-leash area in the upper portion of the park.

I-5 COLONNADE (beneath I-5 south of E Howe Street, between Lakeview Boulevard and Franklin Avenue E, Eastlake; map:FF7) opened in 2005.

JOSE RIZAL PARK (1008 12th Ave S, Beacon Hill; map:II6) has a small off-leash area at the north end of the park.

MAGNUSON PARK (6500 Sand Point Wy, Sand Point; map:EE5) offers the city's largest off-leash area, with water access to Lake Washington in the northeast corner.

NORTHACRES PARK (West of I-5 at N 130th Street, Northgate; map:DD6) features an off-leash playground in the northeast corner of the park.

PLYMOUTH PILLARS PARK (Spans Boren Avenue between Pike and Pine streets, Capitol Hill; map:J3) opened in early 2006 and serves residents of Capitol Hill's Pike-Pine corridor.

REGRADE PARK (2251 3rd Ave, Belltown; map:G7) is a favorite stop for people and dogs who live downtown.

WESTCREST PARK (8806 8th Ave SW, West Seattle; map:KK8) has a dog area nearly 4 acres in size along the southern border of the reservoir.

WOODLAND PARK (N 59th Street and Aurora Avenue N, Green Lake; map:FF7) has a dog area in the park's northeastern portion, west of the tennis courts.

Outside of Seattle, nearby off-leash parks include Mercer Island's **LUTHER BURBANK PARK** (206/236-3545; ci.mercer-island.wa.us; map:II4), **MARINA BEACH** in Edmonds (425/771-0230; ci.edmonds.wa.us), and the Disneyland of all dog parks, **MARYMOOR PARK** (206/296-8687; metrokc.gov/parks; map: FF1) in Redmond, which features a 40-acre off-leash area maintained by local nonprofit Serve Our Dog Areas (425/881-0148; soda.org).

GAYS AND LESBIANS

Seattle is a gay-friendly city. Its large gay community has traditionally been concentrated in the Capitol Hill neighborhood, which offers a variety of gay-focused bars, dance clubs, and bed-and-breakfasts. **SEATTLE GAY NEWS** (1605 12th Ave, Ste 31, Capitol Hill; 206/324-4297; sgn.org; map:GG6) is a weekly community newspaper, available at many shops, bars, and bookstores around Capitol Hill. The GSBA Guide & Directory, a helpful guide to the businesses and services of the gay community, is available at stores in the area or by contacting the **GREATER SEATTLE BUSINESS ASSOCIATION** (2150 N 107th St, Ste 205, Northgate; 206/363-9188; thegsba.org; map: DD7). **BAILEY/COY BOOKS** (414 Broadway E, Capitol Hill; 206/323-8842; baileycoybooks.com; map:HH6) offers a community bulletin board and has a staff that is knowledgeable about local resources and events. The **LESBIAN RESOURCE CENTER** (2214 S Jackson St, Central District; 206/322-3953; lrc.net; map:HH6) provides business referrals, therapy and physician referrals, and housing information. For information on the city's many gay clubs and bars, see the Nightlife chapter.

BEST PLACE
TO HAIL A CAB?

"New York City. No place in the Northwest comes close!"

Herb Weisbaum, consumer reporter, KOMO News

FOREIGN VISITORS

Seattle hosts a number of foreign-exchange brokers and foreign banks. **TRAVELEX** (400 Pine St, Downtown, 206/682-4525, map:J6; and Sea-Tac Airport, main terminal, 206/248-0401, map:OO6; travelex.com) and **THOMAS COOK CURRENCY SERVICES** (10630 NE 8th St, Bellevue; 425/462-8225; thomascook.com; map:HH3) are foreign-exchange brokers. Foreign banks with branches in Seattle include the **BANK OF TOKYO** (900 4th Ave, Ste 4000, Downtown; 206/382-6000; btm.co.uk; map:L6) and **HSBC** (600 University St, Ste 2323, Downtown; 206/233-0888; hsbcusa.com; map:K5). In addition, **WELLS FARGO** (wellsfargo.com) offers foreign currency exchange at its branches, including the Seattle main (999 3rd Ave, Downtown; 206/292-3415; map:L6) and Westlake Center (1620 4th Ave, Downtown; 206/287-0039; map:I6) locations.

A multitude of services are available for the foreign visitor who does not speak English as a first language. **ASSOCIATES IN CULTURAL EXCHANGE** (200 W Mercer St, Ste 108, Lower Queen Anne; 206/217-9644; cultural.org; map:B6) offers language classes and arranges for summertime exchanges and visits by foreigners to American homes. **YOHANA INTERNATIONAL** (5905 190th Pl SW, Lynnwood; 425/771-8465) and the **LANGUAGE CONNECTION** (16436 SE 128th St, Renton; 425/277-9045; map:MM2) provide document translation as well as interpreters in dozens of languages, including those of Africa, Asia, and Europe. The **MILMANCO CORPORATION** (651 Strander Blvd, Ste 100, Tukwila; 206/575-3808; map:OO5) can help those involved in international business and in need of technical written translations (from and into foreign languages); rates vary. The **RED CROSS LANGUAGE BANK** (206/323-2345) provides on-call interpretive assistance at no charge to individuals.

Seattle's importance as a port city has brought it many foreign consulates, though not all are located within city limits. Some consulates are open only part-time, and others are closed to the public, so call ahead for an appointment before you visit.

AUSTRALIA, 401 Andover Park E, Tukwila; 206/575-7446
AUSTRIA, 416-A E Morris St, LaConner; 360/466-1100
BELGIUM, 2200 Alaskan Wy, Ste 470, Downtown; 206/728-5145
BOLIVIA, 15215 52nd Ave S, Ste 100, Tukwila; 206/244-6696
CAMBODIA, 1818 Westlake Ave N, Ste 315, Westlake; 206/217-0830
CANADA, 1501 4th Ave, Ste 600, Downtown; 206/443-1777
CHILE, 700 Sleater-Kinney Rd, Ste B-261, Lacey; 360/754-8747
CYPRUS, 5555 Lakeview Dr, Ste 200, Kirkland; 425/827-1700
DENMARK, 6204 E Mercer Wy, Mercer Island; 206/230-0888
FRANCE, 2200 Alaskan Wy, Ste 490, Downtown; 206/256-6184
HUNGARY, PO Box 578, Kirkland; 425/739-0631
ICELAND, 5610 20th Ave NW, Ballard; 206/783-4100
JAMAICA, 8223 S 222nd St, Kent; 253/872-8950
JAPAN, 601 Union St, Ste 500, Downtown; 206/682-9107
MALTA, PO Box 1104, Duvall; 425/788-3120
MEXICO, 2132 3rd Ave, Belltown; 206/448-3526
NETHERLANDS, 40 Lake Bellevue Dr, Ste 100, Bellevue; 425/637-3050
NEW ZEALAND, 10649 N Beach Rd, Bow; 360/766-8002
NORWAY, 1402 3rd Ave, Ste 806, Downtown; 206/623-3957
PERU, 3717 NE 157th St, Ste 100, Lake Forest Park; 206/714-9037
RUSSIA, 2001 6th Ave, Ste 2323, Belltown; 206/728-1910
SOUTH KOREA, 2033 6th Ave, Ste 1125, Belltown; 206/441-1011
SPAIN, 4709 139th Ave SE, Bellevue; 425/237-9373
SWEDEN, 520 Pike St, Ste 2200, Downtown; 206/622-5640
TAIWAN, 600 University St, Ste 2020, Downtown; 206/441-4586

Web Sites and Blogs

Seattleites are information junkies, and one of their favorite topics is . . . Seattle. So it's little wonder that there are numerous Web sites and blogs that serve visitors and locals alike. Some point the direction to the best seafood in town, and others give live-cam views of the traffic on the floating bridges. See listings within other chapters for specific Web site addresses and the Blog Boom sidebar in the Arts chapter for some of the city's best blogs.

HISTORYLINK.ORG Washington state, King County, and Seattle history
NWSOURCE.COM Seattle events, restaurants, clubs, shopping, attractions, and recreation
SEATTLE.GOV History, tours, city parks, employment
SEATTLEPI.COM *Seattle Post-Intelligencer* daily newspaper
SEATTLEST.COM A Web site about Seattle and everything that happens in it
SEATTLETIMES.COM *The Seattle Times* daily newspaper
SEATTLEWEEKLY.COM *Seattle Weekly* alternative newspaper
SPL.ORG Seattle Public Library
THESTRANGER.COM *The Stranger* alternative newspaper
VISITSEATTLE.ORG Seattle's Convention & Visitors Bureau
WASHINGTON.EDU University of Washington
WSDOT.WA.GOV Seattle traffic updates and cameras at the Washington State Department of Transportation site

Experience Seattle

In decades past, Seattle was considered something of a one-hit—at the most, three-hit—wonder. You came for the seafood, the Space Needle, or to commune with the great outdoors. For a brief period in the early 1990s, you maybe came to rub shoulders with alternative rock gods. But these days, Seattle is truly a renaissance city, and enthusiasts of the arts, music, fine dining, wine, professional sports, and superlative shopping have much to be excited about. So while it's easy to dabble and try a bit of everything Seattle has to offer, it's also fun to specialize and plan an entire trip around whatever you love most. Follow one or two of the themed guides we've assembled below, and you'll realize that Seattle has become a hot ticket no matter what show you've come to see.

CLASSIC SEATTLE: TOURISM'S GREATEST HITS

A young city by almost any measure, the largest city in Washington state has packed some interesting stories into its 150 years. The places and things that are classically Seattle may not be as old as the Liberty Bell or the Eiffel Tower, but they're icons just the same.

PIKE PLACE MARKET is part farmers' market, part tourist attraction, and part shopping mall. Arrive before 9am (8am May through October) to watch the Market come to life: grab a latte from the original Starbucks (1912 Pike Pl; 206/448-8762; starbucks.com) and wander among the farmers and craftspeople as they set up their wares. You'll get first pick of the abundant produce—including berries, peaches, and apples in season—to fuel your progress. Head into the depths of the Market to explore the unusual collection of shops, such as the **MARKET MAGIC SHOP** (206/624-4271), where Harry Potter wannabes can browse props or catch a prestidigitation demo, or **GOLDEN AGE COLLECTABLES** (206/622-9799), a kitschy warren of movie, comic book, and sports memorabilia. Don't miss Rachel, the giant bronze pig, or the entertaining and sometimes unusual street performers. **THE PIKE PLACE MARKET FOUNDATION** (206/774-5249; pikeplacemarket.org) offers hour-long tours that dish up the Market's history, shopping tips, and quirky anecdotes. Reservations are required 24 hours in advance for weekday tours and by 4pm Friday for weekend tours.

Just south of the Market is Seattle's historic district, **PIONEER SQUARE**, which is not so much a square as a neighborhood, centered around a triangular plaza and a two-block-long pedestrian mall and anchored by a 1909 pergola. Here you'll find many of the city's **ART GALLERIES**, as well as totem poles, shops, and restaurants. On weekend nights the neighborhood, with its numerous bars, is a magnet for 20-somethings in search of live music and drink specials. Literary devotees love the independently owned **ELLIOTT BAY BOOK COMPANY** (101 S Main St, Pioneer Square; 206/624-6600; elliottbaybook.com); in a city full of rabid readers, it's considered by many to be Seattle's best bookstore. History buffs shouldn't miss **BILL SPEIDEL'S UNDERGROUND TOUR** (608 1st Ave, Pioneer Square; 206/682-4646; undergroundtour.com), a guided walk beneath Seattle's streets and sidewalks, where the city's original roadways and storefronts were located.

Downtown, at **WESTLAKE CENTER** (5th Avenue and Pine Street, Downtown) you can hop the **MONORAIL** (206/905-2620; seattlemonorail.com), the country's first full-scale system of its kind, originally built in 1962 for the world's fair. The track is 1 mile long, ending at the 74-acre **SEATTLE CENTER** (305 Harrison St, Seattle Center; 206/684-7200; seattlecenter.com), also built for the fair. The monorail operates daily between 11am and 9pm.

At the Center, youngsters love the amusement park rides and games at the Fun Forest, and the smaller among them also enjoy the **CHILDREN'S MUSEUM** (Center House, Seattle Center; 206/441-1768; thechildrensmuseum.org); kids of all ages enjoy the hands-on exhibits and two Imax screens at the **PACIFIC SCIENCE CENTER** (200 2nd Ave N, Seattle Center; 206/443-2001; pacsci.org) and running around the **INTERNATIONAL FOUNTAIN**, which spurts water in time with music. Another absorbing attraction is the two-stage **SEATTLE CHILDREN'S THEATRE** (2nd Avenue N and Thomas Street, Seattle Center; 206/443-0807; sct.org), known for its imaginative performances of old favorites and future classics, afternoons and evenings, September through June.

EXPERIENCE MUSIC PROJECT (325 5th Ave N, Seattle Center; 206/367-5483; emplive.org) is billionaire Paul Allen's ode to American music. Inside the attention-grabbing building, which was designed by legendary architect

UNPLUGGED

Once known for its status as a "wired" city, Seattle now prides itself on its ability to connect sans wires or cables. Wireless Internet access (Wi-Fi) has become ubiquitous in Seattle, and not just at expected locations such as coffee shops. You'll find a gratis connection at a gas station in West Seattle, the entire Columbia City business district, and a posh downtown hair salon. Two **KING COUNTY METRO TRANSIT** (transit.metrokc.gov) routes (48 between Loyal Heights and Rainier Beach, and 197 between the University District and Federal Way) were the first in the country to offer free Wi-Fi on buses and were soon followed by regional bus service provider **COMMUNITY TRANSIT** (commtrans.org), which offers free wireless Internet access on routes 422 (Stanwood to downtown Seattle), 441 (Edmonds to Overlake), and 406 (Seaview to downtown Seattle). **SOUND TRANSIT** (soundtransit.org), too, provides a free Wi-Fi connection on select Route 545 (Redmond to Seattle) buses and on its Sounder commuter rail Everett to Seattle line. The city of Seattle provides free Wi-Fi service at four downtown parks: **OCCIDENTAL** (Occidental Avenue S and S Main Street, Pioneer Square; map:O7), **FREEWAY** (700 Seneca St, Downtown; map:K4), **WESTLAKE** (401 Pine St, Downtown; map:J6), and **VICTOR STEINBRUECK** (2001 Western Ave, Pike Place Market; map:H8). You can also connect at two King County parks (metrokc.gov/parks): **MARYMOOR** (6046 W Lake Sammamish Pkwy NE, Redmond; map:FF1) and **WHITE CENTER** (1321 SW 102nd St, White Center; map:MM7), as well as the Weyerhaeuser King County Aquatic Center (650 SW Campus Dr, Federal Way; map:RR6). Most branches of the **SEATTLE PUBLIC LIBRARY** (spl.org) and **KING COUNTY LIBRARY** (kcls.org) systems offer free Wi-Fi, as does the Center House at **SEATTLE CENTER** (seattlecenter.com). For a comprehensive list of free Wi-Fi spots in Seattle and surrounding communities, visit wififreespot.com.

—Monica Fischer

Frank Gehry, are interactive and interpretive exhibits, including an impressive collection of Jimi Hendrix memorabilia. The building also houses the **SCIENCE FICTION MUSEUM AND HALL OF FAME** (206/724-3428 or 877/367-5483; sfhomeworld.org).

The high point—literally—of Seattle Center is the 605-foot **SPACE NEEDLE** (206/443-2145; spaceneedle.com). If it's a clear day, take a ride to the top, where you can get an unequalled 360-degree overview of the city.

WHERE TO EAT: Pike Place Market's many dining options include the upscale French restaurant **CAMPAGNE** (86 Pine St, Pike Place Market; 206/728-2800; campagnerestaurant.com) and its more casual downstairs sidekick **CAFE CAMPAGNE** (1600 Post Alley, Pike Place Market; 206/728-2233), the charming **MATT'S IN THE MARKET** (94 Pike St, Ste 32, Pike Place Market; 206/467-7909; mattsinthemarket.com), and quaint **LE PICHET** (1933 First Ave, Pike Place Market; 206/256-1499; lepichetseattle.com), the closest you'll get to Paris in Seattle.

WHERE TO STAY: Steps away from the bustle of Pike Place Market is the **INN AT THE MARKET** (86 Pine St, Pike Place Market; 206/443-3600 or 800/446-4484; innatthemarket.com), which affords excellent water views and service. Just south of the Market is **INN AT HARBOR STEPS** (1221 1st Ave, Downtown; 888/728-8910; innatharborsteps.com) a boutique hotel located at the base of a high-rise residential building. **HOTEL 1000** (1000 1st Ave, Downtown; 206/957-1000; hotel1000seattle.com), Seattle's most luxurious new hotel, is located midway between the Pike Place Market and Pioneer Square, and offers impeccable service and a virtual golf course.

GRAPE EXPECTATIONS: CELEBRATE WASHINGTON WINE

Napa, schmapa. Washington is now the second-largest wine producer in the United States (behind California), with a stunning 500 wineries and nine major viticultural areas. It is estimated that the wine industry now has a $3 billion impact on the state's economy. Though the majority of Washington's wineries are located east of the Cascades, there are numerous vintners worth visiting on Seattle's side of the mountains.

WOODINVILLE, just 30 minutes northeast of Seattle, is home to nearly 30 wineries large and small, including the state's oldest and most visited winery, **CHATEAU STE. MICHELLE** (14111 NE 145th St, Woodinville; 425/415-3300; ste-michelle.com); the scenic **COLUMBIA WINERY** (14030 NE 145th St, Woodinville; 425/488-2776; columbiawinery.com), which boasts Washington's largest wine-tasting bar; and boutique favorites such as Betz Family Winery, DeLille Cellars, and Januik Winery.

Two annual, two-day events allow guests to visit all of the region's wineries, many of which are normally closed to the public or open by appointment only. April brings the **PASSPORT TO WOODINVILLE WEEKEND**, while December heralds the festive **ST. NICHOLAS DAY OPEN HOUSE**. Learn more about these events, which sell out far in advance, at woodinvillewinecountry.com.

You'll find an additional 10 wineries within two hours of Seattle on **BAINBRIDGE ISLAND**, **WHIDBEY ISLAND**, and the **NORTH OLYMPIC PENINSULA**. From Seattle, hop a ferry to Bainbridge Island, where Eleven Winery is located about 4 miles from the Winslow ferry terminal. Next, head to quaint Port Townsend and sample the wines of FairWinds Winery and Sorensen Cellars. Stop in at Lost Mountain Winery and Olympic Cellars on your way to Port Angeles, which is home to Black Diamond Winery, Camaraderie Cellars, and Harbinger Winery. On Whidbey Island, don't miss Greenbank Cellars and Whidbey Island Winery. For more information and suggested itineraries, visit northsoundwineries.org.

If you want to experience the best of Washington's wine bounty, but prefer to do so within the Seattle city limits, you're in luck. There's a wine bar in nearly every neighborhood where you can sample the state's ever-growing crop of award-winning wines.

In Pike Place Market, the **TASTING ROOM** (1924 Post Alley, Pike Place Market; 206/770-9463; winesofwashington.com) offers samples of wines from six different Washington wineries, along with a selection of gourmet meats and cheeses. Downtown, **PURPLE CAFÉ AND WINE BAR** (1225 4th Ave, Downtown; 206/829-2280; thepurplecafe.com) offers a massive tasting list along with full lunch and dinner menus. Ballard serves up two wine bars on historic Ballad Avenue: **PORTALIS** (5205 Ballard Ave NW, Ballard; 206/783-2007; portaliswines.com) and **DIVINO** (5310 Ballard Ave NW, Ballard; 206/297-0143; divinoseattle.com). Queen Anne is home to **BRICCO DELLA REGINA ANNA** (1525 Queen Anne Ave N, Queen Anne; 206/285-4900; briccoseattle.com), and Wallingford recently welcomed **SMASH WINE BAR & BISTRO** (1401 N 45th St, Wallingford; 206/547-3232; smashwine.com). Madison Park's **IMPROMPTU WINE BAR CAFÉ** (4235 E Madison St, Madison Park; 206/860-1569; impromptuwinebar.com) features wine, cocktails, and bites from a rotating list of world regions. In West Seattle, newcomer **BEÀTO FOOD AND WINE** (3247 California Ave SW, West Seattle; 206/923-1333; beatoseattle.com) focuses on Italian wines and cuisine.

WHERE TO EAT: BARKING FROG (14580 NE 145th St, Woodinville; 877/424-3930; willowslodge.com) and the **HERBFARM RESTAURANT** (14590 NE 145th St, Woodinville; 425/485-5300; theherbfarm.com) are located just a stone's throw from one another on the grounds of Willows Lodge. Barking Frog serves Northwest-inspired breakfast, lunch, and dinner, complemented by an extensive local wine list. The Herbfarm Restaurant offers one of our region's most creative and decadent dining experiences, with nine-course dinners paired with a handful of perfectly matched wines. See the Restaurants chapter for reviews.

WHERE TO STAY: WILLOWS LODGE (14580 NE 145th St, Woodinville; 877/424-3930; willowslodge.com; see review in the Lodgings chapter) offers Western Washington's only opportunity to slumber in the heart of wine country. The Woodinville Wine Country Package includes accommodations for two, plus wine tasting in the lodge's Fireside Lounge and at two local wineries. In town, at **HOTEL VINTAGE PARK** (1100 5th Ave, Downtown; 206/624-8000; hotelvintagepark.com; see review in the Lodgings chapter) rooms are named for Washington wineries and vineyards, and the industry is celebrated at nightly wine receptions. The hotel will even arrange a customized wine adventure for its guests, such as skydiving with a Washington winemaker.

SEATTLE AFLOAT: NAVIGATING THE CITY'S WATERWAYS

Seattle is a city almost entirely surrounded by water: Puget Sound on the west, Lake Washington on the east, and Lake Union to the north of downtown. You can take in the waterways from shore or from a boat—big or small, powered by a motor, the wind, or you.

At **FISHERMEN'S TERMINAL** (3919 18th Ave W, Interbay; 206/728-3395; portseattle.org) wander the docks and watch the launch of a large portion of the city's fishing fleet. Just over the Ballard Bridge is the **HIRAM M. CHITTENDEN LOCKS** (3015 NW 54th St, Ballard; 206/783-7059; nws.usace.army.mil), where you can watch boats rise and fall as they move between Puget Sound and the inland waterways. In season (generally June and July), don't miss the spectacle of thousands of salmon migrating through the fish ladder on the south side of the locks. Free guided tours are given March 1 through November 30.

For hands-on water work, rent a kayak at the **NORTHWEST OUTDOOR CENTER** (2100 Westlake Ave N, Westlake; 206/281-9694 or 800/683-0637; nwoc.com) on the west side of Lake Union or at **AGUA VERDE CAFE & PADDLE CLUB** (1303 NE Boat St, University District; 206/545-8570; aguaverde.com) on Portage Bay. At either place, staff will offer basic instructions and steer you in the right direction. Paddle past houseboats or through the Montlake Cut, painted with the inspirational slogans of local crew teams. If you prefer a canoe or a rowboat, try the **UW WATERFRONT ACTIVITIES CENTER** (behind Husky Stadium, University District; 206/543-9433; depts.washington.edu/ima/IMA_wac.php). At the south end of Lake Union, experienced sailors can rent a sailboat at the **CENTER FOR WOODEN BOATS** (1010 Valley St, South Lake Union; 206/382-2628; cwb.org), nonsailors can rent rowboats, and landlubbers can admire a collection of boats without getting their feet wet. Not far away is the starting point of the quacky **RIDE THE DUCKS OF SEATTLE** amphibious tours (near Seattle Center; 206/441-3825; rideTheducksofseattle.com). The tour leans toward corny, but the cheap laughs don't diminish the pleasure of cruising Lake Union. **THE ELECTRIC BOAT COMPANY** (2046 Westlake Ave N, Westlake; 206/223-7476; theelectricboatco.com) offers rentals of 21-foot electric boats that comfortably seat 10 adults. Captain the boat yourself, or hire one of the company's experienced skippers.

Downtown, at the waterfront, hop an **ARGOSY CRUISE** (Pier 55/56; 206/623-1445 or 800/642-7816; argosycruises.com) for a harbor tour of the working waterfront or one of the company's other tours. For an unnarrated but cheaper view of Puget Sound, head for the Colman Ferry Dock (Pier 52) and a **WASHINGTON STATE FERRY** (206/464-6400 or 888/808-7977; wsdot.wa.gov/ferries) for the 35-minute crossing to **BAINBRIDGE ISLAND**, where you can spend a few hours strolling its quaint downtown before the next return sailing. Take a seat on the south side of the boat for clear views of Mount Rainier in the distance and to watch the seagulls race the boat.

A few piers north of the ferry dock on the waterfront is the **SEATTLE AQUARIUM** (Pier 59, 1483 Alaskan Wy, Waterfront; 206/386-4300; seattleaquarium.org), with an impressive collection of cold- and warm-blooded creatures, including starfish, jellyfish, and cuddly looking otters. The underwater dome is a visitor favorite.

WHERE TO EAT: Tourists love **RAY'S BOATHOUSE** (6049 Seaview Ave NW, Ballard; 206/789-3770; rays.com) and **PALISADE** (2601 W Marina Pl, Magnolia; 206/285-1000; r-u-i.com/pli), and locals agree these restaurants have two of the city's best waterside views. **PONTI SEAFOOD GRILL** (301

3rd Ave N, Fremont; 206/284-3000; pontigrill.com) is a longtime local favorite with seasonal outdoor dining. Also serving good, fresh seafood is **WATERFRONT SEAFOOD GRILL** (Pier 70, 2801 Alaskan Wy, Waterfront; 206/956-9171; waterfrontpier70.com). In West Seattle, **SALTY'S ON ALKI** (1936 Harbor Ave SW, West Seattle; 206/937-1600; saltys.com) offers a stellar view of downtown and Puget Sound and a plentiful seafood brunch on the weekends. A casual option is **IVAR'S ACRES OF CLAMS** (Pier 54, Waterfront; 206/624-6852; ivars.net) on the Seattle waterfront, where you can opt for inside menu service or order fish-and-chips and sit outside, watching the ferries come and go on Puget Sound.

WHERE TO STAY: If you want to be lulled to sleep by the gentle sound of water, your best bet is the **EDGEWATER HOTEL** (Pier 67, 2411 Alaskan Wy, Waterfront; 206/728-7000 or 800/624-0670; edgewaterhotel.com), overlooking Puget Sound. Across the street to the south is the **MARRIOTT SEATTLE WATERFRONT** (2100 Alaskan Wy, Waterfront; 206/443-5000; seattlewaterfrontmarriott.com), which features a rare-in-Seattle outdoor pool.

THE PACIFIC RIM: DRAGONS AND DIM SUM

Seattle's geographic position on Puget Sound gives it an important role on the world's Pacific Rim. The Pacific Ocean links the city's port—and our culture—with several Asian nations. Their influences can be found throughout the city.

The best place to start is the **CHINATOWN/INTERNATIONAL DISTRICT**. Those expecting a Chinatown like that in other West Coast cities may be surprised by the mix of Japanese, Filipino, Korean, and Southeast Asian cultures. The sprawling **UWAJIMAYA VILLAGE** (600 5th Ave S, Chinatown/International District; 206/624-6248; uwajimaya.com) offers a wide range of Asian specialties, tanks of live fish and rare imported produce, a Japanese bookstore, and wonderful cooking accessories. In the deli and food court, you'll find hot and cold entrées, plus Asian pastries and an espresso counter. Uwajimaya also offers cooking classes.

Venture out of Uwajimaya to stroll the streets and admire the fresh produce and wares. Visit 1-acre **KOBE TERRACE PARK** (221 6th Ave S, Chinatown/International District; 206/684-4075; seattle.gov/parks), where Mount Fuji cherry trees and a 4-ton, 200-year-old Yukimidoro stone lantern were gifts from Seattle's sister city of Kobe, Japan. For a history of Seattle's Chinese immigrants, visit the **WING LUKE ASIAN MUSEUM** (407 7th Ave S, Chinatown/International District; 206/623-5124; wingluke.org), named for the city's first Chinese American City Council member, to see its intriguing permanent collection of photographs and artifacts that integrates the experiences of 10 Asian Pacific American groups. Rotating exhibits also document the Northwest Asian American experience. At press time, the museum was expected to move to its new home in the rehabilitated East Kong Yick Building at Eighth Avenue S and King Street sometime in 2008. Northeast of downtown is the **SEATTLE ASIAN ART MUSEUM** (1400 E Prospect St, Capitol Hill; 206/654-3100; seattleartmuseum.org), in Volunteer Park. Here, the original Seattle Art Museum building holds an extensive collection of Asian art; be sure to check out its Asian art library. Martial arts fans might want to venture into **LAKE VIEW CEMETERY** (1554 15th Ave E, Capitol Hill) next to the park, to find the graves of Bruce Lee and his son, Brandon Lee.

At the **WASHINGTON PARK ARBORETUM**, visit the **JAPANESE GARDEN** (1075 Lake Washington Blvd E, Madison Valley; 206/684-4725; seattle.gov/parks) from late February through November. The authentic garden was constructed under the direction of Japanese landscape architect Juki Iida in 1960. Tours are offered April through October, Wednesdays at 12:30pm, and Saturdays and Sundays at 12:30 and 2:30pm. Plan ahead if you want to attend a tea ceremony ($10) in the garden's teahouse, performed on Saturdays April through October.

Back in the Chinatown/International District, **THEATRE OFF JACKSON** (409 7th Ave S, Chinatown/International District; 206/340-1049; theatreoffjackson.org) offers a variety of cross-cultural programs and hosts the **NORTHWEST ASIAN AMERICAN FILM FESTIVAL** (nwaaff.org) each January.

WHERE TO EAT: For sushi and Japanese cuisine, head to **MANEKI RESTAURANT** (304 6th Ave S, Chinatown/International District; 206/622-2631), a favorite of local critics and residents. For Vietnamese food, visit **GREEN LEAF** (418 8th Ave S, Chinatown/International District; 206/340-1388) or the slightly more upscale **TAMARIND TREE** (1036 S Jackson St, Ste A, Chinatown/International District; 206/860-1404; tamarindtreerestaurant.com). For Szechuan, stop by **SEVEN STARS PEPPER SZECHUAN RESTAURANT** (1207 S Jackson St, Chinatown/International District; 206/568-6446), and for the popular nibbling festival that is a meal of dim sum, head for **JADE GARDEN** (424 7th Ave S, Chinatown/International District; 206/622-8181).

WHERE TO STAY: The historic **PANAMA HOTEL** (605½ S Main St, Chinatown/International District; 206/223-9242; panamahotel.net) was designed by a Japanese architect and University of Washington graduate. The 1910 structure houses the only remaining intact Japanese bathhouse in the United States, though it's for touring only: rooms share a bathroom down the hall.

LISTEN UP: SEATTLE IS FOR AUDIOPHILES

Most local musicians groan if they hear tourists talking about grunge. It's not that they have anything against the bands that made Seattle world famous in the 1980s and '90s; it's just that they know that Seattle music is—and always has been—a lot more.

One music lover (and sometime musician) who recognizes the diversity of the Seattle sound is local billionaire, Microsoft co-founder, and Hendrix überfan Paul Allen, who built a shrine to Northwest music: the **EXPERIENCE MUSIC PROJECT** (see Classic Seattle: Tourism's Greatest Hits).

Seattle rocks at night. Grab a copy of *Seattle Weekly* or *The Stranger* and check out the club listings, or just head straight for some of the city's most reliable nightspots. For jazz, try **DIMITRIOU'S JAZZ ALLEY** (2033 6th Ave, Downtown; 206/441-9729; jazzalley.com) or **TULA'S** (2214 2nd Ave, Belltown; 206/443-4221; tulas.com). At Ballard's **TRACTOR TAVERN** (5213 Ballard Ave NW, Ballard; 206/789-3599; tractortavern.citysearch.com), the music menu could be rock, country, folk, or rockabilly. **THE SHOWBOX AT THE MARKET** (1426 1st Ave, Downtown; 206/628-3151; showboxonline.com), a music staple since 1939, offers live semi-established, semi-alternative bands, plus funk and dance music on alternate nights. The venue recently took over alternative rock club The Fenix and renamed it **SHOWBOX SODO** (1700 1st Ave S, SoDo; 206/621-3151; showboxonline.com). Near Green Lake, the **LITTLE RED HEN** (7115 Woodlawn Ave NE, Green Lake; 206/522-1168; littleredhen.com) is the city's lone country music venue. On Capitol Hill, **NEUMOS** (925 E Pike St., Capitol Hill; 206/709-9467; neumos.com) is one of the city's most eclectic and cutting-edge music venues. For classical fare, try the **SEATTLE SYMPHONY** at Benaroya Hall (200 University St, Downtown; 206/215-4747 or 866/833-4747; seattlesymphony.org) or the **SEATTLE OPERA** at McCaw Hall (321 Mercer St, Seattle Center; 206/389-7676; seattleopera.org).

If you visit Seattle in the summer, plan ahead to get tickets for one of the area's multiple outdoor concerts. The **CONCERTS AT MARYMOOR** (6046 W Lake Sammamish Pkwy, Redmond; 206/628-0888; concertsatmarymoor.com) bring national adult contemporary acts such as Jackson Browne and Tracy Chapman to Marymoor Park. Other places to enjoy music al fresco include **CHATEAU STE. MICHELLE WINERY** (14111 NE 145th St, Woodinville; 425/415-3300; ste-michelle.com) and **WOODLAND PARK ZOO** (5500 Phinney Ave N, Phinney Ridge; 206/684-4892; zoo.org). The summer **KPLU JAZZ AND BLUES CRUISES** (253/535-7758 or 800/677-5758; kplu.org) navigate Puget Sound while offering up live music and a brunch buffet. It's a bit of a haul, but the House of Blues–owned **GORGE AMPHITHEATRE** (754 Silica Road NW, George; 206/628-0888; hob.com) in Eastern Washington, about a three-hour drive from Seattle, is one of the most beautiful spots in the state to catch national headliners such as Dave Matthews and Pearl Jam.

Time your visit around one of the annual festivals held at Seattle Center that sound as good as they look (and taste): the Memorial Day weekend **FOLKLIFE FESTIVAL** (nwfolklife.org) serves up a world view of music and dance; over Labor Day weekend, **BUMBERSHOOT** (bumbershoot.org) is an umbrella for the arts—from dance, film, and theater to visual arts—but has a heavy emphasis on music and consistently draws top national acts.

WHERE TO EAT: Music, not food, is the main attraction at most of these venues, however, the EMP's **REVOLUTION BAR & GRILL** (325 5th Ave N, Seattle Center; 206/770-2777; emplive.com) offers a menu that will hit the spot. Elvis fans flock to **MAMA'S MEXICAN KITCHEN** (2334 2nd Ave, Belltown; 206/728-6262; mamas.com), where an entire small dining room and a burrito are dedicated to the King.

WHERE TO STAY: Hipsters, musicians, and DJs often stay at the **ACE HOTEL** (2423 1st Ave, Belltown; 206/448-4721; acehotel.com), within walking distance of many venues, or the artsy **HOTEL MAX** (620 Stewart St, Downtown; 866/833-6299; hotelmaxseattle.com), just a couple of blocks from the Paramount Theatre.

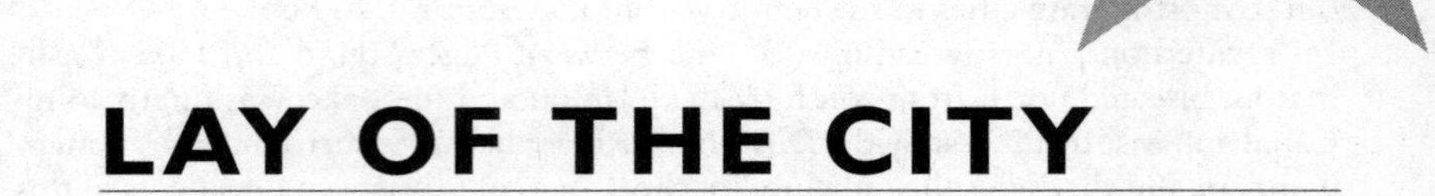

LAY OF THE CITY

LAY OF THE CITY

Orientation

Seattle is like those women that other women want to hate but can't because they're too damned nice. Not only does it have brains—ranking annually as one of the most literate cities in the country—but it's beautiful, to boot.

Situated on a narrow isthmus of land between Puget Sound and Lake Washington, bisected north from south by Lake Union and the Lake Washington Ship Canal and east from west by the Duwamish River, the city is surrounded by watery wonders. But that's not the only lure for the droves of tourists and residents in this city of more than 550,000 people. We've also got mountains aplenty. Directly to the west of Puget Sound loom the Olympic Mountains. East of Lake Washington, the Cascades stretch in a jagged line just 50 miles away. Mount Rainier plays hide-and-seek 67 miles south of downtown, and on clear days you can glimpse Glacier Peak, about 70 miles northeast, and Mount Baker, about 110 miles northeast.

Within the boundaries of these imposing geographic landmarks lies a rapidly growing urban area. Because the city's parts developed in relative isolation—cut off from one another by canals, lakes, and bridges—Seattle boasts a distinct collection of neighborhoods. At the city's heart stands the famous **PIKE PLACE MARKET** (Pike Street and 1st Avenue; map:J8), an authentic smorgasbord of food, flowers, entertainment, and art that has served local residents and visitors for a century. Taking the steps down the steep hill just west of the Market leads you to the **SEATTLE WATERFRONT** (along Alaskan Way; map:K8), brimming with shops, restaurants, and the always busy ferry docks that link the city to Bainbridge Island and other points west. Directly east of the Market is an ever-growing shopping district dominated by **WESTLAKE CENTER** (Pine Street and 4th Avenue; map:I6) and **PACIFIC PLACE** (600 Pine St; map:I5), and fanning out in all directions. Interspersed throughout the shopping area is Seattle's major office and financial district.

At the southern end of downtown lies historic **PIONEER SQUARE** (along 1st and 2nd avenues, between James Street and S Jackson Street; map:N8), the first area of Seattle to be rebuilt after the Great Fire of 1889. In February 2001, a 6.8-magnitude earthquake caused a rain of bricks from crumbling facades and considerable damage to some of the oldest buildings. But most were left intact, including the many shops, bars, and galleries in the area. Just east of Pioneer Square is the **CHINATOWN/INTERNATIONAL DISTRICT** (map:Q6), and just south of Pioneer Square is the newly energized industrial area called **SODO** (south of downtown), home to Qwest Field, the Seahawks' football stadium, and its next-door neighbor Safeco Field, ballpark of the city's beloved Mariners.

Traveling northeast from Pike Place Market through the trendy **BELLTOWN** neighborhood (between Virginia Street and Denny Way, between Western and 5th avenues; map:G7), you come upon the slightly grittier **DENNY TRIANGLE**, also known as the Denny Regrade (the triangle defined by 6th Avenue, Denny Way, and Pike Street; map:H4). Both neighborhoods encompass what used to be steep Denny Hill, which in the early 1900s was leveled along Denny Way from Interstate 5 to the waterfront. Across Denny Way is the sprawling **SEATTLE CENTER** complex (between Denny Way and Mercer Street, between 1st Avenue N and 5th Avenue N; map:B6), home to the Pacific Science Center; Marion Oliver McCaw Hall, the new digs of the Seattle Opera and Pacific Northwest Ballet; Experience Music Project and the Science Fiction Museum and Hall of Fame; and a wide variety of festivals and fairs, as well as Seattle's best-known landmark, the **SPACE NEEDLE**. The Seattle Center is on the lower slopes of **QUEEN ANNE** hill (map:GG7); to the west is **MAGNOLIA** (map:GG8), and in between Queen Anne and Magnolia is the area called **INTERBAY** (along 15th Avenue W; map:GG8). To the east of the Seattle Center, on the northern reaches of downtown, is the newly in vogue **SOUTH LAKE UNION** neighborhood (map:E2); other neighborhoods surrounding the lake are **WESTLAKE** (map:A1) and **EASTLAKE** (map:GG6).

BEST PLACE
TO VIEW ART?

"A screening of just about anything at the Cinerama theater. It beats any moviegoing experience anywhere in the country."

Darryl McDonald, co-founder of Seattle International Film Festival (SIFF)

A few blocks east of downtown, the **CAPITOL HILL** neighborhood (map:K1) rises up from I-5 and is packed with hip people, stores, coffee shops, and nightspots. In addition to its main thoroughfares of Broadway and 15th Avenue E, Capitol Hill encompasses many residential areas mixed with small business and is the central hub of surrounding neighborhoods. Northeast, toward the ship canal, **MONTLAKE** (map:FF6) lies at the northern foot of the hill and **MADISON VALLEY** (map:GG6) and **MADISON PARK** (map:GG5) run down to Lake Washington; southwest, on the edge of downtown, is the **FIRST HILL** neighborhood (map:M2); and southeast, toward Lake Washington, are the **CENTRAL DISTRICT** (map:HH6), **MADRONA** (map:HH6), and **LESCHI** (map:HH6) neighborhoods—a microcosm of the city's diversity.

Southwest of downtown, across the Duwamish River, is **WEST SEATTLE** (map:JJ8), with many residential areas, lush parks, and beaches, as well as thriving commercial centers such as the West Seattle Junction. In the city's south end are the Rainier Valley—including **COLUMBIA CITY** (map:KK5) and **RAINIER BEACH** (map:LL4)—**BEACON HILL** (map:II6), and **GEORGETOWN** (map:KK6), all east of the Duwamish; **SOUTH PARK** (map:KK7) and **WHITE CENTER** (map:MM7) are west of the river. South of Seattle are the suburban cities of **BURIEN** (map:OO7), **TUKWILA** (map:OO5), and **RENTON** (map:MM2); farther south are **SEATAC** (map:OO6), **DES MOINES** (map:QQ7), **NORMANDY PARK** (map:PP7), and **KENT** (map:QQ5); farthest south are **FEDERAL WAY** (map:RR6) and **AUBURN**.

North of the Ship Canal, Lake Union, Portage Bay, and the Montlake Cut, you'll find **BALLARD** (map:EE8) to the west, **FREMONT** (map:FF7) and **WALLINGFORD** (map:FF7) due north of downtown, and the **UNIVERSITY DISTRICT** (map:FF6) and **LAURELHURST** (map:EE5) to the east. Just to the north of Fremont and Wallingford is the **GREENWOOD/GREEN LAKE** (map:EE7) area. In Seattle's expansive residential north end, **CROWN HILL** (map:DD8) and **BITTER LAKE** (map:CC7) north of Ballard in the west; **NORTHGATE** (map:CC6), a busy commercial area, and **HALLER LAKE** (map:CC6) lie north of Greenwood/Green Lake; heading east from the Green Lake area you'll find the **ROOSEVELT** (map:DD7), **RAVENNA** (map:EE6), and **SAND POINT** (map:EE5) neighborhoods, north of the University District. **MAPLE LEAF** (map:EE7), **WEDGWOOD** (map:EE6), and **VIEW RIDGE** (map:EE6) are residential areas to the north of Roosevelt/Ravenna, and **LAKE CITY** (map:DD6) lies north of Wedgwood. (For an artistic but accurate look at the complexity of Seattle neighborhoods, you can order a map from Big Stick Inc. [888/507-0058; bigstickinc.com] for $25.) **NORTH OF SEATTLE** are the suburban cities of **SHORELINE** (map:BB7) in the west, **MOUNTLAKE TERRACE** (map:AA6) along I-5, and **LAKE FOREST PARK** (map:BB6) and **KENMORE** (map:AA5) to the east on the north shore of Lake Washington. Farther north are **EDMONDS**, **LYNNWOOD**, and **EVERETT**.

Formerly composed of bedroom communities that served Seattle's workforce, **THE EASTSIDE**, which is anchored by the city of Bellevue, is now an integral part of the Puget Sound Region, home to some of the area's largest employers and retail centers. East of Lake Washington are **MEDINA** (map:GG4), **BELLEVUE** (map:HH2), **MERCER ISLAND** (map:JJ4), **ISSAQUAH**, and **SAMMAMISH**; to the north and east lie **KIRKLAND** (map:DD3), **JUANITA** (map:CC4), **REDMOND** (map:EE1), **BOTHELL** (map:AA4), and **WOODINVILLE** (map:AA1).

Visitor Information

Seattleites have a well-deserved reputation of being polite and helpful, but not necessarily friendly. Which means you're in luck if you just need directions or a restaurant recommendation, but not so much if you're looking to pad your address book with new acquaintances. More often than not, folks on the street can help you find what you're looking for, but if they can't, try the **CITYWIDE CONCIERGE CENTER** at **SEATTLE'S CONVENTION & VISITORS BUREAU** (710 Pike St, Ste 800, Downtown; 206/461-5800; visitseattle.org; map:J4), part Ticketmaster, part tour guide, and part personal assistant, where you can get pointers on everything from where to find a spa to how to hire a last-minute babysitter.

Savvily staffed **CONCIERGE DESKS** are also available at several downtown shopping locations, including Macy's (1601 3rd Ave; 206/506-6000; macys.com) and Nordstrom (500 Pine St; 206/628-2111; nordstrom.com). The concierges at these locations are exceptionally accommodating and can provide shoppers and tourists with maps and directions to attractions. In Pacific Place (600 Pine St; 206/405-2655; pacificplaceseattle.com) is another useful downtown concierge desk.

The **DOWNTOWN SEATTLE ASSOCIATION** (500 Union St, Ste 300; 206/623-0340; downtownseattle.com) Web site has many helpful links to assist in the navigation of the 275 square blocks of downtown Seattle. Whether you want to know how many vendors set up shop in the Pike Place Market or how many licks it takes to get to the center of a Tootsie Pop, call the research wizards at the **SEATTLE PUBLIC LIBRARY QUICK INFORMATION LINE** (206/386-4636). *The Newcomer's Handbook for Moving to and Living in Seattle* (First Books, Second Edition, 2003) by Monica Fischer and Amy Bellamy is a thorough, reliable resource for newcomers and longtime residents alike.

Getting Around

BY CAR

While mass transit makes navigating downtown Seattle a breeze, if you plan to venture outside the city, traveling by car will offer you the most convenience and flexibility. Most large **RENTAL CAR COMPANIES** have offices at Sea-Tac Airport, in downtown Seattle, and in downtown Bellevue. Some larger ones, such as Enterprise (800/261-7331; enterprise.com) and Budget (800/527-0700; budget.com), have locations in other suburbs and in various Seattle neighborhoods. Hertz (800/654-3131; hertz.com) is the preferred rental car company of AAA Washington (330 6th Ave N, Downtown; 206/448-5353; 800/AAA-HELP, emergency road service).

Centrally located **PARKING LOTS** charge between $15 and $20 a day; lots on the fringes of downtown—Chinatown/International District, Belltown, and lower Queen Anne, for instance—are usually less expensive. Downtown, many parking stalls have a maximum of 30 minutes, and some are off-limits to all but delivery trucks, but if you're lucky enough to get one after 6pm or on Sundays and holidays, they're free. If you ignore the restrictions, or if you park beyond your time limit, expect a $38 parking ticket; parking illegally in a space reserved for the disabled will cost you $250. Large facilities such as Safeco Field, Qwest Field, Seattle Center, and Husky Stadium in the University District generally have their own parking areas.

Except in a few neighborhoods that still have meters, most street parking in Seattle is served by **PARKING STATIONS** that allow you to pay with coins or credit and debit cards. Parking is $1.50 per hour, with a two-hour time limit. The kiosks dispense a sticker that you place in your window; if you don't use all your time at one spot, you can use the remaining time someplace else. Or, if you're feeling generous, leave your sticker attached to the kiosk and let someone else use your unexpired time.

In the city's retail core, the **PACIFIC PLACE PARKING GARAGE** (6th Avenue and Pine Street, Downtown; map:I5) charges $4 for the first hour, $5 for 2 hours, $7 for 3 hours, and $9 for four hours weekdays before 5pm ($3 per hour after four hours); $4 for four hours or fewer after 5pm weeknights; $3 for the first hour on weekends and holidays before 5 pm, $4 for two hours, $5 for three hours, and $7 for four hours; on weekends and holidays after 5 pm, the cost is $4 for four hours or fewer.

For **LOST CARS**, begin by calling the Seattle Police Department's Auto Records Department (206/684-5444) to find out whether your car is listed as towed and impounded. If there's no record, it may have been stolen; call 206/625-5011, or in an emergency call 911.

BY TAXI

Ask Seattleites the best place to hail a cab, and they're likely to answer wearily, "New York" or "San Francisco." It is notoriously difficult to hail a cab here, and at press time the city was considering issuing more cab licenses for the first time in 17 years. Currently, 643 cabs are licensed in Seattle, and the average wait time is nine-and-a-half minutes—and that's if you call a dispatcher. Try your luck on a street corner, and you might wait up to half an hour.

You'll have the best luck hailing a cab near major attractions or downtown hotels. The Westin is a particularly good spot, as is Pioneer Square. There are also a handful of new **TAXI STANDS** that serve the weekend drinking crowd: in Fremont at Evanston Avenue N and N 34th Street; on Capitol Hill at 10th Avenue and Pike Street, and Pine Street and Boylston Avenue; and in Pioneer Square at S Washington Street at Occidental Park, and S King Street at Occidental Avenue.

A cab from the airport to downtown costs about $33, but from the hotel district to the airport it's a flat rate of $28. The standard drop is $2, plus a $1.50 gasoline surcharge, and a meter rate of $2 per mile. Local companies include **FARWEST TAXI** (206/329-7700), **GRAYTOP** (206/782-8294), **ORANGE CAB** (206/522-8800), and **YELLOW CAB** (206/622-6500).

BY BUS

No car? No worries. It's easy to navigate downtown Seattle without a car. **KING COUNTY METRO TRANSIT** (206/553-3000; transit.metrokc.gov) operates more than 300 bus routes, covering more than 2,000 square miles in Seattle and surrounding King County. Many of the coaches are wheelchair accessible, and all are equipped with bike racks (mounted on the front of the bus). Bus stops have small yellow-and-white signs designating route numbers, and many have schedules posted. The fare is $1.50 in the city ($1.75 during peak commuter hours—6am to 9am and 3pm to 6pm) and $1.50 if you cross the city line ($2.25 peak). Exact fare is required. Seniors, youths, and handicapped riders are eligible for discount cards. A Metro Visitor Pass costs $5.50 and buys you unlimited daily travel on all regular and special-event Metro service. The pass is available at Metro's two **SERVICE OFFICES** (1301 5th Ave, Downtown, map: K5; and 201 S Jackson St, Pioneer Square; map:O7) or online at buypass.metrokc.gov. Bus schedules and **MONTHLY PASSES** are also available at the service offices. More than 120 retail locations in Seattle and King County sell bus passes, including many Bartell Drugs stores, or purchase by phone (206/624-7277) or online at buypass.metrokc.gov. **BUS SCHEDULES** are available at a number of downtown office buildings, including the main U.S. Post Office (301 Union St, Downtown; 206/748-5417; map:K6) and the Colman Dock ferry terminal (Pier 52, 801 Alaskan Wy, Downtown; map:M8).

One of Metro's most valued services is the **RIDE FREE AREA** in downtown's commercial core. In the area bordered by the waterfront to the west, 6th Avenue to the east, Jackson Street to the south, and Battery Street to the north, you can ride free on any Metro bus from 6am until 7pm.

For trips from as far north as Darrington in Snohomish County, **COMMUNITY TRANSIT** (425/353-7433 or 800/562-1375; commtrans.org) runs buses on a regular schedule. Fare is $3 per adult to Seattle from any point outside the city; fare within Snohomish County is $1.25.

GRAY LINE OF SEATTLE (4500 W Marginal Wy SW, West Seattle; 206/624-5077 or 800/426-7532; graylineofseattle.com) has the largest fleet of charter buses and competitive prices for sightseeing tours of the city. The company also offers organized tours to destinations such as Mount Rainier, Vancouver, and the San Juan Islands.

BY MONORAIL

The **MONORAIL**, which connects the Seattle Center to the downtown retail district, was a space-age innovation of the 1962 world's fair. The two-minute, 1-mile ride is a great thrill for kids. A smart way to avoid the parking hassle at the Seattle Center is to leave your car downtown and hop on the monorail at Westlake Center (3rd floor, Pine Street and 4th Avenue, Downtown; seattlemonorail.com; map:I6); the station is on a platform outside, just east of the top of the escalator. Adults pay $2 one way, seniors pay $1, and children ages 5–12 pay 75 cents. Round-trip fares are double the one-way price. Trains leave every 10 minutes daily from 11am to 9pm.

BY BICYCLE

Seattle is a bicycle-friendly city. Depending on the weather, between 4,000 and 8,000 bikers commute to work each day. Bike lanes on arterial streets throughout the city are fairly safe routes for cyclists, and bike trails offer a reprieve from huffing and puffing up Seattle's steep slopes. For both commuting and recreation, the **BURKE-GILMAN TRAIL** is the bicycling backbone of Seattle. Extending approximately 15 miles from Kenmore at the north end of Lake Washington through the University of Washington campus to Ballard, and connecting to downtown Seattle via either the Ballard Bridge and 15th Avenue, or the Fremont Bridge and Dexter Avenue, the Burke-Gilman Trail is essentially flat because it follows a former railroad line. The trail connects in Kenmore with the **SAMMAMISH RIVER TRAIL**, which takes riders around the north end of Lake Washington and through Woodinville to Redmond's Marymoor Park on the north edge of Lake Sammamish.

The **ELLIOTT BAY TRAIL** is a scenic 2.5-mile spur running northwest from downtown along the waterfront through Myrtle Edwards and Elliott Bay parks. The rebuilt **ALKI TRAIL** stretches along Alki Beach in West Seattle and connects with the 11-mile **DUWAMISH TRAIL**, which roughly follows the west shore of the Duwamish River south to Kent (where you can pick up the **GREEN RIVER TRAIL**). Recreational riders especially enjoy the **BIKE TRAIL IN**

STREET SMARTS

If you ask for directions in Seattle, you will likely be given an answer that omits actual street names.

Signage in Seattle can be inexplicable, so much so that locals are more apt to tell you to take a left at the auto supply store or a right just before the bridge. Northeast 45th Street in the University District, for example, starts out harmlessly enough, but then begins to vacillate between numbers and names: turning into Sand Point Way NE, then NE 125th Street, Roosevelt Way NE, and NE 130th Street. The key to signage smarts is proper translation—knowing, for instance, that University Way (which everyone refers to as "the Ave," just to further confuse) in the University District is wholly unrelated to University Street, which is downtown. It helps to know that "streets" run east to west and, except for downtown, have a compass direction before the street name or number. "Avenues" run north to south with a compass direction after their name. (Tip: To center yourself downtown, remember the mnemonic Jesus Christ Made Seattle Under Protest—the first letter of each word in the saying reveals the south-to-north order of the main streets: Jefferson and James, Cherry and Columbia, Marion and Madison, Spring and Seneca, University and Union, and Pike and Pine.)

Part of the confusion can be traced to the city's founders. On May 23, 1853, when Arthur Denny, Carson Boren, and David Maynard gathered to file the first plats for Seattle, Maynard felt the grid should be organized according to the points of the compass, whereas Denny and Boren felt the grid should be parallel to Elliott Bay's shore. The muddled streets are a result of their compromise, and the directionally challenged have suffered ever since.

Happily, though navigating the city can be a bit confusing, the destination is always worth the trouble.

—Jenna Land

SEWARD PARK, which circles the wooded peninsula jutting into Lake Washington. The **I-90 TRAIL** takes cyclists from just east of downtown across Lake Washington to Mercer Island. The city's Seattle Bicycling Guide Map shows these trails and cyclists' street routes, including across the lower West Seattle Bridge and south to Sea-Tac Airport; call the **DEPARTMENT OF TRANSPORTATION BICYCLE AND PEDESTRIAN SAFETY PROGRAM** (206/684-7583). Maps include in-depth insets on difficult-to-navigate areas, but they become scarce during summer, so call ahead if you can. For bike maps of Bellevue, call the **CITY OF BELLEVUE TRANSPORTATION DEPARTMENT** (425/452-2894).

If in your travels you come upon a hill or body of water that looms too large, hop on a bus or ferry. All Metro buses come equipped with bike racks on the front, and using them is free, though they hold only two bikes per bus, first come, first served. The only restriction is that you can't load or unload bicycles in the downtown Ride Free Area between 6am and 7pm, except at the route's first and last ride free stop. For more information, call **METRO'S RIDER INFORMATION SYSTEM** (206/553-3000). Taking a bike on most local ferry routes costs $2 on top of the regular walk-on passenger fare. For more ferry information, see the next section.

BIKE RACKS for securing your two-wheeler are conveniently located outside the Washington State Convention & Trade Center (800 Convention Pl, Downtown; map:J4) and can usually be found within a block of most bus stops in commercial areas. In addition, bikes can be parked (as well as repaired and rented) 24-7 at **BIKESTATION SEATTLE** (311 3rd Ave S; 206/332-9795; bikestation.org; map:O7).

To **RENT A BIKE**, try Gregg's Greenlake Cycle (7007 Woodlawn Ave NE, Green Lake; 206/523-1822; greggscycles.com; map:FF7), Alpine Hut (2215 15th Ave W, Interbay; alpinehut.com; 206/284-3575; map:GG8), Recycled Cycles (1007 NE Boat St, University District; 206/547-4491; recycledcycles.com; map:FF6) and, across the street from the busy Burke-Gilman Trail, Ti Cycles (2943 NE Blakely St, University District; 206/522-7602; ticycles.com; map:FF6).

BY FERRY

In the Puget Sound area, ferries are commuter vehicles, tourist magnets, and shortcut alternatives to driving around large bodies of water. You can take a ferry from the downtown terminal at **PIER 52** (801 Alaskan Wy; map:M8) on the waterfront across the Sound to Bainbridge or Vashon islands (many people who live on the islands or the Kitsap Peninsula catch daily ferries into the city), or hop one from Anacortes, 90 miles north of town via I-5, to the San Juan Islands or even Vancouver Island, British Columbia. Travelers headed for the Olympic Peninsula use them as a scenic way to cut across the Sound; some passengers just go for the ride. For complete schedule and route information, call **WASHINGTON STATE FERRIES** (206/464-6400 or 888/808-7977; wsdot.wa.gov/ferries). Schedules vary from summer to winter (with much longer lines in summer); credit cards are not accepted at the Lopez, Shaw, Orcas, and Friday Harbor terminals. For more information on ferry routes, see the Ferry Rides sidebar in the Day Trips chapter.

The **ELLIOTT BAY WATER TAXI** is a cute boat run by Metro that operates every half hour between sunrise and 10:30pm (11pm going from West Seattle back downtown; 6:30pm on Sundays) during the summer to transport people between West Seattle's Alki beach and Pier 54 downtown off Spring Street. Each way on the water taxi costs $3, and bikes can be brought on at no additional fee. The trip takes about 12 minutes, and on Mariners game days the last boat departs from Pier 54 at 10:45pm.

Essentials

PUBLIC RESTROOMS

Public restrooms can be found at the base of the ramp in the **MAIN ARCADE OF PIKE PLACE MARKET** (Pike Street and Western Avenue, Pike Place Market; map:J8), at **FREEWAY PARK** (6th Avenue and Seneca Street, Downtown; map:L5), and on the Main Street side of the **PIONEER SQUARE FIRE STATION** (corner of 2nd Avenue S and S Main Street; map:O8). Five self-cleaning, space-age-looking public toilets are also available at **OCCIDENTAL PARK** (Pioneer Square; map:N7), **HING HAY PARK** (International District; map: Q6), **VICTOR STEINBRUECK PARK** (Pike Place Market; map:H8), **WATERFRONT PARK** (Pier 59, Waterfront; map:J9), and the **1800 BLOCK OF BROADWAY** on Capitol Hill (map:GG6). Public buildings are another option. A few options downtown are the Seattle Public Library (1000 4th Ave; map: L5), King County Courthouse (516 3rd Ave; map:N6), and the Federal Building (915 2nd Ave; map:L7). Downtown shopping centers, such as **WESTLAKE CENTER** (Pine Street and 4th Avenue; map:I6) and **PACIFIC PLACE** (7th Avenue and Pine Street; map:I5), have plenty of restrooms. Many larger parks, such as Volunteer Park on Capitol Hill (1247 15th Ave E; map:GG6) and Gas Works Park in Wallingford (2101 N Northlake Wy; map:FF7), also have public facilities (although most are open only until dusk).

MAJOR BANKS

Money-changing facilities are available at almost every major downtown bank. All of Seattle's larger banks also provide the full range of services, and you can locate neighborhood branches by contacting their downtown headquarters: **WASHINGTON MUTUAL** (1201 3rd Ave; 206/461-6475; wamu.com; map:L7), located in the neoclassical Washington Mutual Tower; **WELLS FARGO** (999 3rd Ave; 206/292-3415; wellsfargo.com; map:M7); **US BANK** (1420 5th Ave; 206/344-3690; usbank.com; map:K6); and **KEYBANK** (1329 4th Ave; 206/447-5769; key.com; map:L6).

POLICE AND SAFETY

In emergency situations, dial 911. In nonemergencies, call the **SEATTLE POLICE DEPARTMENT** (206/625-5011). Seattle is known as a relatively safe city. There are fewer violent crimes here than in many large cities, although pickpockets are a problem in crowded areas such as Capitol Hill and Pike Place Market. As in any large city, be particularly aware of your surroundings when walking around downtown at night. (A fun bit of trivia: Seattle was the first city in the nation to have bicycle cops and, along with Los Angeles, the first in the nation to employ female police officers.)

HOSPITALS AND MEDICAL/DENTAL SERVICES

Seattle has so many hospitals located near the heart of the city that the First Hill neighborhood just east of downtown is known to locals as Pill Hill. One of the best facilities is **HARBORVIEW MEDICAL CENTER** (325 9th Ave, First Hill; 206/731-3000; 206/731-3074, emergency; uwmedicine.org; map:P4), managed by the University of Washington. Originally founded in 1877 as a six-bed welfare hospital in South Seattle (its current name and locale are the result of a 1931 move), Harborview is now the highest-level trauma center for a four-state region. Other hospitals in the neighborhood include **SWEDISH MEDICAL CENTER** (747 Broadway, First Hill; 206/386-6000; swedish.org; map:N2); **VIRGINIA MASON** (1100 9th Ave, First Hill; 206/223-6600; virginiamason.org; map:N2); and a handful of neighborhood clinics. Standing apart from the Pill Hill neighborhood triumvirate is the **UNIVERSITY OF WASHINGTON MEDICAL CENTER** (1959 NE Pacific St, University District; 206/598-3300; uwmedicine.org; map:FF6).

The Seattle–King County Dental Society offers a **DENTIST REFERRAL SERVICE** (206/443-7607) that refers callers to a dentist or a low-cost dental clinic. HealthSouth Medical Clinics (walk-in health clinics) have numerous locations around Puget Sound that can be located on the Web at healthsouth.com.

BEST PLACE
IN THE CITY TO SCORE?

"Seriously, the best place to score in Seattle is at a Long Winters concert. Oh my god, the shows are like Roman orgies, even if you don't like the band."

John Roderick, front man, the Long Winters

POST OFFICE

Downtown Seattle's main **U.S. POST OFFICE** (301 Union St; 206/748-5417; usps.com; map:K6) is open weekdays 7:30am to 5:30pm. Hours at neighborhood branches vary, and some are open on Saturdays, so call ahead.

GROCERY STORES

The closest major grocery stores to downtown are the new **WHOLE FOODS MARKET** (2210 Westlake Ave, South Lake Union; 206/621-9700; wholefoodsmarket.com; map:F4) beneath the Pan Pacific Seattle hotel in South Lake Union, the **QFC** (1401 Broadway, Capitol Hill; 206/860-3818; qfconline.com; map:L1) at the corner of Broadway and E Union Street on Capitol Hill, and two stores on the western edge of Seattle Center: **METROPOLITAN MARKET** (100 Mercer St, Lower Queen Anne; 206/213-0778; metropolitan-market.com; map:A7), which boasts beautiful produce and a knowledgeable staff, and **QFC** (100 Republican St, Lower Queen Anne; 206/285-5491; qfconline.com; map:A7), which is open 24 hours a day.

Safeway has several large locations, such as the **QUEEN ANNE SAFEWAY** (2100 Queen Anne Ave N, Queen Anne; 206/282-8090; map:GG7). The **ADMIRAL METROPOLITAN MARKET** (2320 42nd Ave SW, West Seattle; 206/937-0551; map:II8) in West Seattle and the **QUEEN ANNE METROPOLITAN MARKET** (1908 Queen Anne Ave N, Queen Anne; 206/284-2530; map:GG7) are two of the best grocery stores in the city. The **PCC NATURAL MARKET** in Fremont (600 N 34th St; 206/632-6811; map:FF7) has a nice selection of healthy foods and organic fruits.

PHARMACIES

BARTELL DRUGS is the biggest local drugstore chain in the area, with locations in just about every neighborhood in Seattle. Downtown stores are at 3rd Avenue and Union Street (1404 3rd Ave; 206/624-1366; map:K6), 5th Avenue and Olive Way (1628 5th Ave; 206/622-0581; map:I6), Boren Avenue and Madison Street (1101 Madison St; 206/340-1066; map:M3), and 4th Avenue and Madison Street (910 4th Ave; 206/624-2211; map:L6). The branch on Lower Queen Anne (600 1st Ave N; 206/284-1353; map:A7) is open 24 hours a day. Other 24-hour pharmacies are located in **WALGREENS** stores in Ballard (5409 15th Ave NW; 206/781-0056; map:EE8), Bellevue (647 140th Ave NE; 425/603-1438; map:HH2), and Kirkland (12405 NE 85th St; 425/822-9202; map:DD3). All three Walgreens stores have convenient drive-thru pharmacies. For homeopathic remedies, nutritional supplements, and other holistic remedies, visit the dispensary at **BASTYR CENTER FOR NATURAL HEALTH** (3670 Stone Wy N, Wallingford; 206/834-4100; map:FF7).

DRY CLEANERS AND LAUNDROMATS

Several dry cleaners operate in the city, and many hotels have in-house services. A couple to consider: **A-1 LAUNDRY INCORPORATED** (2401 1st Ave, Belltown; 206/441-1570; map:F8), which offers same-day dry cleaning and laundry, and **ANGE'S FRENCH CLEANERS** (2000 9th Ave, Downtown; 206/622-6727; map:H4), a fixture for more than 50 years that will pick up and deliver.

LEGAL SERVICES

The **KING COUNTY BAR ASSOCIATION LAWYER REFERRAL SERVICE** (206/267-7010; kcba.org) puts clients in touch with member lawyers. For personal injury and workers' compensation cases, the first consultation with the attorney is free; for other matters, the first 30-minute consultation is $35. **COLUMBIA LEGAL SERVICES** (101 Yesler Wy, Ste 300, Pioneer Square; 206/464-5911; columbialegal.org; map:N7) is a program that provides free legal help for clients with very low incomes. **NORTHWEST WOMEN'S LAW CENTER** (907 Pine St, Ste 500, First Hill; 206/621-7691; nwwlc.org; map:J3) provides basic legal information and attorney referrals, as well as advice on self-help methods.

BUSINESS, COPY, AND MESSENGER SERVICES

BUSINESS SERVICE CENTER (1001 4th Ave, Ste 3200, Downtown; 206/624-9188; bsc-seattle.com; map:M6) rents full-time and part-time office and conference space. Another option is **GLOBE SECRETARIAT** (2001 6th Ave, Ste 306, Belltown; 206/448-9441; map:H5); services available include word processing, typing, tape transcription, résumés, 24-hour dictation, copying, and faxing. The University District branch of **FEDEX KINKO'S** (810 NE 45th St, University District; 206/545-7218; map:FF6) is open 24 hours every day and offers copying, in-house computer rentals, videoconferencing, and Wi-Fi Internet access.

FLEETFOOT MESSENGER SERVICE (206/728-7700; fleetfootmessenger.com) has quick-service, radio-dispatched bicyclists delivering packages downtown 24 hours a day, 7 days a week, as well as vehicle delivery of packages up to 250 pounds—or whatever fits—statewide. And there's always **FEDEX** (800/463-3339; fedex.com) and **UPS** (800/742-5877; ups.com).

PHOTOGRAPHY EQUIPMENT AND SERVICES

Seattle's professional photographers swear by **CAMERATECHS** (2034 NW Market St, Ballard; 206/782-2433; cameratechs.com; map:EE8). The shop services all makes and models, usually within 24 hours, and is open Monday through Saturday. For developing, custom printing, and digital outputting, the pros take their film to **IVEY IMAGING SEATTLE** (424 8th Ave N, Downtown; 206/623-8113; ivey.com; map:D3).

BEST PLACE
TO LISTEN TO LIVE MUSIC?

"The Tractor Tavern remains my favorite place to see a show because of their consistent booking, the laid-back vibe, and the fact that the place feels as comfortable as an old boot (many of which hang from the ceiling)."

Charles R. Cross, author of Heavier Than Heaven: The Biography of Kurt Cobain

---

COMPUTER REPAIRS

UP TIME TECHNOLOGY (2408 N 45th St, Wallingford; 206/547-1817; uptimetech.com; map:FF7), open Monday through Friday, 8:30am to 5:30pm, has been serving Seattle since the 1980s repairing PCs and laptops. In-shop repairs are $80 an hour; for house calls, they'll dispatch a technician for $110 an hour. For Mac users, there are several **APPLE STORE** outposts in the area, including University Village (2656 NE University Village St, University Village; 206/524-8100; map:FF6). For repairs, visit apple.com to make a reservation at the Genius Bar.

PLACES OF WORSHIP

Houses of reverence vary widely in Seattle, from classical grandeur to eclectic jumble to tumbledown storefront. Here are a few noted for their architecture, community importance, and welcoming attitudes.

In Islam, the oldest doctrines are those of the Sunnis. North Seattle contains a small, attractive home for local adherents in the form of the **IDRIS MOSQUE** (1420 NE Northgate Wy, Northgate; 206/363-3013; idrismosque.com; map: DD6). The compact dome and minaret-evocative tower, topped with a crescent, routinely slow down traffic.

Synagogues in Seattle serve Reform, Conservative, Orthodox, and Sephardic communities. Freestanding fluted columns lend a Hellenistic air to **TEMPLE DE HIRSCH SINAI** (1511 E Pike St, Capitol Hill; 206/323-8486; tdhs-nw.org; map: HH6), an airy, modern Reform complex.

On the Jesuit Seattle University campus is the breathtaking **ST. IGNATIUS CHAPEL** (901 12th Ave, First Hill; 206/296-6000; seattleu.edu/chapel; map: NN4). The brainchild of renowned architect Steven Holl, it was conceived as "seven glass bottles of light in a stone box," each bottle a vessel of light corresponding to an aspect of Catholic worship.

The twin towers of **ST. JAMES CATHEDRAL** (804 9th Ave, First Hill; 206/622-3559; stjames-cathedral.org; map:N4) announce an elegant and solidly impressive Roman Catholic church that boasts the city's oldest classical New Year's Eve concert and celebration, held at 11pm, featuring cathedral musicians and a chamber orchestra.

ST. MARK'S EPISCOPAL CATHEDRAL (1245 10th Ave E, Capitol Hill; 206/323-0300; saintmarks.org; map:GG6), designed along traditional Gothic lines in the late 1920s, was never finished due to the Depression. After one of many renovations, the interior is now filled with pastel light streaming from a rose window. A popular compline mass is held Sundays at 9:30pm.

The white stucco curves of **PLYMOUTH CONGREGATIONAL CHURCH** (1217 6th Ave, Downtown; 206/622-4865; plymouthchurchseattle.org; map:L5) are both intriguingly intricate and refreshingly simple. Black-and-white abstract crosses dance in starry columns down the sides of the building, inviting passersby

PETS AND STRAY ANIMALS

If you spot a stray animal or lose your pet in Seattle, call the **SEATTLE ANIMAL SHELTER** (2061 15th Ave W, Interbay; 206/386-7387; seattleanimal shelter.org; map:GG7). They hold animals for three working days before putting them up for adoption, so make sure Rover has an up-to-date license.

in for lunchtime jazz services on Wednesdays at noon.

The lofty central dome of the **ST. DEMETRIOS GREEK ORTHODOX CHURCH** (2100 Boyer Ave E, Capitol Hill; 206/325-4347; saintdemetrios.com; map:GG6) is home to Eastern Orthodox Christianity. It stages a Greek Festival in the fall, with everything from dancing to baklava.

FIRST COVENANT CHURCH (400 E Pike St, Capitol Hill; 206/322-7411; seattlefirstcovenant.org; map:K1), with its gold-tipped dome surmounting a heavy classical front, is a roomy space smack in the middle of nightlife-loving Capitol Hill.

FIRST PRESBYTERIAN CHURCH (1013 8th Ave, First Hill; 206/624-0644; firstpres.org; map:L4) is a streamlined sculptural complex dating from the 1960s; the modern architecture hides the fact that, at more than 130 years old, this is one of Seattle's oldest congregations.

Look for the Buddhist festival held every July at **SEATTLE BUDDHIST CHURCH** (1427 S Main St, Central District; 206/329-0800; seattlebetsuin.com; map:R4). The long brick building with upturned roof corners sits across from a park displaying the temple bell (under a canopy) and a statue memorializing the founder of Jodo Shinshu Buddhism.

Red, white, and blue upside-down triangles along the edge of the roof make **MOUNT ZION BAPTIST CHURCH** (1634 19th Ave, Central District; 206/322-6500; mountzion.net; map:HH6) easy to spot, and the church draws congregants from five counties.

A new trend in Seattle is the megachurch, a huge conservative congregation led by a charismatic minister who often holds services at multiple campuses. **MARS HILL CHURCH** (206/706-6641; marshillchurch.org) attracts hundreds of 20- and 30-somethings to its services in Ballard (1401 NW Leary Wy; map:EE8); Shoreline (Schirmer Auditorium, 195th Street and Greenwood Avenue N; map:AA7); West Seattle (Chief Sealth High School, 2600 SW Thistle St; map:KK8); and Wedgwood (3524 NE 95th St; map:EE6). **CHRISTIAN FAITH CENTER** (caseytreat.com), led by husband-and-wife ministers Casey and Wendy Treat, has campuses in South Seattle (21024 24th Ave S; 206/824-8188; map:QQ7) and Everett (13000 21st Drive SE; 206/824-8188).

—Caroline Cummins

For veterinary services, **ELLIOTT BAY ANIMAL HOSPITAL** (2042 15th Ave W, Interbay; 206/285-7387; elliottbayah.com; map:GG8) is recommended by local vets. If your pet needs immediate attention after hours, visit the **EMERALD CITY EMERGENCY CLINIC** (4102 Stone Wy N, Wallingford; 206/634-9000; map:FF7).

Local Resources

NEWSPAPERS AND PERIODICALS

Seattle is lucky to claim two large daily newspapers, though the papers combine their efforts on Sunday. **THE SEATTLE TIMES** (1120 John St, South Lake Union; 206/464-2111; seattletimes.com; map:F2) is locally owned, while the **SEATTLE POST-INTELLIGENCER** (101 Elliott Ave W, Belltown; 206/448-8000; seattle-pi.com; map:B9) is run by the Hearst newspaper group. Both newspapers are delivered in the morning and can be found in nearly every grocery store, bookstore, and coffee shop, and in kiosks on city streets. If you're in search of local flavor, many neighborhoods have their own weekly newspapers, usually available free at grocery stores or in street kiosks.

Weeklies abound here. The free **SEATTLE WEEKLY** (1008 Western Ave, Ste 300, Downtown; 206/623-0500; seattleweekly.com; map:M8) and **THE STRANGER** (1535 11th Ave, 3rd Floor, Capitol Hill; 206/323-7101; thestranger.com; map:HH7), available Thursdays, cover politics, civic issues, and the arts. The pillar of Seattle's gay community is **SEATTLE GAY NEWS** (1605 12th Ave, Ste 31, Capitol Hill; 206/324-4297; sgn.org; map:HH6), which costs a quarter in bookstores (free elsewhere) and comes out on Fridays.

In the glossy publications department, check out the monthly **SEATTLE MAGAZINE** (1505 Western Ave, Ste 500, Pike Place Market; 206/284-1750; seattlemag.com; map:J7), which is packed with insider information about the people and places of the city, and can be found at newsstands and bookstores. Seattle magazine's sister publications, **SEATTLE BUSINESS MONTHLY** and **NORTHWEST HOME + GARDEN**, are also available on newsstands throughout the city. New to the scene is **SEATTLE METROPOLITAN** (1201 Western Ave, Ste 425, Pike Place Market; 206/957-2234; seattlemet.com; map:K7), a glossy monthly from the publishers of *Portland Monthly*. The Pacific Northwest's only monthly multicultural magazine, **COLORSNW** (1319 Dexter Ave N, Ste 250, Westlake, 206/444-9251; colorsnw.com; map:A1), is distributed free in boxes around town, as is **SEATTLE WOMAN** (1752 NW Market St, Ste 400, Ballard; 206/784-5556; seattlewomanmagazine.com; map:EE8), a three-year-old publication that covers careers, health, family, relationships, and finances. **RESONANCE** (206/633-3500; resonancemag.com), which has been giving its hip take on local art, music, and literature since 1994, can be picked up at indie music stores and bookstores. Newcomer **SEATTLE SOUND** (1201 1st Ave S, Ste 309, SoDo; 206/382-9220; seattlesoundmag.com; map: Q9) covers the local music scene, from jazz to rock and hip-hop to honky-tonk. **CITYDOG MAGAZINE** (citydogmagazine.com), the Northwest's only glossy devoted to life with canines, is available quarterly at bookstores and upscale pet supply stores.

PUBLIC LIBRARIES

The Seattle Public Library's **CENTRAL LIBRARY** (1000 4th Ave, Downtown; 206/386-4636; spl.org; map:L5) is an ultracool $156 million structure designed by Pritzker Prize–winning Dutch architect Rem Koolhaas. Built on the same site as its 1960s predecessor, the 355,000-square-foot, 11-level library shows off a gratelike exterior of glass, copper, and steel, with a four-story spiral constructed within to house the nonfiction collection. An underground parking garage makes trips to the castle of books far more pleasant than before, as does the in-library café. The public can reserve time to surf the Web at approximately 130 computer terminals. The main branch also hosts the Quick Information Line (206/386-4636), for answers to almost any question you can think of. Hours at the Central Library are Monday through Thursday 10am to 8pm, Friday and Saturday 10am to 6pm, and Sunday noon to 6pm.

Besides lending books, video and audio recordings, and even artwork, the Seattle Public Library system offers readings, lectures, film screenings, and many other events in 28 branch libraries around the city. Call the individual branches for specific event information. Mobile library service is also available (206/684-4713). The **KING COUNTY LIBRARY SYSTEM** has 43 branches countywide and an answer line (425/462-9600 or 800/462-9600; kcls.org).

BEST PLACE
TO BUY AN UMBRELLA?

"Who buys them? I have 20 in the coatroom at the restaurant."

Mark Canlis, third-generation managing owner, Canlis Restaurant

---

MAJOR DOWNTOWN BOOKSTORES

Seattle's population is legendarily literary, so it's not surprising that the city is filled with bookstores. **ELLIOTT BAY BOOK COMPANY** (101 S Main St, Pioneer Square; 206/624-6600; elliottbaybook.com; map:O8), which celebrated its 30th anniversary in 2003, is the best locally owned bookstore in town. Large chains with downtown branches include **BORDERS BOOKS & MUSIC** (1501 4th Ave; 206/622-4599; map:J6) and **BARNES & NOBLE** at Pacific Place (600 Pine St; 206/264-0156; map:I5). For more bookstores, see the Shopping chapter.

RADIO AND TV

Amid the usual horde of stations offered by the usual nationwide radio conglomerates lie some gems. The University of Washington–owned, student-run KEXP 90.3 FM has had a cutting-edge music and no-commercial format since 1972. For a quick introduction to the issues and politics of Seattle, nothing beats the University of Washington's National Public Radio affiliate, KUOW

94.9 FM, and its daily Weekday program, running every morning from 9am to 11am. Here's a quick guide to the local radio dial.

RADIO STATIONS

570 AM	KVI	TALK RADIO
710 AM	KIRO	NEWS/TALK
950 AM	KJR	SPORTS
1000 AM	KOMO	24-HOUR NEWS
88.5 FM	KPLU	PACIFIC LUTHERAN UNIVERSITY, NATIONAL PUBLIC RADIO, JAZZ
90.3 FM	KEXP	UNIVERSITY OF WASHINGTON, ALTERNATIVE
91.3 FM	KBCS	BELLEVUE COMMUNITY COLLEGE, JAZZ, FOLK, WORLD MUSIC, BLUES
92.5 FM	KQMV	POP, R&B
93.3 FM	KUBE	TOP 40, R&B
94.1 FM	KMPS	COUNTRY
94.9 FM	KUOW	UNIVERSITY OF WASHINGTON, NATIONAL PUBLIC RADIO
97.3 FM	KBSG	OLDIES
98.1 FM	KING	CLASSICAL
99.9 FM	KISW	ROCK
102.5 FM	KZOK	CLASSIC ROCK
103.7 FM	KMTT	ADULT ALTERNATIVE
107.7 FM	KNDD	ALTERNATIVE

TV STATIONS

4	KOMO	ABC
5	KING	NBC
6	KONG	INDEPENDENT
7	KIRO	CBS
9	KCTS	PBS
10	KMYQ	MY Q2
11	KSTW	THE CW
13	KCPQ	FOX

INTERNET ACCESS

Most hotels now offer in-room Internet access for their guests, and many have a business center on the premises (see the Lodgings chapter). The downtown Central Library (see Public Libraries, above) has hundreds of computers available to the public with free Internet access and word processing.

Free wireless Internet access, or Wi-Fi, is available throughout the city at coffee shops, libraries, parks—even on select buses. See the Unplugged sidebar in the Planning a Trip chapter for details or visit seattle.wifimug.org for a list of businesses that offer free, or mostly free, wireless access.

BEST PLACE
FOR A BRAIN FREEZE?

"Red Mill Burgers—from a creamsicle shake."

Tom Douglas, celebrated local chef and restaurateur

UNIVERSITIES AND COLLEGES

The **UNIVERSITY OF WASHINGTON** (Visitor Information Center: Odegaard Undergraduate Library, Ground Floor, University District; 206/543-9198; washington.edu; map:FF6) is the largest of the Washington state public universities and has one of the biggest university bookstores in the country (4326 University Wy NE, University District; 206/634-3400; bookstore.washington.edu; map:FF6). **SEATTLE PACIFIC UNIVERSITY** (3307 3rd Ave W, Queen Anne; 206/281-2000; spu.edu; map:FF8) is a private college associated with the Free Methodist Church. **SEATTLE UNIVERSITY** (901 12th Ave, First Hill; 206/296-6000; seattleu.edu; map:N1) is a private Jesuit school. **SEATTLE COMMUNITY COLLEGES** (206/587-4100; seattlecolleges.com) operate three separate campuses in the city, on Capitol Hill and in Northgate and West Seattle.

Important Telephone Numbers

AAA WASHINGTON	**800/562-2582**
AAA EMERGENCY ROAD SERVICE (24 HOURS)	**800/222-4357**
ALCOHOLICS ANONYMOUS	**206/587-2838**
AMBULANCE	**911**
AMTRAK	**800/872-7245**
ANIMAL SHELTER	**206/386-7387**
AUTO IMPOUND	**206/684-5444**
BETTER BUSINESS BUREAU	**206/431-2222**
BIRTH AND DEATH RECORDS	**206/296-4769**
BLOOD BANK	**206/292-6500**
CHAMBER OF COMMERCE	**206/389-7200**
CHILDREN AND FAMILY SERVICES (TO REPORT ABUSE/NEGLECT)	**866/363-4276**
CITIZENSHIP AND IMMIGRATION SERVICES	**800/375-5283**
CITY OF SEATTLE INFORMATION	**206/386-1234**
CITY PARKS INFORMATION AND SCHEDULING OFFICE	**206/684-4075**
COAST GUARD 24-HOUR EMERGENCY	**800/982-8813**

COMMUNITY INFORMATION LINE	211
CUSTOMS (U.S.)	206/553-6944
DIRECTORY ASSISTANCE (RATES VARY BY SERVICE PROVIDER)	411
DOMESTIC VIOLENCE HOTLINE	800/562-6025
EMERGENCY RESOURCE CENTER (ACTIVATED DURING EMERGENCIES SUCH AS EARTHQUAKES)	206/684-3355
FBI	206/622-0460
FEMA (FEDERAL EMERGENCY MANAGEMENT AGENCY)	800/462-9029
FIRE	911
GREYHOUND BUS LINES SEATTLE TERMINAL	206/628-5526
HIV/STD HOTLINE	206/205-7837
LOST PETS	206/386-7387
MARRIAGE LICENSES	206/296-3933
METRO TRANSIT RIDER INFORMATION LINE	206/553-3000
MISSING PERSONS	206/684-5582
PASSPORTS	206/808-5700
PLANNED PARENTHOOD	206/328-7700
POISON CENTER	206/526-2121
POST OFFICE INFORMATION	800/275-8777
RED CROSS	206/323-2345
SEATTLE AREA TRAFFIC REPORTS	206/368-4499
SEATTLE'S CONVENTION & VISITORS BUREAU	206/461-5840
SEATTLE/KING COUNTY DEPARTMENT OF PUBLIC HEALTH	206/296-4600
SENIOR INFORMATION CENTER	206/448-3110
SEXUAL ASSAULT RESOURCE LINE	888/998-6423
STATE PATROL	425/649-4370
SUICIDE CRISIS LINE	206/461-3222
TICKETMASTER	206/628-0888
WASHINGTON STATE FERRIES	206/464-6400
WEATHER	206/526-6087
ZIP CODE INFORMATION	800/275-8777

TOP 200 RESTAURANTS

Restaurants by Star Rating

★★★★

Canlis
Dahlia Lounge
Georgian, The
Herbfarm Restaurant, The
Le Gourmand
Mistral
Rover's
Tilth
Union

★★★½

Boat Street Cafe and Kitchen
Cafe Juanita
Campagne
Crush
El Gaucho
Harvest Vine
Madoka
Saito's Japanese Café & Bar
Sitka & Spruce
Third Floor Fish Cafe, The

★★★

Assaggio Ristorante
Barking Frog
Brasa
Café Campagne
Carmelita
Cascadia Restaurant
Chez Shea
Elliott's Oyster House
Eva Restaurant & Wine Bar
Flying Fish
The Four Swallows
Geneva
Hunt Club
Il Bistro
Il Terrazzo Carmine
La Carta de Oaxaca
Lampreia
Lark
Le Pichet
Licorous
Metropolitan Grill
Monsoon
Nell's
Nishino
Osteria La Spiga
Pair
Palace Kitchen
Restaurant Zoë
Shiro's
Stumbling Goat Bistro
Tavolàta
Tulio Ristorante
Volterra
Waterfront Seafood Grill
Wild Ginger Asian Restaurant and Satay Bar

★★½

Andaluca
Black Bottle
Cactus
Cafe Lago
Chiso
Crémant
Crow Restaurant and Bar
Daniel's Broiler Prime Steak & Chops
Dinette
Earth & Ocean
El Greco
Frontier Room
Green Leaf
I Love Sushi
Julia's Indonesian Kitchen
La Medusa
Macrina Bakery & Cafe
Malay Satay Hut
Mixtura
Ray's Boathouse
Sazerac
Serious Pie
Shallots Asian Bistro
Shanghai Garden
Shea's Lounge
Sostanza Trattoria
Steelhead Diner
Szmania's
Tango
Tosoni's
Vios Café & Marketplace
Voilà! Bistrot
Yarrow Bay Grill

★★

Anthony's Pier 66
Baguette Box
Barolo Ristorante
Beàto Food & Wine
Black Pearl
BOKA Kitchen + Bar
Brad's Swingside Café
Buenos Aires Grill
Cafe Nola
Chinook's at Salmon Bay
Coupage
Dragonfish Asian Café
Dulces Latin Bistro
El Camino
Etta's Seafood
Fish Club by Todd English, The

Fremont Classic Pizza & Trattoria
Imperial Garden Seafood Restaurant
India Bistro
JaK's Grill
JoAnna's Soul Café and Jazz Club
Kabul Afghan Cuisine
Kingfish Café
La Rustica
Maneki Japanese Restaurant
Maple Leaf Grill
Marco's Supperclub
Marjorie
Market Street Urban Grill
Mashiko
Maximilien in the Market
Oceanaire Seafood Room, The
Palisade
Pink Door, The
Place Pigalle
Pomegranate
Ponti Seafood Grill
Queen City Grill
Ruby's on Bainbridge
Saint-Germain
Salumi
Sea Garden
Seastar Restaurant and Raw Bar
Serafina
Seven Stars Pepper Szechuan Restaurant
Shamiana
Shanghai Café
Sweet and Savory
Szechuan Chef
Tamarind Tree
Tempero do Brasil
Thaiku
Tup Tim Thai
Typhoon!
Via Tribunali
Yanni's Greek Cuisine
Yarrow Bay Beach Cafe

★½

Agua Verde Cafe & Paddle Club
Anthony's Fish Bar
Bell Street Diner
Bis on Main
Blue Onion Bistro
Burrito Loco
Cafe Flora
Cedars Restaurant on Brooklyn
Chandler's Crabhouse
Crave
Ray's Cafe
SkyCity
Tutta Bella

★

Al Boccalino
Bimbo's Bitchin' Burrito Kitchen
Bizzarro Italian Café
Café Happy
Café Stellina
Chinoise Café
Chutneys
Coastal Kitchen
El Puerco Lloron
Endolyne Joe's
Feierabend
5 Spot Café
Fresh Flours
Garage
Greenlake Bar & Grill
Hilltop Ale House
Honey Hole
Joe Bar
Judy Fu's Snappy Dragon
Luau Polynesian Lounge
Luna Park Café
Madison Park Café
Mae Phim Thai
Malena's Taco Shop
Matt's Rotisserie & Oyster Lounge
Medin's Ravioli Station
Mediterranean Kitchen
Mona's Bistro & Lounge
Muy Macho Mexican Grill
Noble Court Restaurant
Olive You
Orrapin Thai Food
Panos Kleftiko
Paseo Caribbean Restaurant
Pontevecchio Italian Bistro
Saigon Bistro
St. Clouds
Samurai Noodle
611 Supreme Crêperie & Café
Tacos Guaymas
Thai Tom

UNRATED

Matt's in the Market

Restaurants by Neighborhood

BAINBRIDGE ISLAND
Cafe Nola
Four Swallows, The
Madoka
Ruby's on Bainbridge

BALLARD
Burrito Loco
India Bistro
La Carta de Oaxaca
Le Gourmand
Malena's Taco Shop
Market Street Urban Grill
Medin's Ravioli Station
Ray's Boathouse
Ray's Cafe
Thaiku
Volterra

BELLEVUE
Bis on Main
Daniel's Broiler Prime Steak & Chops
I Love Sushi
Mediterranean Kitchen
Noble Court Restaurant
Seastar Restaurant and Raw Bar
Shanghai Café
Szechuan Chef
Tosoni's

BELLTOWN
Assaggio Ristorante
Black Bottle
Boat Street Cafe and Kitchen
Brasa
Buenos Aires Grill
Cascadia Restaurant
Dahlia Lounge
El Gaucho
Flying Fish
Frontier Room
Lampreia
Macrina Bakery & Cafe
Marco's Supperclub
Marjorie
Mistral
Palace Kitchen
Queen City Grill
Restaurant Zoë
Saito's Japanese Café & Bar
Serious Pie
Shallot's Asian Bistro
Shiro's
Tavolàta

CAPITOL HILL
Baguette Box
Bimbo's Bitchin' Burrito Kitchen
Café Stellina
Chutneys
Coastal Kitchen
Crave
Dinette
El Greco
Garage
Honey Hole
Joe Bar
Kingfish Café
Lark
Licorous
Monsoon
Osteria La Spiga
611 Supreme Crêperie & Café
Tacos Guaymas
Tango
Via Tribunali
Vios Café & Marketplace

CENTRAL DISTRICT
JoAnna's Soul Café and Jazz Club

CHINATOWN/ INTERNATIONAL DISTRICT
Green Leaf
Malay Satay Hut
Maneki Japanese Restaurant
Saigon Bistro
Samurai Noodle
Sea Garden
Seven Stars Pepper Szechuan Restaurant
Shanghai Garden
Tamarind Tree

COLUMBIA CITY
La Medusa
Tutta Bella

DOWNTOWN
Andaluca
BOKA Kitchen + Bar
Dragonfish Asian Café
Earth & Ocean
Georgian, The
Metropolitan Grill
Oceanaire Seafood Room, The
Sazerac
Tulio Ristorante
Typhoon!
Union
Wild Ginger Asian Restaurant and Satay Bar

EASTLAKE
Serafina
Sitka & Spruce

FIRST HILL
Geneva
Hunt Club

FREMONT
Baguette Box
Brad's Swingside Café
Chiso
El Camino
Fremont Classic Pizza & Trattoria
Paseo Caribbean Restaurant
Pontevecchio Italian Bistro
Ponti Seafood Grill
Tacos Guaymas

GREEN LAKE
Eva Restaurant & Wine Bar
Greenlake Bar & Grill
Luau Polynesian Lounge
Mona's Bistro & Lounge
Nell's
Tacos Guaymas

GREENWOOD/ PHINNEY RIDGE
Carmelita
Fresh Flours
Olive You
Stumbling Goat Bistro
Yanni's Greek Cuisine

INTERBAY/ MAGNOLIA
Chinook's at Salmon Bay
Palisade
Szmania's

ISSAQUAH
JaK's Grill
Shanghai Garden

KENT
Imperial Garden Seafood Restaurant

KIRKLAND
Cactus
Café Happy
Cafe Juanita
Mixtura
Shamiana
Third Floor Fish Cafe, The
Yarrow Bay Beach Cafe
Yarrow Bay Grill

LAURELHURST
JaK's Grill

MADISON PARK/ MADISON VALLEY
Cactus
Cafe Flora
Chinoise on Madison
Crush
Harvest Vine
Madison Park Café
Nishino
Rover's
Saint-Germain
Sostanza Trattoria
Voilà! Bistrot

MADRONA/ MOUNT BAKER
Coupage
Crémant
Daniel's Broiler Prime Steak & Chops
Dulces Latin Bistro
St. Clouds
Sweet and Savory

MAPLE LEAF
Judy Fu's Snappy Dragon
Maple Leaf Grill

MONTLAKE
Cafe Lago

PIKE PLACE MARKET
Café Campagne
Campagne
Chez Shea
El Puerco Lloron
Etta's Seafood
Il Bistro
Le Pichet
Matt's in the Market
Maximilien in the Market
Pink Door, The
Place Pigalle
Shea's Lounge
Steelhead Diner

PIONEER SQUARE
Al Boccalino
Il Terrazzo Carmine
Mae Phim Thai
Salumi

QUEEN ANNE
Canlis
Chinoise Café
Chutneys
Crow Restaurant and Bar
5 Spot Café
Hilltop Ale House
Macrina Bakery & Cafe
Malena's Taco Shop
Orrapin Thai Food
Panos Kleftiko
SkyCity
Tup Tim Thai

RAVENNA
Julia's Indonesian Kitchen
Pair

REDMOND
Malay Satay Hut
Matt's Rotisserie & Oyster Lounge
Pomegranate
Typhoon!

SHORELINE
Black Pearl

SOUTH LAKE UNION
Barolo Ristorante
Chandler's Crabhouse
Daniel's Broiler Prime Steak & Chops
Feierabend
I Love Sushi
Tutta Bella

SOUTH PARK/ WHITE CENTER
Muy Macho Mexican Grill
Tacos Guaymas

UNIVERSITY DISTRICT
Agua Verde Cafe & Paddle Club
Blue Onion Bistro
Cedars Restaurant on Brooklyn
Tempero do Brasil
Thai Tom

VASHON ISLAND
Macrina Bakery & Cafe

WALLINGFORD
Bizzarro Italian Café
Chinoise on 45th
Chutneys
Kabul Afghan Cuisine
Tilth
Tutta Bella

WATERFRONT
Anthony's Fish Bar
Anthony's Pier 66
Bell Street Diner
Elliott's Oyster House
Fish Club by Todd English, The
Waterfront Seafood Grill

WEDGWOOD
Black Pearl

WEST SEATTLE
Beàto Food & Wine
Cactus
Endolyne Joe's
JaK's Grill
La Rustica
Luna Park Café
Mashiko
Tacos Guaymas

WOODINVILLE
Barking Frog
Herbfarm Restaurant, The

Restaurants by Cuisine and Other Features

AFGHAN
Kabul Afghan Cuisine

ASIAN
Chinoise Café
Dragonfish Asian Café
Julia's Indonesian Kitchen
Madoka
Malay Satay Hut
Shallots Asian Bistro
Wild Ginger Asian Restaurant and Satay Bar

BAKERY
Fresh Flours
Macrina Bakery & Cafe
Sweet and Savory

BARBECUE
Frontier Room
Sazerac

BREAKFAST
Andaluca
Chinook's at Salmon Bay
Coastal Kitchen
Crave
Dragonfish Asian Café
Earth & Ocean
Endolyne Joe's
Fish Club by Todd English, The
5 Spot Café
Georgian, The
Hunt Club
Imperial Garden Seafood Restaurant
Le Pichet
Luna Park Café
Macrina Bakery & Cafe

Sazerac
Tacos Guaymas
Tulio Ristorante

BRUNCH

Barking Frog
Blue Onion Bistro
Boat Street Cafe and Kitchen
BOKA Kitchen + Bar
Café Campagne
Cafe Flora
Cafe Nola
Chandler's Crabhouse
Coupage
Crave
Dragonfish Asian Café
El Camino
El Greco
Etta's Seafood
Hunt Club
Joanna's Soul Café and Jazz Club
Kingfish Café
Luna Park Café
Macrina Bakery & Cafe
Madison Park Café
Maple Leaf Grill
Matt's in the Market
Maximilien in the Market
Monsoon
Palisade
Pomegranate
Ponti Seafood Grill
St. Clouds
Sazerac
Serafina
611 Supreme Crêperie & Café
SkyCity
Tilth
Volterra

CARIBBEAN

Paseo Caribbean Restaurant

CHINESE

Black Pearl
Imperial Garden Seafood Restaurant
Judy Fu's Snappy Dragon
Noble Court Restaurant
Sea Garden
Shanghai Café
Shanghai Garden
Szechuan Chef

COMFORT FOOD

Café Stellina
Blue Onion Bistro
Maple Leaf Grill
Marjorie
St. Clouds

CONTINENTAL

Geneva
Georgian, The
Szmania's
Tosoni's

EDITORS' CHOICE

Assaggio Ristorante
Baguette Box
Barking Frog
Brad's Swingside Café
Brasa
Cafe Juanita
Canlis
Carmelita
Crow Restaurant and Bar
Crush
Dahlia Lounge
Flying Fish
Green Leaf
Harvest Vine
Herbfarm Restaurant, The
La Carta de Oaxaca
La Medusa
Lark
Le Gourmand
Le Pichet
Madoka
Matt's in the Market
Palace Kitchen
Rover's
Saint-Germain
Saito's Japanese Café & Bar
Salumi
Shiro's
Sitka & Spruce
Steelhead Diner
Tavolàta
Third Floor Fish Cafe, The
Tilth
Union
Volterra
Waterfront Seafood Grill

FAMILY

Anthony's Fish Bar
Bell Street Diner
Burrito Loco
Cascadia Restaurant
Coupage
Endolyne Joe's
5 Spot Café
Judy Fu's Snappy Dragon
Luna Park Café
Medin's Ravioli Station
Pomegranate
Ray's Boathouse
Ray's Cafe
St. Clouds
Steelhead Diner
Tutta Bella
Vios Café & Marketplace

FRENCH

Boat Street Cafe and Kitchen
Café Campagne
Campagne
Chez Shea
Crémant
Le Gourmand
Le Pichet
Madison Park Café
Maximilien in the Market
Mistral
Pair
Place Pigalle
Rover's
Saint-Germain
611 Supreme Crêperie & Café
Voilà! Bistrot

GERMAN

Feierabend
Geneva
Szmania's

GOOD VALUE

Agua Verde Cafe & Paddle Club
Baguette Box
Bimbo's Bitchin' Burrito Kitchen
Black Pearl
Café Happy
Cedars Restaurant on Brooklyn
Chiso
El Puerco Lloron
Fremont Classic Pizzeria and Trattoria
Fresh Flours
Green Leaf
Honey Hole
Imperial Garden Seafood Restaurant
India Bistro
JaK's Grill
Julia's Indonesian Kitchen
Mae Phim Thai
Malay Satay Hut
Malena's Taco Shop
Maneki
Medin's Ravioli Station
Paseo Caribbean Restaurant
Saint-Germain
Salumi
Samurai Noodle
Seven Stars Pepper Szechuan Restaurant
Shallots Asian Bistro
Shamiana
Sitka & Spruce
Stumbling Goat Bistro
Tacos Guaymas
Tamarind Tree
Tavolàta
Tempero do Brasil
Thaiku
Thai Tom
Tup Tim Thai
Yanni's Greek Cuisine

GREEK

El Greco
Panos Kleftiko
Vios Café & Marketplace
Yanni's Greek Cuisine

HOTEL

Andaluca (Mayflower Park Hotel)
Barking Frog (Willows Lodge)
BOKA Kitchen + Bar (Hotel 1000)
Dragonfish Asian Café (Paramount Hotel)
Earth & Ocean (W Seattle Hotel)
Fish Club by Todd English, The (Seattle Marriott Waterfront Hotel)
Georgian, The (Fairmont Olympic Hotel)
Hunt Club (Sorrento Hotel)
Sazerac (Hotel Monaco)
Tulio Ristorante (Hotel Vintage Park)

INDIAN

Cedars Restaurant on Brooklyn
Chutneys
India Bistro
Shamiana

ITALIAN

Al Boccalino
Assaggio Ristorante
Barolo Ristorante
Beàto Food & Wine
Bizzarro Italian Café
Cafe Juanita
Cafe Lago
Fremont Classic Pizzeria and Trattoria
Il Bistro
Il Terrazzo Carmine
La Medusa
La Rustica
Medin's Ravioli Station
Osteria La Spiga
Pink Door, The
Pontevecchio Italian Bistro
Sostanza Trattoria
Tavolàta
Tulio Ristorante
Via Tribunali

JAPANESE

Chiso
Fresh Flours
Maneki Japanese Restaurant
Mashiko
Nishino
Saito's Japanese Café & Bar
Samurai Noodle
Shiro's

LATIN

Dulces Latin Bistro
Tango
Tempero do Brasil

MEDITERRANEAN

Andaluca
Cedars Restaurant on Brooklyn
El Greco
Macrina Bakery & Cafe
Mediterranean Kitchen
Mona's Bistro & Lounge
Olive You

MEXICAN

Agua Verde Cafe & Paddle Club
Bimbo's Bitchin' Burrito Kitchen
Burrito Loco
Cactus
El Camino
El Puerco Lleron
La Carta de Oaxaca
Malena's Taco Shop
Muy Macho Mexican Grill
Tacos Guaymas

NORTHWEST

Barking Frog
Bis on Main
Canlis
Cascadia Restaurant
Crush
Dahlia Lounge
Earth & Ocean
Eva Restaurant & Wine Bar
Georgian, The
Herbfarm Restaurant, The
Hunt Club
Lampreia
Lark
Maple Leaf Grill
Marco's Supperclub
Market Street Urban Grill
Nell's
Pair
Palace Kitchen
Pomegranate
Restaurant Zoë
SkyCity
Stumbling Goat Bistro
Union

OUTDOOR DINING

Agua Verde Cafe & Paddle Club
Al Boccalino
Anthony's Pier 66
Assaggio Ristorante
Barking Frog
Boat Street Cafe and Kitchen
BOKA Kitchen + Bar
Cactus
Café Campagne
Cafe Nola
Carmelita
Cascadia Restaurant
Chandler's Crabhouse
Chinook's at Salmon Bay
El Camino
El Greco
Elliott's Oyster House
Fish Club by Todd English, The
Hunt Club
Il Terrazzo Carmine
Le Pichet
Luau Polynesian Lounge
Macrina Bakery & Cafe
Madison Park Café
Malena's Taco Shop
Marco's Supperclub
Monsoon
Palisade
Pink Door, The
Place Pigalle
Ponti Seafood Grill
Ray's Café
Rover's
Serafina
Shallots Asian Bistro
Sostanza Trattoria
Steelhead Diner
Tacos Guaymas (some branches)
Waterfront Seafood Grill
Yarrow Bay Beach Cafe
Yarrow Bay Grill

PIZZA

Fremont Classic Pizza & Trattoria
Serious Pie
Tutta Bella
Via Tribunali

POLYNESIAN

Luau Polynesian Lounge

ROMANTIC

Al Boccalino
Andaluca
Barolo Ristorante
Boat Street Cafe and Kitchen

Brasa
Cafe Juanita
Campagne
Canlis
Chez Shea
Eva Restaurant & Wine Bar
Four Swallows, The
Geneva
Georgian, The
Harvest Vine
Herbfarm Restaurant, The
Hunt Club
Il Bistro
Il Terrazzo Carmine
Lark
La Rustica
Le Gourmand
Licorous
Marco's Supperclub
Marjorie
Maximilien in the Market
Mistral
Mona's Bistro & Lounge
Nell's
Pink Door, The
Place Pigalle
Pontevecchio Italian Bistro
Restaurant Zoë
Rover's
Ruby's on Bainbridge
Serafina
Sostanza Trattoria
Tango
Tulio Ristorante
Via Tribunali

SEAFOOD

Anthony's Fish Bar
Anthony's Pier 66
Bell Street Diner
Earth & Ocean
Elliott's Oyster House
Etta's Seafood
Fish Club by Todd English, The
Flying Fish
Imperial Garden Seafood Restaurant
Matt's in the Market
Matt's Rotisserie & Oyster Lounge
Oceanaire Seafood Room, The
Palisade
Ponti Seafood Grill
Queen City Grill
Ray's Boathouse
Ray's Cafe
Ruby's on Bainbridge
Sea Garden
Seastar Restaurant and Raw Bar
Steelhead Diner
Third Floor Fish Cafe, The
Waterfront Seafood Grill

SEE AND BE "SCENE"

Barolo Ristorante
Beàto Food & Wine
Black Bottle
BOKA Kitchen + Bar
Brasa
Crush
Daniel's Broiler Prime Steak & Chops
Frontier Room
Garage
Licorous
Palace Kitchen
Pink Door, The
Queen City Grill
Sazerac
Tango

SMALL PLATES

Black Bottle
Harvest Vine
Lark
Licorous
Marjorie
Pair
Tango

SOUTH AMERICAN

Buenos Aires Grill
Mixtura
Tempero do Brasil

SOUTHERN

Joanna's Soul Café and Jazz Club
Kingfish Café
Sazerac

STEAKS

Buenos Aires Grill
Canlis
Daniel's Broiler Prime Steak & Chops
El Gaucho
JaK's Grill
Metropolitan Grill

SUSHI

Chiso
Dragonfish Asian Café
I Love Sushi
Maneki Japanese Restaurant
Mashiko
Nishino
Saito's Japanese Café & Bar
Shallot's Asian Bistro
Shiro's

THAI

Dragonfish Asian Café

Mae Phim Thai
Orrapin Thai Food
Shallot's Asian Bistro
Thaiku
Thai Tom
Tup Tim Thai
Typhoon!

VIETNAMESE
Green Leaf
Monsoon
Saigon Bistro
Shallot's Asian Bistro
Tamarind Tree

VIEW
Agua Verde Cafe & Paddle Club
Anthony's Pier 66
Beàto Food & Wine
Canlis
Chandler's Crabhouse
Chez Shea
Chinook's at Salmon Bay
Daniel's Broiler Prime Steak & Chops
Elliott's Oyster House
El Puerco Lleron
Etta's Seafood
Eva Restaurant & Wine Bar
I Love Sushi
Matt's in the Market
Maximilien in the Market
Palisade
Place Pigalle
Ponti Seafood Grill
Ray's Boathouse
Ray's Cafe
SkyCity
Sostanza Trattoria
Third Floor Fish Cafe, The
Waterfront Seafood Grill
Yarrow Bay Beach Cafe
Yarrow Bay Grill

RESTAURANT REVIEWS

Agua Verde Cafe & Paddle Club / ★★

1303 NE BOAT ST, UNIVERSITY DISTRICT; 206/545-8570

Even on a gray Seattle day, this bayside cottage with brightly colored walls and stripped floorboards exudes a tropical glow. The menu features Baja classics—fish tacos, salads, ceviche—and plenty of vegetarian plates. The taco de mero, grilled halibut and shredded cabbage with a squirt of fresh lime, is love at first bite. Don't miss the salsa cart, which offers a smoky chipotle and a three-alarm tomato salsa. The crowded cafeteria-style lunch gives way to full service at dinnertime, but table service can be hit-or-miss. Partner any meal with Mexican beer, margaritas, or horchata, a delicious cinnamon-spiced rice and almond drink. Sweet endings come in the form of a quivering coconut flan or a slice of key lime pie. *$; DIS, MC, V; checks OK; lunch, dinner Mon–Sat; full bar; reservations recommended; self parking; aguaverde.com; map:FF7.* ♿

Al Boccalino / ★

1 YESLER WY, PIONEER SQUARE; 206/622-7688

This intimate Italian restaurant has all the trappings of a clandestine meeting place. Guests enter through an iron gate into a small foyer before being ushered into the triangular dining room trimmed in dark wood, brick, and stained glass. Start with zuppa vellutata, starring tomatoes, aromatics, and a touch of cream, and a selection from the rotating antipasti menu. Classic osso buco is a specialty here, as is the pollo trifolato, chicken breast doused in a prosciutto brandy sauce. There are plenty of good pastas: the orecchiette with rapini and bottarga capellini with squid ink are but two. New owner Luigi DeNunzio (who also owns nearby Café Bengodi, DeNunzio Trattoria, and Pastiamo) is well on his way to establishing Little Italy in Pioneer Square. *$$; AE, DC, MC, V; checks OK; lunch Mon–Fri, dinner Mon–Sat; Sun in summer; beer and wine; reservations recommended; street parking; seattleslittleitaly.com; map:N8.* ♿

Andaluca / ★★✯

407 OLIVE WY (MAYFLOWER PARK HOTEL), DOWNTOWN; 206/382-6999

Lovers who love to eat will adore this romantic, informal midtown refuge that goes beyond mere ambience. In the sure hands of chef Wayne Johnson, Andaluca has become a mecca for fine food. Well-informed and lighthearted servers deftly attend to diners in a cocoon of rosewood booths, murals, and textured walls in deep reds and earthy browns. Johnson's seasonal menus emphasize local seafood and produce and include well-considered wine-pairing suggestions from the extensive list. The ever-changing pintxos (small bites) menu, paired with sips of sangria, is perfect for a quick nibble before a show or as a prelude to the main course. Two notable signature entrées are the saffron-scented paella, loaded with shellfish, chicken, and chorizo, and the Cabrales cheese–crusted rare beef tenderloin with grilled pears. *$$$; AE, DC, DIS, MC, V; checks OK; breakfast every day, lunch Mon–Sat, dinner every day; full bar; reservations recommended; valet, self, and street parking; andaluca.com; map:I6* ♿

Anthony's Fish Bar / ★✯
Anthony's Pier 66 / ★★
Bell Street Diner / ★✯

2201 ALASKAN WY, PIER 66, WATERFRONT; 206/448-6688

There's something for everyone at this trio of restaurants on the Bell Street Pier. Upstairs, Anthony's Pier 66 has a spectacular view of Seattle's waterfront, and the Asian-inflected menu of local and regional seafood is priced accordingly. Kick off your meal with the Potlatch, an impressive collection of Northwest steamer clams, mussels, split snow crab legs, and half-shell oysters. Alder-planked wild chinook salmon or Dungeness crab cakes are reliable entrées. For lunch or casual dining, the boisterous Bell Street Diner downstairs is a good choice, offering less formal fare: seafood, chowders, burgers, generous salads, rice bowls, and fish tacos. For a quick, no-frills bite, join the seagulls waterside at Anthony's Fish Bar and chow down on fish-and-chips, chowder, or blackened-rockfish tacos. *$, $$, $; AE, MC, V; checks OK; dinner every day (Anthony's Pier 66); lunch, dinner every day (Bell Street Diner, Anthony's Fish Bar); 2 full bars; reservations recommended for Pier 66; valet (at night) and validated (lunch and dinner) garage parking at Seattle Art Institute; anthonys.com; map:H9.* ♿

CRAZY FOR CUPCAKES

Seattle has **CUPCAKE ROYALE** (2052 NW Market St, Ballard; 206/782-9557; and branches) to thank for the blossoming cupcake craze. Their yummy Lemon Drop bears every semblance of its martini moniker without the hangover, and chocolate cake is paired perfectly with lavender-scented buttercream. **NEW YORK CUPCAKES** (1514 4th Ave, Downtown, 206/326-7900; and 175 Bellevue Square, Bellevue, 425/283-5445) offers a bite of the Big Apple with cupcakes named Manhattan Mint, Long Island Lemon, and Central Park. Seattle's newest cupcake boutique, **TROPHY CUPCAKES AND PARTY** (1815 N 45th, Ste 209, Wallingford; 206/632-7020) combines the finest details—Valrhona chocolate, Madagascar bourbon vanilla, sweet cream butter, and French sprinkles—in one sweet package. At $2.75 a pop, they're not cheap, but they're worth every hip-hugging bite. **DAHLIA BAKERY'S** (2001 4th Ave, Belltown; 206/441-4540) chocolate fancy cupcakes frosted with vanilla "flower petal" icing are so pretty you might not want to eat them right away—but you'll cave eventually.

—Pat Tanumihardja

Assaggio Ristorante / ★★★

2010 4TH AVE, BELLTOWN; 206/441-1399

Assaggio is one of Seattle's best Italian restaurants due in large part to its gracious owner, Mauro Golmarvi, who greets each guest with a hug, a kiss, or a handshake. The menu, which features cuisine from Golmarvi's Le Marche region, is just as genial. Start with simple seared scallops or the pear, apple, and Gorgonzola salad. Primi highlights include the fettuccine frutti di mare, a tangle of imported Italian pasta tossed with a flavorful tomato sauce and brimming with seafood, and the pappardelle al cinghiale: wild boar ragù, Kalamata olives, and roasted red peppers. For secondi, savor the branzino, a Mediterranean white fish roasted whole and expertly deboned tableside. Shipped in weekly from Italy, the limoncello tartufo—a refreshingly light sorbet "ball" encasing a creamy limoncello-spiked center—is divine. *$$; AE, DC, DIS, MC, V; checks OK; lunch Mon–Fri, dinner Mon–Sat; beer, wine, and service bar; reservations recommended; valet, self, and street parking; assaggioseattle.com; map:H6.* ♿

Baguette Box / ★★

1203 PINE ST, CAPITOL HILL; 206/332-0220;
626 N 34TH ST, FREMONT; 206/632-1511

Baguettes beyond your imagination—that's what you'll find at these two storefronts from culinary genius and Monsoon (see review below) co-owner Eric Banh. Banh's take on traditional bánh mì (Vietnamese sandwiches) pairs the loaves with a sophisticated repertoire of fillings. Top of the list is the drunken chicken sandwich, based on Monsoon's very popular deep-fried and glazed chicken (like General Tso's chicken but with the kick of a white wine marinade). The giant meatball sandwich dripping with marinara sauce and the grilled lemongrass skirt steak are also winners. Don't forget an order of truffle fries. Both locales offer the same delicious fare; however, the original Capitol Hill location is more rustic compared to Fremont's mod white interior punctuated with splashes of red. *$; MC, V; no checks; lunch, early dinner every day; beer and wine; no reservations; self and street parking, baguettebox.com; map:GG6, FF7.* ♿

Barking Frog / ★★★

14580 NE 145TH ST (WILLOWS LODGE), WOODINVILLE; 425/424-2999

One of Woodinville wine country's few restaurants, Barking Frog celebrates the senses Northwest-style, with large old-growth beams, wooden tabletops, and an unpretentious staff. Executive chef Bobby Moore's menu changes seasonally, but favored perennial starters are the prawns coated in Grand Marnier aioli, and seared foie gras resting on a savory apple-onion turnover. Both meat and seafood are expertly prepared. Try the seared sea bass paired with ravioli stuffed with lobster meat, mascarpone, and tarragon, or the decadent beef tenderloin (ask if Snake River Farm's Kobe beef is available) with yams, wild mushrooms, and Gorgonzola cream. Dessert does not disappoint—seasonal offerings include a toffee date torte, passion-fruit-poached pears, or an ever-changing crème brûlée. Naturally, the award-winning wine list showcases Washington wines. *$$$; AE, DC, DIS, MC, V; checks OK; lunch Mon–Fri, dinner every day, brunch Sat–Sun; full bar; reservations recommended; self parking; willowslodge.com; map:BB2.* ♿

Barolo Ristorante / ★★

1940 WESTLAKE AVE, SOUTH LAKE UNION; 206/770-9000

Crystal-crusted chandeliers, candlesticks dribbling wax, and white gauzy curtains lend a fairy-tale glow to this modern restaurant in the heart of condo city. The latest venture undertaken by longtime Seattle restaurateurs Leo, Salvio, and Roberto Varchetta offers the rich and earthy cuisine of northern Italy—with a Northwest touch. The broad menu features an extensive antipasti selection, grilled meats, and more than a dozen house-made pastas. Winners include a tuna tartare drizzled with honey and showered with sea salt, tortellini alla Piemontese filled with porcini mushrooms in a creamy truffle-leek sauce, and coho salmon paired with a lusty roasted red pepper purée. The wine list includes more than 300 labels and varietals from around the world and an impressive selection of 30 Italian grappas. *$$–$$$; AE, DIS, MC, V; no checks; lunch Mon–Fri, dinner every day; full bar; reservations recommended; street parking, valet parking (weekends); baroloseattle.com; map:H5.* ♿

Beàto Food & Wine / ★★

3247 CALIFORNIA AVE SW, WEST SEATTLE; 206/923-1333

Beàto has everything you could want in a neighborhood osteria and bar: an inviting dining room, inventive Italian cuisine, and friendly, knowledgeable servers. As soon as you take your seat, fresh-baked bread accompanied by trempette olive oil and an amuse-bouche magically appear. The menu offers a formidable collection of nibblers; don't miss the house-made chicken liver pâté slathered on crostini with tomato jam. Follow with the creamy fontina risotto crowned with foraged mushrooms and truffle-oil-laced fresh arugula, or the exquisite fuchsia-hued beet gnocchi paired with a citrus- and herb-flecked sausage. Sip through weekly changing flights of wines from Umbria to southern Italy. Dining solo? The bar provides the perfect backdrop to survey the room. *$$–$$$; AE, MC, V; no checks; dinner Tues–Sun; beer and wine; reservations recommended; self parking; beatoseattle.com; map:JJ8.* ♿

Bimbo's Bitchin' Burrito Kitchen / ★

1013 E PIKE ST, CAPITOL HILL; 206/329-9978

This tiny taco joint—open to 21-and-older patrons only—serves up great food, an irreverent sense of humor, and delightfully tacky décor. Expect to wait alongside young Capitol Hill hipsters, who can't get enough of the humongous burritos, tacos, quesadillas, or nachos paired with sensational cumin-lime sour cream. Fuel up here, then shuffle over to the adjacent Cha Cha Lounge. It's got the same mood and music as Bimbo's, plus it serves great margaritas with a fresh, homemade sour blend—no bottled mixes. Bimbo's is open till 2am Friday and Saturday, so you can eat there twice in one night—that's a night to remember that you probably won't! *$; MC, V; no checks; lunch, dinner every day; full bar; no reservations; street parking; chachalounge.com; map:GG6.* ♿

BEST SETTING
FOR A CONTEMPORARY TEA PARTY?

"I love Remedy Teas—a very mod and charming tea shop with an amazing selection of teas and treats."

Linda Derschang, proprietor of Linda's Tavern, King's Hardware, Smith, and Viceroy

---

Bis on Main / ★★☆

10213 MAIN ST, BELLEVUE; 425/455-2033

Recently remodeled, a bigger and better Bis on Main boasts a new bar and lounge, plus a second dining room that doubles as a private dining room. Not lost is the intimate setting and personalized service under the direction of owner Joe Vilardi, a warm host well known from his years at Pioneer Square's Il Terrazzo Carmine. With tasteful taupe décor accented by the works of outstanding Northwest artists and crisp white-clothed tables, Bis draws a well-dressed business and social bunch. Longtime Bis fans can rest assured that old favorites such as Dungeness crab cakes and crispy garlic chicken have their place next to new menu items like the garlic sausage and duck confit cassoulet. *$$; AE, DIS, MC,*

V; traveler's checks OK; lunch Mon–Fri, dinner every day; full bar; reservations recommended; valet and street parking; bisonmain.com; map:HH3. ♿

Bizzarro Italian Café / ★

1307 N 46TH ST, WALLINGFORD; 206/632-7277

No restaurant in Seattle is more appropriately named. Rooms are jammed with bizarre kitsch, and the menu, too, proffers quirky delights, including the Forest Floor Frenzy, a mix of shiitakes, portobellos, walnuts, and roasted garlic tossed with rigatoni in sherry cream. Despite all the zaniness, Bizzarro delivers where it counts. All pastas are made fresh daily using organic eggs, and everything from capellini to pappardelle can be paired with the house-made marinara or Alfredo. Recommended are the gnocchi puttanesca, luscious potato dumplings tossed in a spicy tomato sauce with capers and roasted peppers. Wash down the savory Italian fare with a malbec or any one of the house pours. One word of warning: weekend waits can stretch into the hour. *$$; AE, DIS, MC, V; no checks; dinner every day; beer and wine; reservations accepted for 6 or more; street parking; bizzarroitaliancafe.com; map:FF7.* ♿

Black Bottle / ★★☆

2600 1ST AVE, BELLTOWN; 206/441-1500

Black Bottle is the bad boy of Belltown—the one you fall in love with even though you know you shouldn't. It's dark, noisy, and crowded, and service can be sketchy, but you'll nonetheless be seduced by sinfully tempting tapas and healthy pours. Dishes are meant to be shared, but you may find yourself hording the flatbread that oozes with béchamel and prosciutto, the grilled portobellos and butter beans, or the hanger steak and daikon. Other novel creations, such as charred little broccoli heads, will either win you over or turn you off. If you don't like them, trade with those who can't get enough and order more of your favorite $8 and $9 plates. Cocktails are fresh and inventive, and the small but excellent wine list is well priced. *$$; AE, V, MC; no checks; dinner every day; reservations for large groups only; full bar; street parking; blackbottleseattle.com; map:E8.* ♿

Black Pearl / ★★

7347 35TH AVE NE, WEDGWOOD; 206/526-5115;
14602 15TH AVE NE, SHORELINE; 206/365-8989

The house-made, hand-rolled noodles that distinguish this place shouldn't be missed. The Special Chow Mein's plump and plentiful signature noodles are tossed with shrimp, chicken, beef, and seven different vegetables. Another house specialty is the Black Pearl hot pot. Have it with chicken and tofu; with veggies, tofu, and bean threads; with a combo of chickens/prawns/scallops; or with catfish. The young servers are helpful in guiding the newcomer. *$; AE, DC, DIS, MC, V; checks OK; lunch Mon–Sat, dinner every day; beer and wine; reservations recommended for 6 or more; self and street parking; map: EE6, BB6.* ♿

Blue Onion Bistro / ★✯

5801 ROOSEVELT WY NE, UNIVERSITY DISTRICT; 206/729-0579

Decorated in equal parts kitsch and memorabilia, this converted 1950s gas station is a great place to fill up. Comfort food has been zapped into full-flavored, imaginative, new-American fare. The Blue Salad is zesty with apples, chicken, and blue cheese, and the daily soups kick butter. A mean mac and cheese whipped up using a cheddar-Gruyère mix is topped with mounds of blue cheese and green onions; the maple duck is smothered in a delectable sausage-maple glaze; and the chicken-fried steak is just too good to serve at breakfast only. Desserts, posted on a blackboard, change regularly and may include an mmm-inducing bananas Foster. Come for weekend brunch, when you can dig in to hearty American-style breakfasts from biscuits and gravy to inch-high blueberry pancakes. *$$; MC, V; checks OK; lunch Tues–Fri, dinner Tues–Sun, brunch Sat–Sun; beer and wine; reservations recommended; self and street parking; theblueonionbistro.com; map:EE7.* ♿

Boat Street Cafe and Kitchen / ★★★✯

3131 WESTERN AVE, STE 301, BELLTOWN; 206/632-4602

Provence meets Northwest at this little gem wedged into the lower level of Northwest Lofts (go down the ramp to find it) at the awkward intersection of Denny and Western. With whitewashed brick walls, rustic wood floors, and an outdoor garden spilling lavender, the airy, light-filled, French countryside setting is reminiscent of the café's previous incarnation along—where else?—Boat Street. By day, the Kitchen serves bistro fare: perhaps an eggplant sandwich with hot pepper rouille, goat cheese, and basil; plus a revolving menu of seasonal soups and salads. By night, specials such as herb-rubbed pork tenderloin, oyster gratin, and roasted poussin (young chicken) make their appearance. Save room for the amaretto bread pudding served in a pool of rum butter cream sauce. *$$$; AE, DIS, MC, V; no checks; lunch Mon–Fri (Kitchen), dinner (Cafe), brunch Sat–Sun (Kitchen); beer and wine; reservations recommended (dinner); street parking; boatstreetcafe.com; map:C8.*

BOKA Kitchen + Bar / ★★

1000 1ST AVE (HOTEL 1000), DOWNTOWN; 206/357-9000

Like any urban dining room worth its salt, BOKA (an acronym for Bold Original Kitchen Artistry) has a collection of must-try cocktails, including a smoky hibiscus margarita and a white peach cosmo. The restaurant's modern interior boasts a stark palette accented by a reclaimed wood floor, brass tabletops, and backlit walls that shift from hot pink to azure. Every detail spells chic, including the "urban American" menu. Start with a selection of "urban bites" (small plates shrunk down further). The salty-sweet combo of paddlefish caviar on a white chocolate blini or Dungeness crab salad with mango and ginger aioli tucked in a phyllo "nest" will whet your appetite for the main course. Entrées weave modern twists on homespun dishes, such as panko-breaded shake-and-bake chicken, and maple-brined pork chops. *$$$; AE,*

DIS, MC, V; no checks; lunch Mon–Fri, dinner every day, brunch Sat–Sun; full bar; reservations recommended; valet parking; bokaseattle.com; map:L7. ♿

Brad's Swingside Café / ★★

4212 FREMONT AVE N, FREMONT; 206/633-4057

This cramped, funky, homey living room hung with Pittsburgh Pirates memorabilia and pictures of saints is offbeat and charming. Chef/owner Brad Inserra runs the place in an innovative, gregarious, Sicilian way that's made it a beloved neighborhood classic. Though the dining room and kitchen are puny, flavors, portions, and hospitality are huge. You'll find all manner of seafood in pan-Mediterranean styles and aromatherapeutic sauces. Pastas are hard to pass up—especially the aglio e olio, ordinarily simple fare with garlic and olive oil but here an elaborate plateful of linguini lavished with capers, sun-dried tomatoes, anchovies, Marsala, and ground hazelnuts. There's a muscular wine list and a good selection of beers. *$$; MC, V; checks OK; dinner Tues–Sat; beer and wine; reservations accepted for 6 or more; street parking; map:FF8.* ♿

Brasa / ★★★

2107 3RD AVE, BELLTOWN; 206/728-4220

Awash in warm orange tones and amber light, the dual-tiered dining room is sumptuous, while the copper-topped bar is one of the hippest spots in town. From the bar menu (served till 1am on weekends), order Spanish fried squid, a lamb burger with melted feta and garlic aioli, or pizza topped with figs, Serrano ham, and chèvre. Main dishes reflect chef/co-owner Tamara Murphy's belief in sustainable cuisine—she tries to use every part of the pasture-fed animals that are butchered in the restaurant's kitchen. House-cured bacon wraps succulent sea scallops, house-made chorizo shows up in a saffron-scented paella, and roasted pig is scattered with the aforementioned chorizo and clams. Tarry over a glass of red wine from the glass-pour list or shake up the routine with a frozen lemon mousse crowned with raspberries. *$$–$$$; AE, DC, DIS, MC, V; checks OK; dinner every day; full bar; reservations recommended; self and street parking; brasa.com; map:G7.* ♿

Buenos Aires Grill / ★★

220 VIRGINIA ST, BELLTOWN; 206/441-7076

The old Argentine ranch trappings are enchanting, but it's the meat that matters here. Order the parrillada mixta (mixed grill), which features six different cuts of meats from the *parrilla*, a mesquite-fired grill; vacio (flank steak); asado de tira (beef short ribs); entraña (skirt steak); mollejas (beef sweetbreads); chorizo sausage; and chicken. If you prefer a choice cut, the filet mignon is big and chimichurri marinated. The Argentine empanadas (deep-fried turnovers) can be filled with vegetables or with ground lamb, beef, or chicken. Surprisingly, the dessert menu is void of beef, but it does include the festive dulce de leche crepes, filled with liquid caramel and flamed with rum. When crowded, the joint gets very loud. *$$; AE, DC, MC,*

KEEPIN' IT REAL

If you love Mexican food, you may be sorely disappointed by what Seattle has to offer. Though improvement has been seen in recent years—Ballard's La Carta de Oaxaca is a good example—Seattle nonetheless continues to suffer from a dearth of authentic, fresh Mexican cuisine.

Enter the taco truck, a staple in California and Mexico, but a fairly new development in the Pacific Northwest.

There are those who don't trust these roadside stands—often located in rickety old buses—but that just means there are more delicious tacos, tortas, and fresh hot tortillas for the rest of us.

To find a taco stand in your neck of the woods, visit **LOSTACOTRUCKS.COM**, a Web site that pinpoints the region's taco stands on a map—and provides links to their health reports. Below are some of our favorites.

Shoreline can't claim many bests when it comes to dining, but in **TAQUERIA LA GARRETA** (16510 Aurora Ave N) it has a winner. The wet chipotle burrito is filling as hell—and a bargain at less than $5. In a gas station parking lot in Northgate you'll find **TAQUERIA LA PASADITA** (2143 N Northgate Wy). If you're nearby and stuck in traffic, hop off the freeway for a paper plateful of hot tacos. In Rainier Valley is the popular **TACOS EL ASADERO** (3513 Rainier Ave S), which offers a tiny covered outdoor seating area, heated indoor seating, good tamales, and killer mulitas for $1.50. On the Eastside, **TAQUERIA GUADALAJARA** (2421 148th Ave NE) offers quick lunch service at its flip-down counter, where construction workers and Microsoft employees feast on fantastic tortas. Gorditos is a popular Mexican restaurant in the Greenwood neighborhood, and their little wagon in Ballard, **GORDITOS TOO** (1521 NW 50th St), is one of the city's best taco stands. The carnitas tacos are delicious, and the burritos super filling. There's also a six-table outdoor dining area.

—Monica Fischer

V; traveler's checks OK; dinner every day; full bar; reservations recommended; street parking; map:H7.

Burrito Loco / ★☆

9211 HOLMAN RD NW, BALLARD; 206/783-0719

This colorful Crown Hill café plates up sunny Mexican *especialidades*. The huge namesake Burrito Loco is jammed with meat—steak, pork, or chicken—guacamole, salsa, cheese, rice, and beans. We also like the machaca (shredded) beef burrito. Soups are a specialty here, particularly menudo, the tripe-laden morning-after therapy, and the cure-all albondigas with golf-ball-size meatballs marooned in a chipotle-spiked chicken broth. It's a sign of authenticity in any taqueria to see tongue tacos—good news even if you're not adventurous enough to eat them. Order instead the spicy chorizo or barbecued pork tacos *suaves* (soft) and you will know the joys of a perfectly seasoned *parrilla* (grill). There are numerous vegetarian possibilities, including veggie tamales and a spinach enchilada. The new bar serves up south-of-the-border cocktails. *$; MC, V; no checks; lunch, dinner every day; full bar; no reservations; self parking; map:FF6.* ♿

Cactus / ★★½

4220 E MADISON ST, MADISON PARK (AND BRANCHES); 206/324-4140

Bright-painted tables and hanging peppers make Cactus festive; its pioneering tapas menu makes it delicious. Try the Gambas al Diablo, white Mexican prawns sautéed in a smoky and spicy chipotle-agave nectar with mint chimichurri. The usual Mexican entrées are offered, but the more unusual dishes are worth trying, including the butternut squash enchilada, crispy white corn tortillas layered with jack and goat cheeses, spinach, roasted butternut squash, and caramelized onions. To put out the heat, there are plenty of fruit drinks, margaritas, and beers, but the wine list is limited. Bananas dulce and three-milk Cuban flan are must-have desserts. Cactus has been such a hit in Madison Park, it has spawned two more locations: Kirkland (121 Park Ln; 425/893-9799) and Alki (2820 Alki Ave SW, 206/933-6000). *$$; AE, DC, DIS, MC, V; checks OK; lunch Mon–Sat, dinner every day; full bar; reservations accepted for parties of 6 or more; street parking; cactusrestaurants.com; map:GG7.* ♿

Café Campagne / ★★★
Campagne / ★★★½

1600 POST ALLEY, PIKE PLACE MARKET; 206/728-2233;
86 PINE ST (INN AT THE MARKET), PIKE PLACE MARKET; 206/728-2800

Romantic Campagne favors Seattle with an infusion of panache from southern France. Tucked away in a Pike Place Market courtyard, the candlelit room and bar are warmly finished with cherrywood floors, farmhouse-yellow walls, and sumptuous draperies. Chef Daisley Gordon's menu is a passionate union of Northwest and French influences. Start off with gratin of salt cod brandade or the foie gras terrine spread over toasted brioche. For the main event, dishes range from roasted veal sweetbreads on curry cream to roasted guinea hen breast with garlic confit. Save room for dessert: perhaps a cardamom-orange crème brûlée or the tarte tatin. The wine list calls to mind vineyards of France.

Café Campagne, located just below its sibling, offers patrons a slice of French café life morning (on weekends), noon, and night. Weekend brunch is popular; expect to wait for a table or choose a seat at the counter. One bite of brioche French toast fried in bourbon egg batter, or poached eggs resting on garlic croutons marooned in a red wine and foie gras sauce, and you'll be glad you waited. Lunch offers a line-up of croques (Parisian ham sandwiches) and the celebrated lamb burger. Dinners often start with wild Burgundy snails roasted with parsley, garlic, and shallot butter and could end with pan-roasted, boneless trout with steamed potatoes. *$$, $$$; AE, DC, MC, V; no checks; dinner every day (Campagne), lunch Mon–Fri, dinner every day, brunch Sat–Sun (Café Campagne); full bar; reservations recommended; valet and street parking; campagnerestaurant.com; map:I7.* ♿

BEST GROWN-FOLKS BAR?

"Hazlewood in Ballard—this wallet-sized gem eschews shots and high-fives in favor of top-shelf cocktails, intelligent conversation, and the occasional DJ."

DJ Riz Rollins, KEXP, Re-bar, R Place

Cafe Flora / ★☆

2901 E MADISON ST, MADISON VALLEY; 206/325-9100

Cafe Flora is the go-to place for vegetarians across Puget Sound. Salads, like everything here, reflect the seasons—summer offerings might include a strawberry and minted pea salad or organic nectarines tossed with wild greens; in winter, spinach, watercress, and romaine tossed with petite lentils in a tart cherry dressing might tickle your fancy. There are staples on the menu—lest regulars revolt—including the Portobella Wellington: grilled portobello mushrooms, mushroom-pecan pâté, and sautéed leeks wrapped in flaky puff pastry; and the Oaxaca tacos—corn tortillas stuffed with spicy mashed potatoes, cheddar, and smoked mozzarella. Nothing beats sipping a refreshing rosemary lemonade in the lovely covered garden patio next to the gurgling pond. *$$; MC, V; local checks OK; lunch Tues–Fri, dinner Tues–Sun, brunch Sat–Sun; beer and wine; reservations recommended for 8 or more; self parking; cafeflora.com; map:HH6.* ♿

Café Happy / ★

102 KIRKLAND AVE, KIRKLAND; 425/822-9696

Vegetarians and meat eaters alike find themselves inexplicably joyful at the family-run Café Happy, a Taiwanese-style, veggie-only hole-in-the-wall in downtown Kirkland. Instead of meat, freshly made noodle and rice dishes toss in soy-based "chicken" or "beef" with fantastic sauces. While there's no mistaking this faux-meat for the real thing, there's no need—the flavors and textures completely satisfy. Take out or grab one of the two tables to eat in—try the fried rice or one of the marinated tofu sandwiches. *$; V and cash only; lunch and dinner every day; no reservations; street parking; map:DD4.*

Cafe Juanita / ★★★☆

9702 NE 12TH PL, KIRKLAND; 425/823-1505

If there's one reason to brave traffic across the 520 bridge, it's Cafe Juanita—the Eastside's superlative northern Italian dining experience. The excellent service is exemplified by professional servers who deliver elegant cuisine that reflects chef/owner Holly Smith's commitment to fine local produce and artisan products. As a prologue to your meal, the seasonal menu might offer grilled octopus and fennel, or partridge-filled anolini floating in a lemon- and ginger-spiked broth. The signature braised rabbit with chickpea crepes is an evergreen secondo; however, you might fancy a tender saddle of Oregon lamb or quail with mascarpone and balsamico cherries instead. For a formidable epilogue, savor select cheeses or spoon into a velvety vanilla panna cotta paired with local strawberries. The carefully considered wine list comprises Italian and Northwest bottles for varied pocketbooks and tastes. *$$$; AE, MC, V; no checks; dinner every day; full bar; reservations recommended; self and street parking; cafejuanita.com; map:DD4.* ♿

Cafe Lago / ★★½

2305 24TH AVE E, MONTLAKE; 206/329-8005

Locals converge nightly at this wonderful Italian café near the Montlake Bridge. Start with the antipasto plate, stacked with eggplant, bruschetta with olivada, goat cheese, roasted peppers, mozzarella, roasted garlic bulbs, prosciutto, and Asiago cheese (the plate is also available meatless). Try one of the thin-crust wood-fired pizzas, perhaps with salsiccia (sausage), roasted red peppers, marinara, and fontina; or an applewood grilled sirloin steak covered with a balsamic reduction, Gorgonzola, grilled onions, and red peppers. Gnocchi in vodka cream sauce and the locally acclaimed soufflélike lasagna both have one star ingredient: handcrafted pasta. Finish up with a panna cotta infused with Tahitian vanilla and lavender and bathed in orange caramel sauce. *$$; AE, DC, DIS, MC, V; traveler's checks OK; dinner every day; full bar; reservations recommended; street parking; cafelago.com; map:GG6.* ♿

Cafe Nola / ★★

101 WINSLOW WY E, BAINBRIDGE ISLAND; 206/842-3822

This stylish Bainbridge Island bistro was recently featured as the best brunch spot in Seattle on an episode of the Food Network's *Giada's Weekend Getaways*. One bite of their caramel pecan French toast and you'll understand why. The lunch crowd favors hearty soups that rotate daily; the Louisiana gratin of indocile sausage, Yukon potato, okra, and stewed tomato; and the Dungeness crab melt. Dinner hour brings forth pan-seared scallops bathed in roasted-pepper garlic sauce, and lamb osso buco, a petite lamb shank towering over red wine risotto. Not-to-miss desserts include the triple-layer chocolate hazelnut torte. The tight wine list spotlights a "winemaker of the month." *$$; MC, V; local checks OK; lunch Mon–Fri, dinner every day, brunch Sat–Sun; full bar; reservations recommended; street parking; cafenola.com.* ♿

Café Stellina / ★

1429 12TH AVE, CAPITOL HILL; 206/322-2688

Café Stellina's new digs in a 1920s-era garage are a far cry from its original six-table coffee house in the Central District. The light-filled space is laid out with white linens and handsome nature-inspired tableware, and big garage doors roll open in warm weather. The upscale comfort food is well prepared and beautifully presented. At lunch, starters, salads, and sandwiches shine. Shareable plates include roasted beets with feta and fresh mint, and baked polenta with cured salmon. The yam and peanut soup is delightful, as is the roasted eggplant sandwich between molasses brown bread and dressed with a sesame aioli. Service may not be cued for office workers on a one-hour lunch break; come for a leisurely dinner when lamb and fish dishes appear on the vegetarian-biased menu. *$$; MC, V; no checks; lunch, dinner Wed–Sat; beer and wine; reservations available; street parking; map:M1.*

Canlis / ★★★★

2576 AURORA AVE N, QUEEN ANNE; 206/283-3313

For more than 50 years, Canlis has delivered haute cuisine and impeccable service from its perch on the eastern edge of Queen Anne. Guests celebrating their umpteenth whatever still find old favorites, while contemporary foodies soak in the new verve that landed Canlis a top 50 rating from *Gourmet* magazine in 2006. Canlis delivers simply prepared dishes that let local and seasonal ingredients shine. Starters include signature Peter Canlis prawns or Kobe-style Washington beef steak tartare. Mains range from broiler items—salmon, ahi, steaks—accompanied by reliable sides to a more elaborate dish of seared scallops crowned with caviar nestled on truffle-laced edamame purée surrounded by lobster sauce. Be sure to give a half-hour notice for the knockout Grand Marnier soufflé. The much-lauded wine list ranges from a $12,500 magnum to many options in the $30 range. Although a more relaxed vibe has taken over Seattle's most classic dining room, men still wear jackets. *$$$$; AE, DC, DIS, MC, V; no checks; dinner Mon–Sat; full bar; reservations required; valet parking; canlis.com; map:GG7.*

Carmelita / ★★★

7314 GREENWOOD AVE N, GREENWOOD; 206/706-7703

The secret to Carmelita's success is its innovative menu and attention to detail (when the temperature dips, back patio dwellers can bundle up with provided blankets). Not only is the sophisticated, seasonal vegetarian cuisine enticing, but the dining room is gorgeous. Owners Kathryn Neumann and Michael Hughes, visual artists in their spare time, transformed a dilapidated retail space into a theatrically lit, art-filled haven of color and texture. Expect to find such entrées as leek and Gruyère tart, semolina gnocchi baked with ricotta and plum-anise sauce, and polenta cake with saffron sauce. Pizzas are topped with fresh-from-the-farm produce spanning watercress and Gorgonzola to red onion marmalade, fontina, and port-soaked currents. *$$; MC, V; local checks only; dinner Tues–Sun; beer and wine; reservations recommended; street parking; reserve@carmelita.net; carmelita.net; map:EE8.*

Cascadia Restaurant / ★★★

2328 1ST AVE, BELLTOWN; 206/448-8884

Cascadia benefits from a spare but luxurious space and popular chef/owner Kerry Sear, who uses the indigenous foods and flavors of Cascadia (the region he defines as between the Pacific Ocean and Montana) and beyond. The bar offers pocketbook- and palate-friendly noshes ranging from skillet-roasted prawns to miniburgers. The dining room features à la carte exotica such as an appetizer of Kobe saku beef carpaccio with crisp oysters and an entrée of caramelized spice-rubbed wild king salmon with lobster crushed potatoes. Or savor the five-course tasting menu, also available vegetarian; the monthly three-course menu is a deal at $35. The wine list features handcrafted wines chosen for their ability to flatter Sear's cuisine. A kids' menu tested by Sear's young son is available for pint-size foodies. *$$$$; AE, DC, DIS, MC, V; no checks; dinner Mon–Sat; full bar; reservations recommended; street parking; cascadiarestaurant.com; map:G7.* ♿

Cedars Restaurant on Brooklyn / ★★☆

4759 BROOKLYN AVE NE, UNIVERSITY DISTRICT; 206/527-5247

Part Indian, part Mediterranean, the menu may seem schizophrenic, but it's a great solution for diners who can't come to a consensus. At lunchtime, go for the hummus or the baba ghanoush pita sandwiches. Depending on which continent you're leaning toward, you might try the shish taouk, cubed chicken marinated in garlic, oregano, and saffron; or the tender lamb shish kebabs. If you're in the mood for a heartwarming curry, the savory-sweet mango curry or the tikka masala are house favorites. Don't forgo wiping your curry-covered plate clean with some fluffy naan, leavened white bread that also comes stuffed with garlic or seasoned spinach. Service is fast (once you're seated), albeit aloof, and your cup of chai will always be full. *$; AE, DIS, MC, V; no checks; lunch Mon–Sat, dinner Mon–Sun; beer and wine; reservations not accepted; self parking; cedarsseattle.com; map:EE7.*

Chandler's Crabhouse / ★★☆

901 FAIRVIEW AVE N, SOUTH LAKE UNION; 206/223-2722

True to its name, Chandler's menu is crab-centric. Although the crabs may come from as far away as Florida or Australia, the preparations are notably Northwest. Top appetizer choices include crab cakes with curry aioli, and a Dungeness crab and artichoke dip accompanied by cheesy focaccia toasts. Other favorites are the Dungeness crab and bay shrimp Louie brimming with delicious crab meat and large pink shrimp laid to rest over crisp greens, and the whiskey-kissed crab soup. If you're in the mood to get physical, opt for whole or half Dungeness crabs prepared your way and don't mind the goofy bibs. The menu also features surf-and-turf specials and the requisite ahi and salmon dishes. The extensive wine list is heavy on regional labels. *$$–$$$; AE, DC, MC, V; local checks only; lunch Mon–Fri, dinner every day, brunch Sat–Sun; full bar; reservations recommended; valet and self parking; schwartzbros.com; map:D1.* ♿

Chez Shea / ★★★
Shea's Lounge / ★★☆

94 PIKE ST, 3RD FLOOR, PIKE PLACE MARKET; 206/467-9990
Romance is always on the menu at this gem tucked on the top floor of the Corner Market Building, with a view of Elliott Bay through the grand arched windows. There's a seasonal à la carte menu with French flair; or if you're in for a languorous affair, opt for the eight-course tasting menu. Menus reflect the bounty of the season, employing ingredients fresh from the Market below. An early spring meal might begin with Wescott Bay mussels in a saffron and white wine broth, followed by wild mushroom and fennel bisque. Entrée selections usually include fish, meat, and game along the lines of Alaskan halibut with black beluga lentils, and crisp seared pork belly; there's also usually a vegetarian option. Service is sure and gracious. The more casual Shea's Lounge is a sexy bistro wed to Chez Shea by a common door. With a three-course prix-fixe menu that echoes the main room's offerings, it's the perfect place to start a date. *$$$, $$; AE, MC, V; no checks; dinner Tues–Sun; full bar; reservations recommended (Chez Shea); valet parking Thurs–Sat, validation for Market garage, and street parking; dinner@chezshea.com;* chezshea.com; *map:J8.*

Chinoise Café / ★

12 BOSTON ST, QUEEN ANNE (AND BRANCHES); 206/284-6671
Eclectically but assuredly Asian, Chinoise Café is a reliable place for Vietnamese salad rolls, Japanese sukiyaki, Thai curries, Chinese stir-fry, and noodles. The Queen Anne location fills nightly, despite the speedy—some say rushed—service. Nevertheless, the vibrant Vietnamese lemongrass chicken rice noodle salad never fails to drag folks up the hill. For a multicourse meal, start with delicate summer salad rolls or an order of pot stickers and move onto crispy Szechuan chicken or a yakisoba. Chinoise on Madison (2801 E Madison St, Madison Valley; 206/323-0171) is calmer and has a somewhat larger pan-Asian menu. Try the broiled five-spice Cornish hen or the sensational fish of the day, served with Chinese long beans in a tangy tamarind-basil oyster sauce. The Chinoise in Wallingford (1618 N 45th St, Wallingford; 206/633-1160) is a more sophisticated version of its Queen Anne sibling. *$; AE, DC, DIS, MC, V; no checks; lunch, dinner every day; beer and wine; no reservations; street parking; chinoisecafe.com; map:GG8.* ♿

Chinook's at Salmon Bay / ★★

1900 W NICKERSON ST, INTERBAY; 206/283-4665
In the heart of Fisherman's Terminal, this busy restaurant's light-industrial décor—steel countertops, visible ventilation ducts—reflects the bustle of the working marina outside the big windows. You can count on the fish being fresh and the oyster stew being creamy, with wonderful chunks of yearling Quilcene oysters. The regular menu is large and can be overwhelming. Failsafe choices are the tender halibut-and-chips and the mahimahi tacos. The daily special sheet is your best bet, with offerings such as wild king salmon

charred with sun-dried tomato basil butter or garlic-baked prawns with lemon and gremolata. For dessert, try the warm wild blackberry cobbler. *$$; AE, MC, V; checks OK; breakfast Sat–Sun, lunch, dinner every day; full bar; no reservations; self parking; anthonysrestaurants.com; map:FF8.* ♿

Chiso / ★★☆

3520 FREMONT AVE, FREMONT; 206/632-3430

Chiso is one of those very good Japanese neighborhood restaurants that Seattle is known for. The emphasis is on sushi: artful owner Taichi Kitamura is a sushi chef who, sharp knives flashing, always seems to be there, slicing the toro, shaping the nigiri, making rolls and small talk. The hot kitchen does well, too, churning out specialties such as broiled black cod filet and grilled sansho-marinated duck breast. Because they only use the freshest seafood and seasonal items, the menu rotates. You'll be elbow to elbow with Japanese businessmen, chefs taking busman's holidays, Fremont hipsters, construction workers, and sushi cultists who all flock to this busy place. *$$; MC, V; no checks; lunch Wed–Fri, dinner every day; beer and wine; street parking; info@chisoseattle.com; chisoseattle.com; map:FF8.* ♿

Chutneys / ★

519 1ST AVE N, QUEEN ANNE (AND BRANCHES); 206/284-6799

Like any good Indian restaurant, Chutneys' menu spans the continent. For starters, two solid choices are toasted-coriander-and-paprika-dusted calamari with coconut tamarind chutney, and curried mussels with cashew curry wine sauce. Entrées can be ordered with varying degrees of heat, to be chased with an Indian beer or a mango lassi, a sweet fruit smoothie. Try the tender lamb kebab marinated in a mint pesto and flamed in the tandoor, the superhot vertical clay oven, or the boneless breast of chicken simmered in a tangy Alphonso mango curry sauce. Don't forget the Indian breads, such as the Kabuli naan stuffed with nuts, raisins, and cherries. Chutneys Grille on the Hill (605 15th Ave E, Capitol Hill; 206/726-1000) is more laid-back than the bustling Chutneys Bistro at Wallingford Center (1815 N 45th St, Wallingford; 206/634-1000). *$; AE, DC, DIS, MC, V; local checks only; lunch Mon–Sat, dinner every day; full bar; reservations recommended; street parking; chutneystogo.com; chutneysbistro.com; map:GG7.* ♿

Coastal Kitchen / ★

429 15TH AVE E, CAPITOL HILL; 206/322-1145

Peter Levy and Jeremy Hardy—of Queen Anne's 5 Spot Café and Fauntleroy's Endolyne Joe's (see following reviews), among others—conjure restaurants with humor and interesting themes. Coastal Kitchen's quarterly changing menu focuses on the varied coastal regions of the world, with an emphasis on seafood. A Sicilian sojourn may include pan-seared albacore with sausage and white bean ragout, and scallops with gnocchi in a ricotta tomato cream sauce. Or get swept away to the Louisiana Gulf with crawfish crepes. House favorites herb-roasted chicken and charcoal-grilled pork chops are constants on the menu. Neighbors flock in for breakfast, served all day with smoked salmon scrambles, spicy hash browns, and corn griddle cakes, as well as for the key lime pie. *$$; MC, V; local checks only; breakfast, lunch, dinner every day; full bar; reservations recommended for 6 or more; street parking; chowfoods.com; map:HH6.* ♿

Coupage / ★★

1404 34TH AVE, MADRONA; 206/322-1974

At Portland chef Thomas Hurley's first Seattle venture, fusion cuisine is taken to greater heights. Cross-cultural incarnations are apparent in the wild mushroom bi bim bop; a velvety vichyssoise accented by hints of lemongrass and anchored by a Dungeness crab cake "crouton"; and the tumble of mâche greens and maitake mushrooms dressed with a soy black truffle vinaigrette. For entrées, the Coupage burger topped with seared foie gras, red onion kimchi, and tomato confit has reached cult status, and the crispy branzino is simple yet delicious. Don't be put off by the charcoal-colored black sesame crème brûlée—its nutty flavor is quite pleasing. *$$–$$$; AE, MC, V; no checks; dinner every day; brunch Sat–Sun; full bar; reservations recommended; street parking; coupageseattle.com; map:GG7.* ♿

BEST PLACE
TO ELONGATE A PENNY?

"Pirate's Plunder on the Alaskan Way waterfront has a three-die machine. You can get a ferryboat, a miner, or a pirate. Arrr!"

"Awesome," Seattle's premier art-rock collective

Crave / ★½

1621 12TH AVE, CAPITOL HILL; 206/388-0526

The Capitol Hill Arts Center is the perfect backdrop for the creations of Crave founder and executive chef Robin Leventhal, an artist by training and a culinary conjurer at heart. Leventhal's dishes fit right in with the mosaic tabletops and wrought iron chairs that furnish the tiny space. Mac and cheese is jazzed up with New York sharp cheddar and fontina cheeses and studded with shiitake mushrooms, while organic duck confit is served with a mission fig compote and savory bread pudding. At brunch, French toast—sourdough bread soaked overnight in orange custard—served with house-made sweet blue cheese butter, and eggs Benedict (prosciutto or house-made lox—you choose) bathed in a shallot, champagne-orange hollandaise are sure to please. Waits can be long, especially at brunch. *$$; AE, DIS, MC, V; no checks; breakfast and lunch Mon–Fri, dinner every day, brunch Sat–Sun; beer and wine; reservations available; self parking; cravefood.com; map:GG6.*

Crémant / ★★☆

1423 34TH AVE, MADRONA; 206/322-4600

Join the dozens of Seattle Francophiles who have flocked through the cheery yellow door of this cozy Parisian-style bistro. Crémant, named for the French sparkling wine, may be a newcomer, but the kitchen talent has decades of experience. Chef/owner Scott Emerick trained in classic French cooking in Paris and worked at top restaurants in France, as well as Seattle restaurants Campagne and Le Pichet. Dishes are traditional yet creative: Gruyère-glazed onion soup, moules marinière made with crémant, cassoulet à la Toulousaine, saffron-scented bouillabaisse chock-full of fish and shellfish, and a charcuterie selection worthy of any homegrown Gallic establishment—all at neighborhood prices too. Happily, many dishes come with mounds of habit-forming pommes frites. The wine list spotlights affordable French wines, especially crémants. Concrete-clad walls mean decibels can rise, but the exemplary service will keep you happy. *$$–$$$; MC, V; no checks; dinner every day; beer and wine; reservations recommended; self parking; cremantseattle.com; map:GG7.* ♿

Crow Restaurant and Bar / ★★☆

823 5TH AVE N, QUEEN ANNE; 206/283-8800

Bearing no resemblance to its former warehouse self, Crow is adorned with artisan metalwork, an abstract Rothko-esque wall painting, and crimson drapes that soften the cavernous space. The casual bistro/bar is popular with operagoers and neighborhood regulars alike. The bar is a fun way to experience Crow on a whim (read: without reservations). Short and simple, the rotating menu features standouts such as grilled manchego cheese bundled in grape leaves; crispy on the outside, juicy on the inside prosciutto-wrapped chicken; house lasagna with Italian sausage; and a soy-sesame-glazed black cod paired with sticky rice. Tempting dessert options might include a lovely duo of Meyer lemon coconut tart and orange cardamom crème brûlée, or a bittersweet chocolate tart. And then there are a well-balanced wine list, creative cocktails, and friendly, professional servers to round out the dining experience. *$$–$$$; AE, MC, V; no checks; dinner every day; full bar; reservations recommended; self parking; map:B4.* ♿

Crush / ★★★☆

2319 E MADISON ST, MADISON VALLEY; 206/302-7874

Crush's cream-colored interior and attitude-exuding, black-clad servers might take a little getting used to, but chef Jason Wilson and wife and co-owner Nicole have come up with a winning formula: innovative Northwest cuisine plus trendy digs in a converted century-old Tudor equals foodie heaven. Wilson uses seasonal, local, and organic ingredients, so the menu is a surprise every evening, although favorites such as slow-braised short ribs and seared Hudson Valley foie gras with huckleberry sauce are often available. Prettily presented dishes range from a still life of grilled octopus and Merguez sausage surrounded by a moat of chard-speckled broth to seared scallops topped with Fuyu persimmon balanced on a bed of sweet onion risotto. Tables tend to be crammed close together so claustrophobes should ask for a seat on the less stuffy first level. *$$$–$$$$; AE, DIS, MC, V; no checks; dinner Tues–Sat; full bar; reservations required; self parking; crushonmadison.com; map:GG7.*

Dahlia Lounge / ★★★★

2001 4TH AVE, BELLTOWN; 206/682-4142

The very mention of Tom Douglas sends tingles down every Seattle foodie's spine, and the grand dame of his restaurant empire never fails to please. Matching a spirited décor of crimson, gold brocade, and papier-mâché fish lanterns is an exuberant, global approach from the kitchen. Expect appetizers such as roasted mussels in fennel chowder, curried vegetable samosas with tamarind and coriander dipping sauces, and the tempting, seasonally changing Sea Bar Sampler that never fails to include tender chunks of smoked salmon with spicy mustard and some incarnation of tuna. Eclectic entrées range from rotisserie-roasted five-spice Peking duck to lemon green onion Dungeness crab cakes. Don't leave without trying the signature triple coconut cream pie. *$$$; AE, DC, DIS, MC, V; local checks only; lunch Mon–Fri, dinner every day; full bar; reservations recommended; valet parking; tomdouglas.com; map:H6.* ♿

BEST LATE-NIGHT SNACK?

"Nothing provides pure satisfaction like a Bigtop chili cheese dog, a cold beer, and a game of pinball at Shorty's in Belltown."

Buster McLeod, founder, McLeod Residence

Daniel's Broiler Prime Steak & Chops / ★★½

809 FAIRVIEW PLACE N, SOUTH LAKE UNION (AND BRANCHES); 206/621-8262

This classic steak house on the southernmost shore of Lake Union is well appointed with copper, wood, and windows. There's prime seafood on the menu, such as giant Australian lobster tails, salmon, and halibut, but the main attraction is the beef—Midwestern, corn-fed, aged, cut huge, and cooked to order in 1,800°F broilers. We suggest one of the mighty T-bones or the herb-encrusted, cut-it-with-a-fork prime rib. Daniel's also does a great veal chop and French-cut lamb chops. Expect lavish service, a mighty wine list, and all the usual steak house choices—Caesar salads, garlic mashers, or a baked potato the size of your shoe. All three Daniel's Broilers—the others are in Leschi (200 Lake Washington Blvd; 206/329-4191) and Bellevue (10500 NE 8th St; 425/462-4662)—have great views and stellar service. *$$$; AE, DC, DIS, MC, V; checks OK; lunch Mon–Fri, dinner every day; full bar; reservations recommended; valet parking; info@schwartzbros.com; schwartzbros.com; map:HH6.* ♿

Dinette / ★★☆

1514 E OLIVE WY, CAPITOL HILL; 206/328-2282

Snugly sited along Olive Way's plunge into downtown, Dinette's nondescript storefront belies the delights that await you inside. The small dining room swathed in teal is decorated with gold leaf stenciling and chef/owner Melissa Nyffeler's collection of vintage trays. Reflecting its décor, Dinette serves up rustic and unpretentious European-influenced cuisine meant to be shared: from crusty toasts smothered with chicken liver mousse perked up with spicy pickled peppers to a fig-and-walnut spread topped with prosciutto and arugula to a bowl of handmade ricotta gnocchi with wild mushrooms and shallots. Chalkboard specials may announce house-made spiced sausage with French lentil ragout or roasted duck breast with cranberry relish. Dinette also boasts a short yet well-considered wine list, comprised mostly of inexpensive imports. *$$; MC, V; no checks; dinner Tues–Sat; full bar; reservations for 5 or more; street parking; dinetteseattle.com; map:I1.* ♿

Dragonfish Asian Café / ★★

722 PINE ST (PARAMOUNT HOTEL), DOWNTOWN; 206/467-7777

Because of its proximity to the Paramount Theatre across the street, the odd rock star and ensuing entourage frequent this easygoing pan-Asian restaurant, alongside regular Seattleites enjoying preshow drinks, supper, or sushi. Walls are hung with Japanese anime posters; the bar is lined with brightly colored pachinko (Japanese pinball) machines. Two exhibition kitchens—a wok station and a robata grill—contribute to the energetic ambience. The menu specializes in small plates of shareables—dim sum, sushi rolls, and satays, as well as creative entrées such as red Thai curry noodles and shrimp, Szechuan duck breast, or almond-crusted halibut tempura. On the weekend, stop in for a brunch of traditional eggs Benedict or Korean bulgogi hash—grilled bulgogi skirt steak served on a bed of breakfast potatoes. *$$; AE, MC, V; checks OK; breakfast, lunch, dinner every day, brunch Sat–Sun; full bar; street parking; dragonfishcafe.com; map:J4.* ♿

Dulces Latin Bistro / ★★

1430 34TH AVE, MADRONA; 206/322-5453

Dulces is appropriately named—everything about this place is sweet. Immensely popular in its own zip code, the romantic nuevo Latino bistro also draws people from all over the city. "Latino" here is broadly defined—southern French, Spanish, Italian, and regional Mexican flavors and dishes are featured and fused. There is handmade Mexican chorizo ravioli in a cilantro tomatillo cream sauce, braised rabbit with rosemary served over rigatoni, and saffron-infused paella Valenciana. The wine list is a wonder of width, breadth, and affordability—you'll find more than 40 ports by the glass and a fine selection of Portuguese and Chilean wines. They didn't name this place "sweet" for nothing—try the extraordinary pecan pie or the cajeta (Mexican caramel and chocolate tart). *$$; DIS, MC, V; no checks; dinner Tues–Sat; full bar; reservations recommended; street parking; dulceslatinbistro.com; map:GG7.* ♿

Earth & Ocean / ★★☆

1112 4TH AVE (W SEATTLE HOTEL), DOWNTOWN; 206/264-6060

Surf and turf takes on new meaning at Earth & Ocean, the W Hotel's culinary showcase for fresh, organic, and farm-direct produce, meat, and seafood. From the earth comes Anderson Valley lamb kebabs and minty fresh yogurt, Washington Angus rib steak and truffled home fries, and smoked organic chicken. The ocean proffers seared wild Pacific salmon and sunchoke walnut pesto, and diver scallops in a pool of razor clam chowder. The decadent www.chocolate.com cake satisfies many a craving. The dark and clubby dining room provides the perfect backdrop for beautiful, well-dressed patrons. Service is known to oscillate between nice and pampering to snooty and absent. *$$$; AE, B, DC, DIS, JCB, MC, V; checks OK; breakfast every day, lunch and dinner Mon–Sat; full bar; reservations recommended; valet, self, and street parking; earthocean.net; map:L6.* ♿

El Camino / ★★

607 N 35TH ST, FREMONT; 206/632-7303

The bar jumps all night, and the spacious patio sizzles year-round, thanks to reliably smart food from south of the border and superb fresh-juice margaritas. The dining room has the requisite ceiling fan, ceramic tiles, wrought iron, and sequined saints, but the food is more authentically Mexican than most: chicken enchiladas smothered with mole poblano sauce, salmon with tamarind sauce, fish and shrimp tacos with green rice and salsa de tomatillo, thin slices of grilled marinated steak served with cheese enchiladas in spicy salsa coloradita. The ever-changing dessert menu usually includes the signature pecan tart with dark rum or Meyer lemon flan. *$$; AE, MC, V; no checks; dinner Tues–Sun, brunch Sat–Sun; full bar; reservations recommended; street parking; map:FF8.* ♿

El Gaucho / ★★★☆

2505 1ST AVE, BELLTOWN; 206/728-1337

There's a reason why *Playboy* voted El Gaucho one of the country's best steak houses. Liveried captains as servers, flaming sword brochettes, blazing baked Alaska—it's all about the show, baby! The plush eatery is a feast for the senses where cooks scurry at a wood-fired broiler and servers make classic Caesar salads right before your eyes. Patrons seated at comfy banquettes in the senate-style dining room feast on 28-day, dry-aged certified Angus beef or dredge garlic bread in buttery Wicked Shrimp or bite into succulent Chilean sea bass. Bananas Foster is a decadent and sublime capper to the evening. The wine card is formidable, supplemented by a premium reserve list. At press time, a new El Gaucho was scheduled to open in Bellevue in fall 2008. *$$$$; AE, DIS, MC, V; checks OK; dinner every day; full bar; reservations recommended; valet parking; elgaucho.com; map:F8.* ♿

El Greco / ★★☆

219 BROADWAY E, STE 11, CAPITOL HILL; 206/328-4604

Leave the hip grit of Broadway behind and relax in El Greco's cozy azure dining room. Here, the adventurous menu meanders around the Mediterranean with a Greek lamb burger topped with tzatziki sauce; sautéed crispy penne in an eggplant, tomato, Kalamata, and caper sauce; Moroccan spiced chicken with smoked paprika jus; and a rotating risotto of the day. Lines lengthen for the mighty weekend brunch, one of the best in town, with yummy stuff like the El Greco Benedict—poached eggs perched atop potato pancakes and melted Gouda, bathed in sumptuous tomato mushroom sauce; a chorizo, potato, and manchego omelet; and rustic French toast. On warm days, eat outside and witness the splendid, sordid spectacle of Broadway foot traffic. *$–$$; AE, MC, V; no checks; dinner Tues–Sat, brunch Fri–Sun; full bar; reservations recommended; street parking; elgrecorestaurant.com; map:GG6.* ♿

Elliott's Oyster House / ★★★

1201 ALASKAN WY, PIER 56, WATERFRONT; 206/623-4340

Elliott's is the best oyster stop in town, with an extensive selection of the freshest mollusks around, from Westcott Flats to Eld Inlet. Sit at the bar and let the chef pick out the best of the day, or move to one of the cozy tables with a view of the Sound and slurp on creamy, pink-tinged Dungeness crab chowder with a touch of cayenne. The iced shellfish extravaganzas serve two, four, or six people. Whole Dungeness is offered hot and spicy, simply steamed, or chilled with dipping sauces. Dungeness crab cakes are exceptional, with rock shrimp and a crab beurre blanc blended with the juice of blood oranges. The bar offers up a safe, seafood-friendly wine list and an impressive selection of rums, tequilas, and Scotches. *$$$; AE, DC, DIS, MC, V; checks OK; lunch, dinner every day; full bar; reservations recommended; street parking; elliottsoysterhouse.com; map:H8.* ♿

BEST PLACE

TO EAT IN THE SEATTLE CENTER HOUSE FOOD COURT?

"Steamer's Seafood Cafe, in the back left corner. Get the fish tacos with French fries."

"Awesome," Seattle's premier art-rock collective

El Puerco Lloron / ★

1501 WESTERN AVE, PIKE PLACE MARKET; 206/624-0541

This delicious-smelling taqueria hidden midway up the Pike Place Hillclimb serves up the most authentic Tex-Mex that Seattle has to offer. Order by number at the cafeteria-style counter, pick up your food, then fight for a table along with the neighboring workers who line up for the inexpensive but filling fare (and, in nice weather, jostle for the outside tables). Eat the tamales—they're always freshly steamed; the taquito plate with its sliced steak and soft tortillas is the most popular dish, though the machaca beef is a close second; the chiles rellenos are fat and juicy. Most everything is served with rice and beans, and Mexican beers are available. *$; AE, MC, V; business checks only; lunch, dinner every day; beer and wine; no reservations; street parking; map:J8.*

Endolyne Joe's / ★

9261 45TH AVE SW, WEST SEATTLE; 206/937-5637

Endolyne Joe's is a lively, comfortable neighborhood restaurant named for the '40s streetcar "lyne," the end o' which was right here. To keep things popping, the joint is themed differently a few times a year—Key Largo, Little Italy, Route 66—and creates tantalizing dishes to match the rotating local artwork. The regular menu touches on cuisine from the West Coast, the East Coast, the Gulf Coast, and the heartland. A thick-cut pork chop represents the latter, nicely marinated in hoisin and Tabasco. Roasted mushroom ravioli represents our neck of the woods, stuffing rich mushrooms and spinach in locally made pasta pillows. Breakfast—or "blunch" as it's called—is the best meal, with all manner of scrambles and omelets, caramel apple French toast, and fruit parfait. *$; MC, V; local checks only; breakfast, lunch, dinner every day; full bar; reservations recommended; self parking; chowfoods.com; map:LL9.* ♿

Etta's Seafood / ★★

2020 WESTERN AVE, PIKE PLACE MARKET; 206/443-6000

Since the mid '90s, Etta's has been churning out hip, fresh seafood, Tom Douglas–style. For starters, try the crispy shrimp spring rolls or Douglas's Dungeness crab cakes spiked with green tomato relish. For mains, a spice-rubbed, pit-roasted salmon is a Seattle signature. Despite its rep as a fish house, plenty of land options abound, from the Thai fried chicken salad to a pepper-crusted venison loin. Lush desserts come from Douglas's nearby Dahlia Bakery; the coconut cream pie is a local favorite. Locals and tourists descend on Etta's for weekend brunch, so expect to wait for a seat in the small, conversation-friendly dining room or the other larger and much noisier noshery with bar and counter seating. *$$; AE, DC, DIS, MC, V; local checks only; lunch and dinner every day, brunch Sat–Sun; full bar; reservations recommended; street parking; tomdouglas.com; map:I8.* ♿

Eva Restaurant & Wine Bar / ★★★

2227 N 56TH ST, GREEN LAKE; 206/633-3538

Eva is a well-windowed, warm-wooded, if somewhat noisy bistro a few blocks east of Green Lake. Dig into fusiony "firsts" and "seconds" and you might block out the extraneous clanging from the kitchen and replace it with a resounding "mmm." The light, smooth Cabrales flan is a blue cheese blast offset with a tangy-sweet pear relish and anchored to the earth with a buttery walnut cracker. There are basic bistro entrées as well: grilled and roasted fish, steaks, and poultry, all sure to please. Desserts range from new spins on childhood favorites, such as chocolate pudding punctuated with brandy, to more refined seasonal delights. The well-chosen wine list has plenty of bottles in the $30s—and nearly a dozen good half bottles. *$$; MC, V; checks OK; dinner Tues–Sun; full bar; reservations recommended; street parking; evarestaurant.com; map:FF7.* ♿

Feierabend / ★

422 YALE AVE N, SOUTH LAKE UNION; 206/340-2528

You won't find oompah bands or lederhosen at this little German pub in the up-and-coming South Lake Union neighborhood, but you will find a huge selection of German beer on tap, served in its proper, branded glass, as well as a regularly updated menu of creative German food. Find a seat at one of the large wooden farmhouse tables and start with the Bavarian brezel, a large soft pretzel served with a dip of brie and paprika, or the gewertzed gerken, fried thickly cut pickles served with the house special curried ketchup and German-style mustard, before moving on to the Jägerschnitzel, pork loin in a rich mushroom gravy. Show up at happy hour for an even more festive atmosphere and cheap appetizers. *$; AE, DIS, V, MC; no checks; lunch and dinner every day; no reservations; full bar; street parking; feierabendseattle.com; map:G1.* ♿

The Fish Club by Todd English / ★★

2100 ALASKAN WY (SEATTLE MARRIOTT WATERFRONT HOTEL), WATERFRONT; 206/256-1040

Hey Dorothy, you're not in Seattle anymore. The huge, open dining area of the Fish Club feels like something out of new-school Las Vegas. But despite the big décor, service is warm and knowledgeable, and the kitchen specializes in top-of-the-line seafood. Whole salmon twirl around the flames on the "dancing fish" rotisserie, which looks like a medieval torture device. The menu spans the continents with diverse and delicious offerings such as perfectly seared jumbo scallops with a risotto of Israeli couscous; flatbreads with toppings like shrimp mole; and Paella Verde, a melee of lobster, shrimp, mussels, and sausage in a charred green salsa. The full bar mixes some delicious cocktails, including a particularly tasty hibiscus martini. In summer, the sunny patio can be packed. *$$$; AE, DC, DIS, MC, V; no checks; breakfast, lunch, dinner every day; full bar; reservations recommended; valet parking; toddenglish.com; map:D9.* ♿

5 Spot Café / ★

1502 QUEEN ANNE AVE N, QUEEN ANNE; 206/285-7768

Flavor and fun rule at the 5 Spot Café, which wins you over with reasonable prices and neighborly atmosphere. Like most of its sibling Chow Foods restaurants, food festivals celebrating the cuisine of different regions change every three months or so, and 5 Spot's focus is on artisanal cuisines of the United States. In fall, enjoy the Harvest Festival, representing such events as Bradford, Vermont's wild-game extravaganza, though here "wild" translates as hearty venison stew with roasted root vegetables, served with sweet yam dollar biscuits. Favorites include corned beef, sauerkraut, and Swiss stacked high on grilled rye bread and slathered in Russian dressing—served the old-fashioned way with horseradish, cherry peppers, and half a sour pickle. Late riser? No problem: ham and eggs are on the menu until midnight. *$; MC, V; local checks only; breakfast, lunch, dinner every day; full bar; reservations for 6 or more recommended; street parking; chowfoods.com; map:GG8.*

Flying Fish / ★★★

2234 1ST AVE, BELLTOWN; 206/728-8595

Chef/owner Christine Keff knows and loves seafood, and has created a place where ultra-friendly staffers haul platters and plates to exuberant wine-imbibing diners. Even on nights when neighboring Belltown joints are quiet, Flying Fish jumps. A daily changing menu means you get what's fresh and seasonal, and Keff's commitment to organic ingredients adds to the excellence. Small plates and platters are perfect for sharing, while entrée choices let you keep all the deliciousness of dishes such as seared albacore tuna with sweet corn fritters to yourself. The brave should attempt the whole fried rockfish that is sold by the pound; everyone will love the Sister-in-Law Mussels spiced with a gorgeous lemongrass broth and served with chile-lime dipping sauce. The wine list is expansive and accessible. *$$; AE, DC, MC, V; local checks only; dinner every day; full bar; reservations recommended; street parking; info@flyingfishseattle.com; flyingfishseattle.com; map:G8.* ♿

The Four Swallows / ★★★

481 MADISON AVE N, BAINBRIDGE ISLAND; 206/842-3397

The historic William Grow farmhouse, with its warren of mismatched rooms and rural tchotchkes, is home to the charming Four Swallows, a lovely walk on a warm evening from the Bainbridge Island ferry terminal. Italian overtones color the stellar menu. For a light dinner, graze the varied starter list with a glass of wine. Mussels with saffron, leeks, tomatoes, and cream are magical, as are tender spears of asparagus and truffle-y beef carpaccio. Entrées meet expectations too. The rack of lamb with a rosemary port sauce comes with roasted figs and mashed potatoes. The clam linguine is a flavor blast with pancetta and lots of garlic. Large parties, couples, or singles are equally at home in this elegant yet easygoing island eatery. *$$; AE, DC, DIS, MC, V; local checks only; dinner Tues–Sat; full bar; reservations recommended; street parking; fourswallows.com.* ♿

Fremont Classic Pizza & Trattoria / ★★

4307 FREMONT AVE N, FREMONT; 206/548-9411

This popular neighborhood eatery is no longer just a pizza joint, but a righteously creative Italian trattoria. Thin-crusted pizzas, simple pastas, fresh salads, and the laid-back vibe work for both families and couples on a date. A fresh sheet offers seasonal dishes such as fettuccine with fresh chanterelles, roasted pear raviolis with smoked shallots, or 9-inch pizzas with house-smoked chicken sausage. The service is friendly—many servers are longtime employees on a first-name basis with the neighborhood patrons. Don't miss the weekday three-course dinner featuring a seasonal salad, a generous portion of the pasta of the day, and sinful tiramisu. *$; AE, DC, DIS, MC, V; local checks only; lunch Mon–Sat, dinner every day; beer and wine; no reservations; street parking; fremontpizza.com; map:FF8.* ♿

Fresh Flours / ★

6015 PHINNEY AVE N, PHINNEY RIDGE; 206/297-3300

European muffins, shortbreads, and tarts mix it up with Japanese culinary traditions in this tiny, bright café just blocks away from the zoo. The house specialty is matcha, made into green tea and adzuki bean muffins, green tea lattes, or buttery green tea shortbreads. Don't miss the satsumaimo, a Japanese sweet potato tart with the flakiest crust imaginable. For a quick lunch, stop in and indulge in the silky quiche, made daily with seasonal ingredients such as roasted peppers, or a freshly grilled panini, or take your goodies out to one of the nearby parks. *$; V, MC; no checks; open daily; no alcohol; no reservations; street parking; freshfloursseattle.com; map:EE7.* ♿

Frontier Room / ★★½

2203 1ST AVE, BELLTOWN; 206/956-7427

The Frontier Room is a see-and-be-seen Belltown bar and a decent, albeit upscale, late-night barbecue. Dark corners where tanked imbibers once lurked are now lit by a faux fireplace accented by a stack of artfully placed firewood. But don't be put off by all the Western tongue-in-chic: a Southern Pride pit smoker in the kitchen turns out Tennessee-style ribs, pork shoulder, Texas-style beef brisket, chicken, and sassy baked beans cooked low and slow in the smudge of applewood and hickory. The bar gets hoppin' after about 9pm, and the noise makes speaking in a normal tone nigh impossible, so if you're into conversation over dinner, go for lunch or go early. *$$; AE, MC, V; no checks; lunch, dinner Tues–Sat; full bar; no reservations; street parking; frontierroom.com; map:G8.* ♿

Garage / ★

1130 BROADWAY, CAPITOL HILL; 206/322-2296

The Garage is the only restaurant in town with a wine list as long as a bowling lane that actually *has* bowling lanes—14 of them split between two levels of a one-time Plymouth car dealership. There are also 18 full-size billiard tables in the equally funky old repair garage. The dining room is off the billiard room, but runners will carry the peppy tiger prawns in spicy, bacon-enhanced tequila sauce right to your table—or lane. Don't get any of the ever-changing, reliable risotto in the bowling ball's finger holes, and watch that you don't run a cue right through the flash-fried calamari rings and into the honey curry aioli. *$$; AE, MC, V; no checks; dinner every day; full bar; reservations recommended; self and street parking; garagebilliards.com; map:H1.* ♿

Geneva / ★★★

1106 8TH AVE, FIRST HILL; 206/624-2222

The atmosphere at this intimate and demure continental restaurant is dreamy and romantic, and outdone only by the exquisite flavors and aromas of its classic European cuisine. Begin with the lightly sweet Lillet-based Geneva cocktail and the escargot broiled on mushroom caps and go on to signature entrées such as Jägerschnitzel, pork medallions so tender you can cut them with a fork, bathed in a surprisingly light wild mushroom sauce served with a side of delicate buttered spaetzle. For dessert, try the sensational bread-and-butter pudding with vanilla brandy sauce or the bittersweet chocolate mousse and raspberry sauce in a Florentine cookie basket. Service is reverent and pampering. The wine list, with its wide-ranging prices, is a mix of the old world and the new. *$$$; AE, MC, V; no checks; dinner Tues–Sat; full bar; reservations recommended; street parking; genevarestaurant.com; map:L4.* ♿

The Georgian / ★★★★

411 UNIVERSITY ST (FAIRMONT OLYMPIC HOTEL), DOWNTOWN; 206/621-7889

From caviar to crumb scrapers, the Georgian is Seattle's nod to the elegant. Tables are filled with couples celebrating important moments, often same-siding it on the large sofalike bench seat to snuggle close and better view the room. The 1924 Italian Renaissance room with its floor-to-ceiling Palladian windows may take your breath away, but the luxurious service and food are what really sets the Georgian apart. Chef Gavin Stephenson's menus change seasonally; you can't go wrong with the prix-fixe chef's menus of four or seven courses, which will stuff you silly with crab, caviar, truffles, game birds, and other grand ingredients. Each course can be paired with wine for only marginally more, but then, you don't come to the Georgian to scrimp, so be sure to check out the gigantic, well-priced wine list. *$$$$; AE, DC, MC, V; no checks; breakfast and lunch every day, dinner Tues–Sat; full bar; reservations recommended; valet parking validated for dinner only; fairmont.com/seattle; map:EE7.* ♿

Greenlake Bar & Grill / ★

7200 E GREEN LAKE DR N, GREEN LAKE; 206/729-6179

This comfortable Green Lake eatery serves pub food done well. The genteel atmosphere is comfortable both for neighboring families and the buff singles who flock to Green Lake's superbly social shores. Friendly servers are happy to bring you enormous burgers or bowls of hearty pasta, such as the tiger shrimp and chorizo penne, which is creamy without being cloying, and prices are very reasonable. Stop in for happy hour for $2–$3 appetizers served up with microbrews. A brief wine list has good choices, mostly under $30; many are available by the glass. *$$; AE, MC, V; checks OK; lunch, dinner every day; full bar; reservations accepted for large groups; street parking; greenlakebarandgrill.com; map:EE7.* ♿

Green Leaf / ★★☆

418 8TH AVE S, CHINATOWN/INTERNATIONAL DISTRICT; 206/340-1388

Green Leaf doesn't look like much from the outside—if you even manage to stumble upon it tucked away on a side street in the International District. But step inside and you'll feel like you've discovered the city's best-kept secret. Cheerful waitstaff will usher you to a small, shiny black table and quickly set you up with tea while offering assistance with the menu. You won't go wrong with standard Vietnamese dishes such as tender grilled pork, but what sets Green Leaf apart are the specials that you don't find at your average pho joint—dishes like stir-fried jicama, escargot noodles, or the fried flour cake, deep-fried dough with a slightly sweet soy sauce for dipping. You will likely be tempted to tell your friends about the seven courses of beef, but think better of it and keep this gem to yourself. *$; V, MC; no checks; lunch and dinner every day; beer and wine; no reservations; street parking; map:HH6.* ♿

Harvest Vine / ★★★☆

2701 E MADISON ST, MADISON VALLEY; 206/320-9771

Just like it is in his native Basque region of Spain, conviviality is the point of Joseba Jiménez de Jiménez's tiny pintxos (the Basque version of tapas) emporium. The menu is infinitely shareable, and solo diners may strike up a conversation with a neighbor just for a chance to sample a few more bites. Ask for a glass of fino sherry and start with the Plato de Chacinería, one of the best selections of cured meats in Seattle. Simply superb are the grilled sardines with lemon, the lightly pan-fried sweetbreads, and button mushrooms sautéed with garlic and sherry. A seat at the copper-top bar provides a front-row view of Jiménez and his wee crew. Reservations are accepted, but half the seats are set aside for walk-ins. *$$; MC, V; checks OK; dinner every day; beer and wine; reservations accepted; street parking; harvestvine.com; map:GG7.*

The Herbfarm Restaurant / ★★★★

14590 NE 145TH ST, WOODINVILLE; 425/485-5300

Every night from Thursday through Sunday, this culinary shrine in the heart of Woodinville wine country serves up a perfectly paced nine-course meal. A new seasonal menu is featured each month and might include creative, herb-infused treasures such as a bite-size grilled blue cheese sandwich with cherry compote, handmade dumplings with local mushrooms, roasted black cod with burdock, a caramelized fruit soufflé, and lemon-thyme espresso truffles to go with your shade-grown coffee or herbal infusion. The skilled staff attends to every detail, from pouring your wine to clearing away the Christofle flatware after each course. Reservations should be booked months in advance, especially for holidays. While the all-inclusive $175 price tag might initially send your head spinning, by the end of the night, you'll find it was worth every penny. *$$$$; AE, MC, V; checks OK; dinner Thurs–Sun; beer and wine; reservations required; self parking; reservations@theherbfarm.com; theherbfarm.com; map:AA2.* ♿

Hilltop Ale House / ★

2129 QUEEN ANNE AVE N, QUEEN ANNE; 206/285-3877

This Queen Anne watering hole has pub food that's a cut above the usual burgers and deep-fried tidbits. The huge cilantro pesto quesadilla appetizer is crammed with roasted peppers, Monterey Jack cheese, cilantro pesto, and grilled chicken. The spicy Hilltop Gumbo, full of shrimp, chicken andouille sausage, and veggies is hearty, but more Southwestern than Southern. The chicken breast sandwich is a handful, oozing with mozzarella and cream cheese served on toasted rye. This is a noisy, popular joint run by the same owners as the Columbia City Alehouse (4914 Rainier Ave S, Columbia City; 206/723-5123) and the 74th Street Alehouse (7401 Greenwood Ave N, Greenwood; 206/784-2955). The creative fare is but a worthy accompaniment to the real business at hand: the 15 beers and ales on tap. *$; MC, V; checks OK; lunch and dinner every day; beer and wine; no reservations; street parking; seattlealehouses.com; map:GG8.* ♿

Honey Hole / ★

703 E PIKE ST, CAPITOL HILL; 206/709-1399

If ever there were a sandwich worth blogging about, you'd find it at the Honey Hole. Kitschy pop-culture-inspired names, such as the Luke Duke and Buford T. Justice, don't always adequately describe the meatball or pulled-pork contents, but are easily overlooked with the first bite. The monster meat concoctions ooze their stuffing all over your plate and lap, and vegetarian options, such as the El Guapo, stacked with Roma tomatoes, red onions, green bell peppers, Italian herbs, smoked Gouda, and Tillamook sharp cheddar, are enough to convert the most die-hard of meat eaters. The evening menu adds a few personal pizzas, as well as specialty cocktails. *$; AE, MC, V; checks OK; lunch and dinner every day; full bar; no reservations; street parking; thehoneyhole.com; map:K1.*

Hunt Club / ★★★

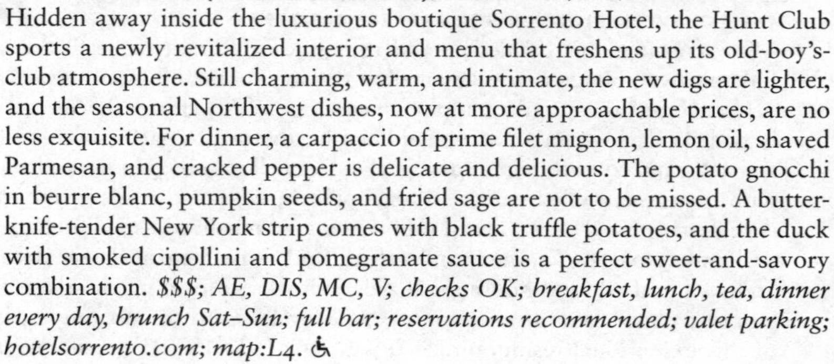

900 MADISON ST (SORRENTO HOTEL), FIRST HILL; 206/343-6156

Hidden away inside the luxurious boutique Sorrento Hotel, the Hunt Club sports a newly revitalized interior and menu that freshens up its old-boy's-club atmosphere. Still charming, warm, and intimate, the new digs are lighter, and the seasonal Northwest dishes, now at more approachable prices, are no less exquisite. For dinner, a carpaccio of prime filet mignon, lemon oil, shaved Parmesan, and cracked pepper is delicate and delicious. The potato gnocchi in beurre blanc, pumpkin seeds, and fried sage are not to be missed. A butter-knife-tender New York strip comes with black truffle potatoes, and the duck with smoked cipollini and pomegranate sauce is a perfect sweet-and-savory combination. *$$$; AE, DIS, MC, V; checks OK; breakfast, lunch, tea, dinner every day, brunch Sat–Sun; full bar; reservations recommended; valet parking; hotelsorrento.com; map:L4.* ♿

Il Bistro / ★★★

93-A PIKE ST, PIKE PLACE MARKET; 206/682-3049

One of the most enduring stars in Seattle's universe of small Italian restaurants, Il Bistro is tucked away under the eaves of the Market. The cozy warren of candlelit rooms is a perfect place to tryst. For tête-à-tête suppers try any of the shareable antipasti—mussels or prawns are fragrant with garlic and basil, and a trio of bruschetta is sure to please. Pasta must-eats are homemade gnocchi in tomato cream or a tangle of linguini in white wine with fresh seafood from the Market. If you're in for secondi, the rack of lamb is heady with rosemary and a sauce sweet with sangiovese, and there's always a memorable cioppino. Save yourself for the Marquis, a chocolate mousse cake so rich it ought to be a controlled substance. The wine list tops 500 choices and can be somewhat daunting. *$$$; AE, DC, MC, V; no checks; dinner every day; full bar; reservations recommended; valet parking Thurs–Sat, street parking; ilbistro.net; map:J8.* ♿

I Love Sushi / ★★½

1001 FAIRVIEW AVE N, SOUTH LAKE UNION (AND BRANCHES); 206/625-9604

This place has been serving wonderful sushi for so long now (since 1986) that many of the younger customers don't get the wordplay in the name. Though it's hard to picture Lucy and Ricky (forget about Fred and Ethel!) at a sushi bar, this would be one of their better bets. The chefs are happy to help guide newbies—and are capable of satisfying diehards. If she didn't order one of the bargain nigiri sushi specials, generously draped in the freshest cuts of the day, Lucy would have some 'splainin' to do. The à la carte dishes, such as flame-broiled mackerel or salmon, are excellent. Two outposts in Bellevue (11818 NE 8th St, 425/454-5706; 23 Lake Bellevue Dr, 425/455-9090) serve Eastsiders. *$$; AE, MC, V; no checks; lunch Mon–Fri (Seattle), Mon–Sat (Bellevue), dinner every day; full bar; reservations recommended; self parking; ilovesushi.com; map:GG7.* ♿

Il Terrazzo Carmine / ★★★

411 1ST AVE S, PIONEER SQUARE; 206/467-7797

Many consider this handsome and romantic restaurant to be Seattle's top Italian eatery. Hidden away in an alley, the airy room and small terrace are a perfect complement to the tempting menu. For a lusty starter there's calamari in padella (frying pan), tender squid in a heady tomato-garlic sauté, or fresh spinach sautéed with lemon and garlic. Cannelloni are creamy and bubbly with ricotta and filled with veal and spinach; wide and tender pappardelle is perfectly paired with braised rabbit and wild mushrooms in a rich version of hunter's pasta. Tiramisu and crème brûlée are appropriately decadent and well crafted, and house-made gelati showcase local fruits in season. A guitarist plays classical music most nights, adding to the dreamy escapism of this exceptional restaurant. *$$$; AE, DC, DIS, MC, V; no checks; lunch Mon–Fri, dinner Mon–Sat; full bar; reservations recommended; valet parking; ilterrazzocarmine.com; map:O8.* ♿

Imperial Garden Seafood Restaurant / ★★

18230 EAST VALLEY HWY, KENT; 425/656-0999

It's quite a drive from Seattle and nearly hidden in a Chinese-themed mall, but the long look for parking should be a hint that many have nonetheless discovered this gem before you. Avoid the rush for weekend dim sum by showing up after 2pm, or brave rush hour and go on a weekday. You'll walk away happily stuffed with lobster dumplings, almond shrimp balls, and pork buns with airy pastry as delicate as any strudel in Vienna. The pork shiu mai with black mushrooms are little satchel bombs of flavor, as are the pan-fried vegetable dumplings or shrimp-stuffed tofu. For dinner, the Peking duck is the house specialty and doesn't require 24 hours' notice. *$; DIS, MC, V; no checks; breakfast, lunch, dinner, dim sum every day; full bar; reservations recommended; self parking; imperialgardenseafood.com; map:PP4.* ♿

India Bistro / ★★

2301 NW MARKET ST, BALLARD; 206/783-5080

The exotic scents of the Malabar Coast and Kashmir waft from a corner of Seattle's old Norwegian neighborhood. The long menu has curries, vegetarian dishes, Indian breads, and meats from the tandoor—the superhot, vertical clay oven. Try the pakoras, little bundles of vegetables, chicken, or fish fried in a lentil-flour batter served with mint chutney. Shareable entrées include kabli masala—delicate garbanzo beans cooked with onions and spices—and lamb vindaloo, a spicy stew with potatoes and a splash of vinegar. The accompanying rice is buttery, flaky, and fragrant. The tender naan is the best way to soak up rich gravies and sauces. Don't miss the $5.95 lunch buffet Monday through Saturday. *$; AE, DC, DIS, MC, V; no checks; lunch Mon–Sat, dinner every day; beer and wine; reservations recommended; street parking; seattleindiabistro.com; map:FF8.* ♿

JaK's Grill / ★★

4548 CALIFORNIA AVE SW, WEST SEATTLE (AND BRANCHES); 206/937-7809

With three locations in the area, JaK's has become the no-brainer neighborhood steakhouse for flavorful, corn-fed, dry-aged Nebraska beef. The steaks are first-rate, but so are the double-thick pork chops marinated in bourbon and brown sugar, glazed with honey and peppercorn. Steaks range from the mid $20s to the upper $30s, but you won't feel nickeled-and-dimed—all meals come with healthy servings of salad, bread, veggies, and your choice of potato. The fried potato pancake option is a great choice. Wines come from California and Washington. Expect to wait for a table, and concentrate on the flavors, not the digs, particularly at the Laurelhurst (3701 NE 45th St; 206/985-8545) and Issaquah (14 Front St N; 425/837-8834) outposts. *$$; DC, DIS, MC, V; checks OK; dinner every day; full bar; no reservations; self and street parking; jaksgrill.com; map:II8.* ♿

JoAnna's Soul Café and Jazz Club / ★★

2514 E CHERRY ST, CENTRAL DISTRICT; 206/568-6300

Down-home and upscale all in one, JoAnna's brings Jim Buchanan's Southern food to the Central District, a Seattle neighborhood on the rise. Start with the Soul Roll, a southern take on the Asian classic, mixing collards, rice, black-eyed peas, and red beans together in a fried spring roll. Then dive into a big bowl of spicy gumbo, a side of mac and cheese, and a basket of honey-sweet cornbread. And by all means, don't miss the sweet potato pie. Show up on Sunday mornings for a sellout buffet brunch starring 10 of the café's specialties, including crisp catfish fillets and collard greens. Live jazz music adds to the lively, inviting atmosphere. *$$; AE, DIS, V, MC; no checks; lunch and dinner every day, brunch on Sundays; full bar; reservations accepted; street parking; map:GG6.* ♿

Joe Bar / ★

810 E ROY ST, CAPITOL HILL; 206/324-0407

Crammed into a tiny space in Capitol Hill's Loveless Building, you'll find Joe Bar, a quaint hipster crêperie and café with a small scattering of tables and frequently rotating artwork. The staff is superfriendly, and while not exactly fast, they're quick enough to stave off much of a line. Food options range from sweet (a PB&J crepe) to savory (a wine-cured salami, Gruyère, and roasted red pepper panini), and a buck gets you a fine sampling of olives. In fall, look for the spiced pumpkin purée, sage, and chèvre crepe. If falling leaves, crisp air, and a roaring fire could be wrapped up in a flavor, this would be it. A terrific selection of beer and wine accompanies the house-blended coffee drinks. *$; AE, MC, V; checks OK; coffee and pastry service all day every day, full menu Tues–Sat evenings, crepes only Sat and Sun mornings; wine and beer; no reservations; street parking; joebar.org; map:GG6.*

Judy Fu's Snappy Dragon / ★

8917 ROOSEVELT WY NE, MAPLE LEAF; 206/528-5575

True to its name, this Maple Leaf house-turned-restaurant serves up some of the snappiest Chinese food around. House-made noodles head the bill here. Don't miss the soft-noodle chow meins or the *jiaozi*, boiled dumplings. Maple Leafers and others flock to the joint, often for takeout. Be sure to order the crispy tea-smoked duck, aromatic fowl served with hoisin and steamed buns. Other big sellers are the spicy-sweet Szechuan favorite, General Tso's chicken; the clay pot stews (especially with shrimp); chicken meatballs; prawns; scallops; and veggies. Almond cranberry chicken is an unusual sweet-sour-savory mélange that makes something lush, complex, and very Chinese out of the simple puritanical New England sour fruit we usually equate with Thanksgiving. *$; AE, DC, MC, V; local checks only; lunch, dinner Mon–Sat; full bar; reservations accepted for 5 or more; street parking; snappydragon.com; map: DD7.* ♿

Julia's Indonesian Kitchen / ★★½

910 NE 65TH ST, ROOSEVELT; 206/522-5528

You won't see lines of sarong-clad servants ceremoniously serving some 40 dishes, as was the tradition during Dutch colonial times, but there are often long lines outside the cozy converted Craftsman waiting to savor Julia Suparman's version of rijsttafel ("rice table" in Dutch). At Julia's, you can dine family-style on your choice of six assorted meat and veggie dishes redolent with the scents and flavors of the Spice Islands. Crowd favorites—based on the same recipes Suparman raised her kids on—include ayam goreng kalasan (sweet fried chicken marinated with Javanese brown sugar and coconut juice), ayam goreng kremes (crispy fried chicken spiced with lemongrass, bay leaves, galangal, lemongrass and red chilies), empal (tender sweet fried beef), and risoles (chicken and vegetables in a béchamel-like sauce wrapped in a pancake, then breaded and fried). Stave off the spice with a dessert drink such as es teler, a milky beverage with bits of avocado, shredded coconut and jackfruit. *$; MC, V; no checks; lunch and dinner Tues–Sun; no alcohol; no reservations; self parking; juliasindokitchen.com; map:EE6.*

Kabul Afghan Cuisine / ★★

2301 N 45TH ST, WALLINGFORD; 206/545-9000

Chef Sultan Malikyar, who emigrated from Afghanistan in the late 1970s, shares his family's recipes, which include his father's kebab and his mother's chaka (garlic-yogurt sauce). He and partner Wali Khairzada make fragrant, elegant food such as crisp bolani (green onion–potato turnovers with chaka for dipping), badenjan borani (sautéed eggplant, with or without meat, in a lightly spiced tomato sauce), and beef, lamb, or chicken kebabs served on perfumed piles of basmati. If you can't choose, try a variety with the $40 dinner for two. The dining room's simple décor is as soothing as the cardamom-and-rose-water custard firni (sometimes known as Turkish Delight) served for dessert. *$$; AE, DIS, MC, V; local checks only; dinner Mon–Sat; beer and wine; reservations accepted; street parking; kabulrestaurant.com; map:FF7.* ♿

Kingfish Café / ★★

602 19TH AVE E, CAPITOL HILL; 206/320-8757

Down-home, sassy goodness practically knocks you over as you step into this Southern-inspired café with creaky, wide-beamed floors and sepia-toned family portraits. When the place is hopping, have a seat at the huge wooden bar and sip on a freshly muddled mojito. In the restaurant, classics such as Jazz It Slow Gumbo loaded with tasso and prawns, pan-fried catfish with grits and collards, and the famous buttermilk fried chicken will more than fill you up, but you'll still want to save room for a slice of the enormous three-layer red velvet cake. Sunday morning brunch, with its crab and catfish cakes topped with a poached egg and hollandaise, always draws a crowd, so be sure to show up early to get one of the coveted tables. *$$; MC, V; checks OK; lunch, dinner every day but Tues, brunch Sun; full bar; no reservations; street parking; map:HH7.* ♿

La Carta de Oaxaca / ★★★

5431 BALLARD AVE NW, BALLARD; 206/782-8722

Some claim great Mexican food is not to be found in Seattle; this small, bustling Oaxacan restaurant with communal tables and black-and-white photographs handily refutes this notion. Start with chips and your choice of dips from the salsa bar. Entrée portions are just larger than tapas size; best bets include halibut tacos, chicken in a sweet mole negro, and sausage and potato molotes (fried tortillas). If you can handle serious spicy heat, look for caldo de pescado, fish soup that's the real deal. Be prepared: Waits can be long. Big margaritas or cerveza from the corner bar help pass the time. *$; AE, DIS, MC, V; checks OK; lunch Tue–Sat, dinner Mon–Sat; full bar; no reservations; street parking; lacartadeoaxaca.com; map:FF8.* ♿

BEST PLACE

TO HAVE A BEER AND WATCH A MARINERS GAME?

"The Roanoke Inn on Mercer Island, where the best sport's timeless delights can be enjoyed in a timeless roadhouse [established 1914]."

—*John Marshall,* Seattle P-I*'s baseball Answer Guy*

La Medusa / ★★½

4857 RAINIER AVE S, COLUMBIA CITY; 206/723-2192

Chef Julie Andres cranks out fresh creative Italian in this burgeoning neighborhood. In summer you might find Andres wandering the aisles of the Columbia City farmers' market, picking out the season's best ingredients for the evening meal. Menus change frequently but might include an oozing cheese-filled flatbread topped with some luxuriously prepared vegetable, or white Spanish anchovies gracing crusty bruschetta. Dishes in the primi course will likely include handmade pastas with traditional tomato sauce, as well as more creative sauces featuring sardines, raisins, favas, nuts, or greens. A daily fish special as well as a tender sirloin are equally innovative. Desserts are house-made—particularly good is the cannoli filled with ricotta and chocolate bits surrounded with Marsala-soaked fruits. Medium-priced wines mainly hail from southern Italy. *$$; MC, V; no checks; dinner Tues–Sat; full bar; reservations recommended for 6 or more; street parking; lamedusarestaurant.com; map:KK6.* ♿

Lampreia / ★★★

2400 1ST AVE, BELLTOWN; 206/443-3301

"Impeccable," "Exquisite," and "Frickin' amazing" are just a few comments you may overhear while you indulge in the gourmet feats of chef/owner Scott Carsberg. The experience begins with a reverential (some say chilly) welcome, an amuse-bouche, and perhaps a glass of champagne to sip as you peruse the menu and settle into the understated dining room. Starters are delicate melodies—the freshest crab rolled in sheer slices of apple with a light sprinkle of smoky sea salt; a gravlax of Kobe beef topped with apple-red wine purée. Mains are a symphony of flavor and texture—a veal chop drizzled with a fonduta sauce, or black bass with pork belly. Artisan cheese, served after a meal, is an end unto itself or a prelude to a white chocolate mousse stuffed with strawberries. Carsberg has developed a near cultlike following, and while some may smirk at all the fuss or fret about the steep prices, there's really nowhere else in Seattle for this experience in excellence. *$$$$; AE, MC, V; no checks; dinner Tues–Sat; full bar; reservations recommended; street parking; lampreiarestaurant.com; map:F8.* ♿

Lark / ★★★

926 12TH AVE, CAPITOL HILL; 206/323-5275

Small plates and big flavors make up this gem of a restaurant in the hot dining corridor of 12th Avenue on Capitol Hill. Plates—expertly prepared from perfectly fresh ingredients—are intended for sharing, but you may want to hoard every bite of dishes such as pommes de terre "Robuchon" (baked mashed potatoes) and roasted eel served with a luscious potato salad. Flowing white curtains can be cleverly arranged to create an aura of privacy in the softly lit, wood-floored open space. Chef John Sundstrom earned a following at Seattle's Earth & Ocean and Dahlia Lounge, and the crowd here is food-savvy and sophisticated. The no-reservations policy (except for large groups) can mean the occasional wait, but relax and let booze infuser Michelle Magidow shake you up a cocktail, such as a delightfully fresh Pear Drop, next door at Lark's little sister, Licorous. *$$$; MC, V; checks OK; dinner Tues–Sun; full bar; reservations recommended; street parking; larkseattle.com; map:M1.* ♿

La Rustica / ★★

4100 BEACH DR SW, WEST SEATTLE; 206/932-3020

Giulio and Janie Pellegrini's pretty little place on Alki Point, with its rough-hewn stone walls and arches, thickets of potted plants, dusty wine bottles, and summer weather al fresco dining, couldn't differ more dramatically from the muscle-beach scene just blocks away. It's a destination for not only its West Seattle neighbors, but also for other city folk savvy enough to know about Giulio's signature osso buco balsamico and his veal-wrapped sautéed prawns in Marsala. Fresh homemade focaccia comes with everything—such as the spaghetti with garlic and mustard greens, or the gnocchi con salsiccia, rich homemade dumplings in tomato sauce with Italian sausage. Janie manages the dining room but doubles as dessert chef, crafting such memorable delectables as bittersweet-chocolate crème brûlée and the best tiramisu west of Belltown. *$$; AE, DIS, MC, V; checks OK; dinner Tues–Sun; full bar; reservations accepted for 6 or more; street parking; map:J9.* ♿

Le Gourmand / ★★★★

425 NW MARKET ST, BALLARD; 206/784-3463

Nestled at the edge of Ballard, far from the neighborhood's other dining hot spots, you'll find this little grotto, where convivial chef/owner Bruce Naftaly prepares exquisite, seasonal, unfussy Northwest/French cuisine. The romantic dining room features a lovely ceiling painted like a clear spring day and a trompe l'oeil of trees, hollyhocks, and lupines. Choose the three-course, prix-fixe menu of appetizer, entrée, and salade après, or linger over the seven-course tasting menu. Naftaly excels at sauces; a creamy one with local caviar graces the sole, and a huskier one with shiitakes, Cognac, and fresh sage accompanies the loin of rabbit. The wine list features notable French, California, and Northwest bottles, with plenty of good midrange price options. Sambar, the tiny attached lounge, shakes up a mean cocktail. *$$$; AE, MC, V; local checks only; dinner Wed–Sat; full bar; reservations recommended; street parking; map:FF8.* ♿

Le Pichet / ★★★

1933 1ST AVE, PIKE PLACE MARKET; 206/256-1499

This narrow *café à vin* near the Market is the closest you'll get to the Rive Gauche in Seattle. Warm overhead lighting, wood-framed mirrors, and a sweet collection of ceramic pitchers create a convivial Parisian ambience. Start your meal with a delicate salad, such as the caille grillée, a succulent half quail nested in a bed of watercress and avocado with a creamy almond vinaigrette. Your next stop on le tour should be the assiette de jambon cru followed by the fish of the day on cockle-warming stewed white beans, cauliflower, and cornichons. The wine list features about 50 labels, mostly French, most under $25, and available by the glass, *pichet* (two-thirds of a 750ml bottle), or *demi-pichet* (two glasses). The petit zinc bar is just long enough to sit a handful of patrons for espresso and brioche in the morning. *$$; MC, V; no checks; breakfast every day, lunch and dinner Thurs–Mon; full bar; reservations recommended; street parking; lepichetseattle.com; map:I8.* ♿

Licorous / ★★★

928 12TH AVE, CAPITOL HILL; 206/325-6947

Everybody loves John Sundstrom's restaurant Lark, and now there's more to adore with next-door Licorous, Lark's lounge-and-small-plates kissing cousin. The name means "tempting to the appetite," and the place delivers with seductive, seasonal cocktails and compelling, creative snacks. The drinks menu helpfully offers pairings—you might find the signature Lark (prosecco, grapefruit, and Campari) coupled with a dish of endive, watercress, and boquerones (Spanish anchovies); or a Ko Samui (mango-infused tequila with lime juice) complementing a Thai tuna tartare. Sweet bites include amazing hazelnut financiers, still warm from the oven. Translucent rose-colored draperies, exposed beams, cozy seating, perfect lighting—life's just prettier (and more delicious, and more fun) here. *$; MC, V; checks OK; dinner Tues–Sat; full bar; no reservations; street parking; licorous.com; map:M1.* ♿

Luau Polynesian Lounge / ★

2253 N 56TH ST, GREEN LAKE; 206/633-5828

In the Tangletown neighborhood just east of Green Lake, you'll find Jessica and Thomas Price's island-themed eatery, where the spirit of aloha greets you at the door like the sweet fragrance of plumeria in Hawaii. Chef Geoffrey Yahn's menu roams the Pacific Rim for pulled pork, pupu platters, pot stickers, sticky rice, and stir-fries, and ambles down to the Caribbean with nods at Mexico and Jamaica, yet still manages to serve a darn good burger. Served with serrano chile corn bread, Big Daddy Mack's smoked Hawaiian-style baby back ribs are made for gnawing to the bone. Late night draws regulars to the bar to spin yarns and sip exotic tropical potables such as the Kaha Mai Tai or the Hawaiian Punch. *$$; AE, MC, V; checks OK; lunch Tues–Fri, dinner every day; full bar; reservations recommended; street parking; luaupolynesianlounge.com; map:EE7.* ♿

Luna Park Café / ★

2918 AVALON WY SW, WEST SEATTLE; 206/935-7250

Decked out in old neon and memorabilia, this West Seattle beanery is named after the "Coney Island of the West," the amusement park that glittered on the northern tip of West Seattle from 1907 to 1913. Simpler times are celebrated with tableside jukeboxes loaded with top 40 hits and retro foods mostly from the 1950s. Weekend brunch is always bustling, but you can get the same old-fashioned—that is to say, large—portions of piles, hobos, and omelets anytime. Lunch and dinner offer up burgers, real malts, grilled sandwiches, meat loaf, prime rib dip, and a popular fresh roasted turkey and Swiss. The diner will flood you with memories of those bygone days, even if you never lived them. In summer, colorful tables and shade umbrellas draw impromptu traffic. *$; MC, V; checks OK; breakfast, lunch, dinner every day; beer and wine; reservations required for 6 or more during the week, recommended on weekends; self parking; lunaparkcafe.com; map:JJ9.* ♿

Macrina Bakery & Cafe / ★★☆

2408 1ST AVE, BELLTOWN (AND BRANCHES); 206/448-4032

Artisanal baker Leslie Mackie has been casting a spell on Seattle for more than a decade, and the enchantment renews each morning as fresh bread, pastry, and the aroma of espresso greet still-sleepy downtown residents and on-the-go commuters. Start your day with homemade bread pudding with fresh fruit and cream, or cinnamon rolls made from Mackie's luscious croissant-style dough. Lunch charms with simple salads, sandwiches, and a meze plate—your choice of three Mediterranean-inspired noshes. Mackie's cookbook (*Leslie Mackie's Macrina Bakery & Cafe Cookbook*, Sasquatch Books, 2003) gives a sneak peak into the magic of the café—but don't pass up experiencing the real thing. Locations on Queen Anne (615 W McGraw St; 206/283-5900) and Vashon Island (19603 Vashon Hwy SW; 206/567-4133) offer even more opportunities to indulge. *$; MC, V; local checks only; breakfast, lunch Mon–Fri, brunch Sat–Sun; beer and wine; no reservations; street parking; macrinabakery.com; map:F8.* ♿

Madison Park Café / ★

1807 42ND AVE E, MADISON PARK; 206/324-2626

Seattle has no shortage of neighborhood bistros, but few are as comfortably refined as the charming Madison Park Café. Chef Amanda Zimlich, a Seattle native and former executive sous chef at Barking Frog, works magic in a kitchen smaller than those in most homes. Expect to find seasonal old-school and new-school French dishes such as citrus-rubbed free-range lamb loin or farro "risotto" with roasted root vegetables and Washington truffles. The charcuterie plate offers locally made salumi and a house-made chicken liver terrine, and the pommes frites cooked in duck fat are not to be missed. Save some room for pastry chef Rich Coffey's incredible homemade glacés. Make outdoor reservations for the cobblestone courtyard on weekends for brunch, which offers such temptations as sourdough waffles and ricotta pancakes. *$$$; AE, MC, V; checks OK; dinner Tues–Thurs, brunch Sat–Sun; full bar; reservations recommended; street parking; madisonparkcafe.citysearch.com; map:GG6.*

Madoka / ★★★☆

241 WINSLOW WY W, BAINBRIDGE ISLAND; 206/842-2448

Just a short (and lovely) ferry ride from downtown Seattle, Madoka's become a destination for diners interested in Asian-fusion cuisine taken to an entirely different, superior level. Chef Alvin Binuya was on the forefront of the fusion movement in the kitchens of several popular Seattle restaurants over the last two decades; now he's created a relaxed yet inspired island haven for it. He elevates something as simple as carrot-parsnip soup with a kick of momiji-oroshi oil and a garnish of toasted sesame seeds, while an applewood-smoked duck breast served with udon noodles in a gingery broth is a treat of the highest order. Service is notably friendly and genuinely helpful; the wine list is brief but thoughtfully assembled, and sake and Japanese tea service are offered as well. *$$$; AE, V, MC; checks OK; dinner Wed–Sun; full bar; reservations recommended; self parking; madokaonbainbridge.com.*

Mae Phim Thai / ★

94 COLUMBIA ST, PIONEER SQUARE; 206/384-2640

The good news is that this exceptionally fresh Thai food is made to order and served up as quick as you can imagine. The bad news is that as you sit there slurping up your tom yum kai, someone else wants your table. Orders are constantly flying at this little hole-in-the-wall Thai café that serves up in-house lunch and dinner, as well as a healthy take-out business, complete with online ordering. Standards such as pad thai and green curry please, as do the less common yum neah, sautéed slices of beef mixed with cucumber, tomato, red onion, and lime juice. Bring cash; Mae Phim doesn't take plastic. *$; cash only; lunch and dinner every day; no reservations; full bar; street parking; maephim.com; map:M7.* ♿

Malay Satay Hut / ★★½

212 12TH AVE S, CHINATOWN/INTERNATIONAL DISTRICT; 206/324-4091; 15230 NE 24TH ST, REDMOND; 425/564-0888

Malaysia meets China, India, and Thailand in this Seattle mini-chain with cafés in Little Saigon and an Eastside strip mall. Both offer the same incredible food, reasonable prices, and kitsched-up charm. It's hard not to be intimidated by the novel of a menu on your first visit, but soon you'll have your own favorites among the Hut's seafood, curries, wontons, stir-fries, and satays, and you'll be ordering like a pro. Try the roti canai, flatbread served with a potato chicken curry sauce; the mild but juicy chicken satay; or Buddha's Yam Pot, a chicken, shrimp, and vegetable stir-fry in a deep-fried basket of grated yams. The service is fast; to-go orders are recommended if you want to avoid the noisy bustle and wait for seats. *$; MC, V; no checks; lunch, dinner every day; beer and wine; reservations accepted for 6 or more; self and street parking; malaysatayhut.com; map:HH6, EE1.* ♿

Malena's Taco Shop / ★

620 W MCGRAW ST, QUEEN ANNE; 206/284-0304; 2010 NW 56TH ST, BALLARD; 206/789-8207

Malena's is the little taco shop that could. Eva Coborubias opened the original Malena's, sandwiched between an upholsterer and a yoga studio on the west side of Queen Anne Hill, in 1997 and has enjoyed a line of devotees spilling out of her petite parlor ever since. As it's a shoebox of a place with only four oilcloth-covered tables and as many counter stools, most folks order to go from the large menu board, with sights set on a park bench. Combination plates come with flaky, lightly seasoned Mexican rice and a heaping spoonful of plump beans, stewed to tender perfection. Favorite combos include carne asada tacos and pork tamales. A second location in Ballard offers the same comforting and reliable food—and four times the seating. *$; V, MC; local checks only; lunch, dinner every day (Ballard location closed Sun); no alcohol; no reservations; street parking; map:GG8, FF8.*

Maneki Japanese Restaurant / ★★

304 6TH AVE S, CHINATOWN/INTERNATIONAL DISTRICT; 206/622-2631

Maneki is Seattle's oldest Japanese restaurant and sushi bar—it is also Seattle's best and most comforting, reflecting the warm personality of owner Jean Nakayama and her loyal staff. What makes Maneki special is simple: perfectly executed food offered without pretension. Sushi and sashimi are impossibly fresh (and an alarmingly good value to boot); don't miss the fresh salmon and yellowtail, the spicy tuna roll, or the horse mackerel special when it's available. Hot food doesn't disappoint, either, particularly tonkatsu, broiled miso black cod collar, or takoyaki (think savory, octopus-filled doughnut holes). All of Maneki's dishes are imbued with undeniable soul, and the dining experience feels timeless. *$; AE, MC, V; no checks; dinner Tues–Sun; full bar; reservations recommended; street parking; map:HH6.* ♿

Maple Leaf Grill / ★★

8929 ROOSEVELT WY NE, MAPLE LEAF; 205/523-8499

Maple Leaf Grill is a quintessential neighborhood eatery. Unless you live nearby, it's unlikely that you've dined in this cozy bungalow on Roosevelt Way. But reliable comfort food, a friendly staff, and Thursday-evening live music should convince you to make a friend in Maple Leaf who you can meet for an amiable meal. Order the house specialty Mars oyster stew full of tasso ham, shallots, artichoke hearts, and spinach, or choose a honey-glazed pork tenderloin or herb-marinated hanger steak, both of which come with a side of yam mashers. The yam fries, too, are a neighborhood favorite. The small, fireplace-warmed bar is a favorite of denim-clad regulars who stop by discuss the news over bowls of Caribbean black-bean soup or some of the best damn sandwiches in town. *$$; MC, V; checks OK; lunch Mon–Sat, dinner every day; full bar; reservations recommended; self parking; mapleleafgrill.com; map:DD7.* ♿

Marco's Supperclub / ★★

2510 1ST AVE, BELLTOWN; 206/441-7801

This funky place was once part of the Belltown renaissance; now it's a Seattle classic. Out front, a few covered tables afford hip sidewalk ambience. Inside, the warm wooden bar topped by paper lanterns feels cozy, though it runs the entire length of the room. Veteran restaurateur Marco Rulff roams the room, greeting regulars and welcoming the uninitiated. While the capable kitchen kicks out bushes and bushes of its signature fried sage leaves to get a meal started, the entrée menu changes regularly—sometimes daily—offering the best of what is market fresh and influenced by diverse cuisines and flavors from around the world. An eclectic collection of European and Northwest wines is available by the bottle or glass. In fair weather, a deck out back doubles the seating capacity. *$$; AE, MC, V; checks OK; dinner every day; full bar; reservations recommended; street parking; marcossupperclub.com; map:F8.* ♿

Marjorie / ★★

2331 2ND AVE, BELLTOWN; 206/441-9842

Donna Moodie gracefully transformed her beloved restaurant Lush Life from dreamy Italian to romantic eclectic, renamed it in honor of her mother, and promised "food for the soul." In bold jewel tones, colorful raw silk, and dynamic metal work, this vaguely Moroccan room is stunning but comfortable. Chef Fernando Martinez makes daily trips to nearby Pike Place Market and showcases the fresh ingredients with a four-course tasting menu offered on Fridays and Saturdays. The menu, divided into "small plates" and "bigger plates," offers seemingly simple but rich and tasty delights such as carpaccio of red and yellow beets, and roast chicken with polenta and grilled chard. Pastry chef Manda Mangrai presents modified classics like brioche bread pudding and chocolate tiramisu, as well as a changing, seasonal "dessert of the moment." *$$; AE, DIS, MC, V; checks OK; dinner Tues–Sun; full bar; reservations recommended; street parking; marjorie@trenchtownrocks.com; trenchtownrocks.com; map:G8.*

Market Street Urban Grill / ★★

1744 NW MARKET ST, BALLARD; 206/789-6766

Market Street Grill owners John and Kendell Sillers, Seattle restaurant veterans, have maintained their own vision of neighborhood fine dining in rapidly developing Ballard, crafting an imaginative menu that changes seasonally. You'll find distinct dishes such as an appetizer of smoked-prawn spring rolls with Asian slaw, fresh crayfish linguine with a napoleon of spring vegetables, a chocolate chip cookie sandwich, or an in-season fruit dessert like the melon tartare with mascarpone and raspberries. *$$$; AE, DIS, MC, V; checks OK; dinner Mon–Sat; full bar; reservations recommended; self parking; map:EE8.* ♿

Mashiko / ★★

4725 CALIFORNIA AVE SW, WEST SEATTLE; 206/935-4339

Mashiko is more than a sushi bar—it's an attitude with a sense of humor. It's flying pigs, strange Japanese windup toys, and real art on the walls. Saltwater fish tanks are filled with unlikely critters fluttering in crystalline waters. Hajime Sato and wife Kirstin Schlecht offer the traditional flavors of Japan in decidedly untraditional fashion—and succeed beautifully. Sato may dance behind the sushi bar to ABBA, juggling knives and ahi loins like a one-man chorus line, while the kitchen serves delectables from a vast hot menu that includes teriyaki and tempura, but also offers such diversities as ceviche or Cajun tuna. *$$; AE, DC, MC, V; no checks; dinner every day; beer and wine; reservations accepted; self and street parking; sushiwhore.com; map:JJ9.* ♿

Matt's in the Market / UNRATED

94 PIKE ST, 3RD FLOOR, PIKE PLACE MARKET; 206/467-7909

At press time, Pike Place Market staple and fresh produce mecca Matt's had just reopened after a major renovation, expansion, and revamping. All this growth bodes well for eaters who have come to rely on Matt's thrillingly fresh food. Just like the old menu did, Matt's new menu promises to showcase the best ingredients the bountiful Market has to offer—smoked catfish salad, baby beets and frisée salad, Penn Cove mussels, oysters on the half shell, roasted duck breast, and pan-roasted wild salmon. No doubt the new-and-improved, more spacious Matt's will be packed with people clamoring for trusted fare and the perfect perch from which to take in the goings-on at Pike Place. *$$; MC, V; no checks; lunch and dinner Mon–Sat; full bar; reservations recommended; street and validated parking in Market garage after 5pm; mattsinthemarket.com; map:J8.*

Matt's Rotisserie & Oyster Lounge / ★

16551 NE 74 ST, REDMOND TOWN CENTER, REDMOND; 425/376-0909

Matt's fills the need for urbane dining in Redmond while at the same time pleasing the varying tastes of shoppers at Redmond Town Center. The space itself—a big, gleaming room awash in deep golds and reds with copper accents—is enough to forget that this rotisserie-cum-oyster-lounge that claims Spanish paella as its house specialty is housed in a suburban mall. Dishes such as salt-and-pepper half chicken; fruitwood-smoked, sweetly glazed baby back ribs; and fish cooked atop the wood-fired grill are tasty and reliable—and the prime rib dinner sells out regularly, for good reason. The oyster bar, filled with regional bivalves flying from the hands of sharp-skilled shuckers, also beckons. *$$; AE, MC, V; checks OK; lunch, dinner every day; full bar; reservations recommended; self parking; mattsrotisserie.com; map:EE1.* ♿

Maximilien in the Market / ★★

81A PIKE ST, PIKE PLACE MARKET; 206/682-7270

Nestled in the Pike Place Market, Maximilien is awash in Parisian romanticism and stunning Northwest views of Elliott Bay, West Seattle, and the Olympic Mountains, the sort of place where couples go to celebrate anniversaries. French classics—onion soup, warm frisée salad with bacon and goat cheese, escargot—should not be missed, and neither should the decadent tournedos de boeuf: beef tenderloin with truffle and Armagnac sauce, served with seared foie gras. Maximilien also now offers a $30 prix-fixe Sunday supper. Lunch features smaller entrée salads and sandwiches, as well as an assortment of tartes flambées and steamed mussel dishes. The French-centric wine list is extensive, with a wealth of midpriced wines and some expensive imports. *$$; AE, DC, DIS, MC, V; no checks; lunch Mon–Sat, dinner Tues–Sat, brunch Sun; full bar; reservations recommended; valet and street parking; maximilienrestaurant.com; map:J8.*

Medin's Ravioli Station / ★

4620 LEARY WY, BALLARD; 206/789-6680

In the funky warehouse-y anti-neighborhood that's not quite Ballard, not quite Fremont, chef/owner Bill Medin serves a steady stream of customers. The bar, always occupied by a regular crowd of wine enthusiasts, has a unique water-heated iron handrail and stools made from train pistons. The big, fat raviolis on the short menu are made using an iron ravioli mold, designed, as is all the ironwork, by Medin, a metal sculptor in his spare time. Ravioli fillings include house-smoked salmon, roasted butternut squash, three cheeses, beef, and spinach. Match your ravioli with one of the sauces—tomato cream, marinara, Alfredo, or roasted red pepper. The low-frills dining room, reasonable prices, casual atmosphere, and the fact that kids love raviolis make this a good place for families. *$; MC, V; local checks only; lunch Tues–Fri, dinner Tues–Sun; beer and wine; reservations recommended; street parking; map:FF8.* ♿

Mediterranean Kitchen / ★

103 BELLEVUE WY NE, STE 1, BELLEVUE; 425/462-9422

Three words: garlic, garlic, garlic. Mediterranean Kitchen is a garlic lover's paradise—and certainly a place not to be missed by any fan of Mediterranean cuisine. The restaurant is very dark and the music very loud, but the hosts and servers are energetic and attentive, and portions are large. Every meal begins with lentil soup and salad. Trusty standbys such as hummus, baba ghanoush, and lamb kebabs should not be missed, but amazingly it's chicken—tangy, marinated in lemon, vinegar, and spices—that steals the show with its incredible depth of flavor. You can't go wrong with the Farmer's Chicken, a pile of grilled wings, smothered in—what else?—garlic sauce, atop a bed of rice. It is the very definition of finger-licking good. *$; AE, DC, DIS, MC, V; checks OK; lunch and dinner Mon–Sat; beer and wine; reservations recommended; self parking; map:GG2.*

Metropolitan Grill / ★★★

820 2ND AVE, DOWNTOWN; 206/624-3287

If the words "Peter Luger Steak House" mean anything to you—and they should—head to the Metropolitan Grill. Much like New York's singular and iconic eatery, at the Met a dry martini and a dry-aged steak will have you feeling like a good ol' boy, laughing in the face of Seattle's earnest progressiveness and cultural sensitivity—if only for an hour or two. Dinner attracts well-dressed folks who want a great meal and are not afraid to pay for it. To miss one of the Met's steaks is to miss the point. The cooked-to-order bone-in New York strip and prime porterhouse are well seasoned and flavorful. Expect to be well cared for by an experienced waitstaff and impressed by the wine list, which is heavy with muscular European and domestic reds. *$$$$; AE, DC, DIS, JCB, MC, V; checks OK; lunch Mon–Fri, dinner every day; full bar; reservations recommended; valet parking; themetropolitangrill.com; map:M7.* ♿

Mistral / ★★★★

113 BLANCHARD ST, BELLTOWN; 206/770-7799

Mistral is widely considered by local foodies to be the best restaurant in Seattle. Executive Chef William Belickis is a man with a singular, passionate, and exacting vision, and his flawless food reflects the best of these traits. An evening at Mistral promises as much a transcendent experience as an exquisite meal. Diners have just three prix-fixe options, all of which feature the freshest local and seasonal ingredients: the nine-course Mistral's Experience menu, the seven-course Chef's Experience menu, and the five-course Market Experience menu. On a recent spring visit, there were impossibly fresh oysters, scallops in pea soup, guinea fowl, foie gras, and lamb chops—nothing short of divine. You can count on knowledgeable servers to guide you through each course and meticulous wine pairing. *$$$$; AE, DIS, MC, V; checks OK; lunch Fri–Sat, dinner Tues–Sat; full bar; reservations recommended; street parking; william@mistralseattle.com; mistralseattle.com; map:G8.* ♿

Mixtura / ★★☆

148 LAKE ST S, KIRKLAND; 425/803-3310

After earning plaudits in Portland, Oregon, with his restaurant Andina, chef/owner Emmanual Piqueras continues his campaign to bring new Andean cuisine to the Pacific Northwest. The atmosphere is warm, sleek, and spacious, and the fusion of modern cooking with native Peruvian and South American dishes is truly intriguing. Lovely presentations and unusual ingredients mark tapas-style mixturas and entrée-size fondos. In the former category, various cebiches delight, as do quinoa-crusted free-range chicken and grilled octopus with Andean pepper oils and botija olive tapenade foam. In the latter category, try seared yellowfin tuna with mashed yucca and guava sauce, or beef entrecôte with pepian sauce (a type of mole made with pumpkin seeds), stuffed piquillo pepper, and tuber chips. A thoughtful sampler lets you nibble on Peruvian desserts, and the Pisco Sour's a don't-miss drink. *$$$; DIS, MC, V; no checks; lunch Fri–Sun, dinner every day; full bar; reservations recommended; self and street parking; mixtura.biz; map:DD4.* ♿

Mona's Bistro & Lounge / ★

6421 LATONA AVE NE, GREEN LAKE; 206/526-1188

Tito Class and Annette Serrano's treasured neighborhood restaurant, named after the lovely Mona Lisa, continues to draw in folks from all around town. The charm of the candlelit dining room is due in part to Serrano's art, which is more Kahlo than da Vinci. The small seasonal Mediterranean menu is reliable and sweet and the food beautifully presented. Ensalada del tomba is a seared, rare, black-pepper-encrusted chunk of albacore, served with a toasted bread salad, light and tangy with tomatoes and basil oil. For heartier appetites, there are classic pork ribs served with sautéed greens and balsamic roasted potatoes. The couple annexed the storefront next door and converted it into a conversation bar that often features live music—a great place for after-dinner drinks or dessert. *$$; AE, DC, MC, V; no checks; dinner every day; full bar; reservations recommended; street parking; map:EE7.* ♿

Monsoon / ★★★

615 19TH AVE E, CAPITOL HILL; 206/325-2111

This small, chicly designed restaurant on a quiet street in north Capitol Hill has developed into a trusted source for modern, sound Vietnamese food. Like the wind after which this sleek restaurant is named, the menu at Monsoon changes direction with the season, blending traditional Vietnamese cuisine with innovative uses of local products. A gleaming open kitchen fills the spare dining room with exotic fragrances. Don't miss signature appetizers such as the crispy spring roll stuffed with Dungeness crab, or duck salad with green cabbage and vermicelli. Entrée portions are ample—share the wokked gulf prawns with dried scallop sauce or crispy drunken chicken. Vegetable dishes are plentiful; the wine list is eclectic and meticulously matched to the food. Upscale weekend dim sum brunch recently replaced weekday lunches. *$$; MC, V; no checks; brunch Sat–Sun, dinner Tues–Sun; beer and wine; reservations recommended; street parking; monsoonseattle.com; map:HH6.* ♿

Muy Macho Mexican Grill / ★

8515 14TH AVE S, SOUTH PARK; 206/763-3484

It's worth a trek to South Park for Muy Macho's amazing traditional Mexican food that oozes homemade flavor. Having outgrown its origins as a parking-lot taco truck, the place remains no-frills and low-key, staying focused on the authenticity and integrity of the food. Burritos are wonderful; tortas—sandwich rolls stuffed with meat, cheese, beans, and vegetables—are incredible; tacos al pastor will blow you away. A house specialty is the classic stew posole, thick, rich broth filled with hominy and tender pieces of pork. If you're feeling bold, sample menudo, a wonderful—and wonderfully spicy—soup with tripe. *$; MC, V; lunch, dinner every day; beer; no reservations; street parking; map:LL7.* ♿

Nell's / ★★★

6804 E GREEN LAKE WY N, GREEN LAKE; 206/524-4044

Nell's is a beloved Seattle restaurant that seems to get better with age. One of the most comforting aspects of dining at Nell's is stealing looks into the pristine glass-encased open kitchen that runs so smoothly. Dishes are artfully prepared and presented, and seasonally changing menus take full advantage of Northwest ingredients. Wonderful flavor combinations might show up in a starter of black cod with tomato salad, romano beans, and pesto, or in the signature entrée of pan-seared duck breast served with baby turnips, wilted greens, and shallot vinaigrette. The tasting menu might travel from lobster broth with Dungeness crab to pan-seared foie gras to Kobe hanger steak. Desserts are dreamy affairs: French toast made with brioche and accompanied by blueberry compote and apricot ice cream is as sensational as it sounds. *$$$; AE, MC, V; checks OK; dinner every day; full bar; reservations recommended; valet and self parking; info@nellsrestaurant.com; nellsrestaurant.com; map:EE7.*

BEST PLACE

FOR ROMANTIC RAW BEEF?

"If you've never thought of raw beef as an aphrodisiac, take a date to Meskel to eat their kitfo, which is chopped, lean steak stirred together with melted spiced butter. It has the most sensual texture you can imagine, plus enough chiles to set off an endorphin spike. Plus nothing smells better on warm flesh than spiced butter."

—*Jonathan Kauffman, food editor,* Seattle Weekly

Nishino / ★★★

3130 E MADISON ST, MADISON PARK; 206/322-5800

At Nishino, the namesake restaurant of Tatsu Nishino, it is best to place your trust in Nishino-san, the chef/owner who worked for five years at the famed Matsuhisa in Los Angeles. You will never go wrong with the *omakase* dinner, a 10-course meal hand-selected by the chef to highlight the freshest and best he has to offer: pristine sashimi, albacore tuna, green-lipped mussels, halibut ocean salad. Regulars at this Madison Park restaurant, beloved for its spare and classic Japanese elegance and modern creative flourishes, know to look to the daily fresh sheet for nightly seafood specials plucked live and direct from the restaurant's tanks. Don't miss the popular banana tempura—caramel drizzled over crispy panko-fried bananas and vanilla ice cream. *$$$; AE, MC, V; no checks; dinner every day; full bar; reservations recommended; self parking; nishinorestaurant.com; map:GG6.* ♿

Noble Court Restaurant / ★

1644 140TH AVE NE, BELLEVUE; 425/641-6011

Noble Court has long been one of the top purveyors of dim sum on the Eastside, drawing particularly long lines on Sundays. It may be best to avoid the crowd and go on Saturday. Steamed shrimp dumplings, pork buns, lotus seed balls, and chicken feet with oyster and black-bean sauce are only the beginning of the movable feast carted from table to table. The regular menu is massive too. There's a live tank with Dungeness and king crabs, lobster, prawns, tilapia, and ling cod, all plucked from the water and served with a choice of sauces. Other seafood specialties include whole flounder and rockfish, geoduck, and abalone. There are hot pots, sizzling platters, and a lot of noodles. You can also get Peking duck without a 24-hour advance order. *$$; AE, MC, V; no checks; lunch, dinner Mon–Fri, dim sum every day; full bar; reservations recommended; self parking; map:GG2.* ♿

The Oceanaire Seafood Room / ★★

1700 7TH AVE, DOWNTOWN; 206/267-2277

The Oceanaire—a local outpost of a national chain—has won the loyalty of independent Seattleites with daily-changing, fresh seafood; huge portions; and—more recently—by hiring Seattle native Eric Donnelly as executive chef. Service is seamless in a room reminiscent of a 1940s supper club, with comfy booths and walls covered in trophy fish. You'll find all the fish house classics—oysters Rockefeller, fish-and-chips—but the best-kept secret is the Kobe beef burger, with crunchy fried onions and blue cheese (available only during lunch). Everything's à la carte, which can make this an expensive outing, but half orders of the immense side dishes, such as au gratin potatoes and green beans amandine, will feed four. Desserts are big, too—from the towering inferno of the baked Alaska to vat-sized portions of crème brûlée. *$$$; AE, B, DC, DIS, JCB, MC, V; checks OK; lunch, Mon–Fri, dinner every day; full bar; reservations recommended; street parking; oceanaireseafoodroom.com; map:J5.* ♿

Olive You / ★

8516 GREENWOOD AVE, GREENWOOD; 206/706-4121

Timur Leno's Olive You is a most welcome addition to Greenwood, providing not only fresh Middle Eastern cuisine, but also a convivial local gathering place. In warm weather, a garage door opens onto the street, and tables and lively conversation spill out onto the sidewalk. The centerpiece of the blue-and-white-tiled interior is a massive cold deli case filled with olives, dolmas, marinated artichokes, grilled eggplant, stuffed squid, hummus, tzatziki, and spreads from which to build meze plates served with grilled pita. Kebabs and generous entrées built around perfectly Mediterranean-spiced lamb, chicken, and seafood are served with heaps of fresh vegetables and rice. Bonus: When you order wine and beer, everything on the appetizer menu is half off. *$; AE, DIS, MC, V; lunch and dinner Tues–Sun; beer and wine; no reservations; street parking; olive-you.com; map:EE7.*

Orrapin Thai Food / ★

10 BOSTON ST, QUEEN ANNE; 206/283-7118

Seattle is filled with Thai restaurants; it takes a special blend of freshness and spice for a restaurant to distinguish itself. Filled with carvings, brilliant fabrics, and antique wall hangings, Orrapin is a serene place in the bustle of the upper Queen Anne restaurant row. But don't go there to meditate, go for the yum gai—sliced grilled-chicken salad with lemongrass, spicy lime juice, red onions, and cucumbers. Rice dishes are especially good here, such as the pineapple fried rice with prawns, egg, nuts, and veggies. House specials are the shoo shee pla, salmon cooked in creamy coconut milk and red curry, or the Jungle Pork, a very hot sauté with lime leaves, lemongrass, green beans, and holy basil. *$; MC, V; no checks; lunch, dinner every day; full bar; reservations accepted; street parking; map:GG8.* ♿

Osteria La Spiga / ★★★

1429 12TH AVE, CAPITOL HILL; 206/323-8881

Even when it was housed in a strip mall, a large and loyal following came to Osteria la Spiga for its beautifully rustic food. La Spiga recently relocated to a gorgeous new space four times the size of its former digs, but its delicious and comforting dishes, thankfully, have not changed. All meals begin with piadini, warm house-made unleavened bread, and should be followed by the house salad—a fantastic blend of frisée, romaine, radicchio, arugula, and shredded carrots slicked with oil and vinegar. Handmade pastas are eggy and toothsome, whether they come with tender wild boar ragù or layered in a dense lasagna. Il mascarpone di Ida, a tiramisulike dessert, is a dreamy puff of mascarpone with a layer of coarsely ground cocoa. The wine list is vast and entirely Italian. *$$; MC, V; local checks only; lunch Mon–Fri, dinner Mon–Sat; beer and wine; reservations recommended; street parking; laspiga.com; map:M1.* ♿

Pair / ★★★

5501 30TH AVE NE, RAVENNA; 206/526-7655

Seattle loves its neighborhood bistros, and with choices like Ravenna's Pair, there is good reason. This homey, light-filled café serves up Northwestern and French dishes the perfect size for pairing and sharing. Flavors on the frequently updated menu are kept simple and fresh, from a green salad of tender butterleaf perfectly dressed in a Dijon vinaigrette to a side of minty snap peas with pistachios to a gorgeously golden roasted half chicken. The Dungeness crab mac, little pasta trumpets lightly tossed in a creamy tomato sauce, brings new meaning to comfort food. Ask the server to recommend wine pairings from their modest but inspired list, and do save room to indulge

IN THE NEIGHBORHOOD

Trends come and go in the Seattle dining scene, but one has stuck around and made itself quite at home—the neighborhood bistro. Just about every neighborhood has at least one little chef-owned-and-operated café that serves fresh cuisine in an unfussy atmosphere.

PAIR (5501 30th Ave NE, Ravenna; 206/526-7655) lies just on the border of the Ravenna and Bryant neighborhoods, and serves up one of the best mac and cheese dishes in Seattle, along with other upscale comfort food. Fremont's **PERSIMMON** (4256 Fremont Ave N, Fremont; 206/632-0760) is as quaint as it is delicious, as is **35TH STREET BISTRO** (709 N 35th St, Fremont; 206/547-9850) just up the road.

Both Phinney Ridge and Greenwood residents get to call **STUMBLING GOAT BISTRO** (6722 Greenwood Ave N, Greenwood; 206/784-3535) home away from home, where they can dine on market-fresh ingredients in a cozy atmosphere.

Just out of sight of the chaos, the Green Lake neighborhood hides a little cluster of shops and cafés, including **EVA** (2227 N 56th St, Green Lake; 206/633-3538), with its Mediterranean-influenced dishes and heavenly desserts. In Wallingford, chef Maria Hines takes the neighborhood bistro organic with **TILTH** (1411 N 45th St, Wallingford; 206/633-0801) in a dining room that feels like home—only

in the lovely cheese selection or one of the seasonal fruit tarts. *$$; V, MC; no checks; dinner Tues–Sat; reservations for 6 or more; beer and wine; street parking; pairseattle.com; map:EE6.* ♿

Palace Kitchen / ★★★

2030 5TH AVE, BELLTOWN; 206/448-2001

An enormous mural, which depicts a lusty, 17th-century scene of scullery maids and castle servants feasting on roast meats while guzzling red wine in the "palace kitchen," cues visitors to Tom Douglas's vision for this busy eatery. Talented cooks staff the palatial open kitchen, and the lively center-stage bar circulates a constant stream of energy. To get in the convivial spirit, order shareable selections such as fat and spicy grilled chicken wings or crispy-fried, semolina-coated anchovies. For a more formal supper, order the plin, tender raviolis plumped with chard and sausage, or one of the night's specials from the applewood grill, including pit-roasted lamb, chicken, or whole fish. The wine list offers well-priced accompaniments, while a knowing crew of bartenders makes some of the best cocktails in town. *$$$; AE, DC, DIS, MC, V; checks OK; lunch Mon–Fri, dinner every day; full bar; reservations recommended; street parking; tomdouglas.com; map:H5.* ♿

with better food. Lower Queen Anne's **CROW** (823 5th Ave N, Queen Anne; 206/283-8800) serves up upscale artisan foods that change with the seasons. East Lake Union's **SITKA & SPRUCE** (2238 Eastlake Ave E, Eastlake; 206/324-0662) is tiny but offers up huge flavors with its big and small plates in an unlikely strip mall location. In Madrona, you'll find **ST. CLOUDS** (1131 34th Ave, Madrona; 206/726-1522), which welcomes everyone as part of the family by sharing delicious, Northwest cuisine. In Columbia City, **LA MEDUSA** (4857 Rainier Ave S, Columbia City; 206/723-2192) serves up lively bistro plates with an Italian influence in a bright and open space.

Eastsiders have their own fair share of neighborhood places. In Bellevue, **PORCELLA URBAN MARKET** (10245 Main St, Ste 101, Bellevue; 425/286-0080) offers bistro fare such as lamb chops and coq au vin and a gourmet market. Redmond is home to **POMEGRANATE** (18005 NE 68th St, Redmond; 425/556-5972) and chef/caterer Lisa Dupar's bright, seasonal French-inspired offerings. Kirkland mixes it up with **MIXTURA** (148 Lake St S, Kirkland; 425/803-3310), a bistro with Peruvian fare worth crossing the lake for. West Seattle residents keep **BLACKBIRD BISTRO** (2329 California Ave SW, West Seattle; 206/937-2875) hopping; heady cocktails play almost as big a role as the organic fare and must-try desserts.

—Lara Ferroni

Palisade / ★★

2601 W MARINA PL, MAGNOLIA; 206/285-1000

Here is one of the most incredible waterfront settings in the area, with a splendid 180-degree view of Elliott Bay, Alki Point, and the Seattle skyline. The view is pretty distracting, especially during long Northwest summer sunsets, but the interior, with its huge beams, Japanese garden with bonsai, and bubbling brook is stunning. Go for an after-work drink and pupu platters of steamed butter clams and Whidbey Island mussels with sun-dried tomatoes and fresh thyme. Chefs use an applewood grill, wood oven, and wood-fired rotisserie for the extensive menu of fish and meat. Seafood is especially good here—giant king crab legs or salmon served on a cedar plank, Dungeness crab cakes, massive grilled prawns. Don't miss the Granny Smith apple tart with cinnamon ice cream and warm caramel sauce. *$$; AE, DC, DIS, MC, V; checks OK; dinner every day, brunch Sun; full bar; reservations recommended; valet and self parking; palisaderestaurant.com; map:GG8.* ♿

Panos Kleftiko / ★

815 5TH AVE N, QUEEN ANNE; 206/301-0393

Eating at Panos is like being at a loud party—in the best possible way. Panos Marina is the chef, host, heart, and soul of this tiny traditional Greek taverna a few blocks north of Seattle Center. Cram your table with mezes, Panos's tapaslike little dishes. They're moderately priced and best accompanied with warm homemade pita bread, hummus, or creamy tzatziki sauce and a glass or three of retsina. Try the melanzane salata, an eggplant salad with good olive oil, tomatoes, and herbs; the baked Kalamata olives; or the meatballs. There are entrées too—spanakopita with fresh spinach layered in crispy phyllo dough or the tender roast lamb with rich, garlicky aioli. Arrive early if you have tickets to a show; Panos encourages lingering and doesn't take reservations. *$; MC, V; local checks only; dinner Mon–Sat; beer and wine; no reservations; street parking; map:B4.* ♿

Paseo Caribbean Restaurant / ★

4225 FREMONT AVE N, FREMONT; 206/545-7440

At lunchtime, don't be surprised to see a line spilling out of a small building made of corrugated metal and painted turquoise and red. If you're tempted to turn away, don't. Let the smoke that fills the air with the intoxicating scent of slow-roasted meat lure you inside. Paseo is by no means fancy (many of the chairs are plastic), but the counter staff is among the friendliest in town, and the sandwiches are to die for. Prawn and chicken sandwiches are stellar, but don't miss the Midnight Cuban, thick slices of moist slow-roasted pork, cilantro, mayo, and an obscene amount of sweet grilled onions—a beautiful sandwich that's as messy as it is satisfying. Be sure to save room for rice pudding! *$; cash; local checks only; lunch and dinner Mon–Sat; beer and wine; no reservations; street parking; map:FF7.*

The Pink Door / ★★

1919 POST ALLEY, PIKE PLACE MARKET; 206/443-3241

The Pink Door is a local institution, a trattoria serving up both "homespun Italian-American" fare and a rollicking, fun-filled atmosphere. The Pink Door recently upped the ante on good times, adding a successful burlesque show on Saturday nights ($12 cover charge). This Pike Place Market fixture is easy to miss, so keep your eye out for the eponymous entrance in Post Alley. In winter the funky dining room, decorated with floral oilcloth table coverings and antique mirrors, grows noisy around a burbling fountain. Come warmer weather, people vie for a spot on the trellis-covered terrace. Whatever the season, everyone grows full on the cherished cioppino, chock-full of seafood and spicy depth, and generous portions of pasta (pappardelle with a Bolognese ragù is unfussy and delicious). The Everything Green salad—Bibb lettuce, English peas and fava beans—is an unexpected delight. The reasonably priced wine list is mostly Italian, and there's free live music most evenings. *$$; AE, MC, V; no checks; lunch Tues–Sat, dinner Tues–Sun; full bar; reservations recommended; street parking; thepinkdoor.net; map:H8.*

Place Pigalle / ★★

81 PIKE ST, PIKE PLACE MARKET; 206/624-1756

Place Pigalle, a hidden jewel tucked beneath the huge clock in Pike Place Market, is the perfect place for an intimate dining experience. Ask for a window table and start with the Montrachet, a twice-baked goat cheese soufflé with roasted oyster mushrooms and port syrup, or the steamed mussels dressed with bacon, shallots, and balsamic vinaigrette. For an entrée, diners are smitten with the sophisticated saddle of rabbit filled with apples, spinach, and blue cheese. There's an excellent, reasonably priced artisan cheese list and, for dessert, the signature brandied apricot almond torte. On sunny days, a small deck is ideal for those anxious to catch every ray of sun. The little bar is perfect for dining solo—or for snuggling up to your choice of hundreds of wines. *$$; AE, DC, MC, V; no checks; lunch and dinner Mon–Sat; full bar; reservations recommended; valet and street parking; map:J8.*

Pomegranate / ★★

18005 NE 68TH ST, REDMOND; 425/556-5972

In Seattle, you won't find the movie and television glitterati of Los Angeles, nor the theater and fashion luminaries of New York. Our celebrities are the talented chefs and caterers who feed us well—and often. Longtime caterer and restaurateur Lisa Dupar, owner of this beloved Eastside bistro, is one such celebrated cook. Her family-friendly restaurant in a Redmond strip mall consistently turns out delicious comfort food (the pine-nut-crusted halibut and baby back pork ribs are seasonal favorites) and one of the most unique views in the Northwest—not of the Olympics or Puget Sound, but the 14,000-square-foot fishbowl kitchen. Pomegranate is also known for its creative libations, especially the signature Pomeria, a pomegranate juice and Cuervo margarita with Grand Marnier and raspberry purée. *$$; AE, DC, MC, V; checks OK; lunch Mon–Fri, dinner Tues–Sat, brunch Sun; full bar; reservations recommended; self parking; lisaduparcatering.com; map:EE1.* ♿

Pontevecchio Italian Bistro / ★

710 N 34TH ST, FREMONT; 206/633-3989

Michele Zacco's bistro, recently expanded from tiny to small and tucked away across the street from Fremont's famous "Waiting for the Interurban" sculpture, is the most deliberately romantic place in town. A Sicilian with the heart of an impresario and the soul of an artist, Zacco can cook too. His panini are fresh, the antipasti generous; his mama's tomato sauce simmers for hours. Desserts are as simple as gelato or cannoli. Try shareable starters, including antipasti of roasted peppers, eggplant croquettes with porcini, and Sicilian hummus, then segue to the gnocchi al Gorgonzola and grilled lamb medallions with fresh rosemary. The menu never changes, but the music does—one night operatic tenor, the next a flamenco guitarist enticing a couple to jump up to dance an ecstatic tango. *$$; MC, V; local checks only; lunch Mon–Fri, dinner Mon–Sat; beer and wine; reservations recommended; street parking; map:FF8.*

PIZZA, PIZZA

Ask any Seattle local where to get the best pizza, and you'll be stepping into the middle of a religious argument that has gone on for years. Some swear by the perfect New York slice, some are all about the authentic Italian experience, and some want it thick and heaping with cheese. Some are all about the perfect toppings, others about the sauce. Crust sparks yet another debate. Whatever your own personal taste, Seattle has a pizza place for you.

For those who swear by the thin-crust New York slice with the Brooklyn fold, a trip to **A NEW YORK PIZZA PLACE** (8310 5th Ave NE, Ravenna; 206/524-1355) is a must for large pizzas with a perfect chew-to-crisp ratio. Sauce has just the right amount of garlic and tomato, and cheese is sparingly applied. For a slice so big you can practically fold it twice, head to West Seattle's **TALARICO'S** (4718 California Ave SW, West Seattle; 206/937-7463) for the gold standard in a cheese slice. It may be out of the way, but it's closer than the Big Apple.

For those seeking wood-oven pizza good enough to be certified, there are several options, most notably **TUTTA BELLA** (4918 Rainier Ave S, Columbia City; 206/721-3501, 4411 Stone Way N, Wallingford; 206/633-3800, and 2200 Westlake Ave N, Ste 112, South Lake Union; 206/624-4422) with three welcoming locations. For the hipper crowd, **VIA TRIBUNALI** (913 E Pike St, Capitol Hill; 206/332-9234; and 317 W Galer St, Queen Anne; 206/264-7768) serves its

Ponti Seafood Grill / ★★

3014 3RD AVE N, FREMONT; 206/284-3000

A local newspaper described Ponti as the "finest waterside dining experience in the city . . . Like a European vacation without the hassles." Over the years, the serene, art-filled dining rooms tucked under the Fremont Bridge have gotten prettier and prettier, and the smart cuisine better and better. Start with the seared weathervane scallops with grilled Walla Walla onions or the famous Dungeness crab spring rolls with Thai red curry aioli. Entrées are ever changing (except for the perennial patron favorite: Thai curry penne); there are savories such as grilled black cod with a lime shallot beurre blanc or a sensational pork loin with a fig balsamic glacé. Ponti has one of the best happy hours in the city (4–6pm and 9pm–close), featuring discounts on top-quality cocktails, wine, and beer, and half-price appetizers. *$$$; AE, DC, DIS, JCB, MC, V; local checks only; lunch Mon–Fri, dinner every day, brunch Sun; full bar; reservations recommended; valet and self parking; pontiseafoodgrill.com; map:FF8.* ♿

Neapolitan pies in a sexy, stylish dining room and shakes up a fine cocktail. Both places offer pizzas with beautifully blistered crusts, San Marzano tomato sauce, buffalo mozzarella, and the freshest of basil, arugula, and other toppings. For a quieter scene and great Italian-style pizza, visit **LA VITA É BELLA** (2411 2nd Ave, Belltown; 206/441-5322) and pick from one of 20 flavor combinations of fresh, thin-crust pies.

Deep-dish pizza lovers shouldn't despair. While thin may be in for most Seattle pizza fanatics, **WALLINGFORD PIZZA** (2109 N 45th St, Wallingford; 206/547-3663), tucked between the Guild 45th movie theaters, serves up superthick individual pan pizzas with a deliciously bready crust as good as any you'd find in Chicago.

Some of Seattle's big names in food have also recently entered the pizza arena. Tom Douglas's **SERIOUS PIE** (316 Virginia St, Belltown; 206/838-7388) can only be described as Northwest-style pizza, combining the best of his local and seasonal sensibilities with slightly chewy, thin artisan crusts baked in a wood-fired oven. **MIOPOSTO CAFFÉ** (3601 S McClellan St, Mount Baker; 206/760-3400), Chow Food's newest neighborhood joint in Mount Baker, also keeps to the Northwest-meets-Italy vibe, with creative toppings such as potato or lamb sausage.

If you can't be troubled to leave the house, **PAGLIACCI PIZZA** (pagliacci.com), delivers to all ends of Seattle with seasonal pizza specials such as pear and blue cheese, as well as great standards.

—Lara Ferroni

Queen City Grill / ★★

2201 1ST AVE, BELLTOWN; 206/443-0975

This venerable Belltown saloon is a favorite of restaurant-industry insiders. The bar and dining room exude masculine elegance, with exposed brick walls, dark wood accents, and straight-backed wooden booths with views of the street. Ask the tenured waitstaff for recommendations from the tried-and-true menu and award-winning wine list. Start with Dungeness crab cakes with a tangy rémoulade or the pepper-encrusted tuna carpaccio with lime, ginger, and tamari dressing. Meat selections are capably executed, but seafood is king. For one-stop Northwest seafood sampling, try the mixed grill with clams, mussels, and chunks of salmon, halibut, or snapper. Sweet tooth? Try the dense, flourless Chocolate Nemesis Cake. Cocktails, not surprisingly, are classic and delicious; the wine list is strong and reasonably priced. *$$; AE, DC, DIS, MC, V; no checks; dinner every day; full bar; reservations recommended; valet parking; map:G8.* ♿

Ray's Boathouse / ★★✯
Ray's Cafe / ★✯

6049 SEAVIEW AVE NW, BALLARD; 206/789-3770

With its unparalleled views and fresh seafood, Ray's has always been the obvious choice for locals to take their out-of-town guests. But what makes Ray's a true landmark is that Seattle residents come on their own, year-round, whether or not they've got visitors to impress. Ray's is quintessential Seattle: a relaxed, laid-back atmosphere where anyone wearing shorts can feel comfortable dining on first-rate local seafood. Grilled Alaskan king salmon (served with an apricot basil sauce) is always a good idea. Rich Chatham Strait sablefish and southeast Alaskan halibut are consistently excellent, as are Dungeness crab cakes and Alaskan red king crab legs. Expect an extensive selection of Northwest wines. Upstairs, Ray's Cafe serves lighter fare and a more casual vibe, though guests are welcome to order from the downstairs menu. Choices include fish-and-chips, burgers, salads, or classic clam linguine. The café's outdoor deck, like its happy hour, is among the best in the city. *$$$, $$; AE, DC, DIS, MC, V; checks OK; dinner every day (Boathouse), lunch, dinner every day (Cafe); full bar; reservations recommended; valet and self parking; rays.com; map:EE9.* ♿

Restaurant Zoë / ★★★

2137 2ND AVE, BELLTOWN; 206/256-2060

With its soft lighting and tall windows, Restaurant Zoë beckons like a warm, safe haven amid the bustle of Belltown nightlife. The food is simple, innovative, and seasonal. The signature grilled romaine salad is a must—whole hearts of romaine, grilled just enough to get a touch of smoke, then dressed with a bacon, apple, and Roquefort dressing. The short entrée list balances sea and land, with equally artful treatments of pepper-crusted yellowfin, pan-seared sea scallops, and troll-caught king salmon, as well as braised veal cheeks, pan-roasted pork tenderloin, and house-smoked hanger steak. Perfect pairings range from Israeli couscous to corn flan. A flaky-crusted lemon tart with in-season fruit, ice cream, and fresh berries is perfectly Northwest. The lively bar and hardwood acoustics can make this place noisy. *$$$; AE, MC, V; checks OK; dinner every day; full bar; reservations recommended; street parking; restaurantzoe.com; map:G7.* ♿

Rover's / ★★★★

2808 E MADISON ST, MADISON VALLEY; 206/325-7442

When asked about culinary loves, a local chef, not surprisingly, replied "Rover's. Rover's is my one true love." Rover's is a destination restaurant for people all over the country who flock to James Beard Award–winning chef and owner Thierry Rautureau's impeccably crafted food. Rover's occupies a quiet spot off Madison Park's main thoroughfare; guests approach through a courtyard that blossoms behind an unassuming arcade. Choose from three prix-fixe menus (one vegetarian) that progress from delicate flavors to bolder expressions with elegant sufficiency. Rautureau is a master of sauces, using stocks, reductions, herb-infused oils, and purées to enhance slices of sturgeon, steamed Maine lobster, wild mushrooms, breasts of quail, and the requisite foie gras. Expect professional service from the loyal staff, and prepare to be dazzled by the 5,500-bottle wine collection. Dining in the courtyard, weather permitting, is an enchanting experience. For a luxurious midday treat, try Rover's Friday lunches, offering a $35 prix-fixe tasting menu or à la carte dishes. *$$$$; AE, DC, MC, V; checks OK; dinner Tues–Sat; lunch on Fri; beer and wine; reservations required; street parking; rovers-seattle.com; map:GG6.* ♿

Ruby's on Bainbridge / ★★

4738 LYNNWOOD CENTER RD NE, BAINBRIDGE ISLAND; 206/780-9303

On a beautiful day, a sunset ferry ride to Bainbridge Island is never a bad idea—especially if it's followed by dinner at Ruby's, a cozy neighborhood bistro housed in a handsome, century-old Tudor manor overlooking Rich Passage. Choose from classics such as French onion soup, pâté, and Caesar salad, or a solid selection of meats—sirloin, tenderloin, and lamb shanks in rich sauces with fresh herbs. Fresh seafood is featured daily and vegetarians will be thrilled with tortino di melanzane, eggplant layered with fresh mozzarella and marinated tomatoes. You can't go wrong with fresh, wood-oven-fired focaccia pizzas with whimsical, daily-changing toppings such as roasted fennel, sweet onions, and cheese. *$$$; AE, MC, V; checks OK; dinner every day; full bar; reservations recommended; self parking.* ♿

Saigon Bistro / ★

1032 S JACKSON ST, STE 202, CHINATOWN/INTERNATIONAL DISTRICT; 206/329-4939; 600 5TH AVE S (AT UWAJIMAYA FOOD COURT), CHINATOWN/INTERNATIONAL DISTRICT; 206/621-2085

Saigon Bistro offers a great selection of reasonably priced Vietnamese standbys. There's a long list of phos, those fragrant, clear-broth, fine-noodle soups with beef, chicken, duck, or tofu, served with a heap of bean sprouts, branches of basil and mint, slices of jalapeños, and lime wedges. Popular with neighborhood day workers are bánh mì, huge sandwiches bursting with grilled meats, veggies, and fresh basil and mint on a baguette for only two bucks! The goi cuon—summer salad rice-paper rolls with vermicelli, shrimp, pork, or tofu—served with peanut dipping sauce are wonderful. Worthy entrées include roasted coconut chicken, clay-pot dishes such as spare ribs or catfish, and a delectably rich casserole of eggplant, tofu, and sea snails. The Uwajimaya Village branch offers only the faster, more portable items from the Jackson Street menu. *$; MC, V; checks OK; lunch, dinner every day; beer and wine; no reservations; self parking; map:P5, Q7.* ♿

St. Clouds / ★

1129 34TH AVE, MADRONA; 206/726-1522

St. Clouds is one of Seattle's great, welcoming neighborhood restaurants where everyone feels at home. The menu is split between "Home for Dinner"

BEYOND COFFEE

Seattle has many monikers related to its cult status as North America's coffee capitol: home of Starbucks, latte land, coffee mecca. And while it's true that there is a coffee shop or cart on every street corner, there are also a slew of coffee alternatives providing delicious drinks for the java-averse.

At cozy **TEAHOUSE KUAN YIN** (1911 N 45th St, Wallingford; 206/632-2055), pink chai is the main attraction. The delicious drink is made from Kashmiri green tea (the tea turns pink through a unique chemical process), spices, and regular or soy milk. **REMEDY TEAS** (345 15th Ave E, Capitol Hill; 206/323-4832) offers 150 varieties of white, green, oolong, black, and herbal teas and maté. The matcha green tea latte is sublime, as is the champagne matcha mojito, a combination of matcha green tea, champagne, and muddled mint. Start or end your workout around Green Lake (or take it with you!) with a decadent hot chocolate from **CHOCOLATI CHOCOLATE CAFÉ** (7810 E Green Lake Dr N, Ste D, Green Lake; 206/527-5467; and branches)—top-quality bitter and semisweet chocolate liquefied and whisked with steamed milk. Warmer weather brings the Frost, a yummy frozen chocolate drink. Taiwanese import "bubble tea," frothy milk tea infused with fruit flavors and chewy black balls made from tapioca (the "bubbles") is a must-try at **POCHI TEA STATION** (5014 University Wy NE; University District; 206/529-1158) and **HONEY MOON TEA CORPORATION** (600 5th Ave S, Ste 101, Chinatown/International District; 206/382-0888). Morning Glory Chai, a locally made spicy black tea blended with Indian spices and Chinese herbs, is available at various locations throughout the city, but only **MR. SPOT'S CHAI HOUSE** (5463 Leary Ave W, Ballard; 206/297-2424) offers offbeat chai concoctions such as Ruby Tuesday (chai, pomegranate syrup, and lemon juice) and Apple Spice Drop (chai and apple cider).

—Pat Tanumihardja

(homey, cheaper) or "Out for Dinner" (fancy, pricier). Happily, ordering from either is a good choice. Typical offerings are roasted chicken and mashers, a rice bowl with ginger-steamed vegetables, or a succulent Parmesan-crusted pork tenderloin. Weekend brunch is known for the Imperial Mix-Up, a semi-legendary jumble of rice, veggies, and Portuguese sausage that might come with white chocolate scones or a sour cream coffeecake. The kids' menu has mac and cheese, spaghetti and meatballs, and burgers. A grown-up crowd gathers in the cozy bar on some weeknights and every weekend for live acoustic blues, jazz, rock, and folk music. *$$; AE, DIS, MC, V; checks OK; dinner every day, brunch Sat–Sun; full bar; reservations recommended; street parking; john@stclouds.com; stclouds.com; map:HH5.* ♿

Saint-Germain / ★★

2811A E MADISON ST, MADISON VALLEY; 206/323-9800

Along a stretch of Madison that just keeps getting more French, Saint-Germain is a marvelous addition. For Gallic-inspired fine dining, there's Rover's; for traditional bistro fare, it's Voila!; for a glass (or three) of wine, a delicious tartine, and an invaluable adjustment in outlook, it's this petite, inexpensive, and entirely delightful café. Tartines are elegant open-faced sandwiches on grilled bread; favorites include Monsieur Seguin (smoky, supple duck breast; goat cheese; garlic) and La Parisienne (mushrooms sautéed in butter, cream, and shallots). Salads, such as butter lettuce with fennel and little cubes of apple, refresh; a few entrées are offered for the hungrier. For dessert, try a poire belle Hélène, the classic ice cream concoction, here served in a sundae glass. It all makes for a divine afternoon respite or salon-style late-night hangout. *$; AE, MC, V; checks OK; lunch and dinner Tues–Sat; beer and wine; reservations for 6 or more; self and street parking; saintgermainseattle.com; map:GG6.* ♿

Saito's Japanese Café & Bar / ★★★☆

2120 2ND AVE, BELLTOWN; 206/728-1333

Sushi enthusiasts—and there are legions in Seattle—flock to this smart Belltown restaurant for Saito-san's sushi, which is arguably the best in town. The fish is super-fresh, buttery-textured, and cut thick. Hot items are innovative—try the butter itame, a geoduck sauté with sugar snaps and shiitakes, or ask about seasonal daily specials, which might include exquisitely presented, utterly tender baby squid. Save room for the house-made ice cream sampler, with green tea, mango, or sweet plum flavors. The large selection of premium sake at the sleek bar is a bonus, as is the contemporary décor and variety of seating options (bar, sushi bar, tables, and snug booths). For the best possible experience, sit at the sushi bar and leave the choices in Saito's expert hands, *omakase*-style. *$$$; AE, DIS, MC, V; no checks; lunch Tues–Fri, dinner Tues–Sat; full bar; reservations recommended; street parking; saitos-cafe.com; map:F8.* ♿

Salumi / ★★

309 3RD AVE S, PIONEER SQUARE; 206/621-8772

Long lines every day mark this cured-meat haven. Armandino Batali, father of world-renowned chef Mario, is a retired aeronautics engineer who after 31 years at Boeing went to culinary school in New York, worked in a salami factory in Queens, and apprenticed with butchers in Tuscany. He cures his own coppa, salami, lamb or pork prosciutto, spicy finocchiona, hot sopressata—and recently, culatello and mole salami. They're cut to order and sold cheaply by the pound, or laid on a crusty baguette slathered with anchovy-rich pesto or garlic sauce. Try the braised oxtail or the amazing meatball sandwich on rosetta rolls piled high with sautéed peppers and onions. Batali's weekly dinners are booked months in advance, but everyone is welcome for lunch at communal tables, with open bottles of wine to be enjoyed on the honor system. *$; AE, MC, V; checks OK; lunch Tues–Fri, dinner Sat; beer and wine; reservations required; street parking; salumicuredmeats.com; map:O7.* ♿

Samurai Noodle / ★

606 5TH AVE S, CHINATOWN/INTERNATIONAL DISTRICT; 206/624-9321

Samurai Noodle is a tiny shop almost hidden on the west side of the International District's Uwajimaya complex, but it packs big flavor, and its noodle and rice bowls have made it a favorite with the area's lunchtime crowd. Samurai's specialty is authentic tonkotsu ramen, a thick, almost creamy pork broth served with egg noodles and moist slices of roasted pork that is downright intoxicating. Those who are especially hungry are wise to order the Armor Bowl, which comes with traditional sides of extra pork slices, a hard-boiled egg, seaweed, flavored bamboo shoots, and green onion that can be added to the soup. For those less enamored of pork, Samurai also offers chicken, fish, soy, and soy/pork broth. *$; MV, V; no checks; lunch and dinner daily; no alcohol; no reservations; self parking; map:P6.*

Sazerac / ★★½

1101 4TH AVE (HOTEL MONACO), DOWNTOWN; 206/624-7755

Named for a New Orleans-invented cocktail that's a wicked blend of rye, Peychaud bitters, and a faux absinthe liqueur, this downtown hotel restaurant is as disarming as it is satisfying. The spacious dining room is lighted by handcrafted, steel-framed chandeliers and brightened by colorful walls. The witty, deep menu reflects the Louisiana roots of chef-partner Jan Birnbaum. Appetizers truly tease: crab cakes with harissa mayo, or andouille sausage pizza pie. The kitchen does well with broiler and smokehouse preparations such as "The Best Fish We Can Catch Today," or the applewood-smoked pork back ribs with molasses barbecue sauce. If you think that's tempting, you'll be bowled over by the warm and gooey chocolate-pudding cake served with its own pitcher of cream. The wine list features midpriced California and Northwest offerings. Servers are funny and capable, and happy hour is always a blast. *$$$; AE, DC, DIS, MC, V; no checks; breakfast and lunch Mon–Fri, brunch Sat–Sun, dinner daily; full bar; reservations recommended; valet parking; sazeracrestaurant.com; map:L6.* ♿

Sea Garden / ★★

509 7TH AVE S, CHINATOWN/INTERNATIONAL DISTRICT; 206/623-2100

Seattle's International District is filled with many stellar Chinese restaurants, but Sea Garden is undeniably the best place to partake of fresh Northwest seafood prepared Cantonese style. The menu is vast—chow mein, congee, sizzling hot pots—and few dishes disappoint, but it's best to order from the seafood tanks at the restaurant's entrance. Crab—the squirming shellfish is brought to your table for approval before cooking—is the best option, whether it comes dressed in ginger and green onions; a crispy salt-and-pepper crust; or the heavenly, pungent black bean sauce. Let go and have fun—Sea Garden's busy dining room encourages family-style sharing and conversation. That it's open until 2am all week (and 3am on the weekends) is just another reason to party while you eat. *$$; MC, V; no checks; lunch and dinner every day; full bar; no reservations; street parking; map:Q5.*

Seastar Restaurant and Raw Bar / ★★

205 108TH AVE NE, BELLEVUE; 425/456-0010

For fresh seafood in swank surroundings, there's no better place on the Eastside that Seastar, owned by celebrated local chef John Howie, who was executive chef at Seattle's Palisade for nearly a decade. Try the multilevel raw-bar sampler: Hawaiian ahi poke, California roll, and scallop ceviche. On the hot side, you'll enjoy flash-seared diver sea scallops with tropical fruit chutney and the Kauai shrimp wrapped in saifun noodles. Howie is also a pioneer of alder- and cedar-plank cooking. Offerings for those more interested in turf than surf—such as a 9-ounce Snake River Farms Kobe beef grilled rib-eye—are also delicious. *$$$; AE, DC, DIS, MC, V; local checks only; lunch, dinner every day; full bar; reservations recommended; self and valet parking; seastarrestaurant.com; map:HH3.* ♿

Serafina / ★★

2043 EASTLAKE AVE E, EASTLAKE; 206/323-0807

Serafina is an unapologetically romantic neighborhood restaurant with undeniably sensual food. Tacchino tonnato, thin slices of delicately poached turkey breast served with a caper-tuna sauce, is a premier example of the restaurant's golden touch with Piedmontese classics, and grilled pork tenderloin with sour cherry chutney and grilled radicchio reflects the eatery's flair for cooking outside the box. Desserts are all amazing, but of particular note is the biscotti and Vigna del Papa vin santo, which makes for an indulgent dipping experience. Live jazz is offered most weekend evenings, occasional Wednesdays, and during Sunday brunch, and goes a long way toward polishing the restaurant's romantic reputation. *$$; MC, V; checks OK; brunch Sun, lunch Mon–Fri, dinner every day; full bar; reservations recommended; street parking; serafinaseattle.com; map:GG7.* ♿

Serious Pie / ★★½

316 VIRGINIA ST, BELLTOWN; 206/838-7388

Forget your thin New York slice. Forget deep-dish Chicago pie. Even set aside the authentic, Naples-blessed rounds. Serious Pie makes artisanal pizza, Tom Douglas–style. Thin-crusted oblong pies with just the right edge of cornmeal crispness are topped with ingredients such as house-made buffalo mozzarella and pancetta, or Northwest specialties like foraged wild mushrooms or local clams. Menus change frequently, but don't miss the shaved celery and anchovy combo or Merv's Washington apple salad with prosciutto and pomegranate when they're available. The no-reservations policy means you may have a bit of a wait in the tiny shop lobby. But you can always grab a glass from the pizza-friendly wine list and watch the action around the pizza oven. *$$; AE, DIS, MC, V; lunch Mon–Sat, dinner every day; wine and beer; no reservations; street parking; tomdouglas.com; map:H6.* ♿

Seven Stars Pepper Szechuan Restaurant / ★★

1207 S JACKSON ST, STE 211, CHINATOWN/INTERNATIONAL DISTRICT; 206/568-6446

You'll be quickly greeted by a server with a smile at this bright and unassuming second-floor restaurant in the Ding How shopping complex. After just a few visits, you'll feel like family. The extensive Szechuan menu cleverly balances hot, sour, salty, and sweet. Hand-shaven dan dan noodles are just the right uneven thickness and bathed in a rich peanut sauce with ground pork. Pot stickers are thick and large but surprisingly light, and will show up somewhere around the end of your meal, even if ordered as an appetizer. Free parking is available belowground in the shopping center, but the lot locks up at 8pm, so opt for free street parking in the evenings. *$$; MC, V; no checks; lunch and dinner every day; beer and wine; reservations accepted; self and street parking; map:HH6.* ♿

Shallots Asian Bistro / ★★½

2525 4TH AVE, BELLTOWN; 206/728-1888

Shallots Asian Bistro is not just a quick combination of kimchi, sushi rolls, and chow mein, like some other so-called pan-Asian restaurants around town. This hip little Belltown gem has a lot of Chinese but also an intriguing mix of Thai, Vietnamese, Cambodian, Japanese, and Korean. Dark wood booths, elaborately folded napkins, tasteful Asian art, and a sweet patio make for agreeable ambience. Portions are generous and well priced. Lunch choices include kung pao chicken, black-bean salmon, or a wok fry of chow fun (wide rice noodles) and seafood. Specialties make Shallots worth seeking out for dinner: try the subtly flavored steamed sea bass, the French Cambodian New York steak salad, or the amazing nine-flavor chicken. *$$; AE, DIS, MC, V; checks OK; lunch Mon–Fri, dinner every day; full bar; reservations recommended; street parking; map:E7.* ♿

Shamiana / ★★

10724 NE 68TH ST, KIRKLAND; 425/827-4902

Shamiana is more than an Indian restaurant in that it's often interpretive, with influences from Bangladesh, Kenya, and Pakistan—a few of the places owners Eric and Tracy Larson spent their youth as Foreign Service kids. Vegetarians do well with such dishes as eggplant bartha or peas and cumin, and vegan options are plentiful. Good rice and grain dishes include dal with red lentils or pulao with fragrant basmati rice. Meat lovers will be pleased too—try the chicken, lamb, and prawns in traditional spicy Pakistani barbecue. Curries and chutneys are made in-house. Consistent winners are velvet butter chicken and the chile fry lamb, chunks of lamb slow-cooked in coconut milk, chiles, and tomatoes. A big draw is the good-value luncheon buffet. *$; AE, DC, DIS, MC, V; checks OK; lunch Mon–Fri, dinner every day; beer and wine; reservations accepted for 6 or more; self parking; shamianarestaurant.com; map:EE3.* ♿

Shanghai Café / ★★
Shanghai Garden / ★★★☆

12708 SE 38TH ST, BELLEVUE; 425/603-1689; 80 FRONT ST N, ISSAQUAH; 425/313-3188; 524 6TH AVE S, CHINATOWN/INTERNATIONAL DISTRICT; 206/625-1689

Shanghai Garden, a luscious pink restaurant in the Chinatown/International District, is most beloved for its soupy buns, little packets of delicate dough twisted at the top that contain combinations of minced pork, shrimp, or crab in a spoonful of hot broth. The flavors explode in the mouth, and even when nibbled carefully, the contents usually also explode on the shirt. Prepare to be wowed by anything made with vivid green, tender pea vines or with the chef's special hand-shaved noodles (rice, corn, or barley), which make the best chow mein you'll ever eat. Seafood shines, as in pepper-salted scallops or shrimp. The Issaquah branch attracts its own lines-out-the-door following; Shanghai Café in Bellevue is similar but smaller. *$; MC, V; no checks; lunch, dinner every day; beer and wine (Seattle and Bellevue), full bar (Issaquah); reservations recommended; self parking; map:II2, Q7.* ♿

Shiro's / ★★★

2401 2ND AVE, BELLTOWN; 206/443-9844

Three decades ago, most Seattleites were in the dark about sushi—until Shiro Kashiba came along to brighten things up, first at Nikko and now at his eponymous Belltown space. In the simple dining room, a small menu offers full-course dinner entrées such as tempura, sukiyaki, and teriyaki. The kasu-style black cod, elegantly marinated and broiled, is not to be missed. But the hundreds of sushi variations are the main event, and the blond hardwood sushi bar is always jammed with Shiro's sushi-fanatic regulars, a mix of Japanese tourists, Belltown hipsters, and business types. There's a great selection of premium sakes, a bar stocked with Japanese Scotches, and inventive desserts such as red-bean ice cream and peeled persimmons. *$$$; AE, MC, V; no checks; dinner every day; full bar; reservations recommended; valet, self, and street parking; shiros.com; map:F8.* ♿

Sitka & Spruce / ★★★☆

2238 EASTLAKE AVE E, EASTLAKE; 206/324-0662

Located in an unlikely spot—next to a Subway in a strip mall—tiny Sitka & Spruce is a pathfinder in local cuisine. The décor is eclectic-minimalist, with pea-green walls and records playing on a turntable; the service is friendly, unrushed. And the food? Eminently seasonal, inspired, and inspiring. Chef/owner Matt Dillon (who has put in time at other bests the Herbfarm and Stumbling Goat) lavishes love upon crazy-fresh ingredients, with uncomplicated results. Depending on the time of year, you'll find morels, fiddlehead ferns, or nettles, while handmade pastas, revelatory vegetable preparations, and delicious, locally sourced meats and fish are standard. Everything comes in two sizes—order a lot (it's a tremendous value) and share it all, or risk some serious food envy. Go early or late (reservations are taken only for five or more), be patient, and enjoy. *$$; MC, V; checks OK; breakfast Sat–Sun, lunch Tues–Fri, dinner Wed–Sat; wine and beer; reservations for 5 or more only; self and street parking; sitkaandspruce.com; map:GG7.* ♿

611 Supreme Crêperie & Café / ★

611 E PINE ST, CAPITOL HILL; 206/328-0292

This Parisian-themed joint wins over the neighborhood's jaded hipsters with a simple menu, cool bar, and romantic décor—bare brick walls, stressed wooden floors, unobtrusive art, and high ceilings. From the open kitchen comes an impressive list of entrée crepes such as cheese, almond, ham, roasted eggplant, and smoked salmon, all with a choice of sauces, or you can create your own crepe from a long list of sexy ingredients. There are tempting salads, like Bibb lettuce with toasted walnuts and bleu d'Auvergne tossed with a walnut oil vinaigrette, and an onion soup full of Gruyère and croutons. Dessert crepes have garnishes such as orange butter and shaved chocolate. A full bar serves pastis, Calvados, Armagnac, and Pernod; the inexpensive wine list is all European bottlings, but even these are mostly French. *$; MC, V; no checks; dinner every day, brunch Sat–Sun; full bar; no reservations; street parking; map:J1.* ♿

SkyCity / ★☆

219 4TH AVE N, SEATTLE CENTER; 206/905-2100 OR 800/937-9582

Seattleites and local restaurant critics don't always agree, but about Sky City they seem to be of like mind: at this revolving restaurant atop the Space Needle, the food and service are nothing to write home about, but the awesome view is one you'll be talking about for months. A meal at SkyCity is an expensive proposition, but if it's any consolation, the elevator ride to the top is free with your reservation. Once you arrive at the restaurant, you'll find a classic Northwest menu adequately executed. Choose from entrées such as wild king salmon, pan-seared halibut, and thick local steaks. The wine list draws heavily—and happily—on Washington wines, and even includes a few affordable choices. *$$$; AE, DIS, MC, V; local checks only; lunch Mon–Fri, dinner every day, brunch Sat–Sun; full bar; reservations recommended; valet parking; spaceneedle.com; map:D6.* ♿

Sostanza Trattoria / ★★☆

1927 43RD AVE E, MADISON PARK; 206/324-9701

It just doesn't seem fair. Not only does the tiny—and tony—Madison Park neighborhood benefit from a stellar location on the shores of Lake Washington, but it also enjoys a preponderance of charming and romantic neighborhood eateries. Case in point is Sostanza, a two-story northern Italian trattoria boasting a skylighted dining room and a balcony with a peek-a-boo view of the lake. Try the beef carpaccio, served with mustard dressing, or the signature veal pappardelle, tossed tableside with mushrooms, goat cheese, tomatoes, fresh basil, and Barolo. Distinctive Italian bottlings join a few domestic favorites on the limited but well-chosen wine list. For winter, there's a fireplace; in summer, enjoy the lakeside patio. *$$; AE, DC, MC, V; no checks; dinner Mon–Sat; full bar; reservations recommended; street parking; sostanzaseattle.com; map:GG6.* ♿

Steelhead Diner / ★★☆

95 PINE ST, PIKE PLACE MARKET; 206/625-0129

The best crab cake in seafood-centric Seattle is a hotly contested debate, but a brand-new contender absolutely takes the prize: the nearly all-crabmeat, jumbo-lump Dungeness version at Steelhead Diner. Chef/owner Kevin Davis first took the city's branch of Oceanaire above and beyond a posh franchise —out on his own, he's taken the concept of diner above and beyond. Steelhead's got booths and kitchen-counter seating, but this sleek, contemporary space isn't about grilled cheese and a shake; it's about caviar pie with a rainbow of delicious roe, organic baby lettuce salad with local cherries (in season, of course), wild salmon (ditto), and a wagyu burger with cheese from Beecher's across the street. Southern accents—gumbo, a "rich-boy" sandwich—pay tribute to Davis's background, but the (already award-winning) wine list is all Pacific Northwest. *$$; AE, DIS, MC, V; no checks; brunch Sun, lunch and dinner every day; full bar; reservations recommended; street parking; steelheaddiner.com; map:J7.* ♿

Stumbling Goat Bistro / ★★★

6722 GREENWOOD AVE N, GREENWOOD; 206/784-3535

If you don't live in this popular bistro's Greenwood neighborhood, you'll wish it lived in yours. The cozy rooms are painted scarlet and forest green with red velvet draperies and vintage 1950s lamps; a beautiful little bar lit with chandeliers is a new, very welcome addition. The kitchen relies on local, sustainable suppliers, so different seasons might bring fresh nettle pasta or squash-blossom fritters to the table. The boneless pan-roasted chicken is always on the menu and not to be missed—it's on an island of rich mashed potatoes in a pond of pan juices and roasted garlic cloves. Desserts also vary with what's freshest and most delicious, but the standby is a chocolate lover's dream: flourless bittersweet brownie cake served with fresh whipped cream and organic strawberry sauce. The wine list is short but well considered. *$$; MC, V; checks OK; dinner Tues–Sun; full bar; reservations recommended; street parking; stumblinggoatbistro.com; map:EE7.* ♿

Sweet and Savory / ★★

1418 31ST AVE S, MOUNT BAKER; 206/325-2900

You won't find yourself overwhelmed by choices at this neighborhood café—the pastry case is filled with just a handful of freshly made individual-sized quiches, tarts, sandwiches, and the occasional cupcake. You won't be disappointed by any of these handmade bites, and if something runs out, you can just wait a bit, sipping on a latte or tea while the pastry for the next batch is rolled out right before your eyes. On weekends, locals line up for freshly made fried egg sandwiches or the French hot chocolate as rich as a molten lava cake. *$; MC, V; no checks; breakfast and lunch Tues–Sun; no alcohol; no reservations; street parking; sweetandsavoryseattle.com; map:II6.*

Szechuan Chef / ★★

15015 MAIN ST, STE 107, KELSEY CREEK CENTER, BELLEVUE; 425/746-9008
In August of 2006, chef Cheng Biao Yang and Hoang Ngo, first lady of hostesses, sold their venerated International District restaurant, Seven Stars Pepper, and set up Szechuan Chef across Lake Washington in Bellevue. Devotees of Yang's authentic, impossibly spicy Szechuan food followed and were rewarded with an expanded menu of more than 200 items, including everything from familiar eggplant with hot garlic sauce to lesser-known specialties such as "intestine + fish in hot & spicy gravy." Now groups flock to Szechuan Chef to cook their own meats and fish at their table in bubbling hot pots. Adventurous eaters should jump at the chance to boil congealed blood and tripe in a hot pot's spicy broth, while those with tamer tastes can stick with Yang's standby standouts like fragrant cumin lamb and hand-shaved dan dan noodles. *$$; MC, V; no checks; lunch and dinner every day; beer and wine; no reservations; self parking; map:GG2.* ♿

Szmania's / ★★½

3321 W MCGRAW ST, MAGNOLIA; 206/284-7305
Magnolia is one of those neighborhoods that you might never visit if you didn't live there. In Szmania's, though, nonresidents will find good reason to visit the community's lovely tree-lined main street. Owners Ludger and Julie Szmania—Ludger is a German-born chef trained in Europe—have created a stylish respite with warm lighting, expert service, and fireside tables. The seasonally changing menu offers a mix of European, Northwest, and pan-Asian cuisines with artful presentation. Homage to Ludger's Düsseldorf roots is paid with the Jägerschnitzel, three thick slices of lightly crusted, crispy pork tenderloin served with red cabbage and the best spaetzle in town. Seats along the entertaining exhibition kitchen counter are favored by neighborhood regulars who like their lunch or dinner with a show. *$$$; AE, MC, V; local checks only; lunch Tues–Fri, dinner Tues–Sun; full bar; reservations recommended; street parking; szmanias.com; map:FF8.* ♿

Tacos Guaymas / ★

6808 E GREEN LAKE WY N, GREEN LAKE (AND BRANCHES); 206/729-6563
Tacos Guaymas is truly a boon: a family-owned restaurant chain that serves high-quality, inexpensive, addictively delicious Mexican food. Locations can be found all over town, including Capitol Hill (1415 Broadway; 206/860-3871), West Seattle (4719 California Ave SW; 206/935-8970), White Center (1622 Roxbury St SW; 206/767-4026), and Fremont (100 N 36th St; 206/547-5110). Excellent soft tacos and burritos come with the usual suspects (beef, chicken, or pork) or more authentic fillings (tripe, tongue, or beef cheeks). The enchiladas are some of the best in the area, as is the chile verde.

On weekends try the menudo, a therapeutic soup for hangovers. The White Center branch keeps a cooler full of ice-cold beer, while Green Lake's has a premium full-service bar. *$; MC, V; checks OK; lunch, dinner every day; beer only (Capitol Hill, Fremont, West Seattle, White Center), full bar (Green Lake); no reservations; street parking; map:LL8.* ♿

Tamarind Tree / ★★

1036 S JACKSON ST, STE A, CHINATOWN/INTERNATIONAL DISTRICT; 206/860-1404

Upscale ambience and buzz-inducing beverages provide big Vietnamese value in the heart of Little Saigon at Tamarind Tree, which is tucked like a hidden treasure in the corner of an unprepossessing parking lot. The modern décor—dark wood with bright punches of color—makes for a refined setting, so you may be surprised to find yourself using your hands as utensils. But that's what makes it so fun. When the wonderful-smelling Thang Long yellow fish comes to your table with all the accompaniments—rice crackers, roasted peanuts, lettuce, carrots, and fresh herbs—don't hesitate to make a little burritolike wrap with a lettuce leaf, condiments of your choice, and the turmeric-seasoned fish. Carnivores should not miss the seven courses of beef, a wonderfully overwhelming experience served for two. *$; MC, V; no checks; lunch, dinner every day; full bar; no reservations; self parking; tamarindtreerestaurant.com; map:R4.* ♿

Tango / ★★½

1100 PIKE ST, CAPITOL HILL; 206/583-0382

Tango stands sexy sentry over downtown, with windows reaching from tiled floor to high ceiling. This is a place to dine in the Spanish shared small-plates tradition. Starting with the ceviche (which changes daily per market offerings) is never a misstep; in summer, it refreshes perfectly, and in colder, damper times, it's a miniature vacation. A traditional tortilla omelet may come stuffed with smoked bacalao salad, while calamari could be sautéed with spinach, garlic, and jalapeño; a half-dozen carne options are inventively prepared with thoughtful side elements. Servers are fun and, better yet, knowledgeable about the menu, the aptly Spanish wine list, and the selection of dry sherries. The sweet-hot El Diablo is arguably the city's best dessert, and Tango's sultry bar is a terrific place to enjoy it. *$$; MC, V; local checks only; dinner every day; full bar; reservations recommended; self parking; tangorestaurant.com; map:J3.* ♿

Tavolàta / ★★★

2323 2ND AVE, BELLTOWN; 206/838-8008

While Union is a shrine for reverent gourmands, chef Ethan Stowell's new place is all about deliciously simple Italian food for the people—many of whom are seated at the namesake communal table. The cavernous, urbane, perfectly lit space is consistently packed (and—be warned—concomitantly loud), but it's very worth the wait. The concise menu offers first courses such as addictive octopus salad with cannellini beans or deep-fried polenta nuggets; pastas, all made on-site and far above par, like rigatoni with sausage and lots of fresh marjoram, or strozzapreti with braised lamb; and just a few entrées, possibly including a mind-bendingly juicy, flavorful pork chop. Zeppole—fresh, hot, superlight doughnut holes with powdered sugar and fresh lemon—have quickly become a favorite local dessert. The kitchen's open until 1am every day. We say: Yum, and hooray! *$$; AE, DIS, MC, V; no checks; dinner every day, kitchen until 1am; full bar; reservations for parties of 6 or more only; street parking; tavolata.com; map:G7.* ♿

Tempero do Brasil / ★★

5628 UNIVERSITY WY NE, UNIVERSITY DISTRICT; 206/523-6229

If there's one thing Seattleites can appreciate, it's a lively restaurant that makes us forget our omnipresent gray skies. Which is exactly what Bahia natives Antonio and Graca Ribeira offer at their sunny eatery. Their partner, sax player Bryant Urban, helps Graca do the cooking, while Antonio tends bar. Bahia's bar/beach/street food is exemplified by tira-gostos (appetizers). The salt cod cakes are served with fresh limes and go great with a beer. The national dish, feijoada, usually available on weekends, is a stew of black beans, long-cooked with ham, garlic, sausage, and beef, and served with couve (julienned collard greens with orange wedges). Weekend evenings there's live music—chef Urban has been known to burst from the kitchen playing his soprano sax. *$; DC, MC, V; no checks; dinner Tues–Sat; full bar; reservations recommended; street parking; temperodobrasil.net; map:EE7.* ♿

Thaiku / ★★

5410 BALLARD AVE NW, BALLARD; 206/706-7807

This Ballard eatery has the atmospherics of an opium den decorated from a Bangkok PTA garage sale. Dark red walls are graced by bright Thai fabric, Indonesian antiques, and the head of a Javanese carnivorous wooden deer. A rubber-tired Jakarta pony cart hangs from the ceiling alongside balloon-tired bicycles. Votives flicker on every surface. The authentic food is as good as ever, with soupy slurp-'em-up noodles such as guay tiow talay; prawns, scallops, squid, and vegetables; or dry stir-fries like the popular classic pad thai or a list of rice dishes. Nang Kwak, the ubiquitous goddess serving Thai businesses, beckons you and prosperity in the door. Her juju seems to be working, though she can't take all the credit—the food and service match the incredible décor. *$; AE, DIS, MC, V; no checks; lunch and dinner every day; full bar; reservations accepted for 6 or more; self parking; thaiku.com; map:EE8.* ♿

Thai Tom / ★

4543 UNIVERSITY WY NE, UNIVERSITY DISTRICT; 206/548-9548

With Thai restaurants outnumbering neckties in this town, why would anyone wait up to an hour for one of the tiny stools wedged next to pizza-box-size tables at Thai Tom? Maybe it's the wacky musical choices, where hair-band jams are interspersed with Far Eastern melodies. Maybe it's the frenzy of pans and sauces, moving from flame to plate in no time flat. Most likely, it's the huge servings of piping hot and perfectly seasoned noodles and seared meats and veggies. Order the Poor Man's or spicy wide noodles with chicken or tofu. Go cautiously on the spicy stars, or your panang beef might have you calling for a glass of milk to put out the burn. You'll need cash on hand, as credit cards aren't accepted, but with nothing on the menu more than about $8, pocket change will probably be enough. *$; cash only; lunch and dinner every day; beer and wine; no reservations; street parking; map:EE7.*

The Third Floor Fish Café / ★★★☆

205 LAKE ST S, KIRKLAND; 425/822-3553

It starts with an office-building elevator ride, but when you get to your third-floor destination, you'll be delighted. A set of well-windowed rooms look out on Lake Washington with views that invite lingering, especially during stunning sunsets. Like the space, chef/owner Greg Campbell's cuisine rises beautifully above expectations here, with the emphasis on perfectly fresh, exquisitely presented seafood. Look for dishes such as sesame-crusted king salmon with ginger beurre soy, Alaskan black cod with shiitake vinaigrette and mango reduction, or grilled prawn skewers with basil tagliatelle. Desserts range from Valrhona bittersweet chocolate banana torte to the café's signature frozen Meyer lemon soufflé. Service is unwaveringly polished and professional; the wine list has both depth and range; and the bar features the coolest piano around. *$$$; AE, DC, DIS, MC, V; local checks only; dinner every day; full bar; reservations recommended; valet parking; fishcafe.com; map:EE3.* ♿

Tilth / ★★★★

1411 N 45TH ST, WALLINGFORD; 206/633-0801

Seattle's first (and the country's second) certified organic restaurant occupies the ground floor of a cozy Craftsman bungalow—and a secure place in locals' hearts. Chef Maria Hines first turned Earth & Ocean into an award-winning destination; her premier independent venture has become a renowned go-to spot, too, with highly seasonal, often playful, always delicious New American cuisine. Don't confuse the sustainable/organic ethos with anything less than indulgent: Tilth won its following with the likes of savory porcini mushroom brûlée and mini duck burgers served on tiny brioche buns with house-made fingerling potato chips, heirloom ketchup, and fig mustard. If pork belly's on the menu, get it. All the dishes come in two sizes, for sharing or conventional courses; expect amuses-bouche and über-knowledgeable service. Brunch at Tilth, offering some of dinner's dishes along with unbelievably delicious breakfast items, is divine. *$$$; MC, V; no checks; dinner every day, brunch Sat–Sun; full bar; reservations recommended; street parking; tilthrestaurant.com; map:FF7.* ♿

Tosoni's / ★★☆

14320 NE 20TH ST, BELLEVUE; 425/644-1668

One of the Eastside's enduring treasures, Tosoni's is known to its many regulars simply as "Walter's place." Look hard or you could miss it, hidden in an Overlake strip mall. But this humble exterior belies the old world delights that await. Chef Walter Walcher works the open kitchen, presiding over a small dining room filled with antique-looking cabinets and armoires. The menu, written on a blackboard hung over the kitchen, tends toward the continental. Meats are a sure bet, and diners are as likely to encounter ostrich or venison as they are rack of lamb. There's also a nice Wiener schnitzel. Look for fresh fish and poultry dishes such as duck or chicken. Choices depend on the season, the night, and Walter's fancy. *$$$; AE, MC, V; local checks only; dinner Tues–Sat; beer and wine; reservations recommended; self-parking; map:GG2.*

Tulio Ristorante / ★★★

1100 5TH AVE (HOTEL VINTAGE PARK), DOWNTOWN; 206/624-5500

This bustling Italian trattoria has a warm and intimate air, with the scent of roasted garlic, a wood-burning oven, and an open kitchen evoking the atmosphere of an entirely welcoming Tuscan villa. Menus change every day or two, reflecting the seasons and chef Walter Pisano's imagination; you might delight in calamari grilled with lavender sausage and chickpeas; chanterelle mushroom risotto; or duck breast with crispy confit, braised brussels sprouts, and golden raisins, scented with orange zest. Focaccia, gelati, granitas, and desserts (the chocolate pudding cake's a local favorite) are all made fresh on the premises daily. Service is swift, knowledgeable, and attentive. When Pisano (Tulio's founding chef) returned after a brief hiatus, his fans rejoiced—he brings a heart and soul to this place that makes it truly special. *$$; AE, DC, DIS, JCB, MC, V; no checks; breakfast, lunch, dinner every day; full bar; reservations recommended; valet parking; tulio.com; map:L6.* ♿

Tup Tim Thai / ★★

118 W MERCER ST, QUEEN ANNE; 206/281-8833

Tup Tim Thai is all about serving inexpensive, well-prepared Thai food to as many people as possible. Some say it's the best Thai food in town (a good way to start an argument in Seattle), and there's certainly no shortage of clientele. Spring rolls or chicken satay are classic starters, and reliable entrée choices include the slightly sweet chicken pad thai, the fragrant red and yellow curries, or sweet-and-sour pork. Try the intensely flavored garlic prawns or local favorite number 69, aka Tup Tim Noodles, pan-fried rice noodles with ground beef, onions, and tomatoes. Extinguish any entrée-induced fires with mango or coconut ice cream, or savor the black rice pudding. Be sure to make a reservation and give yourself time to park. *$; DC, MC, V; checks OK; lunch Mon–Fri, dinner Mon–Sat; beer and wine; reservations recommended; street parking; map:GG7.* ♿

Tutta Bella / ★☆

4918 RAINIER AVE S, COLUMBIA CITY (AND BRANCHES); 206/721-3501

Whether you opt for the warm and cozy Columbia City location, the bright and open Wallingford shop, or the modern South Lake Union outpost, the authentic Naples-style pizza at Tutta Bella is all good. The pizzas, quickly baked in a superhot wood-fired oven, come out beautifully blistered and topped with ingredients such as San Marzano plum tomatoes, fresh whole-milk mozzarella, and fresh basil. Try the prosciutto e rucola pie, a wonderfully fresh cheese and cured ham pizza topped with an arugula salad, or the quattro formaggi, a luxurious blend of four cheeses and garlic. Tutta Bella is a mecca for families with kids, who can order their own pizza bambino, a regular-size pizza with simple cheese and tomato toppings. Save room for an authentically pulled and steamed latte macchiato, one of the best in town, to have along with one of the many daily flavors of house-made gelato. *$$; MC, V; lunch and dinner every day; beer and wine; reservations accepted; self parking (Wallingford location and South Lake Union) and street parking; tuttabellapizza.com; map:KK6, FF7.* ♿

Typhoon! / ★★

1400 WESTERN AVE, DOWNTOWN; 206/262-9797;
8936 161ST AVE NE, REDMOND; 425/558-7666

Typhoon! has a hallowed place in Seattle dining history; it occupies the space of the original Wild Ginger, long since moved uptown to bigger digs. It's nouvelle Thai here, with no sense of obligation to the done-and-done-and-done-again tradition. Monster "superwild" shrimp, served whole, bear a warning: "Not for the faint of heart." Pinecone fish resembles one—little chunks of halibut crispy fried and uniquely clumped together. Grilled beef with grapes is a stunner. The lahd nah features eggs, mushrooms, vegetables, and the lightest of gingery gravies. Coconut milk curries, the mainstay of Thai restaurant cuisine, are velvety and rich but not too heavy handed. The Redmond location in Bella Bottega Center has much the same menu but better parking. *$$; AE, DC, DIS, MC, V; checks OK; lunch Mon–Sat, dinner every day; full bar; reservations recommended; street parking (Downtown), self parking (Redmond); typhoonrestaurants.com; map:I7, DD2.* ♿

Union / ★★★★

1400 1ST AVE, DOWNTOWN; 206/838-8000

It's local-boy-makes-great at Union, downtown's temple to fine dining. Voted Seattle's sexiest chef, proprietor Ethan Stowell's got a set of gold-bling rings that read "CHEFS RULE," but Union's not about glitter. Soaring ceilings, unobtrusive modern lines, and impeccable service set the scene for deep appreciation of an utterly elegant, haute-Northwest menu. Offerings change every day, often made with seasonal-to-the-minute ingredients from Pike Place Market. Expect the likes of kabocha squash soup with poached duck egg; seared hamachi with artichokes, lemon, and shallot; and lumachine pasta with braised veal shortrib. A 200-bottle wine cellar features the best of the region and the world, with at least a dozen selections by the glass. The bar menu offers a taste of Union's glory for those with less advantaged wallets; to experience Stowell's work in more casual environs, head to his also-wildly-popular Italian place in Belltown, Tavolàta. *$$$; AE, DIS, MC, V; no checks; dinner every day; full bar; reservations recommended; street parking; unionseattle.com; map:J7.* ♿

Via Tribunali / ★★

913 E PINE ST, CAPITOL HILL; 206/322-9234;
317 W GALER ST, QUEEN ANNE; 206/264-7768

Owned by the coffee guru behind nearby Caffe Vita, the Capitol Hill outpost of this sexy joint is all about Italian, from ingredients shipped from Italy to the language of the menu (no English translations are provided, so study up or throw yourself on the mercy of your server). Thin-crust pizzas are baked in a wood-burning oven made with bricks formed from the ashes of Mount Vesuvius, and they're certified authentic Neapolitan. Options include the simple Margherita, with hunks of cheese and tomatoes, or the Via Tribunali, with buffalo mozzarella cheese, ricotta, and provolone. A destination for serious pizza aficionados from all over town, a Queen Anne opened in 2007. Neither location takes reservations (except for parties of eight or more), so be prepared to wait. As we go to press, plans are afoot for another incarnation in Georgetown. *$; AE, MC, V; no checks; dinner every day (Capitol Hill), Tues–Sun (Queen Anne); full bar; no reservations; street parking; viatribunali.com; map:GG6, GG8.* ♿

Vios Café & Marketplace / ★★½

903 19TH AVE E, CAPITOL HILL; 206/329-3236

Vios is an airy café and market tucked away in a residential neighborhood on the east slope of Capitol Hill. A few small tables line the windows, while larger community tables fill with foodies and young families who chat and nibble on pita while their rug rats entertain themselves and each other in a "kid pit" complete with its own toy kitchen. Dishes are exceptionally fresh, using seasonal, farmers' market ingredients when available. Start with the pillowy pita with baba ghanoush, tzatziki, or hummus. Pastas, often modern Greek twists on classic Italian dishes such as the hilopites egg pasta with local wild mushrooms and duck confit, are light and satisfying. Save room for a dish of yummy gelato. A small but delightful selection of Greek wines is available by the glass, or pick an inexpensive bottle from the rack and pay retail plus $10 corkage. *$$; MC, V; checks OK; lunch and dinner Tues–Sat; beer and wine; reservations accepted; street parking; vioscafe.com; map:GG6.* ♿

Voilà! Bistrot / ★★½

2805 E MADISON ST, MADISON VALLEY; 206/322-5460

French visitors say that Voilà! tastes just like home. This is a classic casual neighborhood bistro, with Dijon-colored walls adorned with a grand mirror and French posters. Chef/owner Laurent Gabrel sometimes comes out to visit, chatting with neighborhood regulars and destination diners seated at the dozen café-style tables or petite bar; his accent, the room, and the food all charm in that seemingly effortless Gallic style. Try the tagliatelle aux champignons des bois (wild mushrooms and pasta), or excellent versions of French favorites such as coq au vin and beef bourguignon. You can't go wrong ending your meal with a thoughtful cheese course or a stellar crème brûlée. *$$$;*

AE, DC, MC, V; local checks only; dinner Mon–Sat; full bar; reservations recommended; street parking; voilabistrot.com; map:GG6. ♿

Volterra / ★★★

5411 BALLARD AVE NW, BALLARD; 206/789-5100

Ballard's reputation as an in-city Scandinavian fishing village is now way out of date, what with restaurants like Volterra making this North Seattle neighborhood utterly urbane and undeniably world-class. Don Curtiss and Michelle Quisenberry were married in Volterra, Italy; they handle the kitchen and the front of the house, respectively. It's a labor of love that unites Pacific Northwest ingredients, Tuscan-style cuisine, convivial charm, and excellent service in a sweet, bustling, very European setting. Start with seasonally changing chef's antipasti presented on a ceramic palette, or try the heavenly polenta with wild mushrooms; consider grilled pear ravioli for a pasta course; and know that both seafood baked in parchment and organic herbed chicken earn raves. Then there's the roasted wild boar tenderloin with Gorgonzola sauce, one of Seattle's all-time favorite entrées. House-made limoncello punctuates perfectly. *$$$; AE, DIS, MC, V; no checks; dinner every day, brunch Sat–Sun; full bar; reservations recommended; street parking; volterrarestaurant.com; map:FF8.* ♿

Waterfront Seafood Grill / ★★★

2815 ALASKAN WY, PIER 70, WATERFRONT; 206/956-9171

Perched at the end of Pier 70, Waterfront sports sweeping Elliott Bay views from its vast, elegant dining room, while from the 80-foot serpentine bar, patrons drink in a vista of Seattle's new Olympic Sculpture Park. This place is the surf cousin to local steakhouse El Gaucho, so premium meats are offered, but astonishing seafood is what Waterfront's about. Seafood Indulgence is an aptly named starter—a classic presentation of lobster, crab claws, prawns, oysters, and tuna tartare. Entrées showcase that day's very best local and global catches. "Shareable sides" shouldn't be overlooked, either; sweet corn with chipotle lime butter is outrageously tasty, as are lobster mashed potatoes. Servers provide flawlessly for every wish, including torching a version of baked Alaska in a piece of performance art that's worth the price alone (but of course you get dessert too). The wine list is massive and impressive. *$$$; AE, B, DC, JCB, MC, V; checks OK; dinner every day; full bar; reservations recommended; valet and self parking; waterfrontpier70.com; map:D9.* ♿

Wild Ginger Asian Restaurant and Satay Bar / ★★★

1401 3RD AVE, DOWNTOWN; 206/623-4450

This local culinary landmark is still popular with both Seattleites and visitors—especially those going to a Seattle Symphony performance at Benaroya Hall down the street or a show at Triple Door around the corner. The dining room is a huge space with streetside views and an elegant spiral stairway leading up to private banquet rooms. Wild Ginger offers a wide range of multiethnic dishes from Bangkok, Singapore, Saigon, and Jakarta. At the mahogany satay bar, order from an array of sizzling skewered selections such as the mountain lamb and Saigon scallop satay. Indulge in the succulent Singapore-style stir-fried crab, fresh from live tanks and redolent of ginger and garlic; the celebrated fragrant duck served with steamed buns and plum sauce; or laksa, a spicy Malaysian seafood soup whose soft, crunchy, and slippery textures and hot and salty flavors encompass everything good about Southeast Asian cookery. *$$; AE, DC, DIS, MC, V; no checks; lunch Mon–Sat, dinner every day; full bar; reservations recommended; valet parking; wildginger.net; map:L8.* ♿

Yanni's Greek Cuisine / ★★

7419 GREENWOOD AVE N, GREENWOOD; 206/783-6945

Yanni's is a comfortable joint offering the simple goodness of a Greek taverna. Any night will find the place packed with locals (who also stop in to get the spit-roasted chicken to take home). The deep-fried calamari, with perfectly fried, tender squid rings and skordalia dipping sauce, is an appetizer big enough for an entrée. Add a horiatiki salad—a huge pile of tomatoes, cucumbers, feta, Kalamata olives, and a little pita—and you have a meal for two. The huge, seven-page menu encompasses all the classic Greek dishes including spanakopita and moussaka. Yanni's also offers an extensive selection of Greek wines and beers to accompany your meal. *$; MC, V; checks OK; dinner Mon–Sat; beer and wine; reservations recommended; street parking; peo4.com/yannisgreekrestaurant; map:EE8.* ♿

Yarrow Bay Beach Cafe / ★★
Yarrow Bay Grill / ★★☆

1270 CARILLON POINT, KIRKLAND; 425/889-9052

The upstairs grill boasts captivating views and understated, elegant décor—and it's got bragging rights for the remarkable work of chef Vicky McCaffree. She made a name for herself with pan-Asian cuisine, but her inventive, oft-changing menu reflects global influences as well. You'll usually find her beloved Thai seafood stew, with its coconut milk/lemongrass broth, on offer; black cod might be pan-seared with shiitake and soy, sided with Asian slaw. Prosciutto-crusted scallops may boast piquillo peppers and manchego cheese. Ravioli might feature New Mexico corn one day, portobellos and Madeira another. Downstairs, the more casual Beach Cafe turns out great plates, too, drawing inspiration from around the world; options could include New Orleans crab cakes, Thai chicken skewers, or seven-spice albacore tuna. *$$, $$$; AE, DC, DIS, JCB, MC, V; no checks; lunch, dinner every day (Cafe), dinner every day (Grill); full bar; reservations recommended; valet and validated self parking; ybgrill.com; map:FF3.* ♿

LODGINGS

LODGINGS

Belltown/Downtown/International District/ South Lake Union

Ace Hotel / ★★

2423 1ST AVE, BELLTOWN; 206/448-4721

The 28-room Ace Hotel is stylishly spare, with white wood floors, white walls, and mostly white bedding. Fourteen standard rooms have a stainless sink and counter with baths down the hall. Fourteen deluxe rooms have their own bath. With its ultracool location above the Cyclops Café, within walking distance of Belltown galleries and shops, this is the place to experience Seattle's urbane side. Amenities include small TVs, wireless Internet access, CD players, and continental breakfast. There's no room service, but with Belltown's eateries at your command, you can dine around the world during your stay. Rooms on First Avenue can be noisy. Pets OK. *$$–$$$; AE, DC, DIS, JCB, MC, V; no checks, traveler's checks OK; self parking; info@theace hotel.com; acehotel.com; map:F8.*

Alexis Hotel / ★★★

1007 1ST AVE, DOWNTOWN; 206/624-4844 OR 866/356-8894

Long before upstart Hotel Max came to town, the luxurious Alexis was Seattle's most artistic lodging, with original artwork displayed in the guest rooms and throughout the common areas. The boutique hotel has 109 rooms, including spacious executive suites, fireplace suites, spa suites, and one- and two-bedroom suites with kitchens. Themed rooms include the John Lennon Suite, which features reproductions of his artwork and CDs of his music. In the romantic spa suites on the top floor, a giant, two-person tub is surrounded by mirrors. North-facing rooms have a view of Elliott Bay; First Avenue rooms might be a little noisy. Amenities include Internet access, free newspaper, shoeshines, and the Etherea Salon Spa. The Library Bistro serves breakfast and lunch, and offers 24-hour room service. Pets OK. *$$$–$$$$; AE, DC, DIS, JCB, MC, V; checks OK; valet parking; reservations@alexishotel.com; alexishotel.com; map:L7.* ♿

Best Western Executive Inn / ★

200 TAYLOR AVE N, DENNY TRIANGLE; 206/448-9444 OR 800/351-9444

This no-frills, 123-room motor inn provides all the basics and a convenient location. Walking into the comfy, newly remodeled lobby with gas fireplace, you might think you're getting the charm of a rustic lodge experience, but the rooms are pretty basic. No matter, all rooms have views of the city or the Space Needle, just a block away. Hop on the Monorail at the Seattle Center and ride 1 mile to the heart of downtown. The inn has a Jacuzzi and workout room, as well as an informal restaurant and lounge. There's no charge for children 18 and under, and parking is free. Pets OK. *$$; AE, DC, DIS, JCB, MC, V; no checks; self parking; info@bwexec-inn.com; bwexec-inn.com; map:E5.* ♿

Best Western Pioneer Square Hotel / ★★

77 YESLER WY, PIONEER SQUARE; 206/340-1234 OR 800/800-5514

Situated in a turn-of-the-20th-century brick building, this hotel listed on the National Register of Historic Places currently offers the only lodging opportunity in Seattle's historic Pioneer Square neighborhood. The 75 guest rooms are tastefully appointed in period décor but quite small; some have sitting alcoves. The rooms are surprisingly quiet considering the hotel is just one block from the busy Alaskan Way Viaduct and ferry terminal. Amenities include complimentary continental breakfast, access to a nearby health club, and free wireless Internet access. Those looking for great restaurants and bars with a variety of live music will find almost anything they want here. Kids under 12 stay free. No pets. *$$–$$$; AE, DC, DIS, JCB, MC, V; checks OK with 2-week advance deposit; self parking; bestwestern.com/prop_48128; map:N8.* ♿

The Edgewater / ★★☆

2411 ALASKAN WY, PIER 67, WATERFRONT; 206/728-7000 OR 800/624-0670

It may not be the most luxurious of Seattle's hotels—or the newest, or the most plush. But the Edgewater is the only hotel literally over the water (you've probably seen the famous 1964 photo of the Beatles fishing out their hotel window), and its atmosphere is so quintessentially Northwest that you shouldn't miss it. Throw open your window to breathe the fresh, salty air and watch the ferries chug across Puget Sound. The 234-room hotel has a metal log-cabin exterior and a cozy lodge theme inside. All rooms have fireplaces, log bed frames, and furry bears that double as footstools. Second-floor rooms are vulnerable to noise from the lounge downstairs. Splurge for a premium waterfront room to get a luxurious claw-foot soaking tub from which you can gaze upon the Olympic Mountains. The sleek Six Seven Restaurant & Lounge (named for the pier) serves Northwest cuisine with pan-Asian influences. Pets OK. *$$$; AE, DC, DIS, MC, V; checks OK; valet parking; edgewaterhotel.com; map:F9.* ♿

Executive Hotel Pacific / ★☆

400 SPRING ST, DOWNTOWN; 206/623-3900 OR 800/426-1165

Catering to foreign travelers, this 1928-built European-style boutique hotel offers easy access to downtown businesses, entertainment, and stadiums. The hotel's staff includes several Japanese speakers; signs, brochures, and maps are in English and Japanese. The hotel completed a major renovation in 2006, adding business and fitness centers. The 160 guest rooms and suites are simple but comfortable. All rooms are air-conditioned and have 26-inch high-definition LCD TVs, high-speed wireless Internet, and clock radios that play CDs and MP3s. Seattle's Best Coffee is just off the lobby. The hotel's restaurant, Jasmine, serves pan-Asian cuisine. Pets OK. *$$$; AE, DC, DIS,*

SPA TREATMENT

Everyone needs respite from the stresses and strains of daily life—even if you're on a vacation. Fortunately, you don't have to travel far in Seattle to get away from it all. Here are some in- and out-of-city pampering best bets:

Slipped into historic Ballard is local favorite **HABITUDE AT THE LOCKS** (2801 NW Market St; 206/782-2898; habitude.com; map:FF8). Opt for the Under a Northern Rainforest spa package ($240), which includes a sampling of pampering for the whole body. Between services, spagoers are treated to herbal teas, fresh fruits, and nuts. A complimentary cosmetic touch-up is part of the experience; just ask.

Inside tranquil, Asian-inspired environs, **ROBERT LEONARD DAY SPA AND SALON** (2033 6th Ave, Belltown; 206/441-9900; robertleonard.net; map:H5) offers everything from a $35 classic manicure to an eight-hour day of beauty (body polish and massage, facial, manicure, pedicure, scalp treatment and hair styling, makeup, and lunch) for $545.

Owner Nina Ummel conjures a global environment at **UMMELINA INTERNATIONAL DAY SPA** (1525 4th Ave, Downtown; 206/624-1370 or 800/663-4772; ummelina.com; map:K6) with themed "journeys." One such journey, the Equator, makes for a romantic spa interlude where you can spend the day au naturel with your significant other underneath a real waterfall, a gentle rain from the "rain forest," and mud-caked baking in the "desert." Scrub clean with a return visit to the waterfall, all for $190 each. For less adventurous (and less expensive) treatments, choose from the "rituals" (facials, massages, or manicures starting at $50). Book early—appointments are at a premium.

JCB, MC, V; no checks; valet and self parking; resehp@executivehotels.net; executivehotels.net/seattle; map:L6.

Fairmont Olympic Hotel / ★★★★

411 UNIVERSITY ST, DOWNTOWN; 206/621-1700 OR 800/441-1414

It may be a cliché, but "old world luxury" is the perfect description for the Fairmont Olympic, a historic landmark built on the site of the original University of Washington. Impeccable service and pampering are hallmarks of this 1924 Italian Renaissance icon. The opulence extends from the huge chandeliers and rich fabrics of the lobby to the 450 guest rooms (216 of them suites), which feature soaking tubs and terry robes, to the venerable restaurant, the Georgian (see review in the Restaurants chapter). At press time, the hotel had begun a major room renovation. Amenities include 24-hour room service, twice-daily housekeeping, town-car service, high-speed Internet, a

One of three Gene Juarez spas in the Seattle area, **GENE JUAREZ SALON AND SPA** (607 Pine St, Downtown; 206/326-6000; genejuarez.com; map:F9) contains fountains and fireplaces that provide an opulent but cozy atmosphere. You'll move from room to room for services (there are many) like massages, facials, and pedicures. The warm shea butter melt ($135)—a sugar-and-spice scrub followed by a shea butter mask—is the perfect antidote to a chilly Seattle day.

It's convenient—shop, drop, and get a hot-rock massage at **SPA NORDSTROM** (500 Pine St, 5th Floor, Downtown; 206/628-1670; nordstrom.com/spa nordstrom; map:J5). Within Nordstrom's flagship store lies an escape from all those pesky shopping decisions. There are services aplenty, such as body cocoons (aka wraps, $90–$100), mustard baths ($60), and signature facials ($90–$175).

Topnotch treatments for the digits are the forte at the very girly **FRENCHY'S** (3131 E Madison St, Ste 103, Madison Park; 206/325-9582; frenchysdayspa.com; map:GG6). There are no wham-bam-thank-you-ma'am pedicures here. Sink into a cream-colored leather chair to soak your tootsies in style while staff offer coffee and tea. Manicures range from $18 to $30, and a pedicure runs $38 to $47; both use aromatherapy exfoliating scrubs. Get one of their phenomenal facials while your nails dry.

Newcomer **SWOON BOUTIQUE SPA** (1422 E Pine St, Capitol Hill; 206/323-0106; swoonspa.com; map:GG6) is a stylish, super-clean urban spa on Capitol Hill. The plush pedicure station, communal manicure table, and outdoor patio make it a great party destination, and the pedicures ($45–$55) just may be the best in town.

—Kathy Schultz

lounge, a pool, and a health club. Swank meeting rooms and chichi shops flank the lobby. The hotel goes out of its way to accommodate kids, providing them with a welcome bag, loaner Sony PlayStation, cribs, kid-size bathrobes, and babysitting service. Pets OK. *$$$$; AE, DC, DIS, JCB, MC, V; checks OK; valet parking; olympic@fairmont.com; fairmont.com/seattle; map:K6.* ♿

Grand Hyatt Seattle / ★★★

721 PINE ST, DOWNTOWN; 206/774-1234 OR 800/233-1234

The Grand Hyatt offers luxury without pretension, volume without anonymity. An added bonus? Just off the lobby is Seven, one of the city's most cutting-edge hair salons. Warm woods and glass art lend a Northwest aesthetic to the common areas and the 425 guest rooms (including 113 suites). Flip a bedside switch to raise and lower drapes, or change your room's doorbell to a mute "do not disturb" mode. Adjacent to the convention center, the hotel provides a host of large meeting rooms and an amphitheater. Nearly every view in the house reveals at least a sliver of lake or mountain; floors 20 and higher have great views of Elliott Bay or Lake Union. All rooms have high-speed Internet access, separate glassed-in marble showers, and deep bathtubs with cascading faucets. Downstairs, stylish, though not stellar, Ruth's Chris Steak House is open for breakfast, lunch, and dinner. No pets. *$$$–$$$$; AE, DC, DIS, JCB, MC, V; checks OK; valet and self parking; grandseattle.hyatt.com; map:J5.* ♿

Hotel Ändra / ★★★½

2000 4TH AVE, BELLTOWN; 206/448-8600 OR 877/448-8600

Ändra is one of Seattle's most sophisticated hotels, catering to travelers looking for both a prime location and posh accommodations. The lovely 1926 building is located on the border of Belltown and the city's retail shopping district, and the hotel artfully blends Northwest elements with Scandinavian style. The 119 rooms are stocked with high-speed Internet access, flat-screen TVs, and a personal oxygen dispenser for use during your stay. Ändra boasts upper-floor views of downtown, Puget Sound, the Space Needle, Lake Union, and the Olympic Mountains. Two on-site dining options are available: the superb Greek-inspired Lola from local celebrity restaurateur Tom Douglas and an excellent northern Italian eatery, Assaggio Ristorante (see review in the Restaurants chapter). Just down the block is Ralph's, a small, upscale market. Pets OK. *$$$–$$$$; AE, DIS, JCB, MC, V; checks OK; valet parking; hotelandra@hotelandra.com; hotelandra.com; map:I6.* ♿

Hotel Max / ★★★

620 STEWART ST, DOWNTOWN; 206/728-6299 OR 866/833-6299

Artsy, irreverent Hotel Max has replaced the Ace as the favored stop for members of the mod squad. This small boutique-style hotel drips with art and attitude. Trendily furnished rooms are small but cheerful, and each features original artwork from 39 local artists. In the hallways, doors are decorated with striking black-and-white photographs. Photos on the fifth floor depict Seattle grunge icons such as Kurt Cobain and Eddie Vedder. Amenities include menus for pillows and spiritual texts, LCD televisions, high-speed wireless Internet, and small fitness and business centers. Round-the-clock room service is provided by Red Fin, which serves sushi and Asian cuisine in a chic dining room and lounge. Pets OK. *$$–$$$, AE, DC, DIS, JCB, MC, V; no checks; valet parking; info@hotelmaxseattle.com; hotelmaxseattle.com; map:H5.* ♿

Hotel Monaco / ★★★

1101 4TH AVE, DOWNTOWN; 206/621-1770 OR 800/945-2240

The Monaco's bold style is a welcome respite from a gray Seattle day. All 189 rooms and suites are sumptuously appointed in a blend of colorful, eye-popping stripes and florals, which may strike some as busy, others as charming. All rooms have queen- or king-size beds; 10 Mediterranean Suites feature deluxe bathrooms with two-person Fuji-jet tubs. Amenities include free high-speed Internet, 24-hour business services, evening wine tasting, 24-hour room service, leopard-print bathrobes, and a fitness center. Monaco's campy principality extends to the Southern-inspired Sazerac restaurant, named for the bar's signature drink (see review in Restaurants chapter). Pets OK; they'll even provide a loaner goldfish in its own bowl. *$$$–$$$$; AE, DC, DIS, JCB, MC, V; no checks; valet parking; monaco-seattle.com; map:L6.* ♿

Hotel 1000 / ★★★★

1000 1ST AVE, DOWNTOWN; 206/957-1000 OR 877/315-1088

Seattle's newest downtown hotel flawlessly combines luxury and technology in a convenient location close to Pike Place Market, sports stadiums, and the city's financial and shopping hubs. Inspired amenities abound. Each room features 40-inch flat-screen TVs, high-speed Internet access, a courtesy bar that signals the hotel's staff when you run out of your favorite beverage, and a huge pedestal tub that fills via a spout in the ceiling. West-facing rooms offer gorgeous water and mountain views. One floor below the lobby, you'll find a full-service spa, fitness room, and the city's only virtual golf range, where you can tee off at more than 50 of the world's most famous courses. Just off the lobby is sexy BOKA Kitchen + Bar (see review in the Restaurants chapter). Pets OK. *$$$–$$$$; AE, DC, DIS, JCB, MC, V; no checks; valet parking; reservations@hotel1000seattle.com; hotel1000seattle.com; map:L7.* ♿

Hotel Vintage Park / ★★★

1100 5TH AVE, DOWNTOWN; 206/624-8000 OR 800/853-3914

From the lobby's plush velvet settees and leather armchairs to the Grand Suite's double-sided fireplace, the Vintage Park looks like the ideal spot to break out a smoking jacket and a nice Chianti. The 125 rooms (including one suite) are named after Washington wineries and vineyards, with Tuscany-inspired décor. A fireside Washington wine tasting is complimentary every evening. The personable Park offers rooms facing inward or outward (exterior rooms have a bit more space but not much of a view). Amenities include small fitness and business centers and 24-hour room service (including lunch or dinner from the hotel's excellent Italian restaurant, Tulio; see review in the Restaurants chapter). A nearby Interstate 5 on-ramp makes lower floors a bit noisy. Pets OK. *$$$–$$$$; AE, DC, DIS, JCB, MC, V; no checks; valet parking; hotelvintagepark.com; map:L6.* ♿

Inn at Harbor Steps / ★★

1221 1ST AVE, DOWNTOWN; 206/748-0973 OR 888/728-8910

Tucked inside a swanky high-rise retail-and-residential complex across from the Seattle Art Museum, rooms at the Inn are shielded from the surrounding urban hubbub. Harbor Steps offers 28 rooms with sleek furnishings, garden views, fireplaces (excepting five of the rooms, which have two queen-size beds instead), king- or queen-size beds, sitting areas, and fridges with free soft drinks. Deluxe rooms include spa tubs. Double-queen rooms have an angled wall that extends partway into the room, separating the beds for a bit of privacy. Among the amenities are complimentary evening hors d'oeuvres and wine, and a full gourmet breakfast. Guests have access to an indoor pool, sauna, Jacuzzi, and exercise and meeting rooms. Complimentary fresh cookies and computers with Web access in the lobby. No pets. *$$$; AE, DC, DIS, MC, V; no checks; self parking; innatharborsteps@foursisters.com; innatharborsteps.com; map:K7.* ♿

Inn at the Market / ★★★☆

86 PINE ST, PIKE PLACE MARKET; 206/443-3600 OR 800/446-4484

Everything about Inn at the Market oozes quintessential Seattle atmosphere: views of Elliott Bay and the Olympics from most rooms, the proximity to bustling Pike Place Market, and dinner service (5–10pm) from country-French Campagne (see review in the Restaurants chapter). An ivy-draped courtyard wraps around its entrance amid high-end retailers and restaurants. The 70 rooms are handsomely dressed in soft taupe, copper, and green, and have oversize bathrooms, robes, Nintendo, high-speed wireless Internet access, and floor-to-ceiling bay windows that open. West-facing windows have incredible views of the Sound. Rise early to sample the Market's fresh pastries and fruit. Or sleep late and indulge in room service from Bacco in the courtyard. No pets. *$$$–$$$$; AE, DC, DIS, JCB, MC, V; checks OK; valet parking; info@innatthemarket.com; innatthemarket.com; map:I7.* ♿

Mayflower Park Hotel / ★★

405 OLIVE WY, DOWNTOWN; 206/623-8700 OR 800/426-5100

Past and present come together at this handsome 1927 hotel in the heart of the city's retail district. The Mayflower's lobby is decorated with lovely antique Chinese artwork and furniture. The 171 rooms are fairly small but preserve reminders of the hotel's past: elegant dark wood furniture, deep tubs, and double-glazed windows that keep out noise. Twenty suites offer comfortable sitting areas, and most have wet bars. The slightly bigger corner suites have better views; ask for one on a higher floor, or you may find yourself facing a brick wall. Amenities include free high-speed wireless Internet, Nintendo, 24-hour room service, and same-day laundry service. For refreshments, you can't beat Andaluca, an upscale restaurant combining Northwest and Mediterranean flavors (see review in the Restaurants chapter), or you can sip one of Seattle's best martinis at the popular bar, Oliver's. No pets. *$$$–$$$$; AE, DC, DIS, MC, V; checks OK; valet parking; mayflowerpark@mayflowerpark.com; mayflowerpark.com; map:I6.* ♿

Panama Hotel / ★★☆

605½ S MAIN ST, CHINATOWN/INTERNATIONAL DISTRICT; 206/223-9242

This historic European-style hotel with shared bathrooms down the hall was built in 1910 in old Japantown as a workingman's hotel for Japanese immigrants and Alaskan fisherman. All 100 rooms have hardwood floors, antique furnishings, down comforters, single sinks, and free wireless Internet access.

Men's and women's baths are small but clean. Streetside rooms can be a little noisy at times. Ask for a tour of the basement to see the only remaining Japanese bathhouse left intact in the United States. There's no room service, but the adjacent Panama Hotel Tea & Coffee House has yummy snacks and teas. Pets OK, but let them know beforehand. Weekly rates available. *$$; AE, MC, V; no checks, traveler's checks OK; self parking; reservations@panamahotelseattle.com; panamahotelseattle.com; map:P6.*

BEST PLACE
TO LET THE DOG OFF THE LEASH?

"The dog park above Golden Gardens—it's great to be able to have a BBQ and a place for your dog to run around in such close proximity."

Kathy Casey, chef and culinary diva

Pan Pacific Seattle / ★★★

2125 TERRY AVE, SOUTH LAKE UNION; 206/264-8111

The sleek new Pan Pacific anchors the 2200 Westlake complex, a mixed-use retail/condo/hotel high-rise in the red-hot South Lake Union neighborhood. Many of the tastefully appointed 160 guest rooms and suites offer views of the Space Needle, Lake Union, and downtown Seattle, and all feature oversize tubs, plasma TVs, free Internet access, and ridiculously comfortable Hypnos beds (the only beds in the world certified by the Queen of England). A small lounge off the lobby serves snacks and cocktails to both hotel guests and 2200 Westlake residents. Just steps from the hotel's lobby are the sprawling Whole Foods Market, Starbucks, Koots Green Tea, upscale pet supply and home furnishings stores, a spa, and a pharmacy. Pets OK. *$$$$; AE, DC, JCB, MC, V; no checks; valet and self parking; panpacific.com/seattle; map:F3.* ♿

Paramount Hotel / ★★

724 PINE ST, DOWNTOWN; 206/292-9500 OR 800/663-1144

Ideally located for all sorts of diversions, whether it's business, culture, or shopping, the Paramount is kitty-corner from the historic Paramount Theatre, in the lap of posh midtown retailers, and near the convention center. The Paramount's modest size—146 guest rooms and two small meeting rooms—appeals to those who eschew nearby megahotels. Standard guest rooms are prettily appointed, though small, as are bathrooms. Consider splurging for an "executive king," which is always on the corner, quite a bit roomier, and outfitted with a fireplace and a whirlpool jet tub. The tasty pan-Asian-inspired Dragonfish Asian Café (see review in the Restaurants chapter) is adjacent. The Paramount has a 24-hour fitness center and high-speed wireless Internet. No pets. *$$$; AE, DC, DIS, MC, V; checks OK; valet parking; paramounthotelseattle.com; map:J4.* ♿

Pensione Nichols / ★½

1923 1ST AVE, PIKE PLACE MARKET; 206/441-7125

Now nearly 20 years old, the family-owned Pensione Nichols is the only bed-and-breakfast in Seattle's downtown core. Perched above Pike Place Market and furnished with antiques, 10 guest rooms share four bathrooms. Some rooms face noisy First Avenue; others have bright skylights instead of windows and are quieter. Two spacious suites have private baths, full kitchens, and living rooms with jaw-dropping water views. A bountiful continental breakfast—including fresh treats from the Market—is served in a large, appealing common room on the third floor. Couch potatoes be warned: the stair climb from street level is steep. There's a two-night minimum stay on summer weekends; discounts for long-term stays. Pets OK. *$$–$$$; AE, DC, DIS, MC, V; checks OK; self parking; pensionenichols@qwest.net; pensionenichols.com; map:H8.*

Red Lion Hotel on Fifth Avenue / ★★

1415 5TH AVE, DOWNTOWN; 206/971-8000 OR 800/733-5466

All 297 rooms in this former office building provide feather beds, robes, game players, and wireless Internet access. If you move up to one of the suites, you'll have a separate parlor and better views of downtown or the Sound. Rooms higher up are best for people who want to shut out noise from busy Fourth and Fifth avenues. Amenities include room service (7am–10pm), fitness and business centers, and 14,000 square feet of meeting space. The fifth-floor Terrace Garden Restaurant & Lounge serves Northwest cuisine; when the weather is warm, diners can be served on the large outdoor terrace. The British-style pub and restaurant Elephant & Castle is below the lobby, serving fish-and-chips and bangers and mash, in addition to American burgers. Pets OK. *$$$; AE, DC, DIS, JCB, MC, V; checks OK; self parking; redlion5thavenue.com; map: K6.* ♿

Renaissance Seattle Hotel / ★★

515 MADISON ST, DOWNTOWN; 206/583-0300 OR 800/546-9184

This 553-room hotel is aimed mostly at the business and convention crowd, but it doesn't have the carnival atmosphere of some of the busier downtown hotels. Most rooms have great city and mountain views, but avoid rooms on the freeway side—windows are soundproofed but noise still seeps in. Guests enjoy morning newspapers, shoeshines, a rooftop pool, a Jacuzzi, a fitness center, and high-speed Internet. Amenities on the pricey Club floors include free weekday continental breakfast and hors d'oeuvres at the Club Lounge, complimentary wireless Internet, a terrace, and the best views. Pellini, the restaurant on the 28th floor, offers a selection of Italian food and gorgeous views. Dogs OK. *$$$–$$$$; AE, DC, DIS, JCB, MC, V; no checks; valet and self parking; marriott.com/hotels/travel/seasm; map:M5.* ♿

Residence Inn by Marriott Seattle Downtown at Lake Union / ★☆

800 FAIRVIEW AVE N, SOUTH LAKE UNION; 206/624-6000 OR 800/331-3131

Situated on busy Fairview Avenue in the newly cool South Lake Union neighborhood, this Marriott hotel emphasizes longer stays. About half of the 234 rooms are one-bedroom suites, some boasting lake views. Rooms are spacious with fully outfitted kitchenettes. Continental breakfast and a weekly guest social are presented in the lobby—a light- and plant-filled courtyard with a seven-story atrium and a waterfall. The hotel has no restaurant, but several nearby eateries provide room service. Amenities include meeting rooms, a lap pool, an exercise room, a sauna, a business center, and free high-speed Internet. At press time, the hotel was about to embark on a major room renovation. Pets OK. *$$$–$$$$; AE, DC, DIS, MC, V; checks OK; self parking; residenceinn.com/sealu; map:D1.* ♿

The Roosevelt Hotel / ★

1531 7TH AVE, DOWNTOWN; 206/621-1200 OR 800/663-1144

Built in 1929 but updated for the contemporary traveler, the Roosevelt is a lovely bit of architecture, even if some locals still bemoan the loss of the original grand skylighted lobby. Much of that space is now Von's Grand City Café, famous for martinis and manhattans. The hotel's current lobby is still fairly large, with cozy couches and chairs for listening to the piano man playing his nightly jazz. The hotel's 151 guest rooms include Whirlpool Suites with jetted tubs and Roosevelt Suites with separate seating areas. Those are good choices, because the standard rooms are so small you practically have to squeeze around the bed. The hotel has a fitness center, and all rooms have movie and game systems and a separate work area. Pets OK. *$$–$$$; AE, DC, DIS, JCB, MC, V; checks OK; valet parking; reservations@roosevelthotel.com; roosevelthotel.com; map:J5.* ♿

Seattle Marriott Waterfront / ★★

2100 ALASKAN WY, WATERFRONT; 206/443-5000 OR 800/455-8254

As you might expect from one of only two hotels on the Seattle waterfront, the Marriott offers unparalleled views of the Olympic Mountains and Elliott Bay. But many of its guests may be a bit too preoccupied to enjoy the scenery—it's a popular choice for cruise-ship passengers ready to hop the next Alaska-bound ship at Bell Street Terminal. The 358-room hotel has standard rooms and suites; about half the rooms have a tiny balcony. Amenities include 24-hour room service, high-speed Internet access, and a 24-hour fitness center. The hotel also features a Seattle rarity: an indoor/outdoor pool. The surrounding deck has a view of Puget Sound. See the Restaurants chapter for a review of the hotel's restaurant, the Fish Club by Todd English. No pets. *$$$–$$$$; AE, DC, DIS, JCB, MC, V; no checks; valet or self parking; mhrs.seawf.info@marriott.com; seattlewaterfrontmarriott.com; map:G9.* ♿

Sheraton Seattle Hotel / ★★☆

1400 6TH AVE, DOWNTOWN; 206/621-9000 OR 800/325-3535

A megalith looming over the downtown convention center, the Sheraton bustles with business folks morning, noon, and night. Its existing 838 guest rooms are smallish and standard; a second tower under construction at press time promised 415 new rooms. Each room features original artwork from renowned Seattle glass artist Dale Chihuly and high speed Internet access. Once construction is completed, a lounge and new restaurant, the Daily Grill, will be open on the first floor. The 35th-floor health club features a heated pool and knockout city panorama. No pets. *$$$–$$$$; AE, DC, DIS, JCB, MC, V; no checks; valet parking; sheraton.seattle@sheraton.com; sheraton.com/seattle; map:K5.* ♿

Silver Cloud Inn Stadium / ★★☆

1046 1ST AVE S, SODO; 206/204-9800 OR 800/497-1261

Located right across the street from Safeco Field, home of the Mariners, and adjacent to Qwest Field, home of the Seahawks, this new hotel is already a fan and family favorite. The 211 guest rooms and suites all feature free high-speed Internet access, 42-inch plasma TVs, Aveda bath products, refrigerators, and microwaves. The rooftop pool and patio offer glimpses of the action at the baseball stadium and a superb view of Puget Sound and the Olympics. Other amenities include fitness and business centers and free local transportation. Jimmy's on First, a busy restaurant and sports bar, serves breakfast, lunch, and dinner, and provides room service from 6am to 11pm. No pets. *$$$; AE, DIS, JCB, MC, V; no checks; valet parking; info@silvercloud.com; scinns.com; map:Q9.* ♿

BEST PLACE
FOR A ROMANTIC STROLL?

"A stroll through the Olympic Sculpture Park and a kiss near Roy McMakin's sculpture entitled 'Love and Loss.'"

Mimi Gardner Gates, Seattle Art Museum director

Sorrento Hotel / ★★★☆

900 MADISON ST, FIRST HILL; 206/622-6400 OR 800/426-1265

The gorgeous Italianate Sorrento is every bit as grand today as it was when it opened in the first decade of the 1900s. The beauty of the Sorrento is in the details: elegant furnishings, Italian marble bathrooms, and the plush Fireside Room just off the lobby for taking afternoon tea or an evening cocktail while listening to jazz. The 76 rooms and suites are comfortably luxurious in an old-fashioned way but still bow to technology with DirecTV, CD players, and free high-speed Internet. There's also a small exercise room. Top-floor suites make posh quarters for meetings or parties. The Hunt Club serves Northwest and Mediterranean cuisine (see review in the Restaurants chapter). The Sorrento is a short, though hilly, five-minute walk to the heart of the city—perfect for getting away from it all, without being too far away. Pets OK. *$$$$; AE, DC, DIS, JCB, MC, V; checks OK; valet parking; reservations@hotelsorrento.com; hotelsorrento.com; map:M4.* ♿

W Seattle / ★★★½

1112 4TH AVE, DOWNTOWN; 206/264-6000 OR 877/946-8357

The W is in a class all its own: dressed in postmodern art, velvet drapes, plush furniture, and oversize chess sets—and that's just the lobby. Though the all-black-clad staff is hard to see in the much-too-dark hallways, they're friendly and helpful. Rooms are stylishly simple: taupe and black, with stainless-and-glass bathrooms and Zen-inspired water sculptures. Higher corner rooms have impressive downtown views. Goose-down duvets and pillows and an honor bar with wax lips and "intimacy kits" make for a sexy stay. Room service is available 24 hours, as is the fitness room. Each room comes equipped with a 32-inch plasma TV, high-speed Internet access, and CD and DVD players. A Pet Amenity Program provides pet beds and treats for your pooch. You don't have to go far for great food; just cross the lobby to Earth & Ocean (see review in the Restaurants chapter). Pets OK. *$$$$; AE, DC, DIS, JCB, MC, V; checks OK; valet parking; wseattle.whatwhen@whotels.com; starwoodhotels.com/whotels/seattle; map:L6.* ♿

Warwick Seattle Hotel / ★½

401 LENORA ST, BELLTOWN; 206/443-4300 OR 800/426-9280

The Warwick makes up for its dated '70s-era exterior on the inside, which is warm and inviting. The 226 rooms and four suites are large and comfortable, with elegant furnishings, floor-to-ceiling windows, small balconies (ask for a room above the sixth floor for a great view), and marble bathrooms. TVs, movies, robes, and minibars complete the business-friendly rooms. The 24-hour health club includes a short pool, spa, and sauna. The hotel's restaurant, Brasserie Margaux, features Northwest- and French-inspired seafood and local produce. Room service is available 24 hours, as is the business center. No pets. *$$$; AE, DC, DIS, MC, V; no checks; valet and self parking; res.seattle@warwickhotels.com; warwickwa.com; map:H6.* ♿

The Westin Seattle / ★★½

1900 5TH AVE, DOWNTOWN; 206/728-1000 OR 800/228-3000

The Westin's twin cylindrical towers may look outdated, but the spacious rooms provide some of the best views in the city, especially above the 20th floor. The gargantuan size of the hotel (891 rooms and 34 suites) contributes to some lapses in service: the check-in counter can resemble a busy day at Sea-Tac Airport. But rooms are comfortable, and beds have cozy pillow-top mattresses. Hotel amenities are corporate minded: a business center, convention facilities, and a multilingual staff. You'll also find a large pool and Jacuzzi with a city view and an exercise room. On the top floors are some ritzy suites suitable for all manner of CEOs, finance ministers, and sultans. Coldwater Bar and Grill serves fresh seafood and Northwest regional cuisine. No pets. *$$$–$$$$; AE, DC, DIS, JCB, MC, V; no checks; valet and self parking; washi@westin.com; starwoodhotels.com/westin/seattle; map:H5.* ♿

Capitol Hill

Bacon Mansion / ★★

959 BROADWAY E, CAPITOL HILL; 206/329-1864 OR 800/240-1864

Built by Cecil Bacon in 1909, this Edwardian Tudor-style mansion is home to a classy bed-and-breakfast, with lovingly restored woodwork and common areas featuring antique rugs, a grand piano, and a library. Nine rooms in the main guest house (seven with private baths) are appointed with antiques and brass fixtures. The top of the line is the Capitol Suite, a huge room on the second floor with a sunroom, a fireplace, a pine empress bed, sofa sleeper, and a view of the Space Needle. The Carriage House, a separate two-story building with adjoining rooms, is wheelchair accessible and appropriate for a small family or two couples. All rooms have TVs and phones. There's a peaceful flower garden in the courtyard, and the inn is a brief walk to Broadway's numerous restaurants and shops. Pets OK in the Carriage House. *$$–$$$; AE, DIS, MC, V; no checks; self and street parking; info@baconmansion.com; baconmansion.com; map:GG6.*

Gaslight Inn / ★★½

1727 15TH AVE, CAPITOL HILL; 206/325-3654

Not your traditional lace-and-antique kind of bed-and-breakfast, the Gaslight mixes modern elements such as vibrant glass art with period pieces like a stuffed gazelle head mounted over the living room fireplace. Of the eight guest rooms, five have private baths (shared baths are accessed by a staircase), one has a fireplace, and all are gorgeously decorated in a distinct style—some contemporary, some antique, and some Mission. The 1906 Arts & Crafts–style home features an inviting library and living room with fireplace. Sun worshippers gravitate to the outdoor heated swimming pool, open Memorial Day through Labor Day, but if you prefer the shade, head to the cool side garden adjacent to the koi pond. Three-night minimum on summer weekends. No kids or pets (except the inn's dog and cat). *$$–$$$; AE, MC, V; checks OK; self parking; innkeepr@gaslight-inn.com; gaslight-inn.com; map:HH6.*

Salisbury House / ★★★

750 16TH AVE E, CAPITOL HILL; 206/328-8682

This bed-and-breakfast in an elegant turn-of-the-20th-century Capitol Hill home is an exquisite hostelry on a tree-lined residential street near Volunteer Park, one of Seattle's biggest and lushest parks. Glossy maple floors and lofty beamed ceilings lend a sophisticated air to the guest library (with a chess table and a fireplace). Up the wide staircase and past the second-level sun porch are four corner guest rooms, two recently renovated and all with full baths. For longer stays, try the lower-level suite with its private entrance, fireplace, refrigerator, and whirlpool tub (also available for weekly "lodging only" rates). Friendly innkeeper Cathryn Wiese serves a sumptuous meatless breakfast—for a sunny treat, eat on the terrace. Classy and dignified, devoid of televisions (except the suite), the Salisbury is a sure bet in one of Seattle's finest neighborhoods. Two-night minimum during summer, although they can be flexible. No children under 12. No pets (except for the owner's two cats). *$$–$$$; AE, MC, V; checks OK; street parking; sleep@salisburyhouse.com; salisburyhouse.com; map:HH6.*

University District/North End

Canal Cottages / ★

3443 NW 54TH ST, BALLARD; NO PHONE, CELL NUMBER PROVIDED TO GUESTS EN ROUTE; RESERVATIONS VIA E-MAIL ONLY

If you're looking for a true Seattle experience of water and boats, stay at the Canal Cottages. Two bright and cozy renovated cottages on the Ship Canal, near the mouth of Puget Sound, provide privacy, views of the commercial ships and pleasure boats using the Hiram M. Chittenden Locks, and the occasional loud rumble of trains on the trestle overhead. The Boathouse offers one bedroom, a fully stocked kitchen, living room, good-size bathroom, bay window, and a private deck. The spacious Caretaker's Cottage has two bedrooms, a den, kitchen, living room, large bathroom, woodstove, and wraparound deck with outdoor dining table. Cross the bridge and visit Discovery Park, with miles of walking trails, beaches, and breathtaking views of the Sound and the Olympic Mountains. Two-night minimum stay on weekends and holidays; special rates available for extended stays. Closely supervised children 10 and older are welcome. No pets. *$$; no credit cards; checks, traveler's checks OK (half due in advance to hold reservation); self parking; stay@canalcottages.com; canalcottages.com; map:FF8.*

Chambered Nautilus / ★★☆

5005 22ND AVE NE, UNIVERSITY DISTRICT; 206/522-2536 OR 800/545-8459

This lovely 1915 Georgian colonial guesthouse is set on a steep, woodsy hillside just one block below the University of Washington's Greek Row, but unless it's pledge week, you wouldn't know it. Six charming and comfortable guest rooms, all with private baths, share the main house. Four rooms open onto porches with views of the Cascades; the Rose and Garden rooms share a porch. The Crows Nest has a cozy window seat and fireplace. An annex next door houses four University Suites appointed with full kitchens, antique iron queen beds, and sofa couches. Suites are available for long-term stays between October and May. All of the rooms have free wireless Internet, cable TV, robes, antique writing desks, bottled water, gourmet chocolates, and resident teddy bears. A three-course breakfast is included. Kids of all ages allowed in the University Suites, 8 and older in the main house. Pets OK in University Suites. *$$–$$$; AE, MC, V; checks OK; street parking; stay@chamberednautilus.com; chamberednautilus.com; map:FF6.*

BEST PLACE
TO STAGE A PROTEST?

"In front of the Westin Hotel behind sawhorses and police on horses. At least that's the place to be when a visiting head of state comes by."

Charles R. Cross, author of Heavier Than Heaven: The Biography of Kurt Cobain

The College Inn / ★

4000 UNIVERSITY WY NE, UNIVERSITY DISTRICT; 206/633-4441

This is Seattle's best version of a European hostel—27 private rooms in a 1909 Tudor building with Historic Register status. Just steps from the University of Washington, the hotel is appealingly collegial, with locker-room-type facilities for men and women on each floor, an atticlike communal sitting area (where they serve a generous continental breakfast), and a young, knowledgeable staff. No TVs or radios, but all rooms have phones. It can get a little noisy from the street and a café and pub downstairs. For peace and quiet, stay on the third floor. Each room has a sink and desk, and the best of the lot have window seats. There's a high-speed Internet room for guests. Take advantage of the wild and wacky world that is the University District, or hop on the bus for a short ride to downtown. No pets. *$; MC, V; no checks; street parking; mgr@collegeinnseattle.com; collegeinnseattle.com; map:FF6.*

Hotel Deca / ★★★

4507 BROOKLYN AVE NE, UNIVERSITY DISTRICT; 206/634-2000 OR 800/899-0251

This recently renovated and redecorated U District landmark is a supremely appealing boutique hotel built in the 1930s. The 16-story art deco tower encases 158 rooms (including three suites) beautifully styled in yellows, reds, and blues and featuring down bedding, 32-inch flat-screen TVs, iPod docking stations, and wireless Internet access. The octagonal-tower design affords every one of the rooms a bay window with an incredible view of water and/or mountains. Some rooms have refrigerators and microwaves. The swanky, spacious top-floor Presidential Suite boasts a two-sided gas fireplace, wet bar, 1,000 square feet of patio, and a breathtaking view of the Cascade and Olympic mountains—and everything in between. Rates include free parking and a continental breakfast buffet. The District lounge on the lower level is a restaurant and bar with occasional live music, and there's a

Tully's Coffee in the lobby. No pets. *$$$; AE, DC, DIS, MC, V; no checks; self parking; hoteldeca.com; map:FF7.* ♿

University Inn / ★☆

4140 ROOSEVELT WY NE, UNIVERSITY DISTRICT; 206/632-5055 OR 800/733-3855

This is a bright, clean, well-managed establishment. Rooms in the newer south wing are more spacious; some have king-size beds. North-wing rooms are more standard, with shower stalls in the bathrooms (no tubs). Some have small balconies overlooking the heated outdoor pool (open seasonally) and hot tub. All 102 rooms have a cool triangular, floor-to-ceiling bay window nook so you can enjoy the territorial views. Amenities include free wireless Internet access, a complimentary continental breakfast, afternoon snack, morning paper, a tiny exercise room, free off-street parking, laundry facilities, business center, and two conference rooms. The hotel's Portage Bay Café serves up breakfast, lunch, and weekend brunches. Dogs OK. *$$; AE, DC, DIS, JCB, MC, V; checks OK; self parking; reservations@universityinnseattle.com; universityinnseattle.com; map:FF7.* ♿

Watertown / ★★

4242 ROOSEVELT WY NE, UNIVERSITY DISTRICT; 206/826-4242 OR 866/944-4242

This is the upscale sister hotel of the University Inn just two blocks south (see review above). Watertown is more luxurious, with postmodern furniture, bamboo floors in the lobby, and TVs that swivel to face the bathroom if you need your news fix while shaving. One hundred studios and suites come with free high-speed Internet access, microwave, and refrigerator. Suites have a pull-out sofa bed and wet bar. Jacuzzi suites have two-person tubs. The hotel has a fitness center, general store, free underground parking, free local shuttle, and three meeting rooms, and offers free newspapers and a hot breakfast bar, and access to the seasonal pool and spa at University Inn. Thoughtful amenities include loaner bicycles and complimentary "Ala Carts" (push carts filled with board games or spa amenities delivered to your room). No pets. *$$$; AE, DC, DIS, MC, V; checks OK; self parking; reservations@watertownseattle.com; watertownseattle.com; map:FF7.* ♿

Queen Anne/Seattle Center

Hampton Inn & Suites / ★☆

700 5TH AVE N, SEATTLE CENTER; 206/282-7700 OR 800/426-7866

Located within strolling distance from the Seattle Center and Lower Queen Anne eateries, this efficient facility houses 198 rooms and suites. It's a practical, though not luxurious, place to lay your head, and guests here are mostly business travelers and families with full tourist schedules that keep them away most of the day. All rooms are comfortable and include free local phone calls, high-speed Internet access, and satellite TVs. One- and two-bedroom suites feature multiple televisions and a gas fireplace, small kitchen, and balcony. The hotel has free parking in a gated, underground garage, an exercise room, laundry facilities, a business center, and complimentary continental breakfast. No pets. *$$$; AE, DC, DIS, JCB, MC, V; no checks; self parking; hamptoninnseattle.com; map:A4.* ♿

MarQueen Hotel / ★★½

600 QUEEN ANNE AVE N, QUEEN ANNE; 206/282-7407 OR 888/445-3076

Entering the MarQueen Hotel feels like you've stepped into an Edith Wharton novel. The opulent lobby of this 1918 building is lined in dark mahogany wainscoting and stocked with graceful fin de siècle furnishings. Amenities in the spacious 56 rooms include hardwood floors, TVs, minikitchens with a built-in table and benches, coffeemakers, microwaves, refrigerators, robes, a free newspaper, and complimentary overnight shoeshine. Some rooms have full ranges with ovens, and a few have glassed-in parlors. Rooms on the east side are darker than the sunlit rooms facing west. Lunch and dinner room service is available from the nearby Ten Mercer restaurant; breakfast room service is provided by the hotel's bakery and espresso bar, Caffe Ladro. Intermezzo Salon & Spa is located in the lobby. No pets. *$$$; AE, DC, DIS, JCB, MC, V; no checks; valet parking; info@marqueen.com; marqueen.com; map:A7.*

Eastside

Bellevue Club Hotel / ★★★

11200 SE 6TH ST, BELLEVUE; 425/454-4424 OR 800/579-1110

One of the most elegant hotels in the Seattle area, the Bellevue Club is part hotel, part upscale athletic club, part world-class spa. It's hidden inside lush plantings in an office park just blocks from Interstate 405. The 67 rooms feature sunken tubs and original pieces by Northwest artists, as well as cherrywood furniture custom-made on Whidbey Island and luxurious 500-thread-count sheets. Many of the Asian-inspired rooms overlook the tennis courts; Club guest rooms' French doors open onto private terra-cotta patios. The greatest benefit is the attached athletic and spa facilities, including an Olympic-size swimming pool, indoor tennis, racquetball, squash courts, group fitness classes, and a full menu of therapeutic and medical spa services. The club offers fine dining at Polaris restaurant, cocktails at Cosmos, casual fare at Splash Café, and coffee at Luna Express. Small pets OK. *$$$–$$$$; AE, DC, DIS, MC, V; checks OK; valet and self parking; hotel@bellevueclub.com; bellevueclub.com; map:HH3.* ♿

Hilton Bellevue / ★★

300 112TH AVE SE, BELLEVUE; 425/455-1300 OR 800/445-8667

The Hilton Bellevue's 179 recently updated rooms are fairly plain, done up in muted browns and burgundy, but comfortable. All rooms are essentially the same size, although sixth- and seventh-floor executive-level rooms have more work space. However, the hotel's close proximity to the Meydenbauer Center for conferences, plus amenities such as a free shuttle to Bellevue Square, room service, a Jacuzzi, a sauna, a pool and exercise area, cable TV, and a restaurant, make the Hilton a solid lodging bet for business travelers. Working stiffs will appreciate the high-speed Internet access, desks in every room, and a Tully's Coffee in the seven-story atrium. No pets. *$$$; AE, DC, DIS, JCB, MC, V; checks OK; self parking; info@bellevuehilton.com; bellevuehilton.com; map:HH3.* ♿

BEST PLACE
TO SEE A MOVIE?

"The new theatres at Lincoln Center in Bellevue. The seating is great! The chairs are big and comfortable, and you have no problem seeing over the people in front of you."

Herb Weisbaum, consumer reporter, KOMO News

Hyatt Regency Bellevue / ★★☆

900 BELLEVUE WY NE, BELLEVUE; 425/462-1234 OR 800/233-1234

This Hyatt is part of the splashy retail/office/restaurant/hotel/health club complex called Bellevue Place, which in turn is part of the trifecta known as the Bellevue Collection, which also includes Bellevue Square and Lincoln Square. You can't miss the 24-story, 382-room hotel with its two-toned brick exterior. But it's not just big—you get many extras: some great territorial views (particularly south-side rooms above the seventh floor), 32-inch flat-panel TVs, access to a health club, high-speed Internet access, and a free morning newspaper. Guests who book Regency Club rooms on the top two floors get access to a 23rd-floor lounge with continental breakfast and evening hors d'oeuvres. Nearby dining options are numerous, including the onsite 0/8 Seafood Grill and Twisted Cork Wine Bar. The hotel mostly attracts weekday business travelers, so on the weekends, it offers low rates to entice leisure travelers. No pets. *$$$–$$$$; AE, DC, DIS, JCB, MC, V; checks OK; valet and self parking; bellevue.hyatt.com; map:HH3.* ♿

Residence Inn Seattle Bellevue / ★★

14455 NE 29TH PL, BELLEVUE; 425/882-1222 OR 800/331-3131

These 120 condolike suites just off Highway 520 in east Bellevue are a comfortable home away from home for business travelers or families on extended stays. Each unit has separate bedrooms, a living room with fireplace, a full kitchen (they'll even do your grocery shopping), high-speed Internet, and a free evening snack with beer and wine. A complimentary hot breakfast buffet is provided in the main building. Less than 1 mile from Microsoft, the complex has an outdoor pool and Jacuzzis, a workout room, and a sport court. Pets OK. *$$$; AE, DC, DIS, MC, V; checks OK; self parking; residenceinnseattle.com; map:GG2.* ♿

The Westin Bellevue / ★★½

600 BELLEVUE WAY, BELLEVUE; 425/638-1000; 866/716-8126

This sleek new high-rise hotel dominates the downtown Bellevue skyline and anchors Lincoln Square, a posh mixed-use hotel/condominium/retail complex. The 337 spacious and stylish rooms (the hotel also has 28 suites) offer views of the city, mountains, or Lake Washington, and feature 32-inch flat-screen TVs, 24-hour room service, free daily newspaper, and Westin's famously comfortable beds. All guests have access to a heated indoor lap pool with outdoor sun deck, fitness center with whirlpool, running maps, and a 24-hour business center. Northwest cuisine is served at Manzana Rotisserie Grill, and numerous shops and restaurants are just steps from the hotel. Small pets OK. *$$$$; AE, DC, DIS, MC, V; no checks; valet and self parking; westin.bellevue@westin.com; westin.com; map:HH3.* ♿

Willows Lodge / ★★★½

14580 NE 145TH ST, WOODINVILLE; 425/424-3900 OR 877/424-3930

If you're a wine lover, there is no better place to stay than Willows Lodge. Nestled in the heart of Woodinville wine country, this quintessential Northwest hotel blends perfectly with its wooded surroundings. The 88 rooms of the luxe lodge are classified as "nice," "nicer," and "nicest," and even the "nice" rooms are fabulous. Slate bath tile, reclaimed timber shelves, rock-lined fireplaces, DVD/CD systems, free high-speed Internet, lush bathrooms ("nicest" rooms have jetted tubs and heated towel racks), and complimentary breakfast are just a few of the reasons to stay here. Other perks are a spa, 24-hour fitness room, Japanese garden, and evening wine tastings. Even better, Chateau Ste. Michelle, Columbia Winery, and a multitude of small boutique wineries are just a stone's throw away. The Barking Frog restaurant (see review in the Restaurants chapter) serves Mediterranean-influenced dinners and weekend brunch. Guests also have access to nine-course meals at the renowned Herbfarm Restaurant (see review in the Restaurants chapter). Pets OK. *$$$$; AE, DC, DIS, JCB, MC, V; checks OK; self parking; mail@willowslodge.com; willowslodge.com; map:BB2.* ♿

The Woodmark Hotel, Yacht Club & Spa / ★★★

1200 CARILLON POINT, KIRKLAND; 425/822-3700 OR 800/822-3700

The only hotel nestled right on the shoreline of Lake Washington, the Woodmark is tucked inside the elite enclave of Carillon Point on the east side of the lake. The four-story brick hotel is just steps from the marina, shops, and restaurants. One hundred guest rooms, about half with stunning lake views, offer a relaxing retreat of cream-colored furnishings and extras such as minibars, soaking tubs, and comfy robes. Some rooms have balconies with table and chairs; the others at least have doors that open to let in the sound of lapping water. All guests get a complimentary newspaper, free Internet access, and a chance to "raid the pantry" when the restaurant lays out a complimentary late-night buffet. Down the grand staircase is the comfortable Library Bar, with a grand piano and overstuffed chairs in front of the fireplace. The hotel's restaurant, Waters, features Northwest cuisine focusing on local and organic farmers. Pets OK. *$$$–$$$$; AE, DC, JCB, MC, V; local checks OK; valet and self parking; mail@thewoodmark.com; thewoodmark.com; map:EE3.* ♿

Airport Area

Doubletree Hotel Seattle Airport / ★★

18740 INTERNATIONAL BLVD, SEATAC; 206/246-8600 OR 800/222-8733
Guests at this enormous 14-story hotel enjoy the spoils of a well-calibrated operation and, in the east-facing rooms, a view of the Cascades. With 850 rooms and 12 suites, all with balconies, services here are primed to handle scores of conventioneers and business travelers with 24-hour airport shuttle, high-speed Internet access, a notary public, and secretarial service. Diners can choose from a family-style restaurant or sports bar. On-site amenities include a workout room and pool. Pets OK. *$$$; AE, DC, DIS, JCB, MC, V; checks OK; valet and self parking; doubletree.hilton.com; map:PP6.* ♿

Hilton Seattle Airport & Conference Center / ★★

17620 INTERNATIONAL BLVD, SEATAC; 206/244-4800 OR 800/445-8667
In addition to 396 rooms (including seven suites), this well-run hotel directly across from Sea-Tac Airport is home to 39,000 square feet of state-of-the-art meeting and conference facilities and a 24-hour business center. Rooms are set around two landscaped courtyards with a pool and indoor/outdoor Jacuzzi, and include comfortable desks, computer hookups, high-speed Internet access, coffeemakers, and WebTV. The hotel also has a fitness room, and the restaurant, Spencer's for Steaks and Chops, serves all meals. Room service (limited menu midnight to 6am) and complimentary airport shuttle run 24 hours a day. Small pets OK. *$$$; AE, DC, DIS, JCB, MC, V; checks OK; valet and self parking; hilton.com; map:OO5.* ♿

Radisson Hotel Gateway Seattle-Tacoma Airport / ★★

18118 INTERNATIONAL BLVD, SEATAC; 206/244-6666 OR 800/996-3426
Most services and amenities at this slightly more upscale airport hotel are provided with business travelers in mind, but there are nonetheless some thoughtful details in the 204 newly renovated rooms and suites. Rooms feature free wireless Internet access, marbled bathroom floors and granite countertops, pillow top mattresses, and Herman Miller ergonomic chairs.

The hotel also provides free 24-hour shuttle service to the airport, an indoor heated pool and whirlpool, a fitness center, free parking, and more than 4,000 square feet of meeting and banquet space. Gateway Bar & Grill serves breakfast, lunch, and dinner and provides room service from 6am to 11pm. Kids 18 and under stay free. No pets. *$$$; AE, DC, DIS, JCB, MC, V; no checks; self parking; radisson.com; map:OO5.* ♿

Seattle Airport Marriott / ★★

3201 S 176TH ST, SEATAC; 206/241-2000 OR 800/314-0925

The swift service at this 459-room megahotel makes transfer to and from Sea-Tac Airport virtually painless. Convenience doesn't come at the expense of enjoyment, though. The lobby, with its warm Northwest motif, opens into an enormous atrium complete with indoor pool and two Jacuzzis. For slightly higher rates than the standard rooms, five more-spacious, handsomely appointed suites are available, and rooms on the concierge floor include a lounge that serves continental breakfasts and nightly nibbles. All rooms have high-speed Internet, and all guests have access to a well-equipped exercise room. A casual dining room and lounge offer the usual hotel fare. No pets. *$$$; AE, DC, DIS, JCB, MC, V; checks OK; valet and self parking; marriott.com; map:PP6.* ♿

EXPLORING

EXPLORING

Top 25 Attractions

1) PIKE PLACE MARKET

PIKE STREET TO VIRGINIA STREET, BETWEEN 1ST AND WESTERN AVENUES, CENTERED ON PIKE PLACE, DOWNTOWN; 206/682-7453

It's hard to imagine that **PIKE PLACE MARKET**, regarded as the soul of Seattle, was almost torn down in the 1970s to make way for "urban renewal." Opened on August 17, 1907, in response to farmer and consumer complaints about unscrupulous middlemen, the United States' oldest continuously operating farmers' market remains a boisterous bazaar, aggressively eschewing chain stores or franchise operations (except, of course, for Starbucks, which opened its first store in 1971 at the Market). Visit before 9am to watch the Market come alive as the farmers set up, then spend the day meandering its nooks and crannies, nibbling from its astonishing variety of ethnic and regional foods, browsing the shops, and watching the street-corner musicians, puppeteers, and mimes. The official entrance is at the corner of First Avenue and Pike Street, at the volunteer-run **INFORMATION BOOTH** (10am–noon), where you can pick up a map and some advice on sights or a self-guided-tour pamphlet. (The booth doubles as a day-of-show, half-price ticket outlet, called **TICKET/TICKET**, 206/324-2744; noon–6pm Tues–Sat.) **FIRST AND PIKE NEWS** (206/624-0140; firstandpikenews.com), an extensive newsstand carrying national and international newspapers and magazines, anchors this busy corner. So does **DELAURENTI SPECIALTY FOOD MARKET** (206/622-0141; delaurenti.com), a beloved Italian deli/café. Just to the south is the South Arcade, home to modern-looking shops and condos that have spread forth from the 7-acre Market Historic District. Walking west from here, down the covered corridor of the Economy Arcade, you'll chance upon **MARKET SPICE** (206/622-6340; marketspice.com) in the left corner, a market depot for tea, bulk spices, and coffees for more than 90 years. Here, at the elbow of the L-shaped market, you'll find the big bronze pig named Rachel and weekend crowds that delight in the salmon-throwing antics of salespeople at **PIKE PLACE FISH** (206/682-7181; pikeplacefish.com). This is the start of the Main Arcade—the famous neon Pike Place Market sign and clock are just above you—where produce vendors display beautifully arranged international produce and seasonal, regional produce. In the midst of this is a Market institution: the **ATHENIAN INN** (206/624-7166), a working-class café that's been the favorite haunt of Market old-timers since 1909 (and was one of the settings for 1993's *Sleepless in Seattle*). The Main Arcade also has two labyrinthine levels below the street. An outdoor staircase on the Main Arcade's west side leads to the Pike Market Hillclimb, a steep cascade of steps that connects the Market (at Western Avenue) with the waterfront below.

TOP 25 ATTRACTIONS

1) Pike Place Market
2) Seattle Art Museum
3) Space Needle and Seattle Center
4) Olympic Sculpture Park
5) Pioneer Square
6) Safeco Field and Qwest Field
7) Washington State Ferries
8) Woodland Park Zoo
9) Monorail
10) Woodinville Wine Country
11) Seattle Aquarium
12) Seattle Asian Art Museum
13) Pacific Science Center
14) Alki Beach Park
15) Museum of Flight
16) Washington Park Arboretum
17) Ballard Locks
18) Nordstrom and REI
19) Discovery Park
20) Smith Tower
21) Henry Art Gallery
22) Burke-Gilman Trail
23) Gas Works Park
24) Experience Music Project and Science Fiction Museum and Hall of Fame
25) Underground Tour

In summer, the artists' and craftspeople's tables stretch along the Main and North arcades all the way along Pike Place to Virginia Street and **VICTOR STEINBRUECK PARK** (see Parks and Beaches in this chapter), a splash of green that marks the Market's northern border. Across Pike Place from the Main and North arcades, you'll discover shops, ethnic eateries, and the original **STARBUCKS** (206/448-8762; starbucks.com). If you take a short detour here up the wooden stairs to Post Alley, you'll find **THE PINK DOOR** (206/443-3241; thepinkdoor.net), a funky trattoria with terrific summertime porch seating, and **KELLS** (206/728-1916; kellsirish.com), a lively Irish pub and restaurant. Follow Post Alley south, back toward Pike Place; you'll pass the stylish, 70-room **INN AT THE MARKET** (206/443-3600; innatthemarket.com), the Market's only sizable hotel. Back on Pike Place heading south, watch cheese makers at work at **BEECHER'S HANDMADE CHEESE** (206/956-1964; beechershandmadecheese.com) while you enjoy a grilled-to-order sandwich or their self-proclaimed "world's best" mac and cheese. Stop by **MEE SUM PASTRIES** (206/682-6780) for savory Chinese pot stickers, or score balcony seating and a dish of flavorful paella at the **COPACABANA CAFE** (206/622-6359), the city's only Bolivian restaurant. **SUR LA TABLE** (206/448-2244; surlatable.com) is a nationally acclaimed cook's emporium. Inside the Sanitary Market (so named because horses were not allowed inside) is a chaotic jumble of produce stands and eating places, including the **PIKE PLACE MARKET CREAMERY** (206/622-5029), which sells delicious dairy goods; **JACK'S FISH SPOT** (206/467-0514), purveyor of steaming cups of cioppino from an outdoor bar; and **THREE GIRLS BAKERY** (206/622-1045), an excellent

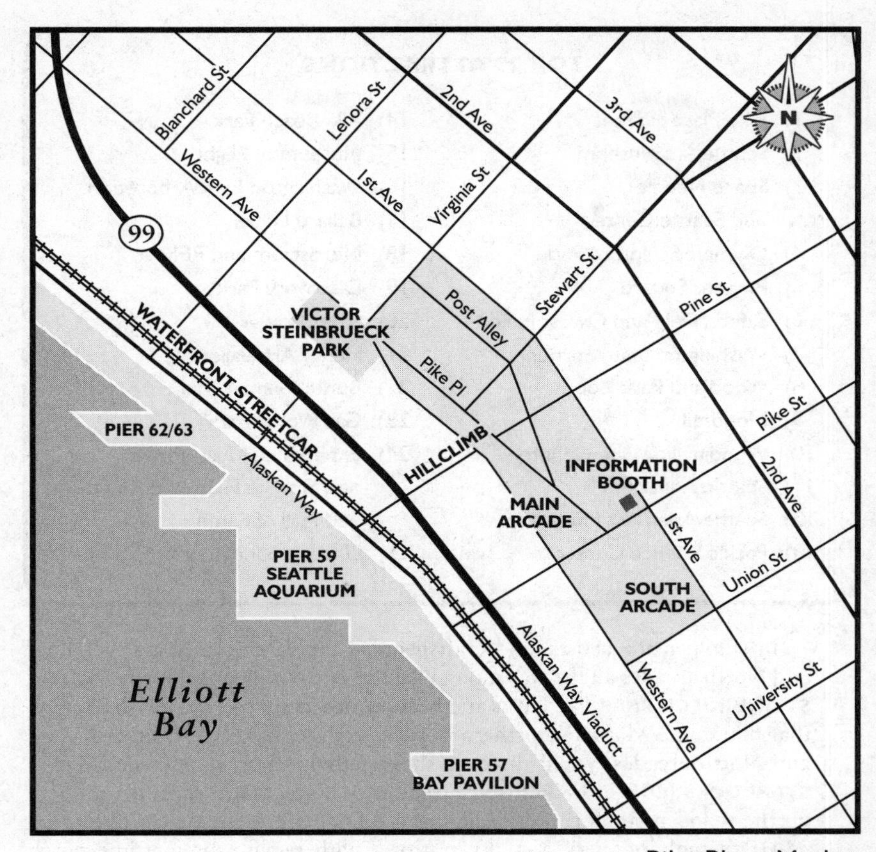

Pike Place Market

sandwich counter that's easily identified by its long line of regulars. Just to the south is the last building in this historic stretch: the picturesque Corner Market houses produce and flower stalls. A couple of restaurants are hidden in its upper reaches: the newly expanded and remodeled **MATT'S IN THE MARKET** (206/467-7909; mattsinthemarket.com), a cozy perch from which to enjoy a lunchtime oyster po'boy; and **CHEZ SHEA** (206/467-9990; chezshea.com), perhaps the most romantic nook in town. Post Alley continues on the south side of Pike Street as it dips below street level and passes the dimly lit Italian restaurant **IL BISTRO** (206/682-3049; ilbistro.net) and the **MARKET THEATER** (206/781-9273; unexpectedproductions.org), home to Unexpected Productions, an improvisational comedy-theater troupe. It's almost impossible to get a parking space on congested Pike Place, so either come by bus or splurge for a space in the 550-slot parking garage on Western Avenue, with its elevator that opens directly into the Market. Alternatively, try one of the lots a little farther south on Western or along First Avenue to the north. *Every day; information@pikeplacemarket.org; pikeplacemarket.org; map:J8–I8.*

2) SEATTLE ART MUSEUM

1300 1ST AVE, DOWNTOWN; 206/654-3100

After a two-year expansion and renovation, the Robert Venturi–designed Seattle Art Museum (SAM) reopened in May 2007 with a new wing, almost doubling its space from 150,000 to 268,000 square feet. With the expansion, SAM now has 70 percent more gallery space for its collection and exhibition programs. Enter through the new public entrance at First Avenue and Union Street or use the former main First Avenue entrance, where you are welcomed by sculptor Jonathan Borofsky's 48-foot mechanical "Hammering Man." The new museum includes two free floors where the public can interact with art. On the second floor, the 5,000-square-foot Brotman Forum is a gathering space for visitors, as well as the site for major rotating contemporary installations such as the inaugural piece, "Inopportune: Stage One" (2004), artist Cai Guo-Qiang's series of nine Ford Tauruses spraying rays of multicolored light as they tumbled across the hallway. The third level emphasizes modern and contemporary art and includes a double-height gallery with flexible spaces to accommodate larger works. The fourth-floor galleries showcase European, African, and Islamic art, among other genres. In addition to a special exhibition space, a gallery dedicated to recent acquisitions has been set aside for the very first time on this level. A lecture room and a 300-seat auditorium lend themselves to talks, films, music, and dramatic performances; there are two art studios for classes and hands-on art making. The revamp also expanded the first-rate museum store and Taste restaurant, which offers creative cuisine with a passion for locally grown foods and artisan products. Every Thursday evening SAM stays open late, with refreshments, live music, and performances; admission is free to all on the first Thursday of the month. General admission is a suggested $13 donation for adults, $10 for seniors, $7 for students and youth (13–19), and free for children 12 and under. (Admission tickets also may be used for entry to the Seattle Asian Art Museum in Volunteer Park—see listing #12 below—within a week of purchase.) *Tues–Sun; seattleartmuseum.org; map:K7.*

3) SPACE NEEDLE AND SEATTLE CENTER

DENNY WAY TO MERCER STREET, 1ST AVENUE N TO 5TH AVENUE N, QUEEN ANNE; 206/684-8582

Seattle Center is the entertainment hub of this city, attracting more than 12 million visitors every year. This 74-acre park north of downtown, at the base of Queen Anne Hill on the edge of the Denny Regrade, is the prized legacy of the 1962 Century 21 Exposition—Seattle's second world's fair (after the 1909 Alaska-Yukon-Pacific Exposition). Today, the center hosts such popular annual events as the Northwest Folklife Festival (Memorial Day weekend), the Bite of Seattle (mid-July), Bumbershoot (Labor Day weekend), and Festál, a year-round series of cultural community festivals dedicated to the celebration of Seattle's rich ethnic heritage and diverse population. In addition, the **EXPERIENCE MUSIC PROJECT** and the **SCIENCE FICTION MUSEUM AND HALL OF FAME** (see listing #24 below) draw crowds year-round.

Legend has it that the city's most recognized symbol, the 605-foot **SPACE NEEDLE** (206/905-2100; spaceneedle.com)—originally called the Space Cage—began as a doodle sketched on a cocktail napkin by world's fair chairman Eddie Carlson. Architects John Graham Sr., Victor Steinbrueck, and John Ridley translated that into a futuristic concept in metal and glass. When King County commissioners refused to fund the project, a private corporation stepped in and completed the work in an astonishing eight months at a cost of $4.5 million. (The Needle is still privately owned.) Anchored to terra firma by almost 6,000 tons of concrete, the tower was built to withstand winds of up to 200 miles per hour and has already survived two major earthquakes (in 1965 and 2001) unscathed. **SKYCITY** restaurant (206/443-2150; spaceneedle.com/restaurant) is located at the 500-foot level and revolves 360 degrees every hour, giving diners and slow sippers in the bar panoramic views of Puget Sound, the Olympic Mountains, and the city center. The 43-second ride up (restaurant patrons ride free) provides panoramic views on clear days for $15 ($13 seniors, $7 youth ages 4–13, free for younger children). New "SkyQ" kiosks on the observation deck showcase the city through interactive plasma screens, exterior high-definition cameras, and interviews with Seattle residents. *Every day; marketing@spaceneedle.com; spaceneedle.com; map:B6.* ♿

Seattle Center visitors who arrive with children head for the **PACIFIC SCIENCE CENTER** (see listing #13 below). Chances are, they'll also visit the **FUN FOREST** (206/728-1585), a small-scale amusement park near the Space Needle that contains 20 rides, including a Ferris wheel, a wild river ride, a roller coaster, and an indoor pavilion offering laser tag and video games. Ride tickets—purchased individually or in discounted packs—are available at booths within the Fun Forest. Just past the Fun Forest is Memorial Stadium, where high school football games and outdoor concerts are frequently held. The **SEATTLE CHILDREN'S THEATRE** stages surprisingly sophisticated youth entertainment. Adults enjoy the performing arts at a string of other stages arranged along Mercer Street at the center's northern edge. The neon-adorned **BAGLEY WRIGHT THEATRE** is home to the **SEATTLE REPERTORY THEATRE** and the **INTIMAN PLAYHOUSE** currently houses the Intiman Theatre. The spectacular $127 million **MARION OLIVER MCCAW HALL** houses the **SEATTLE OPERA**, the **PACIFIC NORTHWEST BALLET**, and the **NESHOLM FAMILY LECTURE HALL**, the new home of the Seattle International Film Festival. With top-of-the-line projection and sound equipment, the theater is slated to be the top screening facility in the Northwest. A good place to get refreshed (especially on a summer day) is the **INTERNATIONAL FOUNTAIN**, near the center of Seattle Center's grounds, which shoots enormous jets of water from a metal dome into the sky, sometimes synchronized with music and lights. Just to the north is the **NORTHWEST CRAFT CENTER** (206/728-1555; northwestcraftcenter.com), displaying a variety of pottery, crafts, paintings, and jewelry for sale year-round. Should you grow hungry, stop in at the nearby **CENTER HOUSE** (206/684-8582), a cavernous structure filled with ethnic fast food, conventioneers, pre-adolescents looking to be seen, and senior citizens. On the lower level of the Center House is the world-class **CHILDREN'S MUSEUM**. There is no charge to get onto the Seattle Center grounds (except during a few major festivals such as Bumbershoot), but parking can be a problem. The cheapest lots are on the east side. For events at McCaw Hall, Mercer Arts Arena, and the Intiman Playhouse, the covered parking garage directly north across Mercer Street from McCaw Hall affords easy access, but the egress can be maddeningly slow on busy nights. One way to avoid the problem is to take the **MONORAIL** from downtown (see listing below), which drops you off at the Center House. (The Monorail stops running at 9pm, however, so you may have to hail a cab back downtown after a late show.) *Every day; seattlecenter.com; map:B6.*

4) OLYMPIC SCULPTURE PARK

2901 WESTERN AVE (AT BROAD STREET), BELLTOWN; 206/654-3180

After almost 10 years in the making, the $85 million Olympic Sculpture Park opened in 2007, transforming downtown's last and largest waterfront property into a vibrant green space that doubles as a dynamic stage for modern and contemporary art. Designed by New York architects Weiss/Manfredi, the 9-acre park integrates architecture, landscape, urban design, and art in a magnificent setting with the Olympic Mountains, Mount Rainier, and Puget Sound as a backdrop. The park is a vital connection between city and waterfront—it's not everywhere that you can dip your toe in the water in the heart of the urban core. No other park in the United States encompasses the topographic variation, the dramatic views, or the 850-foot strip of restored beach that Seattle's park does. On top of that, the park is not exclusive: it's free and accessible to all, thanks to a $20 million endowment from SAM trustees Jon and Mary Shirley. At the main entrance at Western and Broad, the PACCAR Pavilion houses an exhibition and public event space, as well as the Taste Café, while the adjoining Gates Amphitheater hosts performance art and films. From the pavilion at the top, the park descends to Elliott Bay, leading visitors through four ecologically diverse environments along the way and providing safe access to Seattle's waterfront. The main, 2,500-foot-long path zigzags through continuous landscape adorned with native plants and trees, and merges with two bridges traversing the roadway and railroad. The latter bridge features "Seattle Cloud Cover" by Teresita Fernández, a commissioned 200-foot-long glass bridge adornment. Watch people, sky, and skyline flicker in and out as you walk by the glass laminated with a photographic interlayer of brilliantly colored clouds filtered by tiny dots. Fernández's work is joined by more than 20 artworks by some of the 20th century's most seminal artists. "Wake" by Richard Serra comprises five modules of weatherproof steel, 14 feet by 125 feet by 46 feet, arranged in a parallel S-curve. Each massive component of two fused plates weighs 60,000 pounds. Claes Oldenburg and Coosje van Bruggen's

"Typewriter Eraser, Scale X" is a whimsical pop art blast from the past. Art and science intersect in "Neukom Vivarium" by Mark Dion—a slanted greenhouse encloses a 64-foot log supporting a living web of foliage, algae, and insects. Free. *Every day; seattleartmuseum.org; map:D8.* ♿

5) PIONEER SQUARE

S KING STREET TO YESLER WAY, ALONG 1ST AND 2ND AVENUES, DOWNTOWN

The official birthplace of Seattle, Pioneer Square was originally a Native American village before the white pioneers arrived in 1852. After six short (and probably miserably wet and frigid) months along Alki Beach where they landed in November 1851, Arthur A. Denny and his party relocated to a better-protected area across the bay. The Great Fire of 1889 reduced the city's original downtown to cinders. Although rebuilt according to more architecturally coherent—and less flammable—standards, by the 1960s Pioneer Square had become so run down that city officials proposed leveling it. Fortunately, wiser heads fought to save Pioneer Square and turn it into Seattle's first historic district. Accidents and disasters continue to threaten, however; in 2001 a semitruck accident collapsed the square's graceful pergola, and the Ash Wednesday earthquake brought bricks crashing down into the streets. Both the pergola and buildings damaged in the quake have been rebuilt and reinforced. Encompassing almost 90 acres, Pioneer Square is one of the largest historic districts in the nation. It's a busy place filled with bookstores, art galleries, restaurants, antique shops, and nightclubs. Lawyers, architects, and media folk dominate the workforce. Panhandlers and transients are also drawn here by a preponderance of social services (and park benches).

Seattle's earliest intersection, at First Avenue and Yesler Way, is home to triangular Pioneer Place Park. The park's most prominent fixtures—national historic landmarks both—are its iron-and-glass pergola (the 1909 original served as a waiting area during the days of cable cars) and a Tlingit totem pole (a replacement for one originally stolen from Alaska in 1899 by a group of Seattle businessmen). Facing the park is the **PIONEER BUILDING**, designed by Elmer Fisher, a prolific Scotsman who established the architectural vernacular of post–Great Fire Seattle, synthesizing his Victorian philosophies about facades with the weighty Romanesque revival look. The building houses a maze of antique shops on its lower level and is the headquarters of the **UNDERGROUND TOUR**, a fun subterranean prowl through the original streets of downtown (see listing #25 below). In the mid-19th century, greased logs and trees cut in the Seattle hills were dragged down diagonal **YESLER WAY** to feed pioneer Henry Yesler's waterfront sawmill. The avenue quickly became familiar as "skid road" (often mangled into "skid row"), an early-20th-century insult used to describe inner-city neighborhoods that—like Pioneer Square—had fallen on hard times.

Just across Yesler from Pioneer Place is **MERCHANTS CAFE** (109 Yesler Wy; 206/624-1515), Seattle's oldest restaurant. To the west, **AL BOCCALINO** (1 Yesler Wy; 206/622-7688; seattleslittleitaly.com) is a wonderful nook for a romantic Italian meal. First Avenue is the main, tree-lined artery through

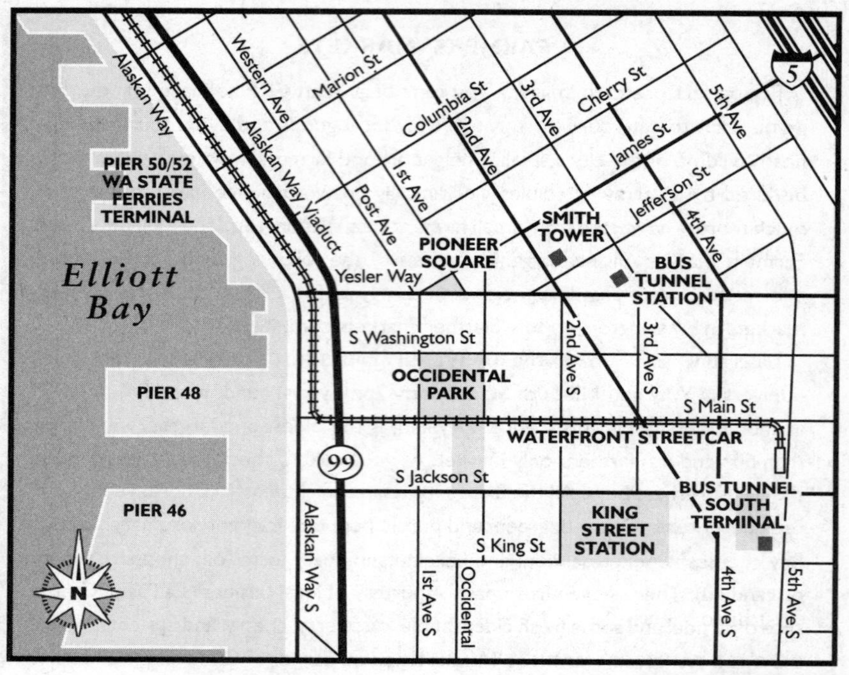

Pioneer Square

the historic district, intersected by streets that terminate at the waterfront a block west. Heading south you'll see the **NEW ORLEANS CREOLE RESTAURANT** (114 1st Ave S; 206/622-2563; neworleanscreolerestaurant.com), a Creole/Cajun eatery known as well for its mint juleps as its Dixieland acts. On the next block is the **GRAND CENTRAL ARCADE.** Opened in 1879 by entrepreneur (and, later, Washington governor) Watson C. Squire, the structure housed Seattle's first real theater. It now contains two levels of eclectic retail, including the excellent **GRAND CENTRAL BAKING COMPANY** (214 1st Ave S; 206/622-3644; grandcentralbakery.com). A few blocks from the Grand Central is the **KLONDIKE GOLD RUSH VISITOR CENTER** (319 2nd Ave S; 206/220-4240; nps.gov/klse), which pays homage to those who headed north during the 1890s in search of gold in Canada's Yukon. Interactive exhibits highlight Seattle's role in this international event, from touch-screen computers that allow you to experience the gold rush through the eyes of actual stampeders, to gold-panning demonstrations and a ranger-led walking tour of Pioneer Square Historic District in the afternoon. The free museum is the southernmost unit for the National Park Service's Klondike Gold Rush historical sites. (Other units are the town of Skagway and the famous Chilkoot Trail, both in southeast Alaska.) At First Avenue S and S Main Street is the renowned **ELLIOTT BAY BOOK COMPANY** (101 S Main St; 206/624-6600; elliottbaybook.com). Since opening in 1973 the shop has

FARMERS' MARKETS

For perfect postcard imagery, you can't beat Seattle's Pike Place Market. But if you want to eat your way through truly local goods and avoid tourist bustle, head to some of the city's smaller neighborhood farmers' markets, where you'll be lured by an array of edibles—organically grown produce, jams, honey, and much more—harvested from small farms across Washington. The Neighborhood Farmers Market Alliance organizes seven of the following markets. For more information, go to seattlefarmersmarkets.org, or for a listing of all the farmers' markets in Washington, go to wafarmersmarkets.com.

Operating since 1993, the **UNIVERSITY DISTRICT FARMERS' MARKET** (University Way and NE 50th St; Sat 9am–2pm, year-round; map:FF6), located at the University Heights Center Playfield, is the oldest and largest (with more than 50 vendors) farmers-only market. As you walk in, check the chalkboard for the day's freshest buys. All the fixings for a same-night feast are here: yellow and red cherry tomatoes; red, green, and purple peppers; fragrant rosemary; Samish Bay cheeses; smoked salmon; and hazelnuts in every form (oil, chopped, sliced, or candied). There's even fresh pasta, courtesy of local business La Pasta. Grab a slice of strudel and some fresh cider (apple, raspberry, cherry, and apricot). **WEST SEATTLE FARMERS' MARKET** (Alaska Junction, corner of California Avenue and SW Alaska Street; Sun 10am–2pm, year-round except March; map:JJ9) is a newer market; you'll see many of the same vendors here as in the U District, selling Walla Walla sweet onions, bunches of fresh basil, artisan breads, goat cheese, and just-caught shellfish. **COLUMBIA CITY FARMERS' MARKET** (Rainier Avenue S at S Edmunds Street; Wed 3–7pm, May–Oct; map:JJ6), located south of Mount Baker and neighbor to the Chinatown/International District, attracts diverse and chatty crowds—from Muslim women wearing headscarves to yuppies in Lexuses. Along with organic seasonal crops, Skagit River Ranch stocks coolers with certified organic meats, from grass-fed-only Angus beef and burger patties to whole chicken. Like Columbia City, **MAGNOLIA FARMERS' MARKET** (2550 34th Ave W; Sat 10am–2pm, June–Oct; map:GG9) truly reflects its neighborhood: in this case, affluent. Pleasantly nestled in the below-street-level Magnolia Community Center parking lot, it tempts with bunches of flowers, honey, fruit and veggie vendors, and slices of pie. Try a few flaky rugelach, a rolled flaky pastry made with cream cheese and filled with nuts and fruit (the currant or chocolate are divine), to fuel your stall

become Seattle's premier independent bookstore, boasting more than 150,000 new and used titles, and readings and signings that draw the nation's most distinguished authors almost nightly. Occidental Avenue S, a sun-dappled, brick-lined cruising. After you've collected your goodies, a prime spot for a picnic is right on Magnolia Bluff overlooking the Sound. The three youngest markets, **BROADWAY** (parking lot behind Bank of America, 230 Broadway E; Sun 11am–3pm, May–Nov; map:GG6), **LAKE CITY** (NE 127th St and 30th Ave NE; Thurs 3–7pm, May–Oct; map:CC6) and **PHINNEY RIDGE** (Phinney Neighborhood Center, 6532 Phinney Ave N; Fri 3–7pm, Jun–Sept; map:EE7) are no less well stocked. They offer items from unusual—such as Greenwater Farm's hardy kiwis (resembling large grapes, they are sweet without the tart edge of regular kiwis) in the fall and Bruschettina's grilled toasts topped with next-door farmer's ingredients (think puréed beets and ricotta cheese)—to everyday: luscious peaches from Rama Farm, Russ's River Organica baked goods, and Loki Fish locally caught salmon. **FREMONT SUNDAY MARKET** (N 34th Street, between Phinney Avenue and Evanston Avenue N; Sun 10am–5pm, Apr–Nov; 10am–4pm, Dec–Mar; 206/781-6776; fremontmarket.com; map:FF8) bills itself as a European-style street market, and you can find anything from old and new furniture to cowboy boots. Goods of the more than 150 vendors range from handcrafted jewelry to hats galore. The year-round **BALLARD SUNDAY MARKET** (Ballard Avenue NW, between 22nd Avenue NW and 20th Avenue NW; Sun 10am–4pm April to November, 11am–3pm December to March; 206/781-6776; ballardsundaymarket.com; map:EE8) is part street fair, part farmers' market. Along with seasonal produce (and, in winter, a smaller selection of hothouse-grown greens) and organic meats and cheeses, find pleasing aromatherapy oils and balms (even get a back massage) or browse handmade jewelry and art (the Chinese silk art is a steal) while being serenaded by Spanish music from a live band. The market's locale makes it doubly fun, situated as it is between the trendy rows of Ballard shops, so you can meander between shops and vendor stalls. This neighborhood market also sells Washington wines. Two more markets have blossomed—one in the heart of **WALLINGFORD** (Wallingford Center parking lot, 1815 N 45th St; Wed, 3–7pm, Jun–Sept; 206/781-6776; seattlemarkets.org; map: FF7) and another in **MADISON/CAPITOL HILL** (Grocery Outlet parking lot, 126 Martin Luther King Jr Wy; Fri, 3–7pm, May–Sept; 206/781-6776; seattlemarkets.org; map:GG6), both offering a wonderful mix of fresh farm produce, natural meats, fresh fish and baked goods, and handcrafted soaps and garden art, among other items.

—Niki Stojnic

pedestrian walkway between First and Second avenues, is studded with galleries, and during the **FIRST THURSDAY GALLERY WALK** (206/667-0687; pioneersquare.org/first_thursday.html), art appreciators swarm Pioneer Square.

Occidental Avenue S segues into Occidental Park, a Northwest attempt at a Parisian park with cobblestones, trees, and totem poles. A more novel park, the **WATERFALL GARDEN**, is tucked into a corner at Second Avenue S and S Main Street (see Parks and Beaches in this chapter).

King Street is Pioneer Square's southern boundary. Look farther south and you can't miss **SAFECO AND QWEST FIELDS** (see listing #6 below). **F. X. MCRORY'S STEAK, CHOP AND OYSTER HOUSE** (419 Occidental Ave S; 206/623-4800; fxmcrorys.com) is the restaurant and watering hole of choice for gamegoers. Just north of the stadiums is **KING STREET STATION** (2nd Avenue S and S Main Street; 206/382-4125). With its striking clock tower, the station opened for business in 1906 and still receives Amtrak trains as well as a commuter train, the Sounder. A $29 million restoration scheduled for completion in 2009 promises to give the station new life and new retail. West on King is **MERRILL PLACE**, a revitalized building that conceals an enclave of apartments, and **IL TERRAZZO CARMINE** (411 1st Ave S; 206/467-7797; ilterrazzocarmine.com), an esteemed Italian restaurant with a romantic bar and a terrace overlooking a fountain—the ideal place to wind up a Pioneer Square tour. *Every day; pioneersquare.org; map:O9–M8.*

6) SAFECO FIELD AND QWEST FIELD

1ST AVENUE S AND S ATLANTIC STREET, SODO; 206/346-4287

When the Kingdome was imploded in 2000, those who considered it an eyesore rejoiced, while others lamented the loss of a homely but loveable landmark. Any disappointment the city may have felt at its loss, however, was amply soothed when the impressive, $517-million Safeco Field was erected. With a retractable roof, comfortable sight lines from just about every seat, public art installments throughout, and more food options than a Vegas-style buffet, the home of the Seattle Mariners is one of the best in the Majors. Even visiting teams agree: in a 2003 survey by *Sports Illustrated*, players tagged "The Safe" as their favorite ballpark. The gates open two hours before each game, and autograph seekers should be among the first inside, since space near the dugouts is limited. If you're looking for a Mariners souvenir, try the **MARINERS TEAM STORE** (1250 1st Ave S; 206/346-4287; seattle.mariners.mlb.com/sea/ballpark/sea_ballpark_teamstores.jsp). To avoid the rush, visit when the team is on the road or down in Peoria, Arizona, for spring training. The store even sells a VIP look at Safeco itself: a one-hour tour of the ballpark is available for $7 (seniors $6, children 3–12 $5, 2 and under free) during the off-season and on days when the Mariners are away. The tour also includes a visit to the new **PACIFIC NORTHWEST BASEBALL MUSEUM AND SEATTLE MARINERS HALL OF FAME**, co-located on the Main Concourse along the third base line, which explores the rich history of baseball in the Pacific Northwest from the 1880s to today. With your ticket, visit on Mariners home game days too. At the bullpens located by left field, fans get up-close looks at what a 90-mile-per-hour fastball looks and sounds like whizzing plateward. The celebrated retractable roof, designed by engineers to cover but not enclose the ballpark, is entertaining in its own right. If you don't get a chance to see it in action during the game, stick around—groundskeepers show off the technology at the end of every game, provided it's not raining too hard. No visit to Safeco is complete without a Mariner Dog and a serving of the park's famously fragrant garlic fries. If you're craving sushi, a stand sells Ichirolls, named after Mariners star Ichiro Suzuki. For those who prefer their fish cooked, try Ivar's Original Acres of Clams. Other options include Bullpen BBQ, serving pulled-pork sandwiches that could tempt a vegetarian. Or show up early for countertop dining at the **HIT IT HERE CAFÉ** in the right-field corner, which has unobstructed views and where all seats become reserved about 30 minutes before game time (season ticket holders have first dibs). Ticket prices range from $7 for center-field bleacher seats to $55 for lower box seats. *Every day; mariners.com; map:R9.* ♿

Adjacent to Safeco Field, **QWEST FIELD** (800 Occidental Ave S, 206/381-7582; qwestfield.com) is home to the city's football team, the Seattle Seahawks. Current Seahawks owner Paul Allen funded about 30 percent of the stadium's $430 million cost out of pocket, and the remainder was paid for by public funds. In addition, a separate $1.75 million Stadium Art Program ensured that a diverse range of artworks by both regional and national artists graced the stadium. Among the dozen works are Claudia Fitch's six "Colossal Heads," each sculpture approximately 6 feet high by 4 feet wide by 4 feet deep.

For a behind-the-scenes look—you'll get to suit up in the visitor's locker room and set foot right on the same next-generation FieldTurf playing surface as your favorite Seahawks players—join a one-and-a-half-hour tour (206/381-7582; $7 adults, $5 seniors and children 4–12). Tours at 12:30 and 2:30pm are available daily (except on game days) from June through August and on Fridays and Saturdays the rest of the year. At the south end, the stadium is connected to Qwest Event Center, which hosts concerts and pregame events for the Mariners and Seahawks. When it's not football season, the Seattle Sounders men's soccer team takes over. The 70-by-110-yard soccer field meets national, Major League, and World Cup soccer field and sight line requirements, and proved good enough even for David Beckham when his former team, Real Madrid, played an international friendly game against DC United in 2006. Tickets to Seahawks games run $33–$360 (888/635-4295 or ticketmaster.com). *Every day; seahawks.com. map:P8.* ♿

7) WASHINGTON STATE FERRIES

COLMAN DOCK, DOWNTOWN (AND VARIOUS LOCATIONS); 206/464-6400

Seattle being surrounded by water, it's not surprising that the Washington State Ferry system is the largest ferry system in the United States, serving eight counties within Washington and the province of British Columbia in Canada. It stretches from as far south as Tacoma to the San Juan Islands and Vancouver Island BC in the north. Now carrying some 24 million passengers every year, the system as it exists today came with the state's buyout of Puget Sound Navigation in 1951. Before that, Puget Sound ferry service was initially provided by a number of companies using small steamers known as the Mosquito Fleet. By 1929, the ferry industry had consolidated into two companies: Puget

Sound Navigation Company and Kitsap County Transportation Company. A strike in 1935 forced Kitsap County Transportation Company out of business and left the Puget Sound Navigation Company, commonly known as the Blackball Line, with primary control of ferry service on Puget Sound. The state's role in providing ferry service began in 1951, when spiraling costs and labor disputes threatened to sink the privately operated Blackball Line, and lawmakers decided government needed to become involved.

WSF provides about 450 daily sailings throughout its system, with its fleet navigating nearly a million miles a year. On most of the ferries you can take your car, driving on in one location and driving off at the next. Rates range from $4.35 one way for foot passengers traveling from West Seattle to Vashon Island, to $55 for a car and driver going from Anacortes to Sidney BC in the summer (note that rates are higher in summer than in winter). The bike surcharge is $1, and passenger fares are collected only on westbound routes (vehicle and driver pay both ways on most routes), so if you're island hopping, head to the westernmost destination first and work your way back. *Every day; wsdot.wa.gov/ferries; map:M8.* ♿

BEST PLACE
TO DINE AL FRESCO?

"Ray's Boathouse, right on the water. A deck, a cocktail, some appetizers, and good friends. Few things can beat that on a clear, warm summer night."

Melanie McFarland, Seattle Post-Intelligencer *TV critic*

---

8) WOODLAND PARK ZOO

5500 PHINNEY AVE N, PHINNEY RIDGE; 206/684-4800

Get deceptively up close to the animals at this superbly designed zoo, one of the oldest on the West Coast. An urban oasis of flora and fauna, the zoo's 92 acres house approximately 1,100 animals, representing nearly 300 species. Occupying what was once the "country estate" of an eccentric 19th-century Canadian real estate baron named Guy Phinney, Woodland Park Zoo has been hailed as one of the nation's 10 best zoological gardens. It has shed its roots as an animals-behind-bars facility in favor of lifelike re-creations of natural habitats ("bioclimatic zones," in zoo lingo) for which the zoo has won five prestigious awards from the Association of Zoos and Aquariums. Among these habitats are a grassy **AFRICAN SAVANNA** populated with giraffes, zebras, and hippos that wallow merrily in their own simulated mud-bottomed river drainage (the lions, though nearby, enjoy their own grassland); **TROPICAL ASIA**, with its Elephant Forest—4.6 acres that include an elephant-size pool and a replica of a Thai temple; and the **TRAIL OF VINES**, an adjoining 2.7-acre exhibit that takes visitors on an imaginary voyage through India, Malaysia, and Borneo with its display of orangutans, siamang apes, Malayan tapirs, and lion-tailed macaques. The heavily planted **LOWLAND GORILLA ENCLOSURES** conceal two brooding troops of adults and their precocious offspring. The exotic **JAGUAR COVE** exhibit, adorned with thousands of tropical plants and a freshwater pool, realistically captures the natural habitat of the biggest cat in the Western Hemisphere. On the tamer side, the **FAMILY FARM** (inside the Temperate Forest) is a wonderful place for human youngsters to meet the offspring of other species. The newest (nonanimal) addition to the zoo, **ZOOMAZIUM**, is an indoor facility that incorporates multimedia features with fun, interactive nature-themed areas devoted to play and learning for children ages 0 to 8. At the indoor-outdoor **RAIN FOREST FOOD PAVILION** (a great place to throw a birthday party), you might not love the food, but the kids, no doubt, will. The zoo also offers a rich schedule of family programming, including orientation walks, classes, sleepovers, and lectures. Its popular **ZOOTUNES** concert series, held outdoors on summer evenings, draws a panoply of top musicians (206/615-0076). Zoo admission is $10.50 for adults, $7.50 for children aged 3–12, Oct–Apr; and $15 and $10 respectively May–Sept. Free for children 2 and under year-round. Seniors and people with disabilities receive a discount. *Every day; zoo.org; map:FF7.* ♿

9) MONORAIL

400 PINE ST, DOWNTOWN, OR THE SEATTLE CENTER; 206/905-2620

Seattle's flirtations with the Monorail started in 1910 when a local inventor named W. H. Shephard suggested that the city construct an elevated monorail network to reduce traffic on its streets. But it was not until Seattle hosted the 1962 world's fair that one was finally erected. Although it cost $3.5 million at the time, it was basically just a space-age gimmick (built by Sweden's Alweg Rapid Transit Systems) that shuttled tourists between downtown and the fairgrounds at what is now Seattle Center. Yet it was so popular that even after the fair closed down, the city continued to operate the Monorail. The elevated trains presently carry about 2.5 million riders each year, making this one of the world's few profitable rapid-transit operations. The Monorail travels 1 mile (a 2-minute ride) between Westlake Center (400 Pine St) and Seattle Center. Tourists are the principal users—except during Bumbershoot and the Folklife Festival (both guaranteed to fill parking lots around the Seattle Center), when many city residents prefer to park downtown and hop the Monorail to the festivities. In a hotly contested 2002 vote, Seattleites approved use of state and city funds to expand the Monorail to encompass a 14-mile route from Ballard to West Seattle at a cost of $1.29 billion. Unfortunately, another vote in 2005 nixed the Seattle Monorail Project. Now, trains depart Westlake and Seattle Center stations every 10 minutes. Fare is $2 one way for adults, 75 cents one way for youth ages 5–12, and $1 for seniors (double the price for a round-trip ticket). *Every day; 11am–9pm; seattlemonorail.com; map:I6.* ♿

10) WOODINVILLE WINE COUNTRY

BETWEEN SR 522 AND I-405, SNOHOMISH/KING COUNTY LINE AND 170TH AVE NE; WASHINGTON SR 202 RUNS THROUGH THE HEART OF WOODINVILLE WINE COUNTRY

Nestled in the lush Sammamish River Valley 25 minutes northeast of downtown Seattle, Woodinville woos oenophiles from Seattle and beyond. This former logging community was once heavily forested—a natural draw for loggers and their families—with the Sammamish River providing a river highway to Lake Washington and Seattle. As more land was cleared, people started farming in the rich soil. More recently, Woodinville's proximity to metropolitan Seattle, as well as its natural wooded landscape and beautiful surroundings, made it an attractive location for wineries. Today, the saw and shingle mills have all but disappeared, and in their place are boutique wineries and a vibrant retail core, although some farmland remains. Woodinville's reputation for fine winemaking was boosted in 2002 when a group of winemakers banded together to form **WOODINVILLE WINE COUNTRY** (woodinvillewinecountry.com), a nonprofit organization working to build awareness for Woodinville wines. More than 30 wineries (and the numbers keep growing!) are located within the tourist district on the southern edge of the city on SR 202 (Woodinville-Redmond Road). Don't expect a Northwest Napa Valley, though. There are no vineyards here—many wineries own vineyards in Eastern Washington—and some wineries are housed in industrial warehouse complexes. But the woodland surroundings are gorgeous enough to keep the romanticism of winemaking alive.

CHATEAU STE. MICHELLE (14111 NE 145th St; 425/415-3300; ste-michelle.com; 10am–5pm daily) was the first to set up shop in 1978. One of the state's oldest and most acclaimed wineries, it is housed in a fairy-tale castle on 87 wooded acres once belonging to lumber baron Fred Stimson. The estate also includes the original trout ponds, a carriage house, formal gardens, and the 1912 family manor house, which is on the National Register of Historic Places. Complimentary tours and tastings are available from 10:30am to 4:30pm daily (425/415-3633). In summer, the winery grounds are a popular venue for concerts that have included Elvis Costello, Lyle Lovett, and Bonnie Raitt. In 1988, **COLUMBIA WINERY** (14030 NE 145th St; 425/482-7490; columbiawinery.com; 10am–6pm daily) followed, establishing its location across the street. In addition to free tours (daily, times vary; 425/482-7490), for $5 visitors can experience what the winery claims is the largest wine-tasting bar in the state. Immediately north, Novelty Hill's (14710 Woodinville-Redmond Rd; noveltyhillwines.com; 11am–5pm daily) destination winery, which opened in 2007, boasts a contemporary design with extensive gardens and a public tasting bar overlooking a barrel-aging room and small-lot fermentation tanks. Other small boutique wineries include **DISTEFANO WINERY** (12280 Woodinville Dr SE; 425/487-1648; distefanowinery.com; noon–5pm Sat–Sun) and **WOODHOUSE FAMILY CELLARS** (15500 Woodinville-Redmond Rd, Ste C600; 425/527-0608; woodhousefamilycellars.com; call for seasonal hours).

During Passport to Woodinville Weekend, held annually in April, all the boutique wineries are open at the same time. For $50, passport-wielding and Woodinville Wine Country glass–toting participants can hop from one winery to another enjoying wine sips and gourmet bites. For the complete Woodinville experience, stay at **WILLOWS LODGE** (14580 NE 145 St; 877/424-3930; willowslodge.com), a rustic retreat with more than just a touch of luxury. Two of the most highly rated restaurants in the Northwest, the **HERBFARM RESTAURANT** (425/485-5300; theherbfarm.com) and **BARKING FROG** (425/424-2999; willowslodge.com), are also on its grounds.

Downtown Woodinville is concentrated along NE 175th Street and offers an array of shopping, restaurants, and business services. Just outside downtown along the Sammamish River, **WILMOT GATEWAY PARK** (17301 131st Ave NE) has a playground and a nice grassy bowl—perfect for a sunny day out. To the east lies **21 ACRES** (13701 NE 171st St; 206/442-2061; 21acres.org), an agricultural and environmental learning center for all ages. *Every day; woodinvillewinecountry.com; map:AA1.*

11) SEATTLE AQUARIUM

1483 ALASKAN WY, PIER 59, WATERFRONT; 206/386-4320

The Seattle Aquarium's summer 2007 expansion promised a fresh new facade and Alaskan Way entrance, a full-service café and gift store, additional ticketing stations, and the Puget Sound Great Hall building, home of **WINDOW ON WASHINGTON WATERS**. This 17-by-39-foot, 120,000-gallon showcase exhibit evokes Neah Bay's rock blades filled with salmon, colorful rockfish, vibrant sea anemones, and other marine life swimming amid a kelp-filled sea; head to the second-floor viewing platforms for a three-dimensional panorama. Elsewhere, the 400,000-gallon **UNDERWATER DOME** continues to rake in crowds of students and travelers. This fish tank causes heads to swivel as they try to take in the myriad king salmon, reef sharks, snappers, and other colorful Puget Sound and Pacific Ocean inhabitants whisking by. Topside tanks are home to seals and sea otters acting clownish at feeding times. Other entrancing exhibits include **LIFE ON THE EDGE**, which allows visitors to experience the tide pool life of Washington's outer coast and Seattle's inland sea while meeting such creatures as aggregating anemones and sunflower sea stars. There are two large exhibit pools, which include touch zones staffed by naturalists and video screens demonstrating the lifestyles of these amazing creatures who thrive in the harsh conditions of Washington's tidal zones. The **LIFE OF A DRIFTER** exhibit stars a giant "Jelly Doughnut," a luminous, 12-foot-high crystal ring filled with dozens of mystical moon jellyfish, as well as a multispecies tank with the giant Pacific octopus and wolf eels. There's also a hands-on area featuring a 13-foot wet table for an interactive experience with juvenile rockfish, sea stars, the life stages of moon jellies, and plankton. Admission is $15 for adults, $10 for youths 4–12, and free for children 3 and under. Senior discount on request. *Every day, 10am–5pm; seattleaquarium.org; map:J8.* ♿

RAINY DAY ALTERNATIVES

So it's raining in Seattle—what else is new? Let's face it, if you wait for the rain to stop, you'll never do anything or go anywhere. But if your umbrella broke or you don't want to ruin your suede sneakers (didn't anyone tell you suede is a no-no in these parts?), there's still lots to do in the city while keeping dry. For a low-key afternoon, head to **ELLIOTT BAY BOOK COMPANY**'s subterranean café (101 S Main St, Pioneer Square; 206/682-6664; map:O8), where the walls are lined with used books. Grab one that catches your fancy and you can read it from cover to cover while nursing that t-a-l-l latte. If you'd rather be surrounded by the grandeur of Italian renaissance architecture, seek refuge from the rain at Seattle's grand dame hotel, the **FAIRMONT OLYMPIC** (411 University St, Downtown; 206/621-1700; map:K6). The hotel's elegant afternoon tea at **THE GEORGIAN** (11:30am to 2:30pm daily; $35 for adults, $18 for children) offers a delightful spread: your choice of finely crafted teas, an assortment of tea sandwiches (think smoked salmon with avocado butter and caviar or Dungeness crab and grapefruit salad), and sweets ranging from fresh fruit tarts and sugared coconut macaroons to currant scones with Devonshire cream and raspberry preserves. Nature lovers can surround themselves with flora without getting

12) SEATTLE ASIAN ART MUSEUM

1400 E PROSPECT ST, CAPITOL HILL; 206/654-3100

Designed by local architect Carl F. Gould, the beautiful art moderne style building housing the Seattle Asian Art Museum (SAAM) sits atop serene Volunteer Park, commanding perhaps the best vista in town. The museum was built in 1931 by Richard Fuller and his mother, Margaret E. MacTavish Fuller, to house their 1,700-piece collection of Asian art before it grew into a more eclectic institution. When the downtown Seattle Art Museum opened in 1991, the original building was renovated to showcase the museum's extensive Asian art collections. Now the carefully lit galleries once again hold the kind of art (the Hindu deities Shiva and Parvati rapt in divine love, for example) that draws you away from daily obsessions and expands your soul. In addition to old favorites from the collection—such as the Fullers' array of elaborate netsuke—don't miss the ancient Chinese funerary art and the collection of 14th- to 16th-century ceramics from Thailand. Reflecting the museum's new commitment, contemporary Asian artwork and videos will change frequently. An Educational Outreach Gallery offers hands-on displays. Admission for adults is $5; $3 for seniors, youths 13–17, and students with ID; free for children 12 and under, and free to all the first Thursday and Saturday of each month. (Admission tickets also may be used for wet at the **VOLUNTEER PARK CONSERVATORY** (1400 E Galer St, Capitol Hill; 206/684-4743; cityofseattle.net/parks/parkspaces/VolunteerPark/conservatory.htm; map:GG7). The Victorian greenhouse modeled on London's Crystal Palace stands at the north end of Volunteer Park. Year-round (daily 10am–4pm, 10am–7pm Memorial Day through Labor Day); you'll be able to explore the conservatory's collections of bromeliads, palms, ferns, and cacti, and a changing seasonal display of plants. Not to be missed is the extensive orchid collection, some of which are rare, restricted species confiscated by U.S. Fish and Wildlife agents. Active types can get their fix by scaling the **PINNACLE AT THE SEATTLE REI FLAGSHIP STORE** (222 Yale Ave N, South Lake Union; 206/223-1944; rei.com/stores/seattle/climbclass.html; $15/per person, per climb, general; $5 members; 10am–6pm Mon, 10am–9pm Wed–Sat, 10am–5pm Sun; map:G1). REI supplies shoes and harnesses for all climbers. Call for reservations. If it's a Saturday, **TOWN HALL** (1119 8th Ave, Downtown; 206/652-4255; townhallseattle.org; $5 adults; free for kids 12 and under with accompanying adult; map:L4) hosts family concerts from storytelling to kiddie pop bands to traditional Japanese koto music. It's a surefire way to keep the tykes entertained and out of the rain.

—Pat Tanumihardja

entry to SAM downtown—see listing #2 above—within a week of purchase.) *Tues–Sun; seattleartmuseum.org; map:GG6.* ♿

13) PACIFIC SCIENCE CENTER

200 2ND AVE N, SEATTLE CENTER; 206/443-2001

Another 1962 world's fair legacy, the Science Center was originally designed by Minoru Yamasaki, the architect responsible for the inverted-pencil Rainier Square tower downtown (as well as New York City's iconic twin-towered World Trade Center brought down in the September 11th terrorist attacks). Since then, more than 30 million people have trooped through the 6 acres of this complex to see hands-on science and math exhibits for school-age children, as well as traveling shows aimed at all age groups. One of several permanent exhibits, **DINOSAURS: A JOURNEY THROUGH TIME**, introduces roaring robotic creatures from Earth's Mesozoic period, including a flesh-eating *Tyrannosaurus rex* and a three-horned, herbivorous *Triceratops*. The **SCIENCE PLAYGROUND** offers a kid-friendly introduction to physics. There are also insect and tropical butterfly exhibits. Outside the center, visitors can take aim with a water cannon, explore their center of gravity on the **HIGH RAIL BIKE**, or interact with live marine animals in the **PUGET SOUND TIDEPOOL**. Year-round, fun rotating exhibits such as **GROSSOLOGY: THE (IMPOLITE) SCIENCE OF THE HUMAN BODY**, where you can be like a dust particle and go exploring inside a giant nose or put a burp machine to work, are sure to delight the young and young at heart. Admission is $10 for adults; $8.50 for seniors 65 and over; $7 for kids 3–12; and free for children under 3, members, and disabled persons. Also in this complex are two IMAX Theaters (206/443-4629), one boasting a six-channel surround-sound system and a 35-by-60-foot screen on which viewers can thrill to experiences such as a climb up Mount Everest. Admission is $8 for adults, $7.50 for seniors 65 and older, $7 for juniors 6–12, $6 for kids 3–5, and free for children under 3. Combination IMAX–Science Center tickets are available. *Tues–Sun; pacsci.org; map:C7.* ♿

14) ALKI BEACH PARK

BETWEEN DUWAMISH HEAD AND ALKI POINT IN WEST SEATTLE, ALONG HARBOR AVENUE SW AND ALKI AVENUE SW

While Pioneer Square likes to be thought of as the cradle of Seattle, the city's real birthplace is in what is now West Seattle. It was there, on November 13, 1851, that a party of Midwesterners led by Arthur Denny stepped off the schooner *Exact*. They dreamed of building a western version of New York City at Alki Point, but it took only six months—including one wind-whipped winter—to convince them to retreat eastward across Elliott Bay in search of more-sheltered ground. Today, however, this migration is often reversed—especially on sunny summer days, as winter-pale Seattleites head to Alki Beach (along Alki Avenue SW). With its numerous in-line skaters, volleyball games, picnicking families, and body-conscious teens, this 2-mile-long stretch of sand is the closest thing we have to California's Venice Beach. The paved path that parallels the beach starts at the Terminal 5 Public Shoreline Access Site and runs around the rocky shoreline all the way to the Alki Point Lighthouse. Heading north and west along the path is Seacrest Park, where the Elliott Bay Water Taxi currently runs shuttles across the bay to Pier 57 every hour on the hour from May through October. (The schedule can change from year to year; check Web site, http://transit.metrokc.gov/tops/oto/water_taxi.html.)

To fuel your fun in the sun, there's **SALTY'S ON ALKI** (1936 Harbor Ave SW; 206/937-1600; saltys.com), **DUKE'S CHOWDER HOUSE** (2516 Alki Ave SW; 206/937-6100; dukeschowderhouse.com), and **SPUD FISH & CHIPS** (2666 Alki Ave SW; 206/938-0606). If you're looking for coffee and a snack, try **ALKI MAIL & DISPATCH** (2536 Alki Ave SW; 206/932-2556; www.alkimail.com), where you can also mail a postcard home. The highlight of Alki Beach comes at day's end, when the sun edges toward the Olympic Mountains to the west and sunbeams shoot across the Sound to reflect off the downtown skyscrapers. On clear nights, you can spot the alpenglow bouncing off the snowy peaks of the Cascade Mountains to the northeast. Most Alki Beach residents plan their entire evenings around these few brief moments. *Every day; map:II9.*

15) MUSEUM OF FLIGHT

9404 E MARGINAL WY S, GEORGETOWN; 206/764-5720

Other than its location at Boeing Field, 10 miles south of Seattle, the museum doesn't actually have a formal affiliation with the aircraft manufacturer. Yet other legacies pop up, including the Red Barn, where Boeing started in 1910, which tells the company's history as well as the stories of other major founders of the American aerospace industry. There are also more than enough flying machines, including a 40,000-pound B-17, to keep even the most passive aviation buffs interested. The museum takes you from the early legends of flying (including a replica of the Wright brothers' original glider) through the history of aviation, with special emphasis on Pacific Northwest flight—military, commercial, and amateur. Highlights include the only Concorde on the West Coast; *Apollo* and *Mercury* space capsules; and the 98-foot Lockheed A-12 Blackbird, the fastest plane ever built (it has flown coast to coast in 67 minutes). Another attraction is the first-ever Air Force One, used by presidents Kennedy and Truman, among others, on display for visitors to walk through at their leisure. The Birth of Aviation exhibit reveals the lives and times of Orville and Wilbur Wright, celebrates their first powered flight on December 17, 1903, and spotlights their unheralded sister, Katharine, after whom the Wrights named their plane, *Kitty Hawk*. The Museum of Flight also offers a variety of workshops, films, tours, and special programs. Children especially enjoy the hangar with three explorable planes, and hands-on learning areas with paper airplanes, boomerangs, and other toys that fly. Admission is $14 for adults, $7.50 for kids 5–17, and free for children under 4; free on the first Thursday evening of each month, 5–9pm. *Every day; museumofflight.org; map:NN6.* ♿

16) WASHINGTON PARK ARBORETUM

2300 ARBORETUM DR E, MADISON VALLEY; 206/543-8800

New York has Central Park; Boston has the Boston Common and Public Garden; Seattle has the Washington Park Arboretum. Set aside as urban wilderness in 1904 and developed beginning in the 1930s, the arboretum is a year-round venue where naturalists and botanists rub elbows with serious runners and casual walkers, for this 200-acre public park doubles as a botanical research facility for the nearby University of Washington. The arboretum stretches from Foster Island, just off the shore of Lake Washington, through the Montlake and Madison Park neighborhoods, its rambling trails screened from the houses by thick greenbelts. More than 5,000 varieties of woody plants are arranged here by family. (Pick up maps or an illustrated guide at the visitors' center if you want to find specific trees.) From spring through autumn, the **SEATTLE JAPANESE GARDEN** (1502 Lake Washington Blvd E; 206/684-4725; seattle.gov/parks/parkspaces/japanesegarden.htm) located in the arboretum is well worth a visit. Just off Lake Washington Boulevard E, which winds north-south through the park, this authentic garden of pruned living sculptures was constructed in 1960 under the direction of Japanese landscape architect Juki Iida. Several hundred tons of rock hauled from the Cascades were incorporated into the design, as were stone lanterns donated by the city of Kobe and a teahouse sent by the governor of Tokyo. The graceful carp pond, spanned by traditional bridges of wood and stone and lined with water plants, is home to numerous carp and turtles. Though the original teahouse was destroyed by vandals years ago, it has since been replaced, and the tea ceremony is still performed on various weekends April through October by members of the Seattle branch of the Urasenke Foundation. Check seattle.gov/parks/parkspaces/gardens.htm for dates and times. Free public tours are available on weekends at 12:30pm and 2:30pm, April through October. Admission is $5 for adults 18–64; $3 youth 6–17, seniors, students with ID, and the disabled. Guided tours are available by arrangement for a fee. Call for event schedules and operating hours; closing time varies seasonally. *Every day; map:GG6.*

Just across the road to the north runs Azalea Way, a wide, grassy thoroughfare that winds through the heart of the arboretum. (No recreational running is permitted on this popular route.) Azalea Way is magnificent in April and May, when its blossoming shrubs are joined by scores of companion dogwoods and ornamental cherries. Drop in on the Joseph A. Witt Winter Garden, especially from November through March, which focuses on plants that show distinctive seasonal bark, winter flowers, or cold-season fruit to attract birds. Side trails lead through the arboretum's extensive camellia and rhododendron groves (the latter collection is world famous).

Follow Azalea Way to the copper-roofed **DONALD A. GRAHAM VISITORS CENTER** (2300 Arboretum Dr E; 206/543-8800), where you can find maps and arboretum guides as well as horticulture-related books, gifts, and informational displays. The arboretum also hosts an annual spring plant sale each April, a fall bulb sale each October, and guided weekend tours. *Every day, 7am–dusk; uwbg@u.washington.edu; depts.washington.edu/wpa; map:GG6.*

17) BALLARD LOCKS

3015 NW 54TH ST, BALLARD; 206/783-7059

The Miraflores and Gatun locks in the Panama Canal may be world famous, but you don't have to travel anywhere near that far to see ship locks in action. The Hiram M. Chittenden Locks in Ballard are always abuzz. Talk of digging a navigable canal between the freshwater of Lakes Washington and Union and the salt water of Puget Sound began shortly after Seattle's pioneers arrived in the 1850s. Numerous engineering challenges ensued: the biggest was the design and construction of locks near the canal's western end that could control the difference in water levels between the Sound and the much higher Lake Washington. (In the end, the latter was lowered by 9 feet, exposing new lakefront property and interfering with salmon migrations.) Not until 1917 was the 8-mile-long Lake Washington Ship Canal dedicated, and another 17 years would pass before it was officially declared complete. In 1936, the U.S. Army Corps of Engineers named the locks in honor of Major Hiram M. Chittenden, who had supervised the canal project. Today around 100,000 pleasure and commercial boats per year go through the canal and what are colloquially known as the Ballard Locks. Couples and families trot down to watch this informal regatta as it works its way through the "water elevator." The descent (or ascent) takes 10 to 25 minutes, depending on which of the two locks is being used. A particularly good people-watching time is during Seafair in July, when boats filled with carousing men and women crowd the locks. Across the waterway in Commodore Park, the fish ladder that bypasses the locks entices struggling salmon bound for spawning grounds in Lake Washington and Cascade mountain streams. You can watch the fishes' progress from a viewing area with windows on to the ladder: sockeye salmon in summer (peak viewing is in early July) and chinook and coho from August to October. Call the visitors' center for tour times (206/783-7059; free daily May–Sept; 10am–6pm Thurs–Mon; 10am–4pm Tues–Wed; closed the rest of the year); there's also an interesting exhibit that explains the use and building of the locks. The green lawns and tree-lined waterside promenade of the park, along with the impressive rose display at the Carl S. English Jr. Botanical Gardens (see Gardens in this chapter), make grand backdrops for summer picnics. *Every day; nws.usace.army.mil; map:FF9.*

18) NORDSTROM AND REI

500 PINE ST, DOWNTOWN; 206/628-2111; 222 YALE AVE N, SOUTH LAKE UNION; 206/223-1944

Seattle is a city of dichotomy, even when it comes to shopping. Whether you're a fashion maven or an incurable gearhead, Seattle's two premier shopping destinations will satisfy. At its flagship store, locally grown retail giant **NORDSTROM** boasts a whopping five spacious floors of clothing, shoes, accessories, cosmetics, fine jewelry, and fabled customer service. Special attractions of this Nordy's include a full-service day spa and a complimentary wardrobe-consulting service; besides the customary café, there's the Nordstrom Grill, featuring fresh market seafood. And the shoes: 150,000 pairs (including hard-to-find sizes, 3AAAAA to 14EE for women) are spread among five departments. Befitting a store that first made its mark in shoe leather, Nordstrom has installed glass cases around the store displaying examples of footwear ranging from turn-of-the-20th-century ankle boots to 1970s ankle-challenging platform shoes. Nordstrom's two-week anniversary sale in late July is a bona fide Northwest event. *Every day; nordstrom.com; map:J5.* ♿

At **REI** (Recreational Equipment Inc.), the nation's largest consumer co-op (89 stores in 25 states), you'll find everything you need for mountaineering, backpacking, camping, cross-country skiing, biking, and other energetic outdoor pursuits. Seattle's high-visibility, two-level location just off Interstate 5 features a 65-foot indoor climbing pinnacle (show up early as there's usually a line), mountain bike and hiking test paths, a children's play area, a World Wrapps restaurant, a coffee cart, and a wide assortment of fleece items, as well as maps, trail food, and outdoor books. For trip planning, **THE OUTDOOR RECREATION INFORMATION CENTER**, staffed by the U.S. Forest Service and National Park Service, is also located here (206/470-4060;

www.nps.gov/ccso/oric.htm). Anyone can shop here, but members (who pay only $15 once to join for a lifetime) usually receive a 10 percent yearly dividend on their purchases. Founded in 1938 by Lloyd Anderson and a group of Seattle mountaineers who wanted to import European equipment, the co-op was presided over for years by Everest conqueror Jim Whittaker, and it is still staffed by knowledgeable outdoorspeople. Outreach programs include a community giving program that benefits local nonprofits, as well as lectures, events, and courses; call for a current schedule. Rentals at good prices too. Smaller branches are in Lynnwood, Redmond, South Center/Tukwila, and Tacoma. *Every day; rei.com; map:H1.* ♿

19) DISCOVERY PARK

3801 W GOVERNMENT WY, MAGNOLIA; 206/684-4075

Old barracks, former military housing, and a training field are the last few vestiges of this park's former incarnation as Fort Lawton Army Base. The city decided to preserve most of the park as open space and nature reserves in 1974, and the collection of early Fort Lawton buildings was declared a landmark district in 1988. (Many old military buildings will soon be converted into another 24 acres of park.)

This densely foliated Magnolia wilderness has been allowed to revert to its premetropolitan natural order. Self-guided interpretive nature loops and short trails wind through 534 acres of thick forests, along dramatic sea cliffs (where powerful updrafts make for excellent kite flying), and across meadows of waving grasses. Discover the park's flora and fauna yourself, or take advantage of the scheduled walks and nature workshops conducted by park naturalists. On weekends the park offers free guided walks and, in spring and fall, bird tours—call ahead to check the schedule, or stop by the visitors' center in the east parking lot, near the Government Way entrance (206/386-4236). Groups can also arrange their own guided walks. Check the tall trees frequently; there's often a bald eagle in residence. Two well-equipped kids' playgrounds are here, along with picnic areas, playfields, tennis and basketball courts, and a rigorous fitness trail. The network of trails is a favorite among runners; the 2.8-mile Loop Trail circles the park, passing through forests, meadows, and sand dunes. The park is also home to the **ENVIRONMENTAL LEARNING CENTER** (open Tues–Sun 8:30am–5pm), offering interactive nature displays for kids; a Discovery Room where kids can color, play, and put on a sea-themed puppet show; and a good collection of hiking, botany, and birding guidebooks for kids and adults. **DAYBREAK STAR CULTURAL ARTS CENTER** (206/285-4425; www.unitedindians.com/daybreak.html) sponsors Native American activities and exhibits of contemporary Indian art in the Sacred Circle Gallery. West Point Lighthouse, built in 1881, is the oldest lighthouse in the Seattle area. *Every day; map:FF9.*

20) SMITH TOWER

506 2ND AVE, DOWNTOWN; 206/622-4004

When Smith Tower first opened in the summer of 1914, this 42-story (522-foot) terra-cotta-and-steel spire was the tallest building west of the Mississippi. It remained the highest in Seattle until 1969, when the old Seattle First National Bank Tower (now the 1001 Fourth Avenue Building) rose to 50 stories, or 609 feet. (The 605-foot Space Needle, finished in 1962, is also taller than the Smith Tower but doesn't usually count in the record books since it isn't a "building," per se.) Today, against the picket fence of skyscrapers that currently make up Seattle's skyline, the Smith Tower looks almost puny, but it is considered the most beloved of this city's cloud-kissing edifices. The building is the legacy of New Yorker Lyman C. Smith, an armaments manufacturer turned typewriter magnate, who commissioned the Syracuse NY architectural firm of Gaggin & Gaggin to design an office structure both distinctive and tall enough that it wouldn't be exceeded in Seattle during his lifetime. He got what he ordered, if not what he intended; Smith died in November 1910, before his skyscraper was finished.

Despite now being an address of choice for high-tech firms, the Smith Tower retains what are reportedly the West Coast's only manually operated elevators—eight brass-caged beauties. Its 35th-floor **CHINESE ROOM**, an elaborate space that's popular for weddings, is surrounded by an observation deck from which visitors can take in magnificent views of downtown for $7.50 adults (cash or check only), $6 seniors, $5 children 6–12. Hours vary by season and private bookings, so call ahead or check the online schedule to be sure you can access the deck. *Every day Apr–Oct; weekends only Nov–Mar; info@smithtower.com; smithtower.com; map:O7.* ♿

21) HENRY ART GALLERY

15TH AVENUE NE AND NE 41ST STREET, UNIVERSITY DISTRICT; 206/543-2280

The University of Washington is fertile ground to nurture the Henry's mission to showcase exhibitions and programs that invite dialogue about contemporary culture, politics, aesthetics, and the traditions of visual art and design of the last two centuries. The Henry's permanent collection of more than 20,500 objects includes late-19th and 20th-century paintings, the extensive Monsen Collection of Photography, and a textile and costume collection, along with a burgeoning collection of cutting-edge works in new media. Founded in 1927, the Henry was the first public art museum in the state of Washington; it underwent a major renovation and expansion that was completed in April 1997, quadrupling the museum's size from 10,000 square feet to more than 40,000 square feet. Today, it continues to forge a challenging identity that builds on its exemplary past, which has brought works by such eminent artists as Maya Lin, Gary Hill, Ann Hamilton, and Doug Aitken. The permanent James Turrell Skyspace, "Light Reign," featuring embedded LED lights, was unveiled in 2003 and continues to draw crowds (especially at twilight), and the Henry retains its national reputation for mounting shows with an eye toward experimental installations, video, and unusual media such as digital art. The expansion in 1997 also added an outdoor sculpture court, a 150-seat auditorium, a café, and an education center. Admission is $10 for adults, $8 for seniors 62 and older, and free for children under 13, UW students, and faculty. *Tues–Sun; henryart.org; map:FF6.* ♿

22) BURKE-GILMAN TRAIL

BETWEEN LAKE WASHINGTON SHIP CANAL (IN BALLARD) AND BOTHELL

The King County Parks System has one of the best trail systems in the nation, with more than 175 miles of trails for hiking, biking, and walking. The trail network spans from Bothell to Auburn, and from Seattle to Snoqualmie. In Seattle, the Burke-Gilman is the undisputed centerpiece of it all. Originally part of a railroad right-of-way, the first 12.1 miles from Seattle's Gas Works Park to Kenmore's Tracy Owen Station were opened as a public trail and named after the founders of the railroad, Thomas Burke and Daniel Gilman, in 1978. Today it runs from Ballard's busy ship canal, past Lake Union, through the University of Washington campus, and along the west shore of Lake Washington to Kenmore's Log Boom Park. From here cyclists, walkers, and runners can continue to Bothell and links to the Sammamish River Trail. The rules of the highway apply—stay to the right—and keep an eye out for crossing rabbits and, at night, feisty raccoons. If you're planning a trip on the trail, bring rain gear, because although the Burke-Gilman enables you to escape automobile traffic, the trail is not immune to Seattle's unpredictable weather. Once you're out there, you'll find ample opportunities to turn off and buy snacks or relax and read a book. If you bring a satchel, you can even use the trail to do major shopping. Just past the University District, the trail runs by University Village, an upscale, open-air shopping mall. *Every day; map:FF7–AA5.*

23) GAS WORKS PARK

2101 NORTHLAKE WY, WALLINGFORD; 206/684-4075

According to NWSource.com, a Web site affiliated with *The Seattle Times*, "Gas Works Park is easily the strangest park in Seattle, and may rank among the strangest in the world." True enough—not every city has a gasification-plant-turned-public-park. This 19.1-acre park on the north shore of Lake Union represents urban reclamation at its finest. A quarter century after the Seattle Gas Company plant shut down here in 1956, landscape architect Richard Haag (who won the American Society of Landscape Architects President's Award of Design Excellence for this project) re-created the industrial eyesore as one of Seattle's most delightful greenswards, with a high grassy knoll for kite flying, a large picnic shelter with reservable space (206/684-4081), a wonderful play barn, and a multitude of front-row spots from which to watch sailboats bounce around on Lake Union. Climb the grassy knoll to enjoy a huge mosaic sundial (created by artist Charles Greening) and a view of the downtown towers just 2 miles south. The threat of lurking pollutants has led to periodic soil cleansings, but risks are few, provided you don't eat the dirt. (Parents with toddlers, beware.) The park has become so popular that in 2003, an unused corner of the park was developed right up to the side of Northlake Way. This green meadow offers a quieter refuge from the sometimes boisterous rest of the park. Cutting east from Gas Works is the Burke-Gilman Trail (see listing #22 above). *Every day; seattle.gov/parks/park_detail.asp?ID=293; map:FF7.*

24) EXPERIENCE MUSIC PROJECT AND SCIENCE FICTION MUSEUM AND HALL OF FAME

325 5TH AVE N, SEATTLE CENTER; 206/770-2777

You can't miss EMP, the giant polychromatic metal blob said to resemble fused electric guitars, designed by Southern California architect Frank Gehry on the southeastern edge of the Seattle Center. The $240 million museum conceived by Microsoft co-founder Paul Allen (originally to be devoted to his boyhood idol, Seattle's own Jimi Hendrix) contains more than 80,000 objects celebrating modern music—mostly rock, but also blues, funk, and the culture that surrounds them all. Memorabilia scattered about the place includes Elvis Presley's motorcycle jacket, Janis Joplin's bell-bottoms, and guitars once played by Hendrix and Nirvana's Kurt Cobain. Visitors tour at their own pace, clutching shoulder-slung digital devices that allow them to access snippets of display interpretation and musical clips. Don't-miss attractions include the Guitar Gallery, featuring versions of the instrument that date back to 1770; the Hendrix Gallery, which recounts that cult guitarist's rise from his days playing teen dances in Seattle to holding forth at the original Woodstock; On Stage, where—with the help of screaming-crowd effects—you can satisfy your childhood dream to be a rock star; and the Sound Lab, equipped with the latest in musical gear and audio technology, where your inner musician can learn a hot guitar lick, mix a platinum record, and even record your very own CD. The new exhibit Sound and Vision: Artists Tell Their Stories allows you to explore EMP/SFM's (see below) collection of more than 450 videotaped oral history interviews. EMP also hosts rotating exhibits (such as Bob Dylan's American Journey and The Art of Modern Rock) and concerts by big-name musicians, from Dave Matthews to Emmylou Harris. In 2004, the **SCIENCE FICTION MUSEUM AND HALL OF FAME** (206/724-3428; sfhomeworld.org) opened next door as a showcase for another of Allen's collections. Devoted science fiction fans flock to the 13,000-square-foot museum chock-full of other-world memorabilia, including rare first editions of Isaac Asimov's and Frank Herbert's books, pulp magazines, and film and television props such as Captain Kirk's command chair from the *USS Enterprise* and light sabers from the *Star Wars* movies. Admission to both museums is $15 for adults, $12 for seniors and students, and $12 for children ages 5–17. All-access nights provide free admission to all galleries between 5pm and 8pm on the first Thursday of every month. *Every day; emplive.com; map:D6.* ♿

25) UNDERGROUND TOUR

610 1ST AVE, DOWNTOWN; 206/682-4646

Beneath those purple cubes of oxidized glass embedded in the sidewalk in Pioneer Square rests a whole other Seattle. Once home to sailors, shysters, prostitutes, and city bigwigs, these remnants of Seattle are the subject of Bill Speidel's Underground Tour—an institution since 1965 when an item in *The Seattle Times* spurred the late journalist Bill Speidel to organize public tours of the subterranean world. Although the 2001 earthquake caused damage to the exterior of some Pioneer Square buildings, it didn't lead—as feared—to the closure of this popular attraction. These tours are mostly one story down—the level of the city before it was rebuilt after the Great Fire of 1889. It's all pretty cornball, but you'll get a salty taste of the pioneers' eccentricities and some historical insights, with plenty of puns from the guides. The 90-minute tours begin at Doc Maynard's Public House in Pioneer Square. The tour operates year-round but varies seasonally. Cost is $14 for adults, $9 for seniors and students, $5 for children 7–12, and free for kids under 6. The tour is first come, first served, so try to arrive half an hour prior to tour start time. *Every day; undergroundtour.com; map:N8.*

Neighborhoods

DOWNTOWN

BETWEEN WESTERN AVENUE AND I-5, YESLER WAY AND DENNY WAY

Seattle's commercial district has shifted over time. Before 1900, most government and business offices huddled in Pioneer Square (see Top 25 Attractions in this chapter), at the south end of today's downtown. After the Great Fire of 1889, crowding in that historic district drove the city's expansion northward.

Today's retail core lies mostly between Third and Sixth avenues from Stewart to University streets. It's anchored by two big department stores—**MACY'S** (3rd Avenue and Pine Street) and **NORDSTROM** (5th Avenue and Pine Street)—as well as two high-end malls. Westlake Center resides at Fourth Avenue and Pine Street, and airy Pacific Place sits two blocks east, at Sixth Avenue and Pine Street. Colorful smaller shops line Fourth and Fifth avenues south to Rainier Square (4th Avenue and Union Street), an elegant three-story atrium at the base of Rainier Tower, a modernist box of a building that's balanced atop a tapered 12-story pedestal. Across University Street to the south is the **FAIRMONT OLYMPIC HOTEL** (4th Avenue and University Street), the grand dame of Seattle hostelries, opened in 1924. It seems as if the city's construction boom, begun in earnest in the 1980s, has yet to hit a speed bump, especially with the numerous condominiums that have been recently raised. Some of the newest buildings downtown include the new **SEATTLE PUBLIC LIBRARY** (4th Avenue and Spring Street), a modern architectural masterpiece designed by Rem Koolhas and completed in 2004, as well as a stunning new **CITY HALL** (5th Avenue between James and Cherry streets) and the **WILLIAM**

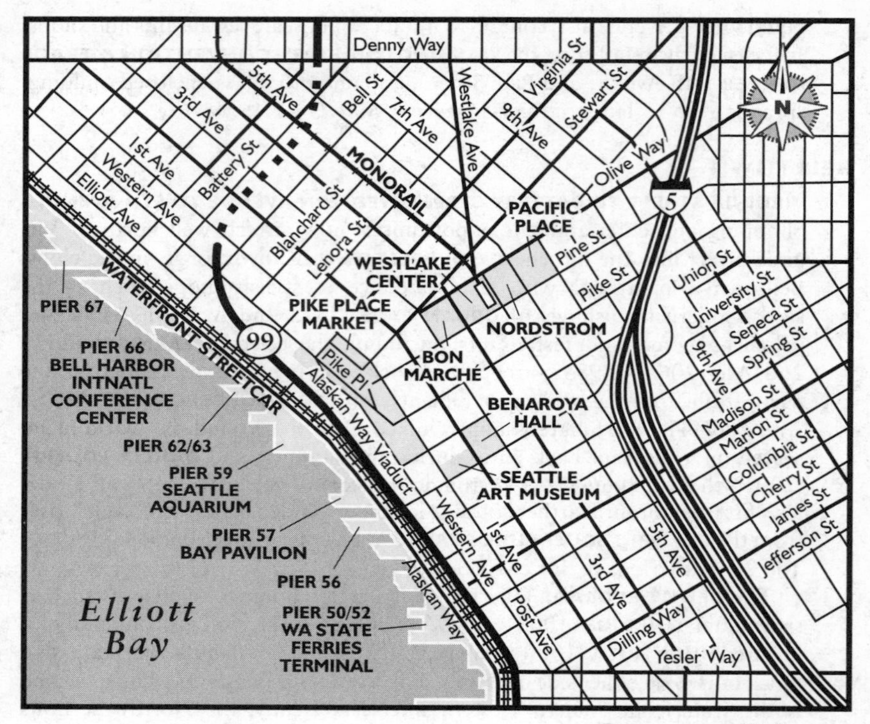

Downtown/Belltown

K. NAKAMURA FEDERAL COURTHOUSE (750 Stewart St). Some of the more eye-catching older buildings include the **1201 THIRD AVENUE BUILDING** (formerly known as the Washington Mutual Tower), a postmodern confection with a stair-stepped profile reminiscent of the Empire State Building's and a covering of pink granite; and **CITY CENTRE** (5th Avenue and Pike Street), with its light-filled lobby, three floors of exclusive shops, and the Palomino bistro. The tallest building downtown is the 76-story **COLUMBIA CENTER**, about six blocks south at Fourth Avenue and Columbia Street. For a grand view, visit its observation platform on the 73rd floor; check in with the security desk in the lobby ($5 adults, $3 students and seniors; Mon–Fri). More interesting are the older towers, such as the 1910 **COBB BUILDING** (4th Avenue and University Street), an elegant 11-story brick-and-terra-cotta structure, and the 1929 art deco, 26-story **SEATTLE TOWER** (3rd Avenue and University Street). Walk west along University Street to reach **BENAROYA HALL** (between 3rd and 2nd avenues), the classy home of the **SEATTLE SYMPHONY**, and the **SEATTLE ART MUSEUM** (between 1st and 2nd avenues; see Top 25 Attractions in this chapter). North on 1st Avenue from the museum is **PIKE PLACE MARKET** (see Top 25 Attractions), popular with both shoppers and people watchers. Leaving its history of strip clubs and pawn shops mostly behind, First Avenue also contains a number of upscale restaurants and shops. Just east of the retail core, the **WASHINGTON STATE CONVENTION & TRADE CENTER** (8th Avenue and Pike Street), a mammoth, glass-enclosed building, sprawls atop 12 lanes of the I-5 freeway. *Map:G3–H8, M8–O5.*

BELLTOWN

VIRGINIA STREET TO BATTERY STREET, WESTERN AVENUE TO 5TH AVENUE

Shopping and entertainment opportunities now stretch well north of Virginia Street into the hip enclave of **BELLTOWN**. Known for its music clubs, Belltown also attracts with an abundance of stylish shops, such as the sleek modern furnishings of **URBAN EASE** (2512 2nd Ave; 206/443-9546; urbanease.com), and restaurants, including the eclectic **MARJORIE** (2331 2nd Ave, 206/441-9842; trenchtownrocks.com), proffering global cuisine using fresh-from-the-market ingredients; **MARCO'S SUPPERCLUB** (2510 1st Ave; 206/441-7801; marcossupperclub.com), with a round-the-world menu served on a pleasant back patio during the summer; and **DAHLIA LOUNGE** (2001 4th Ave; 206/682-4142; tomdouglas.com), celebrity chef Tom Douglas's first restaurant. Farther south, Alexander Calder's crimson "Eagle" rises from the **OLYMPIC SCULPTURE PARK** (2901 Western Ave; 206/654-3180; see Top 25 Attractions in this chapter).

The **DENNY REGRADE** (aka Denny Triangle), home to nightspots such as sister clubs **TINI BIGS** (100 Denny Wy; 206/284-0931; tinibigs.com) and tiki-inspired **HULA HULA** (106 1st Ave N; 206/284-5003; hulahula.org), extends a block or two on either side of Denny Way from I-5 to Western Avenue; beyond is the waterfront. Where Western intersects Denny, the Northwest Lofts Building houses the à la Provence eatery **BOAT STREET CAFE AND KITCHEN** (3131 Western Ave, Ste 301; 206/632-4602; boatstreetcafe.com) and **CANLIS GLASS** (3131 Western Ave, Ste 329; 206/282-4428; canlisglass.com), showcasing J. P. Canlis's signature bamboo glass sculptures. *Map:F6–H5, F8–H7.*

SOUTH LAKE UNION

FROM THE SOUTHERN TIP OF LAKE UNION TO WESTLAKE AVENUE, BOUNDED BY DENNY WAY, I-5, AND AURORA AVENUE N (SR 99)

Seattle pioneer David Thomas Denny was the first to see South Lake Union's potential when he established his sawmill here in 1892. The manufacturing industry followed at the turn of the century, bringing shipbuilding, Boeing seaplane fabrication, and a regional Model T assembly plant to the historic building now occupied by the Shurgard Storage Centers headquarters. Over the century, South Lake Union evolved into an area of industrial and commercial growth, full of small businesses, warehouses and auto-oriented services. In the past decade, South Lake Union has fast developed into a hub for biotech organizations, including Fred Hutchinson Cancer Research Center, ZymoGenetics, Seattle Biomedical Research Institute, Merck & Co., and University of Washington Medicine.

Historically, the Cascade neighborhood east of Fairview Avenue was the only residential pocket in South Lake Union. However, thanks to billionaire Paul Allen and his company Vulcan Inc., many new mixed-use residential and retail projects are redefining South Lake Union as a hip place to live. Combined with numerous eateries, retailers, and tree-lined promenades, South Lake Union is well on its way to becoming a gleaming urban village. Case in point are the sleek new people-movers that comprise the **SEATTLE STREETCAR LINE** (seattlestreetcar.org). Locals may forever refer to the line, which launched in 2007, as the S.L.U.T., thanks to neighborhood coffee shop **KAPOW!** (1165 Harrison St; 206/447-5587; kapowcoffeeshop.com), which unofficially christened the streetcar system as the South Lake Union Trolley. The brightly colored streetcars travel a 2.6-mile, 11-stop route from South Lake Union to Westlake Center (Mon–Thurs 6am–9pm, Fri–Sat 6am–11pm, and Sun 10am–7pm). Adult fare is $1.50, youths, seniors and disabled persons pay just 50 cents, and kids five and under ride free. Riders may also use their Metro bus pass.

BEST PLACE
FOR A COCKTAIL?

"Vito's on First Hill—like a scene from Hitchcock's Vertigo."

Greg Nickels, mayor of Seattle

One of the stops on the Seattle Streetcar line, and the centerpiece of the South Lake Union neighborhood, is Vulcan's **2200** complex (2200 Westlake Ave), comprising the Pan Pacific Hotel (206/264-8111; seattle.panpacific.com), 261 condominium homes, and a miscellany of retail shops including **WHOLE FOODS MARKET** (206/621-9700; wholefoodsmarket.com) and **MARAZUL** (206/654-8170; marazulrestaurant.com), a Latin-Asian restaurant. Begin your exploration of this new urban super-hood at the **SOUTH LAKE UNION DISCOVERY CENTER** (101 Westlake Ave N; 206/342-5900; discoverslu.com), where you'll get a glimpse into South Lake Union's past, present, and future through interactive displays and exhibits. Dining options abound. **SLO JOE'S BIGTIME BACKYARD BBQ** (301 Westlake Ave N; 206/381-9200; slojoes.net) serves a mean pulled-pork sandwich and juicy barbecued ribs. Across the street, **BLUE MOON BURGERS** (920 Republican St; 206/652-0400) has good burgers, and don't miss their onion rings. **FEIERABEND** (422 Yale Ave N; 206/340-2528; feierabendseattle.com) boasts the largest selection of imported German beers on the West Coast—18 on tap! Tuck into some shepherd's pie and a foaming mug of Guinness at **PADDY COYNE'S** (1190 Thomas St; 206/405-1548; paddycoynes.net). Longtime late-night haunt **13 COINS** (125 Boren Ave N; 206/682-2513; 13coins.com) serves familiar comfort cuisine 24-7. **ESPRESSO VIVACE** (227 Yale Ave N; 206/388-5164; espressovivace.com) provides a caffeine fix in the Alley24 apartment building. Alongside longtime landmark retailers **REI** (see Top 25 Attractions in this chapter) and **DAVID SMITH & CO.** (1107 Harrison St; 206/223-1598; davidsmithco.com), newer spots dot the streets. **CHEFSHOP.COM**'s (305 9th Ave N; 206/286-9988; chefshop.com) storefront is a food lover's haven with tasting bars where you can try products, such as Italian balsamic vinegar from Modena, before you buy. Your urban tot will love Alley24's **TOTTINI** (259 Yale Ave N; 206/254-0400; tottini.com), which is filled with stylish bedroom and play furniture, organic bath products, and unique toys. With its wide range of pet accessories and healthy, high-quality pet food, pet boutique **URBAN BEAST** (217 Yale Ave N; 206/324-4400; urbanbeast-seattle.com) is a canine's dream come true. Take a dip at the modern Russian bathhouse **BANYA 5** (217 9th Ave N; 206/262-1234; banya5.com), where three different pools at varying temperatures, and dry and wet saunas do wonders to rejuvenate body and soul. At **URBAN MONKEYS** (1124 Harrison St; 206/262-9282; urbanmonkeys.com), kids have fun at classes such as "Little Lotus Yoga Camp" while urban moms enjoy a soothing on-site Swedish massage or French-tip mani/pedi. *Map:B3–E1, E5–H2.*

BALLARD

FROM LAKE WASHINGTON SHIP CANAL TO 85TH STREET NW, FROM 15TH AVENUE NW TO SHILSHOLE BAY, CENTERED ALONG NW MARKET STREET AND BALLARD AVENUE NW

Ballard began as an industrial burg, full of sawmills, shingle mills, and shipyards, and it has retained its distinctive character ever since (despite its annexation by the city of Seattle in 1907). Much of its current flavor derives from the hordes of Scandinavians who flocked to the shores of Salmon Bay looking for work in the late-19th and early-20th centuries. Traces of the Nordic life show up in the "Velkommen to Ballard" mural at Leary Avenue NW and NW Market Street and in the neighborhood's unofficial slogan of affirmation: "Ya sure, you betcha." In no other corner of town are you likely to find lutefisk for sale. The neighborhood's ethnic history is also apparent along NW Market Street, Ballard's main commercial hub. **NORSE IMPORTS SCANDINAVIAN GIFT SHOP** (2016 NW Market St; 206/784-9420) has more trolls than you would know what to do with, and **OLSEN'S SCANDINAVIAN FOODS** (2248 NW Market St; 206/783-8288; scandinavianfoods.net) sells homemade specialties and imported foods with tastes (and names) that celebrate their foreign roots. The **NORDIC HERITAGE MUSEUM** (3014 NW 67th St; 206/789-5707; nordicmuseum.org) displays textiles, tools, and photos from the old country and the Ballard of long ago. **BALLARD AVENUE NW**, a Historic Landmark District since 1976, gives you an idea of how this area looked a century ago—and how much it is changing now. Small and trendy retailers have moved in, making the street both a good strolling and shopping locale. **CAMELION DESIGN** (5335 Ballard Ave NW; 206/783-7125) sells furniture and artists' wares, **OLIVINE** (5344 Ballard Ave NW; 206/706-4188; olivine.net) deals in very feminine women's clothing, and **SOUVENIR** (5325 Ballard Ave NW; 206/297-7116) specializes in ultrahip handmade greeting cards. **DANDELION BOTANICAL COMPANY** (5424 Ballard Ave NW;

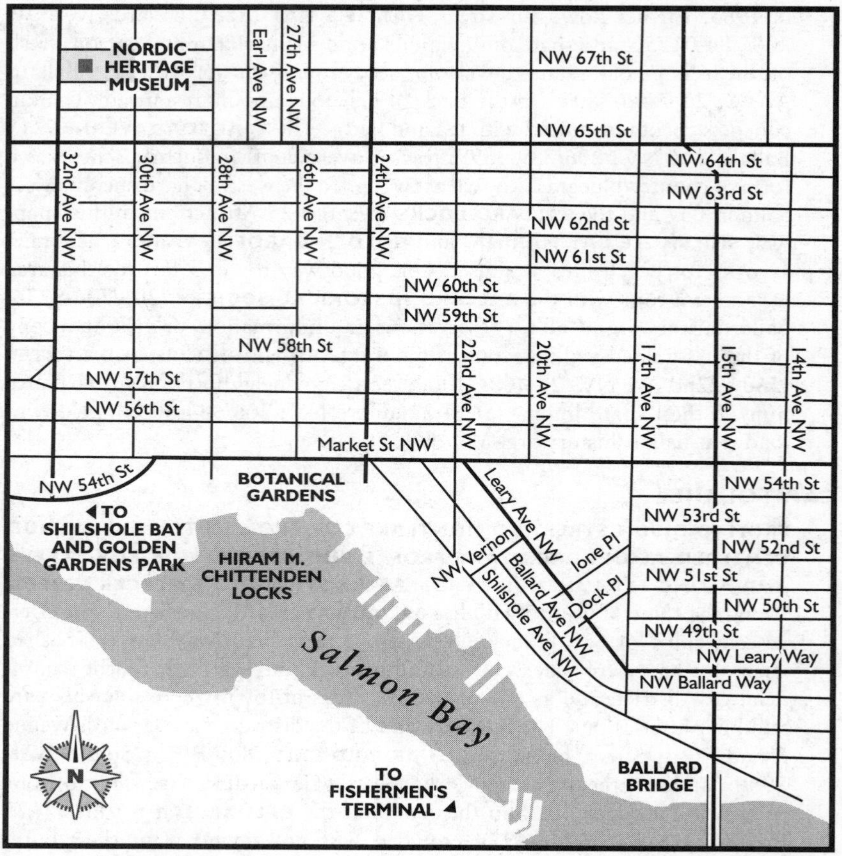

Ballard

206/545-8892; dandelionbotanical.com) is an herbal apothecary specializing in organic and ethically wildcrafted herbs, teas, and tinctures. Shopping make you hungry? Head to **KING'S HARDWARE** (5225 Ballard Ave NW; 206/782-0027; kingsballard.com), housed in a converted—what else?—hardware store, for burgers and beer. **LA CARTA DE OAXACA**'s (5431 Ballard Ave NW; 206/782-8722; lacartadeoaxaca.com) banana-leaf-bundled mole tamales are to die for. Great deep-dish pizzas and the "Orgasm," a sublime skillet chocolate chip cookie, aren't the only reasons to dine at **MADAME K'S** (5237 Ballard Ave NW; 206/783-9710). The sexy servers and scarlet décor are reminiscent of the location's bawdy past as a 19th-century bordello. The most prominent landmark along here is the **BALLARD CENTENNIAL BELL TOWER** (Ballard Avenue NW and 22nd Avenue NW), a cylindrical, copper-topped monument holding a 1,000-pound brass bell that was saved from Ballard's 1899 city hall, which stood on this corner until it was torn down after a severe earthquake in 1965. Farther down the street, **HATTIE'S HAT** (5231 Ballard Ave NW; 206/784-0175; hattieshat.com), with its imposing back bar and patrons fresh off the fishing boat, retains a welcome seedy tone. **FU KUN WU** (5410 Ballard Ave W; 206/706-7807), in the back of delicious noodle restaurant Thaiku, concocts cocktails infused with tea and herbs. The **TRACTOR TAVERN** (5213 Ballard Ave NW; 206/789-3599; tractortavern.com) frequently schedules a form of country/bluegrass known as twang. To the west, Ballard encompasses Salmon Bay and the **BALLARD LOCKS** (see Top 25 Attractions in this chapter), **SHILSHOLE BAY MARINA**, and **GOLDEN GARDENS PARK**, a perennial favorite for beach fires at sunset. One good way to get a feel for this area is to take a tour with the **BALLARD HISTORICAL SOCIETY** (206/706-9236; ballardhistory.org). Call for reservations and information, or pick up a copy of the self-guided walking tour at the **BALLARD NEIGHBORHOOD CENTER** (5604 22nd Ave NW, 206/684-4060; seattle.gov/neighborhoods/nsc/ballard.htm) or the Ballard library (5614 22nd Ave NW; 206/684-4089), or download it at ballardhistory.org. *Map:FF8.*

CAPITOL HILL

FROM MADISON STREET TO MONTLAKE CUT, FROM I-5 TO 23RD AVENUE, CENTERED ALONG BROADWAY FROM E PINE STREET TO E ROY STREET, AND ALONG 15TH AVENUE E FROM E PIKE STREET TO E MERCER STREET

Along the spine of Capitol Hill lies **BROADWAY**, Seattle's answer to the effervescent spirit of San Francisco's Castro Street. Broadway has established itself as a haven for black clothes and pierced body parts, as Seattle's unofficial gay district, and as one of the few areas of town where sidewalks are still busy after 10pm. The northern end of the district is at Harvard Avenue E and E Roy Street, home to the **HARVARD EXIT** (807 E Roy St; 206/323-8986; landmarktheatres.com/Market/Seattle/HarvardExitTheatre.htm), one of Seattle's foremost art-film theaters; and the **DELUXE BAR & GRILL** (625 Broadway E; 206/324-9697), crowded with folks who want their burgers and microbrews served without chichi décor on the side. Up the street, **DILETTANTE**'s (416 Broadway E; 206/329-6463; dilettante.com) truffles and creative cakes and coffee drinks will satisfy any chocoholic's craving. **BROADWAY GRILL** (314 Broadway E; 206/328-7000) is a hip hangout to see and be seen. Capitol Hill's free-stepping spirit is expressed in Jack Mackie's inlaid bronze "Dancers' Series": offbeat public art that appears at intervals as you walk south along Broadway, inviting strollers to get in step with the tango or the foxtrot. Vintage and imported fashion, books, and home accessories are the focus of Broadway's best stores. **BROADWAY MARKET** (between Republican and Harrison streets; 206/322-1610), featuring branches of Urban Outfitters and Gold's Gym, and a giant QFC supermarket, is an imposing symbol of the continuing million-dollar enfranchisement of this once-funky street. On the other side of Broadway are a well-stocked newsstand, **STEVE'S BROADWAY NEWS** (204 Broadway E; 206/324-7323), and a warmly eclectic bookstore, **BAILEY/COY BOOKS** (414 Broadway E; 206/323-8842; baileycoybooks.com). The southern end of the strip bustles with Seattle Central

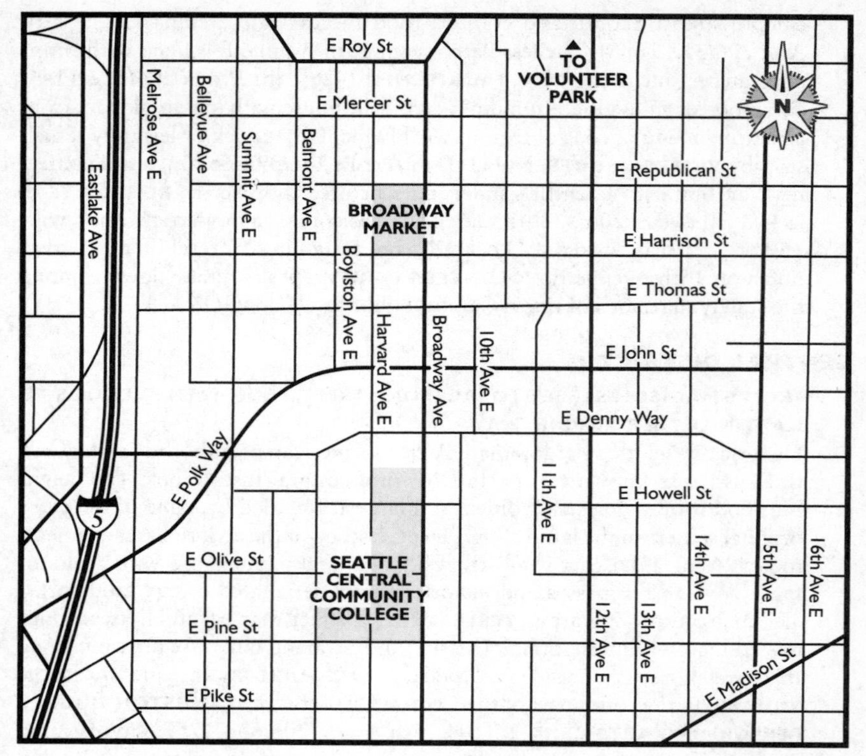

Capitol Hill

Community College's diverse students; across **PINE STREET** from the campus is a second excellent movie house, the **EGYPTIAN** (801 E Pine St; 206/323-4978; landmarktheatres.com/market/Seattle/EgyptianTheatre.htm), perched on the edge of the so-called Pike-Pine corridor. The corridor has become known for its rising housing costs, trendy little shops, restaurants, and nightclubs. Two to look out for are the graceful **CENTURY BALLROOM** (915 E Pine St; 206/324-7263; centuryballroom.com) and **THE BALTIC ROOM** (1207 Pine St; 206/625-4444; thebalticroom.net), a swanky joint frequently packed with the young and beautiful. Distinctly less chic—and proud of it—is the **COMET TAVERN** (922 E Pike St; 206/323-9853), where locals go to play pool and listen to homegrown bands. A burgeoning restaurant row has sprung up along Capitol Hill's 12th Avenue, near Seattle University. The stretch between E Cherry and E Union streets is now home to Italian eatery Osteria La Spiga (1429 12th Ave; 206/323-08881; laspiga.com), chef John Sundstrom's beloved restaurant Lark (926 12th Ave; 206/323-5275; larkseattle.com) and its sexy cocktail lounge sibling Licorous (928 12th Ave; 206/325-6947; licorous.com), the cozy French bistro Café Presse (1117 12th Ave; 206/709-7674;

cafepresseseattle.com), and comfort-food mecca Café Stellina (1429 12th Ave; 206/322-2688). The less flamboyant 15th Avenue E is lined with shops and eateries, including **COASTAL KITCHEN** (429 15th Ave E; 206/322-1145; chowfoods.com), a loud, fun diner-cum-grill-house with kickin' flavors from a rotating menu of coastal regions worldwide. For a quick or leisurely refuel, stop by **VICTROLA COFFEE** (411 15th Ave E; 206/325-6520; victrolacoffee.net), an outpost of Seattle's independent coffee shop scene. **REMEDY TEAS** (345 15th Ave E; 206/323-4832; remedyteas.com) is a modern tea shop with 150 organic teas, spiked tea cocktails, and tasty bites. Several blocks farther north on 15th Avenue E, **VOLUNTEER PARK** drapes its grassy lawns among the stately mansions of north Capitol Hill. *Map:HH6–GG6.*

CENTRAL DISTRICT

FROM E MADISON STREET TO JACKSON STREET, FROM 12TH AVENUE S TO MARTIN LUTHER KING JR. WAY

Historically Seattle's predominant African American neighborhood, the Central District is known for its churches and cultural institutions. The neighborhood is one of Seattle's oldest and largest, founded by some of the city's original settlers in the late 1870s. Once a hotbed of the civil rights movement, today's Central District is mostly residential and interspersed with a mix of family-owned businesses and historic houses designated as city landmarks. The major thoroughfare is **YESLER WAY**, a street that eventually feeds into the Chinatown/International District and straight into downtown. Along this stretch are the residential pockets of **SQUIRE PARK**, and **JACKSON SQUARE**. In the south part of the Central District is the **LANGSTON HUGHES PERFORMING ARTS CENTER** (104 17th Ave S; 206/684-4757; cityofseattle.net/parks/centers/langston.htm) where, on any given day, you might catch a local boys' choir or a performance of a play written by its namesake. Another point of pride is **GARFIELD HIGH SCHOOL**, which has produced the majority of Seattle's National Merit Scholars as well as an internationally known jazz band. The historic **DOUGLASS-TRUTH PUBLIC LIBRARY** (2300 E Yesler Wy; 206/684-4704) houses more than 9,000 items focused on African American literature and history, possibly the largest collection on the West Coast. It reopened in 2006 after a $6.8 million remodel and expansion that included the addition of a sunken reading room. The Central District also claims a burgeoning share of good restaurants. **EZELL'S FRIED CHICKEN** (501 23rd Ave; 206/324-4141; ezellschicken.com), a Seattle institution, is famous for its fried bird. Rumor has it Oprah used to have it flown out to Chicago. For authentic soul food, **JOANNA'S SOUL CAFÉ AND JAZZ CLUB** (2514 E Cherry St; 206/568-6300) has spicy collard greens, jambalaya, and jazz after 8pm, while **CATFISH CORNER** (2726 E Cherry St; 206/323-4330) serves up tasty Creole/Cajun food. For good eats in the south part of the neighborhood, hop in the line forming outside **SEATTLE DELI** (225 12th Ave S, Ste 101; 206/328-0106), where $2 will buy perhaps the best Vietnamese sandwich around. At **CENTRAL CINEMA** (1411 21st Ave; 206/686-6684; central-cinema.com), food and film lovers alike can watch a movie and dine on a sandwich or

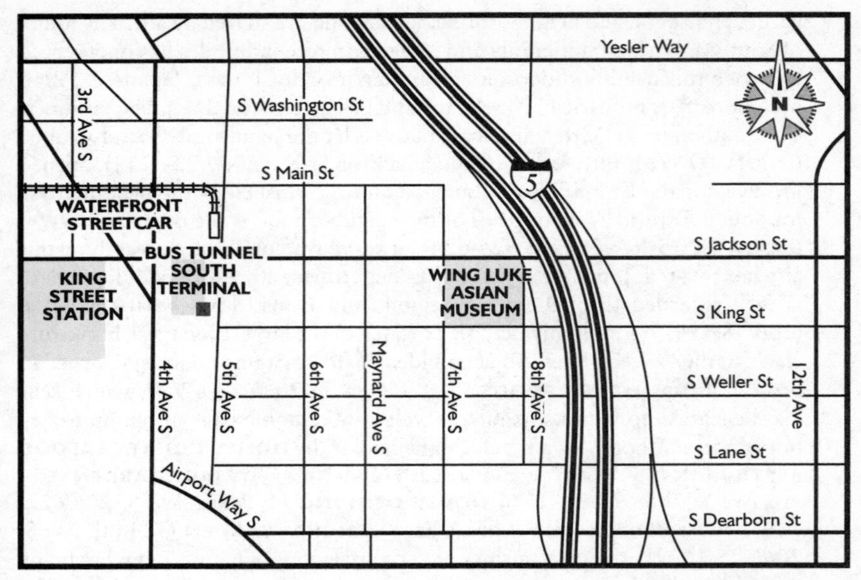

Chinatown/International District

stone-oven pizza. Snackers have a choice of salted edamame or popcorn. Toward the eastern part of the Central District, Sam Smith Park is where you can watch pick-up basketball, soccer, or cricket. *Map:HH7–JJ5.*

CHINATOWN/INTERNATIONAL DISTRICT

S DEARBORN STREET TO S WASHINGTON STREET, BETWEEN 4TH AVENUE S AND 14TH AVENUE S

Seattle's Chinatown first emerged on the eastern fringe of Pioneer Square in the 1880s as immigrant Chinese workers recruited to lay railroads, dig coal mines, and can salmon harvests poured in. Other Asian immigrants soon followed, notably Japanese and Filipinos attracted by the area's inexpensive housing and storefronts for their own businesses and restaurants. By the late 1930s, Chinatown was a distinct neighborhood, along with the West Coast's second-largest Japan Town, which lay adjacent on and around Yesler Way. When thousands of Seattle Japanese Americans were rounded up and interned during World War II, the African Americans who were arriving for military duty and defense work occupied their homes, eventually establishing bistros and dancehalls in the district that became renowned nationwide for jazz, swing, and the blues. Japantown never fully rebounded after the war, and the area's population further diversified as growing numbers of Filipinos, attracted to jobs at Alaska's booming canneries, passed through or settled down. In 1951, the neighborhood was renamed the "International District" to reflect this diversity. Today, Seattle's Chinatown/International District is a collection of distinct ethnic communities and a cohesive melting pot (a community garden, museum, and neighborhood playground are shared by all). The influx of Southeast Asian immigrants and refugees in recent decades has only served to enrich this neighborhood's longstanding mix of Chinese, Japanese, Filipinos, Koreans, and African Americans and has given the "ID" a new vibrancy. The southern edge of this district is marked by the handsome, barrel-vaulted **UNION STATION** (4th Avenue S and S Jackson Street; 206/622-3214), opened in 1911 for the Union Pacific Railroad and refurbished as the headquarters for Sound Transit. A centerpiece of the neighborhood is the emporium **UWAJIMAYA** (600 5th Ave S; 206/624-6248; uwajimaya.com), the closest thing this city has to a real Japanese supermarket/department store—its cooking school is well regarded throughout the region, and it also houses **KINOKUNIYA** (206/587-2477; kinokuniya.com), a branch of the largest Japanese bookstore chain in the United States. To get an idea of the engaging contrasts of the ID, drop in at tiny **HOVEN FOODS** (508 S King St; 206/623-6764), which sells excellent fresh tofu and soy milk as well as take-home bags of plump frozen pot stickers. A honey of a lunch can be had at the **HONEY COURT SEAFOOD RESTAURANT** (516 Maynard Ave S; 206/292-8828). Try **JADE GARDEN** (424 7th Ave S; 206/622-8181) or **HOUSE OF HONG** (409 8th Ave S; 206/622-7997; houseofhong.com) for dim sum. **SHANGHAI GARDEN** (524 6th Ave S; 206/625-1689) offers the cuisines of varying regions of China and what many consider to be the best Chinese food this Pacific Rim city has to offer. The oldest continuously operated Chinese restaurant in town—which is saying something—is **TAI TUNG** (659 S King St; 206/622-7372).

On South King Street, the **WING LUKE ASIAN MUSEUM** (719 S King St; 206/623-5124; wingluke.org), a Smithsonian Institution affiliate dedicated to exploring issues related to the culture, art, and history of Asian Pacific Americans, will settle into its new home in the historical East Kong Yick building in May 2008. Across Jackson Street to the north is the main Japanese district, where you'll find **KOBO AT HIGO** (604 S Jackson St; 206/622-7572; koboseattle.com). Once a pre–World War II Japanese five-and-dime, it was converted to a home and gift store in 2003. The new incarnation still has elements of its past and hosts rotating art exhibitions. The **PANAMA HOTEL** (605 1/2 S Main St; 206/223-9242; panamahotel.net), which houses the oldest Japanese bathhouse in the nation, has a quaint tea- and coffeehouse festooned with historical photographs. Here is also where many of the ID's Japanese restaurants are clustered, including **FUJI SUSHI** (520 S Main St; 206/624-1201), which has fabulous bento boxes, and Seattle's oldest sushi bar, **MANEKI** (304 6th Ave S; 206/622-2631). North on Sixth Avenue and then east on Washington a short way is **KOBE TERRACE PARK**, with a noble stone lantern from Seattle's Japanese sister city of Kobe. Here, too, you'll get a splendid view of the district, including the **DANNY WOO INTERNATIONAL DISTRICT COMMUNITY GARDENS** (206/624-1802). Built in the late 1970s, these gardens were parceled out to low-income elderly inhabitants of the neighborhood, who tend their tiny hillside plots with great pride. East of here on Jackson, the Chinatown/International District takes on a Vietnamese air; the area surrounding 12th Avenue S and S Jackson Street is known as

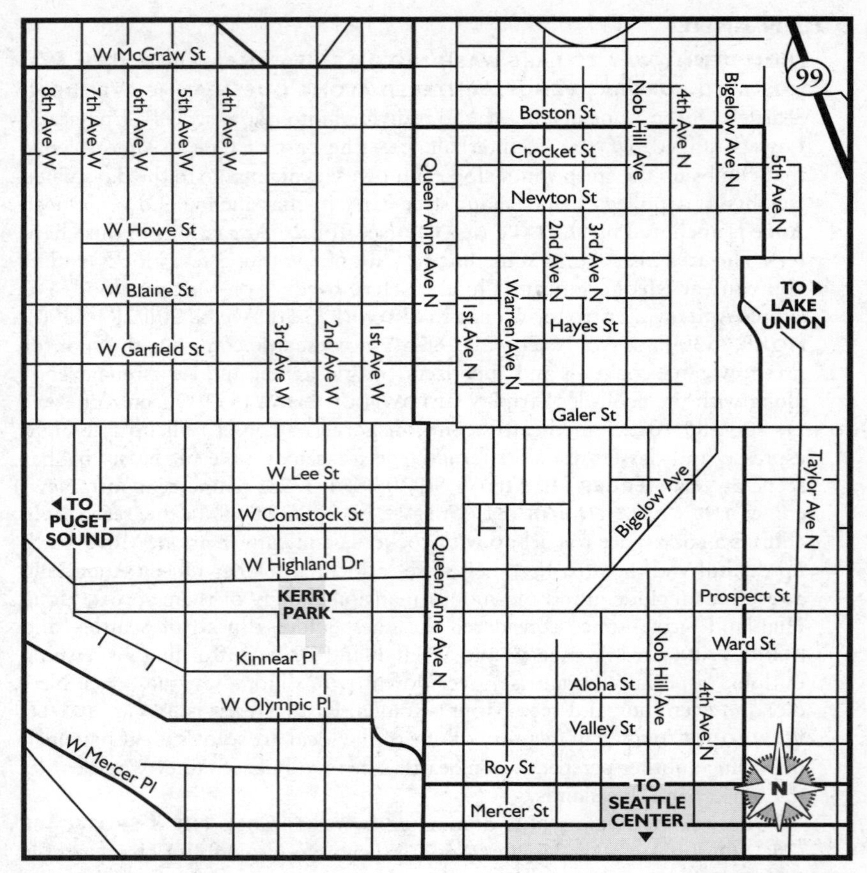

Queen Anne

LITTLE SAIGON. VIET WAH (1032 S Jackson St; 206/328-3557; vietwah.com) provides an excellent selection of fresh and packaged foods at very low prices and the most comprehensive selection of Chinese and Southeast Asian ingredients in town. Seattle has a well-deserved reputation for fine Vietnamese restaurants, and this is where you'll find many of them: **HUONG BINH** (1207 S Jackson St; 206/720-4907), **SAIGON BISTRO** (1032 S Jackson St, Ste 202; 206/329-4939), and **TAMARIND TREE** (1036-A S Jackson St; 206/325-3663; tamarindtreerestaurant.com). Or stop by the **SAIGON DELI** (1200 S Jackson St; 206/322-3700) for spring rolls and grilled beef sandwiches. *Map:O6–R6, O2–R2.*

QUEEN ANNE

FROM DENNY WAY TO LAKE WASHINGTON SHIP CANAL, FROM 15TH AVENUE W TO AURORA AVENUE, CENTERED ALONG QUEEN ANNE AVENUE N
Seattle's Queen Anne neighborhood is divided into two districts—Upper and Lower—joined by "the Counterbalance," the part of Queen Anne Avenue that climbs up the steep south slope and owes its nickname to the days when weights and pulleys helped haul streetcars up that incline. Lower Queen Anne is anchored by **SEATTLE CENTER** (see Top 25 Attractions in this chapter). The area also claims some fine restaurants: within a few blocks' radius you can eat Mediterranean, Chinese, Thai, fondue, or Mexican food. For simple American bistro food, head to **CROW** (823 5th Ave N; 206/283-8800). **MOXIE** (530 First Ave N; 206/283-6614; moxieseattle.com) hits the spot for preshow/game cocktails and appetizers. Seattle Center and KeyArena events, along with the neon-deco triplex **UPTOWN CINEMAS** (511 Queen Anne Ave N; 206/285-1022; amctheatres.com), disgorge patrons to fill up late-night espresso and dessert spots. Alternatively, folks may take in the stylin' bar scene at **TEN MERCER** (10 Mercer St; 206/691-3723; tenmercer.com). Newcomer **THE GREAT NABOB** (819 5th Ave N; 206/281-9850; thegreatnabob.com) is a cozy space to curl up with cocktails and conversation. Move north up the hill and the area becomes more residential. Upper Queen Anne's big attractions include grand old-money mansions, many of them spread along Highland Drive—once considered the finest address in all of Seattle—and **KERRY PARK** (3rd Avenue W and W Highland Drive), affording a smashing outlook (especially at sunrise) over downtown, Elliott Bay, the Space Needle, and even hide-and-seek Mount Rainier. Farther west is **BETTY BOWEN VIEWPOINT** (named in memory of one of the local art scene's great patrons), providing another perspective on Seattle's beauty: Puget Sound, West Seattle, the ferries, and the islands.

Queen Anne Avenue N is dominated by restaurants. **THE 5 SPOT CAFE** (1502 Queen Anne Ave N; 206/285-7768; chowfoods.com) is rich in attitude and American regional cuisines; elegant wine bar **BRICCO DELLA REGINA ANNA** (1525 Queen Anne Ave N; 206/285-4900; bricoseattle.com) has wine and cheese pairings starring both old and new world victuals. At **ORRAPIN THAI CUISINE** (10 Boston St; 206/283-7118), find staples such as pad thai and spring rolls or experiment with off-the-beaten-path items like salmon curry. When the sun sets, head next door to **THE O LOUNGE** (2208 Queen Anne Ave N; 206/352-6594), featuring notable musicians in stripped-down performances. The often-noisy **HILLTOP ALEHOUSE** (2129 Queen Anne Ave N; 206/285-3877; seattlealehouses.com) concentrates on pub grub and beers; **PARAGON BAR & GRILL** (2125 Queen Anne Ave N; 206/283-4548; paragonseattle.com) serves traditional American dishes with elegant twists. Deserving attention, too, is **QUEEN ANNE AVENUE BOOKS** (1811 Queen Anne Ave N; 206/283-5624; queenannebooks.com), strong on fiction and children's lit; **A & J MEATS AND SEAFOODS** (2401 Queen Anne Ave N; 206/284-3885), offering a diverse selection of basic cuts and prepared meals;

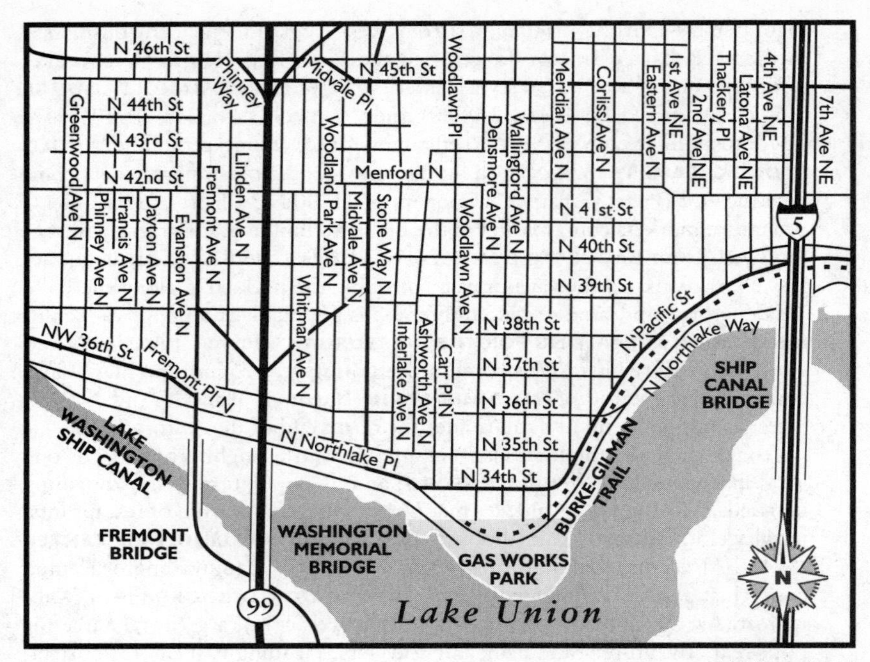

Fremont/Wallingford

and the tempting **MACRINA BAKERY** (615 W McGraw St; 206/283-5900; macrinabakery.com). *Map:GG7.*

FREMONT/WALLINGFORD

NORTH OF LAKE WASHINGTON SHIP CANAL AND LAKE UNION, FROM 15TH AVENUE W TO I-5, CENTERED ALONG FREMONT AVENUE N AND N/NE 45TH STREET

Like so many of the hippies who once gave the neighborhood its funky charm, Fremont seems to have gone mainstream. Yes, it still boldly proclaims itself the "Center of the Universe" and delights in the occasional shock of nude bicyclists in its summer Solstice Parade every June. But the development of new commercial and office buildings on and near Fremont's waterfront—including those that house Adobe software company's Seattle outpost—now clogs surrounding streets and causes observers to worry about the district's eroding soul. Still, streets are filled with highly browsable antique, secondhand, and retro-kitsch stores such as **THE DAILY PLANET** (3416 Fremont Ave N; 206/633-0895) and **DELUXE JUNK** (3518 Fremont Pl N; 206/634-2733). **PORTAGE BAY GOODS** (706 N 34th St; 206/547-5221; portagebaygoods.com) sells cool greeting cards and eclectic gifts, including recycled picture frames made from discarded bike chains. At **DESTEENATION SHIRT COMPANY** (3412 Evanston Ave N; 206/324-9403; desteenation.com), you'll find logo T-shirts sporting original art from West Coast independent businesses including Ballard's Tractor Tavern and the Little Red Hen in Green Lake. Drop into one of the slew of stylish eateries/bars, such as **TRIANGLE LOUNGE** (3507 Fremont Pl N; 206/632-0880) and **TOST** (513 N 36th St; 206/547-0240; tostlounge.com). If you're screaming for ice cream, get in line at **COLD STONE CREAMERY** (624 N 34th St; 206/547-3200; coldstonecreamery.com) near the **PCC** (Puget Consumers Cooperative) (600 N 34th St; 206/632-6811; pccnaturalmarkets.com) market in the Block 40 building. Or grab a gourmet sandwich from **BAGUETTE BOX** (626 N 34th St; 206/632-1511; baguette-box.com). Walk off those calories by strolling the park strip along the Lake Washington Ship Canal or take in Fremont's popular—and populist—sculpture art, such as **"WAITING FOR THE INTERURBAN"** (Fremont Avenue N and N 34th Street), which locals revel in decorating year-round; the huge—and controversial—statue of **VLADIMIR LENIN** (Fremont Place N and N 36th Street); and the Fremont Troll (under the north end of the Aurora Bridge).

To the east lies "the James Garner among Seattle neighborhoods," as one local magazine dubbed **WALLINGFORD**, and its population of mostly young marrieds. Most of the businesses hug N 45th Street. A warren of restaurants, jewelry/clothing stores, and bookshops are inside **WALLINGFORD CENTER** (N 45th Street and Wallingford Avenue N; 206/547-7246; wallingfordcenter.com). Just across Wallingford Avenue is **WIDE WORLD BOOKS** (4411 Wallingford Ave N; 206/634-3453; wideworldtravels.com), a great resource for both real adventurers and armchair travelers. Heading east on 45th Street, you can't miss the very Irish **MURPHY'S PUB** (1928 N 45th St; 206/634-2110; murphyseattle.com), **BOULANGERIE** (2200 N 45th St; 206/634-2211) and their flaky croissants and sweet-tart apple turnovers, and **DICK'S DRIVE-IN** (111 NE 45th St; 206/632-5125; ddir.com), a Seattle classic serving some of the best french fries in town and a parking lot full of teens in lust. Anchoring the south end of Wallingford is **GAS WORKS PARK** on the north shore of Lake Union (see Top 25 Attractions in this chapter). *Map:FF7*

GREENWOOD/PHINNEY RIDGE/GREEN LAKE

ALONG GREENWOOD AVENUE N AND PHINNEY AVENUE N, FROM N 45TH STREET TO N 85TH STREET, AND EAST TO I-5

Greenwood is a burgeoning, though still family-oriented neighborhood that is currently flush with new restaurants and retail. The neighborhood's most interesting stretch runs south from N 85th Street along Greenwood Avenue N. The **PIG 'N WHISTLE** (8412 Greenwood Ave N; 206/782-6044) is a cozy pub and eatery offering fine ribs and ample sandwiches (try the savory meat-loaf variety). For a dollop of attitude with your latte, there's **DIVA ESPRESSO** (7916 Greenwood Ave N; 206/781-1213; divaespresso.com). **YANNI'S** (7419 Greenwood Ave N; 206/783-6945) is one of the top Greek restaurants in the city; **CARMELITA** (7314 Greenwood Ave N; 206/706-7703; carmelita.net) dispenses inventive vegetarian meals; and the **74TH STREET ALE HOUSE** (7401 Greenwood Ave N; 206/784-2955; seattlealehouses.com) is known for its chicken sandwiches and spicy soups. Neighborhood bistro **STUMBLING**

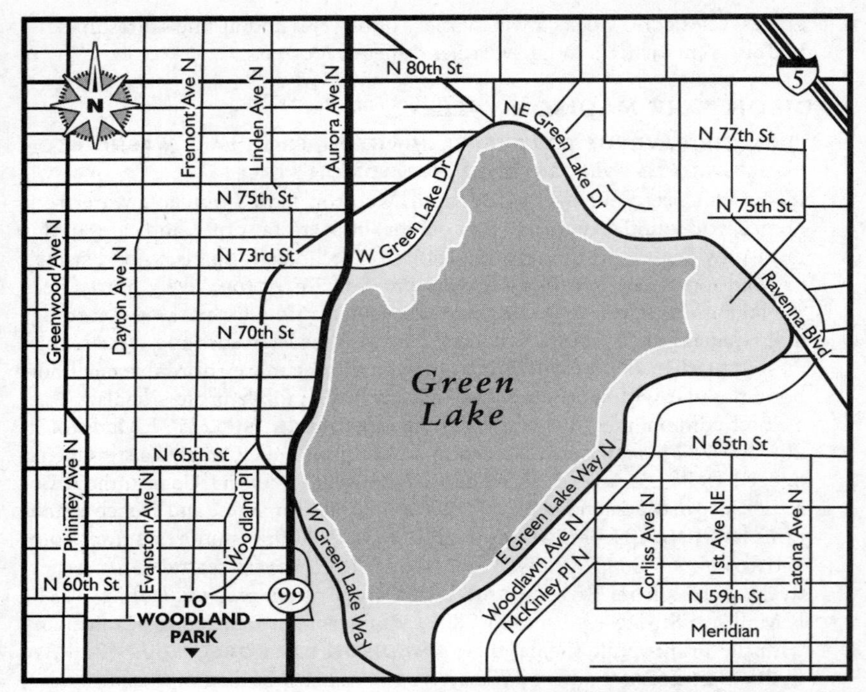

Greenwood/Phinney Ridge/Green Lake

GOAT (6722 Greenwood Ave N; 206/784-3535; stumblinggoatbistro.com) showcases local ingredients in a funky atmosphere, while **OLIVER'S TWIST** (6822 Greenwood Ave N; 206/706-6673) offers creative cocktails and small bites. Traveling south, you'll cross into the Phinney Ridge neighborhood, where Greenwood Avenue N becomes Phinney Avenue N at N 67th Street. That's also where you'll find **RED MILL BURGERS** (312 N 67th St; 206/783-6362; redmillburgers.com), addicting crowds with its wide selection of juicy burgers. Weekends cause a lineup of breakfast aficionados outside **MAE'S PHINNEY RIDGE CAFÉ** (6412 Phinney Ave N; 206/782-1222; maescafe.com). Continue south on Phinney, and you'll hear the trumpeting of elephants and cackling of wild birds that signal your approach to the **WOODLAND PARK ZOO** (see Top 25 Attractions in this chapter). East of Greenwood, the Green Lake neighborhood bustles with runners, walkers, singles on the lookout, and patrons of the many businesses that ring the water. On the lake's east side, **NELL'S** (6804 E Green Lake Wy N; 206/524-4044; nellsrestaurant.com) gives a Mediterranean accent to regional foods such as Columbia River sturgeon and Dungeness crab. **SPUD FISH 'N' CHIPS** (6860 E Green Lake Wy N; 206/524-0565) wraps up orders of flaky fish and greasy fries. **GREGG'S GREENLAKE CYCLE** (7007 Woodlawn Ave NE; 206/523-1822;

greggscycles.com) stocks a wide variety of bicycles and in-line skates for sale, but also rents wheels to fair-weather athletes. *Map: EE7.*

MADISON PARK/MADISON VALLEY

FROM 23RD AVENUE TO LAKE WASHINGTON, FROM LAKE WASHINGTON BOULEVARD TO I-90, CENTERED ON MADISON STREET

If you can peel your eyes away from Madison Park's opulent, waterfront homes, you'll find an entire row of quaint shops, restaurants, and cafés in this ultra-tony Seattle neighborhood. Though it technically spans a good stretch of Madison Street, its main "downtown" consists of four lively blocks near the lake itself. If you're driving here, leave extra time for parking—evenings and weekends, it's not easy to squeeze between the Mercedes and Jaguars. Just west of Madison Park is Madison Valley, a younger, more affordable neighborhood popular with urban families and upwardly mobile professionals.

Both communities offer numerous eateries. Sexy **CRUSH** (2319 E Madison St; 206/302-7874; chefjasonwilson.com), in Madison Valley, created a stir when it opened for its Los Angles–tinged décor and inventive cuisine. Up near the Arboretum, also in Madison Valley, are the incomparable Japanese and French restaurants **NISHINO** (3130 E Madison St; 206/322-5800; nishinorestaurant.com) and **ROVER'S** (2808 E Madison St; 206/325-7442; rovers-seattle.com), respectively. Across from Rover's, **SAINT-GERMAIN** offers *magnifique* bites (2811 E Madison St, Ste A; 206/323-9800; saintgermainseattle.com). Continuing with the Francophile theme, there's **MADISON PARK CAFÉ** (1807 42nd Ave E; 206/324-2626; madisonparkcafe.ypguides.net/), hidden in a small house, serving bistro-style food at bistro-style prices. While in the heart of Madison Park, you'll find young urbanites chowing on tapas and sipping $10 margaritas at **CACTUS** (4220 E Madison St; 206/324-4140; cactusrestaurants.com). If a pint and a burger is more your style, head next door to the authentic pub **ATTIC** (4226 E Madison St; 206/323-3131). An outcropping of appealing shops includes **ROPA-BELLA** (4105 E Madison St; 206/324-7985), purveyor of stylish apparel and accessories; and **PEARSON & GRAY** (4110 E Madison St; 206/322-2765) and **MAISON MICHEL** (4118 E Madison St; 206/325-4600; maisonmichel.com), which both stock a good selection of quality antiques. At the end of Madison Street sits **MADISON PARK BEACH**, one of the city's most popular sunbathing (and singles) spots.

MADRONA/LESCHI

BETWEEN LAKE WASHINGTON AND MARTIN LUTHER KING JR. WAY, E DENNY WAY AND I-90. CENTERED ON 34TH AVENUE, LAKE WASHINGTON BOULEVARD AND LAKESIDE AVENUE

Ethnically and commercially diverse, the Madrona and Leschi neighborhoods paint a picture of contrasts: modest bungalows juxtaposed with grand lakefront mansions and a quaint and quiet small-town feel enlivened by bustling business districts. Some of the city's most dramatic views are found here, as well as lovely parks, beaches, and historic homes.

Like the Central District, Madrona is undergoing transformation. Once predominantly the home of middle-class African Americans, the neighborhood is now increasingly home to white professionals and their families, attracted by (once) low housing prices and proximity to downtown. Madrona's main drag runs along 34th Street E. Only five blocks long, yet it's home to an eclectic collection of businesses, from family-owned and -run **WILRIDGE WINERY** (1416 34th Ave; 206/325-3051; wilridgewinery.com) to **CONROW PORCELAIN STUDIO** (1429 34th Ave; 206/324-0734; conrowporcelain.com). The best breakfast and brunch action is at the **HI SPOT CAFE** (1410 34th Ave E; 206/325-7905; hispotcafe.com); try the Bengal Benedict, a curry-infused variation on the traditional breakfast treat. **ST. CLOUDS** (1131 34th Ave; 206/726-1522; stclouds.com) is popular for dinner and drinks. New kids on the block include **CRÉMANT** (1423 34th Ave; 206/322-4600; cremantseattle.com)—its Gruyère-crusted onion soup never fails to please—and **COUPAGE** (1404 34th Ave; 206/322-1974; coupageseattle.com), with its Euro-Asian fusion cuisine. Other notable establishments include **MADRONA MOOSE** (1421 34th Ave; 206/320-7900; madronamoose.com) and its extensive collections of European and domestic children's apparel and accessories, the **SCOTTISH TEA SHOP** (1121 34th Ave; 206/324-6034; scottishteashop.com) for tea and Scottish paraphernalia, and the **CONLEY HAT MANUFACTURING COMPANY** (1112 34th Ave E; 206/322-1868; halcyon.com/hatter), where Alexander Conley III still makes the same hats his grandfather did. Closer to the water is the well-regarded **SPECTRUM DANCE THEATRE** (800 Lake Washington Blvd; 206/325-4161; spectrumdance.org).

BEST PLACE
TO WATCH PEOPLE AND DOGS?

"Why Green Lake, of course! It's particularly fun to see how much owners and pets look like they belong together."

Dr. Pepper Schwarz, UW sociology professor and relationship guru

---

South of Madrona, Leschi lies along Lake Washington directly east of the Central District. This lakeside neighborhood has served as a recreational hub for Seattleites since the 1890s, when the Yesler-Leschi cable car carried urbanites from Pioneer Square to a lakeside recreational area where a casino, zoo, boathouse, and formal gardens awaited them. Today, the two-block business district still feels like a laid-back beach town. For delicious steaks and a delightful view of Lake Washington, try **DANIEL'S BROILER** (200 Lake Washington Blvd; 206/329-4191; www.schwartzbros.com/daniels.cfm); for casual Pacific Northwest fare, **BLUWATER LESCHI** (102 Lakeside Ave S; 206/328-2233; bluwaterbistro.com) offers grilled salmon and Dungeness crab mac and cheese. If you ride your bike to this neighborhood and you get a flat, fear not—the fellas at **IL VECCHIO BICYCLES** (140 Lakeside Ave; 206/324-8148; ilvecchio.com) will put you back in business.

In addition, the Madrona/Leschi neighborhoods boast a triptych of Frederick Law Olmsted–designed parks linked together by leafy Lake Washington Boulevard. **MADRONA PARK** features a swimming beach, a lakefront jogging path, and a lushly wooded hillside with hiking trails. On any given sunny afternoon, you'll count more nannies with babies than seagulls. If you continue south toward the I-90 floating bridge, you'll hit **FRINK PARK**, a densely wooded ravine winding down to the lake, while charming **LESCHI PARK** is a well-manicured, rolling hillside lawn planted with exotic trees and rose gardens.

UNIVERSITY DISTRICT

FROM PORTAGE BAY/MONTLAKE CUT TO NE 65TH STREET, FROM I-5 TO 35TH AVENUE NE, CENTERED ALONG UNIVERSITY WAY NE

Just 15 minutes north from downtown on the freeway, the 694-acre **UNIVERSITY OF WASHINGTON** campus is the center of a vital and diverse community, as well as the Northwest's top institute of higher learning. The university was founded in 1861 on a plot of land downtown (on University Street) and moved to its present site in 1895. In 1909, the campus hosted Seattle's first world's fair—the Alaska-Yukon-Pacific Exposition—and inherited from that not only some grand buildings, but infrastructure improvements to support the neighborhood's growth. The "U District" is the city's most youth-dominated area, with street life running the gamut from fresh-scrubbed college students to panhandling punk rockers. The **UW VISITOR INFORMATION CENTER** (4014 University Wy NE; 206/543-9198) has maps and information regarding the large, well-landscaped campus. The university's main entrance is on NE 45th Street at 17th Avenue NE opposite **GREEK ROW**, a collection of stately older mansions inhabited mostly by fraternities and sororities. Just inside that entrance, to the right, is the **BURKE MUSEUM OF NATURAL HISTORY AND CULTURE** (17th Avenue at 45th Street; 206/543-5590; burkemuseum.org), displaying Native American artifacts and natural-history exhibits. Wander south past the Burke on Memorial Way to see **DENNY HALL**, the oldest building on campus (circa 1895) and the source of the hourly chimes that ring throughout the district. Continue south through the **QUAD**, where cherry blossoms bloom beautiful in springtime, and you'll find **CENTRAL PLAZA—AKA RED SQUARE**—a striking marriage of brutalist architecture and Siena's town square. Adjacent are **MEANY HALL** and the **HENRY ART GALLERY** (see Top 25 Attractions in this chapter), but most noteworthy is **SUZZALLO LIBRARY** (206/543-9158; lib.washington.edu/suzzallo), the UW's main research library, with a Gothic exterior and stained-glass windows, as well as its modern **ALLEN LIBRARY** addition (donated by Microsoft co-wizard Paul Allen). Walk south between Suzzallo and the adjacent administration building and you'll reach **DRUMHELLER FOUNTAIN** ("Frosh Pond"), a pleasant stopping point, from which (on a clear day) you can see Mount Rainier.

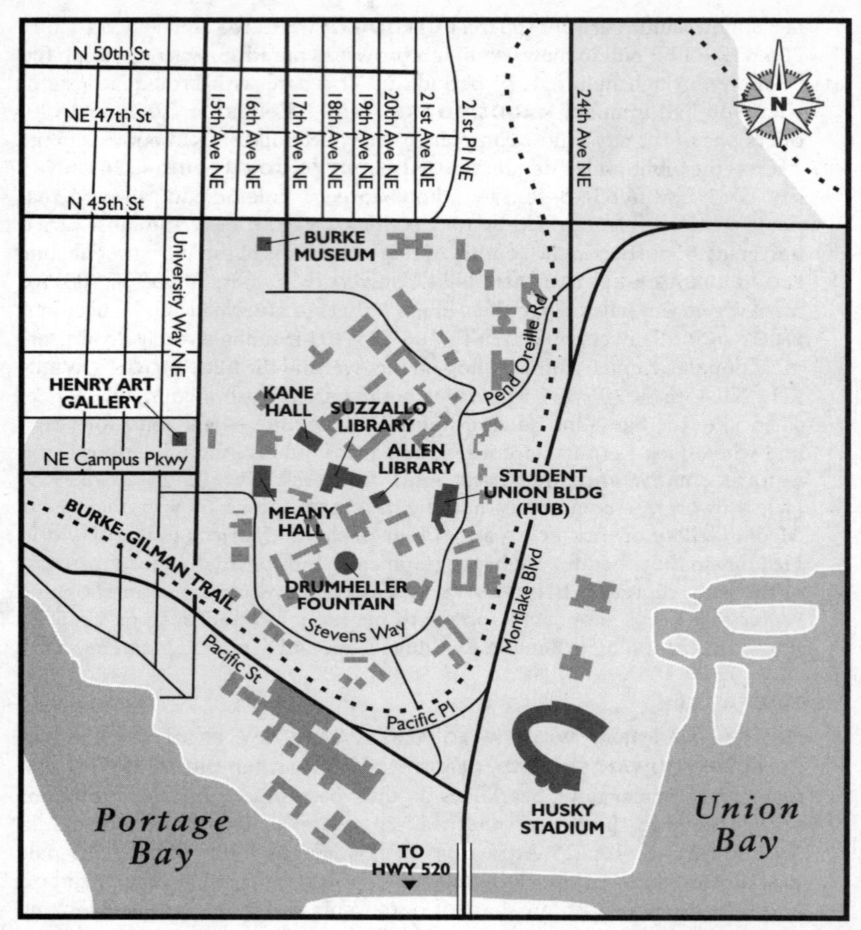

University District

If the university is the brains of this district, **UNIVERSITY WAY NE**, known to all as "the Ave," is its nerve center. In the last decade, the Ave has undergone continual revitalization efforts to try to reverse the damage done by drug dealers and homeless teens who drove out some retailers. More than $8 million was poured into repaved and widened sidewalks, new pedestrian and street lighting, new trees, street furnishings, and public art from Campus Parkway NE to NE 50th Street. The Ave has some distinctly local and often eccentric spots. **BIG TIME BREWERY AND ALEHOUSE** (4133 University Wy NE; 206/545-4509; bigtimebrewery.com) offers good sandwiches and beers made on the premises. Just off the street in an alley you'll find **CAFE ALLEGRO** (4214½ University Wy NE; 206/633-3030), serving excellent espresso in a counterculturish atmosphere. **BULLDOG NEWS** (4208 University Wy NE; 206/632-6397; bulldognews.com) is a browser's paradise, where you can flip leisurely through hundreds of periodicals. If a date with Proust is more of what you had in mind, **MAGUS BOOKS** (1408 NE 42nd St; 206/633-1800) offers one of the city's most comprehensive collections of used books. Up the street is the bibliophile's dream, the **UNIVERSITY BOOK STORE** (4326 University Wy NE; 206/634-3400; www.bookstore.washington.edu), in perpetual rivalry with the Harvard Co-op for the title of biggest, best, and most varied university bookshop in the country. Other must-visits in the U District include **FLOWERS BAR & RESTAURANT** (4247 University Wy NE; 206/633-1903) for tasty vegetarian cuisine (try their lunch buffet) in an eclectic ambience; **RED LIGHT** (4560 University Way NE; 206/545-4044; redlightvintage.com), the most popular vintage clothing shop on the Ave; and the **BLUE MOON TAVERN** (712 NE 45th St; 206/675-9116; bluemoonseattle.blogspot.com), where poet Theodore Roethke—and, later, novelist Tom Robbins—held court for years, and where Jack Kerouac (according to legend) did his inimitable thing. Stop by **JACK STRAW PRODUCTIONS** (4261 Roosevelt Wy NE; 206/634-0919; jackstraw.org), a community audio arts organization, to visit their New Media Gallery or pick up an audio tour of the U District's public artwork. Heading in the other direction (geographically and spiritually), just northeast of the main campus is **UNIVERSITY VILLAGE**, an upscale, open-air shopping center that keeps shoppers happy with big-name vendors such as Crate & Barrel, Anthropologie, Banana Republic, Gap, and Sephora. *Map:FF6.*

WEST SEATTLE

FROM W MARGINAL WAY SW TO ALKI AVENUE SW, FROM SW BARTON STREET TO DUWAMISH HEAD, CENTERED ALONG CALIFORNIA AVENUE SW

On warm summer days, Seattleites do their best impression of Californians when they shed their fleece and head en masse to Alki Beach (along Alki Avenue SW; see Top 25 Attractions in this chapter). But because the pale pastiness of skin kept too long under wraps can be blinding, the neighborhood has developed its fair share of restaurants and shops for those looking to avoid the glare. Along Alki Avenue SW, the **ALKI BAKERY** (2738 Alki Ave SW; 206/935-1352; alkibakery.com) is a popular neighborhood hangout for iced mochas or cinnamon rolls. Pizza lovers can sink their teeth into **PEGASUS PIZZA**'s (2758 Alki Ave SW; 206/932-4849) thick-crusted pies loaded with toppings from the ordinary (pepperoni) to the extraordinary (sunflower seeds). You can't miss the 3-foot-high replica of Manhattan's **STATUE OF LIBERTY**, but if you prefer your landmarks full-size and tourable, check out the **ALKI POINT LIGHTHOUSE** (3201 Alki Ave SW), located at the southern end of Alki Beach. Built in 1913, this 37-foot functioning U.S. Coast Guard facility offers 30-minute guided tours. Continue farther south, along Marine View Drive all the way to Fauntleroy Way SW, and you'll reach Lincoln Park (see Parks and Beaches in this chapter) and the ferry dock where you can hop a boat to Vashon Island. Also worth visiting in West Seattle is an area called **THE JUNCTION** (around California Avenue SW and SW Alaska Street),

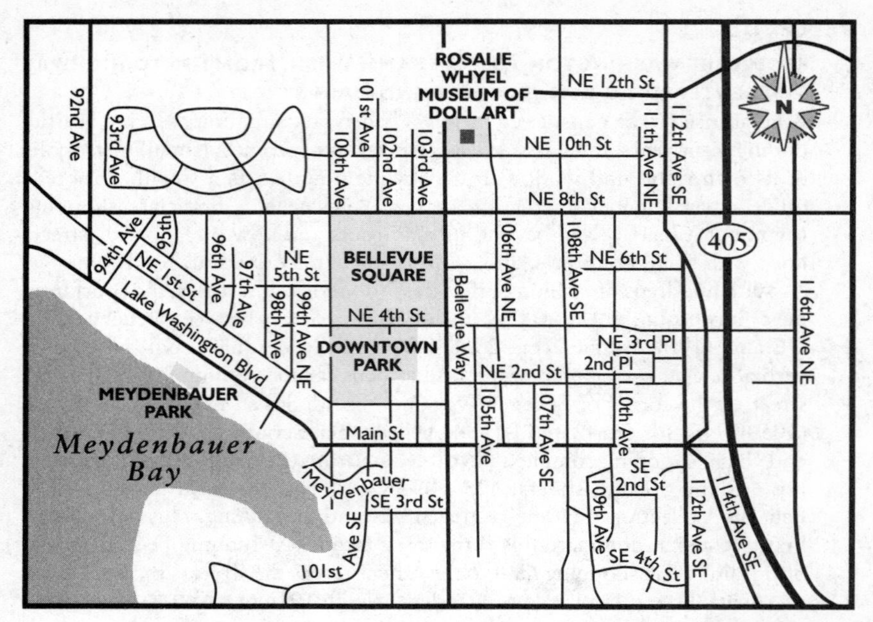

Bellevue

known for its historical murals, as well as the West Seattle Farmers' Market (see the Farmers' Markets sidebar in this chapter). While in the neighborhood, swing by **EASY STREET RECORDS** (4559 California Ave SW; 206/938-3279; easystreetonline.com), which boasts a savvy staff and expansive listening stations; the **ARTSWEST** theater and gallery (4711 California Ave SW; 206/938-0339; artswest.org); and **CAPERS** (4521 California Ave SW; 206/932-0371), a home and gift store with a café known for its scones and quiches. Stock up on gift wrap supplies at **SWEE SWEE PAPERIE** (4218 SW Alaska St; 206/937-7933; sweesweepaperie.com) and stop by **HUSKY DELI** (4721 California Ave SW; 206/937-281; huskydeli.com), famous for its homemade ice cream. For dinner, **TALARICO'S** (4718 California Ave SW; 206/937-7463) features New York–style pizza slices as big as shovel heads in a convivial dining room with windows that open to the street in summer. When you're ready for a nightcap, try **WEST 5** (4539 California Ave SW; 206/935-1966; westfive.com).

To get the best perspective on West Seattle, reach the neighborhood via **WATER TAXI** (206/205-3866). This 8-minute boat ride travels from Pier 54 on the downtown Seattle waterfront to West Seattle's Seacrest Park. The taxi runs seven days a week, May through October. Adults pay $2 (one way), and children under 5 ride free. *Map:JJ8.*

BELLEVUE

FROM LAKE WASHINGTON TO LAKE SAMMAMISH, FROM I-90 TO HIGHWAY 520, CENTERED ON BELLEVUE WAY AND MAIN STREET

Bellevue used to be considered merely a bedroom community serving Seattle, but in recent years, the Eastside's largest city has become a (small) metropolis in its own right, and its downtown skyline now boasts a wealth of hotels, office towers—and construction cranes. Bellevue is a first-class shopping town, but it has evolved beyond its mall roots and now offers parks, streets lined with small boutiques, and a surprising variety of ethnic foods.

With hundreds of fashion outlets, fast-fooderies, and stores, the constantly metamorphosing **BELLEVUE SQUARE** (NE 8th Street between Bellevue Way NE and 110th Avenue NE; 425/454-8096; bellevuesquare.com) is the proverbial one-stop-shopping center and a focus for the community. Across the street, at the corner of Bellevue Way and NE 8th Street, is **BELLEVUE PLACE** (10500 NE 8th St; 425/453-5634; bellevueplace.com), a hotel, restaurant, and chichi shopping complex. **LINCOLN SQUARE** (Bellevue Way NE between NE 6th and NE 8th streets; 425/646-3660) forms the third jewel in "The Bellevue Collection." Home-related stores and fine dining, plus a 16-screen luxury cinema, dominate this three-story facade. A stunning pedestrian sky bridge links one shopping mall to the other. Across the street is the **BELLEVUE ARTS MUSEUM.** On nice days, wander through 19-acre **DOWNTOWN PARK,** also adjacent to the Square, where you'll find a 240-foot-wide, 10-foot-high waterfall; a canal enclosing a 5-acre meadow; and a 28-foot-wide promenade.

Only two blocks from Bellevue Square, **MEYDENBAUER BEACH PARK** (419 98th Ave NE), located on the shores of Meydenbauer Bay, is an immaculately preserved secret—only residents-in-the-know ever find it. Beyond the modern glitz and glamour of the malls, **OLD BELLEVUE** sits in quiet elegance between SE 100th Street and Bellevue Way along what was once a major thoroughfare, Main Street. In recent years, a Main Street revival has seen new restaurants and retail shops. Find delightful French flea market chic at **WATSON KENNEDY FINE LIFE** (10032 Main St; 425/467-1142; watsonkennedy.com) or browse the antique collections of **SOPHISTICATED SWINE** (10230 Main St; 425/452-9300; sophisticatedswine.com). **PORCELLA URBAN MARKET** (10245 Main St, Ste 101; 425/286-0080; porcellaurbanmarket.com) has gourmet edibles to eat in or take with you.

Art-fair lovers shouldn't miss the **PACIFIC NORTHWEST ARTS AND CRAFTS FAIR** (held the last weekend in July), which attracts hundreds of artists from throughout the West. It is said to be the largest crafts fair in the Northwest, and local legend holds that it never rains on the weekend of the fair (Eastsiders plan weddings and barbecues accordingly).

East of town, out SE 8th Street, is **KELSEY CREEK PARK** (425/452-7688), a good place for suburban kids to get a taste (albeit a tame one) of the country. A demonstration farm offers up-close contact with pigs, horses, chickens, and rabbits. Farther east lies **CROSSROADS SHOPPING CENTER** (NE 8th Street and 156th Avenue NE; 425/644-1111), a midsize mall where the emphasis

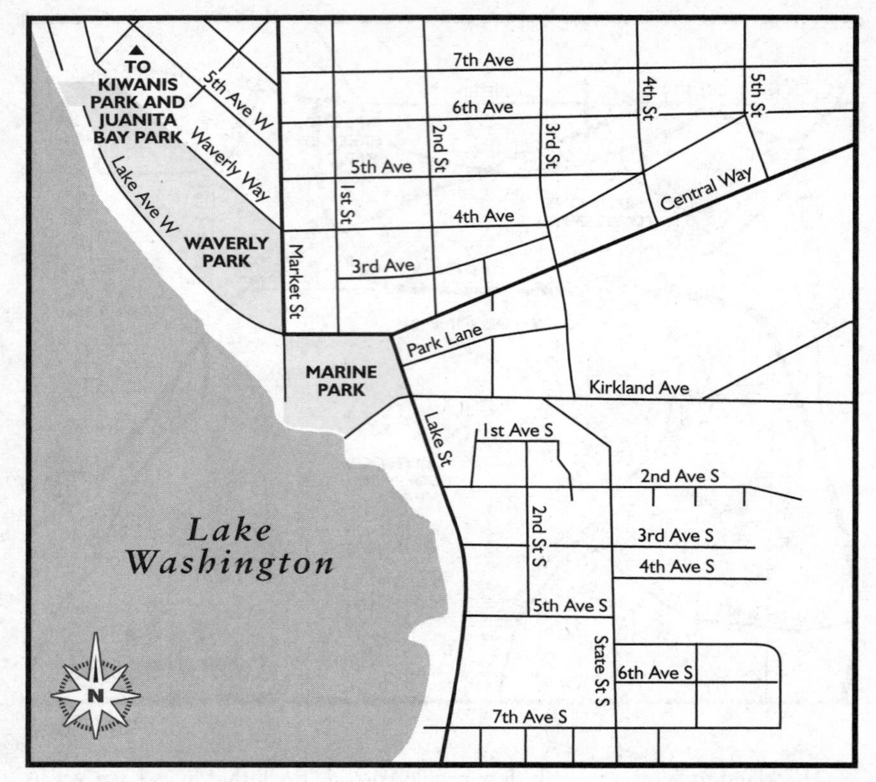

Kirkland

shifts from shopping to community events and ethnic foods. Crossroads sponsors free live musical entertainment—featuring some of the area's most talented musicians playing anything from jazz to polka (the first Thursday night of the month is open mike, for those who dare). *Map:HH3–1.*

KIRKLAND

EAST OF LAKE WASHINGTON TO 132ND AVENUE NE, FROM CARILLON POINT/HIGHWAY 520 TO NE 116TH STREET

This town was supposed to be "the Pittsburgh of the West"—or at least that was the dream shared in the late 19th century by Leigh S. J. Hunt, publisher of the *Seattle Post-Intelligencer*, and Peter Kirk, an English industrialist. They were convinced that an iron- and steelworks could thrive on Moss Bay, just east of Seattle across Lake Washington. However, in 1893, after only a few buildings and homes had been raised in the area, the nation was struck by its worst financial depression. All that remains of Kirkland's campaign to become Pittsburgh are a few handsomely refurbished historical structures, such as the Peter Kirk Building (620 Market St) and the Joshua Sears Building (701 Market St).

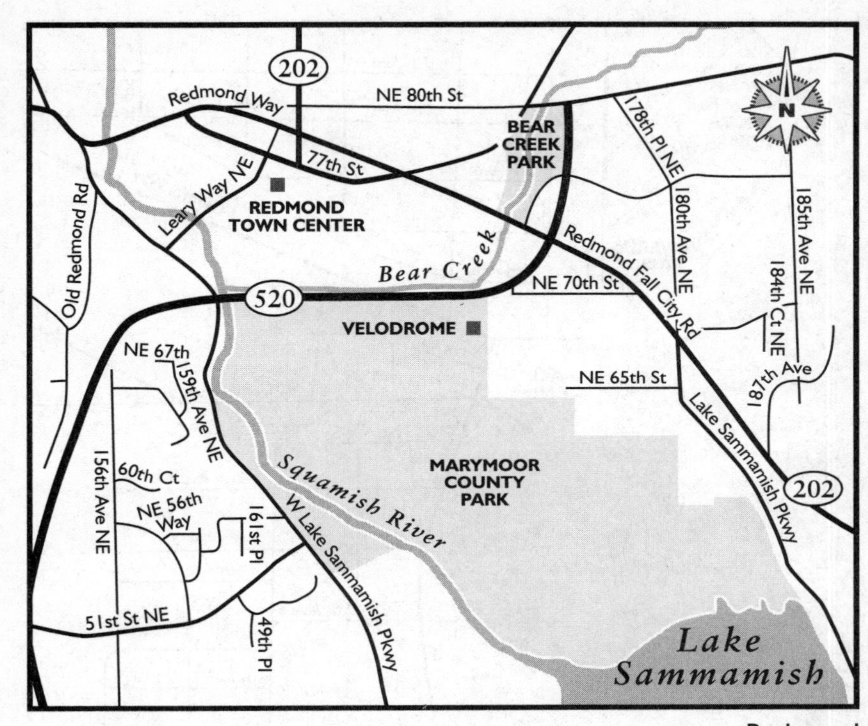

Redmond

Kirkland today is a friendly, low-profile Eastside town that hugs Lake Washington and offers more public access to the water than any other city on the lake's shores. One of the best ways to experience the lake is to head a bit north of Kirkland to Juanita for a visit to **JUANITA BAY PARK** (access is off Market Street just south of Juanita Drive), home to great blue herons, owls, turtles, beavers, and other wildlife. Also strollable is **ST. EDWARDS STATE PARK** (take Market Street north and head west on Juanita Drive), a densely forested park with trails that lead down to lakefront beaches, and **BRIDLE TRAILS STATE PARK** (116th Avenue NE and NE 53rd Street), laced with horse trails. A more urban tour of the town might begin at one of the town's many art galleries, including **HOWARD/MANDVILLE GALLERY** (120 Park Ln; 425/889-8212; howardmandville.com), **KIRKLAND ARTS CENTER** (620 Market St; 425/822-7161; kirklandartscenter.org), **PARKLANE GALLERY** (130 Park Ln; 425/827-1462; parklanegallery.com), and **PATRICIA ROVZAR GALLERY** (118 Central Wy; 425/889-4627; rovzargallery.com). End your excursion at the **KIRKLAND PARKPLACE SHOPPING CENTER** (corner of 6th Avenue and Central Way; 425/827-7789) and its mix of shops and a cinema.

For nourishment, try the northern Italian **RISTORANTE PARADISO** (120 Park Ln, Ste A; 425/889-8601; ristoranteparadiso.com). Or, for smashing lake views, there's **ANTHONY'S HOMEPORT** (135 Lake St; 425/822-0225; anthonys.com) or the **THIRD FLOOR FISH CAFE** (205 Lake St; 425/822-3553; fishcafe.com). If you're in the mood for something more exotic, **MIXTURA** (148 Lake St S; 425/803-3310; mixtura.biz) serves inspiring Peruvian tapas and cocktails. **THE SLIP** (80 Kirkland Ave.; 425/739-0033) located next to the water, is a family restaurant. Nearby **MARINA PARK**, with a sandy beach and public marina, is a venue for summer concerts (425/587-3350). **CARILLON POINT**, south of downtown proper, is a luxury waterfront complex that includes the **WOODMARK HOTEL, YACHT CLUB AND SPA** (1200 Carillon Point; 425/822-3700 or 800/822-3700; thewoodmark.com), specialty shops, waterfront walkways, paths, and benches. Fortunately, the best thing about Carillon Point is free: the view west over the lake toward Seattle. *Map:EE3*.

REDMOND

EAST OF LAKE WASHINGTON, FROM HIGHWAY 520 TO NE 124TH STREET, FROM 132ND AVENUE NE TO 164TH AVENUE NE

Redmond is best known as the headquarters for corporate giant Microsoft. Techies can stop by the **MICROSOFT VISITOR CENTER** (4420 148th Ave NE, Building 127; 425/703-6214; microsoft.com) for a glimpse into the company's history as well as a look at their latest products and prototypes of the future. But there's more to Redmond than Microsoft: Redmond has a bustling downtown shopping mall, **REDMOND TOWN CENTER** (near NE 74th Street and 164th Avenue NE; 425/867-0808; redmondtowncenter.com), with more than 50 stores and the Redmond Town Center Cinemas arranged around plazas and a large open space used for musical performances. This city also offers some more-distinctive delights, including **MARYMOOR PARK** (6046 W Lake Sammamish Pkwy NE; 206/205-3661). Located south of downtown, Marymoor comprises 522 acres of playfields, running and horseback-riding trails, tennis courts, an interpretive nature trail, a 45-foot climbing wall, and the region's best off-leash dog area. This is also where you'll find the **MARYMOOR VELODROME** (2400 Lake Sammamish Pkwy; 206/957-4555; velodrome.org), a 400-meter oval bicycle-racing track that attracts championship riders from around the country and picnickers who come to watch them go round and round. (Spectators pay $3 to attend Friday-night races.) From Marymoor, the **SAMMAMISH RIVER TRAIL** stretches 10 miles north, skirting Woodinville, to Bothell, which lies north of Kirkland and Juanita at the north end of Lake Washington. The trail is a flat but circuitous route ideal for fair-weather bicyclists, runners, and skaters who enjoy views of the surrounding mountains. In Bothell the trail can be linked to the **BURKE-GILMAN TRAIL** (see Top 25 Attractions in this chapter) along the west shore of Lake Washington into Seattle. *Map:EE1–FF1*.

Gardens

Here's the upside to all of that rain that falls on the Pacific Northwest: the region ranks among the world's best places for gardening. The **SEATTLE P-PATCH PROGRAM** (206/684-0264; seattle.gov/neighborhoods/ppatch), a community gardening program begun in 1973, is one of the largest in the country, with 38 sites throughout Seattle. All P-Patch sites are organic and provide gardening space for families and individuals throughout the city. And downtown rooftops and terraces are green with gardens. **FREEWAY PARK** (6th Avenue and Seneca Street) drapes the midcity interchanges with verdant curtains of ivy, the incessant roar of traffic obscured by whispering stands of bamboo. The University of Washington campus is rich with trees; pick up the **BROCKMAN MEMORIAL TREE TOUR** pamphlet for a small fee at the bus shelter across from Anderson Hall (Stevens Wy). **VOLUNTEER PARK** (1400 E Prospect St) on Capitol Hill boasts magnificent specimen trees and a splendid Victorian conservatory overflowing with flowers. The **WASHINGTON PARK ARBORETUM** (2300 Arboretum Dr E; see Top 25 Attractions in this chapter) offers more than 200 acres of wandering trails.

Bellevue Botanical Garden

12001 MAIN ST, BELLEVUE; 425/452-2750

The botanical garden, which sits on 36 acres within Wilburton Hill Park, contains several smaller display gardens. The Waterwise Garden features descriptive signage detailing techniques to conserve water; specially selected plants are labeled to provide ideas for the home gardener. The Alpine Rock Garden boasts a generous display of flora found in rocky alpine settings (visitors are asked not to sit or climb on the rocks). The half-mile trail that rings the botanical garden winds past several other gardens, including the Yao Japanese Garden, a well-executed garden incorporating modern and traditional Japanese features. The trail continues on to the Perennial Border—a 20,000-square-foot mixed planting of perennials, bulbs, trees, shrubs, and grasses. Its largest event, Garden d'Lights, is a holiday light festival that extends from late November through early January nightly. The Shorts Visitor Center, open 10am to 4pm daily, houses a gift shop and provides maps. Docents are available Saturday and Sunday, April through October, and group tours can be arranged by calling ahead. No pets, bicycles, or skateboards are allowed in the garden. Admission is free. *Every day; bellevuebotanical.org; map:HH3.*

Bloedel Reserve

7571 NE DOLPHIN DR, BAINBRIDGE ISLAND; 206/842-7631

Since the late 1980s, this 150-acre Bainbridge Island estate has been open to the public on a limited basis. The manse, which overlooks Puget Sound, is now a visitors' center where interpretive material is available to guide your walk through the property. The parklike grounds contain a number of theme gardens, including a Japanese garden, and nature trails lead through native woods and wetlands. A small pond attracts birds in increasing numbers. This is not a place for a family picnic or a romp with the dog, and reservations for entrance are required (call well in advance during the busy spring months). Guided tours can be arranged for groups, and many of the trails are wheelchair accessible (the reserve has two sturdy wheelchairs available for public use; call ahead). Admission is $10 for adults; $8 for seniors; $6 for children 5–12; and free for children under 5. *Wed–Sun; bloedelreserve.org.* ♿

Carl S. English Jr. Botanical Gardens

3015 NW 54TH ST, BALLARD; 206/783-7059

One of the region's great horticulturists, Carl English made Seattle a horticultural hot spot in the last century through his plant- and seed-collecting efforts. At the Ballard Locks, you can explore 7 acres of his gardens in the romantic English landscape style containing more than 570 species and 1,500 varieties from around the world, including those that made up English's personal arboretum. The gardens are worth a visit even in winter, when the tapestry of bark and berry and the perfume of winter-flowering plants brighten the grayest day. In summer, the Seattle Fuchsia Society's display garden enlivens the spacious lawns, where you can picnic and watch the boats make their way through the lock system that connects Lake Washington to Puget Sound. A summer band concert series and special theme family events, such as Scandinavian Day, provide further entertainment on the weekends. Guided tours of the locks, fish ladder, and garden are held daily in summer (June 1–Sept 30) and on Thurs–Sun the rest of year except for December through February; special in-depth tours can be arranged. (See also Ballard Locks under Top 25 Attractions in this chapter.) Admission is free. *Every day; www.nws.usace.army.mil; map:FF9.*

Kubota Gardens

55TH AVENUE S AT RENTON AVENUE S, RAINIER BEACH; 206/725-5060

This 25-acre Japanese garden tucked away in the Rainier Beach neighborhood at the south end of the Rainier Valley is a surprising oasis, home to such exotics as dragon trees. The large area encompasses many styles, from traditional Japanese garden to expansive lawns perfect for picnicking. The grounds are laced with winding paths that open onto ethereal views framing the many artfully trained pines and pruned plantings. A number of benches provide places for quiet contemplation. The north-central area of the garden is the site of the Necklace of Ponds, a network of waterfalls and ponds with a recirculating water system. The park is open every day during daylight hours, and admission is free. Free tours are available on the last Sunday of each month at 10am, starting in the parking lot, and tours can also be arranged at any time for groups of eight or more. The Kubota Gardens Foundation holds plant sales in May and September, which are open to the public. *Every day; kubota.org; map:MM4.*

Pacific Rim Bonsai Collection

WEYERHAEUSER WY S, FEDERAL WAY; 253/924-5206

The corporate headquarters of the Weyerhaeuser Company, America's biggest timber business, also houses a pair of significant plant collections, both open to the public (see also next listing). Frequently changing exhibits showcase the diminutive gems of the bonsai collection, including a 1,000-year-old Sierra juniper. On alternate Sundays at 1pm, mid-May to mid-September, there are lecture demonstrations on bonsai design, horticulture, and artistic display. Tours are Sunday at noon or by appointment. Admission is free. *Sat–Wed (Oct–Feb), Fri–Wed (Mar–Sept); weyerhaeuser.com/bonsai.*

Rhododendron Species Botanical Garden

WEYERHAEUSER WY S, FEDERAL WAY; 253/661-9377

The Rhododendron Species Foundation's plantings encompass the largest, most comprehensive collection of rhododendron species and hybrids in the world. This is as much a preserve as a garden—more than 60 of the 500-plus species growing here on 22 acres at the Weyerhaeuser Company's corporate headquarters are endangered in the wild. A pair of study gardens are open throughout the year, so visitors can observe the rhododendron family's changing beauties through the seasons; though most are spring bloomers, others peak in winter or in summer, and many deciduous species take on magnificent fall foliage color. The garden has a gift shop and a plant sale pavilion. This is not a garden for picnicking or pets. Admission March through October is $3.50 for adults; $2.50 for students, seniors, and tour groups; and free to children under 12 and school groups. Free to all November through February. *Sat–Wed (June–Feb), Fri–Wed (Mar–May); rsf@rhodygarden.org; rhodygarden.org.*

Seattle Tilth Demonstration Gardens

4649 SUNNYSIDE AVE N, WALLINGFORD; 206/633-0451

Urban gardeners find a world of practical assistance at the Tilth gardens on the grounds of Wallingford's Good Shepherd Center (there's a second garden in Mt. Baker's Bradner Gardens Park, 1733 Bradner Pl S). Self-guided instructional walks lead visitors through the gardens and an impressive array of composting units. The thriving gardens are tended organically and are kept healthy through natural pest controls and environmentally sound horticultural practices. Edible landscaping is a specialty here, but many of the 1,200 plants are also ornamental. This midcity greenery serves everyone from beginners interested in learning how to prepare soil and sow carrots to advanced gardeners who trade heritage vegetable seeds or rare border plants. The Children's Garden, east of the demonstration gardens, lets young green thumbs practice organic and sustainable gardening. The west end of the garden houses the Good Shepherd P-Patch. Numerous workshops and classes are offered. Tilth activities also include a spring plant sale in late April or early May. Admission is free. *Every day; seattletilth.org; map:FF7.*

University of Washington Medicinal Herb Garden

STEVENS WAY AT GARFIELD LANE, UNIVERSITY DISTRICT; 206/543-1126

First established in 1911 by the UW School of Pharmacy on a single acre, the Medicinal Herb Garden currently occupies a little more than 2½ acres on the University of Washington campus. It serves as an accurate specimen garden for botanists, herbalists, medics, and gardeners and covers many healing traditions from various cultures. It is not meant to provide medical information, however, and none is posted. The garden displays more than 1,000 species and is divided into seven areas running west to east. A centrally located office displays a map of the garden and gives descriptions of each "room." Admission is free, and tours can be arranged by appointment for a donation. The garden is located across from the Botany Building and extends east to Rainier Vista. *Every day; map:FF6.*

Woodland Park Rose Garden

5500 PHINNEY AVE N, GREEN LAKE; 206/684-4863

Seattle's premier rose garden offers gardeners a chance to evaluate the regional performance of several hundred kinds of roses. Two acres of permanent plantings hold some 5,000 shrubs, both old-fashioned varieties and modern hybrids. Newest of all are the unnamed roses grown each year in the Seattle Rose Society's trial beds. Here, likely candidates are tested for two years; the best of the bunch will become All-America Rose selections. The Seattle Parks Foundation recently restored several of the garden's historic elements. The Seattle Rose Society offers rose care and pruning demonstrations in the appropriate seasons (call the garden for information). Admission is free. *Every day; zoo.org/zoo_info/rosegarden/rosegarden.html; map:EE7.*

Parks and Beaches

At last count there were 430 parks and playgrounds in the city of Seattle alone; the following are some of the best in and around the area. Find more information about city parks at cityofseattle.net/parks or about state parks at parks.wa.gov. See also Top 25 Attractions and neighborhood write-ups in this chapter for more information.

Alki Beach Park

BETWEEN DUWAMISH HEAD AND ALKI POINT IN WEST SEATTLE, ALONG HARBOR AVENUE SW AND ALKI AVE SW

See Top 25 Attractions in this chapter.

Bridle Trails State Park

116TH AVENUE NE AND NE 53RD STREET, KIRKLAND; 425/455-7010

As its name suggests, this 480-acre park is a densely wooded equestrian paradise laced with horse trails (one links up with Marymoor Park). Though you may feel out of place if you come to do anything but ride, the park also features picnic sites. Warning: The overgrowth is so dense that it's easy to get lost on the trails; also, for obvious reasons, watch where you step. *Map:FF2.*

Camp Long

5200 35TH AVE SW, WEST SEATTLE; 206/684-7434

West Seattle's Camp Long, run by Seattle Parks and Recreation, has a variety of broader functions: a meeting/conference facility (a lodge holds 75 people in its upper room and 35 in the basement), an in-city outdoor experience for family or group use (10 rustic bunk-bed-equipped cabins sleep up to 12 people at $35 a cabin—make reservations at least two weeks in advance), and a 56-acre nature preserve. The park also offers interpretive programs, perfect for school or Scout groups, and family-oriented nature programs on weekends. The lodge and cabins feature 1930s-style log architecture. Climbers can sharpen their skills on a climbing rock and a simulated glacier face. *Map:JJ8.*

Carkeek Park

NW CARKEEK ROAD AND 9TH AVENUE NW, CROWN HILL; 206/684-4075

Carkeek Park is 186 acres of wilderness in the city's northwest corner. Forest paths wind from the parking lots and two reservable picnic areas (206/684-4081) to a footbridge spanning the railroad tracks, and then down a staircase to the broad beach north of Shilshole Bay. (Use caution around the tracks; trains run frequently through the park, and you may not hear them clearly.) Grassy meadows (great for kite flying), picnic shelters, and pretty, meandering Pipers Creek, where volunteers have done much to bring the salmon back, are other good reasons to relax here. *Map:DD8.*

Chism Beach Park

1175 96TH AVE SE, BELLEVUE; 425/452-6914

One of Bellevue's largest and oldest waterfront parks, Chism sits along the handsome residential stretch south of Meydenbauer Bay. There are docks and diving boards, picnic areas, and a playground. *Map:HH4.*

Discovery Park

3801 W GOVERNMENT WY, MAGNOLIA; 206/684-4075

See Top 25 Attractions in this chapter.

Fay-Bainbridge State Park

15446 SUNRISE DR NE, BAINBRIDGE ISLAND; 206/842-3931

About a 15-minute drive from the downtown ferry dock on Bainbridge Island, Fay-Bainbridge is a smallish (17-acre) park known for its camping areas and views of Mount Rainier and Seattle. The log-strewn beach has pits for fires; other features include a boat launch, horseshoe pits, and two kitchen shelters. It's a popular stop for cyclists on their way around the hilly isle.

Gas Works Park

N NORTHLAKE WAY AND MERIDIAN AVENUE N, WALLINGFORD; 206/684-4075

See Top 25 Attractions in this chapter.

Golden Gardens Park

NORTH END OF SEAVIEW AVENUE NW, BALLARD; 206/684-4075

A breezy, sandy beach, nearby boat ramp, beach fire pits, an off-leash area for dogs, a restored wetland, and the pretty—but cold—waters of Shilshole Bay are the park's biggest lures, although fully half of its 88 acres lie to the east of the railroad tracks along the wooded, trail-laced hillside. *Map:EE9.*

Green Lake Park

5200 GREEN LAKE WY N, GREEN LAKE; 206/684-4075

This 188-acre park, a major element of the original 1904 Olmsted park plan, abuts Green Lake on one side and has busy Aurora Avenue running through the middle. On the west side are the rose garden (see listing above in the Gardens section of this chapter) and Woodland Park Zoo (see Top 25 Attractions in this chapter). On the east are playfields, picnic areas, lawn bowling, an off-leash area, a skatepark, and tennis courts. *Map:EE7.*

BEST PLACE
TO FIND INSPIRATION?

"Victrola coffeehouse on 15th because it's like a family rec room—filled with games and interesting people. The only thing missing is bong smoke."

Frances McCue, Richard Hugo House founding director

Hing Hay Park

S KING STREET AND MAYNARD AVENUE S, CHINATOWN/INTERNATIONAL DISTRICT; 206/684-4075

Hing Hay Park (the Chinese words translate as "pleasurable gathering") is a meeting and congregating place for the International District's large Asian community. From the adjacent Bush Hotel, an enormous multicolored mural of a dragon presides over the park and the ornate grand pavilion from Taipei. *Map:Q6.*

Kirkland Waterfront

ALONG LAKE WASHINGTON BOULEVARD, KIRKLAND; 425/587-3300

A string of parks, from Houghton Beach to Marina Park at Moss Bay, line the shore of Kirkland's beautiful Lake Washington Boulevard. Kids feed the ducks and wade (only Houghton and Waverly beaches have lifeguards); their parents sunbathe and watch the runners lope by. *Map:DD4.*

Lake Sammamish State Park

20606 SE 56TH ST, ISSAQUAH; 425/455-7010

The sprawling beach is the main attraction of this state park at the south end of Lake Sammamish just off Interstate 90. Shady picnic areas, grassy play-fields, and volleyball courts are excellent secondary draws. Large groups must reserve day-use areas—the place can be overrun in summer. Issaquah Creek, fine for fishing, runs through the park's wooded area.

Lake Washington Parks

FROM E MADISON STREET AND 43RD AVENUE E, MADISON PARK, TO 5800 LAKE WASHINGTON BOULEVARD S, RAINIER VALLEY; 206/684-4075

This string of grassy beachfronts acts as a collective backyard for several of the neighborhoods that slope toward **LAKE WASHINGTON**'s western shore. Bicycle Saturdays and Sundays take place in the summer, when the route from Colman Park to Seward Park is closed to cars from 10am to 6pm. **MADISON PARK** (E Madison Street and 43rd Avenue E) is a genteel neighborhood park with a roped-in swimming area and tennis courts. If you head east on E Madison Street and turn left onto Lake Washington Boulevard, you'll wind down to meet the beach again, this time at **MADRONA PARK** (Lake Washington Boulevard and Madrona Drive), a grassy strip with a swimming beach, picnic tables, a (summer-only) food concession, and a dance studio. Farther south is **LESCHI PARK** (Lakeside Avenue S and Leschi Place), a handsomely manicured retreat that occupies the hillside across the street from the lake. The park offers great views of the **LESCHI MARINA** and the dazzling spinnakers of sailboats, as well as a play area for kids. Another greenbelt, **COLMAN PARK** (36th Avenue S and Lakeside Avenue S), also with a play area, marks the start of the seamless lakefront strip that includes **MOUNT BAKER PARK** (Lake Park Drive S and Lake Washington Boulevard S), a gently sloping, tree-lined ravine; the hydroplane racing Mecca—once a marshy slough, now a manicured park and spectator beach with boat launches—called **STAN SAYRES MEMORIAL PARK** (3800 Lake Washington Blvd S); and the lonely wilderness peninsula of **SEWARD PARK** (5800 Lake Washington Blvd S; see listing below). *Map:GG5–JJ5.*

Lincoln Park

FAUNTLEROY AVE SW AND SW WEBSTER ST, WEST SEATTLE; 206/684-4075

Lincoln Park, a 130-acre jewel perched on a pointed bluff in West Seattle, offers a network of walking and biking paths amid grassy forests, reservable picnic shelters (206/684-4081), recreational activities from horseshoes to football to tennis, and expansive views of the Olympic Mountains from seawalls and rocky beaches. There are tide pools to be inspected and beaches to roam, and kids delight in the playground equipment. Don't miss the (heated) outdoor saltwater Colman Pool (summer only), which began as a tide-fed swimming hole. *Map:LL9.*

Luther Burbank Park

2040 84TH AVE SE, MERCER ISLAND; 206/236-3545

Occupying a good chunk of the northern tip of Mercer Island, Luther Burbank Park is the Eastside's favorite family park. There are picnic areas, barbecue grills, a swimming area, nicely maintained tennis courts, an outdoor amphitheater for summer concerts, a first-rate playground, several playing fields, docks for boat tie-ups (the haunt of sun-worshiping teens in summer), and green meadows that tumble down to the shore. *Map:II4.*

Magnuson Park

SAND POINT WAY NE AND NE 65TH STREET, SAND POINT; 206/684-4075

This 194-acre park fronts Lake Washington just southeast of now-closed Sand Point Naval Station, with a mile of shoreline, a boat launch, a playing field, and six tennis courts. The Burke-Gilman Trail winds past Magnuson Park, linking it to Ballard and Bothell. Just north of the park is the National Oceanic and Atmospheric Administration (NOAA), where you'll find a series of unique artworks along the beach. Due to security concerns, access to NOAA and the Art Walk has been restricted to Mon–Fri, 9am–5pm. Visitors can walk in but cannot drive in. The back gate is open from 11am to 1pm so visitors can pass between NOAA property and Magnuson Park. No access on weekends. One sculpture, Doug Hollis's "Sound Garden," is fitted with flutelike aluminum tubes that create eerie music when the wind blows. The site is open every day from dawn to dusk and is a hauntingly wonderful spot to sit on a blue whale bench, listening to the wailing wind chimes and watching the sun come up over Lake Washington. *Map:EE5.*

Myrtle Edwards Park

ALASKAN WAY BETWEEN BAY STREET AND W THOMAS STREET, WATERFRONT; 206/684-4075

Myrtle Edwards and adjacent Elliott Bay Park provide a front lawn to the northern section of downtown and a home for the Seattle Art Museum's Olympic Sculpture Park, which opened to great fanfare in January 2007. This breezy and refreshing strip is a great noontime getaway for jogging (the two parks combined form a 1.25-mile trail), picnicking on benches that face Puget Sound, or just strolling. Parking is limited. *Map:B9.*

Newcastle Beach Park

4400 LAKE WASHINGTON BLVD S, BELLEVUE; 425/452-2864

This Bellevue park takes full advantage of its waterfront location with a fishing dock, swimming area, and bathhouse facility (complete with outdoor showers). Walking paths—including a three-quarter-mile loop—weave throughout the 28 acres, and a wildlife area offers the chance to see animals and birds in their natural habitat. *Map:JJ3.*

Schmitz Preserve Park

SW STEVENS STREET AND ADMIRAL WAY SW, WEST SEATTLE; 206/684-4075

Just south of West Seattle's Alki Beach is this 53-acre nature preserve, full of raw trails through thickly wooded terrain. The largest western red cedars and hemlocks here are likely to be about 800 years old. Schmitz creek was recently reopened where it runs through the park. No playgrounds, picnic areas, or other park amenities. *Map:II9.*

Seward Park

LAKE WASHINGTON BOULEVARD S AND S JUNEAU STREET, RAINIER VALLEY; 206/684-4075

This majestic wilderness, occupying a 277-acre knob of land in southeast Seattle, gives modern city dwellers an idea of what this area must have looked like centuries ago. At times the park is imbued with a primal sense of permanence, especially on misty winter days when the quiet of a solitary walk through some of the city's only remaining old-growth Douglas fir forest is broken only by the cries of a few birds. But at other times—hot summer Sundays, for instance—Seward turns into a frenzy of music and barbecues. You can drive the short loop road to get acquainted with the park, past the bathhouse and beach facilities; **SEWARD PARK ART STUDIO** (206/722-6342), which offers classes in the arts; some of the six reservable picnic shelters (206/684-4081); and some of the trailheads, which lead to the fish hatchery and outdoor amphitheater and into the forest preserve. Cyclists and runners can make an even better loop on the scenic 2.5-mile lakeside trail encircling the peninsula. The **SEWARD PARK ENVIRONMENTAL AND AUDUBON CENTER** is a collaboration between the Parks department and Audubon of Washington. *Map:JJ5.*

Victor Steinbrueck Park

WESTERN AVENUE AND VIRGINIA STREET, PIKE PLACE MARKET; 206/684-4075

Pike Place Market's greatest supporter and friend is the namesake of this slice of green at the north end of the market. With the Alaskan Way Viaduct right below, the park can be quite noisy during peak traffic hours. It also tends to be a favorite hangout for street people. Despite those caveats, the park's grassy slopes and tables make a fine place for a Market picnic, and the view of blue Elliott Bay and ferry traffic is refreshing. *Map:H8.*

Waterfall Garden

2ND AVE S AND S MAIN ST, PIONEER SQUARE; 206/624-6096

The waterfall in this tiny Pioneer Square park was built to honor the United Parcel Service, which started at this location in 1907. It does crash (this is no place for quiet conversation), and the benches fill up by noon on weekdays, but the park (on the northwest corner of this intersection) makes for a marvelous little nature fix in the middle of a busy urban day. *Map:O8.*

Organized Tours

To get beneath the city's surface, nothing beats a tour. Clearly fun for visitors, a tour is also a great chance for locals to learn something new about their hometown. Tours can be as informational as one of the **SEATTLE ARCHITECTURAL FOUNDATION'S GUIDED WALKING TOURS** (206/667-9184; seattlearchitecture.org), which examine the mix of art and architecture throughout the city year-round, and as colorful as official "Houseboat Lady" Jeri Callahan's specially tailored seasonal **DISCOVER HOUSEBOATING** (206/322-9157; discoverhouseboating.com) tours-by-water of Lake Union's quirky houseboat neighborhoods. And for $8 for adults and $6 for seniors (55+) and children (under 18), volunteers with the **MARKET HERITAGE TOURS** (206/774-5249; pikeplacemarket.org) reveal nooks and crannies of the Pike Place Market that you might otherwise miss.

AIR TOURS

Kenmore Air

950 WESTLAKE AVE N, SOUTH LAKE UNION; 425/486-1257 OR 866/435-9524; 6321 NE 175TH ST, KENMORE; 425/486-1257 OR 866/435-9524

The largest seaplane operator in the area, Kenmore Air has a fleet of 20 planes that make scheduled and charter flights around Puget Sound and to Victoria BC, from seaports on Lake Union and north Lake Washington. A one-way passage to the San Juan Islands is $129 per person on a scheduled seaplane flight (or $475 for a one-hour charter for one to three people). A two-hour round-trip scenic flyover (standby only) of the San Juans is $75 per person; or sign up for a day-trip package to any of the San Juan Islands for $199. Round-trip all-day excursions to Victoria are $235 per person. The company also offers a flight-seeing 20-minute city tour (which originates from the Lake Union location only) for $75 per person. Be sure to call ahead; several tours are available on a day-of-flight basis only, and advance reservations are required for other trips. *kenmoreair.com; map:GG7, BB5.*

Seattle Seaplanes

1325 FAIRVIEW AVE E, EASTLAKE; 206/329-9638 OR 800/637-5553

Seattle Seaplanes does its main business in charters to Canadian fishing camps but also offers a 20-minute exhaustive airborne tour of Seattle (University of Washington, Lake Washington, the waterfront, Magnolia, the Locks, Shilshole, Green Lake, and back to Lake Union) for $67.50 per person. Consider taking a flight to and from majestic Mount Rainier, Mount St. Helens, the San Juan Islands, or Victoria. Call for pricing and reservations. *info@seattleseaplanes.com; seattleseaplanes.com; map:E1.*

BOAT TOURS

Given Seattle's watery surroundings, it's only natural that waterborne travel is one of the best ways to get a look around the Puget Sound area. Besides customizing your own tour via one of 29 **WASHINGTON STATE FERRIES** (206/464-6400; wsdot.wa.gov/ferries; see Top 25 Attractions in this chapter)—a handful of which leave from downtown's Colman Dock throughout the day en route to Bainbridge Island or Bremerton—there are a boatload of boat tours available.

Argosy Cruises

PIERS 54, 55, AND 57, WATERFRONT; 1200 WESTLAKE AVE N, SOUTH LAKE UNION; 206/623-1445 OR 800/642-7816

Scheduled tours departing from Lake Union include daily, year-round, one-hour narrated cruises along the Seattle waterfront and Elliott Bay ($18.61, Apr–Sept), 2½-hour tours through the Ballard Locks and Lake Washington Ship Canal ($35.62, Apr–Sept), and a two-hour Lake Washington excursion ($27.34, Apr–Sept) featuring peeks at the pricey palaces surrounding the lake—including the 40,000-square-foot Xanadu that Microsoft CEO Bill Gates has erected. Charters for private parties or special events are available for groups of 10 to 400. *sales@argosycruises.org; argosycruises.com; map: L9–K9, A1.*

Emerald City Charters (Let's Go Sailing)

PIER 54, WATERFRONT; 206/624-3931 OR 800/831-3274

Two 70-foot custom-built former racing sloops—the *Obsession* and *Neptune's Car*—cut through Elliott Bay waters from May 1 to October 15. Star of the movie *Masquerade* (along with Rob Lowe), the *Obsession* can comfortably carry up to 49 passengers, who should count on packing their own meals for the scheduled 1½-hour trips that leave from the north side of the pier at 11am, 1:30pm, and 4pm daily. Costs for day cruises are $25 for adults, $20 for seniors, and $18 for children 12 and under. A 2½-hour sunset sail leaves between 6pm and 7pm daily during season and costs $40 for adults, $35 for seniors, and $30 for children 12 and under. Private charters are also available. Times subject to change. Call to check on sailing times and availability. *Reservations recommended; info@sailingseattle.com; sailingseattle.com; map:K9.*

Ride the Ducks of Seattle

5TH AVENUE N AND BROAD STREET, SEATTLE CENTER; 206/441-3825 OR 800/817-1116, RESERVATIONS

See the city's sights by land and sea aboard amphibious vehicles (aka "ducks"). The refurbished World War II landing craft are piloted by Coast Guard–certified sea captains who motor visitors about the streets of downtown, Pioneer Square, and Fremont before launching into the waters of Lake Union for tours past Seattle's houseboats, Pike Place Market, and the Seattle waterfront. The 90-minute rides are $23 for adults and $13 for kids 12 and under. The ducks take off hourly throughout the year and half hourly during summer from the northeast corner of Fifth and Broad (across from the

Space Needle). Drop by that same location for tickets or call for reservations; private duck tours are also available. *info@ridetheducksofseattle.com; ridetheducksofseattle.com; map:C6.*

Tillicum Village Tour

PIER 55, WATERFRONT; 206/933-8600
A Northwest tourist staple, this four-hour narrated voyage from downtown Seattle to nearby Blake Island (reputedly the birthplace of Seattle's namesake, Chief Sealth) has been operating for more than 35 years. The highlight of the hyped-up look at Northwest Indian culture is a salmon bake and a Native American dance. $65 adults, $59 seniors, $25 for kids 12 and under, and free for children 4 and under. *tillicumvillage.com; map:L9.*

MOTOR TOURS

Gray Line of Seattle

4500 W MARGINAL WY SW, WEST SEATTLE; 800/426-7532
This popular bus-touring service offers several choice trips: Mount Rainier (May–Sept, $59 per person), the Boeing plant in Everett ($47 per person), the popular Seattle city tours ($58 per person for seven hours or $32 per person for three hours), overnighters to Victoria, BC, and more. Free pickup at several downtown hotels. *info@graylineofseattle.com; graylineofseattle.com; map:JJ8.*

Private Eye on Seattle

206/365-3739
Brace yourself for a wild ride in Private Eye's ghostly white van as it weaves in and out of some of Seattle's most notorious crime scenes. A Haunted Happenings ghost tour (including a scene-of-the-crime stop at the 1983 Wah Mee Massacre) and Mystery Murder crime tours of Queen Anne and Capitol Hill are both available (famous and infamous locals visited along the way include Kurt Cobain and Ted Bundy). These excursions are recommended for ages 12 and above. Cost for any of the 2½- to 3-hour macabre adventures is $25 per person. Minimal walking required; van picks up guests from downtown hotels or restaurants, or South Lake Union. Reservations required. *jake@privateeyetours.com; privateeyetours.com.*

Seattle Tours

206/768-1234
Ballard's Locks and downtown shops, as well as Fremont, the floating bridges, and more are on the itineraries for these three-hour minicoach tours. Custom-designed coaches hold up to 20 people and cost is $45 per person. Other tours feature a daylong trip to Mount Rainier for $79 per person and a trip to the Boeing assembly plant in Everett for $54 to see where jumbo jets are built and the world's largest building by volume. *info@seattlecitytours.com; seattlecitytours.com.*

Show Me Seattle

206/633-2489

Colorfully decaled vans holding a maximum of 14 looky lous per ride hit downtown Seattle hot spots—the waterfront, Pike Place Market, Chinatown/International District—and do drive-bys of the city's more remarkable neighborhoods, including Fremont (and its lurking Aurora Bridge Troll), Green Lake, Queen Anne, Ballard Locks, and Fisherman's Terminal. The *Sleepless in Seattle* houseboat on Lake Union is an oft-requested stop. Cost is $39 adults, $25 kids 12 and under; reservations required. *geoffb@showmeseattle.com; showmeseattle.com.*

WALKING TOURS

Chinatown Discovery

206/623-5124

Humorous Seattle native Vi Mar conducts four walking tours of the Chinatown/International District, providing a historical and cultural perspective that, in some cases, comes with a meal. For instance, the Chinatown by Day tour features a six-course dim sum lunch; the nighttime tour is an eight-course affair. Reservations required. Rates for adults range from $16.95 to $43.95 and for children from $10.95 to $25.95. Group rates for 10 or more adults are available. *heking@juno.com; seattlechinatowntour.com.*

Seattle Walking Tour

425/885-3173

These tours led by Duse McLean (author of tourist-friendly books such as *Urban Walks* by Thistle Press) concentrate on the architecture and history of downtown. The $15 tours begin outside Westlake Center (400 Pine St) by reservation only. *dusem@seattlewalkingtours.com; seattlewalkingtours.com.*

See Seattle Walking Tours

425/226-7641

Catering to those with no time to waste finding Seattle's favorite sights on their own, these daylong tours take in Pike Place Market, the waterfront, Pioneer Square, Chinatown/International District, and other downtown points of interest. Custom tours are available for groups, including mystery and scavenger hunts. Typical cost is $20 per person (excluding lunch); free for children under 12. Daily except Sunday, will run with at least 6 people; reservations recommended; *walking@see-seattle.com; see-seattle.com.*

Underground Tour

610 1ST AVE, DOWNTOWN; 206/682-4646

See Top 25 Attractions in this chapter.

SHOPPING

SHOPPING

Neighborhoods, Shopping Districts, Malls

DOWNTOWN

No longer second-rate when it comes to sophistication, Seattle is all grown up with lots of places to go, especially when it comes to shopping. The downtown core bustles with restaurants, cafés, and theaters, and nearly every corner sports an impressive national retail destination. At the northeast meeting of Fifth Avenue and Pike Street is **BANANA REPUBLIC**, located in the historic Coliseum movie theater building, while **KENNETH COLE** occupies the northwest corner of Sixth Avenue and Pike. The three-story tabernacle of sneakers and sportswear, **NIKETOWN**, dominates the northeast quadrant of Sixth and Pike, and across the way archrival **ADIDAS** claims the northwest corner of Fifth and Pike. Just down the street where Fifth hits Pine is a confluence of biggies: first you'll come to **GAP** at the southwest corner; then there's the flagship **NORDSTROM** to the northwest; head east and cross the street at the light to Pacific Place and you'll run right into a shiny new **BARNEYS NEW YORK**, while family favorite **OLD NAVY** drops anchor on the opposite corner to the south.

City Centre

1420 5TH AVE, DOWNTOWN; 206/624-8800

You'll find a mix of retailers here, from ritzy Italian handbag purveyor Furla and Facèré Jewelry Art Gallery, to always-appropriate Ann Taylor and the casual attitude of American Eagle and Road men's apparel. To sweeten the appeal there's the posh Palomino Euro-bistro and 1,100 underground parking spots. *Every day; map:J5.*

Macy's

3RD AVENUE AND PINE STREET, DOWNTOWN; 206/506-6000

A staple of Seattle department stores for more than 100 years, the old Bon Marché was bought out by Macy's. However, the corner icon has continued its role of fulfilling clothing, household, and wedding registry needs, and it marks the start of the holiday season with its annual hoisting of the 3,600-bulb Holiday Star. *Every day; macys.com; map:I6.*

Nordstrom

500 PINE ST, DOWNTOWN; 206/628-2111

(See Top 25 Attractions in the Exploring chapter.)

Pacific Place

600 PINE ST, DOWNTOWN; 206/405-2655

Pacific Place shelters a wealth of retailers in its 12,000-square-foot sky-lighted atrium. Among the newish are Barneys New York and Sixth Avenue Wine

Seller, beside longtime residents Tiffany & Co., Cartier, J. Crew, Restoration Hardware, Williams-Sonoma, Pea in the Pod maternity wear, and Barnes & Noble Books. On the fourth floor, there's a Ticket/Ticket outlet offering day-of-show tickets for half price. To ease shopper headaches, the center has 1,200 surprisingly cheap underground parking spaces, several strength-sustaining restaurants, and a state-of-the-art, 11-screen cinema, fashioned after a Northwest lodge. *Every day; pacificplaceseattle.com; map:J5.*

Rainier Square

1333 5TH AVE, DOWNTOWN

Small and special might describe this quiet atrium center with a smattering of notable retailers, including trendsetting David Lawrence, and upscale shops the likes of St. John Boutique, ESCADA, Brooks Brothers, and Nancy Meyer Fine Lingerie. *Every day; rainier-square.com; map:K6.*

Westlake Center

400 PINE ST, DOWNTOWN; 206/467-1600

Westlake Center offers an interesting range of stores, from artsy Fireworks to prom-pleasing Jessica McClintock and Talbot's tailored women's clothing. Noteworthy newcomers are Lush, featuring yummy handmade body cosmetics, and Daiso Japan, a Japanese "dollar" store overflowing with more than 100,000 items at $2 each. If you're on the hunt for Northwest treasures, check out Made in Washington with a plethora of foodstuffs and such and Millstream, carrying the creations of local artisans. An upper-level food court has more than 18 eateries. Boasting the city's largest lighted Christmas tree, complete with Santa pictures, Westlake draws crowds during the holidays. *Every day; westlakecenter.com; map:I6.*

HISTORIC DISTRICTS

Pioneer Square (between 1st and 2nd avenues, from Yesler Way to S King Street, Downtown; pioneersquare.org; map:N8) is where Seattle shopping really got its start in 1852, and today it's chock-full of appealing shops, art galleries, cafés, and bars. Sharing a border to the east is **CHINATOWN/ INTERNATIONAL DISTRICT** (between 5th Avenue S and 12th Avenue S, from S Main Street to S Dearborn Street, Downtown; cidbia.org; map:O6–R6, O2–R2) where you can spend the day poking around in intriguing stores filled with Asian collectibles, gifts, and art while learning a bit about the culture and stopping for dim sum or sushi. **PIKE PLACE MARKET** (between Western and 1st avenues and Pike and Virginia streets, Downtown; every day; pikeplacemarket.org; map:J8–I8), founded in 1907, is the nation's oldest continuously operating farmers' market and a local favorite for fresh seafood, flowers, and produce. A most unusual spot for shopping in town, the bustling bazaar is made up of independent, one-of-a-kind stores packed with vintage apparel, antiques, and arts and crafts.

OWNERS BY DESIGN

True to the pioneer spirit of Seattle, these entrepreneurs not only make the product, they sell it within the walls of their own shop—ensuring that they'll always have an outlet for their creativity. If you want it done right, sometimes you just have to do it yourself.

On the fringes of downtown, you'll find a series of storefronts unified in purveying one-of-a-kind creations with a hefty dose of humor. Of the three—Nancy, Schmancy, and Fancy + Pants—two are owned by artists who started their stores to showcase their own wacky works. **NANCY** (1930 2nd Ave, Belltown; 206/441-7131), brainchild of husband-and-wife team Kate Greiner and Aaron Murray, is a mini gallery featuring their handmade cards, paintings, and miniature animal totem poles, among creations by other artists. **FANCY + PANTS** (1914 2nd Ave, Belltown; 206/443-4621 and 206/956-2945; fancyjewels.com, pantsunderpants.com) is the domain of designer Sally Brock, a jeweler who hand-makes custom creations in sterling silver. While Brock's designs are witty and wholesome, **KIMBERLY BAKER** (617 N 36th St, Fremont; 206/545-1145; kimberlybaker.com) attracts the bad girls (and good girls too) into her enchanted forest boutique, where they covet magical amulets, airy-fairy necklaces, and earrings sporting tiny guns, hand grenades, bunnies, and sparrows. The fanciful shop is the exclusive showcase of the designer's original jewelry, sought after by celebrities from Hollywood to New York.

For Laura Buzzard, her showroom is her workroom, too, the place where she and her staff stitch up multitudes of custom bags for customers all over the country. Her studio, **LAURA BEE DESIGNS** (6418 B 20th Ave NW, Ballard; 206/789-4044; laurabeedesigns.com) is buzzing, filled with bolts of fabric, vinyl, and microsuede; her creations are all made of durable nonleather materials. You'll find a wall of fine examples as well as loads of handcrafted jewelry and handbag accessories. Another bag lady (said in the most complimentary of ways, of course) is Suzy Fairchild, proprietor of **FROCK SHOP** (6500 Phinney Ave N, Greenwood; 206/297-1638;

NEIGHBORHOODS

Along **THE AVE** (University Way NE from NE 41st Street to NE 50th Street, University District; udistrictchamber.org; map:FF6), a stretch of road in the **UNIVERSITY DISTRICT** neighborhood a block from the University of Washington campus, you'll find a typical university mix of stores, including chain and independent coffee, tea, book, and music shops; alternative boutiques; and ethnic restaurants. Recent attempts to reclaim the distinctive student/bohemian flavor have revitalized the lively neighborhood, at one time eclipsed by panhandlers and chain stores, as it slowly spreads north. East down the 45th Street shopfrockshop.com). A prolific creative, she transforms vintage fabric into caps (she calls them cabbies) and handbags, and retro card designs into delightful greetings. All this while keeping her girlie boutique well stocked with affordable fashions and handmade creations from other indie crafty types.

Chris Baumgartner's career started long before the DIY craft movement took root in Seattle. Her discreet shop, **ISTINA** (2804 E Madison St, Madison Valley; 206/322-6527), set back on Madison Valley's neighborhood shopping street, has been around for years. Baumgartner is enamored of rich colors and beguiling textures—loosely a quarter of the lovely creations in her store are her private Istina designs. Inspired by the pleats and performance of Issey Miyake, she turns out modern classics with interesting textures and flowing fit. While Istina caters to the country club set, **VIOLETTE** (212 1st Ave S, Pioneer Square; 206/652-8991; violetteboutique.blogspot.com) aims to please the nightclub crowd. Beth Nielsen, owner of this sweet and simple dress shop, has a great eye for accessible, up-and-coming designers. Perhaps it's because she is one herself, creating new sweaters out of recycled cashmere, handbags of salvaged leather, and skirts of vintage tablecloths. In addition to little-known labels, she carries a sparkling selection of locally made jewels, all at approachable prices.

The ultimate individualist and on a planet all his own is Curtis Steiner, owner, artist, curator, and amazing window dresser of **SOUVENIR** (5325 Ballard Ave NW, Ballard; 206/297-7116) on busy Ballard Avenue. Steiner's acclaim extends far beyond the confines of Seattle with a reputation regarded by the *New York Times*. You'll be intrigued by his eerie and elegant window displays, drawn into the tiny shop-cum-gallery that is all about Steiner's remarkable talent. Although there's an air of "look but don't touch," everything is for sale (except the Chihuahua). Pull out the myriad drawers to explore a treasure trove of old found objects; browse the wall of handmade cards, precious at $12 a piece; or hold your breath while you peruse the ethereal collection of jewelry, made by the hands of the resident artist.

—Lei Ann Shiramizu

viaduct from the UW campus is the casually upscale **UNIVERSITY VILLAGE** (NE 45th Street and 25th Avenue NE; uvillage.com; every day; map:FF6).

Just west from the Ave, the family-friendly **RAVENNA** neighborhood (Roosevelt Way NE from NE 55th Street to NE 70th Street; map:EE6) mixes stores for kids' stuff, specialty foods, videos, and books. **WALLINGFORD** (45th Street from Stone Way N to Latona Avenue NE; map:FF7) combines funky gift and retail shops (such as an erotic bakery) with **WALLINGFORD CENTER** (1815 N 45th St; every day; wallingfordcenter.com; map:FF7)—an old school building converted to house about a dozen shops focusing on home décor, children's books, toys, and fashion for moms and babes.

CAPITOL HILL is the city's apex of the alternative, with lots of piercings, tattoos, and a large gay community, making for a memorable urban experience. The three most concentrated areas for eclectic clothing (especially vintage), eateries, and home stores are **BROADWAY** (E Pine Street to E Roy Street; map:GG6), the **PIKE/PINE CORRIDOR** (Pike and Pine streets between Melrose Avenue up to 14th Avenue E; map:J2), and the walkable **15TH AVENUE E** (Madison Street to Aloha Street; map:HH6). E Madison Street intersects 15th Avenue E on its way from downtown to **MADISON VALLEY** (E Madison Street from 23rd Avenue to 32nd Avenue E; map:GG6): a browsable row of shops for gifts, cards, and home, along with a scattering of bistros. Keep going and you'll run straight into **MADISON PARK** (E Madison Street from McGilvra Boulevard E to 43rd Avenue E; map:GG6). The shopping in this lakeside neighborhood, with stores dedicated to home design, gift items, and high-end fashion, reflects a mix of Americana domesticity and Hollywood glam.

Challenging Capitol Hill for the coolest shopping spot is **BELLTOWN** (Western Avenue to 5th Avenue, between Virginia Street and Denny Way, Downtown; map:G8–D8), full of trendy shops and see-and-be-seen bars and restaurants. Slide east along Denny Way and you'll wind up in **SOUTH LAKE UNION** (Denny Way to Lake Union, between Aurora Avenue and Interstate 5; map:B3–E1, E5–H2), where Northwest stalwart REI shares real estate with shiny new urban boutiques purveying tot fashion and spendy doggy accessories.

BEST PLACE
TO SPEND A RAINY DAY?

"Relaxing in the fireplace lobby at the Edgewater Inn."

Luly Yang, celebrated local couture designer

Trek north and you'll run into **QUEEN ANNE** (Denny Way to the Lake Washington Ship Canal, between Lake Union and Elliott Avenue; map:GG7). At the top of Queen Anne Hill you can experience some of the best views of the city as you wander through a community of restaurants, shops, and grocery stores. Down the northern slope of Queen Anne Hill and over the ship canal lies **FREMONT** (Fremont Avenue N and N 34th Street; map:FF7), otherwise known as the "Center of the Universe"—as residents affectionately labeled it for its unique boutiques, kitschy stores, and some of the city's better pubs. Farther north is the **PHINNEY RIDGE/GREENWOOD** area (from where Phinney Avenue N turns to Greenwood Avenue N between 65th and 80th avenues; map:EE7), fertile ground for indie boutiques mingled with coffeehouses buzzing with Wi-Fi. Take a west turn from Fremont instead and you'll discover family-oriented **BALLARD** (bounded by Salmon and Shilshoe bays and Phinney Ridge; map:FF8), famous for its Scandinavian community. Ballard Avenue, south of Market Street, has morphed into quite the boutique row, home to feminine favorite Olivine and edgy spa/salon/retailer Duque.

SUBURBAN STOPS

Alderwood Mall

OFF I-5 AT ALDERWOOD MALL EXIT, LYNNWOOD; 425/771-1211

A major renovation turned this once-substandard suburban mall into strong competition for newer malls outside the city, especially since it offers more than 175 stores. Highlights include Nordstrom, Apple, Coach, Banana Republic, Borders Books & Music, Urban Outfitters, a collection of enticing restaurants, and an open-air courtyard. *Every day; alderwoodmall.com; map:AA7.*

The Bellevue Collection

NE 8TH STREET AND BELLEVUE WAY, BELLEVUE; 425/453-2431

At the confluence of two of Bellevue's important arterials has arisen a triangle of upscale shopping made up of Kemper Development's properties: Bellevue Place, Bellevue Square, and the newest, Lincoln Square. Together, the trifecta offers major-name retail and one-of-a-kind boutiques, luxury hotels, and a variety of restaurants all just a "walk" sign away.

Across the street from Bellevue Square and anchored by the Hyatt Regency, **BELLEVUE PLACE** (10500 NE 8th St, Bellevue; 425/453-5634; Mon–Sat; map: HH3) is an intimate collection of high-end clothing, gift, and home furnishing shops and a handful of excellent restaurants, some of which occupy the dramatic glass-walled Wintergarden atrium. Still the Eastside's brightest shopping beacon, **BELLEVUE SQUARE** (NE 8th Street and Bellevue Way NE, Bellevue; 425/454-2431; every day; bellevuesquare.com; map:HH3) is constantly adding new attractions for all ages to keep the cars streaming into its mammoth parking garage. Beyond the popular department stores of Nordstrom and Macy's is an ever-expanding coterie of shops, including A/X Armani Exchange, Bose, Coach, Montblanc, Sephora, Tiffany & Co., Crate & Barrel, Pottery Barn, Williams-Sonoma, Lucy, and more, for a total of more than 200 stores and eateries. **LINCOLN SQUARE** (700 Bellevue Wy, Bellevue; 425/453-2431; every day; lincolnsquare.com; map:HH3) houses Thomasville Home Furnishings, Bombay, the Container Store, and Henredon along with wine shop Vino 100, travel clothing experts ExOfficio, and the wondrous world of Paper Source. Tea or coffee? There's Koots Green Tea and a Tully's, too, mixed in with a 16-screen state-of-the-art cinema and the deluxe Westin Bellevue.

Crossroads Shopping Center

NE 8TH STREET AND 156TH AVENUE NE, BELLEVUE; 425/644-1111

With such stores as Party City, Circuit City, and Old Navy, 26 restaurants, a megascreen cinema, a communal giant chessboard, and live music, Crossroads is aptly known as the Eastside's living room. *Every day; crossroadsbellevue.com; map:HH1.*

Factoria Mall

4055 FACTORIA MALL SE, BELLEVUE; 425/641-8282

Just off exit 10 of Interstate 405, this suburban mall is filled with sensible stores—T.J. Maxx, Old Navy, B. Dalton Bookseller, InSpa, Target, plus the Eastside's only Nordstrom Rack. Bring the kids, let them loose, and meet back in an hour at one of the diverse places to eat. *Every day; factoriamall.com; map:II3.*

IKEA

600 SW 43RD ST, RENTON; 425/656-2980

This Swedish-owned warehouse-style store gives Seattleites reason to venture south for home-shopping needs. IKEA's room-by-room showrooms are filled with smartly designed furniture and accessories that can be purchased unassembled, which allows for the lowest prices around. Perfect for the college-bound, newly married, or budget-conscious shopper. *Every day; ikea.com; map:II3.*

Kirkland Parkplace

EXIT 18 OFF I-405, CORNER OF 6TH AVENUE AND CENTRAL WAY, KIRKLAND; 425/827-7789

Parkplace is a community village, with convenient services and shops including Parkplace Book Company, a florist, yoga and martial arts studios, a stationery store, and a shoe repair shop. It's home to Kirkland Cinema 6—where every other Friday morning they feature first-run films for parents with babies and small children—as well as a tasty range of dining options, including the Purple Café & Wine Bar and Rikki Rikki Japanese restaurant. *Every day; kirklandparkplace.com; map:EE3.*

Northgate Mall

N NORTHGATE WAY AND 1ST AVENUE NE, NORTHGATE; 206/362-4777

Boasting the distinction (or shame, depending on your opinion of malls) of being the first mall in the nation when it opened in 1950, the full complement of stores at this no-frills mall includes Nordstrom and Macy's, as well as an excellent food court and newsstand. At press time, a major face-lift was under way, adding more than 100,000 square feet of shopping space to make room for Bed, Bath & Beyond, Ann Taylor Loft, and Barnes & Noble. Right across the street is a Target, Joe's, and Best Buy. *Every day; simon.com; map:DD7.*

Redmond Town Center

16495 NE 74TH ST, REDMOND; 425/867-0808

In yet another villagelike setting, Redmond Town Center (off Highway 520 at W Lake Sammamish Parkway) caters to Eastsiders who wish to stay close to home. The open-air mixed-use mall has an array of retail—Abercrombie & Fitch, Gap, Victoria's Secret, REI, and Macy's, as well as a host of small stores such as the Northwest's first Hush Baby, Louie Permelia, and Eastside Dog. The mall becomes an entertaining nighttime destination as well, flanked by restaurants such as Claim Jumper and Thai Ginger and an eight-screen movie complex. *Every day; shopredmondtowncenter.com; map:FF1.*

Seattle Premium Outlets

10600 QUIL CEDA BLVD, TULALIP, 360/654-3000

If you absolutely adore a bargain—whether it's the real thing or not—you must absolutely make your way north to this mother of all outlets. Wear comfortable shoes for hunting through 100 discount stores, including Coach, Burberry, Chico's, Restoration Hardware, Calvin Klein, L'Occitane, Michael Kors, Sony, Bass, Cole Haan, and Le Creuset. Necessary refueling is on the premises at Starbucks and the convenient food court. *Every day; seattlepremiumoutlets.com.*

SuperMall of the Great Northwest

1101 SUPERMALL WY, AUBURN; 253/833-9500

This supersize mall encompasses discount outlets of popular stores such as Aeropostale, Banana Republic, Eddie Bauer, Old Navy, Marshall's, Bed, Bath & Beyond, and Burlington Coat Factory. An array of eateries, from burgers to Indian food, will fuel your trek. Mall walkers, start your engines. *Every day; supermall.com; map:PP2.*

University Village

NE 45TH STREET AND 25TH AVENUE NE, UNIVERSITY DISTRICT; 206/523-0622

This family-favorite mall has become one of the hottest shopping spots in Seattle. A north-end quadrant includes a parking garage to alleviate the maddening weekend circling, a two-level Crate & Barrel, Storables, and a day spa. Perennial faves such as Restoration Hardware, Pottery Barn, Ravenna Gardens, and Smith & Hawken share open-air space with Aveda, Sephora, Sole Food shoe store, Lucy, and Louie Permelia. There are also more than 17 restaurants—from Atlas Foods to Blue C conveyer-belt-style sushi. *Every day; uvillage.com; map:FF6.*

Westfield Southcenter

633 SOUTHCENTER PKWY; 206/246-7400

Dramatic changes are underway at this South End standard. In addition to the requisite Nordstrom, Macy's, and Sears, the developer is adding 75 new stores, six sit-down restaurants, two covered parking structures, and a modern 16-screen AMC theater. *Every day; westfield.com/southcenter; map:OO5.*

Shops from A to Z

ACCESSORIES, GIFTS, AND STATIONERY

Burnt Sugar and Frankie

601 N 35TH ST, FREMONT; 206/545-0699

Ultra-feminine Burnt Sugar recently merged with Frankie shoes, once a nearby neighbor. Aside from footwear, every corner of the store is filled with delightful doodads—fun lingerie, makeup, charming cheese and dessert plates, bright purses, stylish lamps, and a baby section that is just cause for oohs and aahs. *Every day; burntsugarfrankie.com; map:FF7.*

De Medici Ming Fine Paper

1222 1ST AVE, STE A, DOWNTOWN; 206/624-1983

In a store the size of a postage stamp, the owners of this paperie have covered the walls with exotic, beautiful handmade papers from around the world, along with unique cards and beautiful calendars. Bonus: Exquisite gift-wrapping service is available—simply bring your goods and pay for supplies. *Mon–Sat; map:K7.*

Fini

86 PINE ST, DOWNTOWN; 206/443-0563

At Fini, you'll find glamorama goodies such as cute hats in season, the chicest handbags, handmade greeting cards, and always, an affordable pair of star-quality sunglasses. The hottest items are Jeannine Payer's very special silver pieces, hand-engraved with inspiring and eloquent sayings. Custom orders available—isn't that a sterling gift idea? *Every day; map:I7.*

Fireworks Gallery

210 1ST AVE S, PIONEER SQUARE (AND BRANCHES); 206/682-8707

A favorite with visitors, Fireworks displays a fiery array of ceramics, glass, and other handcrafted wares—from the wild and whimsical to the elegantly functional—plus art jewelry, fiber art, and woodwork pieces. Holidays usher in a surprising number of ways to deck the halls and light up the candles. Other branches are at Westlake Center, Bellevue Square, University Village, and Sea-Tac Airport. *Every day; fireworksgallery.net; map:O8.*

Galactic Boutique

1213 PINE ST, CAPITOL HILL; 206/749-9167

It's a mod, mod world at this itsy-bitsy boutique filled with alluring stuff for body and abode, designed to support local artists (primarily the owner himself, creator of many of the goods) and simply have fun. Everything here pops with color: the prolific purveyor proffers delicious dishes, clever cards, original accessories, and ever-so-slightly-erotic art. *Every day; galacticboutique.com; map:J2.*

George

5633 AIRPORT WY S, GEORGETOWN; 206/763-8100

If you find yourself in the artist-occupied neighborhood of Georgetown, pop into this quirky gift store stocked with irreverent articles: sassy stationery, curious art, cheap and chic jewelry, and T-shirts with cheeky sayings like "Georgetown, not just for hookers anymore." *Mon–Sat; georgeintown.com; map:JJ7.*

Hitchcock

1123 34TH AVE, MADRONA; 206/838-7173

Way off the shopping radar, yet worth a look if you're in the vicinity, is this exquisite gem of a shop, hidden in the tree-lined neighborhood of Madrona. As mysterious as its namesake, its drapes open every so often to reveal a perfectly edited selection of totes, clutches, handmade jewelry, and elegant hats. *Wed–Sun; shophitchcock.com; map:HH5.*

JayWalk

1105 34TH AVE, MADRONA; 206/328-7776

Shoe-box-sized at about 250 square feet, this neighborhood shop packs in plenty of punch per inch. The happy mix of new, used, handmade, and just plain fun gifts ranges from the works of local artists (current count: 60), such as tin collages, paintings, and jewelry, to vintage reproduction linens and aprons, baby bibs, Tibetan prayer flags, scented candles, quirky cards, and random retro home objects. Service is sweet and the attitude definitely local. *Tues–Sun; jaywalkseattle.com; map:HH5.*

Moxie Paper Goods and Gifts

3916 CALIFORNIA AVE SW, WEST SEATTLE; 206/932-2800

It takes chutzpah to open a stationery store off the beaten path. But the owners of this small shop pull it off admirably with a charming blend of greeting and note cards, baby gifts, candles, desk accessories, and delightful discoveries. For those looking for a personal touch, they provide custom invitations and announcements, welcome packets, and gift wrapping. *Tues–Sat; moxiepapergoods.com; map:JJ8.*

BEST

WASHINGTON WINERY?

"Mark Ryan Winery. His wine is delicious, and he is my archenemy at Ping-Pong."

Ethan Stowell, chef/owner of Union and Tavolata

Ottica

2025 1ST AVE, BELLTOWN; 206/443-0320

Men *do* make passes at girls who wear glasses from this glamorous eyeglass store. In fact, Ottica's array of men's specs is pretty eye-catching too. The assortment is plucked from premier designers around the world and includes featherweight frames from Japan. A well-trained and sweetly opinionated staff will assist you in finding the perfect pair to fit your face. *Every day; map:H7.*

Paperhaus

2008 1ST AVE, BELLTOWN; 206/374-8566

Like an architect's pie-in-the-sky supply room, the shelves of albums, portfolios, and (of course) paper at Paperhaus are made by award-winning manufacturers such as NAVA, Pina Zangaro, Prat, and Rexite. The shop also has a wide assortment of sleek pens and vinyl briefcases made in Milan. And the wares here are eco-conscious: paper products are made from recycled materials, leather items from by-products. *Every day; paperhaus.com; map:H7.*

P.W. Kerr's

612 W MCGRAW ST, QUEEN ANNE; 206/285-2467

The owner of this Queen Anne soft spot comes from a long line of independent Seattle home stores. His collection of nifty gifts reflects his well-honed taste for the traditional to the trendy: quirky kitchen items, original wall art, enlightening lamps, unusual handbags, interesting jewelry, and more than you might expect from the small space. As a relied-upon gift shop for the neighborhood, there's plenty with which to celebrate a wedding, anniversary, or birthday—and yes, gift wrapping is provided. *Tues–Sun; map:GG7.*

Real Card Company

2814 E MADISON ST, MADISON VALLEY; 206/325-1854

There are customized cards, and then there are custom-made cards. At this retail shop/design studio you'll find the best of both, along with an assortment of ready-made cards for nearly any occasion. For something truly unique, consult with the graphic designers on hand—they'll pore over books and magazines and swap ideas with you until they come up with something you can call your own. Be warned: all this creativity doesn't come cheap. *Mon–Sat; realcardcompany.com; map:GG6.*

R.E. Load Baggage

1205 E PIKE ST, STE 1D, CAPITOL HILL; 206/329-2946

The smart-looking, utilitarian bags from this Capitol Hill studio are all about you: what size you need, what colors you like, how you carry it, what kind of storage you're looking for—in a word, custom. Designed by real live bike messengers and stitched from scratch by a talented crew (working on the spot) the road-tested bags just keep getting better. Not only are they cool and functional, they're honestly priced too. *Every day; reloadbags.com; map:GG6.*

Silberman/Brown Fine Stationers

1322 5TH AVE, DOWNTOWN, 206/292-9404; 10220 NE 8TH ST, BELLEVUE; 425/455-3665

This refined stationer transcends trend with gracious gifts for the writer within: impeccable writing instruments, leather-bound albums, and classic desk accessories such as inkwells, clocks, and stamp dispensers. Customized stationery and invitations for weddings, graduations, and other occasions are also available. *Mon–Sat; silbermanbrown.com; map:K6, GG3.*

Stuhlberg's

1801 QUEEN ANNE AVE N, QUEEN ANNE; 206/352-2351 OR 888/520-7467

Long the go-to gift store of the Queen Anne set, this already terrific neighborhood store has notched things up by adding a custom stationery section upstairs, creating cards and invitations for every occasion imaginable. The second floor still stocks beautiful linens too; on the main floor you'll find an unfailing selection of candles, infant and layette clothing and toys, dishes, and other delights. *Every day; stuhlbergs.com; map:GG7.*

Swee Swee Paperie and Studio

4216 SW ALASKA ST, WEST SEATTLE; 206/937-7933

The owner's flair for fashion is evident in this pretty paper studio. In the expansive window is a vintage dress form outfitted in the latest of card couture; ribbons flow from a fancy fixture; and paper, like fabulous fabric, lines the walls. Browse the card collection or take a seat in a comfy chair while someone wraps your presents. They also specialize in sourcing and styling corporate gifts to make you look good. *Tues–Sat; sweesweepaperie.com; map:JJ8.*

Watson Kennedy

FINE HOME: 1022 1ST AVE, DOWNTOWN; 206/652-8350;
FINE LIFE: 10032 MAIN ST, BELLEVUE; 425/467-1142;
FINE LIVING: 86 PINE ST, PIKE PLACE MARKET; 206/443-6281

Stroll through the doors and you're quietly transported to a French flea market, Edith Piaf lilting in the background, the air perfumed with lavender, and everywhere you turn, something to intrigue the senses. You'll need to stay awhile to browse the creative collections, arranged to pique your curiosity and please the eye. There are books for the wordsmith; jewels to adorn; soaps and deliciously scented bath, body, and home potions; candles, linens and dishes; and much, much more, all with a subtle French accent. *Every day; watsonkennedy.com; map:I7, GG2, M7.*

ANTIQUES

Ancient Grounds

1220 1ST AVE, DOWNTOWN; 206/749-0747

Only in Seattle could you find a shop to provide you with both your morning macchiato and an ancient Japanese Noh theater mask. And according to aficionados, the coffee is excellent and the antiques equally so. Sip and stroll among the kimonos, Native American masks, and Asian armor and swords; sit in the window and watch foot traffic; or catch free Wi-Fi. *Every day; map:K7.*

Antique Liquidators

503 WESTLAKE AVE N, SOUTH LAKE UNION; 206/623-2740

What Antique Liquidators lacks in ambience, it makes up for in sheer volume. Run by the same family since 1970, the largest antique store in town has 22,000 square feet housing a slew of practical furnishings (mostly Danish and English; lots of chairs and drop-leaf tables). Endless variety and good prices (go ahead and dicker), but don't expect perfect quality. *Every day; antiqueliquidators.com; map:D2.*

Antiques at Pike Place

92 STEWART ST; DOWNTOWN; 206/441-9643

This tidy antique store is not musty or cluttered with junk, which makes for a supremely enjoyable shopping experience. Sure, there are knickknacks, but they are kept clean and behind a case for the most part. The store is large and fun to roam while hunting vintage linens, jewelry, lamps, rare accent furniture, and a whole room filled with aprons. *Every day; antiquesatpikeplace.com; map:I7.*

Bogart, Bremmer & Bradley

8000 15TH AVE NW, BALLARD; 206/783-7333

It's as if you're in a historic museum as you gaze upward at an art deco chandelier or a 1930s carnival glass bowl suspended from the ceiling of this store specializing in antique and vintage lighting. But rest assured, every one of the refurbished, rewired, scintillating fixtures is available for the dazzling right price. As for the furniture, you won't find any projects here: expert hands have carefully restored each piece to its original beauty. *Tues–Sat; bbbantiques.com; map:FF8.*

Collective

5323 BALLARD AVE NW, BALLARD; 206/782-1900

Nearly every day, customers ask if the furniture and collectibles housed in this historic Ballard storefront are new, no doubt because the airy space is a departure from the usual crowded, dusty antique store. Arranged as living areas, presentations mix it up: midcentury modern with 19th-century classic, Asian with European, metal with wood. Staff is kind and knowledgeable; prices are what you'd expect of a hip Ballard shopping street. *Every day; collectiveinballard.com; map:FF8.*

The Crane Gallery

104 W ROY ST, QUEEN ANNE; 206/298-9425

Spare and uncluttered, the Crane's selection speaks to its reputation as a purveyor of fine Asian antiques and artifacts. Paintings, ceramics, bronzes, ivory, jade, prints, netsuke, and furniture from the Orient are museum quality—and priced accordingly. *Tues–Sat; cranegallery.com; map:GG7.*

David Weatherford Antiques & Interiors

133 14TH AVE E, CAPITOL HILL; 206/329-6533; 1200 2ND AVE, DOWNTOWN; 206/624-3514

This antiques seller doesn't muck about with reproductions. Housed in a Capitol Hill mansion, David Weatherford sells exquisite 18th- and 19th-century English and French furniture, as well as Asian collectibles, Oriental rugs, porcelain, screens, and art glass. A resident design team advises clients on integrating antiques with their present furnishings. The downtown location specializes in commercial collections. *Mon–Sat; davidweatherford.com; map:HH6, L7.*

Fremont Antique Mall

3419 FREMONT PL N, FREMONT; 206/548-9140

Enter a bygone era as you descend the stairs into a sea of vintage collectibles, memorabilia, and pop culture ephemera. As you roam the booths and cases, you realize that there are a lot of people out there with very specific fixations. Among the reasonably priced trinkets and treasures you'll find Depression glass, a vintage Kotex tampon dispenser, chrome kitchen tables from the '50s, bell-bottomed jumpsuits and Afro wigs for that '70s party, a Resuscitation Annie CPR doll, and a Styx T-shirt in mint condition. *Mon–Sat; map:FF7.*

Glenn Richards

964 DENNY WY, SOUTH LAKE UNION, 206/287-1877

Laurie and John Fairman's second store (the first is the fine antique gallery Honeychurch), provides 30,000 square feet of Asian antiques. You'll find plenty of ideas in their showroom, complete with a workroom where woodworkers restore and repair. Furniture can be customized and retrofit into media cabinets, storage units, and more. The staff also custom-designs carpets, along with tables that are constructed of rare woods and artifacts by Tibetan refugees in Nepal. Not as pricey as Honeychurch but still fairly spendy. *Tues–Sat; glennrichards.com; map:F4.*

Honeychurch Antiques

411 WESTLAKE AVE N, SOUTH LAKE UNION; 206/622-1225

When out-of-towners seek superior Asian antiques, the Seattle Art Museum has been known to refer them to Laurie and John Fairman's renowned shop—and not simply because Honeychurch stocks museum-quality pieces. The Fairmans' scholarly knowledge of their high-quality wares is paralleled only by their approachability. John's parents opened the original Honeychurch in Hong Kong more than 40 years ago, and he's been doing business in Seattle for more than 25 years. The store's attraction lies in its tasteful blend of Asian fine art, folk art, and furniture, which spans the Neolithic period to the Han dynasty (206 BC) to early-20th-century basketry. *Tues–Sat; honeychurch.com; map:O3.*

Jean Williams Antiques

115 S JACKSON ST, PIONEER SQUARE; 206/622-1110

Family-owned and -operated for more than 35 years, Jean Williams is a well-established place in Seattle selling and restoring authentic antiques. The majority of the collection is 18th- and 19th-century French, English, and Biedermeier furniture in superb condition. They even produce a handmade-to-order drop-leaf walnut dining set that seats 12 to 14. *Mon–Sat; jeanwilliamsantiques.com; map:O9.*

Pacific Galleries

241 S LANDER ST, SODO; 206/441-9990

Whether you're seeking a Qing dynasty money box or a 1940s dressmaker's form, nearly any antique, vintage, or retro treasure you're after can be found in this indoor emporium, a hidden gem in a district of mostly warehouses. The huge room is filled with booths, cases, and kiosks of more than 200 vendors, some with specialties such as seashells, guns, or dishes; others focus on epochs and influences. Auctions are held every Monday at 10am. *Every day; pacgal.com; map:JJ7.*

Sun May Co.

672 S KING ST, CHINATOWN/INTERNATIONAL DISTRICT; 206/624-1467

This matchbox-size shop, secured behind a red iron gate, understands the thrill of the hunt. Cool collectibles—yellowing *Life* magazines, wooden Japanese *kokeshi* dolls, vintage Chinese shop signs—are stacked up and along the walls, hung from the shelves, and strung across the ceiling, with more treasures tucked in every corner. Family-owned, the business has been around since 1911. *Every day; map:Q6.*

BEAUTY, BODY CARE, AND FRAGRANCE

Bliss Soaps

619 BROADWAY E, CAPITOL HILL; 206/322-7627

For more than a decade this Seattle soap works has been hand-making treats for the body and bath out of natural ingredients with no added perfume. So why doesn't anyone know about them? Evidently, fans keep the shop a secret, hoarding every blissful bath bomb, deodorant bar, shampoo bar, and yes, bath soap, to themselves. Check out specialty items that look good enough to eat, such as cinnamon roll soap or bubble bath cupcakes. *Every day; blisssoap.com; map:GG6.*

Dandelion Botanical Company

5424 BALLARD AVE NW, BALLARD; 206/545-8892 OR 877/778-4869

The low lighting and soothing music in this natural apothecary might make you feel healed simply by walking through the door. Since 1996, Dandelion has been offering Chinese and ayurvedic herbs, women's health remedies, and aromatic elixirs, along with classes and books on everything from herbalism to the healing power of animals. *Every day; dandelionbotanical.com; map:FF8.*

Essenza

615 N 35TH ST, FREMONT; 206/547-4895

For beauty lovers with means, this is heaven. The makeup, lotion, and perfume laid out like paint on a palette are impossible to resist. T. LeClerc—a popular makeup line in France—is Essenza's pride, as is the line of all-natural body and hair products called Fresh and body care from Santa Maria Novella of Florence. There are also products for pampering baby and an exquisite assortment of precious jewelry created by local and national designers. *Every day (summer), Tues–Sun (winter); map:FF7.*

Frenchy's

3131 E MADISON ST, MADISON PARK; 206/325-9582

This neighborhood beauty spot is perfect for a girl gathering, with cushy side-by-side chairs that allow for tandem pedicures. After you've finished pampering yourself, you can pick up a few gifts from the wide assortment of body lotions and potions, accessories, candles, jewelry, and high-quality cosmetics. *Every day; frenchysdayspa.com; map:GG6.*

The Herbalist

2106 NE 65TH ST, RAVENNA; 206/523-2600

Even in Seattle, the depth of this natural remedy and health store is difficult to match. You can research an ailment or methodology by browsing its books, or find almost any kind of organic or wildcrafted herb, homeopathic flower essence, or custom herbal tincture. The "herbal tonic bar" supplies good-for-you beverages. *Every day; theherbalist.com; map:FF6.*

Parfumerie Elizabeth George

1424 4TH AVE, DOWNTOWN; 206/622-7212

It can be hard to find this exclusive store inside a downtown office building (between the Red Lion Hotel and a walking-shoe store), but it's open by appointment only, so foot traffic isn't really an issue. Clients are drawn to the shop's reputation for custom- and hard-to-find fragrances, as well as designer-matched scents (less expensive than the originals) and appealing atomizers and bath products. *By appointment; map:J6.*

Parfumerie Nasreen

1005 1ST AVE, DOWNTOWN; 206/623-9109 OR 888/286-1825

If you haven't stayed at the Alexis Hotel, then most likely you haven't seen this tiny parfumerie tucked inside the front door. Just a jewel box, it's large enough to hold more than 800 fragrances, including luxurious imports from all over the world. The crowded stacks of small boxes make maneuvering difficult, but the staff is happy to assist. *Mon–Sat; parfumerienasreen.com; map:L8.*

Passion Flower

2406 NW 80TH AVE, BALLARD; 206/297-6212

A stop into this bright Ballard spot, filled with luscious-smelling aromatherapy kits, handmade soaps, and scented candles, will certainly please your sniffer. But the truly unique aspect of this vintage-dressed shop is that the expert owner will create a custom-made fragrance exclusively for you. *Wed–Sat; passionflowerperfume.com; map:FF8.*

Tenzing Momo

93 PIKE ST, PIKE PLACE MARKET; 206/623-9837

This herbal apothecary and perfumery has been on the same block for the past three decades. In fact, it's the oldest medicinal herbal apothecary on the West Coast. There is a lot of energy in this small shop filled with exotic Tibetan incense, tinctures, massage oils, books, and above all—herbs. Ingredients and products are sourced locally if possible, but otherwise hail from Nepal, India, or Tibet. *Every day; tenzingmomo.com; map:J8.*

Vain

2018 1ST AVE, BELLTOWN; 206/441-3441

There is so much more to this edgy boutique/salon on the fringes of downtown/Belltown than simply another beauty salon selling hair and body products. That's where these purveyors of punk rock style started, and since then they've branched out considerably, carrying everything from fine Italian toothpaste to locally made fashion to alternative art, along with the hair dye, pomade, and putty. *Every day; vain.com; map:H7.*

BOOKS, NEWSPAPERS, AND PERIODICALS

All for Kids Books and Music

2900 NE BLAKELEY ST, STE C, RAVENNA; 206/526-2768

From *Green Eggs and Ham* through young adult novels, there's enough literature here to keep a growing mind occupied. The store stocks plenty of gifts for kids too: wooden toys, blocks, puppets, plush animals, kits, CDs, and activities. There's a weekly story hour on Tuesdays during the school year and plenty of author events. *Every day; allforkidsbooks.com; map:FF6.*

Bailey/Coy Books

414 BROADWAY E, CAPITOL HILL; 206/323-8842

One of Seattle's long-standing favorite local bookshops, this friendly store is geared to the diverse expectations of its neighborhood—from gays and lesbians to punky singles and families with kids. There's interesting reading for all, and the informed staff is happy to make a recommendation. In addition, you'll find greeting cards, journals, and paper gifts. *Every day; baileycoybooks.com; map:GG6.*

Balderdash Books and Art

8536 GREENWOOD AVE N, GREENWOOD; 206/784-4660

Even though the name means "fiddle-faddle," "piffle," and "nonsense," you won't find any of that at this small used bookstore. Along with purveying more than 15,000 preowned fiction books and a wide selection of nonfiction titles, the good-smelling shop is dedicated to supporting artists, showcasing two local artists every two months. Staff is sunny and warm. *Tues–Sun; balderdashbooksandart.com; map:EE7.*

Bulldog News

4208 UNIVERSITY WY NE, UNIVERSITY DISTRICT; 206/632-6397

With one of the fiercest foreign-press selections in town, this venerable newsstand has prevailed in the face of big-name bookstore encroachment. There's a magazine (or newspaper or zine) for any interest here—the mission of the place is to deliver newsworthy material from around the globe, encourage discussion, and provide a comforting cup of coffee to sip over conversation. *Every day; bulldognews.com; map:FF6.*

Cinema Books

4753 ROOSEVELT WY NE, UNIVERSITY DISTRICT; 206/547-7667

Packed with new and used, rare, out-of-print, and collectible books relating to movies, television, and theater, this movie-lover's paradise is aptly located downstairs from the cozy Seven Gables movie theater. You'll also find magazines, screenplays, posters, stills, and technical books for filmmakers. *Mon–Sat; cinemabooks.net; map:FF6.*

East West Bookshop of Seattle

6500 ROOSEVELT WY NE, ROOSEVELT; 206/523-3726 OR 800/587-6002

This store is dedicated to a comprehensive blend of Eastern and Western religions, philosophies, and healthy lifestyles. Those on a spiritual or metaphysical quest will find an array of resources, including classes and workshops. With flute music in the background and wind chimes and other ornamental pieces for sale, it's a peaceful place. *Every day; ewbookshop.com; map:EE7.*

Elliott Bay Book Company

101 S MAIN ST, PIONEER SQUARE; 206/624-6600

This multistoried bookstore has occupied the same corner since 1973. Rickety flooring, high ceilings, and a quiet atmosphere make Elliott Bay feel like a step back in time—except for the exceptional variety of up-to-date books. Travel has its own room; the children's section claims a large area of the store; and the crime fiction department is one of the best in the city. Knowledgeable employees will field questions (be sure to check out staff recommendations), and wrap and ship gifts. Downstairs, readings take place most evenings (also see the Literary section in the Arts chapter). An adjacent storefront boasts an impressive selection of used books. *Every day; elliottbaybook.com; map:O8.*

First and Pike News

93 PIKE ST, PIKE PLACE MARKET; 206/624-0140

This Seattle institution is the city's most bona-fide old-time newsstand, and what better locale than the corner of milling humanity that is Pike Street and First Avenue? The packed stall seems to have a magazine, newspaper, or other publication for each passerby. With some 1,600 publications—from *Money* to *Mother Jones*—it rivals the best stands of its kind in the world. *Every day; firstandpikenews.com; map:J8.*

Flora & Fauna Books

3121 W GOVERNMENT WY, MAGNOLIA; 206/623-4727

Gardeners, biologists, bird-watchers, and naturalists will love this modest bookshop near Discovery Park, which houses more titles on nature than you can shake a stick at. Whether you seek a gorgeously illustrated volume on flowers or birding, or a practical field guide, you're bound to find a new, used, or rare book that will satisfy. *Mon–Sat; ffbooks.net; map:N8.*

Fremont Place Book Company

621 N 35TH ST, FREMONT; 206/547-5970

Locals love this small and special bookstore in the "Center of the Universe," otherwise known as Fremont. As quirky as the neighborhood, the store stocks a well-edited selection of thoughtful, popular fiction and nonfiction, children's books, and poetry. Save yourself some headache by parking in the PCC parking lot, complimentary for 90 minutes while you shop. *Every day; fremontplacebooks.com; map:FF7.*

The Globe Books

5220 UNIVERSITY WY NE, STE B, UNIVERSITY DISTRICT; 206/527-2480; 218 1ST AVE S, PIONEER SQUARE; 206/682-6882

This unstuffy purveyor of new and used books specializes in the humanities (especially literature and reference) and carries a growing section of natural-science books. Don't be intimidated by the esoteric inventory; this is a wonderfully down-to-earth shop. Browse through the antique maps and replicas too. Trades are welcome. *U-District: Tue, Wed, Fri, alternating Sat and Sun; Pioneer Square: every day; map:FF6, N7.*

Horizon Books

425 15TH AVE E, CAPITOL HILL; 206/329-3586; 6512 ROOSEVELT WY NE, ROOSEVELT; 206/523-4217

Readers looking to wax philosophical should swing by Horizon Books, an old-fashioned, independent bookstore (complete with cats) that buys and sells used general books with an emphasis on literature, criticism, history, mystery, and philosophy. The second store is well stocked and eminently browsable. *Every day; map:GG6, EE7.*

Kinokuniya Bookstore

525 S WELLER ST, CHINATOWN/INTERNATIONAL DISTRICT; 206/587-2477

Although part of a large Japanese chain, this Asian-centric bookstore is the only one in Seattle and the best destination for Japanese books, magazines, music, and manga. Books written in Chinese, and children's books, cookbooks, and Eastern medicine volumes, also line the shelves, and it's a favored destination for cute T-shirts, stationery supplies, stickers, movies, and quirky Japanese notebooks. *Every day; kinokuniya.com; map:Q7.*

Left Bank Books Collective

92 PIKE ST, PIKE PLACE MARKET; 206/622-0196

This is a thinking-person's bookshop. Topics you'll find: natural parenting, feminism, anarchism. Topics you won't: setting the perfect table, the adventures of Paris Hilton, winners of *American Idol*. If you're a left-wing warrior looking for fodder to freshen your brain, you must pay a visit to this progressive purveyor. Check out the reading loft upstairs. *Every day; leftbankbooks.com; map:J7.*

Magus Books

1408 NE 42ND ST, UNIVERSITY DISTRICT; 206/633-1800

This Seattle institution has rescued many a starving student from full-price sticker shock with its 70,000-strong used-book inventory. A staple in this student-dominated neighborhood, the store carries everything from classical literature to engineering; it has a large science-fiction selection and tons of CliffsNotes, as well as a poetry section that would do any new-book store proud. *Every day; map:FF6.*

Open Books: A Poem Emporium

2414 N 45TH ST, WALLINGFORD; 206/633-0811

A book store devoted to poetry—what a novel idea. Shelves with books ranging from out-of-print volumes of poetry to new and used titles neatly line each wall. Open Books regularly hosts poetry readings and signings. *Tues–Sat; openpoetrybooks.com; map:FF7.*

Peter Miller Architectural and Design Books and Supplies

1930 1ST AVE, DOWNTOWN; 206/441-4114

For nearly 30 years, this bookstore/architectural supply store has satisfied the needs of a specific—and picky—clientele: those in the realm of design. Along with cubbies filled with beautiful books and glossy magazines covering topics such as sustainable design, architecture, photography, cooking, urban planning, industrial design, landscaping, and gardening, you'll find attractive office supplies, calendars, portfolios, bags, and stationery. The air is serious, the service attentive. *Mon–Sat; petermillerbooks.com; map:I7.*

Queen Anne Avenue Books

1811 QUEEN ANNE AVE N, QUEEN ANNE; 206/283-5624

How this neighborhood bookseller manages to pack in the printed matter without cramping quarters is truly an achievement. Residents of this community are devoted to the family-friendly shop, and the loyalty is reciprocated by an efficient, accommodating staff, ready with savvy reading recommendations. The store often hosts visiting authors. *Every day; queenannebooks.com; map:GG7.*

Ravenna Third Place Books

6504 20TH AVE NE, RAVENNA, 206/525-2347

To call this place a bookstore could be misleading. To describe it as a place for beer, bread (Honey Bear Bakery and Cafe is adjoining), books, and a convivial atmosphere (sometimes with fiddlers) is a more accurate representation. If you're expecting library quiet, you may want to go somewhere else, but return another day when you're looking for books and a brew from the pub downstairs. *Every day; ravennathirdplace.com; map:FF6.*

Seattle Mystery Bookshop

117 CHERRY ST, DOWNTOWN; 206/587-5737

This shop is a sure bet for those who simply must know whodunnit. You'll find new and used stories about suspense, thrillers, detectives, spies, and true crimes. Discover authors ranging from the well known (Lee Child, Elizabeth George, Michael Connelly) to the soon-to-be-known. *Every day; seattlemystery.com; map:N8.*

Secret Garden Bookshop

2214 NW MARKET ST, BALLARD; 206/789-5006

Although it started out as a specialist in children's books, this independent bookstore now includes reading for grown-ups too. In addition to comprehensive parenting and children's nonfiction sections, there is a solid general selection. They also host special events such as musical performances, classes, signings and occasional readings, programs for teachers and parents, and book fairs for local schools. *Every day; secretgardenbooks.com; map:FF8.*

Steve's Broadway News

204 BROADWAY E, CAPITOL HILL; 206/324-7323
There are no frills to this indoor magazine stand, but it's well organized and stocked with magazines, zines, and newspapers from around the globe. In addition, there are eclectic greeting cards, small gifts, and comic books. *Every day; map:GG6.*

Third Place Books

17171 BOTHELL WY NE; LAKE FOREST PARK; 206/366-3333
More than 200,000 new, used, and collectible books, a gift shop, a giant chess set, author readings, kids' activities including children's story telling, live music, dancing, food, and fun, fun, fun make this one of the North End's favorite family destinations. *Every day; thirdplacebooks.com; map:AA6.*

Twice Sold Tales

905 E JOHN ST, CAPITOL HILL (AND BRANCHES); 206/324-2421
Felines rule at this used bookstore, with catwalks overhead so the kitties can people watch. By the time you find what you need among hundreds and hundreds of fairly priced used books in decent shape, you realize that this is an eccentric place and well loved because of it. The Capitol Hill store is open til 2am on Friday. Branches are in the University District and Lower Queen Anne. *Every day; map:GG6.*

University Book Store

4326 UNIVERSITY WY NE, UNIVERSITY DISTRICT (AND BRANCHES); 206/634-3400
Founded in 1900, the University of Washington bookstore is the largest and most respected independent bookseller in the state, offering an impressive selection of more than 180,000 titles in myriad subjects, along with various school, art, and office supplies; UW-logo gear; gifts; and technologic gadgets. Customer service goes far beyond the usual, with free book shipping, gift wrapping, and parking validation; in the rare event that your title is not in stock, staff will promptly special order it. The store often sponsors events and readings in conjunction with the University. Branches are on the UW campus and in Bellevue, Bothell, Mill Creek, and Tacoma. *Every day; ubookstore.com; map:FF6.*

Wessel and Lieberman Booksellers

208 1ST AVE S, PIONEER SQUARE; 206/682-3545
Housed in historic Pioneer Square, this bookstore has the feel of a library, with shelves lined with new, used, and out-of-print-books on everything from the history of the Pacific Northwest and Western Americana to poetry, history, performing arts, and literary criticism. They are happy to work

with individuals and institutions to develop collections, and shipping is free. *Mon–Sat; wlbooks.com; map:N8.*

Wide World Books & Maps

4411 WALLINGFORD AVE N, WALLINGFORD; 206/634-3453 OR 888/534-3453

If travel is on your itinerary, then schedule a stop at this bookstore that focuses on destinations around the world. Plan your trip with books categorized by region: United States, Pacific Northwest and Canada, Australia, Asia, Latin America, Africa, and Europe—the shelf in the back can help you find tour groups and companies. Along with a great deal of information, you'll find travel tools (such as a toiletry kit) for your next adventure, plus maps and bags. *Every day; wideworldtravels.com; map:FF7.*

ETHNIC AND SPECIALTY FOODS

Bella Cosa

1711 N 45TH ST, WALLINGFORD; 206/545-7375

This smallish store is a paradise for those looking to liven up their pantry with enticing imported cheeses, artisanal oils, sauces, fine pastas, honeys, and beverages. Owner Emily Newman picks her favorites from around the world, which are enough to shift anyone's kitchen from drab to dazzling. Cool ergonomic pots and pans, too, from the Culinary Institute of America. *Tues–Sun; bellacosafoods.com; map:FF7.*

Big John's PFI

1001 6TH AVE S, LEVEL B, SODO; 206/682-2022

Just south of Chinatown, this friendly warehouse outlet is where penny-pinching food lovers find imported European, Greek, and Italian specialty foods, many in bulk. Started nearly four decades ago out of the back of Big John Croce's car, the no-frills store has a terrific imported cheese section, barrels of olives, dolmas, sweets, and remarkably low prices. Locals check in regularly to see what new goodies arrived in the latest shipment or to get cooking advice from the staff. *Mon–Sat; bigjohnspfi.com; map:JJ7.*

DeLaurenti Specialty Food Market

1435 1ST AVE, PIKE PLACE MARKET; 206/622-0141

For more than 50 years this Pike Place Market cornerstone has purveyed Mediterranean and international foodstuffs. The slender aisles are dense with canned goods, olives, olive oils, imported pasta, and breads from some of the area's best bakers. The deli has excellent charcuterie and preserved meats and carries more than 200 kinds of cheese. The wine department upstairs is known for its Italian labels and good selection. A sandwich counter facing First Avenue has dandy lunch options and offers good people watching. *Every day; delaurenti.com; map:J8.*

Dish D'Lish

5136 BALLARD AVE NW, BALLARD; 206/223-1848

Local chef and cookbook author Kathy Casey offers a spiffy gourmet food takeout shop with downright sassy party foods, artisan cheeses, specialty items, or simply a hot sandwich. Eat right there or grab one of her tasty ready-to-eat creations to dine like a gourmand without putting in kitchen time. There are also hip salads, dressings, and dips (even cocktail mixes!) at the ready. *Tues–Sun; kathycasey.com; map:FF8.*

El Mercado Latino

1514 PIKE PL, PIKE PLACE MARKET; 206/623-3240

This little store has the essence of a country mercantile in Mexico, with colorful *ristras* (wreaths of chili peppers and garlic) hanging under the arbor out front and plantains in boxes by the door. Inside, there are piñatas, dried fruit, candies, a huge selection of hot sauces, and shelves of canned foods. Caribbean, South American, Spanish, and creole foods are all represented here. *Every day; latinmerchant.com; map:J8.*

From Russia with Love Deli

15600 NE 8TH ST, STE K-16, BELLEVUE; 425/401-2093

Where the expats come for their borsch, handmade piroshki, and vareniki dumplings, this small storefront offers the meal fixin's ripe for washing down with Russian black tea or even kvass, a malt beverage. The long deli case holds smoked fish, cheeses, and delectable Slavic salads. *Every day; frwldeli.com; map:GG2.*

La Buona Tavola

1524 PIKE PLACE, PIKE PLACE MARKET; 206/292-5555

Truffles (the fungi, not the chocolate) are the ticket at this amazing store tucked into the Sanitary Market Building. From fresh and frozen orbs to delicious truffle salts, creams, and oils, it's a quick stop to dress up dinner party fare with something exotic. Owner Rei Hanscomb also stocks unusual Italian pastas, pantry staples, and Italian wine you won't find elsewhere. At lunch there's always a delectable fresh soup to sip at the petite table near the window. The condiment-tasting bar is a fine way to discover just what you want to take home. *Every day; trufflecafe.com; map:I7.*

Market Spice

85-A PIKE PL, PIKE PLACE MARKET; 206/622-6340

One of the longest residents of the Pike Place Market, Market Spice has been selling teas, coffees, cooking spices, and other goodies here since 1911. As well as spices from around the world (everything from chamomile to catnip), there are jellies, cooking utensils, china cups and pots, and tin and pottery tea sets. *Every day; marketspice.com; map:J8.*

The Mexican Grocery

1914 PIKE PL, PIKE PLACE MARKET; 206/441-1147

Come in around lunchtime and you'll see the name the grocery has made for itself with local merchants, who gather for takeout of nachos, sandwiches, burritos, and fresh flan for dessert. The grocery shelves hold bagged Mexican cooking spices, peppers, chili pods, and beans, and the refrigerated case keeps cheeses and salsas fresh. *Mon–Sat; map:J8.*

Pasta & Co.

2109 QUEEN ANNE AVE N, QUEEN ANNE (AND BRANCHES); 206/322-1644

Pasta & Co. is a veritable meal store, a convenient neighborhood source for everyday eats, as well as celebratory ones. For more than 20 years the local icon has been known for its amazing roast chicken and decadent cupcakes, with stylish branches at University Village and in Bellevue and Redmond. *Every day; pastaco.com; map:GG7.*

BEST PLACE
TO SPEND $5?

"On Japanese candy at the checkout aisle of Uwajimaya."

Rachel Hart, Seattle *magazine editor*

Porcella Urban Market

10245 MAIN ST, STE 101; BELLEVUE; 425/286-0080

Porcella is a slice of Paris in the midst of Bellevue. A trip to the market will transport you to a world of cuisine to consume in the café or to impress your guests at home. Shelves are lined with imported salt, olive oil, vinegar, fine wine, and unusual condiments. A charcuterie of house-cured meats, cases of exotic cheeses, and specialty chocolates are all presented in a delicious setting. *Every day; porcellaurbanmarket.com; map:GG2.*

Spanish Table

1426 WESTERN AVE; PIKE PLACE MARKET; 206/682-2827

A move across the street opened up loads of room for this definitive source for Spanish foods. Now the selection of Spanish wines (both esoteric and well-priced), chorizo, Catalan cheeses, and fino sherry is bigger than before, including everything you need for a paella party, plus a pan the size of a car trunk. Cool imported glassware, cookbooks, and music seal the deal. *Every day; spanishtable.com; map:J7.*

Uwajimaya

600 5TH AVE S, CHINATOWN/INTERNATIONAL DISTRICT; 206/624-6248; 15555 NE 24TH ST, BELLEVUE; 425/747-9012

Located in the heart of the International District, this store boasts a vast selection of Asian foods, small electrical appliances (rice cookers, woks), housewares, and gifts. The real distinctions here are the variety of canned goods, depth of choice (one aisle is wholly devoted to rice), fresh seafood (geoduck, live prawns and crabs in the shellfish tanks), and produce department. Check out the pastries at the Yummy House in the food court; the Bellevue store has a fine Asian bakery case. Both branches have in-store cafés with Asian food for eating in or carrying out. *Every day; uwajimaya.com; map:Q7, GG1.*

Zizo Market

10204 MAIN ST, BELLEVUE; 425/646-9496

The air in Tarek Ghaly's sunny, friendly deli on Bellevue's upscale shopping street is perfumed with the scent of spices. Aisles are lined with hard-to-find Middle Eastern foods, both packaged and fresh, and at the deli counter is an array of olives and cheeses and delicious sandwiches for the lunch crowd. Don't miss the unusual salad bar offering more than lettuce: hummus, baba ghanoush, tabbouleh, cucumber/yogurt salad, dolmas, Arabic potato salad, and Greek salad. *Every day; map:GG2.*

FINE JEWELRY

Alexandria Rossoff Jewelry and Rare Finds

402 UNIVERSITY ST, DOWNTOWN; 206/381-3949

Exceptional service, in-depth knowledge, and incredible selection have put this gem of a store on the radar of many a connoisseur. The collection—particularly the bridal and antique pieces from the Victorian, art nouveau, art deco, and Edwardian periods—may have you feeling as if you're browsing a museum of classic jewels, but lucky for us, it all can be had for the right price. *Tues–Sat, Monday by appointment; alexandriarossoff.com; map:K6.*

Alvin Goldfarb Jeweler

305 BELLEVUE WY NE, BELLEVUE; 425/454-9393

Customer service is foremost for this long-standing Eastside establishment. Home to one-of-a-kind sapphires, crystal gift items, sterling watches, jewelry cases, and diamonds, the shop adjacent to a Bellevue strip mall has grown and flourished along with the community. *Mon–Sat; alvingoldfarbjeweler.com; map:HH3.*

Carroll's Fine Jewelry

1427 4TH AVE, DOWNTOWN; 206/622-9191

This classic marble-trimmed storefront has occupied the same location since 1895—no doubt the most established jeweler in Seattle. As specialists in modern and antique settings, Carroll's also offers custom designs and a high-quality selection of watches, silver flatware, and baby gifts. The experienced staff still serves homemade cookies and tea on a silver platter to customers while they browse. *Mon–Sat; carrollsfinejewelry.com; map:K6.*

Crane Jewelers

519 PINE ST, DOWNTOWN; 206/624-1531

This veteran Seattle jewelry store imparts a touch of Northwest class with its grand chandelier, marble countertops, and pre-Columbian artwork. Purveying primarily custom creations, Crane's diamonds come from New York and Chicago and are used both in their new designs and to remake rings and other pieces. You'll also find a selection of pristine estate pieces and a friendly staff. *Mon–Sat; cranejewelers.com; map:I5.*

Facèré Jewelry Art Gallery

1420 5TH AVE (CITY CENTRE), DOWNTOWN; 206/624-6768

You'd never suspect that secreted in the midst of a downtown mall is this tiny shop, chock-full of precious finds gathered from talented artists exclusive to the gallery. You'll find intriguing estate pieces such as Cartier earrings alongside works of wearable art—brushed-metal brooches, colorful beaded link necklaces—from local and international artists. Exhibits and artists' receptions held on occasion. *Mon–Sat; facerejewelryart.com; map:J5.*

Fox's Gem Shop

1341 5TH AVE, DOWNTOWN; 206/623-2528

There's an intimidating hush in this esteemed gold and platinum gallery. Maybe it's the uniformed guard at the door; more likely it's the ooh-inspiring gemstones and dazzling diamonds that sparkle from the glass cases. Highlights of the discerning collection are classic wedding sets, Alex Sepkus originals, and luminous pearls, including unrivaled Mikimoto. For the bride and groom and important anniversaries, there's a gift section with silver serving pieces and an admirable selection of timepieces. *Mon–Sat; foxsgemshop.com; map:K6.*

Greenlake Jewelry Works

550 NE NORTHGATE WY, NORTHGATE; 206/527-1108

Can't find the perfect wedding band or engagement ring? Head to Green Lake Jewelry Works (which used to be located just across the street from Green Lake), where one of more than 30 designers and craftspeople are at the ready to make your vision a reality. They'll use photos and existing examples, draw up sketches, or create a computer rendering to give form to your ideas. *Every day; gljw.com; map:DD7.*

Hannigan-Adams

1260 CARILLON POINT, KIRKLAND; 425/889-9450

Frank Hannigan and Beth Adams, designers/artists/goldsmiths, are known across the nation as luxury jewelers to Saks Fifth Avenue and Nordstrom, yet little word of their talent has crossed the bridge to Seattle. Their collection ranges from sleek, yet somewhat traditional settings of rings, earrings, and pendants, to recent designs weaving dramatic precious stones into modern, handcrafted necklaces. There is plenty of jewelry on hand to choose from, and they'll custom-make anything your heart desires. *Mon–Sat; hanniganadams.com; map:EE3.*

Magnotti Design

709 BROADWAY E, CAPITOL HILL; 206/724-1977

Bruce Magnotti's fine jewelry is sustainability at its most stylish. Using gems from antique or estate pieces, he sets the stone free of its original setting, giving it new life and glamour as the solitary star in a hand-wrought setting atop a hefty hand-forged band. His designs are simple, stunning, and sophisticated, gracing the hand of many a personality—including Sarah Jessica Parker and Paris Hilton. *Tues–Sun; brucemagnotti.com; map:GG6.*

Michael Wm. Farrell Jeweler

5420 SANDPOINT WY NE, SAND POINT; 206/524-8848

Would-be grooms are known to go out of their way to do business with this patient jeweler. If you can't find anything you want from the ready-made offerings, he can custom-make a wedding set (or any other kind of jewelry, for that matter) from traditional materials or even lightweight titanium. If a wedding isn't in your future, there are always vintage editions, signature costume jewelry, and a collection of sterling silver. *Mon–Sat; michaelfarrelljewelers.com; map:EE5.*

Turgeon-Raine Jewellers

1407 5TH AVE, DOWNTOWN; 206/447-9488

Even if you're not shopping for an engagement ring, when you glimpse the unique settings and scintillating shine emanating from these showcases, it may be love at first sight. Flaunt a purchase from Turgeon-Raine, and you'll elicit awe from even the snobbiest acquaintance. In addition to a collection of modern designs, you'll find rare and collectible gemstones, restored estate and antique jewelry, and only two brands of watches: Patek Philippe and Bedat & Co. *Mon–Sat; turgeonraine.com; map:J5.*

FLORISTS, GARDEN SHOPS, AND NURSERIES

Ballard Blossom

1766 NW MARKET ST, BALLARD; 206/782-4213

This Ballard shop has been family run since 1927—its blazing neon sign is a neighborhood landmark. Traditional arrangements are FTD in nature, but the friendly staff presides over a cheerful profusion of fresh, silk, and dried flowers; potted plants; and gift items. Customers can have many selections sent anywhere in the world, while personally chosen arrangements can be delivered area-wide. *Mon–Sat (every day in December); ballardblossom.com; map:FF8.*

Best Buds

411 E BLAINE ST, MADISON PARK; 206/709-3926

If you're a DIY kind of person and all you need is a source for healthy, affordable, fresh flowers; filler; and greens, take a morning jaunt to Madison Park. Tucked on a side street in a charming cottage, you'll find this flower market brimming with (depending on the season) orchids, gerbera daisies, tulips, bedding plants, potted plants, and other delights. Service is neighborly and prices hard to beat. *Every day; map:GG6.*

City People's Garden Store & Mercantile

2939 E MADISON ST, MADISON VALLEY; 206/324-0737; 5440 SAND POINT WY NE, SAND POINT; 206/524-1200

Like the name says, the concept is that of an old-time mercantile—with a modern bent. In the cheery mix of goods for home, garden, and gift giving you'll find kitchen towels and dishes, garden gloves and yard tools, cards and candles (and so much more). The Madison Valley store has a flourishing garden center and plant experts to guide you, while the Sandpoint store is more focused on furnishings for inside and out. *Every day; citypeoples.com; map:GG6, EE5.*

Fleurish

1308 E UNION ST, CAPITOL HILL; 206/322-1602

Sending flowers is a tricky thing. Often you don't know what you're getting—until it's too late. You can rest assured that this modern floral artist will leave a fabulous impression with an arrangement of fresh, exotic flowers and greens presented in an astounding, innovative way. They're consistently a preferred pick of *Seattle Bride* magazine. *By appointment only; fleurish.com; map:GG6.*

Hawaii General Store & Gallery

258 NE 45TH ST, UNIVERSITY DISTRICT; 206/633-5233

If you want to share your aloha spirit with fresh flowers, this island-style destination is about the only game in town. Fragrant leis are flown in every week: garlands of dendrobium orchids, plumeria, tuberose, and maile. Imagine her surprise when you present her with a lei and a kiss, instead of a corsage and a handshake. Prices vary, call ahead to reserve your choice. *Every day; hawaiigeneralstore.net; map:FF6.*

Julius Rosso Nursery & Garden

6404 ELLIS AVE S, GEORGETOWN; 206/763-1888

At this nursery, oddly located in the heart of Georgetown, landscape architects and weekend gardeners alike rub dirty elbows amid blossoming shrubs and ornamental grasses. This is a commercial nursery, not a traditional garden store, so know what you're looking for before you go. Prices are down-to-earth. *Every day; map:JJ7.*

Juniper Flowers

308 W REPUBLICAN ST, QUEEN ANNE; 206/285-2700

Just in case you need a little reminder, this unique flower shop is more than happy to ping you with a heads-up about a birthday, anniversary, or whatever the occasion. Arrangements are lush and artistic, with an emphasis on color, texture, and exotic blooms such as rare orchids, hydroponic roses, and rich berries. Plus, the store supports a number of worthy charities. *Mon–Sat; juniperflowers.com; map:GG7.*

LOCAL FLAVOR

There's one thing we do very well in the Pacific Northwest, and that's eat. We're fortunate to enjoy some of the freshest, finest food around, with many products made by local craftspeople. And because we have so many cultural influences, the flavors are as diverse as the area's population. For the visitor, there's nothing like the taste of Seattle to bring back delicious memories. For those who live here, support your neighborhood and eat close to home with specialty foods made right here in Washington.

Bringing to the city a genuine slice of Italy is **SALUMI** (309 3rd Ave S, Pioneer Square; 206/621-8772; salumicuredmeats.com), established by former Boeing engineer Armandino Batali. Meat lovers return time and time again to savor the seasonal salami, such as hot soppressata, winter salami, and oregano salami, and cured meats like coppa and pancetta. Enjoy a fresh-made sandwich right on the spot. Many fine local restaurants feature Salumi artisan cured meats on their menus too. Replicate the experience at home by ordering a selection to go, thinly sliced and ready to serve. If you have far to travel, opt for uncut and it will keep in the fridge for one to two months.

After studying chocolate making in France and instructing others on how to create luxury treats, Ivy Chan decided to concoct her own line of lovelies. Thank goodness, for today we can indulge in **COCOA CHAI CHOCOLATES** (206/621-7122; cocoachai.com; or Venue, 5408 22nd Ave NW, Ballard; 206/789-3335), truffles with a delectable fusion of Asian and French, like Thai Chili with Lemongrass and Lychee Tea. These delicate works of art are made of the finest dark chocolate sourced from France and Germany by the meticulous owner herself. Further appease your sweet tooth at **THE CONFECTIONAL** (1530 Pike Pl, Pike Place Market; 206/621-7122; theconfectional.com). Dessert maestro Paul B.

Martha E. Harris Flowers and Gifts

4218 E MADISON ST, MADISON PARK; 206/568-0347

Martha E. Harris often fills out her English garden–style arrangements with native evergreens and local flowers. The creators of elegant arrangements work in the back of the eponymous store, past fine accessories, jewelry, and accent pieces for the home. Expect extravagant, dramatic, bountiful arrangements. Parties and weddings are Harris' specialties, and she maintains a bridal registry (upon request). Deliveries worldwide daily except Sunday. *Every day; map:GG6.*

Megan Mary Olander Florist

222 1ST AVE S, PIONEER SQUARE; 206/623-6660

In the heart of historic Pioneer Square is this tiny, sweet-smelling flower and gift shop. Displayed on an antique flower cart are potted plants and delicate

Verono and his staff hand-make the dense, rich individual cheesecakes, beautifully presented, sinfully delicious, and baked fresh every day on the premises. Pick from flavors such as Mochacinno, Seattle's New York Style, and Kahlua White Chocolate (about $3.50 each). If you want to take a few to travel, they'll pack them in a sturdy box and send you on your way.

Smoked salmon is a Seattle classic, and the best can be found far from the tourist crowds at **JENSEN'S OLD FASHIONED SMOKEHOUSE** (10520 Greenwood Ave N, Greenwood; 206/364-5569; jensenssmokehouse.com). A short trip northward rewards you with the just the right amount of smoke and salt in Jensen's salmon. Mike Jensen is the third generation to utilize the family recipe calling for the finest fresh wild king and keta salmon, smoked using special hardwoods, precise temperatures, and perfect timing. You'll also find king candy—smoked salmon cured with extra sugar—and sockeye salmon nova lox (about $7–$22 per pound, depending on variety).

Add a little heat to your smoked salmon with **MAMA LIL'S PICKLED PEPPERS** (206/322-8824; mamalils.com; and De Laurenti, 1435 1st Ave, Pike Place Market; 206/622-0141; delaurenti.com). Picked, packed, and pickled in the Pacific Northwest, these palatable peppers in olive oil (about $7 for a 9-ounce jar) zip up a pizza, pasta sauce, and more. Made by Mama Lil's son, Howard Lev, the condiments come in mildly spicy or kick butt—a great gift for the hot lover in your life.

As a vehicle for these tasty treats, try **LA PANZANELLA CROCCANTINI** (at fine specialty food stores around town, about $5 for a 4.25-ounce bag). A cross between a cracker and crispy flatbread, they hold up well to spreads such as tapenade, goat cheese, sun-dried tomato topping, and of course, smoked salmon. Lightly sprinkled with salt, or infused with rosemary, black pepper, fennel, or sesame, they add subtle texture and taste to hors d'oeuvres.

—Lei Ann Shiramizu

floral finishing touches for the home. Baby clothes on tiny hangers and fragrant French soaps are neatly presented on vintage furnishings. Custom orders are available. *Mon–Fri; map:O8.*

Molbak's Greenhouse and Nursery

13625 NE 175TH ST, WOODINVILLE; 425/483-5000

Since 1956, Molbak's has catered to avid Northwest gardeners with healthy plants that thrive in the Emerald City and environs. Both novice and expert will find plenty to explore among the hundreds of houseplants and the full range of outdoor plants (everything from trees to ground covers) over acres of greenhouses. Molbak's also offers garden-related gifts, a Christmas shop (lavish holiday displays bring visitors here in droves), a garden supply store, and distinctive floral designs. *Every day; molbaks.com; map:BB2.*

Nest Floral and Gift

3256 NE 85TH ST, WEDGWOOD; 206/525-5658

The owner's background in visual merchandising is evident in this charming floral boutique tucked away in a residential neighborhood. With an eye for color and texture, she creates an inviting environment filled with candles, cards, pretty gifts, and of course, beautiful blooms. It's the kind of place that inspires treating yourself. *Tues–Sat, Sunday and Monday by appointment; nestfloral.com; map:FF6.*

Pike Place Flowers

1501 1ST AVE, PIKE PLACE MARKET; 206/682-9797

With buckets of bright flowers spilling over the sidewalk, this is one cheery corner in the bustling Pike Place Market. Stop and smell the roses, or better yet, take a few home. They specialize in spontaneous bouquets or lovely single stems; there are also potted plants for the garden and arrangements for weddings or other occasions, available on request. *Every day; pikeplaceflowers.com; map:J7.*

Sky Nursery

18528 AURORA AVE N, SHORELINE; 206/546-4851

This family-owned "gardeners' garden store" is a perennial favorite among Seattle's serious green thumbs. Whether you're growing vegetables or grooming a lawn, nurturing roses or shopping for sturdy shrubs, it's likely that you'll find what you need on its 4 acres of plants in every size, shape, color, and texture. There are also sensible gardening supplies, along with a staff that knows what they're doing. *Every day; skynursery.com.*

Swanson's Nursery and Greenhouse

9701 15TH AVE NW, CROWN HILL; 206/782-2543

Five acres of annuals, perennials, trees, shrubs, and display gardens make this a worthwhile afternoon for serious gardeners and a decent diversion for those with undeveloped green thumbs. This full-service nursery includes uncommon plants of all kinds and emphasizes choice offerings over sheer quantity. Enjoy a leisurely lunch, desserts, bakery items, and espresso in the recently remodeled garden café and gift shop in the tropical conservatory. The store also offers seminars and garden workshops. *Every day; swansonsnursery.com; map:DD8.*

Wells Medina Nursery

8300 NE 24TH ST, BELLEVUE; 425/454-1853

Many a swanky Eastside home has a landscape graced with flora from this 5-acre nursery nestled in the heart of posh Medina. A favorite among perennial lovers and regionally famed for its variety, this is also the place to buy choice shrubs—the selection of rhododendrons and Japanese maples is unmatched in the area. Look here for unusual vines, bulbs, and ground covers as well, and check out the long demonstration border. The excellent range of plants is complemented by a helpful staff. Prices match the neighborhood (hint: Bill Gates lives here). *Every day; wellsmedinanursery.com; map:GG4.*

HOME FURNISHINGS

Alchemy Collections

2029 2ND AVE, BELLTOWN; 206/448-3309

If you're looking to enhance your environment with a little Asian persuasion, drop by this modern showcase of East-West fusion. You won't find ornamental antiquities, only sleek, modular furnishings—couches, tables, beds, smart storage, and home accents ideal for loft living. *Every day; alchemycollections.com; map:H6.*

Area 51

401 E PINE ST, CAPITOL HILL; 206/568-4782

At one time this favorite urban décor store sold an eclectic blend of retro and current pieces, combined in ways that inspired garage sale-ing. Today the store has grown up to offer strictly new, modernist furniture and accessories, stirring sophisticated shoppers to hand over their credit cards. *Thurs–Tues; map:J2.*

Bitters Co.

513 N 36TH ST, FREMONT; 206/632-0886

This eclectic general store, owned and stocked by sisters Amy and Katie Carson, is a haven of sustainable home style. Weathered walls and flooring and low lighting enhance the mystique of their own line of modern-rustic tables, chairs, and daybeds made from reclaimed wood, as well as bags, pillows, and place mats sewn of abaca, created on nonmechanized looms, and cork bowls and birdhouses from Portugal. *Tues–Sun; bittersco.com; map:FF8.*

David Smith & Co.

1107 HARRISON ST, SOUTH LAKE UNION; 206/223-1598

This Indonesian importer continually fills its mammoth showroom/warehouse with container loads of antique and new tables, chairs, beds, cabinets, and so much more, presented in a way that invites you to linger. Over the years, the store has acquired a lovely patina of age and use, like a well-loved, well-made article of furniture. If you can't afford a hand-hewn teak table, you can bring home the ambience with a hand-woven Lombok basket, batik table runner, or exotically fragranced soy or beeswax candle. *Every day; davidsmithco.com; map:E2.*

Great Jones Home

1921 2ND AVE, BELLTOWN; 206/448-9405

This fabulous store puts shabby chic to shame with a grand mix of vintage and new furnishings blending baroque with boho. Offerings include exquisite candles and chandeliers, impeccably refurbished furniture, and fine china, cards, candleholders, coffee table books, and other unusual and handpicked accoutrements for the home. There's also a lovely linen section in the back where you can choose custom bedding and drapery. Interior design services are available. *Every day; greatjoneshome.com; map:I7.*

Herban Pottery and Patio

3200 1ST AVE S, SODO; 206/749-5112

The outdoor room is well furnished in this lofty old building featuring all things patio, including furniture sets of metal, iron, and teak. Pottery plays an important part in setting the scene with immense pots for plants or garden water features, antique and new pots at surprisingly affordable prices, and a variety of vases. Add finishing flourishes with linens, candles, and other accessories for the garden party. *Every day; herbanpatio.com; map:JJ7.*

Kobo Capitol Hill
Kobo at Higo

814 E ROY ST, CAPITOL HILL; 206/726-0704; 604 S JACKSON ST, CHINATOWN/INTERNATIONAL DISTRICT; 206/381-3000

The original Kobo is a closet-sized shop on Capitol Hill; the second is nearly 3,600 square feet, housed within a historic variety store in the International District. Both locations of Kobo, which translates from Japanese to "artist's workshop," live up to the name, featuring artists from the Pacific Northwest, Japan, and beyond. In-store showings change frequently, from local jewelry to photographic images of Japan's street culture to a display of handmade cups. There's always an array of ceramics and Asian-inspired gifts, from rare and pricey home furnishings to more-thoughtful-than-expensive souvenirs. *Mon–Sat; koboseattle.com; map:GG6, P6.*

Limn Seattle

629 WESTERN AVE, DOWNTOWN; 206/622-2433

Just in time for the unveiling of denser, more designer-ly downtown living comes the arrival of this San Francisco–based lighting and home furnishings showroom. Sleek and chic, the international collection feels modern without being here today, passé tomorrow. The lofty shop also features installations by well-known artists, rotating about four times a year. Staff is well informed and helpful. *Every day; limn.com; map:N7.*

Lucca Great Finds
Lucca Statuary

5332 BALLARD AVE NW, BALLARD; 206/782-7337; 3623 LEARY WAY NW, BALLARD; 206/789-8444

The owners of this tasteful Ballard Avenue boutique keep their shop well merchandised with delightful finds: authentic European gifts of fine stationery, French ribbon, Mariage Frères teas, and bath and body products made in Florence, as well as quirkier gifts such as exotic insects and tin toys. In the garden courtyard, you'll find Lucca's signature statues, ranging from fountains to birdbaths to bookends. Just down the way at Lucca Statuary is a treasure trove of one-of-a-kind statuary, produced and hand-finished on the premises for wholesale and retail. Inside the light-filled conservatory is a tidy presentation of gifts in an uplifting environment. *Every day; luccastatuary.com; map:FF8, FF8.*

Maison Luxe

1123 1ST AVE, DOWNTOWN; 206/405-2828

This store dresses the home as a stylish woman would dress herself: borrow the best from vintage, layer it with modern, add a few thoughtfully chosen accessories, and make sure that everything mixes without being too cutesy. Elegant, eclectic, and approachable makes for a winning combination of furniture and home accents. *Tues–Sun, Monday by appointment; maisonluxe.net; map:L7.*

Milagros Mexican Folk Art

1530 POST ALLEY, PIKE PLACE MARKET; 206/464-0490

Tucked into the Pike Place Market is this fine collection of the best that Mexico's artisans have to offer. Milagros (Spanish for "miracles") is named for the small religious trinkets that many Latin Americans use to petition saints for help. The owners travel frequently to Mexico to bring back Oaxacan wood carvings, authentic dance masks, original Huichol Indian yarn paintings and beadwork, clay figures, and hand-pounded tinwork and Talavera pottery. *Every day; milagrosseattle.com; map:J7.*

Price Asher Garden & Home

3300 1ST AVE S, STE 400, SODO; 206/254-9226

If you've ever said, "That plant looks so beautiful, it can't be real," this place will pique your scrutiny at every turn. Arranged under towering faux foliage is attractive patio furniture and beckoning hammocks, along with other accessories you must have to fashion your outdoor oasis. *Tues–Sat; priceasher.com; map:F4.*

RetroFit Home

1419 12TH AVE, CAPITOL HILL; 206/568-4663

You can find nearly anything to furnish and accessorize your mod, hip, happy home at this fun and functional store on Capitol Hill's expanding 12th Avenue. In addition to stocking the unusual, the usual suspects (couches, tables, chairs, rugs), and all the accomplices (barware, dishes, books), they hold cheerful shindigs with free-flowing wine and exhibits by local artists. *Every day; retrofithome.com; map:M1.*

Square Room

910 E PIKE ST, CAPITOL HILL; 206/329-1214

Square Room is anything but square in its presentation of weird and wonderful goods gathered from hither, thither, and yon. There's exotic art from local and national artists, including mosaic cement bowls, an occasional wool chicken, and a table and hassock made from recycled tires. In the eclectic mix you'll discover handmade jewelry, music, seashells, and artworks by the owners themselves. *Mon–Sat; squareroom.us; map:L1.*

Tableau

2232 NW MARKET ST, STE 101, BALLARD; 206/782-5846

The offerings of this spacious showroom, colored in a restful Pacific Northwest palette, would meld comfortably into nearly any Seattle home. Like any interesting environment, it mixes textures and influences, like a smooth leather sofa set with Asian silk pillows, or wooden salad servers in a glass bowl. There's also a plethora of giftables, including scented candles, cards, and sweet baby things. *Every day; tableaugifts.com; map:FF8.*

Urchin

1922 1ST AVE, DOWNTOWN; 206/448-5800

Now what do you think a store named Urchin would carry? Modern home furnishings and gifts, of course. That, and a selection of darling baby stuff (mobiles, shoes, onesies), a handsome collection of man/computer/diaper/everything bags, exquisite jewelry, lamps, chairs, tables, rugs, and small leather goods, presented in a minimalist setting. The common denominator is great design made for the urban palate. *Every day; urchinseattle.com; map:I7.*

Velocity Art & Design

251 YALE AVE N, SOUTH LAKE UNION; 206/781-9494 OR 866/781-9494

There's an air of cool in this quiet sanctuary of style. And it's not only in the service, a bit aloof behind the counter; it permeates every article. Each carefully chosen piece registers high in hip factor, from bold hand-printed linen pillows and modular sofas to flexible room dividers and colorful clocks. *Every day; velocityartanddesign.com; map:G1.*

Veritables Décor
Veritables Object

2806 E MADISON ST, MADISON VALLEY; 206/322-7782; 2816 E MADISON ST, MADISON VALLEY; 206/726-8047

Veritables Décor is the newest Madison Valley offering from designer Marie Harris, who has owned home accessories shop Veritables Object for more than a decade (though before Décor was born, Object was known simply as Veritables). While Décor features modern, sophisticated furniture, Object focuses on home accents and gifts, such as fragranced candles, handmade jewelry, imported dishware, cashmere and silk wraps, European soaps, and other lovely giftables stacked nearly to the ceiling. *Mon–Sat; veritablesdecor.com; map:GG6, GG6.*

Zanadia

1815 N 45TH ST, WALLINGFORD; 206/547-0884

This Wallingford Center store is stocked floor to ceiling with reliably tasteful furnishings and gifts. You'll find reproductions of large furniture such as armoires and tables of Asian or European origin, along with smaller decorative items like pillows, linens, dishes, and all the accessories of a well-appointed home. A kitchen corner is fully stocked with a mix of beautiful and practical cooking, baking, and dinnerware. On a gift-giving note, this large, sunny store also carries an admirable array of pretty jewelry and one of the best selections of Hobo leather goods in town. *Every day; zanadia.com; map:FF7.*

KIDS AND MATERNITY

Boston Street

1902 POST ALLEY, PIKE PLACE MARKET; 206/634-0580

This filled-to-the-brim shop on the alley carries clothing in sizes from infant to teen, with even a few items for mom thrown into the fashionable fray. In addition to active-and-durable to dressy-and-delicate duds for kids, there's also an assortment of stuffed animals, blankets, hip diaper bags, and other goodies at prices that won't make you wince. *Every day; map:J7.*

Bump Urban Maternity

920 NE 64TH ST, RAVENNA; 206/522-2867

Modern moms-to-be love this chic and sleek (two words not usually associated with an expanding belly) boutique for maternity wear. Lining the walls are sexy dresses, aromatic lotions, feminine underpinnings, attractive jewelry, and more special things to make pregnancy a time to feel pretty. *Every day; map:FF6.*

Flora and Henri

717 PINE ST (ELLIOTT GRAND HYATT), DOWNTOWN; 206/749-9698 OR 888/749-9698

Nearly 10 years ago, a local designer began selling her you-won't-believe-your-eyes cute children's apparel on First Avenue. Since then, she's moved to a more spacious space on Pine Street and opened another shop on New York's Lexington Avenue and in Santa Monica, California. Her designs, in soft, high-quality European fabrics, are stylish enough that Mom might be tempted to ask if they come in her size (select styles do)! *Every day; florahenri.com; map:J4.*

Georgia Blu

4704 CALIFORNIA AVE SW, WEST SEATTLE; 206/935-4499

You'll be drawn in by the beautiful window displays, and once you get through the door, you'll be equally allured. In the baby blue boutique you'll find a selection of kids' clothes from Europe—lovely jackets and little sweaters, precious at $100+ a pop—along with more reasonably priced everyday wear for children from birth to age 6. There are gifts and shoes and everything a tot needs, and then some. A white couch welcomes you to sit down while kids amuse themselves in the play area. *Every day; map:JJ8.*

Mimi Rose

6001 PHINNEY AVE N, PHINNEY RIDGE; 206/361-1834

This combination of designer showroom and sweet boutique is filled with vintage-inspired clothing and accessories for girls and boys: dressy party clothes, picture books, tin toys, hats embellished with old-fashioned roses, and matching shoes. Although the offerings look precious, prices are not, as many are made by the owner herself. *Every day; map:EE7.*

Plum

2913 E MADISON ST, MADISON VALLEY; 206/322-7011

If this tiny shop sold equally cute footwear in adult sizes, they'd be tops on many a Seattle fashionista's list. But here it's all for kids, from toddler to preteen. The focus is on stylish shoes from European designers, sandals, sneakers, Mary Janes, and more. Their mission is to keep Seattle's kids shod in high-quality comfort, while looking darling to boot. Expect to pay a pretty penny. *Tues–Sat; plumshoes.com; map:GG6.*

Pop Tots

6405 ROOSEVELT WY NE, ROOSEVELT; 206/522-4322

Forget pale pink and baby blue—at this store, baby garb is black, leopard spotted, and on the fringe. Impertinent parents will adore cheeky statements on tiny tees such as AB/CD (mimicking AC/DC's logo) and sexist designs from trucker's mud flaps. The rebellious collection is a clash of clothing and accessories, both vintage and from local designers, including products from the owner herself. *Every day; poptots.net; map:EE7.*

Retroactive Kids

4859 RAINIER AVE S, COLUMBIA CITY; 206/932-3154

A recent smart move from West Seattle to Columbia City gained this little store more foot traffic in a kid-friendly community. Located next to a bustling bakery, the new space continues to offer the wares of local artists and craftspeople, vintage-type toys, one-of-a-kind gifts, diaper bags, and blankets, as well as clothing and kid-size accessories. Children are invited to play with toys and even an occasional art project while parents shop. *Tues–Sun; retroactivekids.com; map:II6.*

Rising Stars

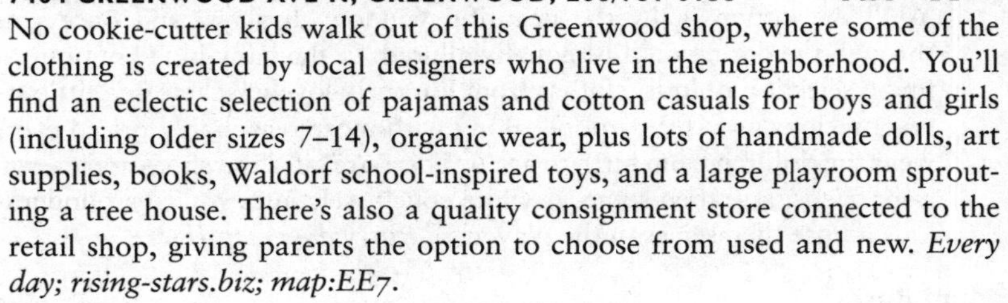

7404 GREENWOOD AVE N, GREENWOOD; 206/781-0138

No cookie-cutter kids walk out of this Greenwood shop, where some of the clothing is created by local designers who live in the neighborhood. You'll find an eclectic selection of pajamas and cotton casuals for boys and girls (including older sizes 7–14), organic wear, plus lots of handmade dolls, art supplies, books, Waldorf school-inspired toys, and a large playroom sprouting a tree house. There's also a quality consignment store connected to the retail shop, giving parents the option to choose from used and new. *Every day; rising-stars.biz; map:EE7.*

Tottini

259 YALE AVE N, SOUTH LAKE UNION; 206/254-0400

In a region popping up with condos, furniture that does double duty is a must—even when it comes to baby's room. At this cheery children's shop serving kids from birth to 10, you'll find modern designs befitting sleek living spaces, such as the Fuji toy box by Argington ($420), an attractive console that doubles as a low table, and bookshelves that blend into a hip home. What's more, many products in the collection of furniture, bedding, bath products, dishes, toys, clothing, and more are recycled, sustainable, and organic. Don't be surprised by the prices, suitable for gifts, grandparents, and well-heeled urbanites. *Every day; tottini.com; map:G1.*

LINGERIE AND UNDERWEAR

Bellefleur Lingerie

720 N 35TH ST, FREMONT; 206/545-0222

Ooo la la, you'll feel delicious in the French finery and lingerie of other European designers from this bodacious boutique. The collection is anything but modest, with sensational scanties, including bras, panties, boy shorts, thongs, cami sets, robes, and luxurious loungewear. Expert fittings are available. *Every day; bellefleurlingerie.com; map:FF7.*

Nancy Meyer Fine Lingerie

1318 5TH AVE, DOWNTOWN; 206/625-9200

If you're looking for a little lingerie therapy, you've come to the right place. This elegant 30-ish-year-old shop continues to blossom with an exquisite inventory of offerings from Italy, France, Spain, Romania, Belgium, and the United States, all top-of-the-line quality. They also carry sleepwear, from fine cotton to sexy silk chemises. Personalized fittings are the standard in this customer-service-oriented boutique. *Mon–Sat; nancymeyer.com; map:K5.*

Pants

1914 2ND AVE, DOWNTOWN; 206/956-2945

You can bet your sweet bippy that the quirky underwear in this store is meant to make a scene and be seen. Adorned with guns, shooting stars, and Western motifs (men's); and polka dots, lace, and bulls (women's), this is not your grandma's underwear. *Every day; pantsunderpants.com; map:I6.*

Undies & Outies

2212 QUEEN ANNE AVE N (QUEEN ANNE MAIL AND DISPATCH), QUEEN ANNE; 206/286-1024

The combination seems so natural at this neighborhood establishment: pick up a package from Auntie, purchase a panty. The assortment of underthings is nicely priced, just like the rest of the interesting merchandise in this funky, friendly place. *Every day; undiesandouties.com; map:GG7.*

Zovo Lingerie

4612 26TH AVE NE, UNIVERSITY VILLAGE; 206/525-9686

Zovo is the brainchild of a woman who found shopping for lingerie a frustrating, unrewarding experience—she decided if she wasn't happy, then there must be others like her. So she created a store filled with comfortable bras, panties, sleep- and loungewear and such, all served up by warm, friendly, and knowledgeable staff. *Every day; zovolingerie.com; map:FF6.*

MEN'S APPAREL

Blackbird

5410 22ND AVE NW, BALLARD; 206/547-2524
The modern Seattle man is willing to drop his grungy jeans for a pair of premium denim—so believes this purveyor of men's products and clothing. One of a new breed of shops, Blackbird focuses on the guy, with an attractive arrangement of shirts, shoes, pants, jackets, grooming goods, jewelry, and man bags. *Every day; helloblackbird.blogspot.com; map:FF8.*

Goods

1112 E PIKE ST, CAPITOL HILL; 206/622-0459
If you can get beyond the attitude, you'll find a good selection of stuff for the skater, including exclusive sneakers, hoodies, hats, jeans, and street-smart art. *Every day; needgoods.com; map:L1.*

Kuhlman

2419 1ST AVE, BELLTOWN; 206/441-1999
Nearly every review of this small store-cum-custom-shop for men gives it stellar ratings for service and style. No doubt it's because whether you want to wear it now or have it tailored in six weeks, you won't leave disappointed. The front of the store is filled with ready-to-wear button-downs, T-shirts, jeans, and furnishings (and a small nod to women's clothes) while the back of the shop is where the magic is made. *Every day; map:F7.*

Marqsmen

1083 BELLEVUE SQUARE, BELLEVUE; 425/679-5610
At last, modern man has his own accessories store, stocking everything a metrosexual may need. From deluxe shaving goods to comfy sleepwear to the quintessential carryall, it's all here in a clean and uncluttered atmosphere. And not to forget the uniform of the Northwest male, there's designer denim and the softest tees too. *Every day; marqsmen.com; map:GG2.*

Oslo's A Men's Store

1519 QUEEN ANNE AVE N, QUEEN ANNE; 206/282-6756
This ballsy boutique has the nerve to cater only to men in an urban environment stocked with stacks of jeans and racks of modish pants, shirts, jackets, and then some. From Friday through Sunday, you can relax with a real-live barber, who will pamper you with an old-fashioned straight-edged shave. *Every day; oslosamensstore.com; map:GG7.*

Utilikilts

620 1ST AVE, PIONEER SQUARE; 206/282-4226

You might say that guys like to hang out at this store, committed to providing men with a comfortable alternative to pants. In an industrial-style environment, they carry only T-shirts and man skirts, otherwise known as Utilikilts. The Seattle original combines the freedom of a kilt with the practicality of pants; available in eight styles depending on your preference for pockets, fabric, and function. Prices range from $130 to $260 ($700 for leather). All are made in the U.S.A. Service is informed and good humored. *Every day; utilikilts.com; map:N7.*

MUSIC (CDS, RECORDS, AND TAPES)

Bop Street Records

5219 BALLARD AVE NW, BALLARD; 206/297-2232

This Ballard record shop has a huge selection of jazz, blues, rock, and funk. At last count: 25,000 78s, 150,000 45s, 8,000 8-tracks, 8,000 cassettes, 10,000 CDs, and 150,0000 LPs. If you're overwhelmed, owner Dave Voorhees is more than willing to help you navigate, just as he has for the British megaband Radiohead, Roots drummer Questlove, and jazz guitarist John Scofield. *Mon–Sat; bopstreetrecords.com; map:FF8.*

Bud's Jazz Records

102 S JACKSON ST, PIONEER SQUARE; 206/628-0445

Even though this store has changed hands, it truly remains an underground Seattle institution. Aside from an astounding collection of CDs, LPs, and videos focused on traditional/Dixieland jazz, blues, Latin, big band, and local jazz, the shop also incorporates visual art into the repertoire. Lining the walls are the works of emerging artists introduced during a gallery opening on the first Thursday of every month. *Every day; map:O9.*

Easy Street Records

4559 CALIFORNIA AVE SW, STE 200, WEST SEATTLE; 206/938-3279; 20 E MERCER ST, QUEEN ANNE; 206/691-3279

If you have a hankering for new and used vinyl and rare imports, or if you're yearning for a diverse collection of new and used CDs—all at a fair and friendly price—go here. The store's sales list is an indie-rock barometer for the Northwest, and the coffee bar and café on-site (at the West Seattle location), plus live, in-store performances, provide yet more reasons to stay. Seattle music luminaries shop here, as do visiting bands. *Every day; easystreetonline.com; map:JJ8, A6.*

Grüv

422 BROADWAY E, CAPITOL HILL; 206/328-6321

Although this store started out specializing in international dance tracks, they've morphed into a 50/50 mix of provocative movies, such as obscure documentaries, and eclectic music. The staff at this crammed Capitol Hill establishment is truly psyched about their esoteric offerings—that's because they have a say in what the store carries. This lends to the ambience, attracting a diverse demographic of intellectuals and independent thinkers. *Every day; map:GG6.*

Jive Time Records

3506 FREMONT AVE N, FREMONT; 206/632-5483; 411 E PINE ST, CAPITOL HILL; 206/329-5168

The sale bin outside this neighborhood record store is acclaimed throughout the city—at least among vinyl junkies looking for a good deal in impeccable condition. For 99 cents, you might find an old Earth, Wind and Fire album; pony up a little more and you can walk away with an immaculate copy of any one of their used rock, punk, soul, or jazz LPs. The specialty here is vinyl; you'll also find a small selection of used CDs; DVDs at the Fremont store. *Every day; jivetimerecords.com; map:FF7, J2.*

MusicWerks

612 E PINE ST, CAPITOL HILL; 206/320-8933

You won't find much mainstream music here (depending on your definition), but that's the point. What you will discover is a copious collection of goth/industrial/noise-related CDs and DVDs and a deeply devoted following. Along with music for your dark side, the store carries an appropriate selection of locally crafted jewelry and tees. *Every day; musicwerks.org; map:J2.*

Silver Platters

9560 1ST AVE NE, NORTHGATE (AND BRANCHES); 206/524-3472

Even in the face of online companies taking over the industry, this music, movie, and more store continues to fiercely maintain its independence while offering the Northwest's largest selection of popular picks. For those who like to recycle, all stores buy and sell used CDs, while for the vinyl junkie, used LPs are available at the Queen Anne store. Branches are located in Bellevue at the Crossroads Shopping Center and at Southcenter Mall in Tukwila. *Every day; silverplatters.com; map:DD7.*

Sonic Boom Records

2209 NW MARKET ST, BALLARD; 206/297-2666; 514 15TH AVE E, CAPITOL HILL; 206/568-BOOM

What makes the thriving independent record store so special is that it caters not only to a specific type of music (rock, mostly), but most of its customers even tune into the same radio station: if something is played on 90.3FM KEXP, this store has it. Sonic Boom also has most things other music stores do—popular titles, a listening station, used albums—but, sorry, no classical music. *Every day; sonicboomrecords.com; map:FF7, FF7.*

Swerve

1535 1ST AVE, STE 8, PIKE PLACE MARKET; 206/382-6151

What started out as an online store now offers a brick and mortar full of everyday deals: new and used CDs, $3.99–$15.99; DVDs, $7.99–$22; videos,

$1.99–$4.99; used video games, $3.99–$19.99; and nice prices on pre-owned vinyl (they buy stuff too). The bright orange walls and upbeat tunes will make you want to swivel your hips through the aisles of this unpretentious corner store, where the service is helpful and GLBT friendly. *Every day; map:J7.*

Wall of Sound

315 E PINE ST, CAPITOL HILL; 206/441-9880

If you're in search of off-the-beaten-path CDs and records, you're in luck. The key word here is "eclectic" (in fact, it's the most common filing category in the store). From French hip-hop to Peruvian percussion, the inventory offers a round-the-world musical tour. Wall of Sound brings its music to life with monthly live music shows at the Rendezvous/Jewel Box Theater (2322 2nd Ave) in Belltown. *Every day; wosound.com; map:J2.*

Zion's Gate Records

1100 E PIKE ST, CAPITOL HILL; 206/568-5446

You may have seen the Zion's Gate name on posters plastered in the area, as they are known to randomly host parties featuring underground dance and reggae music. You'll find vinyl and mostly new CDs, and some used. The small store has a chill atmosphere, with multiple listening stations in the window and racks of graphic tees. *Every day; zionsgate.com; map:L2.*

OUTDOOR GEAR

Alpine Hut

2215 15TH AVE W, INTERBAY; 206/284-3575

This no-frills shop outfits patrons for fun on the water, the slopes, or the trail. Look here for good deals on in-line skates, mountain bikes, ski gear in winter, and bike wear in summer. The owner is friendly and the store aims to please, plus they're excellent at fitting ski boots. *Every day; alpinehut.com; map:EE8.*

Filson

1555 4TH AVE S, SODO; 206/622-3147

Much of the indestructible outdoor wear (heavy wool jackets, canvas hunting coats, oil-finish hats, wool pants) designed by this original Seattle outfitter hasn't changed much over the nearly 100 years they've been in business. In 1914, C. C. Filson sold his clothes to the men headed north to the Alaska Gold Rush; today the quality endures in an attractive, rugged (and rather pricey) collection that also includes handsome luggage and gun bags. *Every day; filson.com; map:R9.*

Elliott Bay Bicycles

2116 WESTERN AVE, BELLTOWN; 206/441-8144

Titanium frames and shop talk rule in this Bentley of bike stores. Regarded as something of a pro shop, it sells bikes to cyclists who know what they're doing and do enough of it to justify paying high prices. Among its other attributes, the shop is home base for Bill Davidson, a nationally known frame builder, whose designs include the aforementioned custom titanium frames. *Every day; elliottbaybicycles.com; map:H9.*

Feathered Friends

119 YALE AVE N, DOWNTOWN; 206/292-2210

Since the '70s, this company has produced the highest-quality down outdoor gear in the world, outfitting expeditions to Nepal, South America, and other mountainous regions. In 2005 the store expanded, doubling its space and inventory of its own line of jackets along with a number of quality outdoor labels. Most of the gear is for those engaged in rock-climbing, camping, backcountry skiing, and such, and for bona fide protection from the elements. However, you can also find durable, stylish pieces from Cloudveil, Ibex, Black Diamond, Patagonia, and Arc'teryx. *Every day; featheredfriends.com; map:H1.*

FootZone

10640 MAIN ST, BELLEVUE (AND BRANCHES); 425/462-7463

While Super Jock 'n Jill reigns in Seattle as the favored shop of runners, FootZone is the undisputed champ on the Eastside. Trained associates professionally assess your gait, then put you in just the right shoes for walking or running. The Bellevue store offers Tuesday evening training runs, the Issaquah branch hosts Saturday morning runs, and the Redmond store offers runs of varying degrees of difficulty on Monday, Tuesday, and Wednesday evenings and Sunday mornings. *Every day; footzone.com; map:GG2.*

Gregg's Greenlake Cycle

7007 WOODLAWN AVE NE, GREEN LAKE (AND BRANCHES); 206/523-1822

Voted one of America's top 100 bicycle stores for 26 years running by bicycleresearch.com, this high-volume Seattle institution stocks bikes, bikes, and more bikes: kids'; all-terrain; Japanese, Italian, and American racing bicycles; and the area's largest collection of touring bikes. The Green Lake location, just yards from the lake's busy bike path, rents bikes, and also carries a large assortment of bike-related clothing, tools, and accessories. Branches are in Bellevue—the second-largest cycle store in the Northwest—and Alderwood Mall. *Every day; greggscycles.com; map:EE7.*

Marmot Mountain Works

827 BELLEVUE WY NE, BELLEVUE; 425/453-1515

This Eastside establishment specializes in excellent equipment for telemarking, backcountry skiing, and alpine climbing and touring. This destination for hard-to-find odds and ends is highly regarded for its knowledgeable, pleasant service. *Every day; marmotmountain.com; map:HH3.*

Outdoor Research Company

2203 1ST AVE S, SODO; 206/971-1496

If you love backpacking but find it back breaking, you'll want to visit this well-rounded gear shop specializing in helping both novices and experts travel light. Along with their own innovative men's and women's apparel, headwear (including a Gore-Tex hat called the Seattle Sombrero, ideal for staving off the elements), gloves, gaiters, and storage and sleeping systems, they're the national representative of Switzerland's Exped tents and sleeping pads and Japan's Snow Peak lightweight and durable titanium cookware. Check out the killer Closeout Corner with discontinued colors and styles. *Every day; orgear.com; map:JJ7.*

Patrick's Fly Shop

2237 EASTLAKE AVE E, EASTLAKE; 206/325-8988
While Patrick's does have a large variety of flies, it's not all the shop offers. Like a veteran fly fisherman, the 60-plus-year-old store can also help with other fly-fishing needs, from what to wear to classes on technique. Gift certificates are available (a great option for the hard-to-shop-for dad) along with supplies and tackle, instructional books, fishing rods, sunglasses, information on local boat shows, and fishing updates. *Every day; patricksflyshop.com; map:GG7.*

BEST PLACE
TO SPEND $5?

"Emerald Downs, where five bucks on a long shot can buy a hundred bucks worth of thrills."

Tom Robbins, author

Perfect Wheels

7009 ROOSEVELT WY NE, ROOSEVELT; 206/522-1933
Larry Naylor is the mechanic, bike fitter, and owner of this tiny bike shop. If you value bicycles as nearly perfect mechanical objects of supreme beauty, this is your place. Naylor is a master wheel builder, and while the bike selection is small, it is perfect—frames from select designer/builders and parts to fit your one-of-a-kind body and riding style. *Tues–Sat; perfectwheels.net; map:EE7.*

R & E Cycles

5627 UNIVERSITY WY NE, UNIVERSITY DISTRICT; 206/527-4822
A stronghold of custom frame-building expertise (the shop has crafted bikes for one-armed customers), R & E specializes in hand-built Rodriguez frames, tandems, racing bikes, and wheel building, and operates Seattle Bike Repair (5601 University Wy NE; 206/527-0360). The shop opens at noon but is open mornings and after hours by appointment. *Tues–Sat and by appointment; rodcycle.com; map:FF6.*

REI (Recreational Equipment Inc.)

222 YALE AVE N, SOUTH LAKE UNION (AND BRANCHES); 206/223-1944
See Top 25 Attractions in the Exploring chapter.

Recycled Cycles

1007 NE BOAT ST, UNIVERSITY DISTRICT; 206/547-4491 OR 877/298-4683

One side of this store sells the bicycles, with a couple hundred on the sales floor at a time, while the other side covers parts and repair. The mix of new and used, both bikes and parts, has no rhyme or reason, they say, so you may have to ask which is which. The waterside store makes a perfect pit stop along the Burke-Gilman Trail and consequently stays pretty busy. *Every day; recycledcycles.com; map:FF6.*

Second Ascent

5209 BALLARD AVE NW, BALLARD; 206/545-8810

Frugal adventurers turn here for a wide range of new and used quality gear for climbing, mountaineering, cycling, paddling, and camping. The store is folksy, with excellent help, and owners know their business, carrying the right products at bargain prices. Buy, sell, trade, or consign—you'll find the best prices, second to none. *Every day; secondascent.com; map:FF8.*

Snowboard Connection

263 YALE AVE N, SOUTH LAKE UNION; 206/467-8545; 118 105TH AVE NE, BELLEVUE; 425/454-1148

Not to say that women and middle-aged extreme athletes won't love this airy, modern store devoted to boarding on snow, street, or water, but it's the 20-something adrenaline boys that feel right at home. Along with a bountiful selection of boards, there's clothing and gear for all seasons and a laid-back, helpful staff. *Every day; snowboardconnection.com; map:G1, GG2.*

Super Jock 'n Jill

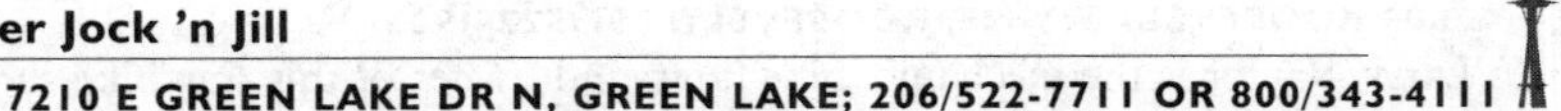

7210 E GREEN LAKE DR N, GREEN LAKE; 206/522-7711 OR 800/343-4111

Pinpoint your gait's trouble spots with analysis from the staff at Super Jock 'n Jill. These salespeople know their metatarsals and their merchandise and understand the mechanics of running and power walking. A podiatrist is in the store once a week to answer questions and help with foot issues. The selection of other merchandise (running gear, bathing suits) is smaller than the footwear choices, but chosen with equal care. This is also a good source for race registration and info, fun runs, routes, and training. *Every day; superjocknjill.com; map:EE7.*

Title Nine

7000 WOODLAWN AVE NE, GREEN LAKE; 206/522-1724; 10237 MAIN ST, BELLEVUE; 425/451-9167

Brilliantly located in the supremely active Green Lake neighborhood, Title Nine, which began as a popular mail order business, sells everything under the sun for women who love to work up a sweat, from sports bras and bathing suits to water bottles and shoes that travel effortlessly from land to water. Complimentary bra fittings are always available. The more spacious Eastside location kicked off Old Bellevue's shopping renaissance. *Every day; titlenine.com; map:EE7, GG2.*

Urban Surf

2100 N NORTHLAKE WY, WALLINGFORD; 206/545-9463

At the state's number one store for the growing adrenaline sport of kiting, you'll find kites and boards, and wisely, lessons for the neophyte. There are wet suits for wind and water protection, and in the board rack, Northwest locals to regional classics. On the lighter side, there's also a selection of in-line skates for those traveling the nearby Burke-Gilman Trail. An expert staff is always on hand to ensure you're appropriately outfitted for your sport. *Every day; urbansurf.com; map:FF7.*

Velo Bike Shop

1535 11TH AVE, CAPITOL HILL; 206/325-3292

There's nothing snobby about this corner shop, where they can fix any make and model of bike, gladly help you unload your current cycle, and assist you in buying a bright, shiny new one. The friendly, knowledgeable staff takes care of the neighborhood like they did before biking became an extreme sport. *Every day; velobikeshop.com; map:GG6.*

Wright Brothers Cycle Works

219 N 36TH ST, FREMONT; 206/633-5132

The front door of this specialty bike repair shop has a sign that reads, "A bad day cycling is better than a good day at work." Only tried-and-true cyclists can appreciate the sentiment behind this message, and that's all you'll find working here. They've been replacing and servicing quality Italian bike parts, and teaching others the fine technique, since 1973. *Tues–Sun, summer; Tues–Sat, winter; wrightbrotherscycleworks.com; map:FF7.*

SEAFOOD

City Fish Company

1535 PIKE PL, PIKE PLACE MARKET; 206/682-9329 OR 800/334-2669

The first fish stand as you enter the Market from the north, City Fish has been in the same stall for 91 years. They put on a show for the mob of tourists that eat it up, working hard to make it, as they chant, a "no line, no wait, no limits" experience. They offer overnight shipping to anywhere in the United States. *Every day; cityfish.com; map:J8.*

The Fresh Fish Company

2364 NW 80TH ST, BALLARD; 206/782-1632

Occupying the space that was once the community's favorite butcher shop is this freshest-of-the-fresh fish spot, recently moved from a long-standing location by the Ballard Locks. Meat is still available from the wholesaler in the back, making this a destination for surf *and* turf. The owners are sticklers for quality, service is neighborly, prices realistic, and a cup of piping hot cioppino is usually on hand to stave off hunger until fish dinner. *Mon–Sat; map:FF8.*

Jack's Fish Spot

1514 PIKE PL, PIKE PLACE MARKET; 206/467-0514

For 28 years, Jack has been selling fresh seafood in the front of his "Spot" and serving fish-and-chips, plus made-from-scratch cioppino and clam chowder, at his bar in the back. Known by locals for friendly service, huge selection, and live crab tanks; prices are reasonable. *Every day; jacksfishspot.com; map:J8.*

Lam's Seafood Market

1221 S KING ST, CHINATOWN/INTERNATIONAL DISTRICT; 206/720-0969

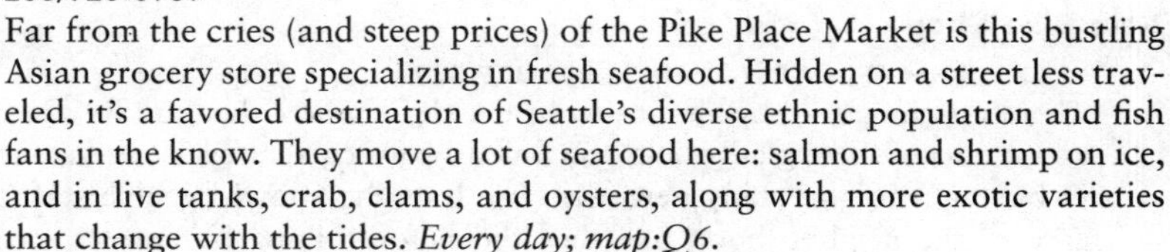

Far from the cries (and steep prices) of the Pike Place Market is this bustling Asian grocery store specializing in fresh seafood. Hidden on a street less traveled, it's a favored destination of Seattle's diverse ethnic population and fish fans in the know. They move a lot of seafood here: salmon and shrimp on ice, and in live tanks, crab, clams, and oysters, along with more exotic varieties that change with the tides. *Every day; map:Q6.*

Metropolitan Market

1908 QUEEN ANNE AVE N, QUEEN ANNE (AND BRANCHES); 206/284-2530

Metropolitan Market stores offer some of the best seafood departments in the Northwest: pristine stock and 20 to 30 kinds of fish and shellfish, from here and all over. They are usually the first to score the sought-after Copper River salmon, available only for a limited time each spring. Savvy cooks call ahead to tailor their menus to what's fresh each day. Special orders welcome; free packing for local travel. Locations in Sand Point (5250 40th Ave NE; 206/938-6600; map:EE5), West Seattle (2320 42nd Ave SW; 206/937-0551; map:JJ8), and Lower Queen Anne (100 Mercer St; 206/213-0778; map:A7). *Every day; metropolitan-market.com; map:GG7.*

Mutual Fish Company

2335 RAINIER AVE S, RAINIER VALLEY; 206/322-4368

Mutual Fish fillets and steaks turn up in many of Seattle's fanciest restaurants—and in the kitchens of the city's more discerning gourmets. This is perhaps the best in town: top quality and a dazzling selection are the result of the undivided attention of the Yoshimura family. Fresh tanks are full of local oysters and crabs, and the seafood cases present the best from the West and East coasts. Seattleites are pleased to find branzino (European seabass) and Maryland soft-shell crabs (in season), and other exotics. Prices are good, and staff will pack for air freight or carry-home. *Every day; mutualfish.com; map:II6.*

Pike Place Fish

86 PIKE PL, PIKE PLACE MARKET; 206/682-7181 OR 800/542-7732

If you've ever been a tourist in Seattle or shown one around, you've been to see these illustrious fish throwers. Aside from offering fresh seafood from wild salmon to scallops, on any given day guys in overalls shout out a ceremonial chant, echoed by more guys in overalls, all watched by a crowd that holds up foot traffic. A fish is thrown overhead, someone pays for it, and the ritual repeats itself over and over again. Think of it as Seattle's changing of the guard. *Every day; pikeplacefish.com; map:J8.*

Seattle Caviar Company

2922 EASTLAKE AVE E, EASTLAKE; 206/323-3005
Owners Dale and Betsy Sherrow sell the finest products from the Caspian Sea and osetra, in addition to Northwest fresh American malossol caviar and all the froufrou accoutrements of serious roe eating (such as pretty mother-of-pearl spoons and caviar *présentoirs*). They'll gladly ready your phone order for speedy delivery at their special pick-up door, arrange beautiful gift packages, and even handle shipping. Stop in for a Saturday caviar tasting. *Mon–Sat and by appointment; caviar.com; map:GG7.*

University Seafood & Poultry Company

1317 NE 47TH ST, UNIVERSITY DISTRICT; 206/632-3900
Drawing not only from the tony Laurelhurst and Windermere neighborhoods nearby, but also from the UW student population, Dale Erickson's shop thrives in the heart of the University District. The selection includes salmon, halibut, lingcod, seasonal treats such as local sturgeon, and an amazing array of caviars—from flying fish to American River sturgeon. Hard-to-find game birds, free-run chickens, and the freshest eggs too. Some prices are not posted but, surprisingly enough, are in line with supermarket prices or better. The fishmongers at the counter are friendly, and all are good cooks with recipes to share. *Mon–Sat; map:FF6.*

Wild Salmon Seafood Market

1900 W NICKERSON ST, INTERBAY; 206/283-3366 OR 888/222-3474;
2401 QUEEN ANNE AVE N; 206/217-3474
Rely on this fishmonger for cheerful service and fresh seafood. In addition to tanks filled with live lobsters, oysters, clams, and mussels, they sell good-looking fish fillets, steaks, and whole fish and shellfish from their large service counters. Crab cakes and salmon cakes are usually available for impressive, quick-to-cook meals. Two locations, one dockside in Interbay's Fisherman's Terminal, the other on Queen Anne, sharing space with A&J Meats and McCarthy & Schiering Wine Merchants. *Every day at Fisherman's Terminal; Tues–Sun on Queen Anne; wildsalmonseafood.com; map:FF8, GG7.*

SHOES

A Mano

1115 1ST AVE, DOWNTOWN; 206/292-1767
Not so long ago, A Mano took over the slim brick-and-wood space occupied by Seattle shoe favorite Ped. Continuing the tradition, A Mano primarily features high-quality leather shoes, bags, and goods made by boutique designers from the United States, Italy, and Spain. With the limited selection of styles

and sizes, you stand a good chance of not passing your purchase on the sidewalk going the other way. Prices keep pace with other fine footwear shops around town. *Every day; shopamano.com; map:J7.*

Capitol 1524

1524 E OLIVE WY, CAPITOL HILL; 206/322-2305

The owner of this sneaker shop is rumored to own more than 400 pairs, so don't you deserve at least a dozen? You'll find that and more in the gallery of new and limited editions, some Euro- or Asia-exclusive, all truly rare on the sneaker scope. Shoe collectors (yes, shoe collectors) visit every month or so to see what's in stock from names such as Nike, Puma, FootAction, and Finish Line. *Every day; capitol1524.com; map:GG6.*

Clementine

4447 CALIFORNIA AVE SW, WEST SEATTLE; 206/935-9400

In the land of heavy foot traffic that is West Seattle's California Avenue, this newcomer is making a splash with an offering of footwear from funky to fabulous independent designers. Although the selection (and the space) is excruciatingly small, everything is well chosen, including the selection of handbags and jewelry to complement the eclectic mix of women's shoes. Prices run the gamut from affordable to up there. *Tues–Sun; clementines.com; map:JJ8.*

Duncan & Sons Boots and Saddles

1946 1ST AVE S, SODO; 206/622-1310

If you are an equine lover, you know that it's not easy to find a good Western store in these parts. Fortunately, Duncan & Sons, established 1898, can take care of all your needs from tackle to boots. They are known for their quality leather goods, including boots for men and women that are mostly handmade in Texas, and good old-fashioned service. For the recycle-minded, they now carry gently used boots for the entire family. *Mon–Sat; map:P9.*

Edie's

319 E PINE ST, CAPITOL HILL; 206/839-1111;
4310 SW ALASKA ST, WEST SEATTLE; 206/937-2029

Edie's isn't your everyday, cram-a-bunch-in shoe store with barely enough room to sit and try on a pair. On the contrary, its interior takes "minimalist" to new heights. Inside its high-ceilinged space on Capitol Hill are displays of brightly colored tennis shoes, such as the popular brands Camper and Asics, along with more classic men's and women's dress shoes, beaded jewelry, and city bags by Nanna and Gravis. The West Seattle store offers an edited selection of favorites from the Capitol Hill location. *Every day; ediesshoes.com; map:K1, JJ8.*

Gotta Have Shoes!

10047 MAIN ST, STE 101, BELLEVUE; 425/460-8316

If you don't look down while cruising Main Street, you'll miss this below-street-level store, a must-stop for the self-proclaimed shoe freak. Packed into the small space you'll find popular brands and every conceivable style at prices to rival the big box (aka Bellevue Square) down the way. The handbag and jewelry selection will leave you exclaiming too. *Every day; gottahave shoesinc.com; map:GG2.*

J. Gilbert Footwear

2025 1ST AVE, BELLTOWN; 206/441-1182

If you're tired of fashionable footwear that hurts your feet, limp on over to this shoe store where everything is about style blended with ease. The good-looking selection is chosen with walking—or dancing—in mind, from strappy sandals to urban boots. Men and women alike will take comfort in the vast array of high-quality shoes from worthy European designers such as Thierry Rabotin, Donald Pliner, and Anyi Lu, prodigy of Taryn Rose. There are also a few judiciously chosen accessories and clothing items, from fantastic handbags to butter-soft leather jackets. *Every day; jgilbertfootwear.com; map:H8.*

John Fluevog Shoes

205 PINE ST, DOWNTOWN; 206/441-1065

One of Seattle's first cutting-edge retailers, John Fluevog Shoes continues to make a statement in Seattle even though other high-end shoe stores have moved in just steps away. Handmade originals for women, from sexy cowboy-style boots to pointy-toed pumps, keep company with stylish men's shoes and earth-friendly veggie loafers. *Every day; fluevog.com; map:I7.*

Market Street Shoes

2215 NW MARKET ST, BALLARD; 206/783-1670

Ballard is an enigmatic enclave that somehow manages to walk the line of kid friendly while at the same time being one of the hippest, hottest hoods in Seattle. This shoe store sits on the community side of the fence, with a comfortable collection for men, women, and children from well-known brands such as Indigo, Naot, Hush Puppies, and Merrell—all served up in a spacious setting. Staff is sweet and service down-to-earth. *Every day; marketstreetshoes.com; map:FF8.*

M. J. Feet

4334 UNIVERSITY WY NE, UNIVERSITY DISTRICT; 206/632-5353; 15 103RD AVE NE, BELLEVUE; 425/646-0416

This dual-location shop cares about keeping your feet healthy. The U District store is a favorite of students in search of campus hiking style, while the Bellevue branch caters to techy types looking for sturdy sandals that are a staple of the Northwest high-tech uniform. It's the place for Birkenstocks, quality repair service, and a thoughtful array of arch supports. *Every day; mjfeet.com; map:FF6, HH4.*

Posh on Main

10245 MAIN ST, STE 103, BELLEVUE; 425/454-2022

Sure it's the Northwest, but you won't find a Mephisto in sight at this lushly appointed shoe salon on Bellevue's new chichi shopping street. In fact, the heels are sky high, and everything has a bit of bling, reminiscent of Hollywood red carpet days and Academy Award–winning nights. In a living-room-like setting, you can slip your feet into Cinderella shoes and dream of Prince Charming to pay the pretty tab. The service and amenities match the class of footwear, with Perrier and chocolates every day. *Mon–Sat; poshonmain.com; map:GG2.*

Re-Soul

5319 BALLARD AVE NW, BALLARD; 206/789-7312

New soles are just part of the offerings you'll find at this Ballard Avenue shop, well regarded for its eye for modern design and selection of must-have accessories for male and female. With its mix of local talent and well-scouted national and even international artists, the collection of jewelry, home stuff, and of course, footwear, is ever changing. *Every day; resoul.com; map:FF8.*

Shoefly

2030 1ST AVE, BELLTOWN; 206/729-7463; 2042 BELLEVUE SQUARE, BELLEVUE; 425/646-1112

Our only beloved local "chain" shoe store, with two locations in Oregon as well as Seattle and Bellevue, this boutique carries footwear for almost any occasion. The recently revealed Belltown spot made room for men's shoes (Shoefly Guy) alongside the in-step assortment of women's. In the mix you'll find a plethora of super-popular designer brands, as well as more unique (such as Cordani) Italian comfort labels. Captivating jewelry and handbags are also perched in the windows, testing the will of passing walkers who have a fetish for more than shoes. *Every day; shoefly.com; map:H7, GG2.*

The Sneakery

612 NW 65TH ST, BALLARD; 206/297-1786

A bit off the beaten Ballard path is a neighborhood store brimming with sneakers, including everything-old-is-new-again PF Flyers. As casual as the footwear they offer, the smart staff will invite you to sit down and try on a pair—you just might fall in love with one of more than 160 styles for men, women, and children. *Every day; thesneakery.com; map:FF8.*

Sole Food

2619 NE VILLAGE LN, UNIVERSITY VILLAGE; 206/526-7184

A move across the courtyard to a corner store has opened up twice as much square footage for this cheery family footwear store—good news for moms, and now dads too. The new space is even more stroller friendly and has plenty of room for the addition of men's shoes. Geared toward fashion-forward parents, the store offers a fun and fitting selection of shoes that are wearable *and* make a statement. However, this is not the place to buy your power pumps or wingtips. *Every day; shopsolefood.com; map:FF6.*

The Woolly Mammoth
5 Doors Up

4303 UNIVERSITY WY NE, UNIVERSITY DISTRICT; 206/632-3254; 4309 UNIVERSITY WY NE, UNIVERSITY DISTRICT; 206/547-3192

Most shoes in the original store are as rugged and weatherproof as their name. The Woolly Mammoth mostly carries sensible European comfort brands such as Josef Seibel, Clarks, Ecco, and Naot. A second store up the street, 5 Doors Up, carries trendier stuff—Steve Madden, John Fluevog, and the like. *Every day; woollymammothshoes.com; 5doorsup.com; map:FF6.*

SPECIALTY SHOPS

Arcade Smoke Shop

1522 5TH AVE, DOWNTOWN; 206/587-0159

Tobacco, pipes, cigars, and accessories are all that you'll find in here, setting it apart from other smoke stores in Seattle. Call them purists. The crystal ashtrays are popular, as are the hand-carved and ivory lighters. There is a humidor in the back containing premium cigars for stogie enthusiasts. *Mon–Sat; map:J6.*

Archie McPhee

2428 NW MARKET ST, BALLARD; 206/297-0240

Pop-culture icons such as the boxing nun puppet and the wiggling hula girl dash ornament get center stage—instead of just a junk-near-the-check-stand nod—at this longtime purveyor of kitsch. Archie McPhee is a great place to stock up on cheap toys and party favors, or just to browse the memorable catalog. Plenty of grown-ups confess shameful inclinations to lose themselves among the windup toys and bendable plastic creatures. Its popularity inspired a sister store next door, filled with party supplies, crafts, lawn ornaments, kitchen and bath accessories, and fabric—all with a prankster twist. *Every day; mcphee.com; map:FF8.*

Babeland

707 E PIKE ST, CAPITOL HILL; 206/328-2914

This well-stocked adult store has a stimulating selection of, shall we say, amusements for women. Whatever your pleasure, you'll find an array of accessories in different kinds of materials, some beautiful enough to be displayed as art (if you dare). You'd be hard pressed to find a better offering of all the extras, and for those in need of enlightenment, there are educational programs too. *Every day; babeland.com; map:J2.*

Ballard Mail & Dispatch

1752 NE MARKET ST, BALLARD; 206/789-4488

Regulars from the neighborhood—which includes blue-haired old ladies, tattooed young men, and everyone in between—call it Sip & Ship. That's because at this eclectic community stop you can grab a drink, mail a package, and gather with your friends. On top of that, there's a fun assortment of small gifts (to be wrapped and sent on the spot), Ballard-centric tees and sweatshirts, free Wi-Fi, a play area for tots in the loft upstairs, and always a friendly buzz. *Every day; www.sipandship.com; map:FF8.*

Byrnie Utz

310 UNION ST, DOWNTOWN; 206/623-0233

There are not many stores these days—in Seattle or across the nation—that specialize in hats. But at Byrnie Utz that's all you'll find: elegant Stetsons, jaunty Kangol driving caps, dapper Borsalino Panama hats—any likely lid you can imagine fills the showcases, boxes, and bins of this store, shading heads since 1934. *Every day; map:J6.*

Dusty Strings

3406 FREMONT AVE N, FREMONT; 206/634-1662

This Fremont institution is *the* place to come for all your stringed instrument needs. Not only will they take in your violin or guitar for careful repair, but the store is the only manufacturer of harps in Seattle. Nowhere else can you find this selection of bagpipes, accordions, banjos, mandolins, and hammered dulcimers, as well as their specific sheet music. Planning an event with live music or want to learn an instrument? Come look through the musician directory or take a workshop. *Every day; dustystrings.com; map:FF7.*

Metsker Maps

1511 1ST AVE, PIKE PLACE MARKET; 206/623-8747 OR 800/727-4430

Seattle's fabled map shop is the perfect place to create dreams or plans of getting out and exploring the world. There are fold-up maps for road trips to wherever your heart desires, maps lining the walls like artwork, world travel books, atlases, and a friendly person behind the counter to lead you in the right direction. *Every day; metskers.com; map:N8.*

Michael Maslan Vintage Posters, Photographs, Postcards, Maps & Ephemera

109 UNIVERSITY ST, DOWNTOWN; 206/587-0187

Since this store moved to new digs across from the Seattle Art Museum, a whole new crowd is discovering its lithographs of jungle scenes, faded portraits of stiff-lipped Victorian-era families, postcards from the 18th and 19th centuries, and enormous stash of vintage posters. Hours vary according to whim (call before stopping in), and prices range from extremely reasonable to heirloom level. *Mon–Fri; map:O8.*

Scarecrow Video

5030 ROOSEVELT WY NE, UNIVERSITY DISTRICT; 206/524-8554

This floor-to-ceiling two-story store carries almost everything ever committed to celluloid anywhere in the world. Although it primarily deals in rentals of movies and equipment, you will find a selection of foreign, boxed sets, and cult films for sale—ideal gifts for the cinema buff in your life. *Every day; scarecrow.com; map:FF6.*

Ye Olde Curiosity Shop
Ye Olde Curiosity Shop Too

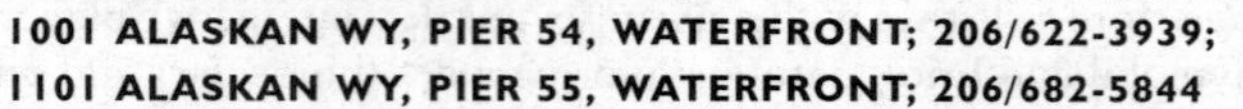

1001 ALASKAN WY, PIER 54, WATERFRONT; 206/622-3939;
1101 ALASKAN WY, PIER 55, WATERFRONT; 206/682-5844

There are few words that adequately describe this Seattle waterfront landmark—around since 1899—but "hilarious," "dusty," and "yuck" come to mind. You'll find something here for those with an appreciation for the stranger things in life. Some of the most notable treasures are Sylvester, the famous desert dummy, and a fortune-telling gypsy machine like the one in the movie *Big*. And of course, it's always stocked with "of the moment" tacky, such as Paris Hilton dollar bills. There's an annex the next pier down with many of the same novelties and curios, distinguishing itself with a zoological section—animal oddities, a seashell area—and homemade fudge. Aptly, the novelty shop has now been immortalized with its own book (*1001 Curious Things*, University of Washington Press, 2001). *Every day; yeoldecuriosityshop.com; map:L9.*

TOYS

Clover

5335 BALLARD AVE NW, BALLARD; 206/782-0715

Stocked floor to ceiling with happy finds of cute clothing, toys, puzzles, cuddly stuffed animals, blankies, and more, this Ballard shop has the air of a European children's store. Tiny dresses and shirts are sewn of beautiful textiles, toys are made of wood and tin, and the atmosphere is intimate and welcoming. Service is friendly, and there's even a shop dog to greet you at the door. *Every day; clovertoys.com; map:FF8.*

The Great Wind-Up

93 PIKE PL, PIKE PLACE MARKET; 206/621-9370

Stocked with more than 350 toys, this store has been devoted entirely to windup toys for more than two decades. The try-before-you-buy table is alive with mechanical animals, battery-operated windups, and tin lunch boxes. Classic toys, such as the clapping monkey, are fun to peruse, and then there's the section of fragile tin collectibles that are just for looking. *Every day; greatwindup.com; map:J8.*

Izilla Toys

1429 12TH AVE E, CAPITOL HILL; 206/322-8697

This family-owned toy store is all grown up, with a recent move to Capitol Hill adding three times the space. But the aim is still the same: to offer kids toys to enrich life's experience and stimulate a sense of wonder about the world. The expanded selection caters to ages 0 to young adult (an audience overlooked by most toy companies), with games, toys, and now a new book section. Helpful and friendly owners assist in the hunt, and a Birthday Club makes your child's birthday extra special with a free gift on the big day. *Every day; izillatoys.com; map:GG6.*

Pinocchio's Toys

4540 UNION BAY PL NE, UNIVERSITY VILLAGE; 206/528-1100

This U Village store sells toys with a purpose: puzzles, interactive play media (such as Playmobil and Brio), nature-exploring aides (binoculars and science workbooks), and a wide variety of paints (nontoxic watercolors and tie-dyeing kits). Books are geared more to adults reading bedtime stories than to older children who read on their own. *Every day; map:FF6.*

Top Ten Toys

104 N 85TH ST, GREENWOOD; 206/782-0098

A good old-fashioned toy store, this North End shop keeps "healthy play alive" with a collection of classic and hands-on toys to inspire creativity and interaction. With more than 7,000 square feet of fun and games, this children's playground has been voted one of the best toy stores in Seattle. *Every day; toptentoys.com; map:EE7.*

VINTAGE/RETRO CLOTHING AND ACCESSORIES

Deluxe Junk

3518 FREMONT PL N, FREMONT; 206/634-2733

Fifties music sets the mood for browsing vintage men's and women's clothes, shoes, accessories, furniture, and a clutter of appealing knickknacks—hence the name. *Wed, Fri–Sun; map:FF7.*

Friday Night Date

2220 MARKET ST, STE 801, BALLARD; 206/783-4409

Don't show up at this underground shopping spot unless you're invited, because it may not be open. To know when the secret Friday night spree takes place, you've got to be on the mailing list. It's worth the wait—when doors do open, the reasonably priced, well-chosen vintage (mixed with some new) clothing, shoes, accessories, jewelry, and more for both men and women fly out the door. *Random Fridays; bonitacomida@yahoo.com; map:FF8.*

Fritzi Ritz

750 N 34TH ST, FREMONT; 206/633-0929

At this veteran of the vintage clothing scene, the focus is on the female, although persistent men just might get lucky. There's no hiding the good deals—price ranges and specials are smartly advertised in clear sight, such as "neckties five for $1." Be warned, they don't keep early hours. *Wed–Sun; map:FF7.*

Isadora's Antique Clothing

1915 1ST AVE, DOWNTOWN; 206/441-7711

Impeccable antique clothing is the rule here. Custom-made in-house wedding gowns, as well as designs by Vera Wang and others, hang in the back among antique Battenburg lace tops, white mink coats, and vintage tuxedos.

An estate jewelry case displays collections from Georgian to retro, and art nouveau to moderne. *Every day; isadoras.com; map:I7.*

Le Frock

317 E PINE ST, CAPITOL HILL; 206/623-5339
Even nonvintage shoppers (both women and men) covet the goods at this store. It's worth combing the racks in search of pre-owned, gently used tees, shoes, dresses, pants, and purses from designers and popular names such as Ann Taylor, Prada, Betsey Johnson, Coach, Laura Ashley, and Anne Klein. *Every day; lefrockonline.com; map:J2.*

Pretty Parlor

119 SUMMIT AVE E, CAPITOL HILL; 206/405-2883
The owner of this passionately pink establishment claims her store is "where Audrey Hepburn meets Jane Jetson." We think it's a must-do destination for any old-fashioned space-age girl worth her crinoline and go-go boots. The bubbly selection of vintage values is dished up in a wonderfully wacky atmosphere complete with house kitty, Vincent. *Every day; prettyparlor.com; map:GG6.*

Private Screening

3504 FREMONT PL N, FREMONT; 206/548-0751
Literally floor to ceiling with clothing and accessories from the '20s through the '70s, this Fremont store is a gold mine for the vintage hunter. You may have to do a little digging to find what you're after, but the owners are super nice, and the collection of jackets, dresses, suits, separates, and accessories is in good repair. *Every day; map:FF7.*

Red Light

4560 UNIVERSITY WY NE, UNIVERSITY DISTRICT; 206/545-4044; 312 BROADWAY E, CAPITOL HILL; 206/329-2200
This place literally rocks, run by polite and pierced young people with the music turned up high. Prices are fairly rock bottom, too, for the floor-to-ceiling collection of used clothing from every era, Victorian to Sid Vicious. Be sure to put it on your list if you're hunting for the perfect getup for a costume party. *Every day; redlightvintage.com; map:FF6, GG6.*

Rhinestone Rosie

606 W CROCKETT ST, QUEEN ANNE; 206/283-4605
Those who know their faux jewels turn to Rosie Sayyah, aka Rhinestone Rosie. The queen of crystal rents, buys, sells, and repairs an inventory of thousands of estate and costume jewelry treasures. Hers is the only store on the West Coast with a rhinestone repair service; she'll search her rhinestone vaults to find replacement stones, convert clip earrings to pierced, or lengthen necklaces and bracelets. She's also an *Antiques Roadshow* appraiser. *Tues–Sat; map:GG7.*

WINE AND BEER

Bottleworks

1710 N 45TH ST, WALLINGFORD; 206/633-2437

This store is dedicated to beer aficionados. More than 850 different kinds of beer are available, and you can buy by the bottle, case, or customized gift pack. Beers, chilled to specified temperatures, along with a selection of beer-specific glassware, allow you maximize the enjoyment of your favorite frothy brew. Imported Belgian and Italian chocolates complement the selection of bottles. *Every day; bottleworks.com; map:FF7.*

City Cellars Fine Wines

1710 N 45TH ST, WALLINGFORD; 206/632-7238

Since 1989, this unpretentious neighborhood shop has kept Wallingford residents abreast of the ever-evolving world of wine. With a passion for European picks and a growing selection of Northwest wines, this shop's almost 700 offerings cover the gamut from 100 under $10 to the Big B's—Barolo, Brunello, Bordeaux, and Burgundy. Friday evening wine tasting for a small fee from 5–7pm, mixed half- and full-case discounts. *Tues–Sun; citycellar.com; map:FF7.*

Esquin Wine Merchants

2700 4TH AVE S, SODO; 206/682-7374 OR 888/682-WINE

While crowded with nearly 4,000 wines—the largest inventory in the city—Esquin still maintains the warmth and attentiveness of a smaller shop. The range is impressive, offering renowned as well as emerging producers from all corners of the world. Everyday to special-occasion wines are well priced, with extensive monthly specials. Twice-weekly tastings, Thursday, 5–6:30pm, Saturday, 1–4pm; case discounts. *Every day; esquin.com; map:JJ7.*

European Vine Selections

522 15TH AVE E, CAPITOL HILL; 206/323-3557

Started in 1972 by friends seeking a solution to the dearth of European wines available in Seattle, this shop has been at its present location in the residential environs of Capitol Hill for 20 years. French wines dominate the inventory, followed by respectable collections of Northern Italian, Spanish, and German wines, and select emerging Northwest producers. This is not the place to hunt trophies, as the focus is on quality at a reasonable price. Every wine is annotated with succinct, often humorous, one liners. The last-Thursday-of-the-month themed tasting with food is as much a neighborhood party as a wine event. Tastings every other Saturday, 2–4pm; mixed case discount. *Every day; evswines.com; map:HH6.*

McCarthy & Schiering Wine Merchants

2401B QUEEN ANNE AVE N, QUEEN ANNE; 206/282-8500; 6500 RAVENNA AVE NE, RAVENNA; 206/524-9500

For more than 25 years, Dan McCarthy (Queen Anne) and Jay Schiering (Ravenna) have set the standard for personalized wine service in Seattle. Loyal customers journey to their two neighborhood locations for their judicious selection of Northwest wines and small-estate wines from Europe and the new world. You can count on the staff as your own sommeliers when orchestrating wine pairings for a dinner party or other special occasion. Saturday in-store tastings, 11am–5pm; mixed case discounts and special rates for members of Vintage Select Buyer's Club. *Tues–Sat; mccarthyandschiering.com; map:GG7, FF6.*

Pete's Supermarket
Pete's of Bellevue

58 E LYNN ST, EASTLAKE; 206/322-2660; 134 105TH AVE NE, BELLEVUE; 425/454-1100

The Seattle location, a 40-year-old store serving the Eastlake area and the houseboats along the eastern shore of Lake Union, is half neighborhood market, half wine shop. The congested wine aisles contain more than 1,000 wines, including extensive selections from California and the Northwest and international wines, as well as great prices on one of the city's best selections of Champagne and sparkling wines. The Bellevue location is exclusively a wine shop with roomier walkways, 2,500 different selections, and a bit more depth in Italian and French wines. Tastings at the Bellevue location every Saturday, 3–6pm. *Every day; petes.cc; map:GG7, HH3.*

Pike & Western Wine Shop

1934 PIKE PL, PIKE PLACE MARKET; 206/441-1307

Anchoring the north end of Pike Place Market for three decades, this shop has provided visitors and locals alike with a considered selection of wine. The Northwest is well represented, as are the major European wine regions. The staff, while not always engaging, is quite knowledgeable when sought out. There are a number of informal to formal themed tastings throughout the year, requiring reservations and a fee. Tastings every Friday, 3–6 pm. *Every day; pikeandwestern.com; map:J8.*

Sixth Avenue Wine Seller

600 PINE ST (PACIFIC PLACE, 3RD LEVEL), DOWNTOWN; 206/621-2669

Given its location in a downtown retail center, this shop does multiple duty as a wine shop, wine bar, wine accessory/gift store, and cigar source. Wines range from single-serving juice box wine to prestigious bottlings. A third of the inventory is from the Northwest, including a good collection of half bottles, while the remainder is split between European and new world wines. *Every day; map:J5.*

West Seattle Cellars

6026 CALIFORNIA AVE SW, WEST SEATTLE; 206/937-2868

This tiny store is truly a neighborhood wine shop, enthusiastically staffed and crammed with eclectic offerings. Choose from solid European and Northwest selections, or be adventuresome and try a wine from Greece, Austria, or Slovenia. Four wine club memberships are available, allowing participants to acquire wines handpicked by the owners. Each club focuses on a range of wine from the everyday to the more exclusive. Tastings every Thursday, 5:30–8pm; mixed half-case discounts. *Tues–Sat; westseattlecellars.com; map:JJ8.*

WOMEN'S APPAREL

Alhambra

101 PINE ST, DOWNTOWN; 206/621-9571

Alhambra's collection of women's clothing, jewelry, shoes, accessories, and home furnishings comes from all over the world, handpicked from designers with an eye for detail. The selection reflects an urban style ranging from feminine to tailored, and there's always an exquisite evening gown or two. To make the indulgence affordable, they also have a warehouse open to the public in the University District (4600 NE Union Bay Pl, Ste C; 206/522-4570; map:FF6). *Every day; alhambranet.com; map:J8.*

Barneys New York

600 PINE ST (PACIFIC PLACE, 1ST LEVEL), DOWNTOWN; 206/622-6300

This is a new location for this posh clothing chain. Though the achingly fashionable staff can be a tad intimidating, it's worth braving the discomfort for designer togs from Diane von Furstenberg, Ella Moss, Juicy Couture, and Velvet, as well as a great selection of shoes, designer denim, and cosmetics. Twice-yearly sales, in summer and winter, offer killer markdowns. *Every day; barneys.com; map:J5.*

Betty Blue

608 2ND AVE, DOWNTOWN; 206/442-6888

Two words: Designer. Discount. Now say them together. This unexpected find on the fringes of Pioneer Square offers some of the most coveted names in couture (who cares if they may be from last season?) in a stunning setting—at 60 to 70 percent off. Clothing, shoes, and accessories from designers from Milan, Paris, New York, Tokyo—everything is in impeccable condition, worthy of wear to the Oscars. *Mon–Sat; shopbettyblue.com; map:N7.*

Bouncing Wall

2225 QUEEN ANNE AVE N, QUEEN ANNE; 206/285-9255

Despite its cryptic name, it's pretty clear what this little store on top of Queen Anne is all about: original, wearable, usable art, all locally made. It's kind of a kitchen sink mix, literally—including silk-screened cotton tea towels—tumbled in with handbags, belts, pillows, jewelry, bath and body products, and clothing for men, women, and kids. The colorful, well-crafted selection is judiciously juried, not ratty rec room chic. *Tues–Sun; bouncingwall.com; map:GG7.*

Butch Blum

1408 5TH AVE, DOWNTOWN; 206/622-5760

Butch Blum sees wardrobes as investments and shies away from trendy fads in favor of classic men's and women's lines from venerated labels such as Giorgio Armani and Comme des Garçons. Recent renovations have added a men's made-to-measure department and a second floor exclusively for the expanded collection of women's clothing, shoes, and accessories from labels like Moschino and TSE cashmere. *Every day; butchblum.com; map:J5.*

Canopy Blue

3121 E MADISON ST, MADISON VALLEY; 206/323-1115

Like a fresh breeze blowing off the water, this shop of powder blue walls and blonde wood provides a cooling, calming effect for the senses. The selection (for the self-proclaimed urban princess) runs from über-soft cotton basics to no-frills feminine jackets and skirts, handbags, jewelry, and other adornments. Voted the best dressing rooms in the city by *Seattle* magazine in its August 2006 shopping issue. *Every day; canopyblue.com; map:GG6.*

Carmilia's

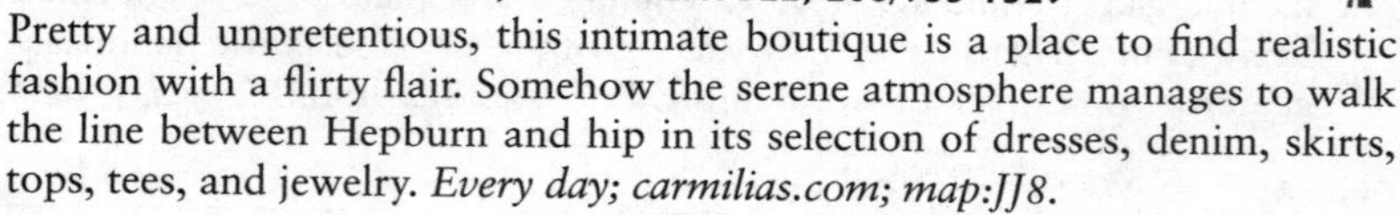

4528 CALIFORNIA AVE SW, WEST SEATTLE; 206/935-1329

Pretty and unpretentious, this intimate boutique is a place to find realistic fashion with a flirty flair. Somehow the serene atmosphere manages to walk the line between Hepburn and hip in its selection of dresses, denim, skirts, tops, tees, and jewelry. *Every day; carmilias.com; map:JJ8.*

Christi's on Main

10149 MAIN ST, BELLEVUE; 425/462-7222

In this sunny corner on Bellevue's happening shopping strip, you'll find a modern interpretation of mother/daughter style. That would be a well-preserved 40-ish mom and fresh-faced 20-something daughter—both with terrific taste and figures, of course. In the mix are supple leather jackets, wrap dresses, cotton tees, sparkly jewelry, and a selection of dainty footwear. *Mon–Sat; map:GG2.*

David Lawrence

1318 4TH AVE, DOWNTOWN; 206/622-2544; 575 BELLEVUE WY NE (BELLEVUE SQUARE), STE 224, BELLEVUE; 425/688-1699

Both David Lawrence stores stock brands with heavy runway presence, such as Dolce & Gabbana, Hugo Boss, and Donna Karan. Smaller dimensions and approachable staff make shopping here a less intimidating experience than at some comparable retailers. *Every day; david-lawrence.com; map:K6, GG2.*

Dream

3427 FREMONT PL, FREMONT; 206/547-1211

The collection of clothing here is attractive—sophisticated standards such as jackets and jeans, feminine tops, skirts, and pants. But the real draw is the jewelry, shimmering like stars in a case that doubles as the wrap desk. You won't find manufactured pieces here: each dangle, bangle, and spangle is crafted individually to add sparkle to your everyday outfit. *Every day; dreamfremont.blogspot.com; map:FF7.*

Encanto Barcelona

1406 1ST AVE, DOWNTOWN; 206/621-1941
Looking for something off the map as far as Seattle style goes? Stop by this lively boutique offering designer clothing and accessories from Spain, for both men and women. True to the Spanish way of dressing, careful attention is paid to body-conscious fit, high-quality fabric and construction, and saturated color. The attitude is urban and the service friendly. *Every day; encantobarcelona.com; map:J7.*

Endless Knot

2500 1ST AVE, BELLTOWN; 206/448-0355
If you're a former hippie or her love child and bohemian style runs in your blood, stop at this corner shop. Once primarily a vehicle for its own brand of loose-fitting, ethnic-inspired clothing, the sunlit store has branched out to include shapely, fluid dresses, and feminine skirts and tops in bright colors and lively prints. There's also a smattering of jewelry and fabric handbags, sold against a soundtrack of world music. Prices are easy too. *Every day; map:F7.*

Ericcé

2345 EASTLAKE AVE E, STE 110, EASTLAKE; 206/325-8882
Despite its location away from any main shopping street, this stylish yet snob-free shop manages to pull in a dedicated following of fashionistas looking for something chicly unique. The designer destination mingles desirable denim from Hudson and True Religion with feminine finds from Milly and Tocca. *Every day; ericce.com; map:GG7.*

The Finerie

1212 1ST AVE, DOWNTOWN; 206/632-4664
This fine store is perfectly situated to take advantage of the downtown boom in urban living. Upscale, yet still approachable, these are the kind of duds you can picture the new citified Seattleite wearing while out for cocktails at nearby BOKA. There's a handsome selection of dress and casual shirts, pants, tailored jackets, and shoes for the nattily attired man, and of course, for his woman, a larger collection of pretty clothing, shoes, and accessories from emerging and established designers. *Mon–Sun; thefinerie.com; map:K7.*

Horseshoe

720 N 35TH ST, FREMONT; 206/547-9639
Some women will be very upset with us for revealing this secret shopping spot. But more will be happy to discover this oasis of urban cowgirl style—tees, tops, great fitting denim, and darling dresses. You can even ride off into the sunset with an embellished belt buckle, handmade sterling silver jewelry, or a softly scented candle. Giddyap! *Every day; map:FF7.*

Ian

1919 2ND AVE, DOWNTOWN; 206/441-4055; 501 N 36TH ST, FREMONT; 206/322-7380
Twenty-somethings (and Peter Pan funky types) who dig the retro-urban look love this store populated with such labels as Ever, Helmut Lang, Paul Smith, Nice Collective, and Diesel. *Every day; ianshop.com; map:I6, FF7.*

Illi

2113 WESTLAKE AVE, WESTLAKE; 206/973-3487
If you can't make it to Italy, find your way to this tiny triangular shop, a stop on the way to the up-and-coming neighborhood of South Lake Union. Targeted at the well-heeled woman are sophisticated sweaters, skirts, and separates; sleek and expensive leather jackets; scintillating handbags; and other styles from high-end Italian designers. *Every day; shopilli.com; map:G4.*

Impulse

3516 FREMONT PL N, FREMONT; 206/545-4854
The most stylish subterranean spot in town, this boutique has matured from its nascent days as an urban art outlet to become a source for some of the most edgy, interesting designers (both local and international) around. Savvy buyers step away from the usual jeans-and-tees crowd to carry drapey dresses and continental cuts of pants and tops along with a unique assortment of bags and jewelry. *Every day; impulseseattle.com; map:FF7.*

In Vogue

800 BELLEVUE WY NE, STE 111, BELLEVUE; 425/468-5765
If this store were a girl you knew in high school, she'd consistently win "cutest smile" in the yearly popularity contest. Tucked away in the heart of Bellevue, this secret shopping spot has secured "Best Boutique" two years running on Seattle's go-to online city guide, NWsource.com. In the stylishly simple space you'll find dangly jewelry, hot handbags, darling tops and bottoms, and the essential selection of sexy jeans. *Mon–Sat; map:GG2.*

Jeri Rice

421 UNIVERSITY ST, DOWNTOWN; 206/624-4000
Jeri Rice exudes exclusivity—in a good way. It's a Seattle original, located off the lobby of the chic Fairmont Olympic hotel, and carries clothes and accessories in the finest fabrics and leathers and by the best designers (with prices to match). In addition to European cashmere and suiting, American designer jeans and casuals, accessories, and shoes, its signature is an amazing collection of evening gowns. *Every day; jeririce.com; map:K6.*

La Ree

11 103RD AVE NE, BELLEVUE; 425/453-7016
Walking into this streetside Bellevue boutique is like entering a sea of tranquil Tiffany blue floating with fabulous frocks. The space is a mix of raw and

refined, the clothing, utterly urbane—a collection of up-and-coming international designers who hail primarily from Europe. Each piece is a rare find, from sophisticated dresses to dreamy tops and premium jeans, and jewelry and handbags to harmonize. The owner has an eye for fabric and pattern, while being a stickler for fit. The styles are spot-on trend, deliberately in sync with the posh shoe store just across the way. *Every day; lareeboutique.com; map:GG2.*

La Rousse

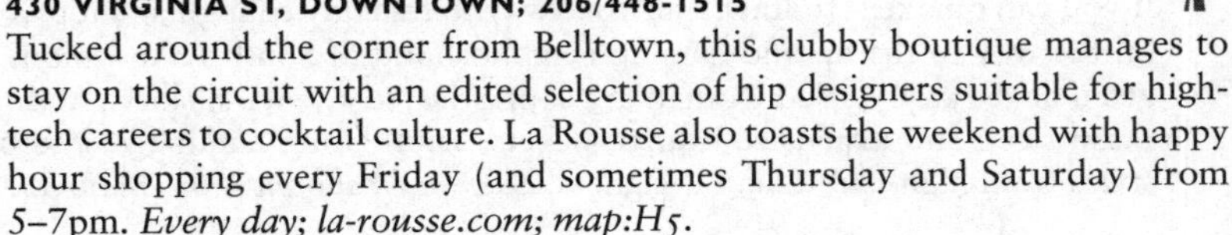

430 VIRGINIA ST, DOWNTOWN; 206/448-1515
Tucked around the corner from Belltown, this clubby boutique manages to stay on the circuit with an edited selection of hip designers suitable for high-tech careers to cocktail culture. La Rousse also toasts the weekend with happy hour shopping every Friday (and sometimes Thursday and Saturday) from 5–7pm. *Every day; la-rousse.com; map:H5.*

BEST SPOT
FOR CHOCOLATE?

"When it's fresh, the devil's cake at the B&O on Olive Street is the absolute best. It's so decadent and delicious it makes my eyes roll to the back of my head."

Cheryl Waters, DJ, KEXP

Lemon Meringue

7720 GREENWOOD AVE N, GREENWOOD; 206/297-6071
Whether you're a stylish young woman, a mom in waiting, a cooing baby, or simply someone who likes a friendly atmosphere stocked with neat stuff, you'll want to make your way to the burgeoning land of Greenwood. Like the namesake pie done well, this store is just the right amount of sweet and tart, topped off with a heavenly lightness. Amid the fun finds are clothing (including infant and maternity wear), lingerie, soaps and lotions, hats, handbags, and even doggie doodads. *Every day; lemonmeringue.us; map:EE7.*

Les Amis

3420 EVANSTON AVE N, FREMONT; 206/632-2877
A forerunner on the boutique scene, this tucked-away trendsetter always manages to walk away with the people's pick prize—and not just for sentimental reasons. Somehow the charming spot manages to stay surprising and consistent, offering clothing lines not represented elsewhere in the area: handmade dresses, beautiful sweaters, fine leathers, lingerie, and handcrafted jewelry. *Every day; lesamis-inc.com; map:FF7.*

Lola Pop

711 N 35TH ST, FREMONT; 206/547-2071

There's a French accent to this tiny shop that got its start selling exquisite footwear. Since then, the offerings have expanded to include accessories and clothing with a unique twist, whether it is beautiful fabrication, intriguing details, or prints that pop. *Every day; map:FF7.*

Luly Yang Studio Boutique

1218 4TH AVE, DOWNTOWN; 206/623-8200

Seattle's queen of couture has a beautiful showroom to match her luxe selection of handmade bridal gowns and evening attire, accompanied by resort wear and a full trousseau for the honeymoon. The diva of design thoughtfully supplies a clubby lounge (the "Library") for the menfolk, replete with handsome accessories and relaxing refreshments. *Every day; lulyyang.com; map:K6.*

Manhattan Boutique

122 LAKE ST S, KIRKLAND; 425/576-1065

If you're cruising for something that's totally *In-Style*, as in the celeb-centric bible, this is a must-stop shop for you. The lakeside boutique is brimming with independent designers and on top of every chic, sexy trend from names like Catherine Malandrino, James Perse, and Juicy Couture—and that's without even mentioning the more than 10 lines of hot denim. *Every day; boutiquemanhattan.com; map:EE3.*

Mario's

1513 6TH AVE, DOWNTOWN; 206/223-1461

When you walk into Mario's, you know you are at the zenith of men's and women's fashion—with pinnacle prices too. The European interior, with white pillars and an iron staircase, is fitting for the labels it houses—Hugo Boss, Ermenegildo Zegna, Etro, Loro Piana, Oscar de la Renta, Dolce & Gabbana, and Prada, not to mention Mario's own label. The store carries luggage, suiting, and shoes, as well as casual, evening, and outerwear, and all the accessories to match. *Every day; marios.com; map:J5.*

Merge

611 N 35TH ST, FREMONT; 206/782-5335

This sophisticated clothing store blends beautiful fabrics and urban styling. Aimed at the woman looking for modern pieces to layer into her existing wardrobe, colors are subdued, and the focus is on fit and fabulous texture. Prices are surprisingly fair for the quality of the apparel and accessories. *Every day; mergeboutique.com; map:FF8.*

Olivine

5344 BALLARD AVE NW, BALLARD; 206/706-4188

It's always a girl party at this boutique on Seattle's historic shopping street, Ballard Avenue. One of the originals in this emerging area, the airy shop consistently delivers the freshest fashions picked with a feminine sensibility. Clothing, shoes, and handbags line the walls; in the center of the warm space are tables displayed with makeup and toiletries, all chosen with as much care as the clothing. *Every day; olivine.net; map:FF8.*

Polite Society

1924 1ST AVE, DOWNTOWN; 206/441-4796
With its clubby atmosphere, you'd almost expect a velvet rope around the sleek doorway of this chic boutique. The focus is on clothing and accessories from emerging designers across the globe, and—as advertised on the Web site—there's something for everyone who's not just anybody. You'll also find home furnishings, antiques, and tea (how apropos!) and will be occasionally offered a beverage while browsing. Price points are aimed at the upper crust. *Every day; shoppolitesociety.com; map:I7.*

Promesse

128 CENTRAL WAY, KIRKLAND; 425/828-4259
Timeless trends may sound like an oxymoron, but it's precisely what this Kirkland boutique promises. True to its name, the store delivers of-the-moment designers that are here to stay for a long time (that would be at least a few seasons in fashion speak). That means sophisticated dresses, tops, jeans, handbags, and more that mix comfortably into your existing closet while adding an instant update. Client relationships are key; wardrobe consulting services are available. *Wed–Mon; shoppromesse.com; map:EE3.*

Rue

611 STEWART ST, DOWNTOWN; 206/264-0788
What can we say about Rue but . . . it's pretty. The clothes are pretty. The owner is pretty. The jewelry and handbags are, well, pretty. And the prices are, take a guess. The lofty space that was once a florescent-lit print shop is much more attractive filled with never-before-seen-in-Seattle brands from the owner's former home, New York. Upstairs in the "walk-in closet," you'll find a selection of gently used vintage clothing. And the service? Pretty sweet. *Tues–Sun; rueseattle.com; map:H5.*

Skookum Clothing Northwest

1629 QUEEN ANNE AVE N, QUEEN ANNE; 206/285-2184
When you hear a customer exclaim "I'm so thrilled!" as she sidles up to the counter at this new-ish store, you know you're in one of Seattle's fresh favorites. Not a surprise, since the sister store on Bainbridge Island has long been a destination for Northwest island style. Lucky for the Queen Anne contingency, they've recently been graced with their own location stocked with classic and contemporary clothing. *Every day; skookumclothing.com; map:GG7.*

Sway & Cake

1631 6TH AVE, DOWNTOWN; 206/624-2699;
201 BELLEVUE SQUARE, BELLEVUE; 425/462-8620

The once overly pink boutique has grown up with two notable locations offering chic and sassy styles to the slim of hip and fat of wallet. Aside from the requisite range of premium denim and tight-fitting tees, there are dresses, jackets, accessories, and footwear, all more NY and LA than NW. *Every day; swayandcake.com; map:J5, GG2.*

Sweetie

4508 CALIFORNIA AVE SW, WEST SEATTLE; 206/923-3533

Don't let the name mislead you—you won't find saccharin style at this neighborhood boutique. What you will uncover is an edgy attitude: a small slice of rocker chick chic alongside wear-to-work clothes and an alluring selection of evening wear. *Every day; sweetieboutique.com; map:JJ8.*

Synapse 206

206 1ST AVE S, PIONEER SQUARE; 206/447-7731

It may look like a mad jumble as you peer in the window, but sally forth and you'll be rewarded with intriguing fashion finds: fascinating skirts, dresses, jackets, and tops, accented with an array of scarves, tights, jewelry, and purses. The proprietor of this unique outfitter seeks standout style from unusual brands and is often approached by local designers to carry their one-of-a-kind creations, making this a get-it-when-you-see-it kind of place. *Every day; synapse206.com; map:N7.*

Tatter's

7605 SE 27TH ST, STE 105, MERCER ISLAND; 206/232-8055

The name of this modest Mercer Island boutique doesn't relay what you'll find inside—a more apt descriptor would be "asymmetrical" or "eclectic." Many of the pieces have uneven hemlines and off-center tailoring intended to be worn in multiple ways, ideal for the creative dresser or world traveler. Gathered from designers across Europe and the United States, the chic collection is more of a style than a size or age. Hard to find elsewhere, the styles do command a pretty price tag. *Mon–Sat; tattersmi.com; map:II4.*

Tininha's Butique de Biquini

617 NE 35TH ST, FREMONT; 206/985-6772

If itsy bitsy teeny weeny is what you're after, get thee to this itty bitty boutique where there's always a warm welcome and a hot selection of swimwear. The specialty of the shop is the Brazilian bikini, famous for its fit. If you're looking for something with a bit more coverage, there's also a sassy array of sarongs and sundresses, yoga wear, and fluttery lingerie, along with colorful totes and candles. *Every day; tininhasboutique.com; map:FF7.*

Tulip

1201 1ST AVE, DOWNTOWN; 206/223-1790
Like a flower blooming in the midst of the city, this girly boutique offers a pleasing respite from the surrounding urban bustle. Organized like the closet everyone dreams of, the limited selection of stylish labels is wrinkle free and categorized by color. Intimate atmosphere, boutique prices. *Every day; tulip-seattle.com; map:K7.*

Tweed

8315 GREENWOOD AVE N, GREENWOOD; 206/784-4444
This is what a neighborhood shop should be: friendly, intimate, and affordable, with an ever-changing assortment of hipster-approved clothing, shoes, and accessories for the cost-conscious customer. The indie denim offerings even include sizes for the shapely. *Every day; tweedboutique.com; map:EE7.*

Velouria

2205 NW MARKET ST, BALLARD; 206/788-0330
Back in the day when Seattle's growing population of do-it-yourself types needed a showroom for their crafts, this Ballard boutique opened its doors. Today it has evolved as a showcase for independent designers, featuring talent from around the country, yet still with a soft spot for local creations. *Every day; shopvelouria.tripod.com; map:FF8.*

Via Lago

129 LAKE ST S, KIRKLAND; 425/893-9191
As you wend your way down Kirkland's waterfront, you may feel like you're cruising an upscale street in California. Everything is clean and contemporary—much like this lakeside boutique. The blonde wood and large windows lend the atmosphere of a comfortable, elegant home, a showroom for the stylish clothing from designers such as Trina Turk, Diane Von Furstenberg, and Elie Tahari, along with accessories and gifts. *Every day; vialago.com; map:EE3.*

What To Wear

2727 78TH AVE SE, MERCER ISLAND; 206/232-2108
Next time you're staring into the black hole of your closet wondering what to wear, maybe it's time to stop by this Mercer Island oasis of fresh, sporty, body-conscious style. The clean and simple shop offers an enormous collection of flattering tees (many from favorite Michael Stars) and jeans in a navigable space, along with belts, bags, shoes, jewelry, and even gifts for baby. *Every day; shopwhattowear.com; map:II4.*

Zebraclub

1901 1ST AVE, DOWNTOWN (AND BRANCHES); 206/448-7452
This urban-wear store is most popular among city men and women in their 20s, although some middle-aged shoppers are hip enough to pull off the look. The clothes are comfortable and sturdy enough for (spoiled) teenagers, with brands such as Paul Frank, Obey, and LRG, and denim from Diesel and J-Brand. *Every day; zebraclub.com; map:I7.*

ARTS

ARTS

Museums

Seattle possesses an enormously vital visual arts scene, with many museums enjoying recent expansions, including most notably the **SEATTLE ART MUSEUM**, which unveiled a newer, spiffier space in spring 2007, boasting more than double the museum's original square footage, an interactive presentation style, many new works on view, and a more open floor plan. Also in 2007, the museum's long-awaited expansion into the outdoors, the **OLYMPIC SCULPTURE PARK** (see Top 25 Attractions in the Exploring chapter), finally opened and immediately became one of the city's premier destinations.

At press time, the **WING LUKE ASIAN MUSEUM** was in the process of moving from its converted garage in the heart of the Chinatown/International District to roomier digs nearby (scheduled to open in May of 2008), and the **MUSEUM OF HISTORY AND INDUSTRY** (MOHAI) has plans to relocate from the U District, though where exactly, and when, is still up in the air. On the Eastside, the Bellevue Art Museum closed, then reopened under a new name, the **BELLEVUE ARTS MUSEUM**, with a focus less on contemporary art and more on arts and crafts.

Bellevue Arts Museum

510 BELLEVUE WY NE, BELLEVUE; 425/519-0770

BAM reinvented itself in 2005 with exhibits that focus on the traditional craft mediums of glass, wood, and metal, from fantastic collections of wooden bowls and shows of delicate contemporary Israeli jewelry to sculptures that are both about and composed of trees. A consistent crowd pleaser is the museum's annual Bellevue Arts Museum Fair, held for three days in July across the street at Bellevue Square. Admission is $7 for adults, $5 for seniors and students, and free for children under 6; free the first Friday evening of the month. *Tues–Sun; bellevuearts.org; map:HH3.* ♿

Burke Museum of Natural History and Culture

17TH AVENUE NE AND NE 45TH STREET, UNIVERSITY DISTRICT; 206/543-7907

The Burke—named in honor of Judge Thomas Burke, former chief justice of the Washington State Supreme Court—is an attention-grabbing place. From its collection of more than 3 million artifacts and specimens, the museum created three permanent exhibits. Life and Times of Washington State looks back over 500 million years of regional history and features the Northwest's only real dinosaur skeleton, a 140-million-year-old, flesh-eating allosaurus. Treasures of the Burke highlights the museum's most unique collections, and best appreciated by adults is Pacific Voices, which delves into the richness of 19 Pacific Rim cultures. A main-floor gift shop sells curiosities; the café is an especially comfy espresso-and-pastries spot. Admission for permanent exhibits is $8 for adults; $6.50 for seniors; $5 for students; and free for children 4 and under, museum members, and UW students/staff; free on First Thursday. Charges for special exhibits vary. *Every day; burkemuseum.org; map:FF6.* ♿

Center for Wooden Boats

1010 VALLEY ST, SOUTH LAKE UNION; 206/382-2628

This maritime museum, which has its own little harbor at the southern tip of Lake Union, celebrates the heritage of small craft before the advent of fiberglass. Of the 75 vintage and replica wooden rowing and sailing boats in the collection, more than half are available for public use. Admission is free. Rentals range from $10–$40 an hour. Lessons in sailing, traditional woodworking, and boatbuilding are offered for all ages. *Seasonal hours; free classic boat rides every Sun 2–3pm; cwb@cwb.org; cwb.org; map:D1.* ♿

The Children's Museum

CENTER HOUSE, SEATTLE CENTER; 206/441-1768

Located on the fountain level of Seattle Center's busy Center House, the Children's Museum stresses hands-on activities and exploration of other cultural traditions. The museum houses a number of permanent features, including a play center, a mountain, and a global village with child-size houses from Japan, Ghana, and the Philippines. The variety of special programs—Mexican folk dancing, Native American games, Chinese storytelling, Japanese kite making—is impressive. The Imagination Station features a different artist every month guiding activities with various materials. The Discovery Bay exhibit is geared to infants and toddlers. Admission is $7.50 per person, $6.50 for grandparents, free for kids under the age of 1. *Every day; tcm@thechildrensmuseum.org; thechildrensmuseum.org; map:C6.* ♿

Experience Music Project

325 5TH AVE N, SEATTLE CENTER; 206/367-5483 OR 877/367-5483

See Top 25 Attractions in the Exploring chapter.

Frye Art Museum

704 TERRY AVE, FIRST HILL; 206/622-9250

After a dramatic expansion and remodel more than a decade ago, this once-stodgy museum (named for late Seattleites Charles and Emma Frye, who made their fortune in meat processing) has become a lively hub of activities, with a pleasant café, poetry readings, chamber music, and other performances in addition to frequently changing exhibits. Since chief curator Robin Held came to the Frye from the Henry Art Gallery in 2004, the museum has been mounting ever more interesting and challenging shows, including exhibits by internationally known artists such as Henry Darger and Erwin Wurm, as well as contemporary local artists like Joseph Park, whose cartoonlike animal paintings possess an erotic charge. Free admission and limited free parking. *Tues–Sun; info@fryeart.org; fryeart.org; map:N3.* ♿

Henry Art Gallery

15TH AVENUE NE AND NE 41ST STREET, UNIVERSITY DISTRICT; 206/453-2280
See Top 25 Attractions in the Exploring chapter.

Museum of Flight

9404 E MARGINAL WY S, GEORGETOWN; 206/764-5720
See Top 25 Attractions in the Exploring chapter.

Museum of History and Industry

2700 24TH AVE E, UNIVERSITY DISTRICT; 206/324-1126
The rambling, amiable MOHAI is a huge repository of Americana, with artifacts pertaining to the early history of the Pacific Northwest. There's an exhibit about Seattle's Great Fire of 1889 (which started in a glue pot on the waterfront), a hands-on history of the fishing and canning industry in the Northwest, and a half-dozen immense wooden female beauties—and one male counterpart—who once rode the prows of ships in Puget Sound. Locally oriented exhibits change throughout the year. At some point, the museum is slated to move, though the location and timing is still to be determined. Admission is $7 for adults, $5 for seniors and children 5–12, and free for kids under 5; free on First Thursday. *Every day; information@seattlehistory.org; seattlehistory.org; map:FF6.* ♿

Nordic Heritage Museum

3014 NW 67TH ST, BALLARD; 206/789-5707
Established in a stately restored schoolhouse, the Nordic Heritage Museum focuses on the history of Nordic settlers in the United States, with exhibits of maritime equipment, costumes, and photographs, including an Ellis Island installation. Periodic traveling exhibits have included a show of 18th-century Alaskan and Northwest Coast Native artifacts from the National Museum of Finland, as well as artworks by contemporary Scandinavian artists. Holidays bring ethnic festivals. Admission is $6 for adults, $5 for seniors and students, $4 for children 5–17, and free for kids under 5. *Tues–Sun; nordic@nordicmuseum.org; nordicmuseum.org; map:EE9.* ♿

Olympic Sculpture Park

2901 WESTERN AVE, BELLTOWN; 206/332-1377
See Top 25 Attractions in the Exploring chapter.

Seattle Art Museum

100 UNIVERSITY ST, DOWNTOWN; 206/654-3100
See Top 25 Attractions in the Exploring chapter.

Seattle Asian Art Museum

1400 E PROSPECT ST, CAPITOL HILL; 206/654-3100
See Top 25 Attractions in the Exploring chapter.

WALK FOR ART

Leave it to health-conscious Seattleites to favor an athletic form of arts appreciation. Nearly every neighborhood, from Ballard to West Seattle to Kirkland on the Eastside, now hosts a monthly art walk.

The granddaddy of all ambulatory art walks is the **FIRST THURSDAY GALLERY WALK**. Centered in downtown Seattle's historic Pioneer Square, it draws milling crowds of sophisticates, posers, and art-loving singles who cruise the area's dozens of galleries, which stay open for extended hours, 6–8pm, and the Seattle Art Museum, which waives its entry fee to certain exhibits for the evening tour.

Other Seattle art rambles include the **BALLARD ART WALK** (second Saturday of each month, 6–9pm; call the Ballard Chamber of Commerce for more info, 206/784-9705) along charmingly historic Ballard Avenue and a segment of Market Street; the **FREMONT ART WALK** (first Friday, 6–9pm); the **CAPITOL HILL ART WALK** (second Tuesday, 6–9pm); the **U DISTRICT ART WALK** (third Friday, 5–9pm; 206/547-4417; udistrictartwalk.org), and the Greenwood/Phinney Art Walk (in early May).

In Kirkland, the Second Thursday Art Walk takes in several closely packed galleries and some quirky public art (6–9pm; free 4-hour parking is available at the Kirkland Library, 808 Kirkland Ave). Another long-standing art walk is the annual **GEORGETOWN ARTS AND GARDEN TOUR**, usually held in July (georgetownneighborhood.com). Georgetown, home to many artists' studios and a small strip of hip bars, also hosts occasional art walks during the rest of the year.

—Shannon O'Leary

Wing Luke Asian Museum

407 7TH AVE S, INTERNATIONAL DISTRICT; 206/623-5124

This museum is scheduled to open in its new, larger location in May of 2008. Named after Seattle's first Chinese American City Council member, this lively museum in the International District is devoted to the Asian American experience in the Northwest. Particularly moving is the exhibit of photographs and artifacts relating to the internment of Japanese Americans during World War II. Changing exhibits are devoted to Chinese, Korean, Filipino, Vietnamese, and Laotian peoples and their often-difficult meetings with the West. Admission is $4 for adults, $3 for seniors and students, and $2 for children 5–12. *Tues–Sun; folks@wingluke.org; wingluke.org; map:R5.* ♿

Galleries

Seattle's vibrant gallery scene is centered near Pioneer Square, and in the past few years a number of smaller, more adventurous galleries have joined longtime heavyweights such as Greg Kucera—most notably in and around the Tashiro Kaplan Building, home to numerous artist live/work spaces. On the first Thursday of each month, this neighborhood thrums with art fans enjoying the **FIRST THURSDAY ART WALK** (6pm–8pm), when new shows are previewed and many galleries stay open late to celebrate. New galleries and alternative art spaces have popped up in other parts of town as well, particularly south of downtown in the SoDo district.

Benham Studio Gallery

1216 1ST AVE, DOWNTOWN; 206/622-2480
From its roots as a photographic exhibition in a passport studio entryway, the Benham has grown into one of Seattle's most recognized photo galleries, representing primarily Northwest photographers, from the well known to up-and-comers, whose work is mounted here in a popular group show in December or January. *Tues–Sat; benham@benhamgallery.com; benhamgallery.com; map:L7.*

Canlis Glass

3131 WESTERN AVE, STE 329, LOWER QUEEN ANNE; 206/282-4428
Husband-and-wife team Jean-Pierre (J. P.) and Leigh Canlis (yes, they *are* related to the venerable Canlis restaurant clan) opened this space near the Olympic Sculpture Park in 2005 to showcase J. P.'s fluid, bamboo-inspired glass art, which also graces numerous local restaurants and retailers. *Tues–Sat and by appointment; canlisglass.com; map:B9.*

Carolyn Staley Fine Japanese Prints

2001 WESTERN AVE, STE 320, PIKE PLACE MARKET; 206/621-1888
The specialty here is fine old prints, including Japanese ukiyo-e woodblock prints, antique maps, and botanical prints. Staley also hosts occasional book-art shows. *Mon–Fri; info@carolynstaleyprints.com; www.carolynstaleyprints.com; map:O8.* ♿

Crawl Space Gallery

504 E DENNY WAY, STE 1, CAPITOL HILL; 206/322-5752
A recently launched gallery run by an artist co-op, Crawl Space is hard to find (hidden behind a fence and tucked into the first floor of a Capitol Hill apartment building), but the work is often worth the trek. Run by a group of recent (mostly University of Washington) MFA grads, the gallery exhibits works in unusual media (such as stick pins tracing the cracks in the wall) by artists you might not see at other venues around town. *Sat–Sun and by appointment; info@crawlspacegallery.com; crawlspacegallery.com; map:I1.*

Davidson Galleries
Davidson Contemporary

313 OCCIDENTAL AVE S, PIONEER SQUARE; 206/624-6700;
310 S WASHINGTON ST, PIONEER SQUARE; 206/624-7684

Davidson Galleries recently opened a second location, Davidson Contemporary, in the Tashiro Kaplan Building and branched out from its usual shows of landscapes and figurative works by contemporary artists. Now you might also find the barest abstractions, multimedia sculptures, and gutsy surveys that include work by internationally known artists. In their Occidental Avenue location, the back gallery features contemporary printmakers from around the world. More challenging—and often more local—work can be seen at the Washington Street venue. *Tues–Sat; davidsongalleries.com; map: O8, O6.* ♿ *(Davidson Contemporary only)*

Foster/White Gallery

220 3RD AVE S, PIONEER SQUARE; 206/622-2833; 1331 5TH AVE, DOWNTOWN; 206/583-0100

Foster/White showcases paintings, sculpture, and ceramics—usually abstract and decorative—by Northwest artists living and dead. The gallery is also one of the major local dealers in contemporary glass by Pilchuck School stars, most notably Dale Chihuly. The downtown branch caters to tourists and shoppers. *Tues–Sat; seattle@fosterwhite.com; fosterwhite.com; map:O8.* ♿ *(Pioneer Square location only)*

Francine Seders Gallery

6701 GREENWOOD AVE N, GREENWOOD; 206/782-0355

In judicious operation since 1966, Seders represents some venerable members of Seattle's art community, including the late Jacob Lawrence, Gwen Knight, Robert Jones, and Michael Spafford. New additions to the stable include a more diverse group of artists, among them painters, sculptors, and assemblagists. *Tues–Sun; sedersgallery.com; map:EE7.*

Gallery4Culture

101 PREFONTAINE PL S, PIONEER SQUARE; 206/296-7580

With a 25-year history of showing local artists, Gallery4Culture (formerly the King County Arts Commission) is a great spot to check out emerging, unsigned artists before they move onto sometimes-prominent art careers. Very often this gallery is home to great exhibitions, showing a wide range of work, from color-saturated paintings of the urban scene to sculptures composed of cathode ray tubes to drawings created with hot glass. *Mon–Fri; 4culture.org/publicart/gallery/info.htm; map:O6.* ♿

BLOG BOOM

Seattle has no end of blogs to peruse and wander, and while some can be indulgent rants, there are a few good ones worth checking out, and even a few you might want to return to, once you've landed back home.

SEATTLE DAILY PHOTO (seattle-daily-photo.blogspot.com) is just that—a daily image of the city, often highlighting quirky or amusing views of Seattle, perhaps suggesting places to visit or offering a virtual tour of the city via some surprising and offbeat images. **SEATTLEST** (seattlest.com) is an opinionated blog, exploring politics, sports, and the arts, as well as the occasional drink recipe. **PIKE/PINE** (pikepine.com) is subtitled "Street Fashion in Seattle + Elsewhere" and offers great photos of fashionable folk in our fair city and beyond. It's a great (vicarious) people-watching site with lovely images and a great eye. **METRO-BLOGGING SEATTLE** (seattle.metblogs.com) offers a slew of content, from arts events heads-ups to quirky posts on the history of the world's fair. **SOUND POLITICS** (soundpolitics.com) focuses on all things political in Seattle and around Puget Sound. One of the better-known Seattle blogs, **NOT MARTHA** (notmartha.org) explores crafty projects, with step-by-step photo instructions, as well as food politics, craft events, and other miscellanea, with entries on such topics as kosher Coca-Cola. A less well-known blog is **ARTDISH** (artdish.com/blog), offering reviews of visual art, theater, and dance.

G. Gibson Gallery

300 S WASHINGTON ST, PIONEER SQUARE; 206/587-4033

Gibson, one of the city's top photography dealers, is located in the Tashiro Kaplan Building, close to Pioneer Square. This is the place to find work by stellar 20th-century photographers such as Imogen Cunningham, Ansel Adams, Jacques-Henri Lartigue, Ruth Bernhard, and Marion Post Wolcott, as well as by adventurous contemporary Northwesterners. *Tues–Sat; gail@ggibson.com; ggibsongallery.com; map:K2.* ♿

Greg Kucera Gallery

212 3RD AVE S, PIONEER SQUARE; 206/624-0770

Smart and outspoken, Kucera maintains a carefully chosen stable of artists, many with national reputations. He has a great eye for emerging talent but also shows editioned works by established blue-chip artists such as Frank Stella, Robert Motherwell, and Helen Frankenthaler. One thematic exhibit each year addresses a touchy topic: sex, religion, or politics. *Tues–Sat; staff@gregkucera.com; gregkucera.com; map:O7.* ♿

Seattle serves up a surprising preponderance of foodie blogs, offering out-of-towners great local advice on where to drink and what to eat, as well as places to avoid. **SEATTLE BON VIVANT** (seattlebonvivant.typepad.com) posts lovely photos, news on new restaurants, and food reviews. **ORANGETTE** (orangette.blogspot.com) offers a chatty narrative with food experiments and recipes. **GLUTEN-FREE GIRL** (glutenfreegirl.blogspot.com) offers a gorgeous daily photo, spelled-out recipes, and the narrative of what sounds like a charmed life. Two lesser-known, funny, and fantastically written blogs are **THE WINE OFFENSIVE** (wineoffensive.com), a smart, in-your-face review of beverages (from beer to wine to port to Jäger) and beverage culture; and **HOGWASH** (jessthomson.wordpress.com), offering a recipe a day, with long entries that offer step-by-step instruction and thoughtful commentary.

And of course, all four major local papers, both the dailies and the weeklies, have their own blogs: **THE SEATTLE TIMES** (seattletimes.nwsource.com/blogs-discussions), **SEATTLE POST INTELLIGENCER** (blog.seattlepi.nwsource.com), **SEATTLE WEEKLY** (seattleweekly.com/blogs), and **THE STRANGER** (thestranger.com/blog). Whatever you want to read up on—from politics to the best new restaurant to which exhibits to visit—you'll find plenty of locally written scrolling type.

—Adriana Grant

Grover/Thurston Gallery

309 OCCIDENTAL AVE S, PIONEER SQUARE; 206/223-0816

In the heart of the gallery district, Grover/Thurston gained considerable status when it picked up one of the region's most popular painters, Fay Jones, just before her 1997 retrospective at the Seattle Art Museum. The gallery also represents esteemed ceramic sculptor Akio Takamori and Oregon painter James Lavadour. *Tues–Sat; mail@groverthurston.com; groverthurston.com; map:O8.*

Howard House

604 2ND AVE, PIONEER SQUARE; 206/256-6399

An ambitious younger dealer with an eye toward the international scene, Billy Howard showcases up-and-coming talent. His stable also includes one of the Northwest's premier ceramic sculptors, former University of Washington professor Patti Warashina, as well as more contemporary artists such as Gretchen Bennett—who creates beauty from stickers—and Victoria Haven, who creates minimalist pen and ink drawings as well as sculptures from rubber bands and nails. *Tues–Sat; info@howardhouse.net; howardhouse.net; map:N7.*

James Harris Gallery

309 3RD AVE S, STE A, PIONEER SQUARE; 206/903-6220

The space is small, and the shows often include just four or five paintings or sculptures, but the offerings at James Harris are always fresh and distinctive. With roots in the San Francisco Bay Area art scene, Harris shows established California artists and emerging talent from the Northwest. *Wed–Sat; mail@jamesharrisgallery.com; jamesharrisgallery.com; map:O7.*

Kirkland Arts Center

620 MARKET ST, KIRKLAND; 425/822-7161

In a historic brick building near the Kirkland waterfront, this publicly funded center puts on several shows each year by Puget Sound–area artists, showing some of the region's most challenging and surprising exhibits. *Mon–Sat; support@kirklandartscenter.org; kirklandartscenter.org; map:EE3.*

Lawrimore Project

831 AIRPORT WY S, CHINATOWN/INTERNATIONAL DISTRICT; 206/501-1231

Run by Scott Lawrimore, formerly of Greg Kucera Gallery, this newest of alternative gallery spaces designed by artist/architect duo Annie Han and Daniel Mihalyo (aka Lead Pencil Studio) boasts some of the bravest and most compelling art on view in the city, in a hard-to-find, nondescript spot. Artists include the trio SuttonBeresCuller, famous for creating and occupying a traffic-snarling island off of the 520 bridge, and Tivon Rice, who does strange and beautiful things with the light emitted from cathode ray tubes. *Tues– Sat; scott@lawrimoreproject.com; lawrimoreproject.com; map:II7.* ♿

Linda Hodges Gallery

316 1ST AVE S, PIONEER SQUARE; 206/624-3034

Hodges shows contemporary paintings, and occasionally photography and sculpture, by artists from Seattle, Portland, and other Northwest burgs. The art ranges from fantasy to realism, with the biggest draw being the zany, countrified mythology of adored Eastern Washington painter Gaylen Hansen. *Tues–Sat; lhodges@lindahodgesgallery.com; lindahodgesgallery.com; map:O8.*

Lisa Harris Gallery

1922 PIKE PL, PIKE PLACE MARKET; 206/443-3315

Above the jostling crowds of the Pike Place Market, this small upstairs gallery can be an oasis of calm. Harris favors expressionistic landscape and figurative works, with several Bellingham artists forming the core of her stable. *Every day; staff@lisaharrisgallery.com; lisaharrisgallery.com; map:I7.*

Martin-Zambito Fine Art

721 E PIKE ST, CAPITOL HILL; 206/726-9509

East Coast transplants David Martin and Dominic Zambito are on a mission to bring recognition to overlooked early Northwest artists, especially women, such as photographer Myra Wiggins, whose work attracted international attention in the early 1900s and then disappeared in the shifting tides of art history. *Tues–Sat; info@martin-zambito.com; martin-zambito.com; map:K1.*

Platform Gallery

114 THIRD AVE S, PIONEER SQUARE; 206/323-2808
An artist-run gallery in the bustling Tashiro Kaplan Building, Platform offers some of the more challenging and inventive exhibits in the city. The gallery's stable of artists includes Jaq Chartier, who creates sensual works using ink tests, employing a meticulous scientific sensibility and a great sense of color and balance. *Thurs–Sat; info@platformgallery.com; platformgallery.com; map:O6.*

Soil Art Gallery

112 3RD AVE S, PIONEER SQUARE; 206/264-8061
The space is unassuming and some of the shows forgettable, but this artists' collective gallery has more than a decade-long history of launching top-notch new artists, many fresh from the University of Washington MFA program. It's usually worth the stroll to check it out. *Thurs–Sun; gallery@soilart.org; soilart.org; map:O6.* ♿

Suyama Space

2324 2ND AVE, BELLTOWN; 206/256-0809
Housed within the offices of Suyama Peterson Deguchi architects, this art space is home to some of the most quietly fantastic works in Seattle. The focus is on installation work, which best uses this barn-like room hidden away from Belltown's urban bustle. From a roomful of inflatable plastic rooms to a sculpture of wires suspended just off the rough-hewn planked floor, the exhibits are consistently surprising and always enjoyable. *Mon–Fri; suyamapetersondeguchi.com/art/; map:G6.* ♿

Western Bridge

3412 4TH AVE S, SODO; 206/838-7444
Art collectors Bill and Ruth True created this gallery to make their sizable and fantastic art collection available to the public. Tucked back from the street (watch for the small orange-lettered sign) in the industrial landscape south of downtown, the gallery is well worth the hunt. You might come across musical installations previously seen at London's Tate Modern, or an exhibit that explores the weather. You'll see artists of international renown in a variety of media, from drawing to installation to video. Check out the artist's residence upstairs. Not only will it give you a voyeuristic thrill to peer into the lives of artists, you'll find art here, too. *Thurs–Sat; info@westernbridge.org; western bridge.org; map:HH7.* ♿

William Traver Gallery

110 UNION ST, STE 200, DOWNTOWN; 206/587-6501; 1821 E DOCK ST, STE 300, TACOMA; 253/383-3645

Glass is the focus at William Traver, and there's always an array of work by local and internationally known talent to choose from. The window-wrapped second-story space in Seattle also showcases paintings, sculptures, photographs, ceramics, and assemblages, mostly by Northwest artists. Also with a Tacoma location. *Tues–Sun; info@travergallery.com; travergallery.com; map:K7.* ♿

Woodside/Braseth Gallery

2101 9TH AVE, DENNY TRIANGLE; 206/622-7243

You'll find strictly Northwest fare in at the city's oldest gallery (founded in 1961), now located in the Denny Triangle neighborhood: paintings by Mark Tobey, William Ivey, Morris Graves, Paul Horiuchi, and a varying selection of midcareer artists. *Tues–Sat; info@woodsidebrasethgallery.com; woodsidebrasethgallery.com; map:J4.*

Wright Exhibition Space

407 DEXTER AVE N, DENNY TRIANGLE; 206/264-8200

Built to showcase the world-class contemporary art collection of Virginia and Bagley Wright, this private gallery also hosts solo shows, including exhibits by Los Angeles artist Ed Ruscha and the late Northwest abstract painter William Ivey. *Limited hours and by appointment; map:D4.* ♿

BEST PLACE
TO TAKE OUT-OF-TOWN GUESTS?

"I always go to the Dahlia Lounge and for dessert insist that we order the doughnuts with the rhubarb jam and mascarpone. Yummy."

Nancy Pearl, author and retired Seattle Public Library librarian

Theater

Aside from its obvious, big-city competitors: New York, LA, and Chicago, Seattle produces more theater in a year than any other city in the country. The reason for this goes back to the early '90s, when Seattle topped "most-livable" lists in national magazines, and fresh talent flocked to the city from all over the country. Young theater artists did not seek to make their homes at the bigger, more staid houses of Intiman, Seattle Repertory Theatre, or A Contemporary Theatre (ACT) but, by and large, began their own companies. Over the next 15 years, there has been an enormous proliferation of fringe theater, produced in venues ranging from leaky basements to a converted funeral home (namely, Richard Hugo House).

Non-mainstream theaters have a tendency to be short-lived, but a few troupes (listed below) have established themselves as long-term successes. (Pick up Seattle's two free weeklies, *Seattle Weekly* and *The Stranger*, for performance listings and smart, critical reviews.) **ANNEX THEATRE** (Gail Stellner Studio, Capitol Hill Arts Center, 1621 12th Ave, Capitol Hill; 206/728-0933; annextheatre.org; map:GG6), once considered the alternative theater in Seattle, produces the long-running monthly cabaret "Spin the Bottle," performed on the first Friday of the months. Annex also puts on more challenging explorations into such topics as politics and humor, like the recent Lenin/Lincoln biographical mash-up, *The Secret Recordings of Lenin*. **THEATER SCHMEATER** (1500 Summit Ave, Capitol Hill; 206/324-5801; schmeater.org; map:GG6) is one of the busiest theaters in town, with one long-running, late-night cash cow: *Twilight Zone: Live on Stage*. This popular series re-creates episodes from the now classic black-and-white series: some performances are all campy fun, while others wear their dated scripts like out-of style, big-shouldered suits. Tickets for those 18 and under are free.

Capitol Hill houses two drama schools, which rent out their spaces to homeless theater companies, and occasionally produce shows themselves. **FREEHOLD THEATRE** (1529 10th Ave, Capitol Hill; 206/323-7499; freeholdtheatre.org; map: GG6) offers courses for actors, directors, and other artists, and runs the Freehold Theatre Lab to develop and support the work of local artists. **THE NORTHWEST ACTORS STUDIO** (1100 E Pike St, Capitol Hill; 206/324-6328; map:GG6) also offers regular classes and features two theaters that supply performance space to smaller companies, as well as showcasing students from the Studio Conservatory. Another group, **THEATER SIMPLE** (various venues; 206/784-8647; theatersimple.org), is unabashedly unmoored, performing as many out-of-town festival shows as they do within the city limits. Theater Simple possesses a history of smart, inexpensive productions that engage the brain as well as the heart, staging a rather broad range of work from Bertolt Brecht to Hans Christian Anderson to Wallace Shawn. The multiethnic **REPERTORY ACTORS WORKSHOP** (various venues; 206/364-3283; reacttheatre.org), under the direction of David Hsieh, produces plays intended to heighten awareness of issues faced by ethnic minorities. The group tackles everything from a musical about the Japanese American internment (*Miss Minidoka 1943*) to the work of Romanian surrealist Eugèene Ionesco, to a stage version of the film *Six Degrees of Separation*.

A Contemporary Theatre (ACT)

700 UNION ST, DOWNTOWN; 206/292-7676

One of the big three theaters in Seattle, along with Intiman and the Seattle Rep, ACT has been in recovery mode in recent years. First, the company flirted with financial ruin in 2003, then in late 2006, artistic director Kurt Beattie, a UW drama grad, was diagnosed with lung cancer. Both Beattie and ACT are now back on their feet, presenting a mix of new work and the occasional American classic. During the Christmas season, ACT stages its extremely popular adaptation of Dickens's *A Christmas Carol. service@acttheatre.org; acttheatre.org; map:K4.* ♿

ArtsWest

4711 CALIFORNIA AVE SW, WEST SEATTLE; 206/938-0339

West Seattle's Junction neighborhood is lucky to claim ArtsWest, a beautiful midsize theater that has steadily evolved from its community-theater roots to become a full-on professional company, with increasingly daring programming choices. *artswest.org; map:JJ8.* ♿

Book-It Repertory Theatre and Seattle Shakespeare Company

CENTER HOUSE THEATRE, LOWER LEVEL OF CENTER HOUSE, SEATTLE CENTER; 206/216-0833 (BOOK-IT); 206/733-8222 (SHAKESPEARE)

Sharing theater and literary ambitions, Book-It produces dramatic adaptations of literary works in an idiosyncratic fashion that's a bit hit-or-miss (some books are best left as books), but generally inventive, while Seattle Shakespeare takes on the Bard with results that vary from uninspired to very good indeed. *book-it.org; seattleshakes.org; map:C6.* ♿

5th Avenue Theatre

1308 5TH AVE, DOWNTOWN; TICKETS 206/625-1900, 888/584-4849

The fabulously opulent 5th Avenue has become the go-to theater for world-premiere musicals hoping to make it big, which is exactly what happened for 2003's *Hairspray*, which went on to Broadway raves and became a Hollywood movie. (*The Wedding Singer* didn't fare as well in 2006.) Designed to resemble the interior of China's Forbidden City, the 5th Avenue is home to its own resident musical theater company, which specializes in revivals of mainstream Broadway musicals, plus one or two Broadway touring shows thrown in to sweeten the mix for subscribers. *info@5thavenue.org; 5thavenue.org; map:L6.* ♿

Intiman Theatre

INTIMAN PLAYHOUSE, 201 MERCER ST, SEATTLE CENTER; 206/269-1900

Adventurous artistic director Bartlett Sher has focused on putting together smart seasons that mix up off-Broadway scripts, unusual takes on classic texts, and the occasional world premiere, such as the Lucas/Guettel musical *The Light in the Piazza*, which went on to win six Tony Awards in 2005. In 2006, Intiman itself won a much-deserved Tony Award for best regional theater, which promises to shine the national spotlight even brighter on the city's best theater company. *tickets@intiman.org; intiman.org; map:A6.* ♿

Northwest Puppet Center

9123 15TH AVE NE, MAPLE LEAF; 206/523-2579

Kids are the target audience for the Northwest Puppet Center, but adults who are dragged along may be in for a pleasant surprise. The resident company, the Carter Family Marionettes, produces some truly charming work (including an oft-revived series adapted from the *Babar the Elephant* books), and also hosts guest artists from around the world. *info@nwpuppet.org; nwpuppet.org; map:EE6.* ♿

On the Boards

BEHNKE CENTER FOR CONTEMPORARY PERFORMANCE, 100 W ROY ST, QUEEN ANNE; 206/217-9888

On the Boards occupies an intermediate place between the fringe and the mainstream theater and has been offering an eclectic blend of dance, theater, and multimedia performance for more than a quarter century (see also Dance in this chapter). Here you'll see both cutting-edge performance art from around the world (Japan, Croatia, Belgium, England—you name it) and new creations by Pacific Northwest artists. The Northwest New Works Festival, held every spring, is a kind of juried fringe festival for locally brewed experimental performance. *ontheboards.org; map:GG8.* ♿

Paramount Theatre

911 PINE ST, DOWNTOWN; TICKETS 206/467-5510

The magnificent Paramount Theatre hosts Broadway musicals, pop headliners, nationally celebrated comedians, silent movies, and the occasional magician (just try to find a restaurant reservation or parking spot when David Copperfield's in town!). You can buy tickets through Ticketmaster or in person at the box office. *boxoffice@theparamount.com; theparamount.com; map:J3.* ♿

Seattle Children's Theatre

201 THOMAS ST, SEATTLE CENTER; 206/441-3322

Seattle Children's Theatre presents several beautifully mounted productions a year for young and family audiences. More than half the performances are world premieres commissioned from leading playwrights and based on both classic and contemporary children's literature. The theater stages several evening and matinee shows per week (with other daytime performances available to school groups). SCT also sponsors a year-round youth drama school for ages 3 through high school, with performances staged in the summer. *boxo@sct.org; sct.org; map:C7.* ♿

Seattle Repertory Theatre

BAGLEY WRIGHT THEATRE, 155 MERCER ST, SEATTLE CENTER; 206/443-2222

The rap on Seattle Rep is that it's become staid, perhaps resting on its laurels as the city's oldest and best-known theater. Productions are generally lavish rather than inspired, and a typical season may not look too different from what Intiman or ACT have to offer. The Rep still manages to pull off a couple of noteworthy shows each season, such as a recent sterling production of *My Name Is Rachel Corrie*, which, though considered controversial in New York City, earned rave reviews in Seattle. *seattlerep.org; map:A6.* ♿

Taproot Theatre

204 N 85TH ST, GREENWOOD; 206/781-9707

Taproot has transcended its church-theater roots to become a critically respected venue for mainstream audiences, featuring a smart mix of contemporary scripts and classic revivals, with an occasional world premiere tossed in. Producing artistic director Scott Nolte knows when to play it safe and when to push the envelope. Particularly worth seeing are the small-cast musicals and the work of associate artistic director Karen Lund, who's adept at mining classical texts for contemporary laughs and drama. *taproot@taproottheatre.org; taproot.org; map:EE7.* ♿

Teatro Zinzanni

222 MERCER ST, SEATTLE CENTER; 206/802-0015

Teatro Zinzanni is one of Seattle's greatest theatrical successes (the dinner theater/cabaret has a successful spin-off in San Francisco). An unlikely cross between Northwest cuisine, cabaret, and European-style circus acts, it's one of the priciest tickets in town, but if the waiting list is to be believed, also one of the most popular. It's a pretty remarkable evening, one that combines comedy, good food, and some truly spectacular moments of theater. If you've got the cash, you can't arrange a better date. *dreams-info@onereel.org; dreams.zinzanni.org; map:A5.* ♿

University of Washington School of Drama

UW ARTS TICKET OFFICE, 4001 UNIVERSITY WY NE, UNIVERSITY DISTRICT; 206/543-4880

The nationally recognized UW School of Drama sometimes presents first-rate productions directed by jobbed-in big-name professionals and featuring students from the school's Professional Actor Training Program. Other productions are all-student work—some outstanding, others less so; inform yourself before you go. Performances are at four theaters on campus. *uwdrama@u.washington.edu; depts.washington.edu/uwdrama; map:FF6.* ♿

Village Theatre

FRANCIS J. GAUDETTE THEATRE, 303 FRONT ST N, ISSAQUAH; 425/392-2202 OR 866/688-8849; EVERETT PERFORMING ARTS CENTER, 2710 WETMORE AVE, EVERETT; 425/257-8600 OR 888/257-3722

The Village is all about entertaining audiences, and they do a remarkably good job of it with a surefire season of classic American comedies and, above all, musicals. The theater has a strong development department dedicated to new musicals, which are workshopped and often make their world premiere at the Village. For lovers of this particular sort of theater, it's worth the trip out to Issaquah (also with performances at the Everett Performing Arts Center). *villagetheatre.org.* ♿

Classical Music and Opera

Classical music has a healthy following in Seattle, with a nationally renowned symphony and opera, and strong local support for chamber music. Excellent early music and choral music groups abound, and several musicians of national and international reputation make their home here and share their musical expertise generously. Seattle is also a regular tour stop for major performers.

Early Music Guild

VARIOUS VENUES; 206/325-7066

Early Music Guild's popular, historically informed International Series comprises five concerts of medieval, Renaissance, baroque, or other classical music, and features top international ensembles. EMG also gives concert assistance to many early-music performers in the area. *emg@earlymusicguild.org; earlymusicguild.org.*

Gallery Concerts

VARIOUS VENUES; 206/726-6088

This plucky group performs baroque and other classical music on period instruments in a variety of intimate spaces. Concerts typically feature heavy-hitters such as Vivaldi, Bach, and Mozart, but include some lesser-known surprises as well. *info@galleryconcerts.org; galleryconcerts.org.*

Mostly Nordic Chamber Music Series and Smorgasbord

NORDIC HERITAGE MUSEUM, 3014 NW 67TH ST, BALLARD; 206/789-5707

Mostly Nordic presents five concerts per season, one for each of the Scandinavian countries. Contemporary and classical chamber music from Denmark, Finland, Iceland, Norway, and Sweden is performed by local (and occasionally Scandinavian) musicians, and is followed by an authentic smorgasbord. *nordic@nordicmuseum.org; nordicmuseum.com; map:EE9.* ♿

Northwest Mahler Festival

MEANY THEATER, UNIVERSITY OF WASHINGTON, UNIVERSITY DISTRICT; 425/591-5329

During the summer, when amateur orchestra players around Seattle are looking for something to do outside of the regular performance season, they band together to play several Mahler symphonies by Mahler and other Late Romantic compositions that require big, noisy orchestras. *info@nwmahlerfestival.org; nwmahlerfestival.org; map:FF6.* ♿

Seattle Baroque

VARIOUS VENUES; 206/322-3118

Seattle Baroque has been winning critical praise since its founding in 1994, scoring broadcasts on public radio and recording several acclaimed CDs. It presents five concerts, presented between fall and spring, most frequently downtown at Benaroya Hall. *info@seattlebaroque.org; seattlebaroque.org.*

Seattle Chamber Music Society

VARIOUS VENUES; 206/283-8710

Seattle Chamber Music Society presents a popular monthlong series in July that showcases local and international talent, another festival in August, and a brief Winter Interlude in January at Benaroya Hall. The performances, which feature the performers' own choices (and often are rarely heard pieces), are spirited, oftentimes exceptional, and almost always sold out. *info@seattlechambermusic.org; scmf.org.*

Seattle Chamber Players

VARIOUS VENUES; 206/286-5052

This group, comprised of flute, clarinet, violin, and cello players, often welcomes guests and soloists to perform chamber music of the 20th and 21st centuries (the latter being newly commissioned works). The players approach the series of six to eight concerts with style, imagination, and occasional humor (a piece entitled "Dead Elvis" featured a hip-swiveling bassoonist). *scp@seattlechamberplayers.org; seattlechamberplayers.org.*

Seattle Men's Chorus

VARIOUS VENUES; 206/388-1400

The Seattle Men's Chorus charms audiences with about 30 appearances a year at local events, plus a subscription series of five concerts: an always-sold-out, family-fun holiday concert in December; a popular-music spectacular during Pride Week in the summer; and three additional performances that vary in content. *info@seattlemenschorus.org; seattlemenschorus.org.*

Seattle Opera

MARION OLIVER MCCAW HALL, SEATTLE CENTER;
206/389-7676 OR 800/426-1619

Seattle Opera made its name with the Wagner's Ring Cycle, but executive director Speight Jenkins, now on the job for more than two decades, doesn't confine himself to Wagner or any other single composer when choosing a season. He's shown himself particularly adept in at programming seasons that mix up the classical canon with more obscure works and, providing a home for commissioned work, such as Amelia, a new American opera. Typical season highlights might include Puccini's *La bohème* or *Tosca*, Wagner's *The Flying Dutchman*, or Leoncavallo's *Pagliacci*. When the *Ring* comes around every six years, though, it's still a major event; tickets generally sell out a year in advance. *seattleopera.org; map:B5.* ♿

Seattle Symphony

BENAROYA HALL, 200 UNIVERSITY ST, DOWNTOWN; 206/215-4747 OR 866/833-4747

Now more than 100 years old, the Seattle Symphony is one of the most vital and stimulating orchestras in the nation, with an impressive track record of supporting classical works by contemporary composers with the help of its composer-in-residence program. As well as its numerous concerts under long-time maestro Gerard Schwarz, the orchestra performs shorter series packaged for every kind of music lover: from pops and light classics to baroque and performances for children. *info@seattlesymphony.org; seattlesymphony.org; map:K7.* ♿

Seattle Youth Symphony Orchestras

VARIOUS VENUES; 206/362-2300

A wealth of talented local musicians have made ours the largest youth symphony in the country, giving three dazzling concerts, plus a benefit performance, during the winter season. Five feeder orchestras train a large number of younger musicians and perform during the summer. *boxoffice@syso.org; syso.org.*

UW International Chamber Music Series
UW President's Piano Series
UW World Music and Theatre Series

MEANY THEATER, UNIVERSITY OF WASHINGTON, UNIVERSITY DISTRICT; 206/543-4880 OR 800/859-5342

The University of Washington's Meany Theater is home to three excellent music series. The popular six-concert International Chamber Music Series features the best of the nation's chamber music ensembles (and an occasional group from abroad), with an emphasis on string quartets and trios. The President's Piano Series attracts pianists of international stature, and the fascinating World Music and Theatre Series features seven famous ethnic performing arts groups from around the world. *ticket@u.washington.edu; meany.org; map:FF6.* ♿

Dance

No longer home to such dance icons as Merce Cunningham, Trisha Brown, and Mark Morris, Seattle has nonetheless become a great place to catch homegrown choreographers, including Pat Graney, Amii LeGendre, Crispin Spaeth, K. T. Niehoff, Wade Madsen, and the Maureen Whiting Company. The best way to see these local superstars at work is to attend On the Boards' popular Northwest New Works Festival. Check out local listings for recitals staged around town, particularly in two popular venues: **VELOCITY DANCE CENTER** (915 E Pine St, Ste 200, Capitol Hill; 206/325-8773; info@velocitydancecenter.org; velocitydancecenter.org; map:HH7) and **BROADWAY PERFORMANCE HALL** (1625 Broadway, Capitol

Hill; 206/325-3113; broadwayperfhall.com; map:HH7). Velocity offers regular classes and is the center of the younger dance community, while the Performance Hall is favored by self-producing companies for its professional facilities.

On the Boards

BEHNKE CENTER FOR CONTEMPORARY PERFORMANCE, 100 W ROY ST, QUEEN ANNE; 206/217-9888

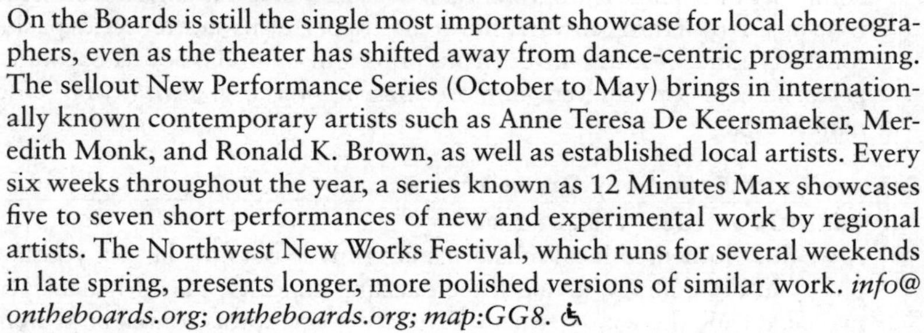

On the Boards is still the single most important showcase for local choreographers, even as the theater has shifted away from dance-centric programming. The sellout New Performance Series (October to May) brings in internationally known contemporary artists such as Anne Teresa De Keersmaeker, Meredith Monk, and Ronald K. Brown, as well as established local artists. Every six weeks throughout the year, a series known as 12 Minutes Max showcases five to seven short performances of new and experimental work by regional artists. The Northwest New Works Festival, which runs for several weekends in late spring, presents longer, more polished versions of similar work. *info@ontheboards.org; ontheboards.org; map:GG8.* ♿

Pacific Northwest Ballet

MARION OLIVER MCCAW HALL, SEATTLE CENTER; 206/441-2424

Artistic director Peter Boal, who took the reins from renowned former directors Kent Stowell and Francia Russell in 2005, has been working to make stronger connections to local artists and showcase work that is less conventional. PNB still mounts a five-show season that features large-scale classical works and story ballets, but with more contemporary offerings by the likes of David Parsons, Christopher Wheeldon, William Forsythe, and Twyla Tharpe. PNB's annual *Nutcracker* is a season favorite, with stunning Maurice Sendak sets and top-quality performances. *tickets@pnb.org; pnb.org; map:B5.* ♿

Spectrum Dance Theater

800 LAKE WASHINGTON BLVD, MADRONA (AND VARIOUS VENUES); 206/325-4161

Spectrum Dance Theater is composed of a professional dance company, a school for students as young as one, and community outreach programs. In 2005, its dance company became the resident dance group of the Moore Theatre, and it often partners with local arts organizations such as the 5th Avenue Theatre and Seattle Opera. Performances are family friendly, and often feature the work of artistic director Donald Byrd. *staff@spectrumdance.org; spectrumdance.org; map:HH6.*

UW World Dance Series

MEANY THEATER, UNIVERSITY OF WASHINGTON, UNIVERSITY DISTRICT; 206/543-4880 OR 800/859-5342

Six international dance groups come to town every year as part of Meany Theater's World Dance Series. The October-through-May series almost always includes such tried-and-true top draws as the Merce Cunningham

Dance Company, the Alvin Ailey American Dance Theater, and Seattle-choreographer-done-good Mark Morris's Dance Group, as well as several non-Western dance groups are usually featured, too, to maintain the promise of "world" music. *ticket@u.washington.edu; uwworldseries.org; map:FF6.* ♿

Film

There was a brief period when Hollywood producers put Seattle on the film-making map, but those days have passed now that big-budget film crews have discovered economically friendly Vancouver BC. But while Seattle is no longer a major movie-making town, it is quite definitely a movie-loving town, as well as a burgeoning mecca for young filmmakers and video artists.

One venue popular with that growing crowd is the well-established **911 MEDIA ARTS CENTER** (402 9th Ave N, South Lake Union; 206/682-6552; 911media.org; map:E3), an independent film and video school that maintains a busy schedule of documentaries and experimental work, as well as open screenings where anyone can show work in progress to an opinionated audience. **NORTHWEST FILM FORUM** (1515 12th Ave, Capitol Hill; 206/329-2629; nwfilmforum.org; map:GG6) is a nonprofit center that offers classes and equipment rentals to local filmmakers, has a venue for films showings, and also operates the **GRAND ILLUSION CINEMA** (1403 NE 50th St, University District; 206/523-3935; grandillusioncinema.org; map:EE6). These venues feature not only local artists, but also regular programs of little-shown underground, avant-garde, foreign, and just plain unclassifiable films.

Mid-May through mid-June, movie lovers go wild for the **SEATTLE INTERNATIONAL FILM FESTIVAL** (various venues; 206/324-9996; boxoffice@seattlefilm.org; seattlefilm.org), now more than 30 years old and one of the biggest movie fests in the country. SIFF also sponsors activities year-round, including the outstanding Women in Cinema Film Festival, which usually takes place in January; Talking Pictures, a series of movies screened with an après-film discussion hosted by critics and directors; and the Screenwriters Salon series, which presents panel discussions and staged script readings at 911 Media Arts Center, with the participation of noted local actors. In March 2007, SIFF opened a new state-of-the art theater at Seattle Center, installing cutting-edge cinema technology to refashion the Nesholm Family Lecture Hall of McCaw Hall, giving SIFF its first non-nomadic film house with the promise of a year-round cinema space.

Curated for more than 30 years by the Seattle Art Museum film department's founder, Greg Olson, the quarterly **SEATTLE ART MUSEUM FILM SERIES** (100 University St, Downtown; 206/654-3100; seattleartmuseum.org/calendar/calendar.asp; map:K7) usually focuses on the work of a renowned actor or director (Cary Grant, Billy Wilder) or on a theme such as French comedy or American film noir. Frequent short programs are featured as well: a few weekends of Yasujiro Ozu, an evening of David Lynch, an afternoon with of Marcel Pagnol. For less polished surroundings, the **FREMONT OUTDOOR FILM FESTIVAL** (3400 Phinney Ave N; 206/781-4230; fremontoutdoormovies.com; map:FF7) screens a purposefully odd mix of flicks, from *Fight Club* to *Casablanca*, in a parking lot across from the old

Trolleyman Pub on North 45th Street. Bring your own seating—movie-themed costume optional.

BEST PLACE
TO FIND A BOOK ON FILM?

"Cinema Books, the small and venerable bookshop run for decades by Stephanie Ogle. Not only does it involve two things I love—books and movies—it has crammed shelves with books spilling out in every direction. Just the way a bookstore should be."

Robert Horton, film critic, The Everett Daily Herald *and KUOW*

At last tally, Seattle was also home to a Polish film festival, a Jewish film festival, a lesbian and gay film festival, an Asian American film festival, a Scandinavian film festival, a human rights film festival, an Arab film festival, an Irish film festival, a couple of different children's film festivals, a short-film film festival . . . well, you get the idea. Check the arts listings in local publications to find out what's playing this week.

In between festivals, film nuts have plenty of year-round viewing options, too. The city boasts a venue—from old movie houses with creaky character and smaller independent theaters to a good number of multiplexes—sure to fit nearly every genre of film fancier. First-run multiplexes include downtown's **MERIDIAN 16** (1502 7th Ave; 206/622-2434; map:J4) and the **PACIFIC PLACE 11** (600 Pine St; 206/652-2404; map:I4) in the Pacific Place shopping center.

The mini-chain **LANDMARK THEATRES** (landmark-theaters.com), which makes its living serving up a mix of select Hollywood films and foreign releases, operates an eclectic collection of theaters throughout the city. The **METRO CINEMAS** (4500 9th St Ave NE, University District; 206/781-5755; map:FF6) offers films on several screens. Capitol Hill's **HARVARD EXIT** (807 E Roy St; 206/781-5755; map:GG6), with its huge lobby and stately air, was founded ages ago by a pair of eccentric film fans. Also on Capitol Hill is the **EGYPTIAN** (805 E Pine St; 206/781-5755; map:GG6), once a Masonic temple. The **GUILD 45TH** (2115 N 45th St, Wallingford; 206/781-5755; map:FF7) is actually two neighboring theaters. The intimate, dreamy **SEVEN GABLES** (911 NE 50th St, University District; 206/781-5755; map:FF6) makes for a very pleasant experience. Also in the U District, you'll find the single-screen **NEPTUNE** (1303 NE 45th St; 206/781-5755; map:FF6) and the three-screen **VARSITY** (4329 University Wy NE; 206/781-5755; map:FF6), where one of the screens offers a repertory of one-night double features of classic and cult movies. In the far north, head to Shoreline for the **CREST** (16505 5th Ave NE, Shoreline; 206/781-5755; map:BB7), where second-run movies are screened at bargain prices ($3 for all shows).

The best place to see first-run movies, as well as occasional revivals of special-effects classics, is on the giant screen of **CINERAMA** (2100 4th Ave, Belltown; 206/441-3080; seattlecinerama.com; map:G6). Local Microsoft mogul Paul Allen bought the landmark movie house in 1998 to screen both 35- and 70-millimeter films and stocked it with state-of-the-art digital sound equipment, a digital projection system (ready for Hollywood's first digital movie), and innovative assistance tools for both blind and deaf moviegoers.

Retro charm is the selling point of Ballard's movie house, the **MAJESTIC BAY THEATRE** (2044 NW Market St, Ballard; 206/781-2229; majesticbay.com; map: FF8), a three-screen gem filled with character—nautical themes in the lobby evoke Ballard's fishy history—and buoyed by digital sound and comfy chairs. Want to see the latest output of Bollywood (as Bombay's cinema is affectionately known)? Cruise down to Kirkland's **TOTEM LAKE CINEMA** (12232 Totem Lake Wy, Kirkland; 425/820-5929; roxycinema.com; map:NN3), which screens first-run Indian movies. The movies are in Hindi, without subtitles; you'll do fine if you just stick to the madcap musical comedies, where the plots are rather obvious and the song-and-dance numbers quite a spectacle.

Literary

A report in 2005 crowned Seattle the nation's most literate city, citing our access to and use of the Internet, as well as our library resources and number of bookstores. But Seattle had become an enclave for the well-read long before that, even claiming a "celebrity" librarian, Nancy Pearl, with her own action figure, a slew of popular books, and a trail of national press clippings. Besides the aforementioned Nancy Pearl shushing librarian action figure (available at local fun shop Archie McPhee), the Puget Sound area is home to a diverse universe of writers, including Ivan Doig, Sherman Alexie, Neal Stephenson, Rebecca Brown, J. A. Jance, and Englishman-turned-Seattleite Jonathan Raban. Touring writers have made Seattle a mandatory stop on the book circuit, and local institution Elliott Bay Book Company practically invented the notion of the author tour. For better or for worse, Seattle-based Amazon.com introduced the world to online bookselling. Naturally, this city of book lovers has page upon page of literary events on offer throughout the year.

ELLIOTT BAY BOOK COMPANY has probably the city's best-known reading series (see listing below). However, a multitude of other Seattle and Eastside bookstores (see Books, Newspapers, and Periodicals in the Shopping chapter) also vie for visiting authors. Among the heavyweights are the **UNIVERSITY BOOK STORE** (4326 University Wy NE, University District; 206/634-3400; ubsbooks@u.washington.edu; bookstore.washington.edu; map:FF6) and Lake Forest Park Towne Centre's **THIRD PLACE BOOKS** (17171 Bothell Wy NE [Lake Forest Park Towne Centre], Lake Forest Park; 206/366-3333; thirdplacebooks.com; map:BB5).

Scores of coffeehouses, cafés, and bars are host to open mikes, poetry slams, and oddball literary happenings. Open-mike poetry generally ranges from rotten to mildly interesting, while the slam scene is either a kick in the pants or a desperate, alcohol-fueled battle of bellowing between audience and performer. The **GLOBE CAFE** (1531 14th Ave, Capitol Hill; 206/324-8815; map:GG6) is home to the granddaddy of the recited poetry scene: Red Sky Poetry Theater, which has been around for more than two decades and features a group of older poets who gather to perform on Sunday night. The Globe's Salon Poetry Series on Tuesday night appeals to the Hill's younger set. At the Northeast Branch of the **SEATTLE PUBLIC LIBRARY** (6801 35th Ave NE, Ravenna; 206/684-7539; spl.org; map:EE6) the long-running **IT'S ABOUT TIME WRITERS' READING SERIES** (206/527-8875; itsaboutimewriters.homestead.com) allows poets and writers of all experience levels to read from their work every second Thursday evening of the month. After trying on various locations over the years, the **SEATTLE POETRY SLAM** (poetry festival.org/slam) now resides at Fremont's ToST lounge on Tuesdays at 8pm (513 N 36th St; 206/547-0240).

Bumbershoot Literary Arts

NORTHWEST ROOMS, SEATTLE CENTER; 206/281-8111

The Bumbershoot arts festival held over Labor Day weekend offers an impressive literary arts program packed with readings, performances, poetry slams, and panel discussions involving world-class authors. The festival's long-running Bookfair boasts the largest West Coast concentration of small presses, which come from around the country to promote and sell their collections of fiction, poetry, nonfiction, hand-set letterpress books, and zines. *info@onereel.org; bumbershoot.org; map:C6.* ♿

Elliott Bay Book Company Reading Series

101 S MAIN ST, PIONEER SQUARE; 206/624-6600 OR 800/962-5311

Elliott Bay Books is a local literary landmark with a well-deserved national reputation for spotting talent: Amy Tan gave one of her first public readings here, as did Sherman Alexie. Elliott Bay's daily reading series annually brings more than 600 authors of national caliber into the cozy brick-walled cavern of the store's basement reading room each year. The bulk of the offerings are free; on rare occasions, typically for special benefit events (or big, big names) tickets cost $5–$10. *elliottbaybook.com; map:O8.*

Richard Hugo House Events

1634 11TH AVE, CAPITOL HILL; 206/322-7030

Named in honor of the late Seattle poet Richard Hugo, this writers' resource center on Capitol Hill offers writing classes, readings, book groups, screenwriters' salons, and other literary programs. Hugo House also maintains a busy schedule of its own events and hosts other arts organizations, including the Stage Fright open mike series for teenagers, held every other Wednesday night. Hugo House's biggest event, the Annual Inquiry symposium, takes place over three days in October and features a full schedule of readings and writers' panels centered around a common theme. Most events are free or low cost. *welcome@hugohouse.org; hugohouse.org; map:HH6.*

Seattle Arts & Lectures

BENAROYA HALL, 200 UNIVERSITY ST, DOWNTOWN; 206/621-2230

At the top of the local literary food chain is this evening lecture series, which runs fall through spring. Whether it be an evening of witty exchanges between a panel of top-drawer writers or strictly a solo affair, the lecturers always manage to surprise (resident writer Sherman Alexie caused a minor sensation with his assertion that writers peak at 25). The list of previous guests reads like a veritable who's who of great modern writers: Salman Rushdie, Michael Ondaatje, Margaret Atwood, Philip Roth, Toni Morrison. Oftentimes the best moments come during the postlecture audience question-and-answer period. Tickets for the seven-event series range from $40–$245; individual tickets cost $18–$23 and are half price for students, though be warned—for popular writers, they can be hard to come by. *sal@lectures.org; lectures.org; map:K7.* ♿

BEST PLACE
TO EAT BREAKFAST?

"If it's a blowout brunch, Salty's on Alki wins hands down. It is the most amazing feast you can imagine. I can't eat for a week after going there!"

Herb Weisbaum, consumer reporter, KOMO News

Seattle Poetry Festival

VARIOUS VENUES; 206/725-1650 OR 800/838-3006

The Seattle Poetry Festival is worthy of notice, bringing poets from across the nation to read in this literature-loving city and offering workshops in topics from revision to bookbinding to using the language of science. Some of the bigger names that have read at this annual festival include Heather McHugh, Christine Hume, Mary Jo Bang, Joshua Beckman and Matthew Rohrer, and G. C. Waldrep. *office@poetryfestival.org; poetryfestival.org.*

Seattle Public Library/Washington Center for the Book

CENTRAL LIBRARY, 1000 4TH AVE, DOWNTOWN; 206/386-4650

The Central Library offers a full plate of free events that include lectures, readings, storytelling, and workshops. Much of this programming happens thanks to the efforts of Nancy Pearl, the director of the Washington Center for the Book. Each year, the library and the Center for the Book undertake the ambitious Seattle Reads program (formerly named If All of Seattle Read the Same Book), in which one lucky author becomes the subject of numerous book groups, lectures, and radio discussions. *spl.org; map:J4.* ♿

Subtext Reading Series

4649 SUNNYSIDE AVE N, WALLINGFORD; 206/547-8127

At press time, Subtext was mid-move, on its way from a long history at Hugo House to a new venue, the Good Shepherd Center. A monthly showcase of local and out-of-town avant-garde poetry readings, with some really fantastic readers—some of which you may never have heard of. *subtext@speakeasy.org; speakeasy.org/~subtext//index.html; map:FF7.* ♿

NIGHTLIFE

NIGHTLIFE

Nightlife by Neighborhood

BALLARD
Conor Byrne Pub
Copper Gate
Cupcake Royale/
Vérité Coffee
DiVino
Fu Kun Wu
Hale's Brewery & Pub
Hattie's Hat
Hazlewood
King's Hardware
Mr. Spot's Chai House
Old Town Alehouse
Sunset Tavern
Tractor Tavern

BELLTOWN
Belltown Billiards
Lava Lounge
Queen City Grill
Rendezvous (Jewel
Box Theater)
Shorty's
Tula's
Two Bells Tavern
Viceroy

CAPITOL HILL
B&O Espresso
Baltic Room, The
Barça
Bauhaus Books and Coffee
Caffé Vita
Capitol Club
Century Ballroom
Cha Cha Lounge
Chop Suey
Comet Tavern
DeLuxe Bar & Grill
Dilettante
Elysian Brewing Company
Fuel Coffee
Garage
Havana
Hopvine Pub
Joe Bar
Liberty
Linda's Tavern
Neighbours
Neumos
Redwood
Remedy Teas
Roanoke Park Place
Six Arms Brewery and Pub
Smith
Top Pot Doughnuts
Victrola Coffee and Art
War Room, The
Wildrose, The

CENTRAL DISTRICT
Twilight Exit, The

CHINATOWN/ INTERNATIONAL DISTRICT
Panama Hotel Tea &
Coffee House

DENNY TRIANGLE
El Corazón
Five Point Café
Re-bar
Tini Bigs Lounge

DOWNTOWN
Brooklyn Seafood, Steak
& Oyster House
Dimitriou's Jazz Alley
Nite Lite, The
Noc Noc
Owl 'n Thistle Irish Pub
and Restaurant
Showbox at the Market
Vera Project, The
Vessel
Virginia Inn

EASTLAKE
Cafe Venus and
the marsBar
Eastlake Zoo Tavern

FIRST HILL
Fireside Room
Vito's Madison Grill

FREMONT
Ballroom in Fremont
Buckaroo Tavern, The
Pacific Inn Pub
Red Door Alehouse
Simply Desserts
ToST

GEORGETOWN
Nine Pound Hammer
Smarty Pants
Stellar Pizza and Ale

GREEN LAKE
Chocolati
Latona by Green Lake
Little Red Hen

Luau Polynesian Lounge
Tangletown
Urban Bakery, The
Zoka Coffee Roaster and Tea Company

GREENWOOD

Diva Espresso
Prost!
74th Street Ale House

MADISON PARK

Attic Alehouse & Eatery, The

MAPLE LEAF

Cooper's Alehouse

MERCER ISLAND

Roanoke Inn

PHINNEY RIDGE

El Chupacabra

PIKE PLACE MARKET

Alibi Room
Kells
Shea's Lounge

PIONEER SQUARE

Club Contour
Comedy Underground
F. X. McRory's Steak, Chop & Oyster House
Last Supper Club
Marcus' Martini Heaven
Pioneer Square Saloon
Temple Billiards
Zeitgeist Coffee

QUEEN ANNE

Caffe Ladro
Caffé Vita
El Diablo Coffee Co.
Mecca Café
Ozzie's Roadhouse
Paragon Bar and Grill
Sitting Room, The
Uptown Espresso and Bakery

RAVENNA

Duchess Tavern, The

REDMOND

Old Firehouse, The

SEATTLE CENTER

SkyCity

SODO

Elysian Fields
Showbox SoDo
Studio Seven

SOUTH LAKE UNION

Feierabend

UNIVERSITY DISTRICT

Big Time Brewery and Alehouse
Blue Moon Tavern
Café Allegro
College Inn Pub
Espresso Express
Giggles
Star Life on the Oasis

UNIVERSITY VILLAGE

Zoka Coffee Roaster and Tea Company

WALLINGFORD

Murphy's Pub
Teahouse Kuan Yin

WEDGWOOD

Fiddler's Inn
Top Pot Doughnuts

WEST SEATTLE

Revolution Coffee & Art
Skylark Café and Club
West 5 Lounge and Restaurant

Nightlife by Feature

BILLIARDS

Attic Alehouse & Eatery, The
Ballroom in Fremont
Belltown Billiards
Blue Moon Tavern
Buckaroo Tavern, The
Café Venus and the marsBar
College Inn Pub
Comet Tavern
Duchess Tavern, The
Eastlake Zoo Tavern
Garage
Linda's Tavern
Owl 'n Thistle Irish Pub and Restaurant
Pioneer Square Saloon

BALLARD RISING

While Ballard has long been home to fishermen and Scandinavians (the city's only Norwegian Independence Day parade is a testament), its nightlife is fast becoming some of the best the city has to offer. With beautiful oak-tree-lined historic Ballard Avenue as the epicenter, the neighborhood boasts music venues of multiple genres, pubs, lounges, and wine bars. It's gotten so high profile, the street even held its own Ballard-themed party at the 2007 South by Southwest music festival in Austin, Texas.

THE SUNSET TAVERN (5433 Ballard Ave NW; 206/784-4880; sunsettavern.com) is an intimate, red-hued room: the perfect place to catch both local and touring acts before they outgrow it. Rock is the primary focus, but everything from alt-country to indie pop makes an appearance now and then. Just down the street is the **TRACTOR TAVERN** (5213 Ballard Ave NW; 206/789-3599; tractortavern.com), a sturdy fixture, like its namesake, on Ballard Avenue. Most nights, the Tractor hosts live shows with roots, country, folk, and Americana leanings. After **HATTIE'S HAT**'s (5231 Ballard Ave NW; 206/784-0175; hattieshat.com) back room underwent a face-lift of sorts (slick booths and a fish tank were added), there was concern among locals that the dusty charm of the place would be lost along with the shag carpet. Not so. The spot has remained as down-home as ever. **MADAME K'S** (5327 Ballard Ave NW; 206/783-9710), nestled in a long, narrow space, is rumored to have been a brothel in the early 1900s, and the quaint restaurant is themed accordingly. Gourmet pizzas are served up alongside standard Italian fare such as lasagna. Topping everything off with an Orgasm (a gooey, house-baked chocolate chip cookie topped with a scoop of vanilla ice cream) is

Re-bar
Roanoke Inn
Temple Billiards
Twilight Exit, The
Wildrose, The

COFFEE, TEA, DESSERT

B&O Espresso
Bauhaus Books and Coffee
Cafe Allegro
Caffe Ladro
Caffé Vita
Cupcake Royale/ Vérité Coffee
Dilettante
El Diablo Coffee Co.
Espresso Express
Fuel Coffee
Joe Bar
Mr. Spot's Chai House
Panama Hotel Tea & Coffee House
Remedy Teas
Revolution Coffee & Art
Simply Desserts
Star Life on the Oasis
Teahouse Kuan Yin
Top Pot Doughnuts
Uptown Espresso and Bakery
Urban Bakery, The
Victrola Coffee and Art
Zoka Coffee Roaster and Tea Company

COMEDY

Comedy Underground
Giggles

highly recommended. **FU KUN WU** (5410 Ballard Ave; 206/706-7807), located in the back of a bustling Thai restaurant, serves up herbal cocktails, some with a one-drink maximum (those with heart problems are warned against imbibing them entirely, increasing the allure 10-fold). **CONOR BYRNE** (5140 Ballard Ave NW; 206/784-3640; conorbyrnepub.com) is heavy on Irish folk and country twang: this cozily lit corner tavern emits a cheery energetic warmth—due in part to the music that rises over the din of voices. **DIVINO** wine bar (5310 Ballard Ave NW; 206/297-0143; divinoseattle.com), with its futuristic ambience, seems to fit right in, despite the contrast with most of the homey spots on the street. **HAZLEWOOD** (2311 NW Market St; 206/783-0478) is a cozy respite from the higher-foot-traffic areas, serving handcrafted cocktails in a low-lit, unassuming atmosphere. The **BALMAR** (5449 Ballard Ave NW; 206/297-0500; thebalmar.com) is another swanky addition, with two pool tables, exposed brick walls, and specialties such as steak and fries. Across the way, **MATADOR** (2221 NW Market St; 206/297-2855; matadorseattle.com) draws big crowds of weekend warrior types and touts a much-raved-about happy hour featuring delectable Southwest-style dishes for a mere $4. Old West flavor abounds at **KING'S HARDWARE** (5225 Ballard Ave NW; 206/782-0027; kingsballard.com), with taxidermy on the walls and whiskey served in jars. A menu heavy on the beef touts adventurous burgers such as the After School, topped with peanut butter and bacon. Should hunger strike after last call, **SNOOSE JUNCTION PIZZA** (2305 NW Market St; 206/789-2305; snoosejunctionpizzeria.com) has the answer (Friday and Saturday nights at least), serving up slices until 3am.

—Aja Pecknold

COUNTRY

Little Red Hen
Tractor Tavern

DANCING

Alibi Room
Ballroom in Fremont
Baltic Room, The
Century Ballroom
Chop Suey
Club Contour
Havana
Last Supper Club
Little Red Hen
Neighbours
Noc Noc
Re-bar
Showbox at the Market
Showbox SoDo
War Room, The

EDITORS' CHOICE

Alibi Room
Bauhaus Books and Coffee
El Diablo Coffee Co.
Feierabend
Fu Kun Wu
Hattie's Hat
King's Hardware
Linda's Tavern
Little Red Hen
Mecca Café
Remedy Teas
Roanoke Inn
Smith
Top Pot Doughnuts
Tractor Tavern
Vessel
Zeitgeist Coffee

FAMILY

Cupcake Royale/
Vérité Coffee
Fuel Coffee
F. X. McRory's Steak,
Chop & Oyster House
Old Firehouse, The
Old Town Alehouse
Remedy Teas
Stellar Pizza and Ale
Studio Seven
Urban Bakery, The
Vera Project, The
Victrola Coffee and Art
Zoka Coffee Roaster
and Tea Company

GAY/LESBIAN

Neighbours
Re-bar
Wildrose, The

GOOD VALUE

Attic Alehouse &
Eatery, The
Big Time Brewery
and Alehouse
College Inn Pub
Cooper's Alehouse
DeLuxe Bar & Grill
El Chupacabra
Five Point Café
King's Hardware
Mecca Café
Nitelite, The
Pacific Inn Pub
Shorty's
Six Arms Brewery and Pub
Stellar Pizza and Ale
West 5 Lounge and
Restaurant

JAZZ

Dimitriou's Jazz Alley
Fireside Room
Latona by Green Lake
Tula's

PUBS

Attic Alehouse &
Eatery, The
Big Time Brewery
and Alehouse
College Inn Pub
Conor Byrne Pub
Cooper's Alehouse
Elysian Brewing Company
Elysian Fields
Feierabend
Hale's Brewery & Pub
Hopvine Pub
Kells
Latona by Green Lake
Murphy's Pub
Old Town Alehouse
Pacific Inn Pub
Pioneer Square Saloon
Prost!
Red Door Alehouse
Roanoke Inn
Roanoke Park Place
74th Street Alehouse
Six Arms Brewery and Pub
Smith
Tangletown

ROMANTIC

Alibi Room
Baltic Room
Barça
Capitol Club
Century Ballroom
Club Contour
Copper Gate
DiVino
Fireside Room
Fu Kun Wu
Havana
Hazlewood
Joe Bar
Rendezvous (Jewel
Box Theater)
Shea's Lounge
Sitting Room, The
Tula's
Viceroy

SPORTS BARS

Attic Alehouse &
Eatery, The
Big Time Brewery
and Alehouse
Cooper's Alehouse
Duchess Tavern
Elysian Fields
F. X. McRory's Steak,
Chop & Oyster House

Music and Clubs

As one of the major hubs in the United States for touring bands and DJs of all kinds, Seattle is a city that knows—and appreciates—its live music. With so many national acts appearing in Seattle, coupled with a thriving local scene, on any given night options abound, from down and dirty garage rock to Beethoven's *5th*. And there are an equal number of quality venues and clubs at which to catch these live acts, from institutions such as the Tractor Tavern to newer, acclaimed spots like the elegant Triple Door.

While a handful listed here will shut down or change format, names, or ownership over time, the capacity for high-caliber nightlife options is certain to endure. In 2005, Seattle followed the examples of California and New York, and all Seattle establishments are now refreshingly smoke free, though a few provide outdoor areas for those who choose to light up.

For current music listings, check the local daily newspapers (weekend happenings appear on Friday), the city's alternative weeklies online or in print (*Seattle Weekly* on Wednesday; *The Stranger* on Thursday), or online entertainment guides such as NWsource (nwsource.com). And what the *New Yorker* reminds readers each week holds true in our fair city too: nightclub owners lead complicated lives; it's advisable to call ahead to confirm engagements.

Baltic Room

1207 PINE ST, CAPITOL HILL; 206/625-4444

Everything at this intimate watering hole feels ethereal, from the ever-present candles and the cloud of butterflies that hang from the ceiling to the sleek and well-dressed patrons who sip exquisite drinks at cushy booths and tables. Though the music is primarily of the DJ variety (theme nights range from dancehall to electronic to Bollywood), hip-hop acts flit through occasionally, and visiting DJs in town from more cosmopolitan scenes in London, Detroit, and Berlin often stop by for one-night stands. *MC, V; no checks; every day; full bar; thebalticroom.net; map:J2.*

Cafe Venus and the marsBar

609 EASTLAKE AVE, EASTLAKE; 206/624-4516

Cafe Venus and the marsBar attract all kinds, from suits to moped clubs to the city's studded-belt punk elite. A diverse array of local bands files across the small stage, and you're practically guaranteed to discover something your friends haven't yet heard of. Arrive early to score one of the glossy black vinyl booths. *MC, V; no checks; every day; full bar; cafevenus.com; map:F1.*

Century Ballroom

915 E PINE ST, 2ND FLOOR, CAPITOL HILL; 206/324-7263

The Century invites the occasional band to its beautiful ballroom, but it's best known for its popular dance classes: salsa and swing-dance nights (with DJs). The light, airy room provides wallflowers and sure-foots alike with one of the best places in Seattle to dance, and lessons are available several nights a week. The lesson and dance are free with the purchase of an entrée from the café. *MC, V; checks OK; Wed–Sun (hours vary according to bookings); full bar; centuryballroom.com; map:L1.*

Chop Suey

1325 E MADISON ST, CAPITOL HILL; 206/324-8000

This red-lit club is a favorite among touring and local bands alike. Decked with Chinese lanterns and an impressive dragon hanging from the ceiling, the stylized Asian-themed club hosts everything from electronic to indie rock acts along with an ample dose of the diverse local scene. *MC, V; no checks; every day; full bar; chopsuey.com; map:HH6.*

Club Contour

807 1ST AVE, PIONEER SQUARE; 206/447-7704

A polished oasis in the desert of Pioneer Square saloons, Contour is primarily a DJ dance venue, though it does occasionally book live music. It's also a place where beautiful people come to sip some of the city's best cocktails and nosh on premier bar food, and where the elegant décor rivals the attractive patrons. It's open until daybreak on Friday and Saturday nights. *AE, MC, V; no checks; every day; full bar; clubcontour.com; map:N7.*

Comedy Underground

222 S MAIN ST, PIONEER SQUARE; 206/628-0303

For 25 years, the Comedy Underground has humbly sent its patrons into fits of giggles, guffaws, and chuckles seven nights a week. Talent can be hit-or-miss—the club considers itself a training ground for new acts—but even a mere titter is worth more when it comes as part of such an enduring tradition. *AE, MC, V; local checks only; every day; full bar; comedyunderground.com; map:O8.*

BEST PLACE
TO PEOPLE-WATCH?

"The window bar at Vessel."

Thierry Rautureau, Rover's "Chef in the Hat"

Dimitriou's Jazz Alley

2033 6TH AVE, DOWNTOWN; 206/441-9729

It really is tucked into an alley, and this sexy venue is one of the best jazz clubs in the nation—not to mention the best in Seattle. Every seat affords an excellent view of international-caliber jazz musicians, as well as blues artists, Latin musicians, big bands, and local artists. Weekends are often packed, so call ahead to reserve tickets. You can guarantee yourself a seat by going early for dinner, although the food isn't nearly as good as the jazz. *AE, MC, V; checks OK; Tues–Sun; full bar; jazzalley.com; map:H5.* ♿

El Corazón

109 EASTLAKE AVE E, DENNY TRIANGLE; 206/262-0482

The walls in this place have seen a lot of rock action through the years—its days as the Off Ramp saw the grunge movement take off with bands such as Nirvana and Soundgarden; as Graceland, indie-rock leanings brought early tours by the Shins. Now remodeled and revamped yet again, El Corazón offers hard rock shows, many of which are all ages. *MC, V; no checks; every day; full bar; elcorazonseattle.com; map:H1.*

Giggles

5220 ROOSEVELT WY NE, UNIVERSITY DISTRICT; 206/526-5653

Name aside, Giggles takes itself seriously as the leading place for edgy, risqué comedy. It draws touring comedians from TV, film, and radio, and almost nothing is sacred on its stage. Like the comedy world in general, bookers seem to prefer the talents of men, though Margaret Cho has dropped in on occasion. *MC, V; no checks; Thurs–Sun; full bar; gigglescomedyclub.com; map:FF6.*

Havana

1010 E PIKE ST, CAPITOL HILL; 206/323-2822

A Cuban-themed oasis on Capitol Hill's strip of rock clubs and dive bars, Havana's potted palms and gold accents step it up a notch. The clientele revel in everything from jeans and Converse to suits and spike heels—making it feel like a place for the people. Handcrafted cocktails along with club nights ranging from alt-country DJs (the tears-in-your-beer Sad Bastard Mondays) to hipster dance parties (Tuesday's Hotel Motel) contribute to the overall vibe of leisure. *AE, MC, V; no checks; every day; full bar; havanasocial.com; map:L1.* ♿

Last Supper Club

124 S WASHINGTON ST, PIONEER SQUARE; 206/748-9975

The big attractions here are the DJs and the mind-bending digital visual effects that accompany them; the club prides itself on "seamless, flawless sets" and technical prowess. Talent is a mix of homespun DJs and occasional touring mixers (the NYC scenesters-cum-DJs MisShapes recently paid a visit), and bookings range from progressive house to trance to dancehall. *AE, DIS, MC, V; no checks; Wed–Sun; full bar; lastsupperclub.com; map:O8.* ♿

Little Red Hen

7115 WOODLAWN AVE NE, GREEN LAKE; 206/522-1168

The Little Red Hen is Seattle's only true honky-tonk. You'll find the largest collection of cowboy boots north of Wyoming ranch country seated in its brown booths and stomping round its huge dance floor. The local country bands that grace the stage are consistently excellent, including local favorites the Swains. Mondays and Tuesdays offer free country-dance lessons; Wednesday is country karaoke. *AE, DIS, MC, V; no checks; every day; full bar; littleredhen.com; map:EE7.* ♿

Neighbours

1509 BROADWAY, CAPITOL HILL; 206/324-5358

Neighbours used to have a monopoly on the gay dance scene, but in recent years similar venues have popped up like molehills in the surrounding area. Still, none spin quite the same blend of high-energy house, disco, and pop; offer such a flamboyant atmosphere; or have the same array of specialty nights. On weekends, it's an after-hours oasis where you can dance till dawn (or 4:30am, at least). *MC, V; no checks; every day; full bar; neighboursnightclub.com; map:L1.*

Neumos

925 E PIKE ST, CAPITOL HILL; 206/709-9467

A rare example of a club that's come full circle: Neumos was originally Moe's, one of Seattle's premier rock clubs in the early '90s. After a few other incarnations (such as the electronic-focused AROspace and Playland), original owner Jerry Everard stepped in and restored the club to its original roots, bringing back rock and the name (in part). Though the ownership has since changed hands again, the "neu" version of Moe's has thrived, consistently booking big-name national acts from indie to hip-hop. *MC, V; no checks; open according to bookings; full bar; neumos.com; map:L1.*

Noc Noc

1516 2ND AVE, DOWNTOWN; 206/223-1333

Part chic art bar, part progressive dance party, Noc Noc is an unpretentious, amusing place to pass an evening, on into the early-morning hours (it was voted best after-hours spot in 2006 by *Seattle Weekly*). DJs spin everything from breaks to house to hip-hop, trance, '80s, goth, and industrial. The city's bike messengers gather here en masse to exchange tips on dodging traffic. Well drinks are $1 during happy hour, which runs from 5–9pm daily. *AE, DIS, MC, V; no checks; every day; full bar; clubnocnoc.com; map:J7.*

The Old Firehouse

16510 NE 79TH ST, REDMOND; 425/556-2370

This all-ages Redmond venue has helped solidify the alternative-rock scene in Seattle's eastern suburbs. For more than a decade, it's been one of the only venues that gives teens a chance to see live bands (the CD compilation *All That Was Built Here*, on Missing Records, documented many of them). It also provides up-and-coming musicians with a place to incubate: bands such as the Blood Brothers got their start on its stage. Shows are scheduled Fridays and Saturdays, with occasional breaks; call to confirm lineups. *Cash only; Fri–Sat (hours vary according to bookings); no alcohol; theoldfirehouse.org; map:EE1.*

Owl 'n Thistle Irish Pub and Restaurant

808 POST AVE, DOWNTOWN; 206/621-7777

Weekend nights can feel a little like a frat party at this boisterous Irish pub hidden on the edge of Pioneer Square, but that's part of the fun. Bookings lean toward Celtic folk bands on weekends and a variety of other music during the week. There's also a small poolroom and a comfortable dining area up front. *AE, MC, V; no checks; every day; full bar; owlnthistle.com; map:N7.*

Paragon Bar and Grill

2125 QUEEN ANNE AVE N, QUEEN ANNE; 206/283-4548

Despite its location on the relatively sedate crown of Queen Anne Hill, the Paragon often bustles just as frantically as any downtown club, particularly on weeknights. Twenty- and thirty-somethings cluster around the long, high bar, jamming to an assortment of live bands that range from pop to singer/songwriter to swing. *AE, MC, V; no checks; every day; full bar; paragonseattle.com; map:GG8.* ♿

Re-bar

1114 HOWELL ST, DENNY TRIANGLE; 206/233-9873

The Re-bar has distinguished itself among the city's many hipster-friendly clubs by playing host to theater events, rock musicals, and performance-art events. Local DJs spin house, old-school, and soul on the off nights, and a light-footed crowd turns up to pack the dance floor. Catch KEXP DJ Riz on Fridays for an eclectic mix of deep, funky house. *AE, MC, V; no checks; open according to bookings; full bar; rebarseattle.com; map:I2.* ♿

Showbox at the Market

1426 1ST AVE, DOWNTOWN; 206/628-3151

This is the grande dame of Seattle music venues. How many clubs can say they've hosted shows by both Captain Beefheart and Pearl Jam? Since a remodel added a measure of comfort to the cavernous space, there's more dance floor, more bar space, and better sightlines, and the national talent that graces the stage is high caliber, whatever the genre may be. The Showbox also occasionally hosts all-ages shows, so even youngsters can see the inside of this institution. The Green Room, a small cocktail lounge in an adjacent space, books mainly acoustic acts. *AE, MC, V; no checks; every day; full bar; showboxonline.com; map:J7.*

Showbox SoDo

1700 1ST AVE S, SODO; 206/382-7877

Formerly the Fenix, this club was taken over in 2007 by the folks who run longtime Pike Place Market venue Showbox, which was subsequently renamed Showbox at the Market. The shiny club books national mainstream rock acts and occasionally hosts parties, local singer/songwriters, and jazz trios. *AE, MC, V; no checks; full bar; showboxonline.com; map:O8.*

Skylark Café and Club

3803 DELRIDGE WAY SW, WEST SEATTLE; 206/935-2111

Just over the West Seattle bridge in the transitional Delridge neighborhood, Skylark is a beacon for folks hankering for live rock shows. Thursday through Saturday nights find quality, up-and-coming local bands still hungry enough to put on a kick-ass show. And while the (free!) shows alone are worth the drive, Skylark's menu is also a draw, with comfort food staples such as chicken fried steak and a weekend brunch that will squash any hangover with stiff bloodies and hearty egg dishes. *MC, V; no checks; every day; full bar; skylarkcafe.com; map:JJ8.*

Studio Seven

110 S HORTON ST, SODO; 206/286-1312

For years, Seattle's all-ages club scene struggled under a restrictive law that forbade kids from dancing in venues that sold alcohol. Studio Seven (which doubles as a recording studio and practice space) is the first attempt at consistently mixing the two (bar available with ID) since the law was lifted in 2002, and so far, it's been a thriving success. The music here is generally loud and hardcore, so if you're worried about early hearing loss, bring your earplugs. *Cash only; open according to bookings; beer and wine; studioseven.us; map:II7.*

Sunset Tavern

5433 BALLARD AVE NW, BALLARD; 206/784-4880

The low ceiling and close quarters at this Ballard dive can be off putting for those not well versed in rock show etiquette. But if you can survive the body heat and jostling crowd, you'll be rewarded with a diverse selection of live music from local and touring acts. Bookings lean toward rock and punk, but country and metal have been known to rear up occasionally. *MC, V; no checks; every day; beer and wine; www.sunsettavern.com; map:FF8.*

ToST

513 N 36TH ST, FREMONT; 206/547-0240

People flock to ToST (pronounced "toast") for its consistent attempts to provide a diverse selection of musical entertainment, unlike other Fremont hot spots. This unassuming space hosts some of the city's finest hipster troubadours seven nights a week. A generous selection of wines by the glass makes for a mellow, intimate evening. *AE, MC, V; no checks; every day; full bar; tostlounge.com; map:FF8.* ♿

Tractor Tavern

5213 BALLARD AVE NW, BALLARD; 206/789-3599

Almost everyone onstage at the Tractor has that windblown look of alternative country—and so do many members of the audience. It's one of the few clubs in Seattle where you can wear cowboy boots, a plaid shirt, and Levi's and fit in. The booking is consistently excellent (rock, rockabilly, bluegrass, Celtic, and folk are featured in addition to alt-country), and the venue itself is intimate without being claustrophobic. *MC, V; no checks; every day (hours vary according to bookings); full bar; tractortavern.citysearch.com; map:FF8.*

Tula's

2214 2ND AVE, BELLTOWN; 206/443-4221

Tula's has quietly grown into a noted jazz club—it even made *Down Beat* magazine's International Jazz Club guide's top 100. Bookings are mostly local musicians, but the jam sessions attract top-rate talent—the legendary Wynton Marsalis has been known to stop by while in town—and it's a great room for music. *MC, V; no checks; every day; full bar; tulas.com; map:G7.*

The Vera Project

SEATTLE CENTER, DOWNTOWN; 206/956-8372

It's one of the seminal all-ages clubs in the city, and in 2007 Vera graduated into a permanent home at the Seattle Center. As much community organization and teen center as it is rock club, with a beautiful new space, the Vera Project will continue to be the all-ages epicenter it's been for years, hopefully long into the future. Kids from all over the area come out as volunteers and run all aspects of the shows—from taking money at the door to providing security to running sound. *Cash only; open according to bookings; no alcohol; theveraproject.org; map:I6.*

The War Room

722 E PIKE ST, CAPITOL HILL; 206/328-7666

This two-story cedar-paneled club on Capitol Hill has diversified since its previous incarnations (Mr. Paddywhacks and Blu were gay clubs). The War Room offers gay dance nights, along with additional fare such as '80s nights, drum and bass, and hip-hop. Inside, hardwood floors, spacious black leather booths, and artwork by Shepard Fairey provide clubgoers with a swank atmosphere. It's home to two of the longest-running club nights in the city: Saturday's Yo Son! hip-hop dance party and the 360 BPM crew's Drum and Bass Tuesdays. *AE, MC, V; no checks; every day; full bar; warroomseattle.com; map:K1.*

Bars, Pubs, and Taverns

Alibi Room

85 PIKE PL, PIKE PLACE MARKET; 206/623-3180

Opened by local Hollywood types (including the ubiquitous Tom Skerritt), the Alibi was conceived as a watering hole for Seattle's burgeoning film set. Unfortunately, that set is fairly small and nowhere to be seen, so the Alibi Room has become a general-purpose bar for a cross-section of Seattleites. The concrete floored basement feels like a secret room, though it gets packed on weekends with DJs spinning everything from hip-hop to house. *DIS, MC, V; no checks; every day; full bar; seattlealibi.com; map:J7.*

The Attic Alehouse & Eatery

4226 E MADISON ST, MADISON PARK; 206/323-3131

The Attic is a friendly neighborhood bar with all the typical accoutrements—darts, pool, comfy booths, and a sizeable collection of draft beers, of both the micro and macro varieties. Like the surrounding Madison Park neighborhood, the bar's constituency seems to straddle the line between rowdy college kids and middle-aged yuppies out for a night away from the kids. *AE, MC, V; checks OK; every day; beer and wine; atticalehouse.com; map:GG6.*

Ballroom in Fremont

456 N 36TH ST, FREMONT; 206/634-2575
This funky club has become one of Fremont's hottest spots for both co-eds and recent graduates. On a good night, entry lines snake out onto the sidewalk, and the boisterous crowd can be heard blocks away. There are nine pool tables, but most people seem more interested in dancing and chatting on the wide patio complete with fireplace. *MC, V; no checks; every day; full bar; fremontballroom.com; map:FF8.* ♿

Barça

1510 11TH AVE, CAPITOL HILL; 206/325-8263
With its outrageous, carnival-like Saturday nights and tasteful European décor, Barça is the Seattle equivalent of a Barcelona bar during the raging months of summer. A diverse crowd gathers to indulge in tasty bar food, a separate vodka bar, and superb service. It's fascinating to watch the servers maneuver through the tightly packed crowd while bearing enormous platters of fine liquor, never spilling a drop. *MC, V; no checks; every day; full bar; barcaseattle.com; map:L1.* ♿

BEST PLACE
TO SAMPLE A MICROBREW OR THREE?

"The Blue Moon Tavern, because a couple of Redhooks in such a genuinely bohemian atmosphere can easily evolve into a metaphysical adventure."

Tom Robbins, author

Belltown Billiards

90 BLANCHARD ST, BELLTOWN; 206/448-6779
Belltown Billiards is a mishmash—part high-tech bar and dance floor, part high-class pool hall, part high-gloss Italian restaurant—but everyone is having too much fun to mind the confusion. The food takes a backseat on weekend nights, when the crowds descend and turn pool into a true spectator sport. *AE, MC, V; no checks; every day; full bar; belltownbilliards.net; map:H7.* ♿

Big Time Brewery and Alehouse

4133 UNIVERSITY WY NE, UNIVERSITY DISTRICT; 206/545-4509
Antique beer ads clutter the walls at the U District's most popular alehouse, where the tasty brews are made on the other side of the wall. Students are the prime clientele, though occasional packs of university faculty can be spotted at the hefty wooden tables, discussing literature or politics over a

pitcher of hand-crafted beer. *MC, V; no checks; every day; beer and wine; bigtimebrewery.com; map:FF6.* ♿

Blue Moon Tavern

712 NE 45TH ST, UNIVERSITY DISTRICT; 206/633-6267

When this seedy lair of legends appeared to be in the path of the wrecking ball, a cry of protest went up, books on its shady history were quickly printed, and demonstrations were organized. A yearlong battle with developers produced a 40-year lease and a collective sigh of relief from the neighborhood pool players, poets, and survivors of the U District's glory days. Tom Robbins put in his time in this crusty joint, and no wonder—the graffiti-covered booths are filled with strange characters who seem to be in search of a novel. Blue Moon funds the literary journal *Point No Point* and holds an annual poetry and fiction contest. *Cash only; every day; beer and wine; bluemoonseattle.blogspot.com; map:FF6.*

Brooklyn Seafood, Steak & Oyster House

1212 2ND AVE, DOWNTOWN; 206/224-7000

If you're looking to meet a lawyer, this is the place: after work, the Brooklyn crawls with suits. On summer weekends, tourists replace attorneys, ooh-ing and aahing at the fresh oyster selection. There's plenty of seating at the wraparound bar, which serves a reasonably priced happy hour menu all day and night—and a good choice of beers, although this is more of a single-malt Scotch crowd. *AE, DIS, MC, V; checks OK; every day; full bar; thebrooklyn.com; map:M7.* ♿

The Buckaroo Tavern

4201 FREMONT AVE N, FREMONT; 206/634-3161

The Buckaroo may have cashed in on its reputation as a grizzly biker bar in the movie *Ten Things I Hate About You*, but celebrity stardom hasn't gone to its head. It really is the city's biker bar, and rows of Harleys are perpetually parked out front. If you have a laptop, leave it at home—the Buckaroo doesn't look kindly on nerdy types, but give them seven days' notice, and they'll give you a cake on your birthday. Free popcorn too! *No credit cards; checks OK; every day; beer and wine; buckarootavern.com; map:FF8.*

Capitol Club

414 E PINE ST, CAPITOL HILL; 206/325-2149

While the mostly young urban professional crowd rubs elbows on the outdoor terrace, serious Capitol Club patrons would be wise to sprawl out on the luxurious benches and embroidered pillows that line the walls of this Moroccan-themed bar. Adventurous drinkers should steer toward the lavish house drinks, which come laced with extravagances such as coconut milk and pomegranate molasses. *AE, MC, V; no checks; every day; full bar; thecapitolclub.net; map:K2.*

Cha Cha Lounge

1013 E PIKE ST, CAPITOL HILL; 206/329-1101

An institution and epicenter for Seattle's rock set (employees have included members of Murder City Devils, Band of Horses, and the Fastbacks), the Cha Cha Lounge was forced out of its original home on Pine Street to make way for condos in 2007. Luckily, it reopened a few blocks away on Pike with a similar red-hued, kitsch-filled, tiki-themed basement bar and a revamped Bimbo's Cantina above. Unfortunately for the kids, the restaurant is now 21-and-over only, but at least it will still be there when they're legal! *MC, V; no checks; every day; full bar; chachalounge.com; map:L1.*

College Inn Pub

4006 UNIVERSITY WY NE, UNIVERSITY DISTRICT; 206/634-2307

You won't find stuck-up intellectuals lingering in the burnished wood booths at the College Inn; this convenient gathering place for university students attracts a low-key crowd. Food is typical pub fare (nachos, sandwiches), and the expansive selection of microbrews on tap and in bottles will help if the conversation turns to postmodernism. *MC, V; no checks; every day; full bar; map:FF6.*

Comet Tavern

922 E PIKE ST, CAPITOL HILL; 206/323-9853

After a recent change of ownership, folks worried that this beloved watering hole (it even made *Maxim*'s top 10 list of dive bars in the country) would lose its down and dirty appeal. Fears were unfounded, however: it's still one of the city's most unpretentious spots. Welcome additions have occurred in the form of a fresh coat of paint, hard liquor, and fantastic live rock shows each week. The heavy wood furniture is still etched and carved by hundreds of hands, and graffiti written by or about one of Seattle's local literary legends remains. *MC, V; no checks; every day; full bar; map:L1.*

Conor Byrne Pub

5140 BALLARD AVE NW, BALLARD; 206/784-3640

Conor Byrne's differentiates itself from the rest of Ballard's pubs by providing an elegant, old-world charm. Giant chandeliers swing lightly above the burnished wood bar, and the exposed brick walls feature local art. The stage generally hosts mellow acoustic folk, traditional Irish music, and various forms of country. *MC, V; checks OK; every day; beer and wine; conorbyrnepub.com; map:FF8.*

Cooper's Alehouse

8065 LAKE CITY WY NE, MAPLE LEAF; 206/522-2923

A mecca for serious brew lovers and home to postgame soccer and rugby bacchanals, this neighborhood pub aims to please in a no-nonsense manner. Patrons can opt for darts or sports on TV, but beer's the main thing, and Cooper's offers 22 taps, most of them dispensing Northwest microbrews. They even hold an IPA fest every year. *MC, V; no checks; every day; full bar; coopersalehouse.com; map:DD6.*

Copper Gate

6301 24TH AVE NW, BALLARD; 206/706-3292

This hot spot oozes Scandinavia, which makes it right at home in Ballard. The bar is beautifully crafted into the bow of a ship (a Viking homage perhaps?), and backlit black-and-white images of fair-haired beauties line the walls. Be warned, most are sans clothing! *MC, V; no checks; every day; full bar; thecoppergate.com; map:EE8.*

DeLuxe Bar & Grill

625 BROADWAY E, CAPITOL HILL; 206/324-9697

The time-honored DeLuxe is where Broadway's most mainstream boulevardiers go for stuffed baked potatoes and electric iced teas. The bar is often crammed, although the retractable wall in front lets you sit on the sidewalk in nice weather and watch the steady stream of passersby. Come early on Wednesdays to snag a table for the ever-popular burger night—$5 will get you more than enough beef in your belly. *AE, DIS, MC, V; no checks; every day; full bar; map:GG7.* ♿

DiVino

5310 BALLARD AVE NW, BALLARD; 206/297-0143

While it seems to be a feat for folks to remember the name of this Ballard Avenue wine bar, the interior is tough to forget. An oft-heard descriptive is "that *Clockwork Orange*–looking bar"—and there's a reason. With its white furniture and minimalist modern décor, the place would fit seamlessly into the film, but with less gore, more grape. *MC, V; no checks; every day; full bar; map:GG7.*

The Duchess Tavern

2827 NE 55TH ST, RAVENNA; 206/527-8606

This is the kind of neighborhood tavern that former university students remember fondly decades after graduation. Today's Duchess has cleaned up its act considerably; it's more open and airy than in the past, and there are 20 beers on tap (more than half are microbrews). The darts, the pool table, and the '60s rock make it the perfect place to stop for a pitcher after the game. *AE, DIS, MC, V; no checks; every day; full bar; map:EE6.* ♿

Eastlake Zoo Tavern

2301 EASTLAKE AVE E, EASTLAKE; 206/329-3277

The Eastlake Zoo is the aging hippie of local bars, still holding tightly to its radical ideas more than three decades after opening its doors: it's a worker-run collective, and the employees have placed an empty water jug on the counter to collect money for the food bank. Along with a solid collection of beer and wine, the bar offers cheap pool, pinball, darts, shuffleboard, and plenty of smoke-stained history on its walls. Sit at the bar and you may get an earful of Marxist commentary. *Cash only; every day; beer and wine; eastlakezoo.com; map:GG7.*

El Chupacabra

6711 GREENWOOD AVE N, PHINNEY RIDGE; 206/706-4889

Named for a mythical Mexican vampirelike creature, El Chupacabra, or "goat sucker" in Spanish, is a like a fiesta set in an old house atop Phinney Ridge. It turns out plates of authentic Mexican favorites such as delectably spicy pork carnitas and enchiladas that will leave you feeling satisfied but not overstuffed. The margaritas, however, pack quite a punch—tangy and stiff, perfectly shaken, and served in pint glasses. Careful though, they're as easy to suck down as goats are for the Chupacabra! *MC, V; no checks; every day; full bar; map:EE7.*

Elysian Brewing Company
Elysian Fields
Tangletown

1211 E PIKE ST, CAPITOL HILL; 206/860-1920; 542 1ST AVE S, SODO; 206/382-4498; 2106 N 55TH ST, GREEN LAKE; 206/547-5929

A low-key combination of brewpub and restaurant, the Elysian Brewing Company often doubles as a meeting place for the jeans and T-shirt Capitol Hill crowd. The grub is delicious (the steak tacos are mouthwatering and the vegan avocado curry will have even carnivores drooling), and the freshly brewed beer even better. With locations in North Seattle (Tangletown) and SoDo (Elysian Fields), you'll never want for a glass of Dragonstooth Oatmeal Stout. *AE, MC, V; no checks; every day; full bar; elysianbrewing.com; map:L1, Q9, EE7.* ♿

Feierabend

422 YALE AVE N, SOUTH LAKE UNION; 206/340-2528

From the owner of popular German pubs Prost! (Phinney Ridge) and Die BierStube (Roosevelt) comes Feierabend, a new watering hole in now-trendy South Lake Union. With 18 thirst-quenching German beers on tap, a tiny patio, and hearty, inspired, Northwest-tinged German cuisine, it's a welcome addition to this burgeoning burg. The Bavarian brezel, a huge warm pretzel served with a mixture of brie, butter, onions, and paprika, just might be the city's best new snack. *AE, DIS, MC, V; no checks; every day; full bar; feierabendseattle.com; map:H1.*

Fiddler's Inn

9219 35TH AVE NE, WEDGWOOD; 206/525-0752

Nearly three quarters of a century old, the Fiddler's Inn feels like a historic space, even though it's officially not. The décor is rustic and homey, with picnic tables and a large patio. Most nights, acoustic singer/songwriters or mellow bands play live music. *MC, V; checks OK; every day; beer and wine; fiddlersinn.org; map:FF6.*

Fireside Room

900 MADISON ST (SORRENTO HOTEL), FIRST HILL; 206/622-6400

The clubby lounge in the lobby of the Sorrento evokes a leisurely world of hearthside chats in overstuffed chairs, an unrushed perusal of the daily newspaper, a hand of whist. It's most pleasant for a late-evening drink, particularly when the piano accompanies the music of many and varied conversations. On Fridays and Saturdays cozy up as live jazz plays in the background. *AE, DIS, MC, V; no checks; every day; full bar; www.hotelsorrento.com/dining-fireside.php; map:M4.*

Five Point Café

415 CEDAR ST, DENNY TRIANGLE; 206/448-9993

Stuffed fish on the wall, nuts in the chairs, rocks in the jukebox—you never know what you'll find here, except extra-strong drinks that have minimal impact on your wallet. With a friendly clientele that ranges from bluehairs and bikers to gays and Rastafarians, the place—despite its divey décor and perma-nicotined walls—gives hope that world peace may be achievable after all. *AE, MC, V; no checks; every day; full bar; map:E6.*

Fu Kun Wu

5410 BALLARD AVE NW, BALLARD; 206/706-7807

Seattle has always prided itself on being a healthy city; Fu Kun Wu takes that to the extreme (a sign over the entry reads "The Doctor Is In"). Working from a Chinese herbalist theme, this classy piano bar creates herbal cocktails designed to improve potency and stamina (some contain the African herb yohimbe). If you have no interest in improving your potency, try the Oolong-tini, a blend of tea, vodka, lemon, and sugar. *AE, DIS, MC, V; no checks; every day; full bar; map:FF8.* ♿

F. X. McRory's Steak, Chop & Oyster House

419 OCCIDENTAL AVE S, PIONEER SQUARE; 206/623-4800

Visiting F. X. McRory's without having just come from a baseball or football game is like eating kielbasa without sauerkraut: still tasty, but lacking that special punch. This old-school bar offers sports fans a raucous atmosphere where they can toss out sports statistics and banter about who's being traded and for what salary. Fresh oysters and a solid beer selection complete the experience. *AE, DIS, MC, V; no checks; every day; full bar; fxmcrorys.com; map:O8.*

Garage

1130 BROADWAY E, CAPITOL HILL; 206/322-2296

The Garage leapt from ordinary pool-hall status (if you can call 18 tables ordinary) to überclub fame by adding a 14-lane bowling alley called Garage Bowl in the adjacent building—Seattle's first new alley in 40 years. Rolling balls around is a surprisingly popular activity: both sides of the club are generally packed with urban hipsters and affluent professionals. DJs spin occasionally, but don't count on live music. *AE, MC, V; no checks; every day; full bar; garagebilliards.com; map:M1.*

Hale's Brewery & Pub

4301 LEARY WY NW, BALLARD; 206/782-0737

This gleaming, spacious brewpub, a showcase for locally renowned Hale's ales, also serves as an oasis of sophistication in the Fremont-Ballard industrial neighborhood. Grab a booth or bring along enough of the gang to fill one of the long tables in the high-ceilinged back room, where live music is performed on weekend nights. At least nine varieties of Hale's pour year-round, as well as a selection of rotating seasonal varieties. *MC, V; checks OK; every day; beer and wine; halesales.com; map:FF8.* ♿

Hattie's Hat

5231 BALLARD AVE NW, BALLARD; 206/784-0175

Hattie's Hat is a Ballard institution that underwent a major renovation several years ago, with a minor refresher recently (the back room now has sleek booths and a fish tank), and now lives on as a hybrid that appeals to both young hipsters and old fishermen. The food is excellent, and the bar is lively even early in the morning. Alt-country superstar Neko Case used to work here, and, if you're lucky, you'll find someone who can tell you about those good old days. *MC, V; no checks; every day; full bar; hattieshat.com; map:FF8.*

Hazlewood

2311 NW MARKET ST, BALLARD; 206/783-0478

Just off the main drag of Ballard Avenue, this tiny two-story gem offers specialty cocktails featuring fresh juices. Owned in part by Soundgarden bassist Ben Shepherd, it's a popular spot for Seattle's rock contingent looking for a quiet night. *MC, V; checks OK; every day; full bar; map:FF8.*

Hopvine Pub

507 15TH AVE E, CAPITOL HILL; 206/328-3120

Another seedy tavern transformed into a clean pub featuring lots of microbrews. There are hop vines stenciled and sculpted on the walls, wooden booths, and tables stained in bright colors. They've grown famous for their soups (the head chef even put out his own cookbook) and offer hearty sandwiches, gourmet pizza, and occasional acoustic shows. *MC, V; no checks; every day; beer and wine; map:HH6.*

Kells

1916 POST ALLEY, PIKE PLACE MARKET; 206/728-1916

Rousing sing-alongs to live Celtic music boom throughout the large pub side of this Irish institution, while couples canoodle in the dark corners of the restaurant side, and regulars belly up to the lamplit bar. Sit near the door in the restaurant and you'll have a breathtaking view of the Olympic Mountains. *AE, MC, V; local checks only; every day; full bar; kellsirish.com; map:I7.* ♿

King's Hardware

5225 BALLARD AVE NW, BALLARD; 206/782-0027
Linda Derschang (owner of Linda's, Smith, and Viceroy) expands her empire into Ballard. The Western-themed establishment is somewhat of a Linda's outpost—the Bloody Marys are still the best in town (though they come in Mason jars, not pint glasses). Burgers are the focus—and they are worth it: try the surprisingly delicious peanut butter and bacon burger. This is also the only joint in town to offer Skee-Ball, a carnival-themed blast from the past. *MC, V; no checks; every day; full bar; kingsballard.com; map:FF8.*

Latona by Green Lake

6423 LATONA AVE NE, GREEN LAKE; 206/525-2238
The Latona is a light, woody, microbrew-and-cheese-bread-lovers' kind of place. Things can get comfortably cozy in this small space, which seems more expansive due to high ceilings. Service is extra attentive and accommodating. Most Friday and Saturday evenings, the pub hosts local jazz and folk musicians. In the summer, it's a perfect place to relax after a walk around the lake. *MC, V; local checks only; every day; beer and wine; latonabygreenlake.lbu.com; map:EE7.* ♿

Lava Lounge

2226 2ND AVE, BELLTOWN; 206/441-5660
This long, skinny Belltown bar sports a kitsch tiki-hut theme, from lava lamps to velvet paintings of bare, busty maidens. While it did without for quite a long time, spirits have been added to the menu—just don't expect to find a frou-frou cocktail menu or paper umbrellas. It's a great place to meet friends before a show at the Crocodile Cafe (see Music and Clubs above). Pinball and shuffleboard provide added amusement. *MC, V; no checks; every day; full bar; map:G7.*

Liberty

517 15TH AVE E, CAPITOL HILL; 206/323-9898
Nestled on Capitol Hill's 15th Avenue, Liberty is the perfect place for an after-work cocktail with friends or a civilized night out. The drinks are handcrafted with care using only fresh-squeezed juices, and the menu offers up—surprisingly—sushi! With rolls named for neighborhood establishments (the Sonic Boom rolls, an homage to the record store across the street, feature spicy tuna and scallops; a California roll is dubbed the Wax On, after next-door WaxOn Spa), the place is homey, comfortable, and locally focused. *MC, V; full bar; every day; libertybars.com; map:HH6.*

Linda's Tavern

707 E PINE ST, CAPITOL HILL; 206/325-1220
Linda's is a hot spot for local musicians and scenesters: on any given night, a covert business transaction seems to take place just one table over. The crowd here is a multiethnic mix of hipsters and plain folks who come to drink or play pool to the strains of alternative music blaring from the stereo, to watch films on the back porch in summer, or to listen to DJ music (Monday and

Tuesday nights). On weekends, they serve up brunch standards, including the best Bloody Mary in town—try the Cody (named after a Seattle drummer, it comes with beef jerky) if you're feeling adventurous. *MC, V; no checks; every day; full bar; map:K1.*

Luau Polynesian Lounge

2253 N 56TH ST, GREEN LAKE; 206/633-5828

At this tiki-themed hideout smack in the middle of a quiet neighborhood, drinks range from the delicious to the downright bizarre, and if you ask nicely, they'll give you an extra little paper parasol. *AE, MC, V; local checks only; every day; full bar; luaupolynesianlounge.com; map:EE7.*

Marcus' Martini Heaven

88 YESLER WY, PIONEER SQUARE; 206/624-3323

The folks at Marcus' Martini Heaven know that there are few things in life more pleasing than a well-mixed martini. Like James Bond, the bartenders like 'em shaken, not stirred. True aficionados may sneer at the array of fruity flavors designed to appease the unconverted, but they shouldn't scoff at the Godiva Chocolate Martini until they've tried it. *AE, MC, V; no checks; Mon–Sat; full bar; marcusmartiniheaven.com; map:N8.*

Mecca Café

526 QUEEN ANNE AVE N, QUEEN ANNE; 206/285-9728

This greasy-spoon/dive bar is home to many a geriatric drinker, but they can usually be found posted up at the bar flanked by young, cool clientele. Take advantage of the hit-heavy jukebox in the corner, and when hunger hits, order the delicious hand-cut fries. Rumor has it that a bartender or two will still let patrons smoke, but you didn't hear it from us. *AE, MC, V; no checks; every day; full bar; map:GG7.*

Murphy's Pub

1928 N 45TH ST, WALLINGFORD; 206/634-2110

As Irish pubs go, Murphy's is a pretty classy place (fireplace, antiques, stained glass). Wallingford residents and others pile in to play darts or give their brains a workout with trivia (on Tuesdays). More than a dozen local brews and stouts are poured on draft, and there's a nice collection of single-malt Scotches and single-barrel bourbons. *AE, DIS, MC, V; no checks; every day; full bar; murphyseattle.com; map:FF7.*

Nine Pound Hammer

6009 AIRPORT WAY S, GEORGETOWN; 206/762-3373

On any given night this Georgetown haunt is full of bikers, blue-collars, and creative types. Its high ceilings and walls filled with historic photographs and antique knickknacks give the place a majestic feel in a quirky, garage-sale-meets-old-West kind of way. Scoop unlimited free peanuts from the stainless steel washtub to go along with one of the local brews on tap. *MC, V; no checks; every day; full bar; ninepoundhammer.com; map:KK7.*

The Nite Lite

1926 2ND AVE, DOWNTOWN; 206/443-0899

The Nite Lite is the queen of retro Seattle lounges. The original décor is from the '40s, with a mind-bending compendium of objects spanning the decades through the '70s. The place was used as a set in the movie *Dogfight* in 1991, and most of the props were kept firmly in place. Look out for that evening's Showbox at the Market headliners—it's often a low-profile postshow stop. Cheap beer specials, stiff martinis, and incredible seasonal decorations make it feel like a perpetual holiday celebration, no matter what time of year. *Cash only; every day; full bar; map:I7.*

Old Town Alehouse

5233 BALLARD AVE NW, BALLARD; 206/782-8323

The Old Town evokes the look of old Ballard, with an ornate antique bar and icebox, exposed brick walls, and old black-and-white photos. The Ballard Wedge sandwiches are tasty—and the fries, seasoned with black pepper and Parmesan that come alongside, are out of this world. *MC, V; no checks; every day; beer and wine; oldtownalehouse.com; map:FF8.*

Ozzie's Roadhouse

105 W MERCER ST, QUEEN ANNE; 206/284-4618

The 2003 demise of Sorry Charlie's Piano Bar left a void in the karaoke landscape of Lower Queen Anne that Ozzie's Roadhouse was happy to fill. This enormous and labyrinthine bar is one of the city's best singing spots, and karaoke nuts fill every booth, cheering and clapping for their favorites. Not just one but two bars offer microbrews on tap and an array of mixed drinks. *AE, DIS, MC, V; no checks; every day; full bar; map:A7.*

Pacific Inn Pub

3501 STONE WY N, FREMONT; 206/547-2967

Should you come for the brew (a dozen on tap, a couple of dozen in bottles and cans) or for the crispy cayenne- and herb-spiked fish-and-chips? Most regulars enjoy both at this workingman's mainstay where Wallingford and Fremont merge. In summer months get there early to snag a much-coveted spot on the lively deck. *AE, MC, V; no checks; every day; full bar; map:FF7.*

Pioneer Square Saloon

77 YESLER WY, PIONEER SQUARE; 206/628-6444

This is one of the few bars in Pioneer Square that doesn't offer live music—and thus doesn't slap on a cover. The clientele ranges from slackers to corporate types, the taped tunes are good, and there's a dartboard in the back. In summer, the patio tables—where you can survey the tourists wandering by—are packed. Between the kindly bartenders, the good (and cheap) wines by the glass, and the unaffected air, this could be the best spot in the city for making new friends. *AE, MC, V; no checks; every day; beer and wine; map:N8.*

Prost!

7311 GREENWOOD AVE N, GREENWOOD; 206/706-5430

Seattle's three authentic German-style beer halls are all owned by Chris Navarra, who spent much of his childhood in Germany. (The others are Feierabend in South Lake Union and Die BierStube in Roosevelt). At Prost!, you may come out smelling like brats and sauerkraut, but the fine imported beers on tap are worth it. Be aware of splashing beer, as enthusiastic Prost!-ing abounds. *AE, MC, V; no checks; every day; beer and wine; prosttavern.net; map:EE7.*

Queen City Grill

2201 1ST AVE, BELLTOWN; 206/443-0975

Fluted lights, flowers, and a rosy glow that bathes the room make this one of Belltown's classiest options. On weekends it gets packed with artists, yuppies, and off-duty bartenders pretending they're in New York or San Francisco; on weeknights sitting at the curved bar can be quietly lovely. *AE, DC, DIS, MC, V; no checks; every day; full bar; queencitygrill.com; map:G7.*

Red Door Alehouse

3401 EVANSTON AVE N, FREMONT; 206/547-7521

During the day, suits, salespeople, and salty dogs stop in to down a cold one with a burger and fries. At night it's so crowded with the fraternity/sorority crowd, you could mistake the place for a J.Crew catalog shoot. There's a wide selection of beers, predominantly Northwest microbrews, to complement some terrific (inexpensive) pub grub. Order a bowl of mussels and eat 'em in the beer garden. *AE, MC, V; local checks only; every day; full bar; reddoorseattle.com; map:FF7.*

Redwood

514 E HOWELL ST, CAPITOL HILL; 206/329-1952

Just off the beaten path of Pine Street, Redwood is a down-home oasis from the madness. Peanut shells litter the floor on a good night, and the jukebox is heavy with '70s rock, roots, and Americana. Try the Micholata—a concoction of Negro Modelo, muddled lemons and limes, soy sauce, and Tabasco, served in a frosty pint glass with a salted rim. During baseball season, post up at the bar (inlayed with spent shotgun shells!) to catch the game on one of the four TVs guaranteed to be broadcasting the sport—much loved by owner and musician Mat Brooke. *MC, V; no checks; every day; full bar; map:I1.*

Rendezvous (Jewel Box Theater)

2320 2ND AVE, BELLTOWN; 206/441-5823

Formerly one of the city's most infamous dives, the Rendezvous has morphed into a slick, glamorous establishment, replete with red velvet booths and well-coiffed servers. The bar originally opened in 1926 as a dinner theater (frequented by Jimmy Stewart when in town), and the new owners have preserved the original screening room, hence the Jewel Box Theater name. Special film events often happen here, as do occasional oddball performance-art and rock shows. *AE, MC, V; no checks; every day; full bar; jewelboxtheater.com; map:F7.*

Roanoke Inn

1825 72ND AVE SE, MERCER ISLAND; 206/232-0800

The Roanoke Inn isn't the kind of place most people will just happen upon. It resides on secluded Mercer Island (and has since 1914), which is usually a destination only for its inhabitants. However, die-hard pub crawlers may want to seek this one out for its history alone. It's known for its somewhat checkered past—apparently the upstairs rooms once housed a brothel of sorts, and the main room was the site of many bloody barroom brawls. Today its biggest draw is the outdoor seating on a generous front porch reminiscent of a Southern estate. *AE, MC, V; no checks; every day; full bar; roanokeinn.com; map:II4.*

Roanoke Park Place

2409 10TH AVE E, CAPITOL HILL; 206/324-5882

A relaxed gathering ground where the junior gentry of north Capitol Hill can feel like just folks. Good burgers and beers, and the new Ping-Pong tables are a welcome addition, but loud music often drowns out conversation. The place is packed with drunken frat boys after Husky games. *MC, V; no checks; every day; full bar; map:GG7.*

74th Street Ale House

7401 GREENWOOD AVE N, GREENWOOD (AND BRANCHES); 206/784-2955

The 74th Street Ale House and its sister establishments, the Columbia City Ale House (4914 Rainier Ave S, Columbia City; 206/723-5123) and the Hilltop Ale House (2129 Queen Anne Ave N, Queen Anne; 206/285-3877), are ale houses in the true sense of the word, with regulars lingering at the bar and taps pouring nearly two dozen brews. The food, however, is more than a cut above pub grub, including a delectable gumbo and several sandwiches and main dishes worthy of a "real" restaurant. All three places are great for after-work meetings or for whiling away rainy Sunday afternoons. *MC, V; local checks only; every day; beer and wine; seattlealehouses.com; map:EE7.* ♿

Shea's Lounge

94 PIKE ST, PIKE PLACE MARKET; 206/467-9990

Don't let the near-hidden location (on the top floor of the Corner Market building) keep you from ferreting out this charming little offshoot of Chez Shea. Seven small tables and a minuscule bar are set in a slender, elegant, dimly lit space with enormous casement windows looking out over market rooftops to Elliott Bay beyond. A nice selection of Italian and Spanish wines is complemented by a short but tasteful, mainly Mediterranean menu. *AE, MC, V; no checks; Tue–Sun; full bar; chezshea.com; map:I7.*

Shorty's

2222 2ND AVE, BELLTOWN; 206/441-5449

Part punk rock, part carnival, Shorty's is home to a bank of pinball machines that are rarely left unoccupied. The PBR flows as freely as the many varieties of hot dogs: if you like spice, break a sweat with the Chicago dog, garnished with tomatoes, onions, hot peppers, and celery salt. *Cash only; every day; full bar; shortydog.com; map:G7.*

The Sitting Room

108 W ROY ST, QUEEN ANNE; 206/285-2830

After taking in a high-minded piece of theater or performance art at On the Boards, a prestigious avant-garde production space, theatergoers can imbibe happily at the Sitting Room. Known for its massive wine list, this glamorous space also features an extensive import and specialty beer menu and an array of delicious snacks and desserts. *MC, V; no checks; Tues–Sun; full bar; the-sitting-room.com; map:GG8.*

Six Arms Brewery and Pub

300 E PIKE ST, CAPITOL HILL; 206/223-1698

Six Arms offers a well-rounded selection of brews, all handcrafted in the tiny room at the rear of the bar. Tasty pub fare rounds out the menu, including innovative items such as perfectly crispy Cajun-spiced tater tots. It's best not to come with extreme hunger—service can be mellow to a fault. Luckily, an assortment of mini statuary (our favorite is the contented sheep), ornamental light fixtures, and the jukebox will keep you entertained till the food comes. *AE, DC, MC, V; no checks; every day; full bar; mcmenamins.com; map:K2.* ♿

SkyCity

SPACE NEEDLE, SEATTLE CENTER; 206/443-2100

If enjoying a truly sensational view means sipping one of the most expensive drinks you'll ever have in your life, cough up $11 for the hop to the top (only restaurant patrons ride free)—and then drink slowly. Or if you're feeling particularly daring, ask to see the wine list. A "cheap" bottle will set you back $30 or $40. For a limited vintage, expect to shell out $250, but fine wines taste better in a restaurant that is rotating very, very slowly. *AE, DIS, MC, V; checks OK; every day; full bar; spaceneedle.com; map:D6.* ♿

Smarty Pants

6017 AIRPORT WY S, GEORGETOWN; 206/762-4777

One of the newest additions to the always-on-the-cusp Georgetown neighborhood, Smarty Pants fits right in. Its charm is rough around the edges, the drinks are strong, and the food will hit the spot—with greasy aplomb. While nights are lively, their brunch alone is worth the trek: it's one of the only spots in town where a Monte Cristo can be wolfed down in all its sweet and savory glory. *MC, V; no checks; every day; full bar; smartypantsseattle.com; map:KK7.*

THE RAINBOW COALITION

Capitol Hill is undeniably the epicenter for gay and lesbian nightlife. It's home to the queen of Seattle's gay dance clubs: the beloved **NEIGHBOURS** (1509 Broadway; 206/324-5358; neighboursnightclub.com), where revelers of all orientations work up a sweat until close to dawn on the crowded floor as video screens broadcast visual delights and DJs spin everything from Top 40 to '80s favorites. The three-tiered **R PLACE** (619 E Pine St, Capitol Hill; 206/322-8828; rplace seattle.com) attracts clientele from all over with DJs, cabaret, pool tables, and karaoke. The top floor gets steamy on the weekends, so dress accordingly—less is more! **PURR** (1518 11th Ave, Capitol Hill; 206/325-3112; purrseattle.com) is just around the corner and offers up karaoke on Tuesday nights. On various nights of the week, **CUFF** (1533 13th Ave, Capitol Hill; 206/323-1525; cuffcomplex.com) offers pool, darts, pinball, karaoke, and dancing.

—Aja Pecknold

Smith

332 15TH AVE E, CAPITOL HILL; 206/709-1900

If anyone has a Midas touch in Seattle, it's bar owner Linda Derschang, whose every watering hole turns to gold, from swanky Viceroy in Belltown to her newest laid-back Capitol Hill pub, Smith. An extensive beer list is partnered with a menu full of comfort food and meat dishes, which diners lustily enjoy while trying to ignore a wall covered with taxidermy. Large windows along the front wall are thrown open on warm days. *AE, DIX, MC, V; no checks; every day; full bar; map:HH6*

Stellar Pizza and Ale

5513 AIRPORT WY S, GEORGETOWN; 206/763-1660

Stellar was originally Stella, but following a dispute with an East Coast joint of the same name, the extra "r" was tacked on. Not much else has changed, thankfully. The pizza at Stellar is delicious; the kid in you will love the no-frills spaghetti and meatballs; and those of age can imbibe the fine selection of beer, wine, and the liquors of the newly added full bar. *MC, V; no checks; every day; full bar; stellarpizza.com; map:KK7.*

Temple Billiards

126 S JACKSON ST, PIONEER SQUARE; 206/682-3242

It's not as glossy as Belltown Billiards, but that's just fine with the youngish crowd that shoots pool at the Temple. Word has it that the regulars here include certain local band members, so keep your eyes peeled if celebrity spotting thrills you. There's a decent selection of beer and wine and some tasty sandwiches. *AE, MC, V; no checks; every day; full bar; www.templebilliards.com; map:O8.*

Tini Bigs Lounge

100 DENNY WY, DENNY TRIANGLE; 206/284-0931

Located on the corner of First and Denny, Tini's adds casual elegance to the KeyArena area. Perch at the bar or grab a more intimate table and dish over a bracingly cold martini (Tini's offers 20 variations). Prices aren't cheap, but the standard's a double; be forewarned—these babies go down smooth. Weeknights are considerably less frantic than Friday, Saturday, and Sonics game nights, when the place packs out in elbow-to-elbow fashion. *AE, MC, V; no checks; every day; full bar; tinibigs.com; map:C8.* ♿

The Twilight Exit

2020 MADISON ST, CENTRAL DISTRICT; 206/324-7462

After moving locations just a half a block down and across the street, the Twilight has, for the most part, remained the same, just in bigger, better digs. The operating theme of this spacious bar is 1970s kitsch, and the ramshackle décor ranges from absurd (a silver mannequin illuminated by blue light) to adorable (blurry family-fishing-trip photos). On any given night, you'll find a diverse mix of people chatting and picking tunes from the well-stocked jukebox. Bring quarters: the Exit features one of the city's only table-style Ms. Pac Man games. *AE, MC, V; no checks; every day; full bar; map:HH6.* ♿

Two Bells Tavern

2313 4TH AVE, BELLTOWN; 206/441-3050

Even the most self-conscious hipster lets it all hang out at Two Bells. There is a good selection of local microbrews and imported gems, plus sporadic but creative bookings of solo guitar acts, unusual art exhibits, and poetry readings. Great burgers and sausage plates and a late-night happy hour complete the experience. *AE, MC, V; no checks; every day; full bar; map:G6.*

Vessel

1312 5TH AVE, DOWNTOWN; 206/652-5222

Step into Vessel wearing casual Pacific Northwest attire and you may feel slightly out of place amid the high ceilings, ornate plasterwork, and sleek crowd. Unlike other overpolished spots that lack soul, however, Vessel is worth a few extra minutes of primp. Cocktails are crafted with care, featuring fresh juices and handmade syrups. All are served with generous 3-ounce pours, so beware: after more than one, you might need another vessel (other than your car) to get you home. *MC, V; no checks; every day; full bar; www.vesselseattle.com; map:K5.*

Viceroy

2332 2ND AVE, BELLTOWN; 206/956-8423

This small, swank cocktail lounge (yet another Linda Derschang brainchild) provides an intimate spot for after-work drinks or a mellow night out. Young professionals lounge on low leather couches alongside hipsters in search of something outside the usual realm. Glasses full of goldfish crackers deck the tables—while they're perhaps not the most sophisticated snack, try resisting a handful (or three). *MC, V; no checks; every day; full bar; viceroyseattle.com; map:F7.*

Virginia Inn

1937 1ST AVE, DOWNTOWN; 206/728-1937

What do you get when you mix artsy Belltown dwellers, chic-seeking suburbanites, and babbling pensioners in a historic, brick-tile-and-avant-garde-art tavern on the edge of Pike Place Market? You get the Virginia Inn, a very enlightened, very appealing, vaguely French-feeling tavern with a fine list of libations (including pear cider) and character to burn. *MC, V; no checks; every day; full bar; map:I7.* ♿

BEST PLACE
TO VIEW ART?

"A hot day on Capitol Hill when the tattoo tribe is walking around."

Sherman Alexie, poet, novelist, and screenwriter

Vito's Madison Grill

927 9TH AVE, FIRST HILL; 206/682-2695

A veritable mishmash of styles (red vinyl booths, shag carpet, etched mirrors, burnished wood), Vito's is a combination of an old Italian eatery (à la *The Sopranos*) and a nightclub. Various club nights rotate through, featuring local DJs. There is occasionally a cover, so bring a little extra cash. *AE, MC, V; no checks; every day; full bar; map:M3.*

West 5 Lounge and Restaurant

4539 CALIFORNIA AVE SW, WEST SEATTLE; 206/935-1966

A vintage feel permeates this bustling West Seattle hot spot—and for good reason: its name harkens back to an era long since past when the telephone prefix WE5 (West 5) would connect you to the area. Bedecked with ancient treasures plundered from Seattle institutions such as Vann's and Gallen Kamp's shoe store, this is a festive, nostalgic spot to revel. Menu favorites include the Astral Mac and Cheese (truly out of this world), and everything will look better after a Chartreuse martini. *MC, V; no checks; every day; full bar; www.westfive.com; map:JJ8.*

The Wildrose

1021 E PIKE ST, CAPITOL HILL; 206/324-9210

The center of the universe for the Seattle lesbian scene, the Wildrose has served as community center, coffeehouse, music venue, pool hall, and just plain great bar since 1984. Tables are just as likely to be filled with women reading alone as those dining with friends or drinking in uproarious groups.

The long-running Taco Tuesday draws in quite the crowd with delectable dollar tacos and $2 Sols, especially in the warmer months. *MC, V; no checks; every day; full bar; thewildrosebar.com; map:L1.*

Coffee, Tea, and Dessert

Thanks to corporate giants (you know who they are), Seattle is a city now known internationally as much for its coffee as its heavy rainfall and grunge superstars. But, though there's a caffeine-slinging franchise on nearly every corner, there's also an ample selection of independently owned coffeehouses, tea shops, and bakeries. And with so many months of the year spent watching rain stream down the windows, we're fortunate to have such warm, cozy places to spend them. These gathering places offer more than just a respite from the rain, however. They're an integral part of Seattle's community and culture, full of students, bookworms, kids and couples alike.

B&O Espresso

204 BELMONT AVE E, CAPITOL HILL; 206/322-5028

Legendary for espresso, extraordinary desserts, and serious conversation, this vigorous Capitol Hill coffeehouse buzzes from morning to 1am (on Friday and Saturday). It's a peaceful place for breakfast and brunch, for a steaming latte and a tart, or for a plate of fried new potatoes with peppers and onions. Lunch and dinner are available, but desserts and coffee are where the B&O really shines; these are some of the best (though they're not the cheapest) homemade desserts in town. *AE, DIS, MC, V; no checks; every day; full bar; map:I1.* ♿

Bauhaus Books and Coffee

301 E PINE ST, CAPITOL HILL; 206/625-1600

At Bauhaus, function follows form. It's a high-ceilinged place with a wall of bookshelves stocked with used art books (Bauhaus doubles as a used bookstore—though we suspect the books actually look better than they sell). Big windows afford a view of the Pike/Pine corridor and the Space Needle, which appears oddly inspiring and appropriate in this context. The wrought-iron fixtures and greenish walls lend style, as does the clientele. *MC, V; no checks; every day; no alcohol; map:K2.*

Cafe Allegro

4002 UNIVERSITY WY NE, UNIVERSITY DISTRICT; 206/633-3030

People who got into the Allegro habit while they were at the University of Washington still find themselves gravitating back. It's hard to pin down the café's appeal. Perhaps it's the moody, dark-wood décor, the cachet of the location (it's not easy to find, set in a U District back alley), or its crowd of serious and interesting international students. You may feel as if you've been left out of a private joke on your first few visits, but it doesn't take long to become a regular. *MC, V; local checks only; every day; no alcohol; map:FF6.*

Caffe Ladro

2205 QUEEN ANNE AVE N, QUEEN ANNE (AND BRANCHES); 206/282-5313

You won't confuse Caffe Ladro with Starbucks, though the local chain now has multiple locations. It's one of the only cafés in the city to serve organic, fair-trade, shade-grown coffee. The sweets and baked goods are delicious—the carrot cake is worth its weight in gold, as are the soups and sandwiches. There is a location on Queen Anne (600 Queen Anne Ave N; 206/282-1549), as well as franchises downtown (801 Pine St; 206/405-1950 and 108 Union St; 206/267-0600); in Fremont (452 N 36th St; 206/675-0854), on Capitol Hill (435 15th Ave E; 206/267-0551), and in West Seattle (7011 California Ave SW; 206/938-8021). *MC, V; checks OK; every day; no alcohol; caffeladro.com; map:A7.*

BEST SPOT

IN THE CITY TO GUARANTEE A HANGOVER?

"The Redwood. I consider it to be the unofficial home of the Trifecta (three parts Guinness, one part espresso, one part Jameson), which is arguably the most dangerously delicious alcoholic beverage of all time. It makes me slap people—and that's not a good thing."

Joan Hiller, publicist, Sub Pop Records

Caffé Vita

813 5TH AVE N, QUEEN ANNE; 206/285-9662; 1005 E PIKE ST, CAPITOL HILL; 206/709-4440

Locals are rabid about this little café tucked in the unlikely neighborhood just north of Silver Platters (former site of Tower Records) and its larger sister establishment on Capitol Hill. All the beans are roasted to perfection, including the well-rounded Del Sol, the Caffé Luna (French roast), and the organic Papua New Guinea. Beware: All espresso drinks are made with double ristretto shots. *MC, V; checks OK; every day; no alcohol; caffevita.com; map:B4, L1.* ♿

Chocolati

7810 E GREEN LAKE WY N, GREEN LAKE; 206/527-5467

Chocolati offers delicious, handmade chocolate (what else?) truffles from its nearby production center. The fruit truffles are a refreshing option and the fish-and-chips—chocolate fish with potato chip crumbles inside—are oddly delicious. An array of chilled, blended drinks ranging from fruity to decadent will cool off ambitious exercisers who choose to jog the lake path in summer. *MC, V; checks OK; every day; no alcohol; chocolati.com; map:EE7.*

Cupcake Royale/Vérité Coffee

2052 NW MARKET ST, BALLARD (AND BRANCHES); 206/782-9557

Even those lacking a sweet tooth have a hard time turning down a fresh-baked cupcake, and the folks at Cupcake Royale have reaped the benefits. They've got their cake-making down to a delectable science using only the freshest ingredients (hormone-free eggs, Mexican vanilla, Belgian chocolate). Each location is paired with a Vérité Coffee, serving up espresso made with Portland-based Stumptown beans, providing a more grown-up beverage to pair with your treat. Don't worry, they've got milk, too. Other locations are in Madrona (1101 34th Ave; 206/709-4497) and West Seattle (4556 California Ave SW; 206/932-2971). *MC, V; no checks; every day; no alcohol; cupcakeroyale.com; map:EE8.*

Dilettante

416 BROADWAY E, CAPITOL HILL; 206/329-6463

The name of this Seattle institution is derived from the Italian word *dilettare*, "to delight." And that's exactly what its sinfully rich truffles and butter-cream-filled chocolates do. No dieter is safe here—if the truffles don't get you, the rich chocolate tortes or crème brûlée, will. Pssst . . . there's a small retail outlet at the candy factory (2300 E Cherry St, Central District; 206/328-1530; map:HH6) with seconds at reduced prices. *AE, MC, V; no checks; every day; beer and wine; dilettante.com; map:GG6.* ♿

Diva Espresso

7916 GREENWOOD AVE N, GREENWOOD (AND BRANCHES); 206/781-1213

This local fave has five locations—it's also in West Seattle (4480 Fauntleroy Ave SW; 206/937-5225), Wallingford (4615 Stone Wy N; 206/632-7019), Lake City (8014 Lake City Wy NE; 206/525-5920) and just south of Shoreline (14419 Greenwood Ave N; 206/632-7019)—and all have excellent coffee and pastries that melt in your mouth. *MC, V; local checks only; every day; no alcohol; divaespresso.com; map:EE7.*

El Diablo Coffee Co.

1811 QUEEN ANNE AVE N, QUEEN ANNE; 206/285-0693

This colorful Queen Anne shop specializes in coffee of the true Cuban variety: dark, full-bodied, and often mixed with a sinful amount of chocolate. Be sure to check out the Love Grotto, a hidden corner of the café where couples can relax on red velvet couches and sip Mexican hot chocolate. Live music of the local, acoustic variety is booked regularly. *MC, V; local checks only; every day; beer and wine; eldiablocoffee.com; map:GG8.*

Espresso Express

6500 15TH AVE NE, UNIVERSITY DISTRICT; 206/524-6326

Believe it or not, this was one of the very first espresso joints in town, on the cusp of the U District and Ravenna, and it's consistently remained one of the finest. Though the ambience isn't fancy, Espresso Express uses some of the finest beans around (shipped from Los Angeles), and the quality of their pulls beats Starbucks hands down. If you want nonfat milk, forget it: they don't think it tastes as good, so they offer only low-fat. *MC, V; local checks only; every day; no alcohol; map:FF6.*

Fuel Coffee

610 19TH AVE E, CAPITOL HILL (AND BRANCHES); 206/329-4700

Further evidence that Seattle can never have enough independently owned and operated neighborhood coffee houses, Fuel Coffee has flourished in the short two-year period since the opening of its first location on Capitol Hill. Clean, stainless steel accents give the place a vintage auto-shop feel, but a homey air prevails in each of its (now three!) locations. The other outposts are in Montlake (2300 24th Ave E; 206/328-0700) and Wallingford (1705 N 45th St; 206/634-2700). *MC, V; no checks; every day; no alcohol; fuelcoffeeseattle.com; map:GG6.*

Joe Bar

810 E ROY ST, CAPITOL HILL; 206/324-0407

Owner Wylie Bush stocks baked goods from the Hi Spot Cafe in Madrona at this comfortable bilevel space across the street from the Harvard Exit movie theater. The crepes, made while you watch, are mouthwateringly delicious. The desserts and good espresso drinks add to the "we're-all-friends-here" atmosphere, fostered by the closely spaced tables and the eager après-film conversation. *MC, V; no checks; every day; beer and wine; joebar.org; map:GG6.*

Mr. Spot's Chai House

5463 LEARY WY NW, BALLARD; 206/297-2424

Chai has become ubiquitous on the menus of many chain coffee shops, but don't consider yourself an experienced drinker until you've tried Mr. Spot's homemade house blend, Morning Glory. Made with "good for you" spices such as astragalus, galangal, cardamom, and coriander, it can be a shock for those accustomed to sugary mixes. Don't miss the chai cheesecake if it's available. Live music happens regularly—call ahead if you're hoping for a quiet night. *AE, MC, V; local checks only; every day; beer and wine; chaihouse.com; map:FF8.*

Panama Hotel Tea & Coffee House

607 S MAIN, CHINATOWN/INTERNATIONAL DISTRICT; 206/515-4000

Once a thriving bathhouse and residence, this hotel's beautiful café has been refurbished around archival photos of Japantown from pre-Internment Seattle. A glass window set in the floor allows you to peer into the basement at items left behind by families forced to move inland during World War II. The coffeehouse has one of the best tea selections in town, and the always-friendly staff is generally willing to explain proper tea-drinking procedures. *No credit cards; local checks only; every day; no alcohol; panamahotelseattle.com/teahouse.htm; map:P6.*

Remedy Teas

345 15TH AVE, CAPITOL HILL; 206/323-4832
Located just a stone's throw from local espresso heavy Victrola, this little tea shop holds its own with a bevy of loose organic herbal and fruit teas. And while she'd probably like it, it's not just your grandma's cup of tea: organic wines, beers, and spiked tea cocktails (the Citra Maté Sake is divine) spice up the menu, especially during the evening hours. Kids will enjoy their own tea service, complete with four delicate PB&J squares. *MC, V; no checks; every day; beer, sake, wine, and spiked tea cocktails; remedyteas.com; map:GG6.*

Revolution Coffee & Art

4217 SW ADMIRAL WY, WEST SEATTLE; 206/932-3661
In addition to local mini chains Caffe Ladro, Uptown Espresso, and Vérité Coffee, West Seattleites now have another independent coffee spot to serve them. A bit more hip than those elder institutions, Revolution is painted a vibrant red, providing a brilliant backdrop for its rotating art. Gems include free Wi-Fi, a walk-up Internet station for those sans MacBook, and complimentary résumé printing. *MC, V; no checks; closed Sundays; no alcohol; revolutioncoffee.net; map:II8.*

Simply Desserts

3421 FREMONT AVE N, FREMONT; 206/633-2671
Simply Desserts cooks up a selection of classic pastries: berry and fruit pies, a white-chocolate strawberry cake that wins raves from everyone, and countless variations on the chocolate cake theme in addition to the lovely chocolate-espresso cake—the most popular being the chocolate Cognac torte and the Bailey's Irish Cream cake. This small spot with an enormous reputation gets plenty busy in the evenings, when chocolate cake fans from across the city sip espresso and enjoy what may be the best desserts around. *No credit cards; checks OK; Tues–Sun; no alcohol; simplydessertsseattle.com; map:FF8.*

Star Life on the Oasis

1405 NE 50TH ST, UNIVERSITY DISTRICT; 206/729-3542
Delicious baked goods of both vegan and nonvegan varieties are the standard at this cafe, which is housed in a ramshackle space adjacent to the Grand Illusion cinema. If you order the black coffee, prepare to stay up way past bedtime—the java at Star Life is famous for its dark, robust roast. *AE, DIS, MC, V; no checks; every day; beer and wine; map:FF6.*

Teahouse Kuan Yin

1911 N 45TH ST, WALLINGFORD; 206/632-2055
Depictions of Kuan Yin, the Buddhist goddess of mercy, preside over the serene atmosphere at this fine teahouse. Kuan Yin offers a full spectrum of teas, including plenty of blacks and greens, a few oolongs, and some herbals. Complementing these is a multiethnic assortment of panini, curry, and samosas, as well as desserts such as green-tea ice cream, pies, and scones. Be sure to chat with the

staff: instruction in the ways of tea drinking is dispensed generously. *MC, V; local checks only; every day; no alcohol; teahousechoice.com; map:FF7.*

Top Pot Doughnuts

609 E SUMMIT AVE, CAPITOL HILL (AND BRANCHES); 206/323-7841

Top Pot offers mouthwatering (and mostly trans-fat-free) fresh doughnuts, delicious coffee, and high-speed Internet in an environment that manages to be both homey and hip. The larger downtown location (2124 5th Ave; 206/728-1966) opened in the fall of 2002 and quickly acquired the nickname of "doughnut central," and a third location recently brought the sugar rush to Wedgwood (6855 35th Ave NE; 206/525-1966). Local (and international) coffee behemoth Starbucks recognized Top Pot's talent for the sweet treats—they now sell its doughnuts at select stores. *MC, V; local checks only; every day; no alcohol; toppotdoughnuts.com; map:GG6.*

Uptown Espresso and Bakery

525½ QUEEN ANNE AVE N, QUEEN ANNE (AND BRANCHES); 206/285-3757

This topnotch coffee hangout turns out a range of superb muffins, scones, and other sweet, semihealthy treats. All four Uptown locations—it's also in West Seattle (3845 Delridge Wy SW; 206/933-9497) and has two downtown locations (2504 4th Ave; 206/441-1084 and 1933 Westlake Ave; 206/782-8853)—are always busy, whether with the quiet postmovie or -theater crowd at night or with louder tête-à-têtes throughout the day. Rightfully so, as these are some of the best espresso drinks you'll find in Seattle. *MC, V; no checks; every day; no alcohol; map:GG7.*

The Urban Bakery

7850 E GREEN LAKE DR N, GREEN LAKE; 206/524-7951

Morning, noon, and night you'll find Green Lake's urban yuppies hanging inside or out of this popular corner spot near the Green Lake shore. Enjoy excellent soups and vegetarian chili, the usual sandwiches and salads, and a world of freshly baked breads, pastries, pies, cakes, and cookies that taste as good as they look. All the requisite coffee drinks too. *MC, V; no checks; every day; no alcohol; map:EE7.*

Victrola Coffee and Art

411 15TH AVE E, CAPITOL HILL; 206/325-6520; 310 E PIKE ST, CAPITOL HILL; 206/624-8204

Bohemians, erudite snobs, and family-oriented yuppies all happily mingle at this homey neighborhood coffee shop. To find out what's going on in the local literary scene, ask any of the frantic laptop clickers to explain his or her current project and its cultural significance. Those a little closer to downtown will be happy about the recent opening of the second Victrola (fondly dubbed V2 by employees) on Pike Street. *MC, V; no checks; every day; no alcohol; victrolacoffee.com; map:GG6.*

Zeitgeist Coffee

171 S JACKSON ST, PIONEER SQUARE; 206/583-0497

Apart from being one of the finest of Seattle's independent coffee roasters, Zeitgeist is also a mecca for the city's long-laboring but under-recognized arts scene. The Pioneer Square storefront has a monthly featured artist, whose work is showcased on the high brick walls, and the coffeehouse occasionally screens independent films. Zeitgeist closes at 7pm most nights but stays open until 10pm on the first Thursday of each month for the art walk. *MC, V; local checks only; every day; no alcohol; zeitgeistcoffee.com; map:P8.*

Zoka Coffee Roaster and Tea Company

2200 N 56TH ST, GREEN LAKE; 206/545-4277; 2901 BLAKELEY ST, UNIVERSITY VILLAGE; 206/527-0990

Owners Tim McCormack and Jeff Babcock bring more than 20 years of experience in the specialty coffee business to this spacious community coffee- and teahouse that recently opened a second outpost in University Village. Zoka roasts its own signature coffees, with the roaster serving as an appropriate backdrop for live acoustic music on Friday and Saturday nights. A variety of loose teas are available by the cup, by the pot, or in bulk. *MC, V; checks OK; every day; no alcohol; zokacoffee.com; map:FF7, EE6.*

RECREATION

RECREATION

Outdoor Activities

Some claim the reason Seattle is ranked among the nation's fittest cities is that gyms and sporting goods stores outnumber fast-food joints; really, it's because Seattleites get their sweat on in the city's parks—which number over 400—and, every chance they get, head out to enjoy the area's easily accessible mountains and waterways. You can walk your dog at a great off-leash city park in the morning, drive up Snoqualmie Pass to ski the slopes in the afternoon, then be home in time for an evening sail on Puget Sound.

If you're unfamiliar with the region, a good place to start planning your activities is at one of the five local branches of **REI** (Recreational Equipment Inc.), the largest of which is its flagship store downtown (222 Yale Ave N; 206/223-1944 or 888/873-1938; rei.com; map:H2). REI has a generous stock of guidebooks for all outdoor sports, topographic maps, and other equipment (see Top 25 Attractions in the Exploring chapter), and hosts numerous clinics, speakers, and other events. The store also rents gear for activities from snowshoeing to camping to paddling. The **U.S. FOREST SERVICE/NATIONAL PARK SERVICE OUTDOOR RECREATION INFORMATION CENTER** located in the downtown REI (206/470-4060; nps.gov/ccso/oric.htm) provides trail reports, weather information, and referrals.

OUTDOORS NW (outdoorsnw.com) is a local publication that provides information about Northwest hiking, mountain biking, climbing, multisport races, and a plethora of other outdoor pursuits. You'll find the free magazine, which includes a comprehensive events and race calendar, at numerous sporting gear and activewear stores throughout the city.

For basic information on some of the city's best—or most accessible—outdoor activities, read on.

BASKETBALL

Seattle offers 58 public courts upon which to practice your jump shot. To find information on those not listed here, visit the Seattle Parks Department Web site (www.ci.seattle.wa.us/parks/athletics/basketba.htm). Two local fitness clubs are also well known for their strong recreational basketball programs: **WASHINGTON ATHLETIC CLUB** (1326 6th Ave; 206/622-7900; wac.net; map:K5) and **SEATTLE ATHLETIC CLUB** (2020 Western Ave; 206/443-1111; twogreatclubs.com; map:G7).

Denny Playfield

WESTLAKE AVENUE AND DENNY WAY, DENNY TRIANGLE

The full court at Denny Playfield is an urban oasis adjacent to a busy street and a good spot to play pickup games—or watch one. Once you've got your hands on the ball, hang on—they've been known to fly into nearby traffic. *Map:F4.*

Green Lake Park

7201 E GREEN LAKE DR N, GREEN LAKE; 206/684-0780
The Green Lake courts are the hottest in the city if you're up for playing with the big boys. There is a fully lighted outdoor court as well as a full indoor court, and there's always plenty to see and do around the lake while you wait your turn to get into the action. *Map:EE7.*

BICYCLING

If you live in Seattle and want to lead an active life, you can't let a little inclement weather get you down. So despite frequent rain and hilly terrain, cyclists persevere, cruising, commuting, and racing all around the city. In fact, city officials recently approved a 10-year plan to designate more than 200 miles of roadway as bike lanes.

If you're just visiting—or just getting your feet wet on a bicycle—many bicycle shops rent bikes for the day or week, from mountain to tandem to kids' bikes. Some even include helmets for free. **ALL ABOUT BIKE & SKI** (3615 NE 45th St, Sand Point; 206/524-2642; allaboutbikeandski.com; map:FF6), **MONTLAKE BICYCLE SHOP** (2223 24th Ave E, Montlake; 206/329-7333; montlakebike.com; map:GG6), **GREGG'S GREENLAKE CYCLE** (7007 Woodlawn Ave NE, Green Lake and branches on Aurora Avenue N and in Bellevue; 206/523-1822; greggscycles.com; map:EE7), and **RECYCLED CYCLES** (1007 NE Boat St, University District; 206/547-4491; recycledcycles.com; map: FF6) are all near major bicycle trails.

BEST PLACE
TO FIND INSPIRATION?

"I love Kerry Park. I took a picture, and it's the screensaver on my computer. Never thought you'd hear that from a born-and-raised New Yorker."

Sue Bird, Seattle Storm guard and WNBA all-star

CASCADE BICYCLE CLUB, the largest bike club in the United States, organizes group rides nearly every day, ranging from a social pace to strenuous workouts. Check out the hotline (888/334-BIKE; cascade.org) for information about cycling in the Northwest and upcoming events. The legendary **SEATTLE-TO-PORTLAND CLASSIC** is a weekend odyssey in which 9,000 cyclists pedal from the University of Washington to downtown Portland in late June or early July, rain or shine. Late February's **CHILLY HILLY**, a 33-mile trek on the rolling terrain of Bainbridge Island, has marked the beginning of the cycling season for the past 35 years. Cascade's hotline has information on both rides.

The city's **BICYCLE SATURDAYS/SUNDAYS** (206/684-7583; seattle.gov/transportation/bikesatsun.htm) are generally the second Saturday and third

Sunday of each month, May through September. Lake Washington Boulevard and Lakeside Avenue, from Mount Baker Beach to Seward Park, are closed to auto traffic, and anyone with a bike is welcome to participate. These pedal-pushing outings offer a serene look at the boulevard and are a haven for cycling tykes not yet street savvy.

The city's **BICYCLE AND PEDESTRIAN PROGRAM** (206/684-7583; seattle.gov/transportation/bikeprogram.htm) provides a biker's map of Seattle that you can order online. (See also the trails listed under Running in this chapter.) **SEATTLE BICYCLE TOURING CLUB** (seattlebiketours.org) is an informal group of recreational cyclists promoting rides and fun for its members. It offers weekly tours and a Web site full of local bicycling resources.

Following are some of the area's favored rides.

Alki Trail

HARBOR AVENUE SW AT FAIRMOUNT AVENUE SW TO FAUNTLEROY WAY SW, WEST SEATTLE

This 8-mile West Seattle route from Seacrest Marina to Lincoln Park comes with impressive views of downtown and Puget Sound. The first half is on a paved bike/pedestrian path along Alki Beach Park to the Alki Point Lighthouse; the remainder is along roads (primarily Beach Drive SW) wide enough for both bikes and cars. The route is crowded on sunny weekends. *Map:II9–KK9.*

Bainbridge Island Loop

Start this hilly and scenic 30-mile bike expedition by taking your bicycle on the ferry (wsdot.wa.gov/ferries) from downtown to Bainbridge Island—porting a bike costs only $1 more than the walk-on fee and lets you bypass the long car-ferry lines. The signed route follows low-traffic roads around the island. Start on Ferncliff (heading north) at the Winslow ferry terminal (avoid Highway 305) and follow the signs.

Burke-Gilman Trail–Sammamish River Trail

8TH AVENUE NW AND LEARY WAY, FREMONT, TO MARYMOOR PARK, REDMOND

The city's most well known and used recreational trail, the Burke-Gilman offers an off-street route for Seattle-area cyclists commuting to downtown, the University District, or Redmond's high-tech campuses. The combined 27-mile path offers great views of the city, waterways, and Lake Washington. Built on an old railway bed, the Burke-Gilman has a trailhead on the Fremont-Ballard border, from which it meanders along the ship canal and Lake Union, through the University of Washington, and along the west shore of Lake Washington. At Bothell's Blyth Park, the trail connects with the Sammamish River Trail, which continues past the Chateau Ste. Michelle Winery (just off the trail at NE 145th Street), Columbia Winery, and the Redhook Brewery. Plans are afoot to extend the western end of the trail into downtown Ballard. (Also see Top 25 Attractions in the Exploring chapter.) *Map:FF7–EE1.*

Lake Washington Boulevard

MADRONA DRIVE, MADRONA, TO SEWARD PARK AVENUE S, RAINIER VALLEY

This serene 5-mile stretch between Madrona and Seward parks is narrow in spots, but bicycles have a posted right-of-way. On Bicycle Saturdays and Sundays, the southern portion (from Mount Baker Beach south) is closed to cars (see introduction above). On other days, riders may feel safer using the asphalt path that follows this portion of the road. Riders can continue south, via S Juneau Street, Seward Park Avenue S, and Rainier Avenue S, to the Renton Municipal Airport and around the south end of Lake Washington, then return via the protected bike lane of Interstate 90. This makes for a 35-mile ride. Take a map with you. *Map:HH6–JJ5.*

Mercer Island Loop

MARTIN LUTHER KING JR. WAY ON I-90 LID, CENTRAL DISTRICT, TO E AND W MERCER WAY, MERCER ISLAND

From Seattle, a bicycles-only tunnel (entrance in I-90 lid park at Martin Luther King Jr. Way) leads to the I-90 bridge on the way to Mercer Island. Using E and W Mercer Way, you'll ride over moderate rolling hills the length of this 14-mile loop. The roads are curving and narrow, so avoid rush hour. The most exhilarating portion of the ride is through the wooded S-curves on the eastern side of the island. Beware speeding teenagers in luxury sedans. *Map:II4–KK4.*

Seward Park Loop

S JUNEAU STREET AND LAKE WASHINGTON BOULEVARD S, RAINIER VALLEY

Take this paved and traffic-free 2.5-mile road around the wooded Bailey Peninsula in Seward Park, which juts out into Lake Washington. The peaceful ride offers a look at the only old-growth forest left in the city and occasional eagles soaring overhead. The loop is popular with runners so keep your eyes on the road. *Map:JJ5.*

Snoqualmie Valley Trail

MULTIPLE ACCESS POINTS

Cycle through this rolling, farm-filled valley just west of the Cascade Mountains as you bike 26 miles between Duvall and North Bend. The crushed gravel and dirt trail meanders past working farms and through lush forests and open spaces. Access the trail at McCormick Park in Duvall (26200 NE Stephens St; 425/788-3434), Rattlesnake Lake Recreation Area (exit 32 off I-90 to Cedar Falls Road), or NE Fourth Street and Ballarat Avenue in North Bend. *metrokc.gov/parks/trails/svt.html.*

FLY FISHING

Anglers from around the world descend on the Pacific Northwest to hook into the area's bountiful salmon, steelhead, and trout. Fly fishing in the rivers and streams near Seattle is increasingly popular, and numerous outfitters offer instruction for beginning to advanced anglers.

The **WASHINGTON FLY FISHING CLUB** (wffc.com) is the area's leading voice for conservation and sportsmanship. It offers public classes in fly tying and fly casting, as well as periodic outings for members and their families on Northwest streams, lakes, and saltwater estuaries. For fly-fishing gear and the wittiest river reports (who knew fishing reports could be funny?), locals rely on **CREEKSIDE ANGLING** (1308 4th Ave, Downtown; 206/405-3474; map: K5; 1180 NW Gilman Blvd, Issaquah; 425/392-3800; creeksideangling.com). Once you've got the rod, reel, and knowledge, head to one of these popular fly-fishing hubs, and remember, patience is the name of this game.

Cedar River

I-405 SOUTH TO EXIT 4/HIGHWAY 169, RENTON

This river is popular for its hungry trout and proximity to Seattle. Urbanites have been known to play hooky from work to get their hook in some Cedar River fish. Weekend crowds fill the shoreline at multiple access points, especially on late-summer evenings when the hatch is thick. *Map:MM2.*

Middle Fork Snoqualmie River

I-90 EAST TO EXIT 34 AND MIDDLE FORK SNOQUALMIE ROAD, NORTH BEND

This picturesque river flows from its snowy headwaters in the Alpine Lakes Wilderness Area down through a deep mountain valley to its mouth near North Bend, where anglers of all levels enjoy the great variety of water features—not to mention brightly colored native cutthroat trout. Catch-and-release fishing with artificial lures and flies only.

Skykomish River

I-5 NORTH TO HIGHWAY 2/CASCADE HIGHWAY, MONROE

City-bound anglers who don't want to cross the Cascades in search of elusive steelhead come to the Skykomish, and they're not alone—all sea-run fish species in the Northwest seek the fresh waters of this mighty river. Good fishing can be found from Monroe to the town of Gold Bar. The staff and river guides at **ALL ABOUT THE FLY** (212 E Main St, Monroe; 360/863-1833; *allaboutthefly.com*) can point you in the right direction.

Yakima River

I-90 EAST 80 MILES, CLE ELUM

Stretching west from Easton through Ellensburg to Yakima, the state's only blue-ribbon trout river is worth the two-hour drive from Seattle. Yakima fishing is solely catch-and-release, which makes this dry-side river a haven for anglers. Head to **THE EVENING HATCH** (2308 Yakima River Canyon Rd, Ellensburg; 866/482-4480; theeveninghatch.com) for local fishing advice or casting tips from the Yakima's most seasoned guides.

GOLFING

There's a golf course for every skill level and wallet size in and around Seattle, and many courses offer spectacular views in classic Northwest settings.

Ballinger Lake Golf Course

23000 LAKEVIEW DR, MOUNTLAKE TERRACE; 425/697-4653
Once in a sorry state of disrepair, this nine-hole comeback course (2,564 yards) was remodeled and reopened in 2005 to rave reviews. It plays short and challenging, with water and wetland hazards. PNGA rating/slope: 32.4/105. *ballingerlakegolf.com.*

Bellevue Municipal Golf Course

5500 140TH AVE NE, BELLEVUE; 425/452-7250
This busy 18-hole course (6,013 yards) is fairly level and easy. Course facilities have recently improved under new management, but the clubhouse still leaves much to be desired. PNGA rating/slope: 68/110. *bellevuepgc.com; map:FF2.*

Foster Golf Links

13500 INTERURBAN AVE S, TUKWILA; 206/242-4221
Following the meandering Duwamish River just south of Seattle, this recently renovated 18-hole course (4,804 yards) has undergone great improvements, and the new 15,000-square-foot clubhouse is one of the best in the state. PNGA rating/slope: 62.8/101. *fostergolflinks.com; map:MM5.*

Golf Club at Newcastle

15500 SIX PENNY LN, NEWCASTLE; 425/793-4653
Rates here are steep, but the view from the two 18-hole courses (7,024 and 6,632 yards) at this hilltop club is impressive; the club also has an 18-hole putting course. PNGA rating/slope: 74.7/142 and 72.3/129. *newcastlegolf.com; map:JJ2.*

Green Lake Pitch & Putt

5701 W GREEN LAKE WY, GREEN LAKE; 206/632-2280
For families and individuals who don't take golf too seriously, Green Lake Pitch & Putt offers the perfect alternative to traditional courses—it's fun, affordable (nine holes cost $6 for adults; $5 for seniors and youths 17 and younger), and beautifully set against the backdrop of the lake. The nine-hole, par-three course, open March through October for pitching and putting only, is busy on summer weekends. *seattle.gov/parks/athletics/golfcrse.htm; map:EE7.*

Interbay Golf Center

2501 15TH AVE W, INTERBAY; 206/285-2200
The best par-three, nine-hole course in the city, Interbay is conveniently located and has a driving range and an 18-hole miniature golf course great for kids, who can rent junior clubs from the shop. The course draws a lot of beginners, so the pace can be slow. *premiergc.com; map:GG8.*

Jefferson Park Golf Course

4101 BEACON AVE S, BEACON HILL; 206/762-4513

Fans of this course boast that it's where Fred Couples grew up. It also prides itself on its recently upgraded, lit driving range with heated stalls; its nine-hole, par-three course; and its 18-hole course (6,200 yards) with sweet views of the city skyline and Mount Rainier. PNGA rating/slope: 67/110. *premiergc.com; map:JJ6.*

Nile Shrine Golf Course

6601 244TH ST SW, MOUNTLAKE TERRACE; 425/776-5154

This lakefront course offers the best beer cart in the area (available Apr–Oct), as well as 18 holes (5,000 yards) that play short with lots of variety, doglegs, and hazards. PNGA rating/slope: 63.7/107. *nilegolf.com.*

Riverbend Golf Complex

2019 W MEEKER ST, KENT; 253/854-3673

The busiest course in the state is becoming better as its trees grow, and the 18-hole course (6,260 yards) has a nice variety of holes. The complex also includes a miniature golf course; a nine-hole, par-three course; and a driving range. PNGA rating/slope: 69.2/116. *www.ci.kent.wa.us/riverbend.*

West Seattle Municipal Golf Course

4470 35TH AVE SW, WEST SEATTLE; 206/935-5187

Tucked into an undulating valley, this good but forgiving course just west of the Duwamish River makes for some surprising lies. Tee times are the easiest to come by in the city, and views on the back nine are spectacular. Eighteen holes, 6,175 yards; PNGA rating/slope: 68.8/116. *premiergc.com; map:JJ8.*

Willows Run

10402 WILLOWS RD NE, REDMOND; 425/883-1200

Willows Run features two 18-hole, links-style courses (5,831 and 6,364 yards), both well designed and well maintained, as well as a driving range, par-three course, and a lit, 18-hole putting course open until 11pm. PNGA rating/slope: 67.3/114 and 69.8/117. *willowsrun.com; map:EE1.*

HIKING

Many Seattleites swear the reason they live here is the city's accessibility to superlative hiking. Day hikers can count on spending just an hour or two in the car before reaching trailheads that lead to alpine lakes, rain forests, ocean cliffs, or mountain meadows. For this reason, the national parks, state parks, national forests, and wilderness areas nearby are heavily used, but conservation efforts have managed to stay a small step ahead of the impact.

Like any outdoor activity, hiking requires a marriage of caution and adventurous spirit. Always carry water and food, and bring extra clothing (wool or synthetics such as polypropylene—not cotton) and rain gear, even if it's 80 degrees and sunny when you set out and you plan only a short hike. Remember, it can rain here almost anytime.

Permits may be required for hiking or camping. Check with the local ranger station before setting out, and buy a trailhead parking permit at a ranger station or outdoor equipment store if necessary; a **NORTHWEST FOREST PASS** (www.fs.fed.us/r6/passespermits) is good at National Forest Service trailheads, picnic areas, and boat launches in Oregon and Washington, and costs $30 per year or $5 per day. In general, national forests require free backcountry permits for hiking, and national parks usually charge fees to enter the park by car but none to hike.

Good hiking guides are published in association with the **MOUNTAINEERS** (300 3rd Ave W, Queen Anne; 206/284-6310 or 800/573-8484; mountaineers.org; map:A9), a venerable outdoors club whose public bookstore has the largest collection of climbing, hiking, mountain biking, and paddling books in the Pacific Northwest. Another reliable information tap to the outdoors is the Seattle branch of the **SIERRA CLUB** (180 Nickerson St, Ste 202, Queen Anne; 206/378-0114; cascade.sierraclub.org; map:FF8). The **WASHINGTON TRAILS ASSOCIATION** (2019 3rd Ave, Ste 100, Downtown; 206/625-1367; wta.org; map:K6), a nonprofit outreach group, welcomes telephone inquiries about hiking, sells maps, and organizes trail-maintenance work parties ranging from an afternoon to a full week. A good source of information in book form is *Inside Out Washington* (Sasquatch Books, 2001) by Ron C. Judd. Here are some popular nearby hiking areas and favorite hikes.

The **ISSAQUAH ALPS** are located 20 miles east of Seattle via I-90. Head out after work to the comely Cascade foothills and get in a great hike before sunset, especially when the snow level is low and you don't want to don a pair of snowshoes to get moving at higher elevations. Dozens of trails—ranging from short and flat to long and steep—weave across these hills. The **ISSAQUAH ALPS TRAIL CLUB** (PO Box 351, Issaquah, WA 98027; issaquahalps.org) organizes hikes every Saturday and Sunday, ranging from short (a good way to introduce children to hiking) to strenuous. When you're pinched for time, **TIGER MOUNTAIN STATE FOREST**, with more than 70 miles of trails, offers the most variety closest to the city, but don't expect much solitude (from exit 20, turn right and right again; drive up to the large parking area for Tiger Mountain hikes). Other popular hikes in the Issaquah Alps include the Red Town Trail in **COUGAR MOUNTAIN WILDLAND PARK** (from exit 13 head south up the hill on Lakemont Boulevard SE; at the hairpin turn after 3 miles, turn left into the parking lot at the Red Town trailhead) and **SQUAK MOUNTAIN STATE PARK'S MOUNTAINSIDE TRAIL** (from exit 17, turn right off the freeway, right again on Sunset Drive, then pass the fish hatchery to Mountain Park Boulevard; turn left on Mountainside Drive and find the trailhead in a quarter mile).

In the **CENTRAL CASCADES**, the best hiking near Seattle is between Snoqualmie Pass (via I-90 due east) and Stevens Pass (via U.S. Highway 2 to the north), one to two hours from the city. The Central Cascades are mainly national forest and wilderness areas, including the scenic Alpine Lakes Wilderness. A gorgeous section of the Pacific Crest Trail cuts through the wilderness along the mountain ridges. The most popular hike in the state is up **MOUNT SI** (exit 32, North Bend), and it's easy to see why when you catch the views of the Snoqualmie Valley from the 4,167-foot peak. Because of its proximity to Seattle, Mount Si Trail traffic is almost as intense as the burning in your thighs as you switchback up this rock. **LITTLE SI**, on the southwest slope of Mount Si, offers a gentler hike than its big, popular neighbor. The trail meanders through mossy forest and rock formations to the 1,575-foot summit. **TWIN FALLS** (exit 32, Edgewick Road) is a favorite for those with a soft spot for waterfalls. Here, the 1.6-mile trail follows the South Fork Snoqualmie River through a cool fern-laden forest up to a 150-foot cascade. When the snow level is high and your hiking legs are in shape, head to the **KENDALL KATWALK** (exit 52, northeast of Snoqualmie Pass), a high-trail section of the Pacific Crest that was blasted from solid rock. The exhilarating 10.5-mile round-trip trail offers great views of distant peaks. Off U.S. Highway 2, **WALLACE FALLS STATE PARK** (Gold Bar, 360/793-0420; www.parks.wa.gov) offers a steep 7-mile trail to the 250-foot waterfalls. To get there, drive 23 miles east on U.S. Highway 2 to Gold Bar and follow signs 1 mile north to the park.

BEST PLACE
TO STAGE A PROTEST?

"Portland, perhaps?"

Greg Nickels, mayor of Seattle

The hiking gets even better farther from the city in the **NORTH CASCADES** (between Stevens Pass and the Canadian border via SR 20, which is closed in winter), with glaciers, summer alpine flowers, and blazing fall colors. Part of this area is in remote and rugged **NORTH CASCADES NATIONAL PARK** (360/856-5700, visitor info; www.nps.gov/noca), which has more than 300 glaciers—more than any other park in the Lower 48. Within the park, the 7.6-mile hike to **DIABLO LAKE** follows a popular, easy, and scenic route with views of the aqua green lake and surrounding jagged peaks. To get there, follow Highway 20 east about 72 miles to the Diablo Dam turnoff, where you head north across the dam and drive just over a mile to the trailhead on the left. Another popular trail, albeit much more strenuous, switchbacks 13.6 miles up from Ross Lake through lowland forest and subalpine meadows to **DESOLATION PEAK**, where the late beat writer Jack Kerouac spent a summer working as a fire lookout. Most Desolation Peak hikers take the **ROSS LAKE WATER TAXI** ($160 round trip for up to six people; 206/386.4437; rosslakeresort.com) from the Diablo Ferry Landing (follow Highway 20 east 68 miles) to the trailhead.

Farther afield, the Olympic Mountains feature **OLYMPIC NATIONAL PARK** (360/565-3130 or 800/833-6388, visitor info; nps.gov/olym) and striking Hurricane Ridge. In the **SOUTH CASCADES** (between Snoqualmie Pass and the Oregon border via U.S. Highway 12 and others), the highlight is **MOUNT RAINIER NATIONAL PARK** (see the Day Trips chapter).

KAYAKING/CANOEING

On a perfect summer day, there is no better way to see Seattle than from a boat on one of its many waterways. Several locations around the city rent canoes and kayaks for day excursions. A good general resource is *Boatless in Seattle: Getting on the Water in Western Washington Without Owning a Boat!* (Sasquatch Books, 1999) by Sue Muller Hacking. **WASHINGTON WATER TRAILS ASSOCIATION** (206/545-9161; wwta.org), which offers access and recreational opportunities for human- and wind-powered watercraft on local marine and inland waters, is another great resource. For those who want instruction on kayaking, one of the oldest kayaking clubs in the nation is the **WASHINGTON KAYAK CLUB** (PO Box 24264, Seattle, WA 98124; washington kayakclub.org), a safety- and conservation-oriented club that organizes swimming-pool practices, weekend trips, and sea- and white-water-kayaking lessons. Several companies rent kayaks by the hour year-round, and some will set you up with a car-top rack for trips farther afield, spring through fall. Here are some favorite places to paddle.

The city's most interesting urban paddle launches from **ALKI CRAB AND FISH** (1600 Harbor Ave SW, West Seattle; 206/938-0975; map:II9), skirts the south shore of Elliott Bay and takes you along giant container ships and under huge construction cranes as you kayak through the industrial Duwamish River Waterway. Rent kayaks from **ALKI KAYAK TOURS** (1600 Harbor Ave SW, West Seattle; 206/953-0237; kayakalki.com; map:II9) or take one of its guided day trips, which cost from $35 to $50. The current is strong at times, but it's not a serious hazard for the moderately experienced.

Green Lake's tame waters are a good place to learn the basics. **GREEN LAKE BOAT RENTAL** (7351 E Green Lake Dr N, Green Lake; 206/527-0171; map:EE7), a concession on the northeast side of the lake, rents kayaks, row-boats, paddleboats, canoes, sailboards, and sailboats. Rates range from $10 per hour for a rowboat or canoe to $14 per hour for a sailboard or boat. Open daily, except in bad weather, May through September.

Kayaking or canoeing on **LAKE UNION** is a great way to get an up-close look at houseboats or to enjoy great views of the city. If you're ambitious, paddle west from the lake down the Lake Washington Ship Canal, through the Ballard Locks (be sure to follow the lock worker's signals), past the clanking of boatyards and the aroma of fish-laden boats to Elliott Bay, or east into Lake Washington. Rent sea kayaks by the hour ($12–$17) or the day ($60–$80) at the **NORTHWEST OUTDOOR CENTER** (2100 Westlake Ave N, Ste 1, Westlake; 206/281-9694 or 800/683-0637; nwoc.com; map:A1) or **MOSS BAY ROWING & KAYAKING CENTER** (1001 Fairview Ave N, South Lake Union; 206/682-2031; mossbay.net; map:D1). Both also offer classes; NWOC recommends reservations on good-weather weekends. On Portage Bay, closer to the Arboretum, **AGUA VERDE CAFE & PADDLE CLUB** (1303 NE Boat St, University District; 206/545-8570; aguaverde.com; map:FF6) rents kayaks hourly ($15–$18), with discounts for multiple hours.

If you want some summer perspective on the bumper-to-bumper commuter traffic on the Evergreen Point Bridge, rent a canoe or a rowboat at the **UNIVERSITY OF WASHINGTON WATERFRONT ACTIVITIES CENTER** (206/543-9433; depts.washington.edu/ima/IMA_wac.php; map:FF6) behind Husky Stadium. Rates are low ($7.50 per hour for nonstudents), and you can cross the Montlake Cut to mirrorlike waters framed by lily pads and marshlands inside the Washington Park Arboretum.

The trip up the gently flowing **SAMMAMISH SLOUGH** is quiet and scenic. Ambitious boaters can follow the slough from the north end of Lake Washington at Bothell all the way to Lake Sammamish, about 15 miles to the southeast, passing golf courses, the town of Woodinville, wineries, and Marymoor Park. In Redmond, you can rent kayaks from **AQUASPORTS PADDLE CENTER** (15143 NE 90th St, Redmond; 425/869-7067; aqua-sports.com; map:EE1).

Seattle's proximity to the open waters and scenic island coves of Puget Sound makes for ideal sea kayaking. The nearby **SAN JUAN ISLANDS** to the north provide endless paddling opportunities, though the currents can be strong, and unguided kayaking here is not for novices. **SAN JUAN SAFARIS** (800/450-6858; sanjuansafaris.com) and **OUTDOOR ODYSSEYS** (800/647-4621; outdoorodysseys.com) are two respected companies that offer guided kayak trips in the islands.

MOUNTAIN BIKING

The growing popularity of mountain biking presents something of a dilemma to environmentalists as well as cyclists. The trails that provide an optimum off-road experience—ones that were once quiet, remote, untouched—are those that often end up closed by the Forest Service because of the damage caused by mountain bikers. The **OUTDOOR RECREATION INFORMATION CENTER** (206/470-4060) provides information on trail closures. The non-profit **BACKCOUNTRY BICYCLE TRAILS CLUB** (206/283-2995; bbtc.org) organizes local rides and trail restoration projects and is adamant about taking care of regional trails. The best local guidebook is *Kissing the Trail: Greater Seattle Mountain Bike Adventures* (Adventure, 2003) by John Zilly. Here are some great mountain-biking options in the region.

Grand Ridge Park

EAST OF SEATTLE OFF I-90, EXIT 20

Once private property, this newly established King County park is close to Seattle and offers something for everyone on its 10-mile trail system. Bike along Issy Creek on a gravel road to access three trail options that have everything from challenging single-track and technical climbs to short, steep descents. *metrokc.gov/parks*.

I-5 Colonnade Park

BENEATH I-5 BETWEEN LAKEVIEW BOULEVARD AND FRANKLIN AVENUE E

At press time, the country's first and only sheltered urban mountain bike trail system was scheduled to open in early 2008. A joint effort of the Backcountry Bicycle Trails Club and Seattle Parks and Recreation, the park includes 2 acres of trails simulating natural terrain. Sharpen your skills over switchbacks, log rides, rock gardens, skinnies, wallrides, and small jumps in this unique, rain-free environment. *bbtc.org/colonnade; map:FF7.*

Iron Horse State Park Trail

EAST OF SEATTLE OFF I-90, EXIT 54; 800/233-0321

This popular trail is bedded on the defunct Chicago, Milwaukee, St. Paul and Pacific Railroad, spanning the Cascades from the western foothills east to the upper Columbia River. There are several trailheads and parking areas to access this wide, packed-gravel trail, which maintains a grade less than 2.3 percent and is perfect for beginning riders or experienced bikers wanting to burn miles. Hyak trailhead at Snoqualmie Pass puts you near the 2.3-mile Snoqualmie Tunnel, which you can ride through in the summer if you're not afraid of cool, dark places—just remember to bring a flashlight or headlamp. *parks.wa.gov.*

Saint Edwards State Park

OFF JUANITA DRIVE NE, KIRKLAND; 425/823-2992

Twelve miles of varied terrain make this enormous park great for all skill levels. At 316 acres, it is the largest undeveloped area on Lake Washington and has 3,000 feet of shoreline. Be wary as you ride among the tall trees and up and down the 700 feet of elevation—the trails become a maze if you don't pay attention. *parks.wa.gov/parkpage.asp?selectedpark=Saint%20Edward; map:CC4.*

ROCK CLIMBING

Several indoor climbing walls and artificial outdoor structures allow rock-climbing enthusiasts to get vertical in and around Seattle.

Marymoor Climbing Structure

6046 W LAKE SAMMAMISH PKWY NE, EAST END OF MARYMOOR PARK OFF HIGHWAY 520, REDMOND; 206/205-3661

Otherwise known as Big Pointy, this 45-foot, concrete structure just south of the velodrome was designed by the godfather of rock climbing, Don Robinson. It features everything from slabs to pockets and boasts walls with angles up to and over 90 degrees. *metrokc.gov/parks/Marymoor; map:FF1.*

REI Pinnacle

222 YALE AVE N, DENNY TRIANGLE; 206/223-1944 OR 888/873-1938

With more than 1,000 modular climbing holds, this 65-foot, freestanding indoor structure (inside the REI flagship store) is very popular. Come early; waits can be as long as an hour and you get only one ascent, but you're loaned a beeper so you can shop while you wait. Members climb for $5; nonmembers pay $15. *rei.com; map:H2.*

Schurman Rock

5200 35TH AVE SW, CAMP LONG, WEST SEATTLE; 206/684-7434

In the 1930s, local Scout leader and mountaineer Clark Schurman designed 20-foot Schurman Rock to incorporate every potential rock-climbing problem. Since then, the erratically shaped rock, set in historic Camp Long, has been challenging beginning and advanced climbers with its varied routes. Open to the public Tues–Sat, 10am–6pm. *seattle.gov/parks/environment/camplong.htm; map:KK8.*

Stone Gardens

2839 NW MARKET ST, BALLARD; 206/781-9828
One section of this indoor climbing gym consists of low overhangs; the rest of the gym offers faces that can be bouldered or top-roped, including a 40-foot outdoor wall with climbs for all levels. You can also rent or buy equipment. Staff members offer helpful advice, or you can take classes ranging from one-on-one beginner instruction to several levels of advanced techniques. You can rent the gym for private parties—including instruction—before or after hours. *stonegardens.com; map:FF8.*

Vertical World

2123 W ELMORE ST, INTERBAY; 206/283-4497; 15036-B NE 95TH ST, REDMOND; 425/881-8826; 2820 RUCKER AVE, EVERETT; 425/258-3431
The new Everett location of this rock gym offers 10,000 square feet of climbing walls with hundreds of lead and top-rope routes and a separate area to tackle bouldering problems. The Redmond and Seattle locations have 7,000 and 14,000 square feet of textured climbing areas respectively, and lessons are offered at all locations. *verticalworld.com; map:FF8, DD2.*

Once you've attained the highest pinnacles indoors and in controlled outdoor settings, take your hardened hands and clenching toes to the great outdoors. **EXIT 38 ROCK** (I-90 east, exit 38) near North Bend is user friendly with well-placed, solid bolts and routes rated 5.5 and above. Before you go, stop at the **MOUNTAINEERS** (300 3rd Ave W, Queen Anne; 206/284-6310 or 800/573-8484; mountaineers.org; map:A9), the largest outdoor club in the region and a superb resource, offering group climbs, climbing courses, and general information.

ROLLER-SKATING/IN-LINE SKATING

In-line skating no longer enjoys the same popularity it experienced a few years ago, but in good weather, you'll still find in-line skaters—and old-school roller skaters—in areas where the pavement is smooth, including the downtown waterfront, the **ALKI BEACH TRAIL**, along **LAKE WASHINGTON BOULEVARD**, and north on the tree-shaded **BURKE-GILMAN TRAIL** that connects with the **SAMMAMISH RIVER TRAIL**, which you can follow all the way to Redmond's Marymoor Park (see Bicycling and Running in this chapter). **GREEN LAKE PARK** (E Green Lake Way N and W Green Lake Way N; map: EE7) is the most popular skate-and-be-seen spot in town, where hotdoggers in bright spandex weave and bob past cyclists, joggers, walkers, and leashed dogs. The 2.8-mile path around the lake is crowded on weekends, but during the week it's a good place to try wheels for the first time. When the wading pool on the north shore of the lake isn't filled for kids or commandeered by roller-skating hockey enthusiasts, it's a good spot to learn to skate backward. The **BITTER LAKE COMMUNITY CENTER** (13040 Greenwood Ave N;

206/684-7524; seattle.gov/parks/centers/bitterlk.htm; map:CC7) hosts a fun family skate every Friday night from 6:30 to 8:15pm. Cost is $3 per skater.

BEST PLACE
TO HAVE A PICNIC?

"Richmond Beach Saltwater Park. West Seattle has Alki, Ballard has Golden Gardens, but a short drive north of the city takes you to this beachfront less traveled. Easy walking trails high above the beach hold the promise of picnic benches, a pavilion, and a panoramic view of Puget Sound."

Nancy Leson, food critic for The Seattle Times

ROWING

Seattle has one of the largest populations of adult rowers in the country, spurring numerous gender- and age-specific clubs that lure enthusiasts out of bed at the crack of dawn. Check out northwestrowing.com for a list of local clubs.

The Seattle Parks and Recreation Department runs two rowing facilities: one on Green Lake, out of the **GREEN LAKE SMALL CRAFT CENTER** (5900 W Green Lake Wy N, Green Lake; 206/684-4074; www.greenlakecrew.org; map:EE7), and the other on Lake Washington, through the **MOUNT BAKER ROWING AND SAILING CENTER** (3800 Lake Washington Blvd S, Rainier Valley; 206/386-1913; seattle.gov/parks/boats/mtbaker.htm; map:JJ6). Both operate year-round, offer all levels of instruction, and host annual regattas.

A handful of boathouses in the Seattle area field competitive teams and also offer introductory rowing programs. These member organizations include the **LAKE WASHINGTON ROWING CLUB** (910 N Northlake Wy, Fremont; 206/547-1583; lakewashingtonrowing.com; map:FF7), the **POCOCK ROWING CENTER** (3320 Fuhrman Ave E, Eastlake; 206/328-7272; pocockrowing.org; map:FF7), and the **SAMMAMISH ROWING ASSOCIATION** (5022 W Lake Sammamish Pkwy, Redmond; 425/653-2583; srarowing.com; map:FF1).

RUNNING

You might think that a city that hosts its annual marathon in November has no love affair with running. But running enthusiasts in Seattle are simply so used to chugging along in a downpour that it seems perfectly reasonable to run 26-plus miles in the wind and rain the Sunday after Thanksgiving. It's easy to find a good running course almost anywhere in the city or its surrounding suburbs, and bike paths often do double duty as flat running trails (see Bicycling in this chapter). The city has a large, well-organized running community that provides company and competition. Pick up a copy of *Northwest Runner* (nwrunner.com) in any running-gear store for information on trails, fun runs, and races.

SEATTLE'S GONE TO THE DOGS

Seattleites, it seems, like dogs more than children—while a mere 90,000 kids reside in the city, an estimated 150,000 dogs strut their stuff through Seattle streets. It's no wonder a plethora of day care, massage, psychic services, raw foods, bakeries, booties, and treats are now at a pooch's disposal anywhere in the Emerald City. Fortunately, there are also plenty of recreational opportunities for Seattle dogs and their owners.

The city has 11 off-leash areas, thanks to City Council member Jan Drago, who introduced legislation back in 1996 to establish the first ones. Citizens for Off-Leash Areas (COLA) stewards the parks and provides the city's best doggy-rec resource (206/264-5573; coladog.org). The biggest and best off-leash area in the city is **MAGNUSON PARK** (7400 Sandpoint Wy NE, Sand Point; 206/684-4075; cityofseattle.net/parks/magnuson; map:EE5), the only Seattle off-leash area with water access. The fenced-in park includes a shelter with running water so you can rinse the Lake Washington seaweed off your pooch before heading home. Every June, Magnuson hosts the Annual Canine Festival with fun runs, dog shows, obedience and agility games, and clinics. Another favorite off-leash area is **GOLDEN GARDENS PARK** (8498 Seaview Pl NW, Ballard; 206/684-4075; seattle.gov/parks/parkspaces/golden.htm; map:EE9), located uphill to the east of the popular beach. This fully fenced park includes a natural slope that's perfect for chasing balls. For info about all of Seattle's off-leash areas and their rules and regulations, go to seattle.gov/parks/parkspaces/yodogs.htm (or see Pet Owners in the Planning a Trip chapter).

On the Eastside, **MARYMOOR PARK** (6046 W Lake Sammamish Pkwy NE, Redmond; 206/205-3661; metrokc.gov/parks/marymoor; map:FF1) is doggy nirvana.

One of the finest running outfitters in town is **SUPER JOCK 'N JILL** (7210 E Green Lake Dr N, Green Lake; 206/522-7711 or 800/343-4411; superjocknjill.com; map:EE7). On the Eastside, **FOOTZONE** (10640 Main St, Bellevue, and branches; 425/462-7463; footzone.com; map:HH2) is the best stop for running shoes and gear. Both stores maintain race calendars on their Web sites. Some of the most popular local races are the St. Patrick's Day Dash and Mercer Island Half Marathon in March; the Nordstrom Beat the Bridge to Beat Diabetes run in May; the Seattle Animal Shelter Furry 5K in June; the Seafair Torchlight Run and Virginia Mason Team Medicine Marathon in July; the Seattle Marathon in November; and December's Jingle Bell Run. Listed below are some popular routes.

The 2.8-mile marked path around **GREEN LAKE** (Latona Avenue NE and E Green Lake Way N; map:EE7) has two lanes: one for wheeled traffic, the other

With 40 acres, including large fields, trails, and water access, Marymoor is the largest and most popular off-leash area in the state. But beware escapees—the area isn't fully fenced, so it's wise to keep your dog leashed when traveling to and from the busy parking lot.

The Seattle area also offers some canine-compatible hikes where you'll want to keep your dog on a leash—or under very strict voice command—at all times. The 3-mile hike to **TWIN FALLS** (see listing under Hiking in this chapter) is a local dog-friendly option, as is **BIG CREEK FALLS** (Taylor River). This old road, less than an hour from Seattle, invites dogs and their owners to walk side by side through lush cathedral forests and past spectacular waterfalls. To get there, drive east on I-90 to exit 34; turn north onto the Middle Fork Snoqualmie Road and continue 12.5 miles; turn left onto Taylor River Road and drive to the trailhead at the road's end.

For friendly four-legged competition, head to **SEATTLE AGILITY CENTER** (19313 Renton–Maple Valley Rd SE, Maple Valley; 425/271-5433; agilityfun.com), which has an indoor arena where students can drop in for agility practice sessions, videotaping, seminars, and workshops. The center hosts monthly Agiligames ($5 for members, $7 for nonmembers), annual Agilympics, and, for the most sporty dogs, a competitive Extreme Agility Team.

With all these options, it's a challenge to keep up with your dog's calendar. Fortunately, **CITYDOG** (citydogmagazine.com), a magazine celebrating life with dogs in the Pacific Northwest, will keep you up to date on local canine events. Whether you and yours are at a furry fun run or strolling First Avenue, remember that dogs are only a hip urban accessory when they're well behaved, which means well exercised—in other words, pooped.

—Yemaya Maurer

for everybody else. There's an unpaved upper path, too, where serious runners avoid the strollers and leashed dogs that can clog the lower path. Early mornings or late evenings, though, it's lovely, with ducks, geese, red-winged blackbirds, and rowers and windsurfers on the lake. The path connects with a bikeway along Ravenna Boulevard.

Various dirt paths cut through thickly wooded **LINCOLN PARK** (Fauntleroy Wy SW and SW Trenton Street, West Seattle; map:KK9), overlooking Vashon Island and Puget Sound. The paved shoreline trail is tucked below a bluff, which blocks the sound of auto traffic.

The 1.25-mile trail from Pier 70 to Pier 86 at **MYRTLE EDWARDS PARK** (3130 Alaskan Wy W, Downtown; map:B9) is a popular lunch-hour and after-work runway for the downtown office crowd.

The **ELLIOTT BAY TRAIL** (Pier 70 to Elliott Bay Marina, Waterfront; map: D9) skirts the Elliott Bay waterfront, passes between the grain terminal and its loading dock, winds its way through a parking lot of just-delivered new cars en route to local auto dealers, and continues to the Elliott Bay Marina. The trail is full of runners at lunchtime.

A striking run in clear weather, the Magnolia Bluff and Discovery Park route (along Magnolia Boulevard W, Magnolia; map:GG9–EE9) offers vistas of the Olympic Mountains across Puget Sound. From the parking lot at Magnolia Boulevard W and W Galer Street, run north along the boulevard on a paved pedestrian trail. Magnolia Park ends at W Barrett Street; continue north for four blocks to Discovery Park, which has numerous paved and unpaved trails where you can easily become lost, if you're not careful.

You can stay on the winding main drive, Lake Washington Boulevard E, or run along any number of paths that wind through the trees and flowers gracing the **WASHINGTON PARK ARBORETUM** (Arboretum Drive E and Lake Washington Boulevard E, Madison Valley; map:GG6). The best Arboretum path leads out to the floating trails on Foster Island, which brings you closer to waterfowl and Lake Washington. Another way to access the lake is back on Lake Washington Boulevard, where you can connect with scenic E Interlaken Boulevard at the Japanese Garden and then wind down to the water. The northern lakeside leg, from Madrona Drive south to Leschi, is popular for its wide sidewalks; farther south, from Mount Baker Park to Seward Park, sweeping views make for a pleasing run.

The Eastside's high-visibility running path stretches along the **KIRKLAND WATERFRONT** (along Lake Washington Boulevard, Kirkland; map:FF3–EE3) from Houghton Beach Park to Marina Park—a little more than a mile one way.

MEDINA AND EVERGREEN POINT (along Overlake Drive and Evergreen Point Road, Bellevue; map:FF4–HH4) offer a scenic run along nicely maintained roads with views of Lake Washington and some of the area's most stunning homes—2.5 miles each way.

SAILING

For all its waterways, Seattle in summer is without an important component of sailing: wind. Thus many local sailors declare that sailing season runs from around Labor Day to the beginning of May. If you're willing to brave the somewhat chilly conditions, there are several local organizations that offer classes and chartered tours.

SAILING IN SEATTLE (2046 Westlake Ave N, slip 28, Westlake; 206/279-9016; sailing-in-seattle.com; map:GG7) offers three different staffed cruises on a 33-foot sailboat: a 2½-hour sunset cruise on Lake Union; an eight-hour cruise through the Ballard Locks to Puget Sound; or five hours on Lake Washington. Rates ($225–$750) are for the entire boat, for up to six passengers. Sit back and enjoy the sights or try your hand at sailing with instruction from the onboard crew. Reservations are a must. Sailing in Seattle also offers courses from beginning to advanced.

No more than a mile across in any direction, Green Lake is the perfect place to learn to sail: it's free from motor cruisers, floatplanes, and barge traffic. For beginners who want to learn to sail in a smaller boat and have a few days to pick up the essentials, the **GREEN LAKE SMALL CRAFT CENTER** (5900 W Green Lake Wy N; 206/684-4074; seattle.gov/parks/boats/grnlake.htm; map:EE7), at the southwest corner of the lake, offers classes. **MOUNT BAKER ROWING AND SAILING CENTER** (3800 Lake Washington Blvd S, Rainier Valley; 206/386-1913; seattle.gov/parks/boats/mtbaker.htm; map:II6), on Lake Washington, also offers sailing lessons in small boats.

Salty dogs who want to be their own skipper should try a classic wooden boat at the nonprofit **CENTER FOR WOODEN BOATS** (1010 Valley St, South Lake Union; 206/382-2628; cwb.org; map:D1). Call and schedule a $10 checkout to show them you know how to tack, jibe, and dock under sail (takes about 30 minutes), then hop aboard one of the fleet of 12- to 20-foot rental sailboats. Sailboat rental rates range from $15 to $46 per hour; viewing exhibits is free. Visitors are encouraged to touch the center's approximately 100 historic boats and to ask questions of the volunteers. The center also rents rowboats (which require no skills demonstration).

SKATEBOARDING

Skateboarding is contentious in Seattle, with pro-boarders lobbying for additional skate parks to meet the needs of Seattle's estimated 26,500 skaters, and anti-boarders claiming Seattle's three public skate parks are more than enough. Although the City Council recently approved a master plan for an ambitious network of skateboard parks, the best of what is currently available is listed below.

Ballard Skate Park

NW 57TH STREET AND 22ND AVENUE NW, BALLARD; 206/684-4075

This free, skate-at-your-own-risk outdoor park officially opened in 2005, thanks to a dedicated group of volunteers who advocated for the park and its improvements. The big, two-level bowl is open daily, 8am–9pm. *seattle.gov/parks/park_detail.asp?ID=4278; map:FF8.*

Liberty Park Skate Park

OFF I-405 AT HOUSER WAY S, RENTON; 425/430-6400

This 8,400-square-foot skate park is a skateboarder's dream and includes two bowls, hips (two ramps meeting at an angle), quarter-pipes, half-pipes, a funbox, and a twinkie (an elongated, curved ramp). Local skaters helped design the park, incorporating skateable artwork that mimics the motion of water. *rentonwa.gov/living/default.aspx?id=2294; map:MM2.*

Marginal Way Skate Park

UNDER HIGHWAY 99 AT S HANFORD STREET AND E MARGINAL WAY, SODO

In 2004 a group of skaters started cleaning up this neglected South Seattle site under a highway on-ramp, turning it from a transients' campground into a well-loved skate park. While it's yet to be designated an official city park, it may be the best skate park around, if not for its covered-bowl-oriented skating elements, then for its celebrated skate jams. *marginalwayskatepark.org; map:II7.*

SNOW SPORTS

Each winter, Seattleites hold their breath in anticipation of the local ski season, which can vary from awesome to awful to somewhere in between. We've seen it all—from record snowfall to a season when local ski areas threw in the towel and failed to open at all. Most years, though, there is good skiing to be had for at least a couple of months in the winter and early spring, and there are numerous spots within hours of the city to get your downhill on.

Several ski areas have weekend shuttle buses leaving from Seattle. If you plan to drive, carry tire chains and a shovel, and inquire ahead about road conditions (206/368-4499 or 800/695-7623; wsdot.wa.gov/traffic). All local downhill ski facilities rent skis, snowboards, and other gear. Many rental outlets are available in the city as well.

Though commercial downhill ski areas have ski patrols, skiers in unpatrolled areas or in the mountainous backcountry should heed the constant danger of avalanche. Conditions change daily (sometimes hourly), so always call the Forest Service's **NORTHWEST AVALANCHE INFORMATION HOTLINE** (206/526-6677) before setting out. Finally, if you are heading off into the backwoods, most plowed parking areas near trailheads and along state highways require a Sno-Park permit (360/586-6645; parks.wa.gov/winter/permits.asp), which costs $20 per vehicle for the winter season. A one-day Sno-Park permit is $8 for all areas ($9 from local retail outlets or online).

Below are the ski areas most accessible to Seattleites, with information about snowboarding and downhill and cross-country skiing. For daily updates on conditions in downhill areas, check out the **CASCADE SKI REPORT** (skireport.com/cascade).

Crystal Mountain Resort

33914 CRYSTAL MOUNTAIN BLVD, CRYSTAL MOUNTAIN, WA 98022; 76 MILES SOUTHEAST OF SEATTLE ON HIGHWAY 410; 360/663-2265, 888/754-6199 SNOW CONDITIONS

Washington's largest ski area boasts 10 chairlifts leading to more than 50 groomed trails on more than 2,600 skiable acres and a 7,012-foot summit. The mountain offers easy access to more than 1,300 backcountry acres, 1,000 of which are lift serviced. Two high-speed six-person chairlifts make getting up the mountain quick and easy for both novice and expert skiers and snowboarders. Nordic skiers will be charmed by Silver Basin's big, broad open area. The ski patrol here monitors your whereabouts if you check in and out. *crystalmt.com.*

I-90 Corridor

EXITS 54 TO 71

The Forest Service offers a wide variety of marked cross-country trails here, which are free and close to Seattle, but you must have a Sno-Park pass to use the parking lots (see introduction above). At **CRYSTAL SPRINGS/LAKE KEECHELUS** (at the top of Snoqualmie Pass, exit 54), Sno-Parks are at either end of an 11.2-kilometer trail that runs along the shores of Lake Keechelus. **CABIN CREEK** (10 miles east of Snoqualmie Pass, exit 63) has 12 kilometers of trails (some of them groomed); the ones on the south side are easy, and the ones on the north side are intermediate, with plenty of turns. At **IRON HORSE SNO-PARK** (exit 71), about 10 miles of easy, flat trails around Lake Easton and Iron Horse State Park are combined with a 12-mile trek from Easton to Cle Elum (not always accessible). For more trails, call the state for a brochure, or contact local outdoor retailers to learn which trails are at their best. Seattle-based **WASHINGTON SKI TOURING CLUB** (wstc.org) is also a great resource, offering cross-country ski trips, training and related activities. *www.fs.fed.us/r6/mbs/recreation/activities/xcountry-i9o.shtml.*

BEST PLACE
FOR FISH AND CHIPS?

"Pacific Inn in Fremont. Nothing fancy; just great food and a real feeling of this town."

Tim Keck, publisher of The Stranger

Methow Valley

NORTH CASCADES SCENIC HIGHWAY 20, 250 MILES NORTHEAST OF SEATTLE

One of the top Nordic ski areas in the country, the Methow Valley offers the charm of Vermont, the snow conditions of Utah, and the big sky of Montana. Too far from Seattle for a day trip, its 200 kilometers of groomed trails make for a great weekend getaway. The valley towns of Mazama, Winthrop, and Twisp offer an ample number of lodges, guides, lessons, and rental shops. Contact **CENTRAL RESERVATIONS** (800/422-3048; methow reservations.com) for hut-to-hut skiing or housing/rental reservations. The nonprofit **METHOW VALLEY SPORT TRAILS ASSOCIATION** (PO Box 147, Winthrop, WA 98862; 800/682-5787; mvsta.com) has more information.

Mount Baker Ski Area

1019 IOWA ST, BELLINGHAM, WA 98226; 56 MILES EAST OF BELLINGHAM, OFF I-5 EXIT 255 TO HIGHWAY 542; 360/734-6771, 360/671-0211 SNOW CONDITIONS

The first area to open and the last to close during the ski season, Mount Baker—which has the highest average annual snowfall (595 inches) in North America—is a terrific weekend destination, though most of the lodgings are in Glacier, about 17 miles to the west. The view is remarkable; the runs are varied but mostly intermediate, with one bowl, two free rope tows, meadows, trails, and wooded areas. Snowboarders (welcome on all runs) test their mettle in the Legendary Banked

Slalom Race, usually held in the first week of February. No night skiing. On the northeastern flank of Mount Baker, Nordic skiers find sporadically groomed trails. Rentals and lessons are available in the main lodge. *mtbaker.us.*

Mount Rainier National Park

ASHFORD, WA 98304; 360/569-2211 EXT. 3314
See the Day Trips chapter for details on Mount Rainier.

Scottish Lakes High Camp

U.S. HIGHWAY 2, 17 MILES EAST OF STEVENS PASS; 509/763-3044
Nestled in a pristine setting at 5,000 feet just east of the Alpine Lakes Wilderness Area, this private backcountry high camp sits at the hub of a 35-mile cross-country and backcountry ski trail network (also accessible in summer and fall). The rustic facilities—with a day lodge, private cabins, hot tub, and sauna—are accessible only via an 8-mile private road. *scottishlakes.com.*

Stevens Pass

SUMMIT STEVENS PASS, U.S. HIGHWAY 2, SKYKOMISH; 78 MILES NORTHEAST OF SEATTLE (NORDIC CENTER, 5 MILES EAST); 206/812-4510, 206/634-1645 WINTER CONDITIONS, 800/695-7623 ROAD CONDITIONS
Challenging and interesting terrain makes Stevens Pass a favorite for many skiers, and it's open daily with seasonal night skiing. Ten chairlifts lead to a variety of runs and breathtaking Cascade views. Snowboarders, welcome on all runs, tend to congregate near the Skyline Express and Brooks lifts, where nearby is a half-pipe and a roped-off terrain park. For Nordic skiing, head 5 miles farther east on U.S. Highway 2 to the full-service Stevens Pass Nordic Center, complete with rentals, instruction, hot food and drink, and 25 kilometers of groomed trails over a variety of terrain. The Nordic Center is open Friday through Sunday and holidays. *stevenspass.com.*

The Summit at Snoqualmie

PO BOX 1068, SNOQUALMIE PASS, WA 98068; 47 MILES EAST OF SEATTLE, OFF I-90 AT EXIT 52; 425/434-7669, 206/236-1600 SNOW CONDITIONS
Consisting of four neighboring sections along I-90—Alpental, Summit Central, Summit West, and Summit East—this complex offers many options for skiers of all abilities. Linked by a free shuttle-bus service (three are also linked by ski trails), all four honor the same lift ticket, but each has its own appeal. Alpental is the most rustic of the bunch and boasts high-grade challenges. Summit Central offers intermediate to expert runs, and most of the mountain is open for night skiing. Summit West's gentler slopes are ideal for children, beginners, and intermediate skiers. Dozens of ski and snowboard classes operate here. Summit East, the smallest, caters to intermediate skiers. The Summit Nordic Center at Summit East has 50 kilometers of trails—some accessed by two chairlifts—to please skiers of any ability level. The center also offers lessons and ski rentals, a yurt, and a warming hut. *summitatsnoqualmie.com.*

SWIMMING

Swimming is a summer thing in Seattle, where natural bodies of water stay frigid year-round. Fortunately, there are eight heated indoor pools managed by **SEATTLE PARKS AND RECREATION** (206/684-4075; seattle.gov/parks/aquatics/pools/index.htm) where lessons are offered, as well as two outdoor pools open during the summer. To cool off during the hotter months, head to one of nine neighborhood swimming beaches, staffed by lifeguards from mid-June through mid-August. The city's most dip-friendly spots follow.

COLEMAN POOL (8603 Fauntleroy Wy SW, West Seattle; 206/684-7494; seattle.gov/parks/aquatics/colman.htm; map:KK8) is the city's only outdoor saltwater pool, which means it's the place to be on a hot summer day. Set on the beach within Lincoln Park, the 85-degree pool offers classic Puget Sound views, along with diving boards, a giant tube slide, and enough salt water to keep you afloat until you shrivel.

GOLDEN GARDENS PARK (8498 Seaview Pl NW, Ballard; 206/684-4075; seattle.gov/parks/parkspaces/golden.htm; map:EE9) offers spectacular views of Puget Sound and the Olympic Mountains from its long, sandy beach. Mornings and early afternoons are the best time to visit for a dip in the chilly salt water: the beach crowd gets rowdy as bonfires light up when the sun goes down.

MADISON PARK (E Madison Street and E Howe Street, Madison Park; 206/684-4075; seattle.gov/parks/parkspaces/madison.htm; map:GG5) is one of the most popular swimming beaches in Seattle, in part because the grassy area above offers great sunbathing with an unbeatable view of Lake Washington. There's a swimming raft, a diving board, and lifeguards on duty during the summer.

MATTHEW'S BEACH PARK (9300 51st Ave NE, Sand Point; 206/684-4075; cityofseattle.net/parks/parkspaces/matthews.htm; map:FF5) on the northwest end of Lake Washington is Seattle's largest freshwater bathing beach and home to the city's Polar Bear Plunge—an annual event drawing more than 800 brave swimmers each January. The water is calm, so it's a great place for tykes to venture beyond the kiddie pool.

TENNIS

Tennis in Seattle has a mostly fair-weather following, but there are plenty of private indoor tennis clubs to serve enthusiasts who can't wait for the next sunny day. Make a reservation far in advance, though, if you're hoping to get one of the 10 courts at Seattle's only public indoor tennis facility, **AMY YEE TENNIS CENTER** (2000 Martin Luther King Jr. Wy S, Rainier Valley; 206/684-4764; seattle.gov/parks/athletics/tennisct.htm; map:II6). Court time lasts one hour and fifteen minutes and costs between $20 and $28. Most public outdoor courts in the city are run by Seattle Parks and Recreation and are available either on a first-come, first-served basis or by reservation for $10 per hour and a half. Players can make phone reservations during the spring and summer up to two weeks in advance (206/684-4062) with a major credit card (AE, MC, V). Otherwise, reservations must be made in person at the scheduling office (5201 Green Lake Wy N, Green Lake; seattle.gov/parks/athletics/tennis.htm; map:EE7). If it rains, your money is refunded. The Eastside's big tennis facility, **ROBINSWOOD TENNIS CENTER** (2400 151st Pl SE, Bellevue; 425/452-7690; www.ci.bellevue.wa.us/robinswood_tennis_center.htm; map:II2), has four lighted outdoor courts (two covered) and four indoor courts that can be reserved in advance for $10 to $30. Following is a list of the best outdoor public courts in the area.

BEACON HILL PLAYFIELD: Two unlighted courts. 1902 13th Ave S, Beacon Hill; map:II6.

BRYANT PLAYGROUND: Two unlighted courts. 4103 NE 65th St, View Ridge; map:EE5.

CAL ANDERSON PARK: Two lighted courts. 1635 11th Ave, Capitol Hill; map:GG6.

GARFIELD PLAYFIELD: Three lighted courts. 23rd Avenue E at Cherry Street, Central District; map:GG6.

GRASS LAWN PARK: Six lighted courts. 7031 148th Ave NE, Redmond; map:EE2.

GREEN LAKE PARK: Five unlighted courts. 7201 E Green Lake Dr N, Green Lake; map:EE7.

HILLAIRE PARK: Two unlighted courts. 15803 NE 6th St, Bellevue; map: HH1.

HOMESTEAD FIELD: Four unlighted courts. 82nd Avenue SE and SE 40th Street, Mercer Island; map:II4.

KILLARNEY GLEN PARK: Two unlighted courts. 1933 104th Ave SE, Bellevue; map:HH3.

LINCOLN PARK: Six lighted courts. 8011 Fauntleroy Ave SW, West Seattle; map:KK9.

LOWER WOODLAND PARK: Ten lighted courts. 5851 W Green Lake Wy N, Green Lake; map:FF7.

LUTHER BURBANK PARK: Three unlighted courts. 2040 84th Ave SE, Mercer Island; map:II4.

MAGNOLIA PLAYFIELD: Four courts (two lighted). 2518 34th Ave W, Magnolia; map:GG9.

MARYMOOR PARK: Four lighted courts. 6046 W Lake Sammamish Pkwy NE, Redmond; map:FF1.

MEADOWBROOK PLAYFIELD: Six lighted courts. 10533 35th Ave NE, Lake City; map:DD6.

MONTLAKE PLAYFIELD: Four unlighted courts. 1618 E Calhoun St, Montlake; map:GG6.

NORWOOD VILLAGE: Two unlighted courts. 12309 SE 23rd Pl, Bellevue; map:II2.

RAINIER PLAYFIELD: Four lighted courts. 3700 S Alaska St, Columbia City; map:JJ5.

RIVERVIEW: Two unlighted courts. 7226 12th Ave SW, West Seattle; map:KK7.

VOLUNTEER PARK: Four courts (two lighted). 1247 15th Ave E, Capitol Hill; map:GG6.

WINDSURFING

A bit of a drive from Seattle but still fondly considered to be in our backyard, the **COLUMBIA RIVER GORGE** (about 200 miles south) is the top windsurfing area in the continental United States (and second only to Maui in the entire country), thanks to the strong winds that blow in the direction opposite the river's current—ideal conditions for confident windsurfers.

Here are some popular locations closer to home. **GREEN LAKE** (E Green Lake Drive N and W Green Lake Drive N; map:EE7) is the best place for beginners; the water is warm and the winds are usually gentle, though experts may find it too crowded. You can take lessons and rent equipment at **GREEN LAKE BOAT RENTALS** (7351 E Green Lake Dr N; 206/527-0171; map:EE7) on the northeast side of the lake. **LAKE UNION** has fine winds in the summer, but you'll have to dodge sailboats, commercial boats, and seaplanes. To launch, head to **GAS WORKS PARK** (N Northlake Way and Meridian Avenue N, Wallingford; map:FF7). Most experienced windsurfers prefer expansive **LAKE WASHINGTON**. Head to any waterfront park—most have plenty of parking and rigging space. **MAGNUSON PARK** (Sand Point Way NE and 65th Avenue NE, Sand Point; 206/684-4946; map:EE5) is favored for its great winds. Choice Eastside beaches include **GENE COULON BEACH PARK** (1201 Lake Washington Blvd N, Renton; map:MM3) and **HOUGHTON BEACH PARK** (5811 Lake Washington Blvd NE, Kirkland; map:FF4). On Puget Sound, tidal-savvy windsurfers (and kitesurfers—who can find more information from the Seattle KiteSurfing Association at seattlekitesurfing.org) head for **GOLDEN GARDENS PARK** (north end of Seaview Avenue NW, Ballard; map:DD9) when there's a good northerly wind or Duwamish Head at **ALKI BEACH PARK** (Alki Ave SW, West Seattle; map:II9).

Spectator Sports

Seattle has a love/hate relationship with professional sports. At press time, the Seattle Seahawks were beloved; the Seattle Mariners were loved one day and reviled the next, depending on the outcome of the most recent game; and the Seattle SuperSonics were either headed to the suburbs—or headed out of town. Some residents are fiercely supportive of expensive new stadiums and willing to pay high ticket prices and extra taxes to fund them; others think public dollars should be used for a host of more important causes. But no matter where you stand, it's hard not to get swept up on the bandwagon of a winning season, and in the past few years, Seattle has had its share of hopeful moments, which had been few and far between since the Sonics' NBA championship in 1979. In 2004, the Seattle Storm brought home the WNBA championship, and in 2006, the Seahawks made their first visit to the Super Bowl, losing a heartbreaker to the Pittsburgh Steelers.

No matter which sport is your favorite to watch, you're likely to find it in Seattle, along with a devoted core of fans, a goofy mascot, great people-watching, interesting food, and some killer scenery.

Emerald Downs

2300 EMERALD DOWNS DR, AUBURN; 253/288-7000 OR 888/931-8400

Emerald Downs is a sweet track in Auburn, 25 minutes south of downtown Seattle, where Western Washington residents can catch the sport of kings. The track has plentiful indoor and outdoor seating, cuisine that goes beyond the usual hot dogs and beer—yakisoba, anyone?—and about 700 color television monitors to ensure that race fans won't miss a thing, plus a sports bar, a gift shop, and an attractive paddock area. Racing season runs from mid-April to mid-September, Thursday to Sunday. General admission is $5, free for children 17 and under; grandstand seating is $2.50, clubhouse seating is $3 (reservations are available). Free general parking is available (catch a parking shuttle); preferred spaces (a shorter walk) are $5; valet parking is $10. *emeralddowns.com; I-5 south to 272nd Street exit, east to West Valley Highway and south to 37th Street N.*

Everett AquaSox

3802 BROADWAY, EVERETT; 425/258-3673 OR 800/GO-FROGS IN WASHINGTON

Real grass, real fans, real hot dogs—the AquaSox have it all, including a lime green frog mascot, Webbly, whose likeness is a globally hot collector's item. Watching this Class-A farm team of the Seattle Mariners is always worth the drive to Everett's 4,500-seat Memorial Stadium. The Sox attract a loyal cadre of fans from mid-June through the first week of September. Tickets can usually be bought at the gate and are also available through Ticketmaster outlets. Tickets are $5; reserved seats are $7–$10. *aquasox.com; 30 miles north of Seattle on I-5 at exit 192.*

Husky Basketball

BANK OF AMERICA ARENA AT HEC EDMUNDSON PAVILION, UNIVERSITY OF WASHINGTON, UNIVERSITY DISTRICT; 206/543-2200

The Husky men's basketball program has recently gone through the roof, and game tickets are some of the hardest to come by in the city. The Husky women's team, though a few years removed from its NCAA tournament glory, continues to put on a great show (the Husky-Stanford duel is always a hot ticket). Dawg basketball teams start play in early November and continue through March. General seating costs $6; reserved seats are $8–$14 for women's games, $25 and up for men's. *gohuskies.cstv.com; map:FF6.*

Husky Football

HUSKY STADIUM, UNIVERSITY OF WASHINGTON, UNIVERSITY DISTRICT; 206/543-2200

Beginning in September, the UW's beloved Dawgs play in the 73,000-seat Husky Stadium. Even in less-than-stellar seasons, tickets are tough to get, so plan ahead, especially for big games; when the Huskies are home, the games are on Saturday. Be sure to pack rain gear, carpool (just follow the cars with the Husky flags), and wear purple. Also, plan to watch game highlights later on TV, as the lovely lake views from the stadium will likely distract even die-hard fans from some of the gridiron action. Tickets are $18–$60. *gohuskies.cstv.com; map:FF6.*

Rat City Rollergirls

MULTIPLE LOCATIONS AROUND SEATTLE

These rough-and-tumble roll models have become the undisputed darlings of Seattle's amateur sports scene. The all-female Roller Derby league comprises four teams that aren't afraid of serious scrapes and bruises as they battle it out on a flat track. Fans flock to the monthly bouts for live punk rock, Pabst Blue Ribbon, and affordable entertainment. The season runs February through August and includes some fun fund-raisers at local bars. Tickets are $15–$20. *ratcityrollergirls.com.*

Seattle Mariners

SAFECO FIELD, BETWEEN ROYAL BROUGHAM WAY AND EDGAR MARTINEZ DRIVE S, SODO; 206/346-4000

In the last few years, the Mariners haven't lived up to their superlative 1995 season, which helped catapult attendance through the Kingdome roof and the M's right into an open-air ballpark (see Top 25 Attractions in the Exploring chapter). But Mariners' fans still love going out to the ball game at Safeco Field, which sports a menu offering everything from California rolls to barbecue ribs grilled in an open pit, several Mariners' merchandise shops, and a baseball museum. The season lasts from early April through the end of September. Individual ticket prices range from $7 for center-field bleachers to $60. The $18 upper-deck seats may be the best in the park, with unobstructed vistas of Mount Rainier, Elliott Bay, and downtown Seattle. *mariners.com; map:R9.*

Seattle Seahawks

QWEST FIELD, OCCIDENTAL WAY S AND S KING STREET, SODO; 888/635-4295

Since the team's thrilling visit to the Super Bowl in 2006, 'Hawk fans have had their hearts set on a title. There's nothing like getting a ticket for one of the 67,000 seats at Qwest Field (see Top 25 Attractions in the Exploring chapter) and cheering along with the loudest crowd in the West, knowing a championship is on the horizon. Your best bet is to take a free Metro bus from downtown—parking near the stadium is an expensive nightmare. The regular NFL season starts in September (preseason games in August) and runs through December. Ticket prices range from $23 to $79. *seahawks.com; map:Q9.*

Seattle Sounders

QWEST FIELD, OCCIDENTAL WAY S AND S KING STREET, SODO; 206/622-3415 OR 800/796-5425

While some American cities are still discovering the world's most popular sport, professional soccer has been kicking around Seattle off and on since 1974, when the Sounders were founded. The 2005 USL Division 1 champions play at the 67,000-seat Qwest Stadium from May through September. Tickets range from $11 to $18. *seattlesounders.net; map:Q9.*

Seattle Storm

KEYARENA, SEATTLE CENTER; 206/217-9622, 877/962-2849

Seattle acquired a Women's National Basketball Association (WNBA) franchise in 2000, and the Storm has strengthened ever since, winning the WNBA championship in 2004. Games are held during the short NBA off-season of late May through mid-August in front of a loyal contingent of fans. Tickets are comparatively affordable at $14 for binocular level to $60 courtside. *storm.wnba.com; map:B7.*

Seattle SuperSonics

KEYARENA, SEATTLE CENTER; 206/283-3865

Since winning it all in the '70s, the Sonics have been an uneven team, especially when it comes to the playoffs. But unpredictability is par for the course in local professional sports, and the Sonics are a consistent winner when it comes to drawing the home crowd. At press time, Starbucks CEO Howard Schultz had recently sold the Sonics to an out-of-state owner, public financing of a new stadium had been rejected by the state legislature, and the team's future in Seattle was uncertain. But at least for the 2007/2008 season, the team will tear up the court from early November to late April, and tickets range from $10 to $150. *supersonics.com; map:B7.*

Seattle Thunderbirds

KEYARENA, SEATTLE CENTER; 206/448-7825 OR 425/869-7825; 206/628-0888 TICKETMASTER

Arguably the best buy in local sports, the Seattle Thunderbirds take to the ice in September and play through March—or early May if they make the playoffs. No one could mistake these young icemen for the NHL, but what they lack in finesse (and years), the 1996–1997 Western Conference champions make up for with sheer energy and some of the most vocal, loyal fans in the region. The T-birds' 36 home games are mostly on weekends; tickets are $12–$20. *seattlethunderbirds.com; map:B7.*

Tacoma Rainiers

CHENEY STADIUM, 2502 S TYLER ST, TACOMA; 253-752-7700 OR 800/281-3834

On clear days at Cheney Stadium, spectacular views of Mount Rainier serve as a stunning background for the Mariners' Triple-A farm club. The Rainiers play 72 home games, from early April to September. Tickets range from $6 to $14. *tacomarainiers.com; about 34 miles south of Seattle on I-5, take exit 132 (Highway 16) west, the 19th street exit east, then turn right on Cheyenne to the parking lot.*

DAY TRIPS

DAY TRIPS

South Puget Sound

BAINBRIDGE ISLAND

Take a Washington State Ferry from downtown Seattle's waterfront at Colman Dock (Pier 52) to Bainbridge Island, about a 35-minute sail. After docking, walk a short distance northwest along Olympic Avenue to the traffic light and take a left on Winslow Way E to Bainbridge's bustling downtown (locals still call it Winslow).

Now that Bainbridge has become a city, locals worry it will lose its flavor. Condos may be moving in, but Winslow still bubbles with arts, crafts, and eateries, and the July festival of flora, **BAINBRIDGE IN BLOOM** (206/842-7901; gardentour.info), is so popular there's talk of a spring version. For information, contact the **BAINBRIDGE CHAMBER OF COMMERCE** (590 Winslow Wy E; 206/842-3700; bainbridgechamber.com). Or just ask the person at the Bainbridge ferry dock for a map of the island and waterfront trails.

If hiking isn't your thing, take advantage of Bainbridge Island's great shopping opportunities. In the last few years, the community has enjoyed an infusion of posh boutiques, saving fashionable island women a trek over the Sound. Pop into **CAKE** (122 Madrone Ln N; 206/842-7200) for trendy (and très spendy) women's clothing, **AMBROSIA BEAUTY** (108 Winslow Wy W; 206/842-5370; ambrosiabeautyllc.com) for luxe cosmetics, and **KENNEDY & KATE** (110 Madison Ave N; 206/780-0515; kennedyandkate.com) for an inspired blend of designer and vintage fashions.

Once you've enhanced your wardrobe, don't miss the wide selection of new and used volumes at **EAGLE HARBOR BOOKS** (157 Winslow Wy E; 206/842-5332; eagleharborbooks.com) or the sculpture, glass, ceramics, and jewelry at nonprofit **BAINBRIDGE ARTS & CRAFTS** (151 Winslow Wy E; 206/842-3132; bacart.org).

Winslow may be small, but it's got lots of restaurants. Chef Alvin Binuya's pan-Pacific dishes have been wowing critics since he opened **MADOKA** (241 Winslow Wy W; 206/842-2448; madokaonbainbridge.com) just a few years ago, focusing on wild seafood and hormone- and antibiotic-free meat. Likewise, locals love the ribs and salmon at **BAINBRIDGE ISLAND BARBEQUE** (251 Winslow Wy W; 206/842-7427). **CAFÉ NOLA** (101 Winslow Wy W; 206/842-3822; cafenola.com) offers hearty soups and sandwiches at lunch and more formal fare at dinner on its pretty patio. You can pack a picnic at **TOWN & COUNTRY MARKET** (343 E Winslow Wy; 206/842-3848) or roam the **BAINBRIDGE FARMERS' MARKET** in City Hall Park's Town Square (206/885-1500; bainbridgefarmersmarket.com) Saturdays from April to October, 9am to 1 pm. There's also a winter market November through December, 10am to 3pm at **EAGLE HARBOR CHURCH** (105 Winslow Wy W).

Downtown is walkable, but you'll need a car or another set of wheels to maneuver the hills that crisscross the island. Bike rentals are available at **B.I. CYCLE SHOP** (162 Bjune Dr; 206/842-6413; b-i-cycle.com).

Use your wheels to visit one of the island's picnic spots. **FORT WARD STATE PARK**'s beach (2241 Pleasant Beach Dr NE; 206/842-4041) on Bainbridge's south end is ideal for picnics, walks, or fishing. **FAY BAINBRIDGE STATE PARK** (15446 Sunrise Dr NE; 206/842-3931 or 360/902-8844) is easier to find and has a playground, picnic shelters, and the island's only campground. From Winslow, take Highway 305 north to the turnoff at Day Road E and follow the signs. On the way, visit **BAINBRIDGE ISLAND VINEYARDS AND WINERY** (8989 Day Rd E; 206/842-9463; bainbridgevineyards.com) for weekend tastings and a self-guided tour. Wine lovers don't have to leave downtown for tastes, though. **ELEVEN WINERY** (278 Winslow Wy E; 206/780-0905; elevenwinery.com), whose wines, surprisingly, are produced in the owners' two-car garage, has opened a tasting room downtown and is rapidly gaining a following. Another newcomer is **PERENNIAL VINTNERS** (8840 Lovgren Rd; 206/780-2146; perennialvintners.com; by appointment).

Save two hours for roaming the **BLOEDEL RESERVE** (7571 NE Dolphin Dr; 206/842-7631; bloedelreserve.org), the estate of timber magnate Patrice Bloedel, which features Japanese gardens, a moss garden, and a bird sanctuary. Open Wed–Sun; reservations are required and can be made online.

CHIEF SEATTLE'S GRAVE is on the Kitsap Peninsula, a short distance north of the island past the Highway 305 bridge over Agate Passage and up Suquamish Way, and offers a view of the Seattle skyline. For more information about Seattle's namesake, return to Highway 305 and visit the **SUQUAMISH MUSEUM** (15838 Sandy Hook Rd; 360/598-3311; suquamish.nsn.us/museum).

Finish your day with dinner off the beaten path on the southwest side of the island at **TREEHOUSE CAFÉ** (4569 Lynwood Center Rd; 206/842-2814), a café-turned-pizzeria, then follow it with a film at the retro 1936 **LYNWOOD THEATRE** (4569 Lynwood Center Rd NE; 206/842-3080; lynwoodtheatre.com).

If you want to make a night of it, you could stay in the Main House or the Cottage Apartment at **TWIN ROSE GUESTHOUSE** (5257 Lynwood Center Rd NE; 206/855-9763; guesthouseonbainbridge.com), three blocks away from the theater. Other lodging options include the **EAGLE HARBOR INN** (291 Madison Ave S; 206/842-1446; theeagleharborinn.com), a boutique hotel in downtown Winslow with five bedrooms and three townhouses; **WATERFALL GARDENS PRIVATE SUITES** (7269 NE Bergman Rd; 206/842-1434; waterfall-gardens.com), a private reserve on 5 acres filled with birds and wildlife; and a slew of bed and breakfasts.

VASHON ISLAND

Take a Washington State Ferry from the Fauntleroy dock in West Seattle to Vashon Island; the crossing is approximately 15 minutes.

Artsy Vashon Island is less than an hour from West Seattle, but the countryside and Mount-Baker-to-Mount-Rainier views make it seem hundreds of miles away—it even snows regularly in the winter. Vashon is 12 miles long

FERRY RIDES

No activity better captures the spirit of Seattle than a ferry ride—both for commuters who use them for transportation and for sightseers who want to simply enjoy the sunset or the city skyline from an unobstructed vantage point.

Most of the ferries on Puget Sound are run by **WASHINGTON STATE FERRIES** (206/464-6400 or 888/808-7977; wsdot.wa.gov/ferries). The largest ferry system in the country, it operates 10 routes serving 20 terminal locations and transporting some 24 million passengers a year. On weekend and evening runs, ferries often don't have room for all the cars, so be prepared to wait unless you walk on or ride your bike (fare is much cheaper for pedestrians and cyclists). Wi-Fi service is also offered for $6.95 a day or $29.95 a month.

Ferry rates range from $4.35 one way for foot passengers traveling from West Seattle to Vashon Island to $55 each way in the summer for a car (under 20 feet long) and driver going from Anacortes to Sidney, British Columbia (RV and trailer drivers, take note: beyond 20 feet, the fee goes up and is determined by vehicle length and height; check the Web site for pricing). The bike surcharge is $1 from Seattle to Bainbridge, Vashon, or Bremerton. Passengers pay both ways to Canada but stateside pay only on westbound ferries except on the Port Townsend route, where passengers pay each way (so if you're island hopping, head to the westernmost destination first and work your way back).

Three ferry routes leave downtown from the main Seattle terminal at Colman Dock (Pier 52, Alaskan Way and Marion Street; map:M9). The small, speedy walk-on ferry takes mostly commuters to **VASHON ISLAND** (Monday through Friday only; 25 minutes). Tight budgets mean that it is the sole remaining passenger-only ferry, having avoided the ax thanks to the pier protests of some die-hard riders. The car-ferry trip to **BREMERTON** takes an hour. The **SEATTLE–BAINBRIDGE ISLAND** run takes 35 minutes. If sightseeing is your objective, take the Bremerton trip. It's a bit longer, but the scenic ride crosses the Sound, skirts the south end

and 6 miles wide including Maury Island, which is joined to the larger island by a mudflat. For information on visiting, contact the **VASHON–MAURY ISLAND CHAMBER OF COMMERCE** (206/463-6217; vashonchamber.com).

Long country roads through dense forests and peaceful pastures make it a favorite of bikers—once they make it past the killer hill near the ferry dock. You can bring your own bike or rent one at **VASHON BICYCLES** (9925 SW 178th St; 206/463-6225; vashonislandbicycles.com) after riding a Metro bus 4 miles from the ferry dock (206/553-3000; transit.metrokc.gov). Bus service stops at 7pm and doesn't run on Sunday.

of Bainbridge Island, and passes through narrow Rich Passage into the Kitsap Peninsula's land-enclosed Sinclair Inlet.

In recent years, the population of Bainbridge and Vashon islands has increased, and more folks are commuting by ferry. As a result, drive-on passengers should arrive early, especially when traveling during peak hours (mornings eastbound, evenings westbound; summer weekends: Friday and Saturday westbound, Sunday eastbound). Schedules and fees vary from summer to winter (with longer lines in summer). Americans traveling to Canada should bring a passport. Other major Puget Sound routes are listed below.

Edmonds–Kingston (30 minutes)

Kingston, close to the northern tip of the Kitsap Peninsula, is reached from Edmonds, about 15 miles north of Seattle (take the Edmonds/Kingston Ferry exit, exit 177, from I-5 and head northwest on Hwy 104).

Fauntleroy–Vashon Island–Southworth (15 minutes to Vashon plus 10 minutes to Southworth; 35 minutes from Seattle to Southworth)

Vashon, an idyllic retreat west of Seattle, can be reached via passenger ferry from downtown Seattle, Monday through Friday, or every day via car ferry from the Fauntleroy ferry dock in West Seattle (exit 163 off I-5; map:LL8). Vashon is the first stop on a trip from the Fauntleroy terminal to Southworth on the Kitsap Peninsula (see Vashon Island in this chapter). There are also some direct trips to Southworth.

Vashon–Tacoma (15 minutes)

At the southern end of Vashon Island is the Tahlequah ferry dock, from which the ferry departs for Point Defiance Park, on the northwest edge of Tacoma.

Mukilteo–Clinton (15 minutes)

From Mukilteo, 26 miles north of Seattle (exit 189 off I-5), a ferry goes to Clinton on pretty Whidbey Island (see Whidbey Island in this chapter).

Keystone–Port Townsend (30 minutes)

From Keystone, 25 miles up Whidbey Island from Clinton, a ferry reaches

Most island beaches are private, but Maury Island's **DOCKTON COUNTY PARK** (9500 SW Dock St) is a nice rest stop with a view of Quartermaster Harbor and Vashon's southeast shore. An early-20th-century lighthouse rises from the lonely beach, and a loop trail at Point Robinson on the eastern tip of Maury looks out on Des Moines. Hikers also have access to a sliver of beach along the forest trail at **BURTON ACRES PARK** (on the Burton Peninsula, which extends into Quartermaster Harbor), where relatively warm waters make for good swimming . . . if you're acclimated. You can rent kayaks from **VASHON ISLAND KAYAKS** (206/463-9257; pugetsoundkayak.com) at Jenson

Olympic Peninsula's Port Townsend, one of the most enchanting towns in the state (see Port Townsend in this chapter). This route is subject to cancellation due to extreme tidal conditions. If you're prone to seasickness, this is not the route for you. On the plus side, it does offer views of the widest range of wildlife, including orcas and eagles.

Anacortes–San Juan Islands–Sidney BC (crossing times vary)

The remote San Juan Islands are reached by ferry from Anacortes (82 miles northwest of Seattle, exit 230 off I-5). There are 743 islands at low tide, but only 172 have names. Gene Hackman owns one, and only four have major ferry service: the boat stops on Lopez, Shaw, Orcas, and San Juan islands. Once a day (twice a day in summer), the ferry continues on to Sidney on British Columbia's Vancouver Island, just 30 minutes north of Victoria by car. It returns in the early afternoon. During the summer, you can reserve space for your car on this crowded run. You also pass Butchart Gardens.

Seattle–Victoria BC (2 hours)

The Victoria Clipper fleet (206/448-5000 Seattle, 250/382-8100 Victoria, or 800/888-2535 outside Seattle or BC; victoriaclipper.com) offers the only year-round ferry service to Victoria from Seattle. The waterjet-propelled catamarans carry foot passengers only between Seattle and Victoria three times a day from mid-May to mid-September, and once or twice a day the rest of the year. Reservations are necessary. (See Victoria in this chapter).

Port Angeles–Victoria BC (1½ hours)

The privately run Black Ball Transport's (360/457-4491; cohoferry.com) **MV COHO** makes four daily runs in summer and two runs daily in spring and winter (with an extra run for a few days in October for Canadian Thanksgiving Day and U.S. Columbus Day) from Port Angeles, on the Olympic Peninsula, to Victoria, on Vancouver Island.

Point Boathouse and tour the inner harbor; staff also lead tours. The island is the home of the roastery originally used by Seattle's Best Coffee before it was assimilated by Starbucks. It's now home to **VASHON ISLAND ROASTERIE** run by **MINGLEMENT MARKET** (19529 Vashon Hwy SW; 206/463-9672; tvicr.com and minglement.com). Visitors can tour the roasterie and buy organic foods, teas, and local crafts. People who consider coffee a religion will take comfort knowing that monks at the **ALL-MERCIFUL SAVIOUR MONASTERY** (9933 SW 268th St; 206/463-5918; vashonmonks.com) make Monastery Blend Coffee and offer tours of the grounds; call in advance.

Much of the island's cultural life is based at **BLUE HERON ARTS CENTER** (19704 Vashon Hwy SW; 206/463-5131), which includes an art gallery and events sponsored by **VASHON ALLIED ARTS** (206/463-5131; vashonalliedarts.org), including literary readings, folk music, and plays on weekends from September to June. It also features kids' programs, classes, and works-in-progress.

The island's biggest event is early July's **STRAWBERRY FESTIVAL** with music, crafts, and a parade featuring the Thriftway Marching Grocery Cart Drill Team (206/408-8057; vashonchamber.com).

The only screwdrivers at **THE HARDWARE STORE** (17601 Vashon Hwy SW; 206/463-1800; thsrestaurant.com) can be found in the full bar of this historic home-supply-store-turned-restaurant with an art gallery in back. Down the street, a group of caterers who've learned the likes and dislikes of islanders spice up the dining scene at intimate, dimly lit **GUSTO GIRLS** (17629 Vashon Hwy SW; 206/463-6626; gustogirls.com), serving an eclectic mix of Northwest specialties. After being closed for two years, the landmark **BACK BAY INN** (24007 Vashon Hwy SW; 206/463-5355; backbayinn.net), once Vashon's most formal dining spot, let down its hair with an expanded menu that still features rack of lamb, but also fish-and-chips. The Inn offers four rooms upstairs if you feel a case of food coma coming on. Island B&B options range from remote farmhouses to restored Edwardians. Call the **LODGING RESERVATION SERVICE** (206/463-5491; vashonislandlodging.com/castlehill.html).

TACOMA AND GIG HARBOR

Take Interstate 5 south of Seattle 30 miles to exit 133, approximately 45 minutes. Gig Harbor is about 10 miles northwest of Tacoma via Highway 16 (exit 132 off I-5).

It has taken Washington's third-largest city a while to live up to its moniker "City of Destiny," but in the last few years, Tacoma, a formerly blue-collar burg—once known for the aroma from its paper mills—has built beautiful museums; opened high-end restaurants, spas, and boutiques; and gotten part of its light rail system up and running. The city insisted on preserving its old buildings in the process, saving many architectural reminders of days gone by, including City Hall's Renaissance clock and bell tower and the 92-year-old copper-domed Union Station, which is now a **FEDERAL COURTHOUSE** (1717 Pacific Ave; open to the public during business hours). The station's interior is worth a visit just to see works by glass artist and native son Dale Chihuly, who, legend has it, worked his first job here—as a shoeshine boy. Cell-phone-toting visitors can punch in numbers on their keypads to learn about the artworks.

The brick of Union Station stands in stark contrast to the boxy stainless steel of the **TACOMA ART MUSEUM** (1701 Pacific Ave; 253/272-4258; tacomaartmuseum.org; $7.50 adults), but blends perfectly with the facade of the **WASHINGTON STATE HISTORY MUSEUM** (1911 Pacific Ave; 888/238-4373; washingtonhistory.org), which features lively exhibits detailing Washington's past, including a film on the history of the Columbia River and a fascinating scale reproduction of rail lines running through Tacoma in the

1950s. Between the Federal Building and the History Museum is the 500-foot-long Chihuly Bridge of Glass, a combination outdoor gallery of works by the artist and link to the **MUSEUM OF GLASS** (1801 E Dock St; 866/468-7386; museumofglass.org; $10 adults), where the 90-foot-tall, stainless-steel-wrapped cone that holds the Hot Shop Amphitheater has become a distinctive part of the city's skyline. In addition to being able to watch glass artists in action, children can participate in the Design Your Own Vessel program by drawing a sculpture they'd like to see the artists make. Two versions of the winning entry are made on the last Sunday of the month, with one going to the young designer. Midweek is the best bet for the budget-conscious, with admission to all three museums $18 for adults on Wednesdays.

The newly remodeled **WORKING WATERFRONT MUSEUM** (705 Dock St; 253/272-2750; fosswaterwayseaport.org; $3 adults), which focuses on the waterfront's history while teaching maritime skills to a new generation, is slated to reopen in 2008 as part of a redevelopment effort, but **AMERICA'S CAR MUSEUM** may steal its thunder when it opens in the Tacoma Dome parking lot by early 2010. Looking like a car dealership showroom on steroids, with a glass roof evoking the curves of a car's hood, the museum will house part of the 2,000-plus classic car collection of waste disposal magnate Harold LeMay. Until the move, part of the **LEMAY COLLECTION** (325 152nd St E; 253/536-2885; lemaymuseum.org) will be available for tours Tues–Sat on the grounds of a former military school in South Tacoma.

Classic theater houses are also part of downtown's rebound. The painstakingly restored 1918 **PANTAGES THEATER** (901 Broadway; 253/591-5894; broadwaycenter.org) has gone from showing movies to hosting dance, music, and stage shows while the smaller, refurbished **RIALTO THEATER** (310 S 9th St; 253/591-5894; broadwaycenter.org) hosts more intimate shows. Both regularly feature shows put on by the **BROADWAY CENTER FOR THE PERFORMING ARTS** (901 Broadway; 253/591-5890; broadwaycenter.org). **THEATER ON THE SQUARE** (905 Broadway; 253/591-5890; broadwaycenter.org) is another local venue.

On Tacoma's northwest side, it's hard to find a prettier place with a better view than **POINT DEFIANCE PARK**, 700 acres strong, with 550 acres of forest overlooking Puget Sound. Point Defiance's **FIVE MILE DRIVE** provides eye-popping views of the Olympic Mountains, Vashon Island, and Gig Harbor. Other highlights include a rose garden, Japanese garden, beach, reconstruction of Fort Nisqually, ferry dock, railroad village with working steam engine, and the **POINT DEFIANCE ZOO AND AQUARIUM** (5400 N Pearl St; 253/591-5337; pdza.org). Its newest exhibit is an Asian Forest Sanctuary featuring endangered Asian mammals, including elephants, tigers, and gibbons.

THE RUSTON WAY WATERFRONT is a 6-mile mix of parks and restaurants filled with people in any weather. **WRIGHT PARK** (Division Avenue and S "I" Street) is a serene in-city park with many trees, a duck-filled pond, and a beautifully maintained classic glass and steel conservatory built in 1908.

Garden lovers and park fans may recognize the influence of urban planner Frederick Law Olmsted and landscape architect Thomas Church at **LAKEWOLD GARDENS** (12317 Gravelly Lake Dr SW, off I-5 at exit 124;

253/584-3360; lakewoldgardens.org), a 10-acre estate 10 minutes south of Tacoma. Recognized as one of the country's outstanding gardens, it has one of America's largest rhododendron collections.

Tex-Mex restaurant and tequila bar **THE MATADOR** (721 Pacific Ave; 253/627-7100; matadorseattle.com) is one of the latest additions to the area's night scene. Other standbys include **ENGINE HOUSE NO. 9** (611 N Pine St; 253/272-3435; ehouse9.com), a beer lover's neighborhood brewpub near the University of Puget Sound, and the **SPAR** (2121 N 30th St; 253/627-8215; the-spar.com) in Old Town, the city's oldest saloon, which recently added a family section. If you're looking for food with a view, check out Italian restaurant **ALTEZZO** (1320 Broadway; 253/572-3200) on the top of the Sheraton Hotel or the commanding view of Commencement Bay from the **CLIFF HOUSE** (6300 Marine View Dr; 253/927-0400; cliffhouserestaurant.com). **THE SWISS** (1904 S Jefferson Ave; 253/572-2821; theswisspub.com), a pub in a former Swiss lodge, remains popular with local lawyers and politicians thanks to its food and insider atmosphere. Don't miss the art by local artists, including the ubiquitous Dale Chihuly. Beautifully hung red drapes, rich cherrywood, and brick are part of what make Thai fusion **INDOCHINE** the area's hottest new restaurant (1924 Pacific Ave; 253/272-8200; indochinedowntown.com). The intimate two-level theater district eatery **OVER THE MOON CAFE** (709 Opera Alley, Court C; 253/284-3722; overthemooncafe.net) features great bistro food, interior accents by the **RUBY COLLECTION** (711 Opera Alley; 253/383-6384; rubycollection.com) next door, and a women's bathroom that shouldn't be missed. Classic Tacoma eatery **STANLEY & SEAFORT'S STEAK, CHOP AND FISH HOUSE** (115 E 34th St; 253/473-7300; stanleyandseaforts.com) has a panoramic view of city, harbor, and mountains; the **DASH POINT LOBSTER SHOP** (6912 Soundview Dr NE; 253/927-1513; lobstershop.com) and its sister **LOBSTER SHOP SOUTH** (4013 Ruston Wy; 253/759-2165) are old standbys. Lest you think the museum district is getting too stuffy, **HARMON'S** (1938 Pacific Ave; 253/383-2739; harmonbrewing.com) offers old standards—burgers, homemade microbrews, and absolutely no Chihuly art.

Tacoma's top lodging options include **CHINABERRY HILL** (302 Tacoma Ave N; 253/272-1282; chinaberryhill.com), a B&B with wraparound porch, Jacuzzi tubs, and bay views (ask for the Pantages Room); the **VILLA BED & BREAKFAST** (705 N 5th St; 253/572-1157; villabb.com), a five-bedroom Italian Renaissance mansion in the north end; and the **SHERATON TACOMA HOTEL** (1320 Broadway Plaza; 253/572-3200; sheratontacoma.com), next to the Tacoma Convention Center with views of Commencement Bay and Mount Rainier. Adjacent to the hotel is the supremely indulgent **SAVI DAY SPA** (1320 Broadway Plaza; 253/627-2000; savidayspa.com), Tacoma's best spot for relaxation and rejuvenation. In addition to providing superb skin scrubs, facials, and pedicures, the spa hosts popular girlfriend parties in conjunction with the hotel.

Seattle demolished the Kingdome years ago, but the **TACOMA DOME** (253/272-3663; tacomadome.org) stands strong. The country's largest wooden domed stadium hosts expos, concerts, monster trucks, and sporting events. The city's best outdoor game is at Tacoma's **CHENEY STADIUM** (2502

S Tyler St; from Seattle, take I-5 south to exit 132/Highway 16 west), the home of the **TACOMA RAINIERS** (253/752-7707; tacomarainiers.com), the Seattle Mariners' Triple-A affiliate. Now that singer Nick Lachey has purchased a part interest, you never know who's going to sing the national anthem.

OLYMPIA

Take Interstate 5 south of Seattle 60 miles, approximately 1½ hours.

Life is finally back to normal in the state's seat of government, though Olympia residents won't soon forget the destruction caused by the Nisqually Earthquake of 2001. The **LEGISLATIVE BUILDING** (14th Avenue SW and Capitol Way; 360/902-8880) reopened following a $100 million renovation, and legislators are back in permanent offices. Late winter is the best time to see the legislature in action. Visitors can take guided tours of the building and the verdant grounds of the capitol campus (360/902-8880) every hour on the hour from 10am to 3pm daily. It's also possible to do a self-guided tour and take in the plant conservatory, Tivoli Fountain, and Temple of Justice along the way. There are also guided tours of the **TEMPLE OF JUSTICE**, home to the **WASHINGTON STATE SUPREME COURT** (must be booked in advance). Tours of the **GOVERNOR'S MANSION** are available most Wednesdays (call 360/902-8880 for reservations). The buildings are a study in classical architecture ranging from Beaux-Arts to the modernist **JOEL PRITCHARD LIBRARY BUILDING**, which recently became a government office building. It still houses a cafeteria and a Kenneth Callahan mural depicting different stages of Washington history. The mural is now in a locked meeting room, but visitors can call to arrange a viewing (360/902-8881). The **WASHINGTON STATE VISITOR INFORMATION CENTER** (14th Avenue SW and Capitol Way; 360/586-3460) has additional information about the campus.

BEST PLACE
TO PARK DOWNTOWN?

"Pacific Place—central and still pretty cheap."

Rachel Hart, Seattle *magazine editor*

South of campus, the **WASHINGTON STATE CAPITOL MUSEUM** (211 21st Ave SW; 360/753-2580; washingtonhistory.org/wscm) is a museum stuffed into a mansion featuring memorabilia from the state's early days. Kids can enjoy the capitol, too, at the **HANDS-ON CHILDREN'S MUSEUM** (106 11th Ave SW; 360/956-0818; hocm.org), which features a variety of interactive exhibits including a large tree house and an animal rescue station where children can nurse stuffed animals back to health.

Downtown is home to offbeat shops, galleries, entertainment venues, and cafés. **BATDORF AND BRONSON COFFEE ROASTERS** (516 Capitol Wy; 360/786-6717; batdorf.com) is a 3,000-square-foot coffeehouse with a wide range of coffees, teas, and espresso drinks, plus occasional live music. Its

ROASTERY (200 Market St NE; 800/955-5282; dancinggoats.com) has twice-daily tours and a tasting room. On Capitol Way, **SYLVESTER PARK** hosts concerts, holiday lights, and protests under the watchful gaze of the old stone Capitol Building, originally the Thurston County Courthouse. A boulder at the corner of Capitol and Legion ways marks the end of the Oregon Trail. Grab a sandwich or a slice of cake at **WAGNER'S EUROPEAN BAKERY AND CAFÉ** (1013 Capitol Wy S; 360/357-7268). **THE URBAN ONION** (116 Legion Wy; 360/943-9242; theurbanonion.com), right across the street in the **HOTEL OLYMPIAN** apartment building, draws lunch crowds with its signature sandwich, the Haystack—sprouts, tomatoes, guacamole, olives, and melted cheese piled high on whole-grain bread. The venerable **MCMENAMINS SPAR** (114 4th Ave NE; 360/357-6444) has seen changes under new ownership. Portland brewer McMenamins kept the historic photos and oyster stew, but added a microbrewery and elements of its own pub menu, and expanded food service until midnight. Another increasingly popular lunch spot is the **BREAD PEDDLER** (222 Capitol Wy N; 360/352-1175), an artisan bread maker featuring pastries and sandwiches made by a French baker.

Olympia isn't a city that never sleeps, but it doesn't quite roll up the sidewalks after business hours, either. **THE WASHINGTON CENTER FOR THE PERFORMING ARTS** (512 Washington St SE; 360/753-8586; washingtoncenter.org) offers dance, music, and theater performances, and the **CAPITOL THEATER** (206 E 5th Ave; 360/754-5378; olyfilm.org) is a revitalized vaudeville theater that hosts film festivals, concerts, and alternative-music performances. On weekends from June through December, the **OLYMPIA FARMERS' MARKET** (700 Capitol Wy N; 360/352-9096) sells produce, flowers, and local crafts. Nearby is **PERCIVAL LANDING** (at the foot of State Street), a waterfront park with a tower providing views from Budd Inlet and the capitol dome to the snowcapped Olympic Mountains. To the west of town, **EVERGREEN STATE COLLEGE** (2700 Evergreen Pkwy; 360/867-6000; evergreen.edu), one of the country's top liberal arts colleges, boasts a woodsy campus with an organic farm, a rock-climbing wall, and 3,000 feet of waterfront.

Not far from downtown there are several spots to appreciate nature, including **TUMWATER FALLS** and **CAPITOL LAKE** to the southwest. Five miles farther south off Pacific Highway SE is **WOLF HAVEN** (3111 Offut Lake Rd, Tenino; 360/264-4695; wolfhaven.org), a conservation organization fostering wolf appreciation with hourly tours 10am–3pm (noon–3pm on Sundays) and a howl-in with its wolves (Saturday nights July through September; reservations required). Closed in February, open weekends only in winter, closed Tuesdays in summer.

The **NISQUALLY NATIONAL WILDLIFE REFUGE** (100 Brown Farm Rd; 360/753-9467; fws.gov/nisqually; $3 per family), 10 miles north of Olympia off I-5, exit 114, offers a 5.5-mile bird-watching hike through its wetlands sanctuary.

If you're looking for food with a view, try Falls Terrace Restaurant (106 Deschutes Wy, Tumwater; 360/943-7830; fallsterrace.com; reservations recommended), an upscale steak and seafood restaurant overlooking Tumwater Falls and the Deschutes River.

Snoqualmie Valley

Take Interstate 90 east of Seattle approximately 30 miles to exit 27, Snoqualmie–Fall City, about 40 minutes.

As Seattle suburbs have edged east, sleepy farm towns have disappeared, but Snoqualmie Valley's relatively bucolic stretch of cow country just west of the Cascades is still great for weekend biking or driving, especially if you like U-pick farms, roadside stands, and local cafés.

From the town of Snoqualmie off I-90, Highway 202 heads south to North Bend and north to Fall City, then Highway 203 takes over heading north through Carnation and Duvall—both highways are crisscrossed by a web of back roads leading to dairy farms, quiet lakes, and beaches along the Snoqualmie River. Cyclists should stick to back roads to avoid weekend traffic. Mountain bikers, hikers, and horseback riders can hit the Snoqualmie Valley Trail, a 31-mile old railroad right-of-way with a short on-road segment that runs from Duvall to past North Bend. In Fall City, the Tokul Trestle provides stunning views of Snoqualmie River Valley.

Head into downtown Snoqualmie and climb aboard the **SNOQUALMIE VALLEY RAILROAD** (38625 SE King St; 425/888-3030, fares and schedules; trainmuseum.org) for a scenic upper valley tour. The museum also has a Santa Train on early December weekends (reservations required), numerous railroad artifacts, and a train restoration center. If you're hungry, head to **ISADORA'S** (8062 Railroad Ave SE; 425/888-1345), a cozy café and funky store with used books and all manner of stuff. It now serves beer and wine. Farther south, the **FACTORY STORES AT NORTH BEND** (461 South Fork Ave SW, exit 31 off I-90; 425/888-4505; factorystoresatnorthbend.com) outlet mall is North Bend's main attraction.

Continue north on Highway 202 to the 268-foot-high natural wonder, **SNOQUALMIE FALLS**. The **SALISH LODGE** (6501 Railroad Ave SE; 425/888-2556 or 800/272-5474; salishlodge.com), adjacent to the falls, is an upscale hotel with a spa. You can see the gorge from the restaurant—while gorging yourself on its famous four-course breakfast (reservations recommended)—but not the falls. You can marvel over them from a cliffside gazebo or hike down the gorge for a closer look.

To the northwest, Fall City has **SMALL FRYES (**4225 Preston–Fall City Rd; 425/222-7688), a burger stand with seasoned French fries and tasty shakes that make it the ideal lunch stop for an active day in the valley.

From Fall City, take Highway 203 north (Highway 202 heads west to Redmond). The **TOLT RIVER–JOHN MACDONALD PARK** (31020 NE 40th St; 206/296-2964), at the confluence of the Tolt and Snoqualmie rivers south of Carnation, is perfect for a picnic. Reserve a shelter, play Frisbee, float the Tolt, camp, or watch teenagers dive from the Tolt River Bridge. The park also has six yurts that sleep up to six people. Mountain bikers can hit a spur of the Snoqualmie Valley Trail here, meander over the Snoqualmie River into the Tolt River Campground and through part of the Snoqualmie Valley, and see awe-inspiring views of the Cascades and Mount Si along the way.

Carnation's **REMLINGER FARMS** (32610 NE 32nd St; 425/333-4135 or 425/451-8740; remlingerfarms.com) sells farm-grown produce (U-pick or not), baked goods, gift items, and canned foods. It's also a theme park with rides, a petting zoo, and a restaurant that serves lunch and desserts. Open May through October.

BEST PLACE
TO LUNCH DOWNTOWN?

"Salumi, at Third and Main, for home-cured meats and homemade mozzarella cheese. The lamb prosciutto is sent from heaven each day and blessed personally by God."

Greg Kucera, owner of Greg Kucera Gallery

From Carnation, Highway 203 follows the Snoqualmie River west, then north to **DUVALL**, which has preserved its small-town storefronts in the face of commercial growth fueled by Microsoft employees, who have moved there en masse in the last few years. **DUVALL SMITHY** (26331 NE Valley St; 425/844-4039; duvallsmithy.com) is part horse-shoer, part equine-themed gift shop, with metalwork items made from horseshoes. **THE DUVALL GRILL AND TAP ROOM** (15602 Main St NE; 425/844-1430; duvallgrill.com) serves a standard mix of sandwiches during the day, but offers European-influenced food with a dash of creole thrown in at night. Meat loaf is the signature dish—with a port wine demi-glace, of course.

At the end of the day, continue north on Highway 203 to U.S. Highway 2 at Monroe, from which you can head east toward Everett on US 2 or southwest to Seattle on Highway 522 for a loop tour.

North Puget Sound

SNOHOMISH

Take Interstate 5 north from Seattle to exit 186; then take WA 96 E to Highway 9 and take the ramp toward Snohomish. Turn right onto 2nd Street and left onto Avenue C. Approximately 31 miles north of Seattle, a 40-minute drive.

Originally the seat of Snohomish County, this little lumber town was left in the dust when Everett emerged as the area's port and shipping powerhouse, but not before its early settlers built handsome homes in a variety of architectural styles. A **WALKING-TOUR BROCHURE** is available at the **SNOHOMISH VISITOR CENTER** (1301 1st St; 360/862-9609; snohomishvic.com). These days, antiques are the town's main attraction. While downtown is filled with antique malls such as the five-level **STAR CENTER MALL** (829 2nd St; 360/568-2131; myantiquemall.com/starcenter.html), packed with so many items it's impossible to see them all, **BLACK CAT ANTIQUES** (1234 1st

St; 360/568-8145; blackcatantique.com) stands out because it's easy on the eyes: items are well organized, and it focuses on larger items such as desks, pool tables, and even the occasional sports car. **PEGASUS THEATER SHOPS** (1003 1st St; 360/568-8815) is a high-octane mix of petroliana, car collectibles, and other items that probably aren't antiques. The owner of **BRASS LAMP ANTIQUES** (901 1st St; 360/568-1614) has an odd sense of humor, a keen eye for improbable matches of lamps and shades, and a corner on the market for Rise-n-Fall lamps. **CASA E CUCINA FRANCESCA** (1112 1st St; 360/563-9440; atouchofvenice.com) doesn't sell antiques but is worth a look for the Italian imported items on one side of the store and work by Northwest artists on the other.

If the thought of all that shopping makes you hungry, start your day at **TWIN EAGLES RESTAURANT** (1208 1st St; 360/568-0535), which serves a mighty hearty breakfast for a place that's rumored to be haunted. Stop in for a coffee and maybe even the chili of the day at family-owned **JAVA INN** (1102 1st St; 350/568-8254; javainn.com). Have a midday cookie or a slice of apple pie at **SNOHOMISH PIE CO** (915 1st St; 360/568-3589), a local favorite that's now owned by a woman who used to work at the bakery after high school; then round out the day with a meal at the Mediterranean restaurant **MARDINI'S** (101 Union Ave; 360/568-8080; mardinis.com). Save a little bit of room for after-dinner coffee and music at **WIRED AND UNPLUGGED** coffee house (717 1st St; 360/568-2472; wiredandunplugged.com). If you're too jittery after all that caffeine, you can spend the night at the **COUNTRYMAN B&B** (119 Cedar Ave; 360/568-9622; countrymanbandb.com) just a block away.

WHIDBEY ISLAND

Take Interstate 5 north about 25 miles, past Lynnwood, then take Highways 526 east and 525 north about 5 miles to Mukilteo; driving time is about 45 minutes. Then take a Washington State Ferry from Mukilteo to Clinton; the crossing is approximately 20 minutes.

When Seattleites plan an island escape, they generally turn first to the San Juan Islands. But Whidbey Island's pretty towns, majestic views, beautiful beaches, and rolling farmland are much closer, and it's a great place to take the family for beachcombing, clam digging (call 800/562-5632 for red tide warnings), touring, or biking.

Once the ferry reaches the island's south end at Clinton, drive north on Highway 525 and Langley Road to **LANGLEY**, 10 minutes from the ferry dock. First Street is a small-town shopper's dream, filled with galleries and stores. Trade tales with Josh Hauser at **MOONRAKER BOOKS** (209 1st St; 360/221-6962); buy adornments and elegant clothing at **THE COTTAGE** (210 1st St; 360/221-4747); check out Asian and American wares at **VIRGINIA'S ANTIQUES** (206 1st St; 360/221-7797); wander through restored and unrestored furniture at **WHIDBEY ISLAND ANTIQUES** (115 Anthes Ave; 360/221-2393; whidbeyislandantiques.com); or check out the **STAR STORE** (201 1st St; 360/221-5223; starstorewhidbey.com), a mercantile outpost with groceries, gifts, and gadgets. As its name suggests, **THE PRIMA BISTRO** (201½ 1st

St; 360/221-4060; primabistro.biz) upstairs is a French-inspired eatery with Northwest influences, a great wine list, and wine dinners.

Don't miss the town's fine galleries. The **ARTISTS' GALLERY COOPERATIVE** (117 Anthes Ave; 360/221-7675; whidbeyartists.com) features works from more than 30 island craftspeople and artists, while **MUSEO** (215 1st St; 360/221-7737; museo.cc) focuses on local and regional glass artists but also offers art in all media and rotating exhibits from national artists. **HELLEBORE** (308 1st St; 360/221-2067; helleboreglass.com) features glass art made in its studio. Many area galleries are open late on the first Saturday of the month. **KARLSON/GRAY GALLERY** (302 1st St; 360/221-2978; karlsongraygallery.com) specializes in original Northwest art and fine crafts. Just down the street, the funky 1937 movie house, the **CLYDE THEATRE** (217 1st St; 360/221-5525; theclyde.net), is the cheapest ticket in town, with first-run movies at $5 and popcorn for $1.

Accommodation options include the two beautifully furnished suites at Linda Lundgren's **GARDEN PATH SUITES** (111 1st St; 360/221-5121; gardenpathsuites.com), **HOME BY THE SEA** (2388 E Sunlight Beach Rd; 360/321-2964; homebytheseacottages.com), or a room with a view at the intimate **INN AT LANGLEY** (400 1st St; 360/221-3033; innatlangley.com).

CAFE LANGLEY (113 1st St; 360/221-3090; cafelangley.com) specializes in Northwest and Mediterranean dishes. The classic local dive **DOG HOUSE TAVERN AND RESTAURANT** (230 1st St; 360/221-4595) is where natives go for microbrews and pub food. If the weather is nice, pack a picnic and head to the unspoiled shoreline of **DOUBLE BLUFF BEACH** northwest of town and have a romantic stroll, take in a sunset, watch bald eagles, or fly a kite with the kids. It's also a great place to clam, depending on the tides. A mile south of town, **WHIDBEY ISLAND VINEYARDS AND WINERY** (5237 S Langley Rd; 360/221-2040; whidbeyislandwinery.com) does small bottlings of estate-grown grapes, a full line of Washington-grown varietals, and rhubarb wine.

Head west and north on Highway 525 and you'll pass Freeland at Holmes Harbor and the road west to South Whidbey State Park. Halfway up the island's narrowest section is **GREENBANK FARM** (corner of State Highway 525 and Wonn Road; 360/678-7700; greenbankfarm.com), a community gathering place that hosts weekend events and a farmers' market from 10am to 4pm on Sundays from April to November. You can also buy loganberry jams, jellies, and liqueurs, and 36 regional wines in Greenbank's store and tasting room.

Continue north to Keystone, where Highway 525 ends and Highway 20 begins; follow 20 north into **COUPEVILLE**, Washington's second-oldest incorporated town. It began as a farming community in 1853 and added a fort after Indian scares. The **ALEXANDER BLOCKHOUSE** remains on Alexander Street and is open for tours. The **ISLAND COUNTY HISTORICAL MUSEUM** (908 NW Alexander St; 360/678-3310; islandhistory.org) has the largest collection of mammoth artifacts in Puget Sound.

Downtown is populated by souvenir stands, antique shops, and restaurants. The **JAN MCGREGOR STUDIO** (19 Front St; 360/678-5015; whidbey.net/mcgregor) specializes in Japanese furniture, handwoven silk, and pottery

McGregor makes with rare porcelain techniques (open weekends in winter, daily June–Oct). **TOBY'S 1890 TAVERN** (8 NW Front St; 360/678-4222; tobysuds.com) has Penn Cove mussels, burgers, beer, and pool. The **KNEAD AND FEED** (4 Front St; 360/678-5431; kneadandfeed.com) offers homemade breads, pies, and soups, or you can join locals for coffee at **COUPEVILLE COFFEE HOUSE** (12 Front St; 360/678-5358; coupevillecoffeehouse.com). Annual community events include the **PENN COVE MUSSEL FESTIVAL** the first weekend in March and the **COUPEVILLE ARTS & CRAFTS FESTIVAL** the second weekend in August (Whidbey Island Visitor Center; 360/678-5434; centralwhidbeychamber.com).

BEST PLACE
TO SEE AND BE SEEN?

"Pike Place Market, because shopping for fruit and vegetables is both a sensual and a reasonable thing to do."

Frances McCue, founding director of Richard Hugo House

You can ride the bike lane on Engle Road 3 miles south to **FORT CASEY STATE PARK**, a decommissioned fort with beaches and commanding bluffs. The Washington State Ferry (206/464-6400 or 888/808-7977; wsdot.wa.gov/ferries) to Port Townsend leaves from Admiralty Head in Keystone, just south of Fort Casey (see Port Townsend section).

Other exploring options include the bluff and beach at 17,000-acre **EBEY'S LANDING** and **FORT EBEY STATE PARK** northwest of Coupeville. Highway 20 winds north around Penn Cove to Oak Harbor. The Whidbey Island Naval Air Station's air base for tactical electronic warfare squadrons in Oak Harbor acts as a magnet for active and retired military folk. There's something for everyone at **BLUE FOX DRIVE-IN THEATER** and **BRATTLAND GO-KARTS** (1403 Monroe Landing Rd; 360/675-5667; bluefoxdrivein.com). If you want dinner before the show, try **FRASER'S GOURMET HIDEAWAY** (1191 Dock St; 360/279-1231; frasersgh.com), a popular local restaurant with a classically French-trained chef cooking Asian-influenced dishes with Northwest flair in an open kitchen. Fried frog legs with chipotle rémoulade, anyone? Reservations recommended.

Another big draw is **DECEPTION PASS STATE PARK** at the island's north end with its 2,300 acres of prime camping, forests, and beach. Don't let the beauty fool you. The currents in the gorge are highly dangerous, so the water is best enjoyed from afar. The bridge over Deception Pass links Whidbey to Fidalgo Island and the mainland via Highway 20 to I-5; or take Whitney–La Conner Road south to La Conner in the Skagit Valley.

SKAGIT VALLEY

Take Interstate 5 north of Seattle 60 miles, then take exits 221, 226, or 230 west to La Conner; approximately 1½ hours.

Motorists may rush by the Skagit Valley most of the year, but colorful blooming tulips draw huge crowds in spring to the **SKAGIT VALLEY TULIP FESTIVAL** (360/428-5959; tulipfestival.org), creating gridlock most weekends in April. Fortunately, many of the roads are level, so biking is a good way to skirt traffic. There are plenty of parking lots at nearby I-5 exit ramps where you can hop a shuttle. Or you can completely avoid the crush by taking a **VICTORIA CLIPPER TOUR** (206/448-5000 or 800/888-2535 outside Seattle; clippervacations.com). The excursions leave Seattle's waterfront on selected weekend mornings during the festival, dock in La Conner, and take visitors on a bus ride through the countryside. There's still plenty to see after the tulips are cut. Swarms of tourists descend upon U-pick farms starting during the June strawberry season and continuing with blueberries, raspberries, and sweet corn, ending with pumpkins in October. Roadside fruit stands offer a variety of fresh produce and honey.

Turn right off exit 226 and you'll be in **MOUNT VERNON**, which passes for the big city in Skagit and Island counties. Despite being a small town, good restaurants outnumber taverns and video stores. It's also a college town (even if it's only small Skagit Valley College) and a major retail center now that outlet malls with stores such as J Crew and Coach have taken up residence between Mount Vernon and Burlington.

Exit 230 to **LA CONNER** will send you through Conway, where locals eat pan-fried oysters, burgers, and onion rings at the classic **CONWAY PUB** (18611 Main St; 360/445-4733). Five miles west of town, **SNOW GOOSE PRODUCE** (15170 Fir Island Rd; 360/445-6908) is a monster produce stand open late February to mid-October, where you can buy fresh Hood Canal shrimp, local fruit, pasta, cheese, wine, and ice cream.

Much of La Conner seems unchanged from 1867 when John Conner founded the trading post. Back then, the community relied on water transport for its trade. Train and interstate auto travel turned the town into a backwater, but today it's a quaint destination. First Street has the feel of an American bazaar. **TWO MOONS GALLERY** (620 S 1st St; 360/466-1920; twomoonsgallery.com) has a mix of whimsical works from local and regional artists. **CATTAILS AND DRAGONFLIES** (608 S 1st St; 360/466-1046) specializes in garden art. **EARTHENWORKS** (713 S 1st St; 360/466-4422; earthenworksgallery.com) has a lovely sculpture garden out back.

Longtime local institution Tillinghast Seed Company at the town's southern entrance has been sold, but its former home, the **TILLINGHAST SEED COMPANY BUILDING OF LA CONNER** (623 Morris St), has been converted into a shopping center that includes the home accessories store **TILLINGHAST FLOWERS AND GIFTS** (360/466-3329; tillinghastflowersandgifts.com), **SEEDS BISTRO** (360/466-3280), a shoe store, and a bridal shop. **GO OUTSIDE** (111 Morris St; 360/466-4836) is a small garden accessories store. **GACHES MANSION** (703 S 2nd St; 360/466-4288; laconnerquilts.com; $5 adults, free for members and children) is an American Victorian home with a widow's walk outside, period furnishings, and one of only 12 quilt museums in the country (open Wed–Sun). The **MUSEUM OF NORTHWEST ART** (121 S 1st St; 360/466-4446; museumofnwart.org; $5 adult) features the work of regional artists. On the edge of town, the **HERON INN AND WATERGRASS DAY SPA** (117 Maple St; 360/466-4626 or 877/883-8899; theheron.com) has pretty-as-a-picture rooms and a hot tub in the back.

BELLINGHAM

Take Interstate 5 north to Exit 250; 87 miles north of Seattle, approximately a 90-minute drive.

Bellingham isn't one of those towns that's so small, if you sneezed you'd miss it, but it's located so close to the Canadian border on the route to Vancouver BC that you could speed past it on Interstate 5 without giving it a thought. And that would be a shame. The college town that some have dubbed "Berkeley North" is well worth a visit, even if you're a conservative.

FAIRHAVEN is a good first stop. A once and former 20th-century boomtown that went bust when Seattle became a major rail terminus, the area that was once a hangout for loggers and cannery workers is now home to boutiques, bookshops, and galleries. **ARTWOOD** (1000 Harris Ave; 360/647-1628; artwoodgallery.com) features beautiful handcrafted furniture by Northwest woodworkers; glass works and jewelry are on offer at **RENAISSANCE CELEBRATION** (915 Harris Ave; 360/647-4592); and **ARTESANO'S** (1010 Harris St; 360/647-4373) sells a fun mix of jewelry, home décor, and geegaws and doodads of all sizes. One of the area's top independent bookstores, **VILLAGE BOOKS** (1200 11th St; 360/647-4592; villagebooks.booksense.com) has a great selection and frequent author readings.

AVENUE BREAD (1135 11th St; 360/676-1809) is a popular stop for artisan breads, breakfast, and lunch, but bibliophiles who don't want to stray far can always get a snack at the café in Village Books, **BOOK FARE** (360/734-3434), or sup on soup at the **COLOPHON CAFE** (1208 11th St; 360/647-0092; colophoncafe.com) and sit on the outside patio next to **VILLAGE GREEN** (Mill Avenue and 10th Street), where the **FAIRHAVEN OUTDOOR CINEMA** shows movies against a building on Saturday nights in summer. Get a sweet dessert at **SIRENA GELATO CAFE** (2925 Newmarket St; 360/752-0023; sirenagelato.com), then return in time for the movie. **FAIRHAVEN VILLAGE INN** (1200 10th St; 360/733-1311; fairhavenvillageinn.com) across the street may well have the best view of the movies from its second-floor porch. Bayside rooms have a view of Bellingham Bay and the area's working harbor. Another boutique hotel nearby, the **CHRYSALIS INN** (804 10th St; 360/756-1005; thechrysalisinn.com), has spacious rooms with window seats, views of the bay, a day spa, and an impressive wood-beamed lobby.

From Fairhaven, you can board an **ALASKA FERRY** (800/642-0066) at the **CRUISE TERMINAL** (355 Harris Ave; 360/676-8445) and ride all the way up to Skagway; hop one of the **VICTORIA–SAN JUAN CRUISES** (800/443-4552; whales.com) for a day trip to Victoria BC, the San Juan Islands, or just a whale-watching tour; book passage on **AMTRAK** for points north or south; or hit curvy **CHUCKANUT DRIVE** and enjoy a meandering 10-mile scenic drive overlooking Bellingham and Samish bays. If you're looking to stay local, you can also take the 7-mile **INTERURBAN TRAIL** to **LARABEE STATE PARK** and enjoy views of the bay on the 2-mile **SOUTHBAY TRAIL** to downtown.

The central district's main draws are its small museums. **THE AMERICAN MUSEUM OF RADIO AND ELECTRICITY** (1312 Bay St; 360/738-3886; amre.us/site; $5 adults) features a large hands-on collection of vintage radios and traces the development of radio back to the 1600s; **MINDPORT** (210 W Holly St; 360/647-5614; mindport.org; $2) is a tiny museum and gallery focusing on imagination, with an eclectic mix of hands-on exhibits; and the **BELLINGHAM RAILWAY MUSEUM** (1320 Commercial St; 360/393-7540; bellinghamrailwaymuseum.org; $3 adults) is a train lover's paradise. There's also the **WHATCOM MUSEUM OF HISTORY & ART** (121, 201, 206, and 227 Prospect St; 360/676-6981; whatcommuseum.org), which is part of a four-building complex that includes the **CHILDREN'S MUSEUM** ($3.50; other museums free) and **ARCO EXHIBITS BUILDING.**

The central area also has numerous places to eat or get a snack. **THE BAGELRY** (1319 Railroad Ave; 360/676-5288; thebagelry.biz) has soups, bagels, and a fun mix of flavored cream cheeses. With pizzas named Greek Havoc, Major Grigio, the Sofa, and Pizza Diablo, it's obvious **LA FIAMMA WOOD FIRE PIZZA** (200 E Chestnut St; 360/647-0060; lafiamma.com) doesn't take itself too seriously, but it serves seriously good pizza. **ROCKET DONUTS** (306 W Holly St; 360/671-6111; rocketdonuts.com) is a good place to stop for a round snack, but hands down the best place for dessert is **MALLARD FRESH MADE ICE CREAM** (1323 Railroad Ave; 360/734-3884) where the flavors range from staid vanilla to Earl Grey Tea to Spontaneous Human Combustion Cinnamon (with a touch of cayenne), and the tastes come on real spoons, not dinky pink plastic ones.

If the weather holds and you want more time outdoors, follow curvy North Shore Drive to the **NORTH LAKE WHATCOM TRAILHEAD** for a 6-mile walk along the lake. On the return trip, turn right on Alabama Street and right on Sylvan Street to see the **BIG ROCK GARDEN**, a hidden 2.7-acre garden with a variety of sculptures mixed in with trees, plants, and shrubs. Follow Alabama back to Electric Avenue, turn right and follow the signs to **WHATCOM FALLS PARK**, one of the city's best parks, with pretty waterfalls and a stone bridge over the Works Progress Administration–era bridge over Whatcom Creek. Turn left on Lakeway Drive and follow it around past Euclid Avenue and you'll come to **SCHNAUZER CROSSING** (4421 Lakeway Dr; 360/734-2808 or 800/562-2808; schnauzercrossing.com), a B&B with a tiny Japanese tearoom, a large lawn sloping down toward the lake, and a schnauzer presiding over the property.

Kitsap and Olympic Peninsulas

HOOD CANAL

Take a Washington State Ferry from Colman Dock (Pier 52) in downtown Seattle to Bainbridge Island; crossing is approximately 35 minutes. From the Bainbridge ferry dock, take Highway 305 north across Agate Passage and through Poulsbo to Highway 3; driving time approximately 45 minutes. South leads to the east shore of Hood Canal; north leads to the Hood Canal Bridge at the mouth of the canal, with its crossing to Highway 104 and U.S. Highway 101, which in turn meanders south along the west shore of the canal—your return route.

Hood Canal, a 65-mile-long, fishhook-shaped inland waterway, lies west of Puget Sound, between Kitsap Peninsula and the Olympic Peninsula. The eastern arm of Hood Canal extends from Belfair southwest along Highway 106 to Union. The area is filled with mansions and homes built by urbanites seeking summer getaways with Olympic Mountain views and is the site of the gracious, recently renovated Alderbrook Resort. From Union, the canal turns north at the Great Bend; US 101 follows the west shore of the less domesticated western arm, which has long stretches of forested slopes and accessible beaches. Three rivers that plunge down from the Olympics to Hood Canal's western arm offer trail access to the mountains: the **DUCKABUSH**, the **HAMMA HAMMA**, and the **DOSEWALLIPS.** US 101 and Highway 104 lead north and west to the mouth of Hood Canal, closing the loop tour described below.

From Highway 3 just outside Poulsbo, head south toward Silverdale and follow signs west to Seabeck. On the Kitsap Peninsula's west shoulder is **SCENIC BEACH STATE PARK**, with picnicking, campsites, and a view of the Olympics.

To reach the peninsula's southern tip, follow back roads south through Holly and Dewatto to reach the Belfair-Tahuya Road or return to Highway 3 and drive south to Belfair to Highway 300 southwest, which follows the north shore of the canal's east arm. At the tip of the peninsula, overlooking the canal's Great Bend, sprawling **TAHUYA STATE FOREST** embraces beach and forest and is sought out by mountain and dirt bikers, hikers, and horseback riders.

Returning north on Highway 300, **BELFAIR STATE PARK**, three miles south of Belfair, is one of the peninsula's busiest parks. Campers must reserve in summer (888/226-7688). You can swim, fish, or dig clams. Just north of the state park, South Belfair's **THELER COMMUNITY CENTER AND WETLAND TRAILS** (E 22871 SR 3; 360/275-4898; thelercenter.org) features 3.8 miles of wheelchair-accessible trails through marshes, woods, and the Union River estuary. A wooden causeway over a tidal marsh provides a view of the head of the canal's expanse. The interpretive center gives insight into the value of wetlands.

From Belfair, continue south on Highway 3 a short way to Highway 106 and follow it southwest. Renovated in 2007, **TWANOH STATE PARK** on the south shore of Hood Canal's eastern arm has a big shallow pool that makes it popular with families and a newly spiffed up fast-food concession. Farther southwest, the **UNION COUNTRY STORE** (E 5130 Hwy 106; 360/898-2641) offers exotic groceries, produce, wines, and wonderful fresh-daily dips (free tastings). Open seasonally. In the off-season, try the pub menu at **ROBIN HOOD** (E 6790 Hwy 106; 360/898-4400; therobinhood.com) or enjoy a stellar view of the canal and fine dining at the **RESTAURANT AT ALDERBROOK** (10 E Alderbrook Dr; 360/898-2200 or 800/622-9370; alderbrookresort.com). Continue west to cross the Skokomish River and meet US 101, where you turn north to follow the canal's west shore.

POTLATCH STATE PARK, three miles south of Hoodsport, is a good stop for a picnic or refreshing dip. At low tide, you can gather oysters on the beach. **HOODSPORT WINERY** (23501 N Hwy 101; 360/877-9894; hoodsport.com), a mile south of Hoodsport, will pair its wine with your oysters. Sample fruit wines, white varietals, or the legendary Island Belle, made from grapes grown on nearby Stretch Island. Open daily.

Hoodsport serves as the gateway to the Lake Cushman area. Just west of the lake's development and a mile west of the Olympic National Park Boundary you'll find a ranger station, campground, picnicking, and trailheads. The short **STAIRCASE RAPIDS TRAIL** along the upper Skokomish River is a pleasure. From Hoodsport to Quilcene, Hood Canal's west arm boasts many recreational areas in the **OLYMPIC NATIONAL FOREST** and **OLYMPIC NATIONAL PARK**, but some are hike-in only. Ranger stations along US 101 provide all the information you need to visit.

The Hoodsport Ranger Station is now the **HOOD CANAL VISITORS CENTER** (just off US 101 on Lake Cushman Dr; 360/877-2021), but it still has single-sheet maps for hikes along the canal's southern sector.

Public beaches where oystering is permitted along the canal's west reach include Cushman Beach, Lilliwaup Recreational Tidelands, Pleasant Harbor State Park (near the mouth of the Duckabush River), Dosewallips State Park (a choice stop, with 425 acres of meadows, woodlands, and beach), and Seal Rock Campground. Most have clam beds. North of Seal Rock, Bee Mill Road heads eastward from US 101 to the Point Whitney State Shellfish Laboratory, with an interpretive display and a good oyster and swimming beach. Check the state hotline (800/562-5632) for red tide warnings. North of Hoodsport and just south of the Hamma Hamma River, shucked and whole oysters may be purchased at **HAMA HAMA OYSTER COMPANY SEAFOOD STORE** (35846 N US 101; 360/877-5811; hamahamaoysters.com).

WHITNEY GARDENS in Brinnon, between Dosewallips State Park and Seal Rock, is part nursery, part tourist attraction, where visitors can see a rainbow of colors from blooming rhododendrons, azaleas, and camellias or roam among the 7-acre facility's corridors filled with weeping spruces, maples, and magnolias. The company also has a mail-order catalog business and ships plants all over the United States. Open daily (small fee). You can picnic at the gazebo or eat at folksy, unassuming **HALFWAY HOUSE** (US 101 at Brinnon Ln; 360/796-4715) and rub elbows with the locals.

Just 5 miles south of Quilcene off US 101, 2,750-foot **MOUNT WALKER** is one of the canal's most spectacular viewpoints, providing views of Seattle, Mount Rainier, and the Cascades. You can reach it by driving up a 5-mile dirt road that snakes around the mountain (summer only) or hiking up the 2-mile trail (year-round). Also worth a stop is the **WALKER MOUNTAIN TRADING POST** (near the Mount Walker turnoff from US 101; 360/796-3200), which crams antiques and collectibles into a pioneer home. On the highway's west side, 1 mile north of the Mount Walker turnoff, **FALLS VIEW CAMPGROUND** is a short hike from a lovely waterfall on the Quilcene River.

THE QUILCENE RANGER STATION (295142 Hwy 101 S; 360/765-2200; www.fs.fed.us/r6/olympic), south of Quilcene, has information about outdoor recreation on the canal's north end, including shellfishing advice. **QUILCENE** has the world's largest oyster hatchery and perhaps the purest saltwater in the West. The mellow **WHISTLING OYSTER** (294903 Hwy 101; 360/765-9508; whistlingoysterbar.com) is where locals go for food, darts, and shuffleboard. In the middle of town, the **TWANA ROADHOUSE** (360/765-6485) features fresh soups, sandwiches, homemade pies, and quick service.

Pearls aren't the only thing that's cultured in these parts. There's also the **OLYMPIC MUSIC FESTIVAL** (north of Quilcene just before the US 101–Highway 104 junction; 206/527-8839; olympicmusicfestival.org) in a turn-of-the-20th-century barn/concert hall (2 pm on Saturdays and Sundays, late June through mid-September). The classical music concerts are held at a working farm, and kids are encouraged to pet the animals. The music is heavenly and performed by a variety of string quartets and guest artists from all over. Reservations advised.

Head east on Highway 104 and cross the Hood Canal Bridge to close the loop at Highway 3 south of Port Gamble. Or continue north on US 101 to Discovery Bay and Highway 20 north to Port Townsend.

PORT TOWNSEND

Take a Washington State Ferry from Colman Dock (Pier 52) in downtown Seattle to Bainbridge Island; crossing is approximately 35 minutes. From the Bainbridge ferry dock, head northwest on Highway 305 to Highway 3. Follow Highway 3 north to the Hood Canal Bridge and cross it to continue west on Highway 104, turn north onto Highway 19, which merges into Highway 20. Follow Highway 20 north into Port Townsend, 50 miles northwest of Seattle (approximately 2 hours).

It may be a staid Victorian town today, but in Port Townsend whiskey once flowed freely, brothels flourished, and sailors were shanghaied. The seaport is still a magnet, but the mid-1800s architecture and waterfront are the big attractions. Instead of spending hours roaming the streets seeking parking during festivals, stop at the **PARK AND RIDE** (at Haines Place near Safeway, as you enter town) and ride the shuttle, which runs every 20 minutes to uptown (Lawrence Street) and downtown (Water Street), for $1.25.

While you wait for the shuttle, you can take in the hidden treasure of **KAH TAI LAGOON**, a popular spot with bikers, birders, and waterfowl. Other parks in town include diminutive **POPE MARINE PARK** at the end of Adams Street, with picnic tables and playground equipment, and **UNION WHARF**, a 130-year-old fixture with views of Mount Baker and Mount Rainier.

Wander along Water Street downtown and enjoy a combination of Victorian architecture and 21st-century consumerism in the city's shops, galleries, and eateries. *Niche* magazine rated **EARTHENWORKS** (702 Water St; 360/385-0328; earthenworksgallery.com) one of the top 25 craft galleries in the country. **THE ANTIQUE MALL** (802 Washington St; 360/379-8069) holds 35 shops offering a hodgepodge of old and new, as well as Port Townsend's version of Underground Seattle: a display of artifacts from PT's old Chinatown, which was destroyed by fire at the turn of the 20th century. The items were discovered when the mall basement was excavated. **PACIFIC TRADITIONS** in the lobby of the **WATER STREET HOTEL** (637 Water St; 360/385-4770; pacifictraditions.com) sells serigraphs, carvings, Cowichan sweaters, and goods made by Olympic Peninsula artists. **IMPRINT BOOKSTORE** (820 Water St; 360/385-3643) has a mix of classics, contemporary literature, and regional guidebooks. Across the street, **WILLIAM JAMES BOOKSELLER** (829 Water St; 360/385-7313) sells used and rare books. **APRIL FOOL & PENNY TOO** (725 Water St; 360/385-3438; aprilfoolandpennytoo.com) focuses on whimsical cards, collectibles, and jewelry. The new location of **THE WINE SELLER** (1010 Water St; 360/385-7673; ptwineseller.com) is an art loft offering wine tastings and a large selection of wine, beer, and coffee.

BEST PLACE
TO MEET A STRANGER?

"Rachel the pig, at Pike Place Market."

Tom Douglas, celebrated local chef and restaurateur

The community fixture **ELEVATED ICE CREAM COMPANY** (627 Water St; 360/385-1156; elevatedicecream.com) has a sundeck overlooking the bay and a wide range of flavors, including local favorite Swiss Orange Chocolate Chip. **FIN'S COASTAL CUISINE** (1019 Water St; 360/379-3474; finscoastalcuisine.com) features a fresh menu daily, European-trained chefs, and a balcony view. **BREAD & ROSES BAKERY AND DELI** (230 Quincy St; 360/379-3355) serves artisan bread, pastries, and light lunch with open-air seating. **SALAL CAFÉ** (634 Water St; 360/385-6532) has breakfast and cleverly conceived meals. At the classic **ROSE THEATRE** (235 Taylor St; 360/385-1089; rosetheatre.com), contemporary American and foreign films are still introduced by a staff member.

Uptown is just a stair climb away at Taylor and Washington streets, or you can drive past the old Episcopal church and red **OLD BELL TOWER**. Venerable Victorian mansions populate a residential area just blocks from Lawrence Street's cafés and galleries. It took two years to rebuild after a fire, but **ALDRICH'S** (940 Lawrence St; 360/385-0500; aldrichs.com) is back in business with its eclectic mix of groceries, gourmet foods, wine, a bakery, and a deli. **PROVISIONS** (939 Kearney St; 360/385-4541; provisionspt.com) offers specialty meats and ready-made takeout, or you can cut out the middleman and go to the **PORT TOWNSEND FARMERS' MARKETS** (Tyler and Lawrence streets, Saturdays, May to mid-November; Lawrence and Polk streets, Wednesdays, mid-June to late September; 360/379-9098; ptfarmers market.org). Take your takeout to **CHETZEMOKA PARK** at Jackson and Blaine streets and enjoy the rose arbors and beach access. You can even dig clams (call 800/562-5632 for red tide warnings).

A visit to **FORT WORDEN STATE PARK** could easily take an entire day, which is why it's a good thing the old army base has inexpensive lodgings that are great for families or people attending events put on by the Centrum Foundation, including summertime concerts, plays, and music workshops. For a taste of history, visit the **COMMANDING OFFICER'S QUARTERS** (360/344-4452; commandingofficersquarters.org) to see how a turn-of-the-20th-century officer and family lived, then go to **ARTILLERY HILL** to explore the gun emplacements and bunkers. The area may look familiar to film buffs—for good reason. Parts of *An Officer and a Gentleman* were filmed here. Grab a meal in the Servery (in the heart of Fort Worden; 360/385-9950), the park's buffet-style dining facility, then head back out to the beach's **PORT TOWNSEND MARINE SCIENCE CENTER** (360/385-5582; ptmsc.org), which has touch tanks and aquariums for kids (closed in winter; call for hours) and a natural history exhibit that's open on weekends in winter.

You can get a glimpse of PT's tawdry past at the **JEFFERSON COUNTY HISTORICAL SOCIETY MUSEUM** in City Hall (540 Water St; 360/385-1003; jchsmuseum.org), which includes the original courtroom, jail, and a reproduction of a Victorian bedroom. The 130-year-old Greek Revival **ROTHSCHILD HOUSE** (360/379-8076, group tour reservations) at Jefferson and Taylor streets features original furnishings and family artifacts, as well as herb and rose gardens. If you want to see more, come for PT's annual **HISTORIC HOMES TOUR** (Port Townsend Visitors Information Center, 360/385-2722; ptchamber.org), held every September, or experience history up close by staying at the turreted Victorian **OLD CONSULATE INN** (313 Walker St; 360/385-6753 or 800/300-6753; oldconsulateinn.com), which features a seven-dish, three-course breakfast.

Port Townsend also has two downtown marinas and a Washington State Ferry dock. From here, you can take a short ferry ride across Admiralty Inlet to the Keystone ferry dock on Whidbey Island. PT's annual **WOODEN BOAT FESTIVAL** (360/385-3628; woodenboat.org/festival) on the first weekend after Labor Day is centered at Hudson Point at the end of Water Street. Attractions include concerts, entertainers, and, of course, boats. And don't miss the annual **KINETIC SCULPTURE RACE** (360/379-4972; ptkineticrace.org) in early October, when locals race anything they can get to move in land, on water, and through a mud bog.

Mount Rainier and Mount St. Helens

MOUNT RAINIER

Take Interstate 5 south from Seattle to exit 142; then take Highway 161 south through Puyallup, Graham, and Eatonville; head east on Highway 7 to Elbe. Take Highway 706 east through Ashford to the park's southwestern (Nisqually) entrance; 100 miles southeast of Seattle, approximately 2½ hours.

At more than 500 feet tall, the Space Needle may be impressive, but it's got nothing on Mount Rainier. Called "Tahoma" by Native Americans, the dormant, 14,410-foot volcano is an awe-inspiring landmark that creates its own weather and magnetically draws people from all over the globe.

A day of nature appreciation can start long before the park with a visit to **NORTHWEST TREK WILDLIFE PARK** (11610 Trek Dr E, Eatonville; 360/832-6117; nwtrek.org; $13.50 adult) 55 miles south of Seattle off Highway 161, about 60 miles from Rainier's Nisqually entrance. Visitors can ooh and aah over bison, moose, and elk as naturalists narrate an hour-long, 5.5-mile tram trip.

The closest lodging to the park's Nisqually entrance is around Ashford. **WELLSPRING SPA AND RESORT** (54922 Kernahan Rd E, Ashford; 360/569-2514) boasts two spas surrounded by evergreens. If your massage (or hour-long hot tub soak for $10) has rendered you too mellow to travel, spend the night. **ALEXANDER'S COUNTRY INN** (37515 Hwy 706 E, Ashford; 360/569-2300 or 800/654-7615; alexanderscountryinn.com) is a turn-of-the-20th-century inn offering modern comforts, including a full-service spa, a full-course breakfast, and B&B-style rooms. The inn also serves an upscale dinner—including pan-fried trout from the holding pond out back (reservations suggested). **MOUNTAIN MEADOWS INN B&B** (28912 Hwy 706 E, Ashford; 360/569-2788; mountainmeadowsinn.com) is closer to the park and has six large guest rooms, a private outdoor 23-jet Jacuzzi spa, and a mile-long nature trail. The 24-room **NISQUALLY LODGE** (31609 Hwy 706 E, Ashford; 360/569-8804; escapetothemountains.com) may offer a reasonably priced respite for people who favor charm over a phone, TV, and air-conditioning, but it's not a complete escape: it now offers wireless and DSL connections.

A mile past the park's Nisqually entrance is Sunshine Point Campground (open year-round) and 6 miles farther is the village of Longmire and the **NATIONAL PARK INN** (360/569-2411; guestservices.com/rainier), a wildlife museum, hiking information center, and cross-country skiing rental outlet.

A major winter storm in November 2006 inflicted a great deal of damage on **MOUNT RAINIER NATIONAL PARK**. At press time, park officials expected that most areas would reopen soon but urged visitors to call ahead or check the Web site (360/569-2211; nps.gov/mora).

The 235,625-acre park is a lushly forested reserve surrounding Mount Rainier. You can tour by car, hike or snowshoe, ski nearby, or climb to the summit.

The most popular (and lowest-impact) option in summer is to drive a loop around the mountain. Follow the road from Longmire to Paradise (you can use it during daylight hours in winter, but it's best to carry tire chains and a shovel and check conditions beforehand on the 24-hour information line, 360/569-2211) to Highway 123 over Cayuse Pass to Highway 410 just west of Chinook Pass (both passes are closed in winter), then take the road west to Sunrise (open only when it's snow free, usually July 1 through early October). This route was closed at press time but was scheduled to reopen in 2008, with the segment of Highway 123 from Ohanapecosh north to Highway 410 slated to open in late 2007. Call the park or check the Web site.

The park road winds past **COUGAR PARK CAMPGROUND** (reservations required, 877/444-6777), scenic viewpoints, and waterfalls on its climb to **PARADISE.** At 5,400 feet on the mountain's south side, it is the park's most visited destination because of its sheer beauty. It also offers the most complete services in the park, including rustic accommodations at **PARADISE INN** (mid-May to October; 360/569-2413; guestservices.com/rainier), which at press time was under renovation and expected to reopen in May 2008. A new visitor's center next to the Inn was under construction and expected to be complete at the end of fall 2008. The area also has a network of hiking trails perfect for cross-country skiing, inner tubing, or snowshoeing in winter.

The park road continues east to Highway 123 at the Stevens Canyon entrance; head north over Cayuse Pass at Highway 410, then continue north to Sunrise Road at the White River entrance: White River Campground is on the way up to Sunrise. About 1,000 feet farther up, the **SUNRISE** visitor area offers views of the peak from the northeast. It's the highest point open to cars and is only open in summer. A number of naturalist talks are offered daily; check at the visitor center or the Web site for a schedule.

There are 305 miles of trails within the park, including the 90-mile Wonderland Trail, which circles the mountain. A few sections of the trail were closed at press time but were expected to be back in service in 2008. Backcountry permits are required for camping and are available at ranger stations and visitors' centers. The campgrounds at Ohanapecosh (just south of the Stevens Canyon entrance) and Cougar Rock require reservations (877/444-6777), while sites at White River, Ipsut Creek (on the park's northwest corner), and Sunshine Point are first come, first served. At press time, Sunshine Point was closed but was to reopen in 2008.

Skiers may enjoy the **MOUNT TAHOMA SKI HUTS**, a hut-to-hut trail system south and west of the park run by the Tahoma Trails Association (PO Box 206, Ashford, WA 98304; 360/569-2451; skimtta.com). There are more than 75 miles of trails, three huts, and one yurt. Not far away, the rooms at **WHITTAKER'S BUNKHOUSE** (30205 Hwy 706; 360/569-2439; whittakersbunkhouse.com) are basic and cheap. Another skiing option is **CRYSTAL MOUNTAIN** (33914 Crystal Mountain Blvd, Enumclaw; 360/663-2265; skicrystal.com), near Sunrise Road on Highway 410, which is said to have the state's best skiing (see Recreation chapter).

Or you can climb the mountain with a concessioned guide service such as **RAINIER MOUNTAINEERING** (30027 Hwy 706 E, Ashford; 888/892-5462; rmiguides.com) or with your own party. If you're on your own, you must register at a park ranger station and pay $30 for a year pass. The guide service offers a number of programs with a range of training requirements. It's possible to climb year-round, but late May to mid-September is the best time to go. It's also advisable to climb with a guide unless you're qualified to do it solo. Rainier is as dangerous as it is beautiful.

To complete your loop around Mount Rainier, continue north and west on Highway 410 through Enumclaw back to Highway 161. Or return to Elbe on Highway 7 and turn south to Morton on U.S. Highway 12 to reach Mount St. Helens from the north.

MOUNT ST. HELENS

Take Interstate 5 south from Seattle to exit 49, then follow signs east via Highway 504; approximately 150 miles south of Seattle, a two- to three-hour drive.

After years of relative quiet since Mount St. Helens' eruption in May 1980, an increase in seismic activity in late 2004 prompted worries about another possible blast. The crisis passed, but a new lava dome continues to grow inside the crater, and a small eruption occurred in 2006. Nonetheless, the mountain is worth a day trip, especially on a clear day when you can see how the mountain has recovered from the 1980 blast.

BEST PLACE
TO FIND INSPIRATION?

"At a beach burn at Golden Gardens Park. Someone's usually staging one on any given weekend over the summer, but the best are thrown by Burning Man tribes—dementia set to a glorious inferno. Leave the kids at home."

Melanie McFarland, former Seattle Post-Intelligencer *TV critic*

Take I-5 exit 49/Castle Rock to Highway 504 (the Spirit Lake Memorial Highway) to start your visit to the five interpretive centers that put the blast into perspective. The Washington State Parks and Recreation Commission's **MOUNT ST. HELENS VISITORS CENTER** (milepost 5; 360/274-0962) features a walk-through volcano, historical photos, exhibits about the blast, and a film. Cowlitz County's **HOFFSTADT BLUFFS VISITOR CENTER** (milepost 27; 360/274-7750; mt-st-helens.com) has a memorial to those who died in the blast and, in summer, a glass blower who makes Mount St. Helens ash-blown glass. This stop has a restaurant, gift shop, and helicopter tours. The Weyerhaeuser-operated **FOREST LEARNING CENTER** (milepost 33; 360/414-3439; weyerhaeuser.com/citizenship/publicoutreach/sthelens/anniversary.asp) covers the impact of the eruption on forest management. The Forest Service's **COLDWATER RIDGE VISITOR CENTER** (milepost 43; 360/274-2114; www.fs.fed.us/gpnf/mshnvm) offers awe-inspiring views of the black dome in the middle of the 2-mile-wide steaming crater and of Coldwater and Castle lakes (both created by massive mud flows), and focuses on the landscape's stunning biological recovery. The **JOHNSTON RIDGE OBSERVATORY** (milepost 52; 360/274-2140; www.fs.fed.us/gpnf/mshnvm) provides a view directly into the crater and looks at the eruption, how geologists monitor volcanoes, and what has been learned since the eruption. Admission to each Forest Service visitor center is $3 per adult ($6 for more than one center, free for children under 4).

There are viewpoints along the roads approaching the mountain (from the south, Highway 503 via Woodland and Cougar; from the north, U.S. Highway 12 east to Randle, then Forest Roads 25 and 99), but all of the visitors' centers are on Highway 504. Although there's no camping in the Mount St. Helens National Monument, the nearby 1.3-million-acre **GIFFORD PINCHOT NATIONAL FOREST** (360/891-5001; www.fs.fed.us/gpnf) offers more than 50 places to fish and pitch a tent. Call ahead for road and camping conditions.

Budget at least 7 to 10 hours if you plan to climb the mountain. Reservations can be made online. In-person registration should be done the day before you plan to climb. In either case you'll need to get a permit for $15. You can sign in at **JACK'S STORE AND RESTAURANT** (23 miles east of Woodland on Highway 503 just west of Cougar; 360/231-4276). Consider it a winter climb from November 1 to late spring and a summer one July through October. In either case, bring good hiking boots, drinking water, sunscreen, sunglasses, crampons, and an ice ax.

Extend your mountain sojourn by staying at the moderately priced, 49-room **SEASONS MOTEL** (200 Westlake Ave, Morton; 360/496-6835 or 877/496-6835; whitepasstravel.com) halfway between Mount St. Helens and Mount Rainier on US 12.

British Columbia

VICTORIA

The oh-so-international city of Vancouver may be a popular getaway for Washingtonians, but it's more of a weekend escape; for details, pick up *Best Places Northwest, 16th edition* (Sasquatch Books, 2007). Victoria, on the other hand, is doable in a day. The passenger-only Victoria Clipper from Pier 69 in downtown Seattle takes only 2½ hours.

A city that mixes the old-world charm of Britain with new-world experiences, Victoria is gaining a reputation as a soft adventure destination and for its culinary scene. The Cousteau Society rates it as home to the world's second-best winter diving, making it a big diving destination, while the Island Chef's Collaborative has made local restaurants something to write home about.

First, you have to get there. The **VICTORIA CLIPPER**'s high-speed foot ferry (206/448-5000 Seattle, 250/382-8100 Victoria, or 800/888-2535 outside Seattle and BC; clippervacations.com) takes passengers to this highly walkable city three times a day from May to September and once or twice a day in the off-season. You can also fly **KENMORE AIR** (425/486-1257; kenmoreair.com) from Lake Union to the Inner Harbor starting at $200 round trip or **HORIZON AIRLINES** (800/547-9308; horizonair.com) from Sea-Tac Airport.

TOURISM VICTORIA (812 Wharf St; 800/663-3883; tourismvictoria.com) is a good first stop for information on where to go hiking, biking, diving, or sightseeing. **CYCLE BC RENTALS** (950 Wharf St; 250/380-2453 or 866/380-2453; cyclebc.ca) is a block away, and the 78-mile (125 km) **GALLOPING GOOSE TRAIL** is just across the Johnson Street Bridge. Diving is just a 10-minute walk or short bicycle cab ride to the **OGDEN POINT DIVE CENTER** (199 Dallas Rd; 888/701-1177; divevictoria.com), where you'll be outfitted and in the water in nothing flat.

If atmosphere is your thing, hop on one of **TALLY HO**'s (250/514-9257 or 888/383-5067; tallyhotours.com) horse-drawn carriage tours. The most popular route starts at the **PARLIAMENT BUILDINGS** (Belleville and Menzies streets) and meanders through Beacon Hill Park to the waterfront and James Bay. **THE ROYAL BRITISH COLUMBIA MUSEUM** (Belleville and Government streets; 250/387-3701; rbcm.gov.bc.ca; adults $25.50, seniors $19.50, students with I.D. and youths 6–18 $17.50, children 5 and under free; all prices Canadian) isn't as stodgy as it sounds, with lively exhibits including reconstructions of Victorian storefronts and another detailing global warming's impact on the region. The Rockland neighborhood mansion that houses the **ART GALLERY OF GREATER VICTORIA** (1040 Moss St; 250/384-4101; aggv.bc.ca) has been restored to its original Queen Anne colors and includes an Emily Carr exhibit, Asian art, and North America's only Shinto shrine. It's a 10-minute walk from downtown and not far from **CRAIGDARROCH CASTLE** (1050 Joan Crescent, off Fort Street; 250/592-5323; thecastle.ca), an opulent mansion built by coal tycoon Robert Dunsmuir, who died before it was completed. Open daily.

Old-home buffs will find plenty to like, such as five **VICTORIA HERITAGE HOMES** (admission varies; seasonal closures) downtown, including **HELMCKEN HOUSE** (behind Thunderbird Park, east of the Royal BC Museum), **POINT ELLICE HOUSE** (Bay and Pleasant streets), **CRAIGFLOWER MANOR** (110 Island Hwy), **CRAIGFLOWER SCHOOLHOUSE** (2765 Admirals Rd), and painter Emily Carr's childhood home, **CARR HOUSE** (Government and Simcoe streets).

If you only have time for one grand old building, make sure it's the **FAIRMONT EMPRESS** (721 Government St; 250/384-8111 or 250/389-2727, tea reservations; fairmont.com/empress). Hotels may come and go, but this century-old Edwardian in its commanding location across the street from the water *is* Victoria and the place to go for afternoon tea at 12:30pm (summer only), 2pm, 3:30pm, and 5pm. (For other afternoon tea locations, see Tea Time in Old Town sidebar, this chapter.) The **BENGAL LOUNGE** down the hall from the tearoom is famed for its curry buffet and martinis. The **MCPHERSON PLAYHOUSE** (3 Centennial Square; 250/386-6121 or 888/717-6121; rmts.bc.ca), a former vaudeville house, still hosts a variety of shows. The free **MONDAY MAGAZINE** contains the city's best weekly calendar of events.

The city has more to offer than old buildings. **BEACON HILL PARK**'s 177 acres south of downtown offer water views, beautiful landscaping, and

TEA TIME IN OLD TOWN

Aah, tea. Such a civilized beverage. Sure, there are plenty of places to grab a cup of coffee in Victoria BC, but there's something about tea's very nature that makes it a slower drink. There's the sitting while waiting for the steeping and all the trays filled with all those finger sandwiches. And what place could possibly be more perfect for such a traditional afternoon repast than this far-flung outpost of the British Empire?

Afternoon tea at **THE EMPRESS** (721 Government St; 250/389-2727; fairmont.com/empress/GuestServices/Restaurants/AfternoonTea.htm) may be a must for visitors who remembered to make reservations far enough in advance, but $40 (in summer; $27.50 in winter) for crustless sandwiches and a pot of Empress tea can put a major dent in anyone's wallet. Fortunately, there are other options for people who want to have an oh-so-Victorian experience without breaking the bank.

At the **WHITE HEATHER TEA ROOM** (1885 Oak Bay Ave; 250/595-8020) you can have full tea service for half the Empress's price—and you may have more fun. Local character and owner Agnes Campbell offers the Wee Tea (approximately $10), the Not So Wee Tea ($13), and the Big Muckle Giant Tea for Two ($31.50), which Campbell guarantees will make you "cuddlier." Reservations required.

THE BLETHERING PLACE (2250 Oak Bay Ave; 250/598-1413 or 888/598-1413; thebletheringplace.com) may use traditional Royal Doulton China, but it's

BEACON HILL CHILDREN'S PETTING ZOO, a mini-zoo with a petting corral. **ABIGAIL'S HOTEL** (906 McClure St; 250/388-5363 or 800/561-6565; abigailshotel.com), a 23-room Tudor manor, is also close to the park.

Shopping is another important part of any visit. The area near the Empress is great for window-shopping. **W&J WILSON CLOTHIERS** (1221 Government St; 250/383-7177), the oldest family-owned clothing business in Canada, sells Scottish cashmere sweaters. **SASQUATCH TRADING COMPANY** (1233 Government St; 250/386-9033) specializes in Native art and Cowichan sweaters. **OLD MORRIS TOBACCONIST** (1116 Government St; 250/382-4811 or 888/845-6111; oldmorris.com) carries pipes, tobacco, and Cuban cigars, and **MUNRO'S BOOKS** (1108 Government St; 250/382-2464 or 888/243-2464; munrobooks.com), in an early 1900s bank building, is one of Canada's largest independent booksellers. Sweet lovers should pick up Victoria creams at **ROGER'S CHOCOLATES** (913 Government St; 250/384-7021 or 877/663-2220; rogerschocolates.com); Pontefract cakes, Australian licorice, and bon bons at the **ENGLISH SWEET SHOP** (738 Yates St; 250/382-3325; www.englishsweets.com); and beautiful Belgian chocolates at not fussy. There are lots of little tables with mismatched chairs; visitors can order full tea service for $13–$15.30 or order à la carte; and there's no dress code. Older residents love it because servers take time out to visit, and it reminds them of the England they left behind.

At $30, tea at the **HOTEL GRAND PACIFIC** (463 Belleville St; 250/380-4458) comes dangerously close to prices at the Empress, but it offers a different take on the much-loved repast: a West Coast theme, featuring Bodum tea pots, such savory treats as five-spice scones and cucumber wasabi cream cheese, alternative Asian tea selections, and even a dim sum menu. Available from 2 to 5pm, Thursday through Sunday. Reservations recommended.

SILK ROAD AROMATHERAPY AND TEA COMPANY (1624 Government St; 250/704-2688; silkroadtea.com) doesn't exactly offer afternoon tea service, but it does offer tea tastings and educational workshops, and plans to offer a tea tasting bar where people will be able to sample the classic drink and learn about it the same way wine lovers try new varietals on for size.

Of course, if none of those work, one local wag mentioned another option. Go to **MURCHIE'S TEA & COFFEE** (1110 Government St; 250/381-5451; murchies.com) a few blocks from the famed hotel, buy a cup of tea, carry it to the Empress, and walk through the lobby as you drink it. Then you'll be able to tell your friends you had tea at the Empress, and no one will ever be the wiser.

—David Volk

BERNARD CALLEBAUT CHOCOLATERIE (621 Broughton St; 250/380-1515; bernardcallebaut.com).

A restored 19th-century courtyard-turned-mall, Market Square (between Wharf and Store streets on Johnson Street) boasts three floors of eateries and stores, including the gardening shop **DIG THIS** (560 Johnson St; 250/385-3212). **CHINATOWN** is just a few blocks north on Fisgard Street at the Gate of Harmonious Interest, but boutiques, lofts, and non-Chinese eateries have begun nibbling into an area that was once the turf of Chinese restaurants and greengrocers. Once a hidden passage into Chinatown's gambling parlors and opium dens, **FAN TAN ALLEY** is the narrowest street in North America listed on a map even though you can't drive on it. Shop for your home at **PANACEA THE FURNITURE ART COMPANY** (532 Fisgard St; 250/391-8960) while sipping a bubble tea—a neon mixture of tea and your favorite flavor with chewy tapioca pearls at the bottom. Sip slowly, though. If you drink through the straw too quickly, you'll end up getting a pearl in the back of your throat. Round out your visit to the neighborhood with a Chinese dinner at **WAH LAI YUEN** (560 Fisgard St; 250/381-5355).

Antique Row is east of downtown along the 800 to 1100 blocks of Fort Street ending at **FAITH GRANT THE CONNOISSEUR SHOP** (1156 Fort St; 250/383-0121; faithgrantantiques.com). **BASTION SQUARE** (bounded by Yates and Fort streets and Wharf and Langley streets) is home to sidewalk restaurants, art galleries, and the **MARITIME MUSEUM OF BRITISH COLUMBIA** (28 Bastion Square; 250/385-4222; mmbc.bc.ca; adults $8, seniors and students $5, kids 6–11 $3) where Victoria's old gallows were located. It has become prime real estate for ghost sightings. You can find out about other spooky locales on a **GHOSTLY WALKS TOUR** (250/384-6698; discoverthepast.com). Led nightly from mid-June to mid-September, weekends during the Ghosts of Victoria Festival in October, and Saturdays the rest of the year. Tours start at the Visitors Information Centre and wind through alleys, squares, and Olde Town's other happy haunting grounds. $12 for adults. The company also offers Chinatown Walks every Saturday year-round.

Although it's ostensibly geared to kids, the **VICTORIA BUG ZOO** (631 Courtney St; 250/384-2847; bugzoo.bc.ca) also appeals to adults who love creepy-crawlies. Why else would only adults be allowed to hold the tarantula during a guided tour of the storefront menagerie?

BUTCHART GARDENS (800 Benvenuto Ave, Brentwood Bay; 250/652-5256; butchartgardens.com) is Victoria's other must-see attraction. Even if you aren't a big botanical garden fan, this landmark 13 miles outside town is stunning. What started as Jenny Butchart's plan to reclaim her husband's limestone quarry became 50 acres of impressively manicured formal gardens. Aim for early in the morning when the dew is on the grass or late summer afternoons after the tourist buses have left. Afternoon tea and light meals are served in the garden's teahouse. Entertainment and fireworks on Saturday nights in late summer (admission fee; open daily).

There are plenty of great places to grab a bite to eat. For breakfast, try **MO:LE** (544 Pandora St; 250/385-6653), a happening early-morning spot featuring such dishes as a curried squash omelet and French toast with wild flowers and honey-roasted pears. The **BROUGHTON STREET DELI** (648 Broughton St; 250/380-9988) is a great stop for a quick Montreal smoked beef sandwich, while **NOODLE BOX** (818 Douglas St; 250/384-1314) is a street-food-vendor-turned-restaurant that offers fast sit-down service. Dinner offerings range from fish and pub food at local institution **SPINNAKERS** (308 Catherine St; 250/386-2739; spinnakers.com) and the ambience of a brick converted power plant at **CANOE BREW PUB, MARINA AND RESTAURANT** (450 Swift St; 250/361-1940; canoebrewpub.com) to the French country-style dishes at **BRASSERIE L'ECOLE** (1715 Government St; 250/475-6260; lecole.ca), in a former Chinese schoolhouse in Chinatown.

Index

C

L

M

Best Places Seattle Report Form

Based on my personal experience, I wish to nominate the following restaurant, place of lodging, shop, nightclub, sight, or other as a "Best Place"; or confirm/correct/disagree with the current review.

(Please include address and telephone number of establishment, if convenient.)

REPORT

Please describe food, service, style, comfort, value, date of visit, and other aspects of your experience; continue on another piece of paper if necessary.

I am not associated, directly or indirectly, with the management or ownership of this establishment.

SIGNED

ADDRESS

PHONE **DATE**

Please address to *Best Places Seattle* and send to:

SASQUATCH BOOKS
119 SOUTH MAIN STREET, SUITE 400
SEATTLE, WA 98104

Feel free to email feedback as well: **BPFEEDBACK@SASQUATCHBOOKS.COM**